D0086939

PEABODY COLLEGE

PEABODY COLLEGE

From a Frontier Academy to the Frontiers of Teaching and Learning

PAUL K. CONKIN

VANDERBILT UNIVERSITY PRESS • *Nashville*

First Edition 2002

This book is printed on acid-free paper.
Manufactured in the United States of America

Library of Congress Cataloging-in-Publication Data

Conkin, Paul Keith.
Peabody College : from a frontier academy to the frontiers of teaching and learning / Paul K. Conkin.— 1st ed.
p. cm.
Includes bibliographical references and index.
ISBN 0-8265-1425-1 (cloth : alk. paper)
1. Vanderbilt University. George Peabody College for Teachers. I. Title.
LB2193.N297 C66 2002
378.768'55—dc21

2002011656

I dedicate this book

to the corps of Peabody-trained teachers.
From the first thirteen young women who enrolled
in a new State Normal College in December 1875
to the present, thousands of women and men,
teachers or prospective teachers, have come to Peabody
to gain needed skills in their chosen calling.
They have eschewed wealth or the lofty status
that too often attaches to high incomes.
They have left Peabody, not only well prepared
to teach or to assume leadership positions in education,
but with a heightened idealism and
a stronger commitment to a life of service.
More than anyone else,
they embody the Peabody ideal.

C O N T E N T S

Contents

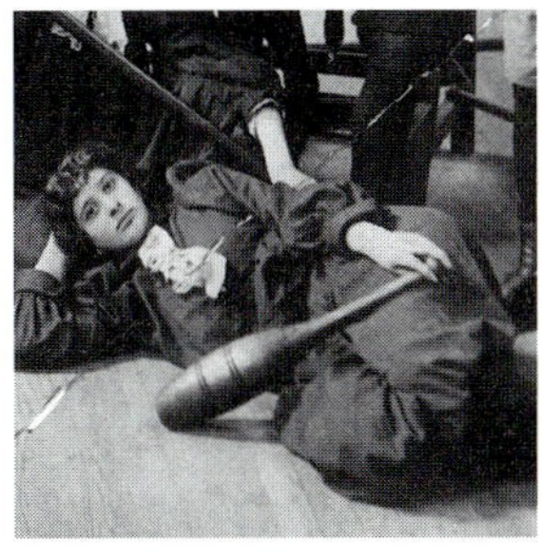

TIME CAPSULE
1980

1785
1985
EABODY

ILLUSTRATIONS

PREFACE AND ACKNOWLEDGMENTS

This is a history of George Peabody College for Teachers and its many predecessor academies and colleges. It is an unusually complex history, for Peabody has a distinctive position in American higher education. In its past was a frontier academy, a pioneer college in Nashville, and the multifaceted University of Nashville, which included at various times a four-year college, a medical school, a military institute, and a state-owned but privately funded normal school. In 1909, the assets of the University of Nashville helped fund the George Peabody College for Teachers, which for the next seventy years was the only private independent teachers' college in America. In 1979, it became a college within Vanderbilt University.

Colleges and universities, as much as cities and counties, or churches and corporations, gradually gain distinctive identities. All are collections of people joined in pursuit of certain goals. Most of us participate in several communities, and derive part of our sense of self from each such community. As time goes on, succeeding generations in each such community are shaped by beginnings, by the beliefs and values of founders, by the achievements and the frustrations of prior generations. They are shaped by what came before whether or not they are aware of this past. But awareness, historical consciousness, can heighten appreciation as well as provide a departure point for critical re-evaluation and the development of new goals.

Colleges, perhaps more than any other institutions in our society, cultivate historical self-consciousness. They have compelling reasons to retain the loyalty and gain the financial support of alumni. One of their purposes is to transmit the deepest values of society. They are, today, the major custodians of records from the past and scholarship about it. But to talk about Peabody's past is to invite confusion, for it has lived so many lives, seen so many new beginnings and so many endings. Like phoenixes, its predecessor institutions stumbled and often died, only to rise again in some new form. Only legal continuities and a few assets (a small part of its present endowment and some library books) connect the Peabody of today with its earliest predecessors. Thus, this is more a genealogy than an institutional biography, at least for the part of the story that precedes 1875.

This is a long story. For those at Peabody whose memories of the institution stretch back a half century or more, what will be most apparent is what is not here—the numerous faculty who contributed so much and who appear, if at all, only in a brief reference; the critical decisions that I reduce to a page; the student leaders and board of trust members whose names never appear. Many have already told much of the Peabody story. I was often pleasantly surprised by how many historical memories have remained alive and influential at the college. In part, this was the result of crises, endless self-studies, never-ending efforts to define Peabody's identity or to chart its future mission. At the same time, some critical aspects of the Peabody past are all but dead to the present generation. The most significant contribution of this history may be to illumine the now dark corners, the beliefs and values forgotten or repudiated. All along, I have tried to serve two goals—to write a story that is inherently interesting, something that at least Peabodians will like to read, but at the same time to complete a reasonably complete book of record, a reference book that will be useful in the future to those who want specific information about Peabody.

I could not have told this story without help. Most critical was the excellent work of Douglas Kasischke, who served as a research assistant in 2000–2001. He compiled the notes for all but one chapter. He carried hundreds of boxes, helped find documents, corrected mistakes in the text, and provided encouragement when I almost floundered in all the records. In a year haunted by health problems, I could not have kept going without his help. It is his book almost as much as mine.

I want to offer all possible praise for the staff of the Jean and Alexander Heard Library. I enjoyed the use of a convenient office and had the consistent and generous help of the staff in Special Collections. They granted my every request, sought out records, and did it with grace and kindness. Sara Harwell, then associate archivist in Special Collections, was my guide to the Peabody records, which she knew better than anyone. Strawberry Luck helped me select most of the photographs for this book. Phillip Tucker, editor of the Peabody Reflector, provided back copies of the Reflector and photographs. John M. Lyda of Campus Planning and Construction supplied maps and plats of the Peabody campus.

Interviews were indispensable to my research, particularly for the very recent period. For formal, extended interviews, I thank Jack Allen, Camilla Benbow, Kimberly Bess, Thomas Burish, Joseph Cunningham, James Guthrie, Robert Innes, Ann Kaiser, John Robert Newbrough, Raymond Norris, Ida Long Rogers, Howard Sandler, and Robert Stovall, who also read the chapter on merger and offered invaluable advice and information. I enjoyed more brief telephone conversations with James Pellegrino, Emmett Fields, and Alexander Heard.

PEABODY COLLEGE

C H A P T E R O N E

Davidson Academy and Cumberland College

FROM SMALL ACORNS LARGE OAKS GROW. THROUGH A SUCCESSION of legally connected charters, by the passing on of such assets as land and libraries, a small academy in a new village in western North Carolina would become in 1826 the University of Nashville, a corporate entity that exists today. This University would provide the facilities for a state normal college in 1875, and in time transfer most of its assets to a new George Peabody College for Teachers. This chapter involves the earliest progenitors of the present Peabody College.

BEGINNINGS

In December 1785, the State of North Carolina approved a charter for Davidson Academy. The small academy opened in 1786, with Thomas Craighead as president and sole teacher. He held classes in the small, just completed stone meeting house of the Spring Hill Presbyterian congregation, six miles northeast of the little settlement of Nashville. James Robertson, the leading founder of Nashville and an elected delegate to the North Carolina Assembly from the newly formed Davidson County, secured not only a charter for the new academy, but also a 240-acre land grant from the North Carolina legislature. (This land would remain tax free for ninety-nine years.) Perhaps more important, a small number of families formed a Presbyterian congregation and committed the resources to persuade Craighead to move to Nashville as their pastor. This was the first organized religious congregation in the five-year-old settlements around Nashville.

The setting was inauspicious for an educational institution. For its first nine years, frequent Indian attacks interrupted the small academy's efforts. Until the virtual cessation of Indian warfare in 1795, it was not possible to plan for any stable institution of higher education in the Cumberland basin. In this sense, the academy was a pledge for the future, a small, ill-funded, and sparsely attended school for boys, some of whom could attend only sporadically. A French visitor in 1802 reported only seven or eight boys in Craighead's little church.[1]

In 1786, when Craighead opened his school, his small stone church, twenty-four by thirty feet, was the most solid and impressive building in the Cumberland area. No other facility could have accommodated the academy. This would remain true for the next ten years. But the area around the church and school remained largely rural, and by 1795 its location had become a distinct disadvantage, as the early history of the Cumberland settlements reveals.

The first enduring settlements in the Nashville area began in late 1779. But a few families had settled there briefly in the preceding decade, and there a French-

Where it all began. This is the exact location of the former Spring Hill church and Davidson Academy. The inscription on the stone monument at the back of the old foundations suggests that the cemetery began soon after the building of the church in 1785. In 1813 a board of commissioners designated it as a perpetual burying site called the Craighead Spring Hill Cemetery. Thomas Craighead is buried near this site. His tombstone is still intact. Courtesy of Paul Conkin.

man, Timothy Demonbreun, had for years operated a trading post. Settlers moved permanently to what would become upper east Tennessee as early as 1769, leading to a thriving Watauga settlement by the beginnings of the American Revolution. The most important leader in settling the Cumberland basin, James Robertson, was one of the signers of the Watauga Compact and had served as an effective but unofficial agent in dealings with the Cherokee Indians. But at first even Robertson, who would later own one-fifth of the land in the Nashville area, took second place to another entrepreneur, Richard Henderson.

In 1775, Henderson and other land speculators from Virginia came to Watauga with a fantastic scheme. They met with a delegation of Cherokee chiefs and used abundant gifts or bribes to extract from them an informal treaty and land transfer. Henderson "bought" from these Cherokees a huge block of land that covered most of present-day Kentucky and much of the Cumberland area of middle Tennessee. The trouble was that Henderson had no authority from Virginia to negotiate such a treaty. At the same time, the Cherokees did not have any clear claim to this land. They had no settlements close to it and at most had used it as a hunting area, along with other tribes. Who cheated whom is an open question. But in the wake of this "sale," Henderson moved into western Virginia (later Kentucky), established a new colony he called Transylvania, ratified a constitution, and, above all, set up land offices and began to sell his new land to a rush of settlers. Virginia, when it learned of this daring bid for an independent nation largely on its own western lands, of course repudiated Henderson's claim, leading to unclear titles and decades of land litigation in the later state of Kentucky. After losing title to these lands in Kentucky, and helping survey the western boundaries between Virginia and North Carolina, Henderson hoped to collect on the lands south of the Virginia (Kentucky) border and thus by 1779 was recruiting possible settlers for the Cumberland basin. Out of his prompting came the first large and enduring settlements in the Cumberland. James Robertson, at Watauga and a friend of Henderson, was tantalized by the prospects Henderson offered far to the west.[2]

The move to Nashville has become a Tennessee legend. Robertson and a few other men came to the Great Salt Lick and the Sulphur Spring on the Cumberland in the spring of 1779. They planted corn and built fences; much of the land was open and thus easily plowed. Robertson returned in the fall, leading a group of families overland through Kentucky and picking up additional families along the way. They arrived at what would become Nashville on Christmas Eve, 1779, crossing the frozen Cumberland in one of the bitterest winters in American history. Back in Watauga, other families, including Robertson's wife and children, joined a second party, led by John Donelson from Virginia, another land speculator. This group boarded boats, one rather large, on the Holston, and in the winter and spring of 1780 made it all the way to Nashville via the Tennessee, Ohio, and Cumberland Rivers. By the time they arrived in April, Henderson had come down from central

Kentucky with a well-developed plan. He helped organize the family heads, drafted a Cumberland Compact for them to sign, established an informal government with elected magistrates, and set up a system of courts. Most important for Henderson was that the compact, modeled on a constitution he had written in Kentucky, provided for a land office and a scheme for selling land to later arrivals. But for those already there, his friends and even fellow conspirators, he granted a provisional title to designated and loosely surveyed land for only ten dollars per thousand acres. To his credit, the purchasers did not have to pay until some jurisdiction granted clear title. In this way, at least 150 founding families gained large estates around the largest fort, which they established near the Great Salt Lick and soon named Fort Nashborough. Unlike the fiasco in Kentucky, these land sales did not lead to a legal quagmire, for even though the State of North Carolina later repudiated Henderson's claim, it granted preemption rights for up to 640 acres to all those who had signed up for their land before May 1780—almost all the first settlers. In effect, their large farms cost them nothing. Later arrivals had to purchase their land, albeit for very low prices, from North Carolina.[3]

The free land was hardly worth the risks of occupying it. The problem was the almost continuous Indian raids, which led to the death or capture of thirty or forty settlers each year. The little settlement barely survived. Over the next three years, many of the original settlers, despite their land, fled temporarily to central Kentucky, including John Donelson and his extended family (one daughter, Rachel, would later marry Andrew Jackson). The Indian problem was unanticipated, for no Indian villages or towns were even close to Nashville, since the Shawnees had moved north decades before. But the Cumberland basin, because of its very lack of habitations and its lush vegetation, its many springs and salt licks, open land, and plentiful game, was a fabulous hunting preserve. Shawnees came back to hunt, while Chickasaws to the west (near Memphis), and Creeks and Cherokees from the east and south, resented the new settlements, continued to send hunting parties into the area, and found a new source of wealth in the horses of the whites, which they stole with abandon. Provocations came from both sides. Some of the interactions were peaceful, particularly with the Chickasaws. But each year, the Indians took their toll, not through open warfare but continuous harassment. Small bands of Indians hid in forests or the numerous canebrakes (stands of native bamboo) and attacked outlying farms, killing a few people at a time, creating great insecurity, and making it almost impossible for these new landowners to settle on their farms. Ironically, the very lack of clear Indian claims to the area caused the problem. Robertson, an expert in Indian bargaining, had no single nation to deal with. Negotiated agreements did not bind all the Indians. Soon, the settlers could not always identify the tribe of invading Indians, but after 1785 most were Creek or renegade Cherokees.

By 1782, it seemed unlikely that the small settlements around Nashville would survive. Had it not been for the difficult logistics of moving back east, the beleaguered settlers might have given up by 1783. As it was, they had to accommodate the new challenges. Not only did they build a central fort, Nashborough, where the men elected as guardians in the informal system of government met, and where militia units assembled, but they raised smaller forts in eight and more outlying areas, stretching from Donelson's large landholdings in the Clover Bottoms to near Gallatin. They called these small forts "stations." The local farm families fled to these stations for safety during Indian raids. One station, six miles northeast of Nashborough on the west bank of Pennington Bend, was early on referred to as Fort Union Station, and later as Hays Station. It was named after one of the more prominent original settlers, Robert Hays, who was also one of the nine original trustees of the nearby Davidson Academy. This area retained the name Haysborough (today Haysboro), but in the early years it never became a significant village. In 1786, as the Indian raids continued, Thomas Craighead moved to his farm near this station and undoubtedly fled to its safety dozens of times during the next decade. The present Spring Hill Cemetery is the best guide to the site today.[4]

In 1783, the State of North Carolina agreed to assume direct jurisdiction over the Cumberland settlements. It established Davidson County and set up the first county court system. In the next year, it created the town of Nashville, with commissioners and a grant of two hundred acres (roughly the land north of present-day Broadway, stretching west from the fort to the gulch). When the town began selling lots in 1785, the village contained not more than twelve permanent homes, all small and built of logs. New settlers, or those who fled from nearby farms in times of emergency, camped in tents or gathered in the small cabins within the palisades of the fort. The new town had no commercial establishments, although it would soon have at least one saloon, and in 1786 its first dry-goods store. But even in 1784 it had a thriving land office. Notably, it did not yet have a single church.

In this turbulent, violent setting, it is remarkable that a few of the leading families took time to establish a Presbyterian congregation at Spring Hill. We have no record of their deliberations. Presbyterian migrants to the Cumberland basin, as in almost all western settlements, often yearned for the type of church life they had enjoyed back in Virginia or North Carolina. This was particularly true of women. Thus, all the eastern presbyteries were besieged with pleas from settlers in Watauga and central Kentucky to send ministers to serve their new congregations in often unruly, and as yet unchurched, settlements. We can only assume that some like-minded families joined to form the Spring Hill congregation and beseeched James Robertson, as he took the long journey east as a delegate to the North Carolina Assembly, to search out a minister willing to come west. Presbyteries did not recognize or absorb such groups until they had a settled minister. Given the danger, it must have seemed unlikely that any would accept such a call.

We do not know exactly how the negotiations began with Thomas Craighead. According to later memory, Robertson met him while attending the assembly and learned that he was considering a move to Kentucky, where open congregations were begging for ministers. Before moving to the Nashville area, he visited congregations in the Kentucky settlements and there married Elizabeth Brown. Robertson persuaded him to settle on the Cumberland. Some of the families in the Nashville basin may have known him or his father back in North Carolina and thus wanted him as their minister. What probably clinched the deal was the promise that he would head a new academy and thus have an assured and handsome income. In any case, to induce Craighead to join them, twenty men subscribed more than nine hundred English pounds, to be paid in annual installments. They agreed to buy him 640 acres of land and pay him fifty pounds a year as salary during the first three years, both as pastor and teacher. The land, often referred to as Buchanon Spring, had been owned by one of the subscribers, John Buchanon, who sold it for 640 pounds hard money, one English pound per acre. It adjoined a trail that would later become Gallatin Pike. In fact, the subscribers would never pay Buchanon the full sum, and he later had to sue to get the balance. Craighead eventually built a large home on this land, across the pike and a bit south of the church, where he lived until his death in 1824. Some of his family lived in the home until the Civil War. Maps from the 1850s identify a small branch that flowed into the Cumberland as the Craighead Spring Creek.[5]

Thomas Craighead's father, Alexander, may have passed on to his son a bent for independence and for controversy. The son of an early immigrant from Ulster, Alexander Craighead grew up in Pennsylvania, qualified as a Presbyterian minister, and settled in Virginia, but in 1741 he withdrew from his presbytery and denomination. He soon joined a few scattered ministers in Pennsylvania, members of a tiny Reformed Presbyterian movement (Covenanters, or the Reformed Synod) that had originated in Scotland. Its intent was to adhere to the Solemn League and Covenant of 1643, which had briefly committed the churches of both England and Scotland to a national covenant that united in purpose state and church. Since the monarchs of the United Kingdom had rejected this covenant, Alexander Craighead published a testimony that in effect denounced the existing British government. This promised great embarrassment to the regular Presbyterians in America and led to a strong denunciation from his former Philadelphia Synod. But, ever changeable, Alexander repented of his action and regained ministerial fellowship in the larger church by 1750. He accepted a pulpit in Bath County, Virginia, and apparently took an oath of allegiance to the king to refute charges of treason. In 1558, Craighead moved with many families in his congregation to Mecklenburg County, North Carolina (the present Charlotte area). Here he continued to resist any complicity with the colonial government and its unwanted Anglican establishment, refusing to accept land grants from the royal governor. His ministry was cut short by his death in 1766. But many of his defiant congregants would sign the 1775 Mecklenburg declaration of independence, one of the earliest colonial bids for complete independence from Britain.[6]

Alexander Craighead's son Thomas was born in Virginia in 1750 and moved with his father to Mecklenburg County as a child. He probably attended a local academy, Queen's College, which won a colonial charter but then lost it when the assembly learned that it was really a Presbyterian institution, despite the appointment of an Anglican as its head. As a matter of course, after academy work, he attended the College of New Jersey, graduating in 1775. He then moved from licensed minister to ordination in 1780. For ten years before moving to Kentucky and then to Nashville, he headed three congregations in Virginia and North Carolina, reflecting an unusual mobility among Presbyterian ministers. It is possible that his later somewhat erratic behavior in Nashville was a family inheritance. David Caldwell, who married Thomas's sister, had several children who suffered from various forms of mental illness.

PRESBYTERIANISM AND CLASSICAL ACADEMIES

The Davidson Academy began as dozens, possibly even a hundred, earlier Presbyterian schools and academies, which by 1785 dotted the country from New Jersey and Pennsylvania to South Carolina and Georgia. In the colonial period, most academies originated with individual Presbyterian ministers. In rural areas and small villages, they were often the only persons with classical educations, the equivalent of college degrees. They rarely received large salaries from congregations, which often did not even fulfill the contracted salary mandated by the assigning presbytery. Thus, they needed the fees paid by parents for young boys to attend a common school or an academy to supplement their income. The better academies offered a type of secondary or higher education to male youth, something desired by parents and highly valued in the Scotch-Irish culture of American Presbyterianism. As in Puritan New England, parents accepted a responsibility to teach their children to read and calculate, beginning as early as age three. But few parents had the education to go further, particularly into the classical languages. Few could afford tutors, even if tutors were available. Thus the need for schools. In almost all Presbyterian academies, the teacher taught boys from around age eight to fourteen or fifteen, and in the very best until seventeen or eighteen. In the more famous academies, many boys came from other, even distant, congregations and boarded with the teacher's family. The younger boys enrolled in elementary or preparatory classes and eventually moved into the academy proper.

The best Presbyterian academies, in their most advanced classes, reached a level of study that approximated the second year in degree-granting colleges. Their graduates often had enough classical learning to gain a license to preach in Presbyterian congregations, although the road to ordination might take years of study under the guidance of other ministers or, when possible, completion of a college degree. For a graduate not headed into the ministry, a diploma or certificate from a good academy almost assured one's status as a gentleman, easily prepared one for apprenticeship training in law or medicine, and qualified one, almost without exception, as a teacher in an academy or in lower schools for both boys and girls.[7]

It was the Scotch-Irish Presbyterian culture that led to Davidson Academy and that shaped its early orientation. But, perhaps unfortunately for the life of the mind in middle Tennessee, this culture did not remain dominant for long. Yet the struggling successors of Davidson Academy (Cumberland College and the University of Nashville until 1850) continued to adhere to the founding ideals and the demanding academic standards these required.

The story of this distinctive culture goes back at least to 1560, to John Knox and the Scottish Reformation.[8] One of the early goals of the Church of Scotland was universal literacy, for reading and understanding the Bible was critical for all lay persons. Within a century, Scotland was one of the most literate countries in the world, and by the eighteenth century it had, arguably, the world's best universities. This led to a flowering of culture, the Scottish Enlightenment, which also involved transplanted Scottish Presbyterians who settled in Ulster in the northern counties of British-controlled Ireland. Notably, the Church of Scotland soon enforced the highest educational standards for ordination of its ministers of any branch of Protestantism, except possibly for New England Puritans. When the first, largely Scotch-Irish settlers reached the Nashville area in 1780 and signed Henderson's compact, all but one of the 256 could sign their own names.

In the eighteenth century, the Ulster Scotch moved in large numbers to the American colonies. Many families had maintained the Scottish culture in Ulster for more than a century before they migrated.[9] The Scotch-Irish at the beginning of the great migration had hoped to find a welcome among New England Puritans, who adhered to similar doctrines. One of these migrants was the grandfather of Thomas Craighead. When New England proved inhospitable, most Scotch-Irish landed at Philadelphia and soon flourished in religiously tolerant Pennsylvania, moving in large numbers to Lancaster county. From here, a growing number of Scotch-Irish families moved to western Pennsylvania, and then by 1736 down the Shenandoah Valley in Virginia. After 1847, an able Presbyterian missionary converted many Anglican families in central Virginia and soon established a group of churches and a presbytery. This opened central and southern Virginia to more Scotch-Irish migrants from Pennsylvania. Gradually, these Presbyterians moved down the Piedmont to South Carolina and Georgia, easily outnumbering Anglicans in many counties, particularly in North Carolina. Just before the Revolution, the Scotch-Irish made up the majority of early settlers in the valley of what later became east Tennessee.[10]

Wherever they settled, the Scotch-Irish established schools and, in fortunate locations, rather advanced academies. It was no longer feasible for young men committed to the ministry to go back to Ulster or Scotland. A few attended Harvard and Yale, but most could not afford to do so. Thus, most would-be ministers attended the best available academy. Most such academies remained local and unrecorded, ending with the death or removal of a pastor. A few gained regional fame and became, in effect, substitutes for colleges. In time, several matured into more than twenty Presbyterian colleges, including four in Tennessee. Davidson Academy fit this pattern, but because of the setting and the role of Thomas Craighead, it would evolve in its own way and make the present Peabody College unique among the modern offspring of eighteenth-century Presbyterian academies.

Yet these early academies provided a model for Davidson Academy. The first enduringly famous and influential Presbyterian academy, founded by William Tennett in 1726 at Neshaminy in Bucks County, Pennsylvania, soon earned the affectionate name of Log College. Here, Tennett's four sons, and soon a coterie of Log College men, helped lead a revivalist faction in the Philadelphia Synod. One son, Gilbert, who went on to get a master's degree at Yale, became one of the two or three most influential preachers in what we now call the Great Awakening. The Log College men, referred to as New Side Presbyterians, soon triggered a temporary split in American Presbyterianism. The New Siders welcomed a new revival style that encouraged such physical manifestations as swooning, and its ministers were less rigid in doctrine than Old Side ministers, some just over from Ulster. In 1745, the Old Side expelled the New Side ministers from the Philadelphia Synod. The two sides reunited in 1758, but during the split it was the New Siders, or, as they were sometimes called, the evangelicals, who grew most rapidly. And, as always, the more evangelical faction had a greater commitment to education. Just after the break, in 1746, the New Side and its New York Synod fulfilled a long-term goal, establishing the first four-year Presbyterian college in America—the College of New Jersey (renamed Princeton University in 1896). It hoped to compete with Yale. It began classes in homes and churches, first in Elizabeth and then Newark and New Brunswick, before the completion in 1756 of a huge college building, Nassau Hall, on donated land in Princeton. This college long remained the pride of American Presbyterians. Soon, every aspiring Presbyterian minister who could afford to came to old Nassau Hall, which briefly served as the capitol of the new United States. After 1736, ministers who established regionally famous academies almost all had degrees from the College of New Jersey, as did Thomas Craighead. Mother to a majority of early colleges in the mid-Atlantic and southern states, its role in American higher education was immense.[11]

Even before the College of New Jersey, Presbyterians had founded academies that matured into colleges. In 1749, ministers at a new Presbyterian congregation in the valley of Virginia founded Augusta Academy. This became Liberty Hall during the fervent patriotism of the Revolution, Washington College after George Washington saved it from bankruptcy in 1796 with an unprecedentedly large gift of $50,000, and finally Washington and Lee after Lee served as its president at the end of the Civil War. After the success of the college at Princeton, its graduates founded an academy in the Pittsburgh area (later Jefferson College), and then Hampden-Sydney College in southern Virginia. In North Carolina, at least five major academies were in operation before the Revolution. David Caldwell established the most famous and influential of these near Greensboro in 1766. Caldwell attended a small academy in Pennsylvania and then completed his studies at the College of New Jersey. He moved to North Carolina, helped found the Orange Presbytery, taught dozens of future ministers, and trained almost all the early Presbyterian ministers in middle Tennessee except an older Thomas Craighead, who was his brother-in-law. Of the two, David Caldwell would have a larger, although indirect, impact on middle Tennessee than Craighead, and his students would contribute directly to Craighead's sad religious fate in Nashville.[12]

Davidson Academy was not the first academy or emergent college in what became Tennessee. Samuel Doak founded Martin Academy in Washington County in 1785 (later Washington College), a year before Davidson Academy opened. Doak grew up in the valley of Virginia, studied at Liberty Hall, took his degree at the College of New Jersey, served as a tutor at Hampden-Sydney, and then moved to east Tennessee as the first settled Presbyterian pastor. He later moved near Greeneville and established another academy, Tusculum. In 1794, a Presbyterian minister in Greeneville, Hezekiah Balch, chartered Greeneville College, although nothing suggests that this school offered more than academy-level work. It would be the first academy in the South to admit a black student. Subsequently, Greeneville College and Tusculum would merge as Tusculum College, which still claims to be the oldest college in the state. In 1794, only a week after the chartering of Greeneville College, another Presbyterian minister and friend of Balch, Samuel Carrick, helped charter Blount College in Knoxville, which for years remained all but moribund. Eventually, it became East Tennessee College and, after the Civil War, the University of Tennessee. In the new century, a Presbyterian seminary in Maryville eventually became today's Maryville College. Thus, all the pioneer founders of higher education in Tennessee were Presbyterians, part of the Scotch-Irish tradition. Later, Methodists, Baptists, Episcopalians, and Disciples would found denominational colleges in Tennessee, but they were all latecomers.[13]

Although Greeneville and Blount Colleges adopted the pretentious label, "colleges," neither came close to offering college-level training in their first incarnations. In Tennessee, Davidson Academy's successor—Cumberland College—would offer the first rigorous four-year degree program. In this sense, Peabody, through its legally connected progenitors, can claim to be the oldest effective college in the state, the second-oldest college west of the Appalachians (Transylvania in Kentucky was first), and by some counts the eleventh-oldest college in the United States.

FINANCING AND GOVERNING DAVIDSON ACADEMY

Thomas Craighead alone determined the nature of Davidson Academy. Unfortunately, we know little of these beginnings. Because of Indian raids, he could not have held regular terms. The academy awarded no degrees. In the subsequent history of Nashville, we have no records of people who claimed to have graduated at Spring Hill, but only a list of textbooks purchased for the academy (standard texts in Greek, Latin, and mathematics) and one undated report on some of the boys who attended. In 1859, a Nashvillian, Albigence Waldo Putnam, published a history of middle Tennessee largely devoted to the career of James Robertson. In it, he recorded the memories of one E. H., who had been a student in the early academy under "Parson Craighead." E. H. tells of boys, apparently of elementary-school age, who paid their four English pounds in annual tuition and walked to the academy from as far as Nashville after crossing the ferry (before 1795, this would have been dangerous and thus unlikely). They came barefooted or in moccasins. Craighead, as they remembered him, frequently wielded a cane or switch. The boys carved their names on trees, talked about politics and girls, and wrote poetry. They had to take good care of their precious textbooks, and after classes were dismissed they often drove their cows home for milking. These almost romantic memories at best document the probability that most of the early students were not old enough to have advanced to academy-level instruction. This was, in fact, the only school of any type available, but in those turbulent times, it is doubtful that many boys attended for long.[14]

Craighead's friends or parishioners largely made up the academy's early board of trustees, an elite group of founding families. Robertson, the academy's long-time protector, grew up almost illiterate until educated by his wife. Craighead became an esteemed local citizen, an example of the gentility and classical learning that might grace this small cluster of villages sometime in the future. One of the best-trained ministers in the West, he was by all reports an eloquent but cold or rational preacher if compared to Methodists. Tall, sandy-haired, and blue-eyed, Craighead would be remembered as serious, devout, stubborn, and courageous. We know little about his public role. He seems to have demanded his full salary, and for one brief period he operated a distillery, a possibly lucrative business because imported whiskey cost a small fortune. In the wake of the later revivals, such an occupation seems odd for a clergyman, but the temperance movement lay in the future. Even later, it would be the evangelical faction among Presbyterians that fought to suppress strong drink, not the more traditional and orderly Presbyterians like Craighead.[15]

What is odd about the records of the work of the trustees of the academy (thanks again to Putnam) is that almost none refer to education, which the trustees left to Craighead. They struggled, from the beginning, to raise enough money to pay his authorized salary. For more than fifty years, the finances of the academy and its successors were so complex that no one can understand the whole story, which largely involved land, as was true for most western academies and colleges. In a sense, the board of trustees became land speculators, at times not clearly separating their own schemes from those of the academy. Nothing suggests any chicanery. If anything, the trustees ended up committing private funds to the academy, but to keep it going they sometimes bought land in their own names and held it for the school. Sometimes they bought land on speculation, not to use for a campus but to earn needed money. The academy's only original asset was the 240-acre land grant. But early on, the academy sought subscriptions from benefactors, and some of these involved gifts of land, which was inexpensive and plentiful. Also, North Carolina eventually gave the academy at least two sections of outlying land plus two salt licks, all of which the trustees sold to raise money.[16]

At its first meeting, the board of trustees had to make choices about the 240 acres of land, which, like the open pages of a book, faced the land just deeded to the town of Nashville. Trustees and commissioners surveyed the joint boundary. Although the land grant did not specify that the future academy occupy a part of this grant, this must have been the early assumption. Even as Craighead began teaching up at Spring Hill, the trustees opened a ferry across the Cumberland that docked at the low land (now Riverfront Park) on the northeast corner of the academy grant. This allowed Nashvillians to travel back and forth to the academy. For the next twenty-eight years, the trustees owned the ferry, leased it to various operators, and apparently made money from it. In all the board's subsequent land deals, the trustees retained ownership of the dock area. Otherwise, they soon began alienating most of the original grant, either by leasing farm land or selling residential lots (at first, for from three to six dollars an acre, but soon for as much as a hundred dollars). What they protected, with a future campus in mind, was the highest land in the grant, now about five blocks south of Broadway between Second and Fourth Avenues. Eventually, this would be known as College Hill (today, as Rutledge Hill). The trustees even donated three acres of choice land for the construction of Broad Street. By 1796, the board retained only about seven acres of the original grant, including the ferry dock, College Hill, and a street or right-of-way to it from Broad Street. (This entrance road would later become College Street and today is Third Avenue.) But they held notes on dozens of lots and over the next few decades would have to foreclose on and resell several of these. The trustees were, in fact, the main real estate agents in the growing Nashville. Their lots were in great demand because, for ninety-nine years, they were tax-exempt. In 1791, among the new trustees who replaced those who died or resigned, was a rising young lawyer, Andrew Jackson.[17]

Meanwhile, the political and military situation changed rapidly. North Carolina had in 1784 voted to cede its western lands to the federal Congress, but soon repealed this act. Thus, the Cumberland settlements remained part of that state until 1790. In fact, for over a year, they were part of the independent nation of North Carolina, for in its first convention North Carolina refused to ratify the federal constitution of 1787. In a second convention in late 1789, it reversed itself, ratified the federal constitution, and rejoined the Union. As a condition of ratification, North Carolina ceded its western lands to the federal government. Unfortunately for the western settlers, before the cession, North Carolina sent commissioners west to locate large chunks of the best unsold land and used them to reward revolutionary veterans. Some of these warrants for veterans were for lands still controlled by Indians, among them parts of what is now west Tennessee.

To govern these newly ceded lands, Congress established the Territory South of the Ohio River, following an earlier pattern for the Northwest Territories but with added provisions to protect slavery. George Washington appointed a prominent North Carolinian and Revolutionary veteran, William Blount, as governor and commissioner of Indian Affairs for the new territory. A major land speculator in the tradition of Henderson and Robertson, Blount established his capital in Sullivan County but soon moved to a village he named Knoxville (after his superior in Indian Affairs, Secretary of War Henry Knox). Belatedly, in 1793, Blount first established an elected territorial assembly, which met in Knoxville, with delegates from the three counties in the Cumberland basin—Davidson, formed in 1783; Sumner, formed in 1786 to the northeast of Davidson, and by 1793 the most populous and wealthy county in the western areas; and Tennessee, formed in 1788 and including land from present-day Clarksville west to the Tennessee River. Such an assembly was the last step to statehood, which came in 1796. Those who drafted the new state constitution chose the name Tennessee for the new state (a division of the former county of Tennessee vacated the name). These changes placed the fate of Davidson Academy under a government that, as territory and then state, met in east Tennessee, usually in Knoxville. Only in 1826 did Nashville become the state's permanent capital; for several preceding years, the assembly met in Murfreesboro.[18]

More important for the fate of Nashville and Davidson Academy was the virtual end of Indian hostilities by 1795. In 1794, General James Robertson, as head of the western militia, conducted an unauthorized military campaign against the renegade western Cherokee (or Chickamauga) towns in the area near present-day

Chattanooga. He won a decisive victory and burned the towns. Because he had acted against orders from Governor Blount, he soon had to resign his commission, but the raid had its intended effect. In 1795, the Cherokee nation (a confederation, not a single tribe) signed a new peace treaty, and this time it held. Both sides wanted peace and were willing to submit future provocations, most of white origin, to the courts. In 1795, a treaty with the Creek tribes to the south led to peace in the Cumberland. For the first time, families could move away from the now dozens of stations, create permanent homes on their own land, and gradually develop a thriving agricultural economy. Nashville, on its way to becoming a shipping port and commercial center for the whole central basin, enjoyed its first period of rapid growth. Finally, a great religious revival swept the area in the heady years at the turn of the new century.

This was a challenging but anxious time for Davidson Academy. With the Indian problem settled, it now seemed appropriate to establish a real academy, or even a degree-granting college, on the remaining land facing Nashville. In April 1796, some concerned Nashvillians persuaded their delegates to the first general assembly of the soon-to-be-admitted State of Tennessee to pass an act, probably without legal authority to do so, that added ten new trustees to the academy (in effect giving a majority voice to new members), appointed three auditors, and stipulated that the trustees build a new academy building on College Hill. This would have meant, in effect, a takeover of the academy by outsiders. The old board of trustees resented this action, with its implied censorship of the work of the existing nine trustees, and successfully denied the state any authority over Davidson. But it did begin planning a new campus on the designated land. The process was slow, and one can imagine that old Craighead wanted it that way, for he continued to teach in his small church. Also, in the next few, exciting years, Craighead became as much of an obstacle to a new academy as a resource for it, the result of both his religious and his educational roles.[19]

With the end of Indian warfare, settlers flocked to the Cumberland area, most from Virginia and North Carolina. At least half were Scotch-Irish Presbyterians, who began forming new congregations in the larger Nashville area. Such congregations, from 1796 to 1800, attracted five new ministers from North Carolina, all of whom had attended David Caldwell's academy near present Greensboro. Beginning in 1797, these ministers were able to lead a revival of religion in the Cumberland area. Two of the ministers, including the most effective preacher, James McGready, settled in Logan County, Kentucky, two more in adjoining Sumner County, in the new state of Tennessee. The religious stirring began in the weekend-long summer communions, a Scottish tradition. Families from nearby congregations came to these sacramental meetings and received home hospitality from local church members. By 1800 these scheduled sacraments became larger and more fervent, with more and more physical exercises occurring during the preaching services. New converts helped speed the formation of new congregations and provide young men anxious to become Presbyterian ministers. In 1800, in Logan County, many families, anxious to be present at all the evening excitement, came prepared to camp on the grounds of the Gasper River congregation. Soon most such communion gatherings had camping, or the beginning of a camp meeting tradition. At first, Thomas Craighead had welcomed a religious revival, and even hosted a stirring communion in his own church. But, as many of the older Presbyterian ministers in the west, he was soon horrified by the physical excesses. He wanted an orderly form of preaching. His was soon a minority in this view.

Because of all the new congregations forming each year, the new Kentucky Synod created a separate Cumberland Presbytery in 1802. Led by McGready and the revival faction, it soon began licensing young ministers who lacked the classical Latin and Greek that had long been a requirement of Presbyterian ordination. Of greatest concern to the synod, most of these young men were also doctrinally suspect, for they subscribed to the Westminster Confession with reservations about the doctrine of double predestination, the belief that God ordained both those he would save and those he would damn. Craighead was horrified at revival excesses and disorder, but not, it turned out, by free-will doctrines. He protested the disorder to the Kentucky Synod. In Sumner County, he also formed a small, dissenting congregation that had split from the Salem church, probably the largest Presbyterian church in Tennessee, and one which had joined enthusiastically in the new revival culture. His protests to the synod led to a complicated series of events—a synod investigation, demands that all the young ministers submit to a synod exam, their refusal to do so, the suspension of the Cumberland Presbytery, and, after almost a decade of conflict, the formation of a new Cumberland Presbyterian denomination in 1810. In the process of the investigations, it became clear that Craighead was, doctrinally, even more opposed to most key Calvinist doctrines than were the exuberant young ministers.

In 1805, some members of Craighead's orderly Presbyterian congregation in Sumner County became concerned about his orthodoxy. This led to a widely aired charge of Pelagianism, or the most extreme free-will doctrines. Craighead could not accept the coherent, logical Calvinist system in which God alone chose those destined for salvation. In an examination before his synod in 1805, he failed to satisfy his examiners. The next year he preached a sermon on regeneration in which he aired his views about the necessary human role in conversion. These views were as clearly heretical as any ever preached in the Presbyterian Church. Once again, he faced a synod examination, but he survived (the synod was reluctant to lose ministers with Craighead's ability). Then, in 1809, as if to throw salt on a festering sore, Craighead published his regeneration sermon. He must have realized that the church could no longer suffer his views. The sermon led to an 1810 exchange of letters, all published, between Craighead and an accusing minister,

John Campbell. His presbytery cited him for heresy. When he did not appear for trial, the presbytery had to recommend his suspension from the gospel ministry. The Kentucky Synod suspended him in its next meeting, in October 1810, a terrible blow to the sixty-year-old Craighead. Embarrassed by the controversy, he had already resigned as president of what was by then Cumberland College. He now had no secure source of income, and by some reports he became almost destitute. He kept appealing his suspension. In a hearing held at his request in 1816 before a synod committee, he tried to justify his doctrinal views, possibly retreated a bit from his earlier position, but was too honest to concede the major issues. Only in 1824, based as much on procedural and humanitarian as doctrinal grounds, did his synod decide that his views, although erroneous, by the most favorable interpretation were not of fundamental importance. It remanded the case to his presbytery (by then the new West Tennessee Presbytery), which restored him to the gospel ministry. He died before the year was out, with at least some sense of vindication after almost twenty years of doctrinal controversy.[20]

CUMBERLAND COLLEGE

What happened to his academy may have caused Craighead almost as much grief as the battles within his church. In 1785 no one knew that Nashville would eventually become the commercial hub for the rich agricultural lands of the central basin. Most of the early trustees were from Craighead's congregation, six miles from Nashville, and at least some lived in the area of his farm and church building. In time, the location so far from Nashville became a liability. This led the trustees in 1796 to commit to a new building and a new campus. Even before the building effort began, it was clear that many prominent citizens in Nashville wanted a "college," whatever that label meant. Some supported a new Federal Academy in Nashville, a threat to the future of Davidson Academy (the two later merged). At least three other educational institutions in Tennessee already had the impressive name of "college," though none offered anything on the level even of a standard B.A. program. In 1803, without consulting the trustees, the Tennessee General Assembly changed the charter of Davidson Academy to rename it Davidson College. The academy trustees rejected the name change, along with the assembly's right to make such a unilateral alteration to the charter. Craighead led the opposition, probably because the school had insufficient resources to create a legitimate, degree-granting college (he had as his model the College of New Jersey), and possibly also because such a change, if effected, would end his small academy and diminish his role. It was by then clear that the view of the trustees, including a majority who remained loyal to Craighead, was out of line with public sentiment in Nashville.[21]

In 1806, a federal land grant enticed the trustees to accept a name change.

Under the terms of the cession of its western lands to the federal government, North Carolina had stipulated that the citizens in these western areas enjoy the same privileges and benefits offered to those in the Northwest Territory, including public land for the support of education. Congress, undoubtedly pressed by Tennessee representatives, granted 200,000 acres of federally owned land, most of it recently acquired from the Cherokees, for the support of education in the young state. This land (described as south of the Holston and French Broad and west of the Big Pigeon Rivers) was mainly in present-day Sevier and Blount Counties. Half was to help fund academies in each county, the other half to support colleges in both east and west Tennessee (what we now call middle Tennessee). The state, as custodian of this grant, was to sell the land for not less than two dollars an acre, except to those already settled on the land, who could pay only one dollar an acre. East Tennessee College, although scarcely functioning at the time, bid successfully for the eastern grant. Nashville wanted the western half, and so did the trustees of Davidson Academy. The Tennessee General Assembly once again changed Davidson Academy's charter, this time transforming the school into Cumberland College, and thus secured the land grant. The new charter stipulated not only a name change, but also the officers for a degree-granting institution.

The land grant marked the beginning of an agonizing era in the history of the college and the later University of Nashville. As one would expect, before the state even tried to sell the land, most of it was already occupied. The squatters soon gained strong political support and kept getting legislative permission to postpone payment for their land. Most never paid in full. And Cumberland College and its successors never received, directly, even half of the money intended by this federal grant.[22]

With all deliberate speed, the trustees did build a new college, but on a shoestring budget. In 1803, before the name change, the trustees had appointed Robertson and Andrew Jackson to superintend the construction of the new academy building. Despite inadequate funds, by 1806 the trustees had nevertheless contracted for a $10,890 building. In 1805, Robertson resigned from the board. A new generation was taking over. Not until 1808 did the trustees complete the three-story brick building, only seventy by forty feet, barely larger than some homes. It was located just west of what would later be Third Avenue, between today's Peabody and Franklin Streets. When the University of Nashville opened in 1824, this became the west side of a building approximately three times its size.[23]

Thomas Craighead was appointed president of the newly chartered Cumberland College in 1807. Most of the older trustees remained. Classes opened in the new brick building in the fall of 1808. To give some credibility to the school's new status as a college, Craighead and the trustees hired William Hume as a second and very able professor—the academic title stipulated in the new charter, along with a never honored requirement that professors and students wear academic gowns. Hume came to America in 1801 from Scotland as a missionary of the small Seceder Presbyterian sect in his home country (officially the Associate Synod). Its members, like the earlier and closely related Covenanters, wanted to maintain a pure Calvinist church, and in America they strongly resisted such new innovations as revivals. A few Seceder families had already moved to Nashville and in 1798 organized a small congregation. Hume acquired one of the lots sold by Davidson Academy and erected a small brick church building on it early in the new century, the home of the first Presbyterian congregation in the city. Although regular Presbyterians would not join this small congregation, many attended its services and came to admire Hume. Perhaps few Nashvillians cared about the doctrinal differences that separated this small sect from the larger Presbyterian Church. In time, it seemed, neither did the mild and beloved Hume. In 1818, he sold his church and lot, joined the Nashville Presbyterian Church founded in 1814 (later the First Presbyterian Church) along with the remaining Seceder members of his congregation, and served for a time as its minister. A former student at the University of Edinburgh, Hume was admirably qualified to become a professor of ancient languages at Cumberland College, and his orderly approach to worship made him congenial to Craighead. In addition to Hume, the trustees appointed a tutor to teach preparatory classes, undoubtedly the best attended of all.[24]

Cumberland College struggled from the first. The expected funds from the land grant had created hope for a solvent school. Without that money, the college had only small sums from local land transactions, in some years a profit from its ferry (this it sold in 1813 for just over $7,000), and small tuition payments by students—not enough. Craighead remained as president for only a year. It is not clear that he even made the trip to the new college to do his teaching. The announcement for 1908 mentioned only classes by Hume, and these were at the preparatory level. Suspended by his church in the next year, Craighead gave up his long connection with higher education, although his term as a member of the board ran for three more years, and a son and grandson would later serve on the board. In fact, Craighead soon resumed private teaching at his Spring Hill church, for we have at least one travel report about his students. He needed the fees to survive. He apparently continued to preach, at least monthly, to his small congregation, which supported him in his battles with the synod. After the organization of the Presbyterian church in Nashville in 1814, Craighead frequently preached in its pulpit, defrocked or not.

To Craighead, the old Scotch-Irish culture must have seemed doomed in Tennessee by 1810. The new Cumberland Presbytery had to relax its ministerial requirements, moving closer to the Baptists and Methodists by accepting candidates with no college education. Its doctrines were softer and more sentimental than the older and rigorously logical forms of Calvinism. Meanwhile, more and more English and other non-Scottish families moved into the region, none with the same commitment to classical literacy. As the McGready revivals reinvigorated Presbyterians in the West, new Methodist itinerants began establishing Methodist circuits (one in the Nashville area as early as 1786), and these soon outgrew even the Cumberland Presbyterians. The Methodists had almost no educational requirement for ordination; they soon capitalized on camp-meeting revivals and created a much more sentimental religious culture. It took the Methodists decades to create even weak colleges, and only in 1875 with Vanderbilt did the southern branch of Methodism gain its first university. Gradually, waves of Baptists, most of English roots, expanded into middle Tennessee, and they too accepted untutored young men as ministers. What Craighead stood for—not only classical literacy but also logic and order—was out of fashion. He and his immediate successors in Cumberland College and the University of Nashville tenaciously held to the traditional ideals, resisting the dilution of the classical curriculum, but with less and less public support.

As the ascendancy of the Cumberland Presbyterians and the rapid growth of Methodism weakened the Presbyterian denomination in the old Southwest, Davidson Academy would have been expected to become a denominational college. That it did not had major implications for its future. Who owned Cumberland College? Was it a Presbyterian college? An independent private college with Presbyterian roots? A public college? No one knew, and the ambiguities about its status would linger for more than a century. Although Davidson Academy was Presbyterian in origin, no presbytery or synod ever adopted it or any of its successors or provided any funds to support it. Thus, the church never owned it. Soon, even its Presbyterian leaders would emphasize its nonsectarian status. At various times, legislatures in North Carolina, in the Southwest Territory, and in Tennessee intervened in its affairs. The federal government, indirectly, gave it a land grant to be administered by the state. In this sense, it resembled a public university. But never before 1880 did Tennessee appropriate one penny for its support. At best, it was a hybrid. But the lack of clear ownership or affiliation meant that it never had a distinct constituency. No one took responsibility for it or wanted to lend it financial support.

In its first incarnation, Cumberland College lasted only from 1808 to 1816, with a brief but abortive attempt to resume classes in 1820–21. Succeeding Craighead as president was another Presbyterian minister, James Priestley, who completed his college work at Liberty Hall in the Valley of Virginia but did not earn a degree. He had taught in, or headed, numerous academies before taking the position in Nashville. Felix Grundy, later a senator from Tennessee, had taken courses with him in an academy in Bardstown, Kentucky, and probably helped lure him to Nashville. Priestley was a rather eccentric man, somber and stern but with flashes of brilliance. He did not have the talent for raising enough funds, or luring enough students, to make the college solvent. He carried on a running battle with the state legislature because of its failure to sell the federal land and thus provide an endowment for his college.

By the standards of the time, Hume and Priestley made up a reasonably well-qualified faculty, able to teach an array of courses, primarily in classical languages, mathematics, and moral philosophy. They had only a few students at the college level. They conferred the college's first, lone bachelor of arts in 1813 and by 1816 had graduated only nineteen students with a bachelor's degree. These fully earned degrees, bestowed only after a rigorous series of courses and long public examinations, were the first such quality degrees awarded in Tennessee. As in all U.S. colleges at the time, classes required textbooks and daily recitation. Of the few graduates, all among the local elite, two later became senators, including the influential John Bell; three became representatives.[25] But the college simply could not make it financially and had to suspend classes in 1816, although Hume and others taught preparatory classes in the college hall. Few students attended the reopened college classes in the fall of 1820, just three months before President Priestley died. With no president and insufficient funds, the college had once again to suspend classes, at least until the trustees could find new sources of income and hire a new president.[26]

THE REVIVAL OF CUMBERLAND COLLEGE

It was not clear in 1821 that Cumberland College would survive. The trustees had already sold most of the original land grants and had no early prospects of realizing much income from the federal land granted the college in 1806. The one small campus building, with only twenty-two dorm rooms and a few recitation areas, was already in poor repair, its chimneys about to tumble onto the roof. The college had no endowment and, without students, no tuition. Its academy-level courses meant that the campus was never vacant, but the survival of Cumberland College depended on a repaired and much enlarged hall, new sources of income, and a faculty distinguished enough to attract able students. Because of the trustees' commitment, ability, and eminence, combined with a bit of luck, they rose to the challenge by 1824.

The Cumberland trustees clearly wanted to create a quality college. It was a matter of regional pride and perceived need. The times were auspicious. Nashville had, by 1820, grown to near 4,000 inhabitants, the county to more than 20,000, and Davidson plus five contiguous counties to more than 110,000. The central basin had become one of the prime agricultural areas of the nation. Briefly, before the opening of the Midwest, Kentucky and Tennessee were the country's largest producers of corn, wheat, and hogs. North of Nashville, tobacco culture thrived. To the south, cotton prevailed. In fact, the Deep South by 1820 enjoyed a great cotton boom, made possible by the cotton gin and power looms. The rich black soil of

Alabama, Mississippi, and Louisiana supported a booming cotton empire, which included some of the wealthiest counties in the nation. These cotton areas provided a market for the horses, mules, and cattle of the Nashville basin. Politically, too, Nashville was thriving, gaining national attention and respect. Andrew Jackson, a trustee of Cumberland College, was the hero of New Orleans, the architect of successful campaigns against the Creeks and Seminoles. His military victories made possible the annexation of Florida in 1819. In 1824, as he helped revive the college, he won a majority of the popular vote for president of the United States but lost in a runoff election in the House of Representatives. Already, he was building a political movement that would win him the presidency in 1828. Jackson and his Jacksonian movement would dominate American politics for the next twenty years.

In 1822, the college received a small and unexpected windfall. Before North Carolina had surrendered its western lands, it not only had rewarded Revolutionary veterans with land warrants in what became Tennessee. It now decided to grant any unclaimed warrants to the new and struggling University of North Carolina, the first state university to hold classes. Many veterans with warrants died intestate, before they had located and won title to any land. In some cases, the state could not even locate holders of warrants. Why not use such escheated lands to support higher education? This was not welcome news in Tennessee, which challenged the UNC claims. Among other problems, this land was tax-exempt. In a compromise settlement with North Carolina and the university, Tennessee finally agreed to honor these claims and even defer taxes on them until 1850, if North Carolina would give 60,000 acres of the land to the two chartered colleges in the state. East Tennessee College was, at the time, little more than a charter without a campus, and Governor William Carroll was a committed trustee of Cumberland College. So, in the agreement, North Carolina granted only 20,000 acres to what would later be the University of Tennessee, and 40,000 to Cumberland College. The two colleges quickly gained title to this land, all west of the Tennessee River. By 1827, an agent had located the Cumberland College plots, and very shortly, the trustees put the first parcels up for sale. More important, as early as 1823, they could use the land as an inducement in recruiting a new president for the college.

Spurred on by this gift, the trustees initiated the most concerted subscription effort in the college's history. Agents, working on commission, began soliciting gifts as far away as New Orleans and by 1824 had pledges of more than $7,000. Not all donors would pay up, and many would delay payments for years, but new subscriptions augmented this original campaign, meaning that the college could expect at least $3,000 or $4,000 in gifts over the next two years. Meanwhile, it continued to collect payments on older land sales and to resell land it had recovered for defaulted notes or mortgages. And, contrary to its public complaints, it did receive on occasion payments from farmers on the East Tennessee lands, even though the state continued to allow such squatters to remain on their land without title. The college suddenly seemed more solvent than ever before. It was also more involved in complex land purchases and speculation. This included a nice 120-acre plot bought by 1825, and just south of the older land grant. This land included the post-1850 campus of the University of Nashville and from 1912 to 1925 the campus of the medical and dental colleges of Vanderbilt University. Soon after this purchase, the trustees began planning for a new campus. But they seemed more motivated by the prospect that land on the outskirts of the small town of Nashville would rapidly increase in value, enriching the college when they later sold the land.[27]

The trustees had also identified the man they wanted to preside over the revived college. They first contacted Philip Lindsley in 1823, when he was acting president of the College of New Jersey at Princeton. He was not interested. The trustees had simply joined a lineup of suitors. Both Transylvania University and Ohio University had already elected him as their president, but he refused in each case. In 1823, he had also declined the offer of the presidency of the College of New Jersey. But in April 1824, after years of protesting that he desired only to remain in teaching, Lindsley traveled to Nashville to talk to the trustees. He shortly accepted an offer that involved several specific commitments to him by the board. One factor in his decision may have been the proximity of 2,560 acres of land in nearby Wilson County that Lindsley's wife had inherited from her father, who had gained it as a bounty based on his service as an officer in the Revolution. Much later, in 1851, Lindsley's son, Nathaniel, would open an elite academy for girls on part of this land.[28]

Back at Princeton, Lindsley began soliciting gifts for Cumberland College in the greater New York area. He and his family finally arrived in Nashville on Christmas Eve, 1824, exactly forty-five years after James Robertson's settlers had crossed the Cumberland to found Nashville. To anyone acquainted with American higher education, this was a remarkable coup by the trustees, for Lindsley was one of the most respected educators in America and in his lifetime probably turned down more offers of presidencies than anyone in the history of higher education in America.

Subsequent scholars have debated and puzzled over Lindsley's decision. Why did he select a suspended college in Nashville over Princeton? It seemed to make no sense. In fact, it made very good sense, and Lindsley made the correct decision, although in later years of frustration, he may have briefly questioned his sanity back in 1824. What most people in Nashville did not realize is that he had as much push as pull. He left his beloved Princeton when its college was in almost as much trouble as the one in Nashville. As an expression of that love, he created a reformed Cumberland College that was, in almost every detail, an exact copy of the College of New Jersey that he had known as a student early in the nineteenth century. Also, in 1826, he and his board of trustees lobbied the Tennessee Assembly into awarding a charter for a new institution, the University of Nashville. It is not clear that Lindsley intended that the new title replace Cumberland College, a name he and others used with less and less frequency over the next two or three years. His understanding was that Cumberland College was to become just one in a complex of colleges and professional schools that he believed would justify the title "university." But soon the name disappeared, replaced by the grand but in many respects never justified title "university."

CHAPTER TWO

The Educational Mission of Philip Lindsley

PHILIP LINDSLEY WOULD BECOME THE MOST EMINENT EDUCATOR in the history of Nashville. His achievements were, for the time and place, exceptional. But what most distinguished Lindsley was not what he achieved in Cumberland College and the University of Nashville, but his aspirations for the University he led, the eloquence with which he communicated these aspirations, and the unmet challenges he offered to Nashville and the State of Tennessee. If any one person, in the long history of Nashville colleges and universities, deserves a full chapter in a book, it is Philip Lindsley.

LINDSLEY AND THE COLLEGE OF NEW JERSEY

Philip Lindsley was born near Morristown, New Jersey, on December 21, 1786. His ancestors, back several generations, were English Presbyterians who first migrated to the American colonies in the seventeenth century, before any organized presbyteries or synods. While at Princeton, and even more in the South, Lindsley was a minority among the Scotch-Irish that dominated his church.

Some enduring traits were visible very early in Lindsley's life. His mother was his first teacher. He early learned to read, and never stopped reading the rest of his life. In a sense, this was his first profession. He soon read up to several books a day and remembered it all. He became a walking encyclopedia, informed on almost all subjects but least addicted to the speculative subjects, such as theology and philosophy. In an age when this was at least remotely possible, he read every new book he could acquire for his library or college library. This insured that the professors at the University of Nashville used the very latest texts.

At the age of 13, Lindsley began his formal schooling, in a new Presbyterian academy taught by Robert Finley (in the last year of his abbreviated life, Finley became president of the University of Georgia). Except for winter months, Lindsley did not board in Finley's home but walked the three miles to the academy. In one winter, he took courses closer by, in Morristown, in an academy owned by James Stevenson. In three years, he completed the most advanced work in these academies. In 1802 he moved on to the College of New Jersey, where he enrolled as a junior (not unusual) and graduated in two years, when he was not quite eighteen. Although he began theological training at Princeton and announced plans to become a minister, his calling was teaching. Stevenson brought him back as tutor in his academy for a year and taught him French on the side. Lindsley then taught for two years in Finley's growing academy.

When Lindsley enrolled at Princeton in the fall of 1802, President Samuel Stanhope Smith became his mentor and the one person who most shaped his beliefs and values. On almost no issue did the two disagree, even on their conceptions of higher education. But behind Smith, and a vital indirect influence, was Smith's mentor, until this time by far the most successful and influential president of the College of New Jersey, John Witherspoon. Smith had matriculated at Princeton just a year before Witherspoon arrived from Scotland in 1768 to take charge of a college that had suffered from the untimely deaths of all its early presidents, including the most famous, Jonathan Edwards, America's first and greatest philosophical theologian. Until his encounter with Witherspoon, Smith had been under the sway of those who still honored Edwardian theology, and with it a type of philosophical idealism. The New England intellectual influence had been dominant among the faculty. Witherspoon reoriented the intellectual outlook toward Scotland and hired a new faculty to reflect it. Lindsley, later, would absorb this outlook, and he would reflect little knowledge of, or sympathy with, the Edwardian tradition.

In Scotland, Witherspoon had supported an evangelical or conservative position in the Church of Scotland, which made him acceptable at Princeton. But he was a product of the Scottish Enlightenment, and of a somewhat varied philosophical position today called commonsense realism. Witherspoon was not a philosopher. He eschewed metaphysical issues. But, all too loosely, he accepted the key position of these Scottish realists, which they traced back to John Locke: Through their senses, humans could frame true accounts of the natural world and intuitively had a sense of what was right and wrong (a moral sense). This was, in many ways, an irenic position—a view that favors moderation and conciliation—that reflected the common understanding of people untutored in speculative philosophy. Witherspoon saw no opposition between empirical science and the revealed truths of Christianity, and he tried to move Princeton toward a balanced curriculum. He particularly emphasized the sciences, political thought, and moral theory, with a somewhat lesser emphasis on the ancient languages. Above all, Witherspoon was a fervent American patriot. He signed the Declaration of Independence and was a longtime delegate to the federal Congress. He helped turn the College of New Jersey away from its early role of training ministers to its developing role as a school for statesmen. As the proportion of divinity students fell from near 50 to only 13 percent during Witherspoon's tenure, almost all Princeton men became active in politics, including a large array of judges, congressmen, and even one president, James Madison.[1]

Samuel Stanhope Smith became president of the College of New Jersey in 1794 upon the death of Witherspoon. Smith reinforced the changes inaugurated by Witherspoon and was himself a scientist of some renown, as well as a Presbyterian minister. He was handsome, charismatic, even elegant. His speeches were polished gems. He exerted a powerful influence on all he knew, although critics found his impeccable dress and bearing a bit pompous. Like his student Lindsley, he had matriculated as a junior at age sixteen. As much or more than Witherspoon, he stressed the nonsectarian nature of the college, flirted with some heterodoxy as a professed Calvinist (he espoused a degree of human agency that seemed, to some, to challenge divine omnipotence), and devoted even more time than had Witherspoon to the advancement of mathematics and the physical and biological sciences. He desperately tried to find money to buy physical apparatus from Europe and to develop cabinets of exhibits in natural history, paying $3,000 for one such cabinet imported from England. As enthusiastic a patriot as Witherspoon, Smith always correlated republicanism with an enlightened Christianity. For half a century, the Fourth of July was the greatest holiday at Princeton and public service the highest calling. Smith was a scholar who wrote first in the field of physical anthropology (Lindsley would follow), publishing a book on the reasons for racial diversity. He affirmed the orthodox, and biblical, theory of unitary origins, and attributed later changes in humans to the effects of climate and social organization. He also published a two-volume text on moral theory—he adhered to the moral-sense position of the Scottish philosopher Thomas Hutchinson and came close to denying human depravity—and a book on natural theology.

Smith was not successful as president of the College of New Jersey. Unruly students were his undoing. Boys, who entered the college at fifteen to seventeen, resented the tight rules embodied in what the college called the *Laws,* a student manual and catalogue all in one. The boys had few outlets for their physical exuberance, and almost half were from the South, bringing with them a prickly sense of honor. In 1807, the students rebelled. The College suspended 126, which left only 35 in good standing. When the expelled students rioted, breaking down doors and windows, the trustees closed the college. In the following years, enrollment sank to half its former level (under a hundred until 1812), and the faculty, because of the lack of fees, shrank from five to two. Not for thirty-three years would Princeton again graduate the number it had in 1806. Smith was embarrassed, and after further disorder, resigned in 1812.[2]

In 1807, the College of New Jersey invited Lindsley back as a tutor, just after the worst student violence. For the next three years he taught the ancient languages and had to live, as a monitor, in Nassau Hall. He earned his license to preach in 1810 at age twenty-four, and for two years he left Princeton to accept scattered preaching assignments. In 1812, at the time Smith retired as president, Lindsley moved back to Princeton, where he stayed until he came to Nashville twelve years later. He remained a tutor for only a year before becoming a professor of languages, which meant teaching Latin and Greek. In 1913 he married Margaret Elizabeth Lawrence, the daughter of the attorney general of New York. In the next four years he served for a time as librarian (a part time job) and as something that resembled a modern dean. In 1817 he became vice president and in the same year was ordained in the New Brunswick Presbytery. He became acting president of the college in 1822–23, having declined to be a candidate for the presidency. This meteoric rise may be deceiving, for these were turbulent years at Princeton, with continuous student violence, low enrollments, only two or three professors each year, ineffective leadership, and an often divided board of trust. Princeton aspired to be at least the third-best college in America, behind only Harvard and Yale, but in these years it did not deserve this ranking.[3]

Smith's successor as president, Ashbel Green, less an intellectual and more pious, tried to tie the college more closely to the Church. Over half of the ministerial trustees—thirteen of twenty-five—worried that the college was training too few ministers. They wanted to move the college toward a more sectarian orientation, to repudiate the nonsectarian position of Smith and Lindsley. A religious revival ended the student violence, but for only two years. In 1817, students led another nasty revolt. They complained about the rigor of the *Laws* and the severity of discipline in what they saw as a near monastery under the pious Green. The boys took over Nassau Hall, locked out the faculty for four days, and brandished pistols. The college had to call in local constables to arrest some leaders and expelled twenty-four students. Most of the remainder went home, leaving only thirty at the college. By then, Lindsley was vice president and much more effective in working with students. When a beleaguered Green resigned as president in 1822, everyone assumed that Lindsley would replace him, but he chose instead to serve for the peaceful year of 1822–23 as acting president.[4]

In 1823, when Lindsley turned down the presidency, the position was not the plum it seemed. The college, after years of turmoil, was at a low ebb. In his year as acting president, Lindsley was the only professor. He had to make do with four tutors. Enrollment was low, and some trustees were not supportive of Lindsley. Back in 1811, when the church established an independent theological school at Princeton, Lindsley had ridiculed the ignorance and bigotry of many ill-trained ministers in the church. He was never tactful. In 1824, he accepted the offer in Nashville in the belief that he would have the strongest possible backing of his trustees, be an honored and unusually eminent educator in the West, avoid any religious control over his school, and above all have the freedom to build not just a college, but a university that met his impossibly high standards. Princeton students in the fall of 1823, his last year there, planted a bomb in front of Nassau Hall that blew down the door and broke many windows. For years in Nashville, Lindsley lived in fear of student disruptions. Remarkably, few if any consequence occurred.[5]

A portrait of Philip Lindsley completed in his final years at Princeton. From a portrait owned by Peabody College.

Lindsley drove a hard bargain with the trustees in Nashville. He had to assure that he and a growing family (four children) would not suffer financially from the move. Thus, he received a very large salary for the era: $2,500, or much more than he had received at Princeton. In addition, Cumberland College paid all moving costs, and promised him a new house (until completed, he received free rent). Beyond this, the trustees later authorized him to receive different fees from students, including the charges for a diploma (Lindsley refused most such gifts). In effect, Lindsley became one of the more affluent citizens of Nashville. Until he resigned from the University of Nashville in 1850, Lindsley collected his salary and enjoyed other amenities. In the last few, declining years of his university, he accepted a salary reduction to $2,000. But to cite his salary is to conceal a very complex financial situation during his tenure. He sometimes had to accept notes in payment of salary. At other times he used his own funds to buy land from the university (the money was needed to pay debts or other professors) and held this in trust until the university could redeem it at cost plus a very low interest; this represented a concealed gift, since land values continued to climb. He still held some such lots when he resigned, and thus he or his heirs benefited from what turned out to be good investments. No one will ever be able to trace the complicated financial transactions between Lindsley and his board, but he was never suspected of improprieties. He expected the trustees to live up to their commitments to him and his family, and they did.

The second commitment by the trustees involved the campus buildings. When Lindsley visited in the summer of 1824, he must have been horrified at the campus, although he always thought buildings of minor importance to a college. The only building, with its twenty-two student suites, was in terrible repair, but work was already under way on additions that were completed in 1825, after Lindsley was in charge of Cumberland College. These involved a matching three-story dorm to the east, similar to the original building, and a connecting center wing with a two-story chapel, classrooms, and on the third floor two large rooms for two literary societies and their libraries. The rectangular, unadorned brick building, 180 feet long, had rooms for eighty-eight students. (Today, Third Avenue bisects what had been the center of this building.) Visitors who noted the lack of adornment compared the main hall to a cotton mill. In 1823, before Lindsley accepted the offer, the trustees had constructed a two-story steward's house, which included in the rear a long one-story dining room for students. The board insured these two buildings for $20,000. To fulfill another critical commitment to President Lindsley, the college in 1826 completed a one-story laboratory, ninety by thirty-seven feet, the largest such building on any American campus. Finally, in 1827, the trustees built a large, imposing president's home for $7,000, located not on the campus but on the

120 acres of land the college owned to the south, only about three blocks from the main college. Unmentioned in the records were the necessary auxiliary buildings, such as stables and large privies.[6]

Lindsley, like his mentor Samuel Stanhope Smith, wanted his students to have access to the best scientific training. In fact, what most distinguished Lindsley's college was its scientific faculty and equipment. Thus, he asked the trustees for only $1,500 for new library purchases and other expenses, but more than $5,000 for physical apparatus for the laboratory. An expert on what was needed, he ordered this from London and Paris. (Princeton had wrestled with this issue for the preceding twenty years.) The apparatus soon arrived in Nashville and became the pride of the college. No one has listed the individual items, but if typical these included at least one microscope, one or more telescopes, globes, barometers, thermometers, quadrants, surveying equipment, electromagnetic machines and Leyden jars (batteries), scales, air pumps (to create vacuums), and several machines for use in physics courses. In addition, any science program needed cabinets for mineralogy and natural history, containing rocks, fossils, stuffed fish, birds, and mammals, and possibly dried plants. Lindsley would get such cabinets when Gerard Troost joined his faculty in 1828.[7]

One promise proved deceptive. When Lindsley accepted the offer in 1824, Cumberland College seemed solvent, with enough land to provide it a continuing income. Lindsley later stressed that he was misled on this issue. For the twenty-six years he presided over the college and then the university, he had to struggle each year to find enough funds to pay a faculty and maintain the campus. He did not blame the trustees, who did what they could to raise funds. Instead, he increasingly blamed the citizens of Nashville, the state government, and, as the frustrations mounted, the anti-intellectual culture of the South. In the end, a lack of support destroyed his educational experiment in Nashville. Perhaps sadder still, he could never implement the almost utopian hopes he had for a great university in the Southwest, possibly the first real American university, one comparable to those in Germany.

At his inaugural on January 12, 1825, Lindsley outlined his educational philosophy and his dreams for what he already referred to as the future University of Nashville. He had obviously spent months composing this three-hour speech. He offered, if the trustees wished, to write and deliver it in Latin, a tradition in eastern colleges. They chose English, although Lindsley continued to award degrees in Latin. The speech inspired his audience and surely thrilled the trustees, who immediately ordered a printing of two thousand copies (this was, in fact, to be Lindsley's longest publication). His short-range goal was clear—to establish a college comparable to his alma mater at Princeton. But this was to be only a beginning, for ahead lay a great university. He sought only two immediate changes from the Princeton model (to a large extent, also the model of Harvard and Yale). First,

Cumberland College was to be completely free of sectarian control. Lindsley had not come to Nashville to head a Presbyterian college, or to report to a board of trust dominated by ministers. Second, he was determined to prevent the type of student violence that had all but destroyed the College of New Jersey and that disrupted all the northeastern colleges.

In his inaugural, Lindsley tried to win a broad a base of support in Nashville and the South for what he referred to as a great educational experiment. His long-term goal was state support for a public university modeled after but more ambitious than those in North Carolina and Virginia. He knew that it would take years of work and evidence of great accomplishment to win tax support, and thus he made his immediate appeal to the affluent citizens who could, through gifts, nurture the experiment. Possibly they could help move Nashville and the area around it to a culture closer—in literacy, in scientific inquiry, in literature and the arts, and in a balanced and prosperous economy—to that of Scotland and New England. He was not openly patronizing, but he had clearly come south as a cultural missionary.

Lindsey opened, as one might expect, with a long defense of education, but his approach had novel elements. Typical of those influenced by the Scottish philosophy and by Locke, he stressed that humans had no innate skills or knowledge. Children were plastic, open to shaping influences. Any degree of intellectual excellence, any strong character, depended on education, and thus on those who supervised and trained youth. As he put it, even a child of the great Francis Bacon, if not educated, would end up as much a savage as the rudest Hottentot of Africa. Lindsley had read all he could find about educational theories. He had learned all he could about European universities. He wanted to borrow from them all, including a few laudable innovations in America (he referred to West Point). He advocated not uniformity but diverse approaches, all finally adapted to the genius and character of people, and to location. What followed was unique: an odd, detailed, and informed detour into what Lindsley was most interested in at this point in his career—the history of the ancient world.

At Princeton, under the guidance of Samuel Stanhope Smith, Lindsley had first developed an interest in human origins and in the growing archaeological knowledge about the ancient Near East. Unlike most scholars, for whom the great problem was tracing and explaining the development of civilization from its primitive beginnings, Lindsley became convinced that human history had largely been a decline from an earlier splendor. The more he immersed himself in the achievements of Ancient Egypt and Mesopotamia, the more certain he was that humanity had begun with a high level of civilization. Although in a few areas of the world this civilization had survived, in most it had not. So-called primitive peoples, as in Africa and the Americas, had thus become that way through time, as they had wandered away from the civilized points of origin. Lindsley assumed as beyond doubt the biblical story of human origins and a human history of only a few thousand years.

Adam, said Lindsley, had been the literate and knowledgeable parent of humankind, an educator of his many descendants over the nearly one thousand years he lived. God had imbued him with knowledge and wisdom. Noah, after the deluge, had begun the educational process all over again. And the distance from Noah to the great Near East civilizations could be only a few centuries. Abraham lived during a golden age in Egypt. From the ancient Near East came the civilizing influences that redeemed the early, barbaric Greeks and Romans. And thus on to Western Europe. Elsewhere, as humans wandered, they lost the skills, arts, and knowledge that constituted civilization and sank into savagery. Humans were prone, not to progress, but to degeneracy. Only unremitting attention to the education of each new generation could preserve the fragile flower of civilization. Implicit in this, but of course not stated, was a widespread concern of both churchmen and educators in the Northeast, particularly among Congregationalists and Presbyterians, that conditions west of the Appalachians, and most of all in the slave-owning parts of the old Southwest, would be conducive to cultural and moral decline. Lindsley's theory of civilizational decline thus gave added urgency to his educational experiment in Nashville. Much was at stake.

With all his celebration of ancient civilizations, Lindsley admitted that each had a fatal flaw. Only a few elites gained the education required for civilized life. All other people were subordinate. Not so in America. Lindsley was a great patriot, proud of the new American republic and its political liberty. But it was not the first to move toward this degree of enlightenment. He praised Scotland, Switzerland, and Holland as earlier experiments in republicanism. He castigated the failure of Spain, Portugal, Russia, Turkey, and even France to gain freedom for all. But for a republic to survive, all citizens had to be as literate and enlightened and virtuous as possible. Colleges could not be just for the rich. Lindsley recognized that not everyone could attend a small college in Nashville, but he held up as a model the State of Massachusetts and its common schools. Tennessee needed a system of public education, which required educated teachers. He deplored the relative ignorance of most who taught in America's elementary schools. Here was a key mission for a restored Cumberland College.[8]

To a receptive audience, Lindsley stressed that a wide range of other occupations depended on higher education, including farming and the industrial arts. He advocated liberal learning for farmers and laborers and dreamed of tax support, paid by the affluent, that would make it possible. He cited a famous industrial school in Switzerland that served mechanics. (At various times he would try, without success, to get a working farm or shops, so that poor boys could work their way through the university.) As his climatic goal, he referred to a new age: "How different an aspect would human society present were every farm-house and cottage supplied with useful books and every inmate a reader? Intelligence would then beam from every eye; and home—sacred home—would be the scene of the purest pleasures. Contentment too would smile on every countenance—with pious hope animating every bosom, and virtue gilding the pathway of life's humble pilgrimage to brighter mansions in the skies! Thus would be realized on earth the poet's golden age, and the Christian's millennial Elysium. Whenever science and religion shall have gained universal dominion, then peace and happiness will crown the lot of every mortal."[9]

Even with such soaring hopes, Lindsley tried to set some practical guidelines for the just reopened Cumberland College. After his experience at Princeton, he emphasized that the college would be Christian and republican, but in no sense sectarian. No college president ever did more to fulfill such a commitment. He begged support from all sects or persuasions. Not that Lindsley did not favor the beliefs and the polity of Presbyterianism; he eloquently defended both in church councils and had negative attitudes toward some Christian denominations, particularly Roman Catholicism. But he never allowed these personal beliefs to invade his campus. One of the early affiliated preparatory schools of the university, for example, rented the new Catholic church in Nashville for its classes. In 1834, Lindsley said of his students: "They may be Methodists, Presbyterians, Baptists, Episcopalians, Roman Catholics, Quakers—Whigs, Democrats, Federalists, Conservatives—we care not—so that they are Christians and patriots."[10] Soon, the members of his board of trust represented a spectrum of denominations. Graduation exercises moved from church to church each year. The faculty, who had to meet no religious test, soon represented several Christian confessions. Of course, from a contemporary perspective, even the Christian identity might seem sectarian. No one so viewed it at the time, and as far as the records indicate, all students were at least nominally Christian. While plenty of students resented the required chapel services, even these were broadly ecumenical.

As in all contemporary degree-granting colleges, the classical languages would remain the educational core of Cumberland College. But Lindsley always wanted the languages to be a tool, not an end in themselves. They were to reveal the ancient world, the beauties of past cultures, and introduce students to the best of philosophy, the arts, and history. It was in this sense that they would be liberating. But Lindsley was even more enthusiastic about the sciences. He wanted a university with such an array of able professors, libraries, apparatus, cabinets of natural history, botanical gardens, and astronomical observatories as to match the best of the older universities of Europe. Beyond the classics and the sciences would be the courses he would himself teach in what we now refer to as the social sciences. He was particularly interested in political and moral theory, and in the new "science" of political economy.

After his Princeton experience, it is no wonder that Lindsley spent so much time talking about student culture. He knew the college would quickly fail if it suffered the extent of violence he had known at Princeton. How could the college deal with late adolescents from various backgrounds, with no prior parental guidance? He was never able to implement the physical education program he proposed to give the boys an outlet for their energy. He talked of sports and games, a gymnasium, and work assignments, all to keep the boys from idleness, card games, drinking. Supplementing this would be the courses in moral philosophy, the parental guidance of faculty, instruction in the Bible (in the same sense, he said, that Moslems read the Koran). He had a message as much for his faculty as for parents and students: The professors should be kind and understanding, serve as older brothers, teach duty and honor, use enormous tact. As at Princeton, he wanted not less discipline, not fewer rules, but a softer, more humane way of enforcing them. Largely, he succeeded. The discipline at the University of Nashville, rigorous on paper, would be flexible in implementation.

Lindsley's final clue about the future direction of Cumberland College involved academic standards. He would not compromise his understanding of what a higher education demanded of faculty and students. The admission standards, too low in an ideal world but as high as circumstances allowed, required applicants to be proficient in the English language, skilled in elementary subjects—geography, English grammar, arithmetic—and thoroughly grounded in the elements of Latin and Greek. Because of the deficiencies of most common schools and academies, this was all one could demand. At the college, students would pursue the three main areas of instruction—classical languages; mathematics and the natural sciences; and belle lettres, which included political and moral philosophy. No student could excel, or even advance very far, in all subjects. The curriculum and the faculty would have to be flexible enough to encompass individual differences. Thus, Lindsley stressed an aroused curiosity, a sense of what the various disciplines were about, and the less definable but critical results of living and learning in an intellectual environment. The college could support selective depth in some fields and provide some sense of beauty and virtue, of what is excellent and proper. On the criteria for admission and graduation, Lindsley's university would never compromise, even as all the colleges springing up in middle Tennessee compromised from the beginning. This non-compromising commitment to standards distinguished the University of Nashville, at least in the South, but also helped spell its doom by 1850.

In his annual baccalaureate addresses to his graduates, and in occasional speeches or letters to newspapers, Lindsley kept boosting his college. In 1826, as part of a larger petition to the state legislature involving federal lands, the trustees asked to change the name of the college to the University of Tennessee. This involved, as one opponent in the legislature correctly argued, a long-term bid for state financial support. Lindsley and his trustees wanted a university like those already funded in Virginia, Georgia, and North Carolina and soon chartered in Alabama. Apparently, some legislators from east Tennessee also objected to the new name. The trustees in Nashville denied that they were attempting to outmaneuver East Tennessee College; they said they were willing to accept the designation West Tennessee University, noted the need to change the name because of confusion with a new Cumberland Presbyterian College in Kentucky, and eventually accepted as a compromise title the University of Nashville, a name Lindsley had suggested more than a year earlier. For Lindsley, the name change meant that Cumberland College would soon be the literary college of a cluster of schools or colleges that, by European precedent, would collectively constitute a true university. Called a visionary in Nashville, and often loved for it, Lindsley was deadly serious about his educational dream, and for more than a decade he believed he could achieve much of it.[11]

WHAT A GREAT UNIVERSITY ENTAILS

In his 1826 baccalaureate address, Lindsley stressed that the newly purchased 120 acres just south of the campus offered an opportunity to expand to six scattered but associated colleges. Each would have its own classrooms, steward's house and dining room, houses for professors, and a hundred students. In all, he contemplated six hundred students and twenty-five professors, the largest university in the United States. He did not propose an array of professional schools, but colleges more like those at Oxford, each with a classical orientation. But he believed at least one of the colleges should emphasize agriculture and another serve as a great training school for teachers—not what would soon be called a normal school, which trained teachers at the secondary-school level at best, but a full-fledged and demanding college. In this proposal, he anticipated the twentieth-century George Peabody College for Teachers. To facilitate agricultural training, he wanted the trustees to buy an additional hundred acres as a farm for the students. He was so committed to this vision of a great university that he begged for legislative support. Short of that, he hoped that inspired southerners would contribute the required $200,000. If no one gave, he contemplated borrowing the money. Surely, once in place, such a university would prove so useful and profitable that it would attract the needed support.[12]

At the next baccalaureate, in 1827, Lindsley raised the stakes. The whole American system, the great experiment in self-government, was at risk. If a sovereign people could live in peace and safety, and in freedom, then the American system would become the system of the world. The grand instrument for carrying it to perfection was, and would ever be, education, and education for all the people. This was revolutionary, for in most of the world the great mass of people had no rights and no political power and were incapable of mental enjoyments above those of savages or brutes.[13]

By 1829, Lindsley saw that what America lacked was not a growing number of so-called colleges, but a few colleges of the highest quality. Even the best in the East, his models for the University of Nashville, barely approached the level of great European universities, and then only in what he called the liberal arts. He believed that his struggling University of Nashville matched these eastern colleges in its standards, even as it lagged in assets. But in the West, the University of Nashville had to compete with more and more less-demanding colleges (soon three in the counties surrounding Nashville) and, not incidentally, much cheaper ones. Lindsley blamed the multiplication and dwarfish quality of western colleges and universities on the diversity of religious denominations. Each sect had to have its own college. In Ohio, Kentucky, and Tennessee, only two or three were nonsectarian, and the sectarian schools were little better than impositions on the public; they represented a grievous and growing evil. Colleges had no better reason to be sectarian than had canals or banks. The purpose of a college was instruction in the arts and sciences, not in the dogmatic theology of any sect or party. Mathematics and the various sciences were not sectarian but common to all humans.

Sects controlled colleges for one reason—to promote a sectarian position. Whenever he considered the sectarian impostures that drew away support from his own university, Lindsley fell into his most satirical and passionate language: "Let any religious sect whatever obtain the absolute direction of a college—located in a small village or retired part of the country—where their religious influence is paramount, perhaps exclusive—where the youth must necessarily attend upon such religious instructions and exercises and ceremonies as they shall prescribe—where, in fact, they can witness no other—where every sermon and prayer and form, where all private conversation and ministerial services proceed from, or are directed by, the one sect—and, is it possible that youth, at the most susceptible period of their lives, should not be operated on by such daily influences, during a period of two, four or six years? How long will the people be gulled by such barefaced impudence—by such unreasonable and monstrous pretensions?"[14]

Lindsley did not necessarily win support by such denunciations. But he was in part angered by sectarians who denounced the location of the University of Nashville because it was in a growing and increasingly diverse city, exactly where Lindsley believed a university should be. His polemic possibly had the desired effect on more cosmopolitan parents or non-Presbyterians who feared sectarianism even at the University of Nashville. He spoke as eloquently as any educator in America on these themes. He was indeed a Christian; his university would be Christian. But, as he put it, "Science and philosophy ought to know no party in Church or State. They are degraded by every such connection." Such a position was not unchristian. Just the opposite, for Christianity, "if rightly interpreted, breathes a pure angelic charity, and is as much a stranger to the strife, and intrigue, and rancor, and intolerance, and pharisaism of party, as science and philosophy can be. But as long as men are not content to be honest Christians, but will be zealous Presbyterians, Episcopalians, Methodists, Baptists, Quakers or Romanists, we must so organize our *public* seminaries of learning, as that all may intrust their sons to them without fear of danger to their religious faith."[15]

Implicit in all such pronouncements was a belief of Lindsley's drawn from the Scottish philosophy he learned from Samuel Stanhope Smith, that nature was as much a revelation of God as the Bible. If understood correctly, these two sources of truth could not be in conflict. Thus, Lindsley saw truth-seeking inquiry as itself an expression of piety, and truth as an eventual solvent of sectarian differences and intolerance. To be fully scientific in outlook was to be a good Christian. He witnessed the development of mind-stretching new theories in geology and read about early evolutionary theories but never recognized in them any threat to his irenic vision of one truth. He denounced as mere speculation theories that seemed to challenge the biblical cosmology. The same was true of the subversive forms of biblical scholarship emanating from Germany: It was also speculative, not empirically based or proven. As far as one can tell, Lindsley died in 1855 with his own certainties still in place, even as new intellectual discoveries had made them seem almost as illusioned as the more overtly biased views of the unwashed American multitudes. In particular, he never gave up on his theory that early humans were civilized, a completely untenable position by 1850. In 1852, three years before his death, he wrote to a ministerial colleague that Adam and Eve were in the image of God, perfect specimens of humanity in both beauty and culture. He noted that his belief, borrowed from Stanhope Smith, that the earliest peoples were civilized was "a doctrine which I have taught and published and battled for, during some fifty years past—both at Princeton and Nashville."[16]

The year after the University of Nashville reached its peak enrollment (126 in the summer session of 1836) and enjoyed its full complement of professors, Lindsley used a special commencement address to offer his fullest views on the status and prospects of the university and on higher education in America. In part, Lindsley did what he had to do every year—defend the college against those who charged it with elitism, those who wanted it to reflect sect or party, those who saw Nashville as a cesspool of iniquity. But on this occasion, he revealed his own critical perspective in a remarkably well-informed and critical survey of higher education in both Europe and America. He delivered this speech, which reflected the magnitude of his dream for the future, just as his beloved university began to gradually decline toward its virtual death in 1850.

Lindsley emphasized that his continuing pleas for support of his university were really aimed, not at the often flawed present, but at what the school ought to be—a real university. He defined this as "the species of institution where the largest amount and extent of liberal and useful knowledge may be acquired, under the most auspicious circumstances, and with the surest guaranty to the public against imposition and charlatanry." The University of Nashville was but a mere atom, a foundation, a nucleus, a cornerstone of this ideal, a first essay "toward the glorious consummation and perfection of my own cherished hopes and anticipations."[17] He could say the same about all American colleges or universities. All were infants or at best in their early youth; only growth and maturation would earn them the right to the title of university. He noted that the same course of study prevailed in all the credible undergraduate colleges. In this area, Nashville came close to the best and maintained as high standards as any.

Other American universities had professional schools, he said, but none at the level of European universities. Even the two great English universities with their undergraduate colleges, despite their rich resources and great libraries, were not much ahead of the best American colleges in the education they furnished their undergraduates. For undergraduates, large libraries and numerous faculty were not necessary, just a dozen or so professors and tutors for each hundred to two hundred students, a few thousand library books, and suitable scientific apparatus or museums. After all, English and American bachelor's degree graduates were only beginning their higher education at the age that European students began their university studies. That some believed their education finished at this young age was almost criminal. What should follow this beginning, as it did in the best Scottish and continental universities, was a period of advanced work by now legal adults, and not in the paternal, boarding-type undergraduate colleges that still prevailed in America. But if one recognized that the University of Nashville was still only an undergraduate college and fit one's expectations to that status, it had been a modest success. Lindsley then compared its faculty and curriculum with its older peers, such as Harvard, Yale, and Princeton. He did not claim equality but noted that Nashville had almost as many faculty in the liberal arts as did these American leaders. What it did not have were courses in law, medicine, and divinity. But, in every case, American professional schools were so inferior to European models, so much a deceitful cover for mediocrity, that the University of Nashville lost little but pretense by not establishing such schools. Lindsley could barely conceal his intellectual contempt for what passed for legal and medical training in America. He had little more respect for most denominational divinity schools.

Lindsley wanted to continue to improve the common colleges, even as he tried to improve his university. But what was needed, at least in each large state, was a comprehensive university on the continental model. This was a goal of at least twenty-five years, maybe fifty or five hundred years. What is remarkable is how much he knew about such universities, all from reading. He never toured Europe yet could give a detailed description of every cultural resource in Paris. He held up as models the universities of Berlin, Munich, Gottingen, Leipzig, Copenhagen,

Vienna, Halle, Leyden, Paris, Moscow, and St. Petersburg. He lauded the ability of the little republic of Geneva to support a model even though small university, something that the people of Tennessee, more numerous and more wealthy than those of Geneva, could easily emulate had they but the wisdom and the will. Even these great European universities were not static or perfect. They continued to add to their libraries of 100,000 to 500,000 volumes, while the United States had not a single respectable library. Lindsley then spelled out what a true state university should entail: a library with a copy of every published book in every language; specimens of every vegetable, animal, or mineral on earth; observatories, botanical gardens, models of all machines and useful inventions; the great works of art, or copies of them; museums of gems, statues, pictures, medals, monuments; and collections from all the ancient civilizations. Paris had most of these.

The faculty of a university should represent every discipline, Lindsley told his audience. Notably, he ended an exhaustive list of fields of study with biblical literature. To ensure the highest level of teaching, each professor should be able to limit himself to one speciality. Lindsley ridiculed modern-language professors who taught five or more languages, when it was impossible to be an expert in all of these. In America, the national government should fund such a great university, but it would not, and Lindsley lamented that his dream would remain a castle in the air unless the American people, and particularly rich people, embraced the dream and made it a reality. So far, Tennessee had refused support (Lindsley berated its legislators until many despised him), and the people had not filled the vacuum.

In his speech, Lindsley linked true universities with professional schools. He was not opposed to these as part of the University of Nashville, but everywhere he looked in America he found a growing number of law, medical, and divinity schools, none at a university level. He would not allow this at his University of Nashville, despite growing local support for medical and law schools. He was, however, open to an engineering professor for the University of Nashville, for the usefulness of his instruction. As for medicine, neither the United States nor England had a medical college comparable to those in the best German and French universities. The University of Paris, for example, had a medical faculty of fifty-eight; admission required a B.A, and the four-year course of study ended with a rigorous examination. No wonder, he noted, that poorly educated American physicians, already in possession of an M.D. degree (a joke, he said), studied at Paris to bring their skills up to date. If anything, Lindsley was even more contemptuous of what passed for law schools in America, and of the overall ability of lawyers.

As for theological schools, "the least said or done, the better." Such schools, almost by necessity sectarian, had no place in Lindsley's model university. But he had a happy and prescient idea: Various denominations might establish theological schools adjacent to a great university. The religious sects would own and control their schools and pay for them. He envisioned Episcopal, Methodist, Presbyterian, and Baptist schools all clustered around the "great literary Headquarters," with their faculties freely "associating, studying, conversing and disputing with each other." They would never agree to think alike, but they might "acquire a more tolerant, indulgent, catholic spirit; and agree to differ, with sentiments of mutual respect, good-will and Christian charity. They might learn that the worst heresy is uncharitableness; and that a holy life is the best, if not the only, evidence of orthodox principles."[18] In these suggestions, he anticipated the present clusters of denominational theological schools around such major universities as the University of Chicago and the University of California, Berkeley.

LINDSLEY AS CITIZEN AND CLERGYMAN

One might assume that these almost utopian dreams of a great future university in Nashville would have caused practical Nashvillians to view Lindsley as an airy intellectual, completely out of contact with reality. Not so. He was possibly the most respected man in the city, gracing Nashville with his learning. The newspapers, at least in his early years, celebrated his reputation and even exaggerated it. He seemed to be awesomely informed, a cosmopolitan critic, and a great scholar. Even newspaper editors who disagreed with the policies of the university bowed before his great erudition, his worldwide reputation. His dignity, his demeanor, his eloquence, and his superb speaking ability set him apart. No one called him by his first name. Without intent, he was his own best press agent.[19]

The elevated descriptions were only half correct. Lindsley was a noted educator. His essays on educational issues were as informed, and at times as daring, as those of any other college president. But a great scholar he was not, at least in the modern sense of the word. He read in all fields and had imposing critical skills. A generalist at its best, he was able to synthesize enormous amounts of information and communicate it to others. He was thus a great teacher. Before coming to Nashville, he had two sets of lectures almost ready for publication, but never completed them. He never had time for serious inquiry, never did any of the archaeological digging that lay behind his fascination with the ancient Near East. And he never had much time for probing philosophical or theological analysis. Any beliefs that challenged his worldview he deemed either speculative, and thus beyond proof, or simply misinformed.

Lindsley became a community asset in Nashville, much valued for his contributions to the city and state. He was quite simply the ablest serious lecturer in the area. His speeches at the university, at local churches, or before public audiences were often three hours long, all carefully written and so delivered as to hold large audiences captive. For any great public event, Lindsley was the person to engage for a speech. Thus, he gave an address to commemorate George Washington's hundredth birthday in 1832. When the aged and famous Pierre Lafayette visited Nashville in 1825, Lindsley prepared an appreciative tribute. He soon became president of the State Lyceum, was much in demand for sermons in various Nashville churches, and held honored positions in his own Presbyterian denomination. He served as president of the local branch of the American Bible Society, was a leading supporter of the Tennessee Colonization Society, and became a spokesman for temperance reform (he denounced distilled liquors, but not wine). He regularly contributed articles to local newspapers, some in defense of his university, some witty or satirical in nature. His was a unique niche, but all in all he was one of the most famous and respected citizens of Tennessee, a good counterpart to the state's notable political heroes.

Yet, Lindsley was never a member of the local gentry. He was an alien from the North and, more important, aloof, dignified, and in time even a quaint anachronism. Political economy, one of his favorite subjects, became more important to him in Nashville. He did not hesitate to speak out on policy issues, even though, as university president, he insisted on complete neutrality. He did not want to offend Whigs or Democrats, remained a close friend of Andrew Jackson, and worked with trustees from both parties. But privately, he was the perfect Whig. He supported a balanced economy, defended protective tariffs, denied any basis in America for class conflict, and wanted a positive government to assure needed moral and economic progress. His ideal society was that of Massachusetts. He deplored political conflict and scolded abolitionists on one hand, secessionists on the other. He disliked slavery and considered the slave trade one of the great injustices of all time, but he favored gradual emancipation. In all ways he was cautious, moderate, and in his last years considered by almost everyone a model conservative, one who valued order as the basis of a free society.

Lindsley continued to play a significant role in his church, even after moving to Nashville. He attended two critical meetings of the General Assembly of the Presbyterian Church in the United States of America and served as moderator in 1834, just before the split into Old School (legally, the continuing denomination) and New School in 1837. He deplored the controversy, but in the crunch adhered to the Old School, as did most southern Presbyterians and those with a strong attachment to Princeton. Typically, he was most resistant to New School deviations from what he saw as the policy and discipline of the church, not the anti-slavery stand of many of the New School presbyteries. In all his sermons, he was nominally orthodox. He never directly challenged any of the tenets of the Westminster Confession and always affirmed its doctrines, the central doctrines of all the Reformed churches, as the most coherent and logical of all the major traditions, but not thereby exclusive or alone consistent with a reasonable understanding of the Bible. He deplored the ugly and mistaken stereotypes by then attached to the label "Calvinism" but admitted that even this most logical of Christian confessions involved several issues beyond human understanding. He acknowledged that the Bible offered no exact prescriptions for either church polity or the content of worship, but he did believe the republican polity of Presbyterianism was most consistent with the political institutions of the United States.

Yet, this overt orthodoxy concealed what most typified Lindsley's approach to controverted doctrinal issues. His views remained close to those of his mentor, Samuel Stanhope Smith. He simply refused to become involved in complex theological issues, resting his case on common sense and speculative restraint. He affirmed the leading doctrines of the Reformation but would not try to unravel what remained for him, and he believed for any human, paradoxes and even contradictions that one must leave to God. He was in temperament the opposite of the leading New England theologians of his day, beginning with Nathaniel Taylor and what many referred to as the Yale school. These latter-day disciples of Jonathan Edwards erected elaborate structures of rationalizations to justify the ways of God with humans. Lindsley found these unconvincing and certain to lead to novelties, modernized updates of traditional doctrines, that would divide and subvert the church.

Lindsley illustrated this restraint in two sermons, one that he probably used several times at ordinations, and an 1851 sermon preached after he left Nashville.[20] He noted that much in nature we observe and describe but cannot fully understand, and the same is true of the Bible. Christians accept, on the basis of revelation, that their God created the visible universe, but they do not know how he did it. They know that God will raise the dead to life at the resurrection, but they cannot conceive how. They know that human and divine nature join in the Christ, but they do not know how. The trinity involves one God and three persons, but this truth lies beyond human understanding. He extended such reasoning to the most lofty and difficult doctrines of the Church. Evil, crime, pain, misery prevail in this world, which God created as it is. Yet, we know from revelation that God cannot sin, cannot be guilty of any crime. Thus, how is it that a perfect God permits evil? Lindsley's answer: "*How* this can be—how God could make a world with sin in it, or with the certainty or even possibility of sin's ever entering it, and yet not be sinful, or the author of sin, we are not informed."[21] Likewise impossible to understand is how Jesus can be the son of an eternal God, yet himself also eternal. Finally, and this he frequently admitted, God elects humans to salvation, and as the creator and sustainer of all things, his will is implicated in all that humans do. He is the ultimate cause, with full foreknowledge of all that takes place. Yet, in a seeming contradiction, we also know that humans are free agents, fully responsible for what they choose and do. How can this be? No human knows.

A willingness to accept such opposed dualities as givens meant that Lindsley was willing to affirm all the central doctrines of evangelical Christianity, but in no theoretical sense to defend them. He would not argue the issues, take sides among contending Christians. He advocated an unusual degree of tolerance. As he put it, "A bigot or a persecutor cannot be a Christian. . . . Christ denounced every symptom of a persecuting spirit in his disciples."[22] He quoted Paul in Galatians: "But the fruit of the Spirit is love, joy, peace, long-suffering, gentleness, goodness, faith, meekness, temperance." It was this approach that made him such an enemy of narrow sectarianism, so open to other Christians who were, after all, part of one church. His preaching was usually practical and moralistic, not doctrinal. As late as 1833, he used an ordination sermon to talk about the polity and creed of his own church for the first time. In outlook, he was closest to Thomas Campbell, the father of Alexander and the grandfather of the Restoration Movement. But Lindsley, although intellectually in favor of a unified Christianity, or even of making the Bible the only creed of the Church, noted that those who emphasized a creedless church, or the Bible only, soon turned this position into an exclusive point of doctrine, a creed of creedlessness. He doubted any strategy would dissolve all the divisions in Christianity. He honored his own tradition. The answer was openness to others, generosity, a type of ecumenism that led, not to one church or one creed or lack of creed, but cooperation across denominational boundaries.

Although unwilling to indulge in doctrinal debate, Lindsley was a sharp, pungent, and courageous preacher. He was as prophetic as Jeremiah. He revealed this in an installation sermon he delivered at the Nashville Presbyterian church in 1833. In this more than three-hour-long address, he challenged the new pastor as no one had before. He noted that Christians, since the days of Luther, had become more sensitive to worldly evils, more decent if not more heavenly. He thought the new moral philosophy, which he taught to his students in the University of Nashville, had helped create a new level of moral sensitivity. He thus offered his litany of former evils accepted and perpetuated by Christians. For his Nashville audience, he began with slavery. "After having stolen and forced from their native home, and transported across the ocean or buried beneath its waves forty millions of our African brothers; of whom and their descendants scarcely six millions remain as the fragments and witnesses of our Christian charity; we are just beginning to boast of our Christian chivalry in attempting to close the floodgates of this long-continued and more than fiendish contempt of the most obvious dictates of justice and humanity."[23]

Lindsley's views on slavery were complex and not always consistent. He denounced slavery in his farewell address at Princeton, which students published. Much later, Lindsley dropped the section on slavery from a compilation of his manuscript sermons, suggesting some modifications of his sharp denunciations of 1824. In the address, he asked when Christian charity would awake to the tears and groans and cries and suffering of the two million Africans dragged from their distant homes by Christian avarice. Even the tenderest mercies shown such Africans in America were a cruel mockery of treatment harsher than Moslems ever inflicted on Christians, the bitterest cup ever presented to the lips of humanity. The Old World had never known the level of ignorance and depravity exhibited in America, particularly in the South. He supported colonization as worthy in itself but knew it would never touch the problem of most blacks in America. Most African slaves would have to be emancipated on the soil they cultivated. How? He had no answer.

Once in the South, he eventually concluded that precipitous emancipation would cause more problems than it cured. He blamed such slavery on Christianity as a whole, not just on slave owners, whom he knew in many cases to be honorable people trapped in a tragic situation. As he aged, he hoped for gradual measures, such as opportunities for slaves to earn their freedom; laws that gave the status of fathers, not mothers, to children; laws forbidding internal slave trade; the repeal of all laws against the education and emancipation of slaves; and appropriations by both federal and state governments to aid blacks who wished to emigrate to Liberia. He always argued that the education of blacks, even helping them read the Bible, would lead them to demand freedom. He also suggested that, as cotton culture spread to other lands, and southern planters lost a near monopoly, southerners would have to diversify their economy, and in such a mixed economy, without artificially high cotton prices, slavery would no longer be profitable and would thus gradually disappear. Yet, he feared that blacks and whites could not live together in peace, and viewed blacks as culturally inferior to whites.[24]

His denunciations of slavery, and above all of the slave trade, were only a beginning for Lindsley. "Nor has Africa wept alone under the scourge of Christian barbarism. Where are the millions of red men who once held undisputed dominion over this mighty continent, form pole to pole, and from ocean to ocean? The meek, peaceful, self-denying, benevolent Christian, of another hemisphere, whose heroic creed is, to do to others as he would have them do unto him, has kindly undertaken the management of all these fair lands upon his own account.—After having exterminated the aboriginal possessors, by means and with views, which he dares to parade upon the pages of history, as disinterested, magnanimous, philanthropic, Christian!" Next: "How have the Jews been treated among Christian nations and by Christian churches during the last fifteen hundred years? How are they treated *now* in almost every Christian state and city under heaven?" He followed with a similar statement about Moslems. Then he broadened out: "Look at the history of European colonization and commerce in an every quarter of the globe. Alas, what a debt does Christendom owe to pagan Asia, to pagan Africa, to pagan America! Will it ever be repaid?" Wherever Christians have colonized, they have invariably "made the natives worse instead of better, " and created among them a "hatred and aversion to Christianity."[25]

After such cosmic evils, Lindsley listed some less comprehensive ones, all aimed at a Nashville audience: whiskey drinking (a nation of drunkards was as unseemly as a nation of robbers), dueling, horse racing ("the most destructive and pernicious species of gambling, dissipation, and reckless knavery, ever yet contrived by the ingenuity of man or demon,") and acquisitive business practices.[26] He also cited local violence, the evils of warfare, intolerant bigotry (he listed martyrs from both Catholic and Protestant societies), and the pernicious effects of a union of church and state (separation was a near crusade on the part of Lindsley). He concluded that every national church is and "must be antichristian," including the churches of Scotland and England. He begged the new pastor to go beyond orthodoxy, beyond sermons against doctrinal errors, beyond exhibitions of theological profundity, in order to preach against habitual practices and indulgences.[27]

Half of these evils applied directly to his Nashville audience. At times, he seemed to be preaching at some of his board of trust—those who drank whiskey, raced horses, dueled, bought slaves, suppressed Indians, or exhibited religious intolerance. In fact, President Andrew Jackson, the most famous trustee of all, must have been uneasy if he sat in that Nashville church in 1833 (he was most likely in Washington). This was Lindsley at his moral best and political worst. He could not for long resist bouts of honesty and truth-telling. He continuously created enemies, even as he tried to gain support for his university. He was a local Jeremiah or Savonarola, and he suffered from his role. Yet, most of Nashville as a whole continued to respect him even when it did not heed him, to celebrate his educational visions even when it had not a dime to spare to support them.

Lindsley often suffered alienation in Nashville and in the South. He was far from the culture, even the climate, for which he now felt nostalgia. Even as he defended Nashville as a perfect location for a southern university (just far enough north to escape the diseases of the cotton belt), he privately fretted at the awful weather. Nashville endured a series of very cold winters with subzero temperatures he had never experienced in New Jersey. Yet, the summer heat and occasional drought could be worse. A gardener, he lamented his inability to grow good vegetables—no good fruit, melons, potatoes. He could not buy good butter and cheese, pumpkin pies, or even beef and mutton. Only the resented tobacco and cotton grew well in such a climate, and these were not worth growing. In one only partly whimsical essay, he argued that everything degenerated in Tennessee. Physicians were made by a guess (no real medical education), lawyers by magic, parsons by inspiration (a dig at the type of hot Christianity that offended him), legislators by grog, merchants by mammon, farmers by necessity, and schoolmasters by St. Nicholas, to do penance for the sins of their youth. Even charitable acts were never open and direct, for the strange people of Nashville had to give a party or a ball or a dance as an inducement to give money to others. But most bitter was his very personal comment: "Our colleges and schools are like fires kindled upon icebergs—their light is scarcely visible before they are extinguished." This sad reflection is an excellent introduction to the fate of that great experiment, Philip Lindsley's University of Nashville.[28]

CHAPTER THREE

Princeton West

IT HAD A RELATIVELY BRIEF CAREER OF ONLY A QUARTER OF A century. Yet, Philip Lindsley's University of Nashville first justified the reputation of Nashville as a center of higher education in the South. It was his Princeton in the West. In 1835 he also referred to Nashville as the "Athens of the West." It all ended in 1850. Never again would the University of Nashville be able to sustain a college of arts and sciences. It tried, and in brief interludes claimed such a status, but never with the faculty or educational standards that justified the claim.

ACADEMIC CULTURE

In almost all respects, the college that Lindsley inherited in late 1824 had already followed a pattern common in the United States. Lindsley only added some emphases that had distinguished Princeton (the code of laws, unusual stress on the sciences, and an emphasis on educating political leaders). It was, nominally, a four-year undergraduate college leading to a bachelor of arts. As did all such colleges, its curriculum had at its core Latin and Greek. Supplementing these were broader cultural studies of the ancient world; courses in what then was denominated natural philosophy (natural sciences); advanced mathematics; belle lettres (literature, philosophy, some ancient history, political and economic theory, and often religion); and skills in writing and declamation.

This description conceals the many compromises, which Lindsley constantly regretted, that imperiled such a traditional college program. First, colleges could not enforce high entrance requirements for fear of losing students to competitors. In fact, they could seldom keep boys for all four years. And "boys" is the correct term, for, as Lindsley's own career illustrated, most entered college around the age of sixteen. Even then, few entered as freshmen, which would have meant a loss of face for the academy or preparatory school that trained them for college. At Nashville, as at Princeton, Lindsley almost had to admit up to half of his students to the junior class. This meant graduation at the age of eighteen or nineteen, and a pattern of immaturity in his students that he deplored. Few students, or few parents, wanted to pay for four years of college, and there were always small colleges that would gladly admit boys to advanced status rather than lose enrollment and tuition. Soon, it became almost necessary for colleges to work with preparatory schools, as did the University of Nashville. Colleges would approve their curriculum, publicly announce their willingness to accept the schools' graduates, and try to use this informal certification system to recruit students. Admission to a college and class placement had to depend on entrance exams, as they did at Nashville. Students at times struggled to advance too quickly, and some had to accept demotion, typically from junior to sophomore standing.

The University of Nashville was a residential college. Given the age of its students, it almost had to be. Tuition was twenty-five dollars a session (later briefly raised to thirty), fifty dollars a year, but room rent was only two dollars a session, as was the right to use the library. Firewood, laundry, and servants cost extra. Local boys could live and board at home (no reduction in tuition), but even they had to make a small contribution for firewood to heat the classrooms. Parents could allow their sons to live with Nashville relatives or in rare cases even arrange off-campus housing and board. At up to two dollars a week, board was the most expensive item for students. They had to contract board with the steward, who furnished meals in the small dining room attached to the steward's house. This arrangement led to student discontent, and at least one near riot. The university did not pay wages to the steward but leased the house and dining room to the family who offered the highest bid. The steward bought all supplies and paid all servants. The university contracted this yearly and often changed stewards in a losing attempt to hire someone who met the student expectations. In all, a student needed about $150 a year to meet his minimal expenses, more than nearby denominational schools charged, less than Harvard or Princeton.

The college followed the then standard calendar. The first or winter session lasted from November until April, the summer session from May to commencement in early October. At first, the college observed no holidays, but in the last years before suspension in 1850, students often had a week-long holiday from Christmas to New Year's. Always, July 4 merited major celebrations. The students' two annual vacations occurred in the four or five weeks between sessions.

Classes met six days a week, with most students and full-time faculty in class five or six hours a day. The few freshmen, along with the sophomores, devoted much of their time to Latin, Greek, and mathematics, moving through algebra, geometry, trigonometry, and on to calculus if they were able. The classical studies climaxed in the junior year with logic, rhetoric, political and economic philosophy, astronomy and physics, and chemistry and natural history, with courses in moral philosophy or evidences of Christianity in their last two years. The mode of instruction was conventional—text and recitation. Faculty members lectured on occasion, but lectures were supplemental to regular coursework and often open to larger audiences. Above all, students were privileged to hear, on special occasions, Lindsley's long, carefully written, and eloquently presented lectures. In each discipline, a student was expected to master a text, with more demanding texts in the junior and senior years. These were classic works in a field, some written for lay people, particularly in political philosophy and political economy. The university did not have a catalogue, but in the *Laws* that governed all aspects of university life, published an imposing list of books that students were to master before graduation. In each session they would try to absorb the content of at least one book per course, with the professor's help. Almost daily, they had to recite what they had learned. This at times meant scheduled written reports delivered orally, with frequent criticism from professors or other students. The low enrollment meant that most classes were small and resembled seminars. By the testimony of later graduates, the plan worked well. Above all, it forced students to write and speak often, and in time, fluently. In addition, all students, on a rotating basis, had to present evening orations in the chapel before the whole student body.[1]

Grades and competition were largely absent at the University of Nashville. For entrance exams, professors assigned number grades and at times may have listed such grades for students in their courses. But progress toward graduation largely involved mastery of a text, and thus a body of knowledge, to the satisfaction of the professor who made up what the university called a department. The system did not include failure; students who did not attend classes or complete assigned work were routinely asked to leave the university, at any time during a session. But students who could not quickly master some subjects or complete some texts simply had to remain longer and gain competence in some fields. In a few cases, they had to drop down to a lower class. By a decision of the earlier students, the university did not award honors at graduation, a move Lindsley applauded. It distinguished the University of Nashville from northeastern colleges. (The university violated this decision in a few years.) Each student who completed a degree was honored equally at commencement. Most offered orations, which meant the celebrations sometimes lasted for five hours or more.

Examinations, in the modern sense, were not part of the system. Because students recited almost daily, they were thus continuously in the spotlight, their weaknesses known to professors. The goal, for each student, was to progress toward a standard of competence and intellectual engagement that justified a bachelor of arts degree, a standard higher than that of any other southern college and comparable to Princeton's. More than half of the enrolled students never made it to graduation. This was not necessarily a mark of failure, for some never intended to stay that long and gained much from their study. The serious students had the advantage of daily, often informal, interaction with an unusually able and cosmopolitan faculty. As Lindsley often boasted, students were plunged into an intense intellectual environment which was as important as any completed courses. Students could enroll at any time, even in the middle of a session, simply paying a prorated tuition. They could also skip a session and then resume their work.

The climax of each session, the closing exercises, were not exams in the modern sense, but public demonstrations of competence that extended for up to ten days. Nothing in the record suggests that students ever failed these exercises, even if they performed poorly. Through daily evaluations, professors had already determined which students would perform during the exercises—and "performance" was the correct word. Everyone in Nashville was invited—parents; young ladies from the excellent Nashville Female Academy; common school students; and anyone else who wanted to come—to hear the long speeches on assigned subjects, or readings in Latin and Greek, all tied to courses taken during the preceding session. Each of the four classes performed, but at different levels of expectation. The exercises served several purposes. They forced students to do their best possible work, were part of the students' training for subsequent leadership roles, and allowed the university to demonstrate its achievement to the larger community. In the early years, from 1825 to 1835, the exercises were generally well attended, although many dragged on all day and must have bored audiences. Great public festivals they were not.

The exercises culminated in more of the same. On Commencement Day, after a grand academic procession to a Nashville church (the college chapel was too small), most graduating seniors performed again in sessions that lasted, often without a break, for four or five hours. This was a well-advertised public event well attended in early years. After 1826, when the state assembly was in session in Nashville, it always suspended its business so that legislators from across the state could attend the university commencement and take pride in the caliber of education available in Nashville.[2]

FACULTY

The glory of the University of Nashville was its able faculty and high standards. Its undoing was its failure to achieve financial solvency and a suitable campus and buildings. At first, the successes overshadowed the failures. But after 1845, the struggle to make ends meet, to win outside support, and to make do with a poorly maintained physical plant slowly took its toll.

For an excellent undergraduate program in 1825, a college needed at least five professors and enough tutors to meet the instructional load dictated by enrollment. As was then a standard practice, a college appointed only one professor in each discipline or cluster of disciplines. At the University of Nashville, he headed a department. Tutors were responsible for extra teaching, if needed. They had little status and low salaries, $500 or $600 a year plus room and board. As Lindsley reorganized Cumberland College in 1825, he contemplated only five departments: ancient languages; mathematics and physics; chemistry and natural history; moral, intellectual, and political philosophy; and modern languages. This division of disciplines would change only slightly, to accommodate the interests of faculty. For Lindsley, having so few departments was a compromise dictated by financial necessity. He always bemoaned the diversity of courses taught by individual professors, and the lack of specialization and expertise this entailed. In his dreams for a great university, the undergraduate program would have had at least ten professors and ten departments. As it was, the university maintained a regular faculty of four professors throughout its history, with at least two tutors in periods of peak enrollment. Except for one brief interval, it never paid the fifth professor—in modern languages. This was an American pattern, again made necessary by a lack of funds. In most years, someone taught at least French and a second language (German, Spanish, or Italian) on a proprietary basis. The university approved but did not pay such professors, who lived on student fees. Financially strapped students could not take a modern language, and none was required for graduation.

Whatever the financial straits, Lindsley kept his full faculty together, year after year, even when the enrollment did not justify it. This meant an annual expenditure of around $7,000 including his salary of $2,500, a salary of $1,000 to $1,500 for each of the three other salaried professors, $1,000 for two tutors, and small sums for a part-time treasurer and a few servants to maintain the classrooms. Even as the campus buildings decayed around him, Lindsley refused to cut instructional costs.[3]

Largely because of its professors, the University of Nashville could claim an eminence that rivaled its parent and model, Princeton. First among these professors was Lindsley himself. His national recognition added luster to the university. While at Nashville, he turned down at least four offers to head other universities. His breadth of knowledge, his strength in political and economic theory, his brilliance in the classroom, and his moral example made an indelible impact on students. He did not want to remain active in classical studies and gladly handed over instruction in Latin and Greek to other professors and tutors. Correctly, he prided himself on his teaching of moral philosophy, in all of its dimensions. In this, he was typical of an emerging cadre of college presidents.

The drudge work of any college was the endless effort to advance students in Latin and Greek. No college could survive without a competent professor in this area. Lindsley could take over these classes briefly, but he preferred not to. For more than half of Lindsley's presidency, Nathaniel Cross served, first as tutor for two years and then as professor of ancient languages. Although he added no distinction to the school, Cross was highly competent, admired by his students, and at least as able as most of the dozens of classical teachers serving in American colleges. Like almost all professors at the time, he had earned only a bachelor of arts. He was in Nashville in 1824 when Cumberland College reopened, and he was on the faculty when it closed in 1850, the only professor who could claim this distinction. But in 1826, he resigned his position over a matter of unequal salaries and opened a classical academy of his own. He returned in 1838 and remained until the end, when he again opened his own academy. The university hired, in succession, two tutors and two relatively undistinguished classicists to teach the ancient languages during the twelve years that Cross was absent. It was Lindsley's fame, not his teaching, that maintained the reputation of the university in classics.[4]

It would be the sciences that would distinguish the university. Few eastern colleges rivaled the University of Nashville in this area that was so important to Lindsley. The first professor of mathematics and natural philosophy, who preceded Lindsley's tenure, resigned in 1827. His replacement was George Hamilton, a Princeton graduate soon much loved by Lindsley, the board, and students. He served from 1827 until his death from cholera in 1849, which helped insure a suspension of classes in 1850. Although his own illness, or illness in his family, forced Hamilton to leave his position on two occasions, for a total of six years, in each case the board worked to get him back. A great mathematician he was not. The range of subjects taught allowed him no time for research, even had he been so inclined.[5]

The other early scientist, George T. Bowen, showed great promise when Lindsley recruited him. He had completed an undergraduate degree and postgraduate work with Benjamin Silliman at Yale, then the best-known scientist in America. Bowen's field was chemistry and natural philosophy, and it was he who pushed for a new laboratory and carried on research intended for publication. He died tragically at the age of twenty-six, in October 1828.[6] His replacement was the most eminent professor ever connected with the University of Nashville, Gerard Troost, who had already joined the faculty in February 1828. He had a special appointment, and only a part-time appointment after 1831, when he became the first state geologist of Tennessee. Because of his special talents, he took the title of professor of chemistry, mineralogy, and geology, but he also took over some of the courses taught by Bowen. Unlike other professors, he was not required to live near campus or take responsibility for monitoring students outside the classroom. In most years, he was absent during part of at least one session, as he carried out detailed geological surveys to present to the Tennessee General Assembly; he completed ten reports by his death, and once almost drowned while crossing a mountain stream in east Tennessee.

That someone like Troost would relocate to Nashville and grace the university with his services was even more unlikely than Lindsley's unexpected acceptance of the presidency of Cumberland College in 1824. Troost moved to the city in 1827 at the age of fifty-two. He was still at work in his laboratory the day before he died in August 1850. Born in Bois-Le-Duc in the Netherlands, he earned a medical degree at Leyden through an apprenticeship program. He later did advanced work in chemistry, which earned him a certificate in pharmacy at Amsterdam in 1801. This provided him more rigorous scientific training than was available in any medical school in America.

Troost became a distinguished scientist in Europe, for a time practicing pharmacy in Amsterdam. In the turbulent Napoleonic Wars, he twice entered the army of the Netherlands, then under French control, and was wounded, apparently while serving as a medic. In 1807, Louis Napoleon, the puppet king of the Netherlands, sent him to Paris to extend his scientific studies and to collect minerals. For two critical years, he studied and worked in the Museum of Natural History of France, where he became an admiring disciple and student of Abbe René-Just Haüy, head of the museum, the first great modern mineralogist and the author of the first comprehensive classification scheme for minerals. Troost adopted this scheme and in frequent trips throughout Europe began collecting every mineral specimen he could find. He also completed his first publications, including a Dutch translation of some of the books of Alexander Humboldt, the great geographer and explorer, who became his correspondent and friend.

In 1809, Troost joined a French-Dutch expedition to Java as its scientist. To avoid the English blockade, the party boarded an American ship, which was captured by the French and brought to port at Dunkirk. Under arrest until he could identify himself, Troost had to return to Paris, where in 1810 he was elected a corresponding member of the French Museum, a diploma he proudly displayed later in Nashville (this was his Ph.D.). In the same year, he escaped the turmoil of Europe and moved to Philadelphia, married Margaret Tage in 1811, and would soon have a son and daughter. His wife died in 1819, and Troost remarried in 1825; his second wife already had children. In Philadelphia, he helped found the Academy of Natural Sciences in 1812 and for several years served as its president. He lectured, traveled widely to do geological surveys and add to his growing collection of minerals, became a professor in a new college of pharmacy, and taught in the Philadelphia Museum. But, as so often in his life, he made some poor decisions, particularly in the unfamiliar area of economic entrepreneurship. He helped launch a firm in Maryland, near Annapolis, to manufacture alum, a valued emetic and astringent. It soon failed, stripping him of all his assets. In 1825, Troost and his new wife joined other American intellectuals at the new socialist colony at New Harmony, Indiana, the first of Robert Owens's communal colonies in America. Troost went as an invited scientist and taught in the colony's adult school. Like other New Harmony colonists, he soon suffered from the internal conflict and the early end of the communal aspects of this much publicized experiment. His Catholic wife was unhappy there, and his daughter of fifteen eloped in an unfortunate marriage that Troost had annulled. In 1827 he fled New Harmony and, for reasons unclear, came to Nashville. He apparently thought he could find a position; possibly he hoped to serve as state geologist or as a professor in the newly thriving university. Nashville, the closest sizeable city to New Harmony, was growing rapidly. Such was the bulk of Troost's cabinets that he must have loaded down two or three wagons for this difficult move.

Nashvillians must have been puzzled by Troost when he first arrived, an aging Dutchman who spoke English with a heavy accent. They may have suspected him of being a charlatan or an early P. T. Barnum when he rented space above a store to display his cabinets. In an early lecture at the Masonic Hall, he described what he had spent his adult life collecting— the largest mineralogical collection in America, fossils that marked the age of various rocks in Tennessee, and a huge assortment of marine and freshwater shells. He had on order from Philadelphia a collection of fish and reptiles (he collected snakes and astonished visitors by his calm handling of rattlesnakes). Finally, he had the largest library on natural history west of the mountains. It took time for the locals to grasp what Troost was all about. His goal was to establish the kind of natural science museum in Nashville that he had known in Paris and Philadelphia. He solicited gifts to create it (donors could visit free) but never won much local support for his scheme. So Troost sought a position at the university and began lobbying to become, in 1831, the state geologist. Neither job paid well. In view of his state post and his paid lectures to local audiences, the board briefly reduced his university salary to $500 a year, and it was never more than $1,000. Every surplus dollar he raised went for new specimens from Philadelphia and Europe and for books.

Troost's arrangement with the university allowed him to retain ownership of all the cabinets, which nonetheless became a boasting point for the school. No other university had such collections. At Troost's death in 1850, after thirty yeas of collecting in Europe and America, his cabinets held 13,582 identified minerals, in all probability the largest such collection in the world. (A later catalogue of these minerals created by the Free Public Library of Louisville, which bought the collection from Troost's heirs for $20,500, ran to 1,400 pages.). Troost was, according to one visiting English naturalist, unkempt in dress, disorganized, and always short on funds. At his death, he was so poor that the university board had to appropriate funds to give him a decent burial in the city cemetery, while the State of Tennessee provided a small marker.[7]

Troost was lonely in Nashville. To compensate for having no one to talk to in his areas of specialization, he continued to correspond with everyone in the fields of mineralogy, crystallography, paleontology, chemistry, and geology. One of some ten scientists around the world who became an expert on meteorites, he collected at least two in Tennessee and submitted both to qualitative and quantitative chemical analysis. He also speculated wisely about their source—clearly celestial and not terrestrial, and of unknown origin but possibly from the breakup of a planet. He regularly sent articles and specimens to European journals or to the new Smithsonian Institution. As state geologist, he surveyed as many counties as possible, dutifully searching for minable minerals (he first identified the rich zinc deposits of Jefferson County), but he could not resist his own research, which primarily involved fossils in different geological strata. In almost all his geological reports, he worked with a publisher to include handsome color maps with hashes to indicate elevations, topographic overviews with elevations, and printed names. A few days before his death, he sent to the Smithsonian a manuscript on encrinites he had found in Tennessee. These were early invertebrates with a lilylike shape. As always, he sought a local artist to make careful drawings based on collected specimens in his cabinets. After Troost died, a curator at the Smithsonian did not publish the monograph but stole from it for his own publications. Only fifty years later did the Smithsonian discover the injustice and publish Troost's essay. Later, a geologist at Peabody Normal College and another at Vanderbilt offered appreciative evaluations of his pioneering work, pointing out in what areas geologists had improved upon it.[8]

On every possible occasion, Troost showed off his cabinets or offered what he called popular lectures on his sciences. While his humor amused local audience, each lecture soon soared well beyond their competence. Even Lindsley could not begin to keep up with Troost, and possibly for good reason (his geology, and his evolutionary theories, would have challenged the orthodoxy of Lindsley). Upon arriving in Nashville, Troost gave a series of lectures on natural history that were marvelous in the knowledge they revealed, particularly in the history of several scientific disciplines from antiquity to 1827. Even today, these lectures, written carefully in a notebook, deserve publication. He kept up with recent research, read every book in the broad area of natural history, and knew the work of every prominent scientist. For example, just after publishing his first full geological survey of Tennessee in his fifth report to the general assembly in 1839, Troost read some new books from Europe, including a new and better classification system developed by Adam Sedgwick in England. In his sixth report, he carefully explained the new information and updated his earlier survey to reflect it.[9] After Troost's death, Lindsley appropriately remarked: "We should never look upon his like again."[10]

Troost was religious, in his own way. His background was in the liberal Remonstrant or Arminian faction of the Dutch church. His work led him to reject almost all of the biblical cosmology. He laughed at lingering theories of a worldwide flood and lamented the scholastic forms of orthodoxy that had retarded advances in the geological and biological sciences. He emphasized the vast age of the earth; charted the eons before life emerged as revealed in what he called primeval or non-fossil-bearing rocks, some exposed in the high Smokies of east Tennessee; and traced, as carefully as stratified fossils allowed, the emergence of new life forms and the extinction of many past forms. Although the geologic column was now reasonably clear, he could not explain, empirically, the emergence of new species. Like so many idealists or transcendentalists, he attributed it all to a divine plan that led to the eventual emergence of humans. This causal reference to a mind behind the process, about all that kept Troost close to Christian orthodoxy, was enough to satisfy the always generous Lindsley.

Troost attracted few disciples among students. The most interested was John Berrien Lindsley, the son of the president. But Troost was a popular teacher in chemistry and geology, and the boys found him memorable. He could be patronizing even to adults, often prefacing a long explanatory section in his Tennessee reports with the warning that no one not abreast of the latest research, mostly from Europe, could fully understand the import of his surveys. As Lindsley remembered him, a mild-mannered man completely immersed in his own research, Troost exhibited a different face when confronted with what passed for science in the denominational colleges that surrounded Nashville. He had an eye for charlatanry and for ill-concealed religious apologetics. He knew, even if people in Nashville did not, that he was the only scientist in the Southwest on the frontiers of knowledge, and that in America only Silliman at Yale, or later the Swiss immigrant Louis Agassiz, was his peer. He corresponded with both, in the case of Agassiz even before either he or Troost had immigrated to America.[11]

Troost exemplified both the strength and the weakness of the University of Nashville. He enabled students to confront a truly cosmopolitan intellectual, but he did not offer what most students wanted, or what seemed to meet their practical goals. He could not boost the university. Though much honored in Nashville, he was not understood. Everyone conceded or even exaggerated his eminence but scarcely knew what to make of his cabinets or of his research and publications. What Nashvillians wanted was a medical college, boarding students, and income for local businesses. Even Lindsley had few political skills. He was too given to sarcasm and sermons. Thus, no one on the faculty was well equipped to promote the university or to win the funds to pay for it. This task, by default, rested on the board of trust.

STUDENTS

Despite disclaimers by Lindsley and the board, the University of Nashville was an elite institution. Lindsley tried but could never afford to offer scholarships or work assignments to poor boys. The university did offer one-half tuition to prospective ministers, regardless of sect. Even the minimal $150 in annual fees represented the average income of small farmers. So the students came from affluent homes and from families who owned slaves, the economic aristocracy. And the strongest support for the university came from an economic, cultural, and political elite. No university in American history had a more distinguished board, at least in terms of political influence. Early in Lindsley's tenure, one university committee included Andrew Jackson, president-elect; Felix Grundy, U.S. senator; and John Bell, U.S. representative (and later senator). At the graduation exercises in 1828, Governor Sam Houston and soon-to-be-president Andrew Jackson were both present. Andrew Jackson Jr., an adopted son, was one of the graduates. The governor was an ex officio member of the board, which meant, later, that James K. Polk also served—two U.S. presidents during Lindsley's regime. The board also reflected continuity among the founding families. Felix Robertson, son of Nashville founder James Robertson and the first of his children born in the Nashville area, not only served on the board but also became its president, just after Philip Lindsley resigned. David Craighead, son of Thomas Craighead, the founder of Davidson Academy, was active on the board under Lindsley, while his son, also Thomas, served on the board after the Civil War. Other board members included representatives of such leading Nashville-area families as the Ewings, Leas, McGavocks, and Overtons. The board members selected its successors from among the most prominent men in middle Tennessee, and at least during most of Lindsley's tenure, membership was a social and political asset.

Lindsley hoped that his university could replace Princeton as the college of choice for the soms of affluent southern planters, particularly those west of the mountains. He briefly attained this goal, but mostly for students relatively close to Nashville. Nashville students did not dominate the student body. The more distant boys traveled in from plantations or from professional families in small towns—the two overlapped to a large extent, for prominent lawyers and physicians often owned farms or plantations. Yet few of the boys were accustomed to work in the fields, and Lindsley regretted the lack of good work habits, a lack tied to the slave economy. The membership rolls of the two student literary societies, roughly one-half of the students in each, often included home addresses. In the two sessions of 1841–42, for example, the Erosophian Society (until 1831 the Carroll Society) listed seventy members, including some students present for only one session and possibly a few recent graduates who still came to meetings. Twenty-three of the seventy were from Nashville or Davidson County and twenty-seven from other Tennessee counties, with twenty of these from middle Tennessee, six from west Tennessee, and only one from east Tennessee, and this from Bradley County, a county with a high slave population. Twenty were from outside Tennessee, all from the South: Alabama (nine), Mississippi (four, with three of these from Natchez), Kentucky (one), and Virginia (two).[12]

The literary societies were vital to student culture. Every college worth its salt had such societies, which provided students an opportunity for debate or forensic displays. College boards and presidents encouraged these clubs and provided rooms for their gatherings and libraries. Each society scheduled meetings and debates at a set time each week. At the University of Nashville, these were usually on Saturday morning or early afternoon. But the rooms, with their libraries, were open throughout the week and served as gathering places. Lindsley never achieved his hoped-for gymnasiums and organized outlets for boyish energy. The era of social fraternities and secret societies still lay ahead, and these were forbidden at the university. The societies offered the only authorized social outlet, although the boys also played games with balls and marbles, wrestled, swam in the Cumberland, and, against the rules, played cards. The minutes of every meeting of each society remain the most detailed record of the university. The societies soon ran out of current issues to debate, including a few debates on slavery, but despite often silly topics, the boys seemed to take the debates seriously, week after week. Records of positions taken show no end of flowery speeches and at times very well developed arguments. These debates further strengthened the university's emphasis on public speaking and political careers.

The literary societies played a role similar to that of a modern college library, for the university library primarily served the faculty or offered recreational reading to students who paid for the privilege. Most students probably did not pay the optional two-dollar fee. But fees, and fines, paid a librarian to open the university library for borrowing at least one period each week and to keep records, collect fines, and maintain subscriptions for periodicals. The university subscribed to the leading reviews in both England and America.[13] Money for new books was scarce, but the library received books as gifts. In 1825, it had about 1,500 books, most recently purchased by Lindsley, and eventually nearly 3,594, which fit easily into one room in the main building.[14]

Students had little leisure time, save on Sunday. Even then, they were required to attend a church of their choice, although this rule was never rigidly enforced. On weekdays, they had to attend brief morning prayers, stay in their rooms and study from sunrise to breakfast, and then be either in recitations or in their rooms at study (nine to twelve, two to five, and in winter from eight to the final bell). The only breaks were meals, chapel services, and a brief time before final prayers. Students routinely violated these strict rules, and at least in the evening often visited families, or even young ladies, in Nashville. But the authorized fun time was limited to the scheduled literary society meeting each week, and to the socializing at meals or just after lunch. Such a full schedule was a deliberate tactic to keep boys out of trouble.[15]

Rules for students were strict as published in the *Laws* that each student had to buy on matriculation, but lenient in application. Professors or tutors monitored the mandated attendance at recitation, chapel, and final examinations. A long list of student actions led to reprimands, public confessions, suspension, or expulsion, depending on the severity of the crime. Such serious offenses as theft, forgery, challenges to or participation in duels, and cock fighting led to immediate expulsion but did not preclude readmission for repentant students. Students were not allowed to bet money; fight or insult each other; lie, cheat, or play cards; drink intoxicating liquors; visit taverns or houses of ill repute; resist the authority of professors and tutors; conspire with other students to challenge faculty authority; attend balls, theater, dances, or horse races; travel more than two miles from campus without express permission; deface buildings or property; play musical instruments during study hours or after the evening bell; or bring dogs, weapons, servants, or horses on campus. Neglect of studies led to dismissal. The faculty would later make a few exceptions to these rules, such as permitting students to attend carefully chaperoned dances at commencement time, or selected programs at the downtown theater.

These rules, which closely followed those at Princeton, reflected a fear of student disorder. They also represented a broader Protestant, Evangelical culture. Lindsley greatly feared certain patterns of conduct widely identified with the South, such as cock fights or duels, and what he soon observed to be slovenly habits. His boys had a keen sense of personal honor, which meant frequent quarrels and fist fights, and on two or three occasions attacks with guns or knives. Fighting without weapons rarely led to expulsion, but rather to efforts to shame the protagonists or to get them to reconcile.

The punishment of students required wisdom. Lindsley, after his experience at Princeton, was determined to provide the type of nurturing that would prevent widespread student alienation. He succeeded. The mischief on campus never elicited broad student support, but every year at least a few students faced either suspension or expulsion. Some suspensions were inevitable. A few boys could not adjust to the university and simply left without permission. Some could not adjust to the heavy schedule of studies and faced charges of indolence or idleness. In one year, several students, without permission, joined the militia. In such cases, students who wanted to come back would almost always be readmitted in a subsequent session. In fact, Lindsley seemed at times to use suspension as an excellent tool of moral education. The embarrassed student faced parental wrath and usually reformed. Also, Lindsley, with great kindness, counseled boys in trouble or those devastated by disciplinary action. This led to even greater respect for the often lofty and awe-inspiring president. But these kindnesses also had a pecuniary motive: The university desperately needed students. Also, the derelict boys were usually from prominent families, including in a few cases those of board members or their friends. Thus, in 1838, the board set up a board committee to approve all suspensions. This move did not seem to reduce their number, but the board usually offered suspended or expelled students the right to reapply for admission. In most cases, the names of punished students appear later on lists of students or on graduation lists.

The most serious student crimes led to immediate expulsion by the faculty or, later, by the board of trustees, which in most cases reaffirmed faculty action. Over twenty-five years, such serious offences occurred every three or four years. An early incident involved a student who fired a pistol at a fellow student. He was probably never readmitted. Another student caught with a pistol in his possession was expelled but later readmitted. Five drunken students who broke windows and fought in downtown Nashville were also suspended but later readmitted. When a student seriously wounded another with a cane in a brawl, the board negotiated a reconciliation between the two and readmitted both. In all such cases, readmission meant penitence, confession, and often long, tearful sessions with Lindsley.

Even the most serious misbehavior was mild compared to the mayhem Lindsley had known at Princeton. The most grievous offenses at the University of Nashville included an attack on a servant in the dining hall, six students who were drunk and riotous, six others who were not only drunk on Sunday but beat on doors and windows and fired a pistol, seven students who battled each other with knives and brandished pistols, and a single student who exploded gunpowder at the door of a tutor. But even many of these miscreants later returned. Most feared by Lindsley were widespread student rebellions or riots. None occurred. The closest approximation came in 1840, when a group of young men, including both students and townspeople, attacked the main college building, destroyed seven windows and two doors, and injured a tutor with a thrown stone. In this case, the university prosecuted anyone who could be identified and of course expelled the students, although only a few seem to have been involved. Toward the end of Lindsley's presidency, as the west and center wings of the main building deteriorated and campus morale plummeted, students in 1847 did serious damage to the dorm rooms. All students had to pay an extra fee to cover the repairs. Notably, this occurred when Lindsley was on leave. Then in 1848, during vacation, students seriously damaged books, shelves, and furniture in Agatheridian Hall. The culprits were not caught, but the board of trust enacted tougher admission standards. Lesser offenses, if not part of a pattern or in conjunction with more serious misdeeds, usually led only to a reprimand. These included card playing, drinking, and even fist fights without deadly weapons.[16]

The best window into daily life at the university comes from a rare artifact, a student diary for the academic years 1841–42 and 1843–44 written by Jethro Peyton Gatlin, who enrolled in 1841 as a sophomore. From Tippah County in northern Mississippi, he had nearby relatives on a farm outside Nashville, where he spent the weeks between sessions. He arrived at a good time. The peak of enrollment had just passed and all the core faculty were on campus (Cross, Hamilton, Lindsley, and Troost) along with one live-in tutor. Gatlin boarded nearby in his sophomore year but lived on campus as a senior. These years were as close to normal as any in the history of the university. And, by all the evidence, Gatlin was a somewhat better than average student.

Gatlin recorded an educational experience that, while intense, was tedious and lacked excitement. Week after week, he attended recitations—but not always. If ill, or possibly even tired, he would skip classes, particularly in the sciences. Yet he was a more conscientious student than most of his thirty-three sophomore classmates. An avid reader, he at times felt guilty for spending too much time on novels. Candlelight reading almost every evening strained his eyes. On some days when he was well prepared, he lamented that the professor had not called on him. In a few cases, he lamented being called on when not prepared, and making a fool of himself. In two years of almost daily entries in a diary, he recorded only one significant student prank—hitting the door of a classroom with rocks. He denounced not only the ones who threw the stones, but also students who did not rush to identify and punish the guilty. In his sophomore year, a fire broke out in a student room, burned a hole in the floor, and destroyed the contents of two rooms. The fire department quickly extinguished it, but one student was left with no clothes and another lost his precious books. Gatlin's main recreation was reading and participating in his literary society. Only two sophomores had not yet joined one of the two competing groups. Every Saturday after morning recitations, Gatlin joined his Erosophian brethren in conversation, debate, and oratorical contests. For one session, he was his society's librarian.

Gatlin, even in these most private comments, showed great respect for his four professors. He usually studied conscientiously and condemned those who did not. He listed all thirty-three fellow sophomores, their homes, and even their ages and physical appearance. But for each, the most telling judgment involved the calibre of his scholarship. He identified about ten good or very good students. Most of the others were indifferent, lazy, or dull. One Baptist minister, the oldest sophomore at twenty-two or twenty-three, was, by Gatlin's description, about the worst in the class. The younger students were fifteen or sixteen, mere boys. Gatlin never recorded his age, but he voted in a city election in his senior year. If Tennessee enforced voting-age requirements, which is doubtful, he would have been at least twenty-one in his last year. Of the thirty-four in his sophomore class, seventeen took their bachelor of arts two years later, a higher than average retention rate. This helps account for the twenty-five graduates in 1844, the highest in the history of the University of Nashville. It also means that eight students not in the sophomore class graduated in 1844. Some undoubtedly entered as juniors; a few may have been kicked back a year, which was the case with two of Gatlin's classmates.[17]

Despite all the rules, Gatlin seemed unusually free or unsupervised. He was a good young man and probably valued by his professors. He frequently, even on weekdays, went downtown, attended legislative sessions, observed court cases, or visited friends. At times, he accumulated debts, but sooner or later his father sent plenty of money to cover them. In his senior year, he spent some evenings visiting young women, including the steward's daughter. But above all, he was serious and continuously involved in a lofty intellectual dialogue. He read all the great philosophers, became an expert in rhetoric and political theory, and was fluent in Greek. For pleasure, he read the *Edinburgh* or *North American Review.* He carefully wrote his prepared speeches and rendered detailed evaluations of preachers or orators he heard. He sought out public speakers, trying always to develop his own oratorical gifts.

Unfortunately, Gatlin grew increasingly ill. He coughed, even spit up blood, and thus suspected consumption. By his senior year, the certainty that he would soon die may have heightened his piety. He prayed, read his Bible, and usually attended Lindsley's Bible lessons at three o'clock every Sunday afternoon. Yet, perhaps consistent with the nonsectarian claims of the university, he did not seem to have any church of his own. He rotated from one congregation to another, often to evaluate the preaching skill of the pastor. A strong temperance advocate, he appreciated a nearby Methodist congregation. He also attended and commented on a Disciples of Christ church (Vine Street), First Baptist, Trinity Episcopal, and the Roman Catholic church (twice, once to hear good Christmas music, again to observe a regular Sunday worship service in order, he said, to satisfy his curiosity about "the worshipers of the beast," a deprecating comment, not on Catholicism, but on the prejudices of Protestants). By the summer session of 1844, his last, he was often too ill even to remain on campus, and he last appeared in the records of his literary society in August. But he graduated and lived at least two more years, when he received his master of arts in course(a courtesy degree which required no additional course work).[18]

Some of Gatlin's entries suggest why Lindsley's university faced ongoing criticism because of its location. Even to have a university in a city scandalized some parents, who feared both disease and dissipation. In its publicity, the university tried to allay these fears. Even Lindsley, who knew better, sometimes referred to Nashville as the healthiest city in the country. It was far enough north to escape the worst of what we now know to be mosquito-borne diseases such as malaria and yellow fever. The relatively warm winters were considered healthful, and no one seemed concerned with the boiling heat of summer, at the heart of one university session. But Nashville suffered a cholera epidemic every three or four years, some so serious as to cause a suspension of classes or reduced enrollment. Cholera, as we now know, reflected hygienic deficiencies and was a direct result not of Nashville's climate, but of the close human contacts in a city or on a campus. Since cholera is a bacterial intestinal infection that leads to debilitating diarrhea, it spreads by direct contact with infected food or water. The communal drinking buckets, unclean hands at meals, and shared privies at the university almost guaranteed its spread. Some believed the swampy bottomland just south of Broad Street, between the campus and the town, contributed to cholera. It did not, but it could have harbored the mosquitoes that caused the infrequent cases of malaria. At least on this issue, rural colleges might have had an advantage.

The problem of an immoral city environment proved intractable for the university. For more than a century, the low area south of Broad was Nashville's red-light district, home to most of the city's taverns and brothels and the destination of many visitors. Saloons flourished less than a block from the north boundary of the campus, and the number of students punished for visiting them or houses of ill repute reflected a problem the university was loath to admit. At intervals, the campus joined nearby homeowners in efforts to clean up the area, but this always proved a temporary fix.[19] The local environment, more than any other factor, led the trustees to consider moving the campus to a new location as early as 1831, and frequently in the years that followed. And the sense of a temporary campus contributed to the relative neglect of the buildings. The area was also uninviting to faculty, who by their terms of employment had to live on or next to the campus (the university eventually owned faculty homes and counted rent as part of salaries).

FINANCIAL PROBLEMS

If the university was to move, it needed more money, always in short supply. The University of Nashville was an anomaly in higher education by 1830. By Lindsley's choice, it was in no respect a Presbyterian college. He never wanted or sought support from a synod or general assembly. He wanted a major state university modeled on Virginia, North Carolina, and Georgia. But he was never able to gain even a single appropriation from the Tennessee General Assembly. By 1850, Tennessee was the only southern state that had not appropriated any money for higher education. The state at times even worked to prevent the university from realizing its income from a federal land grant. Thus, the university was on its own, with no clear constituency save possibly its growing group of distinguished alumni.

The university had three sources of funds: tuition and fees, gifts, and the land it owned, some by earlier grants, some by purchase. If tuition were to pay even the instructional costs of $7,000, the university needed around 140 students each session. Its maximum enrollment, in 1836, was 126 students; the average over twenty-five years was just under 80, with a rather abrupt decline after 1848. This meant that tuition covered only the salaries of Lindsley and one other professor. The enrollment seemed low in comparison to competing colleges, but almost all of them listed preparatory students along with fully qualified college students, which Lindsley never did. Even the two or three times the university tried to launch an in-house preparatory department, without success, it listed only fully matriculated students. Its faculty was about right for 100 students, and it had only forty-four dorm rooms, which would accommodate a maximum residential student body of 88. A higher enrollment would have required more dorms and classrooms, neither of which it could afford.

Fees added a small amount to the tuition total. Desperate for money, the board required both a matriculation and a graduating fee, at first dedicated to Lindsley, who always turned these over to the university. Like almost all American colleges, Lindsley's university offered several honorary degrees, each with an appropriate fee. Most of these were "in course" master's degrees offered to any graduate on request after three years (later two years). This questionable tactic ensured that almost all college faculty in America listed an M.A. after their name, but in 1825 almost none were earned.

During Lindsley's presidency, the university had 3,971 class registrations. He kept a careful list. But this enrollment figure does not reveal the much smaller number of matriculates, approximately 410. This seemed a small return for twenty-five years, but the graduates of the University of Nashville were exceptionally able and successful, comparable to graduates of major eastern colleges. At least half these graduates who lived long enough (many died young) would hold major public office: senators and representatives, governors, state legislators, judges, and military officers. Lindsley conducted a school for statesmen.[20]

Subscriptions were critical for university finances from 1824 to about 1830, when the board began appointing fewer and fewer agents to solicit funds. Lindsley hated the begging game but had to keep it up until his last years in Nashville. The system of fund-raising was universally well established by 1825. Colleges hired agents, some professional fund-raisers, who accepted as their pay about 20 percent of the gifts they solicited. The system could be a bit porous; many people pledged gifts on the installment plan and never paid up. In some cases, the university even used such promises as security for loans. Some agents proved untrustworthy. As gifts declined, the board tried a second common strategy, a lottery. The state assembly approved it, the university contracted with a company to run it, but it sold too few tickets even to pay the promised awards.[21] One of the university's last financial hopes lay in its increasing number of alumni. A new alumni association, in the later years of Lindsley's tenure, began an ambitious project to raise enough funds to endow a professorship. It never met this goal, and the fund accumulated interest through the Civil War years.

This left land. Had Davidson Academy and the early Cumberland College not sold off the original 240-acre land grant from North Carolina, the university would have been wealthy by 1825, since its former land became about half of downtown Nashville. But it had to alienate its land to survive. As Lindsley took over in 1825, the college had the campus, which had shrunk to about seven acres, deeds to several nearby lots sold on credit, and the newly acquired but widely scattered parcels in west Tennessee (the University of North Carolina warrants). It still held legal claim to something less than the original 50,000 acres of land in the area south of the French Broad in east Tennessee, which derived from the 1806 federal land grant. But collecting payments for this land proved endlessly frustrating.

In 1825, in a brief period of successful fund-raising and budget surpluses, the trustees bought 120 acres just south of the original land grant for only $7,245, a third of what the land would soon be worth. The board began building the president's home on this land and carefully preserved 30 adjoining acres for a future campus. But the board could not afford to hold the rest and began to sell large lots almost immediately. It eventually received at least $17,000 for approximately 90 acres. This began a pattern of land purchases, in part for speculation and almost all on credit. Board members signed personal notes at the time of purchase and held the land until the university could retire what amounted to an interest-free loan. As far as the records reveal, none lost money from such generosity, but a few board members and Lindsley later had to accept title to lots as payment for their loans. During Lindsley's tenure, land speculation was probably the largest single source of income for the university. By 1850, the surviving 30 acres from the original 120 had an estimated value of $30,000.[22]

Another series of transactions proved even more lucrative, acre for acre. In 1845, a board member and board secretary lucked on to a great opportunity. In the name of the university, they bought some lots just south of the campus for $3,450. They sold half of them in 1848 for $6,600, and the other half was worth at least $6,000. On the basis of the accrued value of these lots, the trustees in 1847 bought from General William Harding of Belle Meade fame what they called the south field, a plot of land with 348 feet fronting Franklin Pike (soon to become Spruce Street, and today Eighth Avenue) at the point it intersected Demonbreun Street—choice land, near downtown and only five blocks west of the land the university already owned. For the next two years, the board hoped to make this land the site of a new campus, in such an upscale and densely occupied neighborhood that nearby boarding houses could substitute for dorms. This would end the problems with stewards and with dorm mischief. The board paid Harding only $11,000 for a plot with an estimated value of at least double this price a few years later (the university eventually sold it for more than $30,000). Once again, board members signed the notes. Such land deals meant that, at almost any time, the university had an outstanding debt of $15,000 or more, but it was a debt largely owed to Lindsley and other board members.

The debt would have been much greater except for income from the sale of the lands from the University of North Carolina warrants, about 30,000 acres widely dispersed in west Tennessee counties. But, as usual in such cases, the university had to hire an agent to locate, survey, and sell the lands, for which he received the going commission of 25 percent. Early estimates of the value ranged up to $65,000, but sales were difficult. Eventually, the agent bought much of the land, after casting lots to determine his one-fourth. No chicanery seems to have occurred, but the university recouped only about $30,000, all of which went into the university's operating expenses or helped pay off notes held by trustees. The university did not have the financial strength to convert the money into an endowment.

In 1838, the University of Nashville finally received its first and only endowment, the result of the settlement of an ongoing dispute with the state that reached back to the federal land grant of 1806 (see chapter 1). This was the 50,000 acres granted to both East Tennessee University and Cumberland College, land south of the French Broad River in Cocke, Sevier, and Blount Counties. Even at only one dollar an acre, the federal government seemed certain to give Cumberland College at least $50,000. But the state, as the final custodian of the land, could set the terms for sale. It allowed settlers to survey the land and establish claims, requiring them only to pay local taxes. But to gain title they had to pay the purchase price and accumulated interest to the two colleges, which had to sign over the deeds to the purchasers. This meant that the colleges held what amounted to liens or mortgages on lands eventually owned by at least two hundred farmers.

What happened after 1806 was complex and opposed to the interest of the colleges. In 1807, the state postponed to 1809 the due date for the first payments by settlers for the land (in this and all subsequent payment plans, the settlers could make payments over several years). In a near ritual, every two years the general assembly again postponed payment on the principal but at times still required that settlers pay the accumulated interest. A few did. In 1811, the assembly began postponing payment of interest, and in at least one case forgave interest already due. This pattern continued until November 1823, when the assembly forgave one-third of the accumulated debt (by then the interest often exceeded the principal) but required that the settlers finally pay the two colleges the remaining two-thirds of principal and interest, in installments. By May 1, 1824, they were to pay one-fifth of this debt, and then over the next six years make payments on the rest on each May 1. This act seemed finally to assure that the University of Nashville would have money for an endowment, for the sum owed it was still large, despite the forgiveness of one-third (probably $150,000, had every settler paid in full). With this heady prospect in mind, the trustees had begun the new building program and recruited Lindsley as president. In good faith, they had assured Lindsley that a revived Cumberland College would have the means to become a great university. When the plan fell through, the trustees felt embarrassed and betrayed, and Lindsley remained bitter about the treatment by the State of Tennessee until he died.

What the university did not make public was the amount it did receive from these east Tennessee lands. In 1824 and into 1825, a probable majority of settlers made their first payment of one-fifth of what they owed. Agents commissioned by East Tennessee College, who were close to the lands dedicated to both colleges, collected these payments. Some records indicate that, in total, the University of Nashville received around $30,000, which went to retire old debts and build the campus, as well as to pay the salaries of the new faculty. Because the university spent these funds and saved none for an endowment, it violated the intent of the federal grant. In all probability, with Lindsley on board, the installments over the next six years would have become an endowment. But in 1825, the by now well-organized and politically potent "poor" settlers refused, almost to a person, to make the second payment. In fact, they never resumed the payments and eventually won title to their land anyway, with the complicity of the Tennessee assembly, which never forced payment or began foreclosure procedures.

Not surprisingly, Cumberland College and then the University of Nashville felt cheated. The state had acted in bad faith and had sabotaged the clear intent of Congress. Lindsley was sharp in his criticism of the assembly, and eventually his attacks infuriated legislators, especially those from east Tennessee. The Nashville trustees, almost all well placed politically, worked to get some resolution, as did representatives from the Nashville area. The university had one strong bargaining point: It had to sign over the deeds to the settlers' lands. Thus, as the university lamented its lost income, insecure settlers feared that the university would never grant them titles. They both feared and resented the elite university in far-off Nashville.

In 1825, with the first default, the trustees petitioned Congress to redress the wrong inflicted by the State of Tennessee. Since it had not received the intended funds, it asked Congress to award it an equally valuable grant in lands to be deeded over by the Cherokees to the south of the old grant, in what was soon referred to as Ocoee lands, to the east and north of Chattanooga. This appeal over the heads of the state assembly involved risks. The university knew that the assembly hoped for a major federal land grant to fund Tennessee schools. The broadest public support involved academies or elementary (common) schools. The state, for the first time, envisioned a state-supported school system like those emerging in New England. Obviously, such use of the land had broad appeal. The university had no real support outside the Nashville area, if federal grants to it diminished the money available for "democratic" schools for everyone. It is doubtful that the trustees expected to win in the Congress. The general assembly, in fact, directly instructed its representatives and senators to oppose any land grant to the university.

By 1828, committees from both East Tennessee College and the University of Nashville began complicated negotiations with the assembly. In 1830, the assembly offered a deal: If the two colleges would surrender all claims to the old grant, the state would give each one-half of a township in the Ocoee district. This 11,520 acres seemed a poor offer, since the university would relinquish claims to the unpaid debt on at least 30,000 acres in a much better developed agricultural area. The University of Nashville board rejected the offer; East Tennessee College accepted.[23]

In 1834 and again in 1836 the trustees filed their final appeals to Congress and lost; in 1835, the federal government took over the Cherokee lands. By 1837, in debt and desperate for money as always, the trustees began bargaining in good faith. They offered a clear title on the lands if the general assembly would guarantee an annual income of $3,000 to the university plus title to one-fourth of a township. The state stuck to its offer of one-half a township.

In 1838, the university capitulated. The state grant stipulated that the money gained from sale of the township land go into an endowment to support the university. Once again, the university had to hire an agent to survey and sell these lands. Luke Lea took the job and earned a large commission; his family owned a large estate south of Nashville and would later become influential in the city. Lea eventually sold the land for a net sum to the university of almost $40,000, the largest return yet from the various land transactions. Unfortunately, he was unable to turn all the money over to the university and had to execute a note for the final $5,000, an asset listed by the university up to the verge of the Civil War. By the terms of the deal, the university invested most of the remaining money in state bonds and soon had an income from them of about $2,000 a year.[24]

THE SAD ENDGAME

By 1845, the University of Nashville faced an overwhelming array of challenges. The campus itself presented problems. By 1831, the board had already envisioned a new campus on the thirty acres that included the president's house. It appointed a committee in 1835 to consider a new campus and the sale of the old one. In 1836, an even larger building committee began developing plans for the new campus, with the authority to sell all or part of the old campus to raise the needed funds. But the university had not yet worked out the compromise on the Ocoee lands, apparently received few local gifts, and thus backed off the plan. Enrollment had peaked in 1835 and 1836, briefly filling all forty-four dorm rooms. Thus, beginning in 1837, the university added a new wing to the old building, an ell to the east along Market (Second Avenue). It contained extra dorm rooms, classrooms, and a room for the library. It replicated the old building (three stories, only seventy-six by forty-five feet) but was apparently built of better brick and mortar. It alone survived the eventual suspension of classes in 1850 to become the home of the new University of Nashville Medical Department and later also of the Vanderbilt University Medical Department.[25]

The new building added space but did little to improve the overall campus. By the accounts of every visitor and of local newspapers, the original building, with its plain walls of locally fired red brick, was as ugly as unadorned brick could be. And no efforts at moral reform could clean up the red-light district just in front of the campus (ironically, on land formerly owned by Davidson Academy). The new building, which opened in June 1839, was already redundant, since enrollment had declined from its peak—in part because of a tuition increase from $25 to $30, and the admission of fewer students who did not seek degrees. By 1840, the average enrollment had shrunk to around eighty, and by 1845 to an average of seventy. By then, it was clear that, sooner or later, the university had to move. But even with the Ocoee endowment, the school could barely meet its annual expenses, although the value of its assets continued to grow because of higher land values. As events proved, the university could not afford to keep classes going in the old building and at the same time build a new campus.

The university's mood also changed. The board met less often. The core faculty—now the big four: Hamilton, Cross, Lindsley, and Troost—were all old men in precarious health. Lindsley clearly lost heart, almost stopped delivering his carefully prepared addresses, gave up on further fund-raising, and let things drift. In 1844, his youngest son and his only child born in Nashville, died unexpectedly at age nine. Grief devastated him and his wife, who herself died the next year. Lindsley had to take sick leave in 1846. By the time he returned, the university was increasingly under attack by local populist newspapers. Newer and cheaper colleges abounded, including Cumberland University in Lebanon with its popular law school. The high standards of the University of Nashville, its gradually declining enrollment, and the comparatively high salaries of Lindsley and his professors invited such attacks. The ugly campus did not help. It seemed to outsiders that Lindsley had used all the funds to pay salaries and had neglected the buildings, which in a sense was correct. But the most telling criticism involved the apparent resistance of Lindsley and his board to what Nashville most craved—a medical school and a law school. Nashvillians assumed that the prestige of any professional school required an affiliation with the university.

By his second year in Nashville, Lindsley had revealed his dreams for a great university that would include schools of law and medicine. In 1835, the board even announced it would establish such schools as soon as possible. By 1843, it seemed on the verge of appointing a law faculty and in 1844 appointed a committee to inquire into the feasibility of a medical school. Local physicians, led by Thomas Jennings, were clearly behind these proposals, and several board members joined in the effort to found a school. Within a few weeks, even Lindsley asked approval from the board for a medical school, and the board appointed a medical and law faculty—hopeful planning, at best. But Lindsley set terms unacceptable to local physicians and business backers. He had always condemned the level of medical education in America, had held up a European model as alone acceptable for a true university, and in the board resolution insisted that graduates of a University of Nashville medical school be twenty-one and enter with a bachelor's degree or its equivalent. No medical school in America approached such admission requirements. Minimal literacy in English and an elementary education gained one admission to most early and, lamentably, later proprietary schools. A proprietary school was all that the University of Nashville could consider, for it had no funds, and no American precedent, for a university-funded school. All proprietary schools reflected the efforts of entrepreneurial physicians who sought profits and added prestige by becoming part of a medical faculty. Lindsley's impossible terms, and his outspoken criticism of the existing American schools for quacks, made him look like the major obstacle to what had become a high-priority civic project in Nashville.[26]

A major crusade for a medical school, and a less prominent push for a law school, began in 1849. Once again, university trustees were much involved in the effort. A group of committed physicians, now led by an ambitious and able Charles Caldwell, convened public meetings, offered sample lectures, and built what seemed to be universal support. A medical school promised to lure three or four times the number of students in the existing university. Such students would all board in Nashville, boosting the local economy. Besides, Nashville was falling behind Louisville and Cincinnati, as well as Memphis and Lexington, each of which had a proprietary medical school. Newspapers believed the university was dragging its feet on the school and fanned public resentment against an elitist university, particularly the salaries of professors ($7,000 in all) in contrast to the few students and even fewer graduates. The aging professors made a good target. A lively newspaper battle ensued; the more populist and Democratic press opposed the university, and the one Whig newspaper, supported by the leading citizens, defended it, carrying some articles ghosted by Lindsley. Few dared criticize Lindsley's academic credentials, but held against him his northern birth and his now much moderated opposition to slavery.

The criticism wounded Lindsley. He probably decided to resign as president in 1849, during the newspaper war, in part for personal reasons. At the same time, the board finally began planning a new campus and announced its early intentions to tear down part of the old building—the west wing and the center or chapel section, which the city now wanted cleared in order to extend College Avenue to the south. Critics of the university, along with boosters of new law and medical schools turned the muted but still promising negotiations into a bitter battle. Perhaps led by Caldwell, some supporters of a medical school sought help from the Tennessee assembly in a campaign that involved an open and cruel repudiation of Lindsley. In November 1849, the assembly chartered a medical school, and in December a law department, both listed as part of the University of Nashville. The legislation provided for separate boards for each new entity, and in a direct slap at Lindsley provided that no faculty member, in any branch of the university, could serve as president of the board of trust of the university as a whole. This law, if constitutional, would have required Lindsley to withdraw as board president. In February, the trustees of the new medical college asked for a joint meeting of the three separate boards to plan a new organization. The legislation had required that all general issues be decided by a majority of the combined boards. More revealing, the medical board noted that neither of the two new boards were fully acquainted with real estate and "personal assets" belonging to the university, which suggested not only designs upon university assets, but also an implied accusation that individuals, probably meaning Lindsley, held in their own names some of those assets. In a subsequent statement that responded to challenges to the medical board's legality, the medical board offered its legal opinion that the assembly, based on a series of charter amendments in the past, had the right to make such a drastic alteration in the university's governance.

Three days later, Lindsley resigned as president. He pointed out that he had never opposed the establishment of medical and law schools in the university (true, but the statement disregards the conditions he had set for such schools), and that he regretted that the charter for the University of Nashville had specified that the president of the university also be president of the board of trust. Perhaps as he expected, this forced an early resolution of the legal status of the new boards. A frightened senior class begged Lindsley to rescind his resignation, sensing that their degrees might be in jeopardy. Board support followed, and at its next meeting, on March 25, 1850, the board tabled Lindsley's resignation. At the board's request, Lindsley withdrew his resignation, subject at any moment to reconsideration if the board changed its mind. Lindsley intended only to finish out the year so that seniors could graduate. He had remarried in April 1849, choosing the widow of the benefactor who had helped establish a Presbyterian (Old School) seminary in New Albany, Indiana. He was already planning to move there and accept a professorial post in the seminary.

Despite several requests, some accompanied by polite overtures, the old board of the University of Nashville refused to recognize the constitutionality of the action taken by the assembly. It would not cooperate with the two new boards (echoes of the Dartmouth College Case of 1819). A battle seemed to be brewing when a member of one of the new boards argued that the reinstatement of Lindsley was illegal because all the trustees had not been involved. But the old board and the two new boards did agree to submit the issue to the state supreme court. As anyone might have predicted, the court, not in a formal decision but in an advisory opinion, sided with the old board. The University of Nashville was a private, not a public, university. Tennessee had never contributed any money to its support. The two new boards, although they could continue to act in behalf of their respective schools, were not legally connected to the University of Nashville, whose board had not approved such a connection. The new boards did not survive this decision.[27]

The legal victory did not end the dilemma faced by the now beleaguered university. During the battle over charters in the spring of 1850, enrollment sank to only thirty-nine, among them at least fifteen seniors. Uncertainties, the ongoing demolition of more than half of the main campus building, and another cholera epidemic had taken their toll. Lindsley probably anticipated suspension after commencement in the October term. In June 1849, the beloved mathematics professor James Hamilton died. This was a serious but not fatal blow to the school. The death of Gerard Troost in August 1850 was the final blow, particularly since the board knew that it would have no alternative but to accept Lindsley's resignation at the end of the summer session. Of the regular professors, only Cross would be left at the end of the term in October. Briefly, the board announced a winter session for 1850–51, even though the center and west wings were gone. In the spring and summer session of 1850, all classes had to move into the surviving east wing, and all students had to move to boardinghouses. For this reason, most of the last students were local. It soon became obvious to the board that the university would have to suspend classes until completion of the new academic building about three blocks south of the old campus. The suspension did not reflect a worse than usual financial situation. By the board's careful and fair estimation, the university had assets of between $130,000 and $150,000 as it began its new campus, with debts of only about $15,000.[28]

Gloom pervaded the campus during final exercises in September 1850. It was clear that, at the very least, this phase in the life of the University of Nashville was ending. Fourteen seniors would graduate, but the few lower classmen were not sure they would be able to complete their work and receive a degree. On September 21, just before finals, the boys in the Agatheridian Society held their last meeting of the year. Twelve members attended, the only members left, most from the Nashville area. The names were familiar: Ewing, McGavock, Harding, Hays. Thomas Craighead, grandson of the founder, was present. The occasion invited flowery and sad speeches, one by a graduate so moving that the boys sat for a long period in silence. The secretary noted that this was "perhaps the last occasion on which we should assemble together," and that this ended "the ties which have so long bound us together as a band of brothers." (In fact, four of the members present, including Craighead, would be back in 1854 to reorganize the society in the stone castle on the new campus.)[29]

Lindsley, who would begin teaching in New Albany in January 1851, stayed on to the bitter end. His great educational dream had collapsed in controversy and ill feeling. Everyone awaited his final address; in the previous five years, he had delivered none of his famous policy statements. The topic he selected seemed odd: "Discourse on the Life and Character of Professor Gerard Troost, M.D." In the long, moving speech, he did not directly address the events that led to his resignation. He did not chart any plans for the new campus. He offered no final comments on American higher education.

But he did what he wanted to do, with passion and a bluntness rare even for

Lindsley. He used Troost's life and career to illustrate scholarly commitment and intellectual integrity. Troost symbolized what the university had been at its best: no sham, high standards, no compromise with mediocrity. In stinging words, Lindsley indicted the critics of the university, and of Troost, whom newspapers had ridiculed and critics had called a humbug, laughing at his silly cabinets in a dingy laboratory. In its preceding session, the state assembly had abolished Troost's position as geologist. Lindsley compared "the impudent, selfish, swaggering, successful careers of the brazen-faced and iron-hearted popular demagogues" in Nashville—those who had tried to destroy his beloved university—with the "calm, subdued, patient, humble, retiring, modest course of the laborious, philosophical pioneer" Gerard Troost. It was an old story, the persecution of great scientists by ignorant and intolerant and often sectarian demagogues.[30] Thus, Lindsley had the last word on the troubled but in many ways successful career of the first incarnation of the University of Nashville. It would have at least four more lives, but none as distinguished. No subsequent president of the University of Nashville, or for that matter of the later George Peabody College, would enjoy the eminence of Lindsley. No scientist would approach the stature of Troost. No body of graduates would go on to such distinguished careers.

C H A P T E R F O U R

Crisis Years for the University of Nashville, 1850–1875

THE TWENTY-FIVE YEARS FROM 1850 TO 1875 WERE CRISIS years for the United States, for the South in particular, and thus for the struggling University of Nashville. During this quarter of a century, the university supported a series of educational activities, but only a proprietary medical school endured, and—except for ownership of the campus and buildings—the university had no direct control over it. When the university tried to reestablish a semi-proprietary literary department on a new campus in 1854, it barely survived for one academic year. In 1855, the university leased its new campus to the Western Military Institute, which for the next seven years offered both preparatory and college-level instruction, but not up to the standards of the old university under Philip Lindsley. The Civil War caused the final suspension of WMI in February 1862.

In the financially beleaguered years after the war, the University of Nashville finally reopened in 1867 as a preparatory academy partly endowed by Montgomery Bell and named after him. Attempts to glue collegiate work onto the academy largely failed, although two former Confederate generals leased the campus and the academy in 1870 and tried to reestablish a credible military college. It attracted few college-level students and by 1875 was floundering and in debt. The frustrations of this effort led to plans for another client for the campus and buildings, a new normal school chartered by the state but largely funded and supervised by the Peabody Education Fund.

JOHN BERRIEN LINDSLEY AND THE UNIVERSITY OF NASHVILLE MEDICAL DEPARTMENT

Even as the board of trustees arrived at the difficult decision to suspend the literary department after commencement exercises in October 1850, it had to respond to new proposals for a medical school. Efforts in 1849 led by Charles Caldwell had failed after the Tennessee Supreme Court deemed unconstitutional a medical school charter with imposed ties to the University of Nashville. But everyone in Nashville wanted a medical school, and for the first time, the university had an empty building—the rather new east wing of the old campus. It was the obvious place for a school, particularly one that needed ties to a university.

The leading architects of the medical school were two new allies, John Berrien Lindsley, the youngest surviving son of Philip Lindsley, and William K. Bowling, who had just moved to Nashville from nearby Logan County, Kentucky. Both had M.D. degrees, but Lindsley, unlike Bowling, would never develop a medical practice; he had too many other irons in the fire. Bowling, who had built up a practice in Logan County, was a graduate of the Cincinnati Medical College. He had long wanted to establish a medical school, preferred Nashville as a site, and believed it would be possible to create a stronger school than any short of Philadelphia. Quality medical instruction proved an almost impossible goal, given the competition. Bowling, in part as a medical journalist, deserves the reputation as the first able medical reformer in Tennessee or even the old Southwest. He found a critical ally in John Berrien Lindsley, who could take care of negotiations with the university board and had superb political skills.

Young Lindsley quickly became the new leader of the University of Nashville and was responsible for its survival in the hard years after 1850. The trustees made him curator of the suspended literary department, in charge of maintaining the library and scientific apparatus, until they could complete a new college building. It would be near the president's home on a block of land that stretched east from the present-day Second Avenue past Academy Street, and south from Middleton to Lindsley. Lindsley also became the first dean of the new Medical Department.

Lindsley contributed almost as much to the University of Nashville as had his father, and a great deal more to the city and state. One of the most accomplished and versatile men in the history of Tennessee, he ranks among the leading reformers in both public education and public health in nineteenth-century America. Born at Princeton, he was two when his parents moved to Nashville in late 1824. Although he would be the Lindsley most involved with the university, his older brother, Adrian Van Sinderen Lindsley, a successful Nashville lawyer, served on the board of trust from 1839 until his death in 1885. A.V.S., or Van, was quiet, in no sense a leader, but served as secretary of the board throughout these forty-six years, meticulously keeping the minutes of each meeting. John Berrien—who was usually called Berrien, the family name of a maternal great grandfather—revealed a curiosity about all subjects as a boy, was carefully tutored in the Lindsley home, and at fourteen entered the University of Nashville as a sophomore. He graduated in 1839 and in course received his master of arts. (One of his classmates and longtime close friends was William Walker, later an adventurer or filibuster in Central America, killed in Honduras in 1850.)

Two years after receiving his bachelor's degree, Berrien Lindsley apprenticed himself to a local physician, and then in the fall of 1841 enrolled in the Louisville Medical School, remaining for only the first year of the two-year course. In 1842, he moved to the Medical School of the University of Pennsylvania, the oldest and best in the United States. After only one annual course of lectures, the school awarded him the M.D. degree—to his surprise, it gave him credit for the year in Louisville. Back in Nashville, he was not content simply to practice medicine. He had several interests. He studied geology and paleontology for at least two years with Gerard Troost and accompanied him, in the summer of 1848, on an extended geological survey throughout the Northeast and North, where the two no doubt collected mineral and fossil specimens for Troost's cabinets. For years, on most of his trips in Tennessee, Lindsley searched for the early invertebrate fossils that Troost

A portrait of John Berrien Lindsley. From a portrait owned by Peabody College.

had written about. He became so involved with this pursuit that his friends expected him to succeed Troost as state geologist. After Troost died, Lindsley carefully preserved his cabinets, although the Troost heirs owned them and fought over ownership rights. The State of Tennessee, in 1860, had considered an appropriation to buy the collection as a nucleus of a state museum but voted down the bill. Finally, in 1874, Lindsley helped sell the precious cabinets for only $20,500—perhaps a third of their value—to the Polytechnic Society of Louisville for a museum in what became the Free Library of Louisville. Earlier, Benjamin Silliman had traveled to Nashville, spending three days with the collection. He urged its preservation.[1]

During the same years, Lindsley studied theology with his father in preparation for entering the ministry. In 1845, he received a license to preach from the Nashville Presbytery, and he preached at the Tulip Grove congregation next to Andrew Jackson's Hermitage. According to his father, he was present before and at the death of Andrew Jackson in June 1845, possibly as both physician and minister. In 1846, Berrien spent six months at a church in Symrna and in October was ordained at the First Presbyterian Church in Nashville. His presbytery assigned him to do mission preaching among blacks and the poor. Apparently his education, his ability, and possibly his father's eminence accounted for the unusually short period between licensing and ordination. After these first two years, Lindsley accepted only short preaching assignments or attended revivals or camp meetings but never served as a full-time pastor. He simply did not have the time.

In 1857, Lindsley married red-haired Sarah (Sally) McGavock, daughter of Jacob McGavock, an affluent member of the university board of trust. Her grandfather, David McGavock, was an early settler of Nashville, a friend of James Robertson, and a successful land speculator, who joined the board of trust of Davidson Academy in 1805, just before it became Cumberland College. Sarah's mother was the daughter of Senator Felix Grundy. The marriage secured Berrien Lindsley's status among the most affluent and socially prominent families in middle Tennessee. With his parents dead, Lindsley identified closely with the McGavock family and in 1863 suffered with them when a favorite and gifted son, a founder of charitable institutions in Nashville, died in battle as a Confederate officer.

After the war, Lindsley in 1869 left the Presbyterian Church, USA, to join the regionally strong Cumberland Presbyterian Church, in which he retained his ministerial fellowship until his death. After the Civil War, his Old School denomination reunited with the New School, forming what became largely a northern denomination except in such former unionist areas as east Tennessee. Most Old School Presbyterian congregations in the South had formed a separate denomination during the Confederacy, which after the war became a separate southern denomination. Lindsley apparently did not want to be part of either sectional church. The Cumberland Presbyterian denomination, which did not divide over slavery or during the war, was strong in the Nashville area. Lindsley's openness to this denomination suggests that he was as nondoctrinaire as his father, since the Cumberland Presbyterians repudiated such distinctive Calvinist doctrines as complete depravity and irresistible grace. Lindsley became an early historian of the church and contributed frequently to its publications. In fact, he was one of the most able early historians in the state, and a charter member of the Tennessee Historical Commission. In 1886, he published as author/editor the nine-hundred-page *Confederate Military Annals of Tennessee,* which he planned as part of a three-volume encyclopedia on Confederate Tennessee until low sales discouraged its completion. He also projected but did not complete a history of medicine in Tennessee.[2]

Bowling and Lindsley, who met in 1850, joined with four other local physicians to plan their medical school. They departed slightly from the usual pattern of American medical schools, most of which, if they survived, established ties to a college or university. All were, and would long remain, proprietary—individual physician's salaries came from fees paid by students. Usually, the sponsoring university retained some control over faculty appointments and educational standards. Lindsley wanted no university control. Thus, he and Bowling asked for a twenty-year lease of the east wing of the old campus. They offered no rent but promised to improve and maintain the facilities, insure them, and add needed wings or new buildings. This at first involved a commitment not only to convert the old building to new uses, but to add a west wing to contain the large lecture theaters demanded by medical schools. The faculty would control the school, including the selection of faculty, the election of a dean and other officers, the formulas for dividing up the income, and all decisions about adding new facilities. The university board forced the school to take good care of the campus, which it still owned, and had to respond to future requests for lease extensions. The success of the school—technically, the medical department of the University of Nashville—depended entirely upon its faculty. Because of this arrangement, the medical department had no charter from the State of Tennessee and no supervisory board. Legally, the six original faculty, shortly to become seven, were equal partners in a profit-making enterprise. After paying all costs, they would share the annual income.

The school, in terms of student enrollments, growth in facilities, and local popularity, was an early success. Within three years, Dean Lindsley and other faculty boasted that it was the best medical school in the Southwest. It undoubtedly was. But if so, this only further testified to the scandalous nature of medical education in America. The Nashville school lived on its student fees, wanted to maximize enrollment, and never enforced admissions at even a high school level. It advertised some requirements: Students had to be literate, to be twenty-one years of age by the time they graduated, and to have three years of prior study with a physician (part of the old apprenticeship system). But the school relaxed the requirements for both age and prior experience. The ability level of students varied enormously; only a few arrived with college degrees. Essentially, any young man could enroll who could pay $105 in fees for a four-month series of lectures and limited lab and clinical experience. If students repeated the same series of lectures a second time and passed an oral exam by their professors, they received an M.D., a degree less demanding by far than a high school diploma or a certificate from a classical academy. No one failed. For eight years, as a gesture to the medieval tradition of the M.D. as a scholarly degree, the school asked each student to write a thesis on any medical subject he chose. It is doubtful if the professors read, let alone evaluated, all these twenty- to thirty-page theses. Eventually, the school dropped this requirement as a useless burden for students. (The theses, all 495 of them, are in the Biomedical Library at Vanderbilt University.)

The only excuse for such a nondemanding education was that all competing schools had almost the same requirements. The proprietary system made any higher standards unrealistic, for any school that demanded more, such as extended sessions or a graded curriculum (a different, and more demanding, set of courses for the second year), would have had to charge more tuition and thus risk losing all its students. The system placed a premium not on substance but on show—well-stuffed medical museums, publicized innovations by prima donna surgeons, plenty of cadavers for the anatomy laboratory. For the professors in Nashville, all but Lindsley practicing physicians, the academic work was soon routine. Each professor, in one of the six standard specialties (chemistry and pharmacology, materia medica, anatomy, the practice of medicine, obstetrics and gynecology, and surgery), lectured to all the students for one hour four days a week over a four-month period each year. In the case of anatomy and surgery, the students often observed the professors at work; surgeons performed the more daring operations on a marble table before up to four hundred students in the anatomy theater. From the beginning, the school had agreements with nearby hospitals and soon had its own dispensary or outpatient clinic. Here the hundreds of students could at least observe some clinical practice. Their numbers, and the limited number of indigent patients, made it impossible for students to have any but cursory hands-on experience with patients. At least in theory, they had already worked as apprentices and thus had clinical experience. During the eight months between sessions, they could continue their medical practice, for even one year of medical school, limited as it was, gave would-be physicians a competitive edge over those without formal training.

For the next quarter century, this pattern of training did not change. In 1874, Vanderbilt University adopted the school for its own students, but by then the school had fallen behind many competitors. The winds of change had finally begun to waft through medical education. The new American Medical Association had begun to certify medical schools and very gradually to raise requirements. For example, by 1850, it demanded two terms, spread over two years, for an M.D. The

AMA, plus such medical reformers as Lindsley and William Bowling, wanted much more, but the competitive proprietary system remained an obstacle to higher standards. To its credit, the Nashville school tried to lead the way. It had an unusually able faculty, offered a month of access to its labs and a few free lectures before the regular term began, and added a summer term with a limited array of lectures. None of these extra courses were required for the degree, and they entailed added fees, so few took advantage of them. As Bowling lamented, no medical student would pay for more than two four-month terms, whatever the incentives. If Nashville demanded more, they would go elsewhere. When the AMA so recommended, the school in 1871 added a speciality in psychological medicine, a position closely tied to the state insane asylum. For a period, its labs and museum outshone those of nearby medical schools. If they wanted to take advantage of the extra courses, students could attain as sophisticated a medical education in Nashville as anywhere in the United States.

The Medical School faculty included Nashville's best-trained physicians. All had college degrees. Three of the first six professors had graduated from the University of Pennsylvania Medical College. Bowling and two other early faculty members eventually served as presidents of the AMA. One faculty member, before the opening, toured Europe and bought needed apparatus. Lindsley toured all the eastern schools before launching his own and in 1852 and 1859 toured, and attended lectures in, the best European medical colleges, including that at Paris. (The detailed journal of his first trip is in the biomedical library; on both trips he called on the wealthy expatriate American merchant George Peabody while in London.) Paul Eve, a widely known surgeon, joined the faculty soon after the school opened and helped establish its reputation. He also had an M.D. from Pennsylvania, served in the Polish army during the Polish revolt, and attended lectures in Paris and London. He was egotistic, often contentious, but as eminent as any contemporary American surgeon. He would later serve as president of the AMA. He wowed students with innovative and often risky surgery, such as the removal of brain tumors. Fortunately, by the Medical School's founding in 1850, ether or chloroform had been routinely used in such surgery for four years. Aseptic precautions still lay years ahead. The greatest contribution of the school, at least to medical practice, was a journal launched at its founding by Bowling, the *Nashville Journal of Medicine and Surgery,* which provided a continuing education for literate physicians in much of the South. Bowling wrote editorials, reported on new research, and published articles, letters, and reviews.

These achievements demonstrate that the abysmal quality of medical education was the fault of the system and not distinctive to Nashville. Both Lindsley and Bowling were aware of the deficiencies of American medical schools and in rare unguarded moments confessed the gap that separated their school from those in Europe. Gradually, after 1875, pressured by the AMA, the best American medical schools extended the course of study to three years, adopted a graded curricula, and enforced higher entrance requirements (at least a high school education), as did the University of Nashville–Vanderbilt University Medical Department. But only in 1893 did the Johns Hopkins University first break completely from the weak proprietary system with its built-in incentives for mediocrity. Johns Hopkins introduced a university medical school with salaried professors, a B.A. requirement for entry, four years of graded course work, and extensive clinical training in a large and innovative hospital.

The pre–Civil War medical department seemed a great success. Nashvillians loved it. The faculty gained both prestige and, in most years, a good income. Even during its first session, in 1851–52, it attracted 121 students. The number rose rapidly to an average of 400 between 1856 and the war, making it one of the five largest schools in the United States. Most students came from four states—Tennessee, Kentucky, Alabama, and Georgia. The students who completed two sessions or their equivalent earned the M.D.; an experienced physician had to attend only one session. The number of M.D.s awarded each year averaged over 100 in the five years before the war and peaked at 141 in 1861. After the war, enrollment settled down to a more manageable average of 200, the number of graduates to about 65. The large income from tuition allowed the faculty to improve and expand facilities, even eventually to add hospital wings to its soon somewhat rambling building, yet the school never had adequate clinical facilities. Every available boardinghouse catered to the prewar flood of students, and Lindsley and other faculty liked to boast of the great impact of the school on the Nashville economy. What all the celebrations ignored was the lack of standards. Everything that old Philip Lindsley had charged about the sorry state of medical education in America lay revealed in the medical department. About all one can say in its favor is that it was one of the best of a sorry group. Thus, in some sense it was both the greatest popular and economic success story in the complicated history of the University of Nashville, and the greatest blemish on its academic reputation.[3]

THE LITERARY DEPARTMENT AND THE WESTERN MILITARY INSTITUTE

While the medical department boomed, the literary department remained suspended. The board no longer had the old campus to sell. It had the $2,000 annual income from its endowment, which accumulated interest for the four years of suspension. The board made Berrien Lindsley its agent to seek subscriptions, but as usual few were forthcoming. Still, the university had land. Briefly, it had intended to build the new college building on the south field, along what is now Eighth Avenue. But it soon decided to move three blocks south on Market (Second) to the land around the president's house and sell some of the valuable lots in the south field to raise the money for a new building. In 1852, the board hired an outside architect who developed plans for a magnificent college hall, but the projected costs soared to $70,000. Finally, after almost three years of delay, the board secured a local architect who designed a more modest building. Construction began in the summer of 1853 and would be complete by the projected opening in October 1854. The board decided to use stone, not brick, for the building (154 by 54 feet), which survives to this day. But along the way, it had to drop two end wings from the original plan to limit the cost to about $30,000, all it could fund. The cornerstone laying in 1853 for the building that would become a Nashville landmark involved a huge procession and numerous speeches.

Another, even more elaborate, ceremony marked the opening of the literary department in October 1854. The castlelike stone building was a hit. The six local newspapers reported the largest procession yet in Nashville. Legislators attended, although the now famous alumnus John Bell was too ill to speak. The times seemed auspicious. Nashville, with a population of twenty thousand, had become the leading commercial center of the upper South. The railroad was on the way. The beautiful state capitol building was almost complete, although its famous architect,

A contemporary picture of the Stone Building, or Castle, completed in 1854 as the home of the literary department of the University of Nashville. Later, this historic building would serve as home of the Western Military Institute, Montgomery Bell Academy, the State and then Peabody Normal College, the Medical School of Vanderbilt University, and the Children's Museum of Nashville. Its external dimensions are unchanged from 1854. Confusingly, today it is referred to as Lindsley Hall, or the earlier name for a barracks and dorm just to the north of this building. Courtesy of Paul Conkin.

William Strickland, had died earlier in the year (he was entombed in the walls of the capitol, his last architectural masterpiece). Felix Robertson, president of the university board, sat for a daguerreotype; photography had arrived in Nashville.

Unfortunately, the new building had absorbed all accumulated income from the endowment and from the sale of some of the university's most valuable land, leaving no reserve to pay a new faculty. The board, guided by Berrien Lindsley, recruited three local ministers as professors at $500 per year and tried to make do with a semi-proprietary system. The Presbyterian minister became president of the new and soon contentious faculty. Lindsley, one of four regular faculty, asked for no additional salary beyond his deanship in the medical department. By the plan, each of the three paid professors would, after necessary expenses, share the tuition income to complete their salaries. As before, a professor of foreign languages had to live entirely on special fees. No one, save possibly Lindsley, was an experienced professor or had any notable qualifications except a college degree. At the same time, the board announced the opening of a new law school with two proprietors, housed in the courthouse. It floundered before even one student attended class. And within three months, the literary department all but collapsed.

This effectively ended an ambitious plan, supported by Lindsley. He wanted to make the reopening literary department a part of the new and popular Nashville public school system, which supported one of the first and best public high schools in the South—Hume School (today Hume-Fogg), named after the son of William Hume, one of the first two professors of Cumberland College. As Lindsley envisioned it, the University of Nashville was to serve as the college, and capstone, for a comprehensive free school system rivaled by no other in the country. He offered students selected and sponsored by the board of education entry into the literary department at two-thirds the normal tuition, and graduates among such students free tuition in the medical and law departments. The city government approved this arrangement for a brief period, but we have no record of any special city students enrolled in the first and only year of the revived department.

Few college-level students enrolled in October, 1854. Literary society records suggest no more than thirty. The professors were soon unhappy and fighting with each other. By February, the three regular professors and Lindsley resigned, leaving no faculty. Students despaired, even as the board briefly negotiated with the Nashville free school system to accept their students as transfers to Hume High, which suggests that the remaining students were largely in preparatory classes. But Lindsley would not give up. He had already hired, as a replacement, A. P. Stewart, formerly at Cumberland University, and borrowed a Latin and Greek teacher from the public high school. These two, plus Lindsley, who rejoined the new faculty, finished out the year but could not continue. On paper, this briefly revived literary department seemed a rough equivalent of the old university. The course of study was just as rigorous, tuition was $75 a year, and the new two-semester calendar, with the summer off, replaced the old winter-summer sessions. But the new campus had no dorms or boarding facilities. That students had to find room and board in the area may have deterred students from outside the Nashville area, for most of those in the literary societies were local. We have no records of any degrees conferred at the end of this one frustrating year.[4]

After the faculty resignations, the board decided to appoint Lindsley chancellor of the entire university (medicine, literary, and anticipated law departments), with almost dictatorial powers. He made his first report in March 1855. His aspirations rivaled those of his father in 1825, although he was less eloquent and visionary. He was a forceful, clear writer and had great political skill. Thus, he did not give up on the literary department but wanted to organize it like the medical department, as fully proprietary. He had just completed the first negotiations with a military institute seeking a new campus. In his speech, he argued that the medical department was the best on the North American continent, save Pennsylvania. The literary department, with its wonderful new building, could soon be the strongest in the Southwest, besting the twenty-five or thirty competitors. He referred to his father's vision, and to his desire to bring his father's work to completion. Under the proprietary plan, the literary department could soon duplicate the success of the medical department and have the income to build great libraries and laboratories. In the future, the University of Nashville could rival great universities ancient and modern, and Lindsley named the best in Europe plus Harvard and Princeton. Meanwhile, he asked the board to organize a new subscription drive to fund a dorm or barracks for a military institute.[5]

After some tough bargaining, the board signed an agreement with the Western Military Institute (WMI). It would take over the campus and operate a college with almost complete freedom—but not quite the freedom the board had granted the medical faculty. Some board members opposed any surrender of the board's responsibility to operate a college for undergraduates. It forced the two leaders of WMI to give the board authority to approve all faculty appointments and to award degrees. The plan worked, but not without continued negotiations over funding. Within two years, WMI had won as much enthusiastic local support as the medical department. From the perspective of Berrien Lindsley, this was another great success story. The reality would be a combination preparatory school and undergraduate college that matched others in the South but that never had the quality of faculty, or of students, that had marked the old University of Nashville. It did not have a Philip Lindsley or a Gerard Troost. Its graduates would not be as eminent, although the Civil War's devastating impact on almost all the boys who attended WMI from 1855 to 1862 may account for this.

Military academies and colleges were increasingly popular after 1840, particularly in the South. The preparation of soldiers was not their major role and almost incidental to the perceived benefits of military discipline—order and good character. In the South, at least half of the early state universities eventually converted to a military system, including Georgia, Virginia, and the predecessor of the University of Tennessee. In 1860, beset by discipline problems, Langdon C. Garland, who would later become the first chancellor of Vanderbilt University, imposed a military regimen on the University of Mississippi. Virginia Military Institute, chartered by Virginia in 1839, became famous for the later military success of its graduates, as did the Citadel (1842) in South Carolina. The festering sectional conflict, and a militant and defensive stance in the South, added appeal to a military regimen after 1850.

The University of Nashville ended up with a better than average military institute. Assuring this was the leadership of Bushrod R. Johnson, who founded WMI in Georgetown, Kentucky, in 1847, and his second-in-command, Richard Owen, who joined him in 1850. Johnson was a graduate of West Point and a master teacher of the physical sciences. Owen was a cosmopolitan intellectual, a well-informed but speculative geologist, and a former soldier and officer in the Mexican War. In spite of his background and originality, he was not a Gerard Troost, but like Troost, he reflected a broader culture rare in Nashville. He also opposed slavery and supported the Union in the developing sectional struggle.

Also like Troost, Owen seemed an unlikely migrant to the old Southwest. Born in 1810, he was the son of Robert Owen, the famous textile manufacturer in New Lanark, Scotland, who founded a new socialist or communal system. In 1825, Robert Owen came to the United States, purchased an older village from a German communal sect, the Harmonists, and established the well-publicized New Harmony on the Wabash River in extreme southwestern Indiana, the colony that Gerard Troost had joined. One Owen son, Robert Dale, accompanied his father, but the younger son, Richard, did not, for he was still in Europe completing his education. His main college work, when he was only in his late teens, was at a famous educational experiment at Hofwyl, Switzerland, a college for artisans operated by Emmanuel Fellenberg. Philip Lindsley had applauded this college in his inaugural address of 1825. In Switzerland, Owen married the daughter of Joseph Neef, an associate of the great educational reformer Johann Pestalozzi. It was probably from Owen that Berrien Lindsley first learned of the Pestalozzi system, which he later tried to graft onto the Nashville public schools. Owen studied geology and reported attending later lectures on the subject at the University of Glasgow. He joined his family in New Harmony in about 1829, after the failure of the socialist experiment and just after a disappointed Gerard Troost had moved to Nashville. In America, Owen seems to have floundered for awhile. He assisted his brother, Robert Dale, in some geological work, fought in the Mexican War, and then joined Johnson at WMI, feeling that he had not lived up to the standards of his more famous father and brother.

Owen had an irenic personality and related well to boys at WMI. In addition to instruction in chemistry and geology, he taught tactics and commanded the cadets in their daily drill. He was also the only teacher at WMI with scientific ambitions. For years, he had worked at a great new system of geology, and he published his masterpiece, *Key to the Geology of the Globe,* while in Nashville, in 1857. Though it brought him neither fame nor fortune, it remains a fascinating, and in a quite literal sense, fantastic book. In a subtitle, Owen made clear that his three hundred-page book would prove that certain fixed laws designed by the Creator of the universe shaped all the geological features visible on the earth's surface, even as analogous laws shaped all organic life. In other words, this was a complete new key to the mysteries of geology. Owen referred to it as a dynamic geology to replace the static geology that had so far prevailed. He was knowledgeable in the field and in his book cited almost every important geologist.

Key to the Geology of the Globe began with an argument that has gained Owen a footnote in geological history, and that might allow Peabody boosters to claim that one of their own invented plate tectonics. Owen argued that the Western Hemisphere was long ago conjoined to Europe and Africa. The proof was in coastal configurations and shared flora and fauna. His broader argument was that landmasses move about the surface of the earth. But his explanation was murky at best, completely mistaken at worst. Owen believed that the earth had expanded from a much smaller primordial state, and that the layers of sediment that accumulated under the oceans and on the continents fit regular patterns. What determined these patterns, including the orientation of mountains, the paths taken by rivers, the configuration of coasts, and even continental shifts, were subterranean force fields tied to electrical and magnetic activity under the surface. So far, this seems almost consistent with convective currents in the mantle, and thus modern plate tectonics. But Owen had a fanciful explanation. He believed that lines of energy circled the globe, and at their points of intersection defined a group of spherical triangles, most oriented at the top to a slowly oscillating north magnetic pole. The lines of divergence (fault lines or the intersection of plates, today) and the various orientations of geological phenomenon were tied to these lines and triangles. He worked out maps of the globe to reveal these lines. Almost all that exists on earth depended on this base geology. Drawing from Louis Agassiz, Owen argued that the pattern of emergence of new species depended on the level of development of the earth's geology. Each new age prepared the way for new species, all according to the creative plan of a deity. Unlike Troost, Owen still adhered to much of the biblical cosmology, even explaining some deposits by Noah's flood. By the time he finished, he had correlated his new geology with flora, fauna, the emergence of humans and various races of humans, all the way to the evolution of ethical systems and higher civilizations. Gerard Troost surely turned over in his grave when his first real successor in geology at the university fell prey to such wild, unproven speculation.[6]

When the literary department failed in its first year on the new campus, the partnership with WMI was a godsend. Lindsley leaped at the opportunity but had to prepare his board carefully to accept the new plan. The board once again would have to surrender its authority to someone else. In fact, with the opening of WMI in the fall of 1855, the board had few remaining responsibilities. It owned two campuses but functioned largely as a landlord. The founders of WMI also offered what they had been seeking—stability. The institute had never settled into a permanent home after leaving Georgetown in 1849, spending a year in Blue Lick Spring and a second in Drennon Springs, in each case occupying resort hotels during the winder months. By 1853, Bushrod Johnson wanted to find a permanent home in Tennessee; he visited Nashville in late 1854, where he organized a local board to seek a site and petition the Tennessee assembly for a new charter. This charter made student cadets part of the state militia, awarded suitable rank to Johnson and Owen, and provided state support in the form of rifles and other military gear. But the only location available in Tennessee was another hotel watering place—Tyree Springs in Sumner County, twenty miles north of Nashville. WMI conducted its 1854–55 sessions there while it solicited offers for a better site. For a time, the institute almost joined with East Tennessee University in Knoxville.

As it became clear early in 1855 that the University of Nashville would have to suspend its literary department, Lindsley began serious negotiations with Johnson and Owen. He reached a speedy agreement with them in early March and by April 4 had persuaded his board to go along. A little more than a month later, Philip Lindsley, in Nashville for the general assembly of his church, died at the home of his daughter-in-law. In a late letter, he made clear that he was not enamoured by the idea of a military school, although the agreement with WMI was widely praised in Nashville. The board granted WMI free rental of the campus but assumed no responsibility for salaries, which would come entirely from student fees. Like almost all military schools, WMI operated a store for student supplies, beginning with the required blue uniforms. Owen and Johnson had a right to 10 percent of all profits from the store, which did make money. Additional profits were to retire deficits or buy equipment. The professors were to divide whatever tuition and fees remained after Johnson and Owen received their guaranteed base salaries of $1,750. The two men would get raises when enrollment reached 150 and 200 students.

For their part, Lindsley and the board had to promise to complete, as quickly as possible, a dorm or barracks to hold the cadets. Lindsley's new subscription drive fell well short of the required $32,000. He gave his own note to make up the difference, a personal debt that the board finally redeemed after the Civil War, not without some ill will. The three-story barracks, with a mess and rooms for 150 students, was not ready until the fall of 1856. Hastily constructed of brick, it was

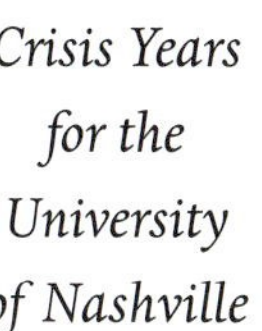

Barracks completed in 1856 for the boys in the Western Military Institute. Later named Lindsley Hall, it was demolished in 1911. [GPCR]

northeast of the classroom building. By the second year, the popular WMI had two hundred students, almost evenly divided between preparatory students (thirteen or older) and college students. It remained full until the war. The two main proprietors—Colonel Johnson as superintendent, Lieutenant Colonel Owen as commandant of cadets—plus at least two other professors lived in apartments in Philip Lindsley's old home, now with new wings. Johnson wanted a gym and a second barracks for a total residential student body of three hundred, plus faculty residences. The board supported such expansion but never had the funds. It had to sell some South Field lots to loan funds to the medical faculty for necessary expansions and resented the constant barrage of pleas for financial help from its two lessees.

WMI maintained a standard liberal-arts curriculum, scarcely changed since Philip Lindsley's era. Because of the number of students, it eventually employed eight or nine faculty, none distinguished, apart from the two commanders. Drill and tactics joined the standard five fields of ancient languages, math and physics, chemistry and geology, belle lettres, and fee-based courses in modern languages. The residential cadets had to observe full military discipline. Their day began with reveille and roll call at daybreak, breakfast at 7:00, study and recitations in the morning and afternoon, dinner at 1:00, and drill an hour before sunset, followed by supper, study, tattoo at 9:30, and taps at 10:00. Students had no free time during the day and had to attend a church of their choice on Sunday. The rules were strict, and even minor violations led to demerits; accumulated demerits led to serious discipline or even expulsion. The cadets trained with real rifles but could not take guns into the barracks or keep private firearms. Some day students did not have to wear uniforms or attend drill but were in a sense second-class citizens. From all the evidence, the boys loved their uniforms and took to the military regimen. Otherwise, campus life was much as it had been before 1850. The literary societies continued. The former library, except for medical books, found a home in the new college building, along with the laboratory apparatus and Troost's cabinets. From Berrien Lindsley's perspective, WMI was almost as successful as the Medical School. He still yearned for a matching law school and tried but failed to establish a scientific school closely tied to the Medical School (it advertised for students for one year). From 1857 to 1860, it seemed to Lindsley that the University of Nashville was finally approaching his and his father's dream of a truly great southern university.[7] Then came the war.

The B.A. graduates of the Western Military Institute (their degrees were from the University of Nashville) in 1860. Within the next year, most would become Confederate soldiers. Photographic Archives of Vanderbilt University.

Crisis Years for the University of Nashville

The developing sectional conflict had already cast a dark shadow over the University of Nashville, and particularly WMI. Sectional tensions led to the only major controversy that involved students; it contributed to Richard Owen's resignation in 1858. In the fall of 1857, a troubled year marked by a few cases of yellow fever in Nashville and a brief suspension of classes, the WMI faculty expelled seventeen students on charges of an "unlawful combination." Its exact nature is not clear, but it involved a "point of honor" among students who defended slavery, which the University of Nashville board later asserted was a common view in the South. What seems most likely is that some southern young men met as a club to defend what they perceived as southern views, perhaps in reaction to either policies or beliefs expressed by some faculty. Owen was the likely target of their distress. His attempt to keep political issues off campus may have triggered the student initiative. The suspended students denied the charges and appealed their suspension to the board of the University of Nashville. It is not clear that this board could interfere with disciplinary procedures in the institute, but board members were deeply concerned and had earlier attended faculty meetings on campus to gain an understanding of the conflict. Some of the expelled students were sons of board members, including the son of board president Felix Robertson. A concerned board considered several motions and amendments but eventually, in a divided vote, upheld the faculty's move to expel the students, at the same time making it clear that the students, if penitent, should be eligible for readmission. The board believed that both students and faculty had erred, and that much of the controversy sprang from misunderstandings. In any case, Owen and Johnson were by now on opposite sides in the developing conflict. Their disagreements made it impossible for both to continue, and Owen chose to leave. According to Lindsley, the parting was amiable and the situation at the college less tense after Owen left.[8] Owen rejoined the U.S. Army at fifty-two and during the Civil War commanded a prisoner-of-war camp. His generosity and kindness to Confederates captured at Fort Donelson led some of them, after the war, to erect a monument in his honor. He would spend his postwar career as state geologist of Indiana.

Tennessee was a reluctant convert to the Confederate cause. An overwhelming majority of voters rejected a secession convention in February 1861, after states to the south had already seceded. Most blacks, of course, were slaves and could not vote. But after Lincoln decided to reprovision Fort Sumter in April, sentiment at least among the governing white elite in middle and west Tennessee shifted rapidly toward secession. A majority of those voting endorsed a declaration of independence on May 6 and in June ratified a new Confederate constitution. John Bell, a popular University of Nashville alumnus, won Tennessee's electoral vote in 1860, as a candidate of a new Constitutional Union Party committed to some compromise to preserve the Union. In the wake of Sumter, even he and many other Whigs who had formerly opposed secession supported it. But more than any other Confederate state save Virginia, Tennessee was divided. Most counties in east Tennessee remained loyal to the Union, which meant that Tennessee furnished almost half as many troops to the Union as to the Confederacy. In no sense was the war, at least in Tennessee, between North and South; it was between unionists and secessionists. Clearly, if one included blacks, most Tennesseans opposed the Confederacy. But in middle and west Tennessee, and particularly in areas with large slave populations and a planter elite, such as the central basin around Nashville, most whites were pro-Confederate. So was the governor. Wealth and power were on the side of secession; blacks and many less affluent, particularly non-slave-owning, whites remained loyal to the Union. For this reason, the war was truly a civil war in Tennessee, which, next to Virginia, suffered more battles and casualties than any other state. In most such battles, regiments from Tennessee fought against each other.

At the University of Nashville, the early months of the war seemed calm. The Confederate state government tried to organize a defense for Tennessee. Bushrod Johnson resigned to join the Confederate army. Lindsley took charge of the college, and he and four professors continued the military system. Nineteen students received the bachelor of arts or science in June 1861, but by then many of the older students had joined the army, most on the Confederate side. In the fall of 1861, Lindsley opened WMI as usual, with sixty students. Until then the Medical School had continued to boom. No major battles had yet occurred near Nashville. But in the fall, Confederate officials asked for hospital space for ill soldiers (not yet for wounded). The WMI students then passed a resolution in which they offered to evacuate their campus if military authorities needed it, and even offered their blankets and mattresses. It was clear, by then, that the remaining students were Confederate sympathizers. This was a typical student gesture, but only the board of trust could donate facilities to the military, and it did not do so until February 12, 1862, when it had little alternative. Presumably, classes continued until that date. The Medical School never closed. Because all the graduates of WMI had just left school and were still young, none became famous military commanders during the war, but one of the last students in WMI, Sam Davis, became locally famous as "the boy hero of the Confederacy."[9]

No southern university fared better during the Civil War than the University of Nashville, in part because of luck and location, and in part because of the dedicated work of Berrien Lindsley. His consuming goal after 1862 was to protect two campuses, two libraries (one in the Medical School), and the laboratory equipment and medical museum. In the darkest days of 1863–64, he was able to retain a few students in the Medical School, in part to have on-site protection for buildings and equipment. Many of the rooms served as a federal hospital, and for a brief period the students had plenty of clinical opportunities.

Lindsley held complex political views about the war. Like John Bell, he had been a strong Whig and unionist until 1861. He deplored the secession movement and would always believe that irresponsible southern hotheads had brought on the awful destruction that befell the South. But with Fort Sumter, he reluctantly chose to support what he saw as alone defensible, the right of self-determination for southern states. Although a slave owner who believed forced abolition would be disastrous for both races, Lindsley acknowledged that the denial of self-determination to four million Africans also violated U.S. constitutional principles. This explained why Europeans eventually refused to support the South. As the war developed, and the cruelty and suffering became almost unbearable, Lindsley sometimes took a fatalistic view. As so many Tennesseans in the middle of an unwanted conflict, he blamed the war on political incompetents on both sides and wondered why God had allowed the glorious American Republic to sink so low. But European countries had survived worse fratricidal conflict. Lindsley hoped that after the horrible testing, God had ordained a new and glorious future for his country. His brother, Van, remained a strong unionist, and thus the two chose opposite sides. By 1863, Berrien's southern loyalties became more intense as he suffered the inevitable frustrations of military occupation, but by then he most of all wanted the war to end. In 1863, he and his wife's family, the McGavocks, all took an oath of loyalty to the Union and posted bond for their good behavior. The military governor, Andrew Johnson, forced the oath upon prominent citizens with known Confederate sympathies. Johnson, as a prewar governor of Tennessee, had been an ex-officio member of the board of the University of Nashville. Taking the oath allowed Lindsley, as a U.S. citizen, to negotiate with federal officers, and to file substantial claims for damages to, and rent of, university buildings. Except for wear and tear and some destroyed fencing, the campus suffered no structural damage; it lost not a single book or museum exhibit. But the vacant, deteriorating old laboratory, the beloved former domain of Troost, burned. It was no great material loss, however, as insurance more than covered its value. This would be the only significant fire in the history of the University of Nashville and Peabody College. Few other universities have been so fortunate.[10]

What saved the university and made possible continuous financial gain during the war was a federal victory in 1862. On February 5, Ulysses Grant captured Fort Henry on the Tennessee River and then laid siege to the well-defended Fort Donelson on the Cumberland, just south of the Kentucky border at Dover. Gunboats joined troops in the battle, and in a controversial decision, the Confederate commander surrendered on February 15, creating the first large pool of Confederate prisoners. Albert Sydney Johnston, the western commander for the Confederacy, felt he had no alternative but to move his troops south of Nashville. Thus, federal troops and gunships captured or liberated Nashville—depending on one's political views—without a fight. Retreating Confederates set fire to one bridge and destroyed military equipment. Nashville would remain within the Union for the rest of the war. Few southern cities fared as well. With its railroad connections (the Louisville and Nashville), Nashville became a major supply center for Union armies throughout the western theater. Business and population boomed. Freed blacks flocked to the city and helped build Fort Negley just south of the campus. To Lindsley's despair, some black workers briefly occupied the two main college buildings. His response reflected not only a concern for the buildings, but a typical racism. The most committed Confederates, if they had the means, fled Nashville. New, often entrepreneurial types moved in. To an extent later denied by older families, a surprising number of business people in Nashville decided the best policy was to cooperate with federal authorities. Less appealing businesses developed to cater to federal soldiers, including a plethora of bars and eventually even legalized brothels. Perhaps most important, Nashville banks, which held the bonds and other investments of the University of Nashville, remained under U.S. control, with a federal rather than a depreciating and eventually worthless Confederate currency as the medium of exchange.

It was during the siege of Fort Donelson that Lindsley had to surrender his main campus for hospital use. At first, it served wounded soldiers from the battle. Briefly, the Confederates remained in control and appointed Lindsley as interim post surgeon. His two weeks in this position qualified him later as a Confederate veteran. In a time of fear and near chaos, he persuaded the Confederate officials not to house soldiers in campus buildings, but to keep them for hospital use. Up to five hundred men briefly filled the barracks, including wounded federal prisoners. Lindsley desperately sought food for them all. The legislature had fled, no one was in control, and local supplies were subject to looting.

Lindsley must have welcomed the restored order imposed when federal troops moved, without resistance, into Nashville on February 24. He surrendered his hospital to federal surgeons and earned their recognition for his kind and equal treatment of hospitalized federal soldiers. The Federals apparently did not consider him a prisoner, given the circumstances. Now, wounded federal troops gradually replaced the remaining Confederates who were too ill to move with the retreating army to the Murfreesboro area. Lindsley worked with federal army surgeons and found some of them very decent. In this chaotic time, he seemed to minister to the wounded with little regard to their allegiance. By March, the campus buildings held more than seven hundred patients.

In September 1862, federal officials, fearing an attack on Nashville, began building fortifications at Fort Negley and for a time stationed troops and black workers in campus buildings. Lindsley worked frantically to box books and apparatus and secure them in homes or locked rooms in the main building. In June 1863, he boxed the medical library and brought it to the same safe storage, finally adding Troost's cabinets in December. With the nearby construction completed, the campus became, once again, a hospital and remained so until the end of the war. At various times, federal troops encamped on university land and used fences for firewood. Later, in a process that continued long after the war, the university successfully prosecuted claims for such damage and, beginning in 1864, received both retroactive and continuing rent for the buildings. One can only imagine how different the scenario would have been had Nashville remained under Confederate control.

The climax of the war, at least for Nashville, came late—in December 1864. It was now clear that the Confederacy would lose. Sherman had marched through Georgia. But in a final, desperate tactic, a Confederate army under General John B. Hood moved north into middle Tennessee to attempt to retake Nashville and cut off supply routes to federal armies to the southeast. Hood prevailed (to say he won is misleading) in one of the war's bloodiest engagements, at nearby Franklin, on November 30, 1864. He then marched his weary troops on heavily fortified Nashville. The city prepared frantically for battle, which took place on December 15–16. Entrenchments passed through part of the south campus, just northeast of Fort Negley. Had Confederate troops prevailed or even been able to penetrate federal defenses as far north as Fort Negley, campus buildings would have come under fire and could have been badly damaged, even destroyed. Had the Confederates taken Nashville, the fighting would have involved both campuses. More critical, the now tattered Confederate army might have suffered a Union counterattack, and Nashville itself could have suffered the fate of Atlanta. But the federal defenses held, and the Confederate army withdrew, in effect marking the end of the fighting in Tennessee. In the calm that followed, Lindsley began rebuilding fences and repairing buildings. But the hospitals in Nashville were flooded with wounded, and the federal authorities retained control of campus buildings until September 1865.[11]

The medical department alone remained intact at war's end, although one professor had been killed in battle. Within a year the school was back to normal, with about 200 students attending each session (192 in 1866–67). Its course of study, except for the addition of work in psychiatry, would remain the same until its adoption by Vanderbilt University in 1874. It faced a minor crisis in 1868, when an increasingly unstable professor, Thomas Jennings, apparently became incensed at assessments levied by his partners, withdrew from the faculty, and sued for his share of the assets. In effect, he tried to end the partnership and in fact did force a resignation of the faculty and a reorganization. But his action, joined by two colleagues, did not significantly damage the school. What grew increasingly difficult was gaining access to clinical facilities. After unsuccessful efforts to get the city to build a hospital, the medical faculty decided to go it alone. In 1875, it received a final lease extension to 1905 from the university board and used its own funds to add two hospital wings to its main building. Without such planned facilities,

Vanderbilt University would probably not have adopted the school as its own in 1874.[12]

The university delayed restoring the literary department for reasons that remain unclear. The campus was intact, and Lindsley saw to its full restoration after the war. The stone castle awaited residents. Unlike so much of the South, Nashville and the surrounding counties had suffered limited destruction. But times were hard. Another cholera epidemic hit the city in 1866. Lindsley doubted that the university, with no public funding, could attract college-level students in the confused postwar environment. He had hoped that the university could tap into federal funds and tried to explore ways to become the recipient of land grants under the Morrill Act of 1862, but the school was ill prepared to bid to train students in either agriculture or engineering.

Postwar Tennessee faced enormous social and economic problems. Most sections of the state were much worse off than Nashville. After 1867, and particularly after 1873, land prices plummeted. Although Tennessee ratified the Fourteenth Amendment in 1866 and won full readmission to the Union without coming under federal occupation and the various Reconstruction acts, it still struggled through a turbulent political interlude. The deep divisions of the war continued. With many Confederate supporters disenfranchised, the Republican Party won control of state offices. It bestowed votes on blacks (a lasting and controversial issue) and found its strongest base of support in unionist east Tennessee. But its soon notorious governor, "Parson" William G. Brownlow, from Knoxville, managed to alienate a majority of whites. When the Democrats regained power in 1869, they convened a new constitutional convention, and citizens ratified the new constitution despite its retention of black suffrage. Thus, what some would call Reconstruction in Tennessee ended early, with no lasting shift of political power away from the older, more affluent white families.

But the state, as well as the South as a whole, faced intractable economic problems. Tennessee's main economic sector, agriculture, recovered much of its prewar prosperity in the interlude from 1866 to the panic and depression of 1873, and then remained stagnant. Public services, including education, lagged far behind those of northern states. Away from the larger cities, public schools remained closed; a generation of Tennesseans grew up illiterate. By 1880, per capita incomes in Tennessee and the South as a whole were only half the national average, and they remained at that low level for more than fifty years. The tiny manufacturing sector grew fastest after the war, but a paucity of human skills, high rail rates, and a low level of public services led to labor-intensive, low-wage industries. Of vital concern to the University of Nashville, the state came close to repudiating its state debt and for several years was unable to make interest payments on it bonds, including those owned by the university.

Crisis Years for the University of Nashville

With control of the campus back in his hands in the fall of 1865, Berrien Lindsley began talking to board members. Many had fled Nashville during the war, and almost all had pressing personal and family problems to deal with. Meanwhile, Nashville newspapers that had inquired about plans to reopen the college blamed the board for delays. After all, Cumberland University in Lebanon, despite a burned-out campus, had already reopened. On June 21, 1867, at the first board meeting since the war began, Lindsley briefly recounted his wartime activities and recommended that the campus reopen as a first-class grammar and preparatory academy, not as a college. Correctly, he sensed that the university did not have the resources to succeed in the difficult postwar environment. Few students could pay the tuition required to support a college-level faculty. The university's tiny endowment, still mostly in Tennessee state bonds, had grown only to about $45,000. But the state could neither redeem nor pay interest on the bonds and soon contemplated repudiation. In effect, the university had no sure income at all. Eventually, the state issued new bonds to reflect accumulated interest and redeemed all bonds owned by charitable or educational institutions at full value (not so those owned by banks or corporations).[13]

The university did have enough money to open an academy. Montgomery Bell, who had grown wealthy mining and smelting iron ore in Dickson County, had died in 1855 and left a special bequest of $20,000 to the University of Nashville. His instructions were detailed and specific: The university was to invest this fund in state bonds or other secure instruments and use only the interest to support a Montgomery Bell Academy for the education of boys, beginning at the age of ten to fourteen and continuing until the age of eighteen. Bell also prescribed the basic curriculum—English, reading, writing, arithmetic, and geography—with courses in higher math and languages determined by the academy. The main object of his gift was to provide free tuition in such an academy for a suggested twenty-five boys from families unable to afford such an education (the university would always accept this number). He even specified his preferred geographical distribution of these boys—ten from Davidson, and five each from Williamson, Dickson, and Montgomery Counties.

The problem with the gift was that the income each year from $20,000 (at most $1,200) was far too little to establish an academy. In 1855, a board committee was unable to recommend acceptance of the gift. Fortunately, Bell's will did not require immediate implementation, which meant the fund could grow. In 1856, Lindsley, as chancellor, strongly recommended acceptance. Since WMI already accepted boys of thirteen for preparatory work, Lindsley wanted to fold Montgomery Academy into WMI, with no extra faculty and a room in the stone building dedicated to these impoverished boys. To reject the gift would discourage future benefactors. After formal acceptance by the board, the funds went into state bonds. No one did anything to establish such an academy, and then the war intervened.

In one of the rare investment triumphs of the University of Nashville, an official at Planters' Bank kept reinvesting this fund during the wartime inflation. By 1867, the $20,000 had more than doubled to $46,000 (yielding $2,600 annually), more than enough to cover the tuition of twenty-five needy boys. Beyond the scholarship students, Lindsley anticipated a local demand for quality elementary and high school education, particularly for those families just outside Nashville whose children could not attend the free public schools of the city; the county, as yet, provided no public schools at all. The board appointed teachers for the Montgomery Bell Academy (MBA) in July 1867, and it opened in the fall in the south wing of the stone building. The principal was Le Roy Halsey, an alumnus of, and briefly tutor in, the University of Nashville and a fervent admirer of Philip Lindsley; he would later publish a three-volume edition of Lindsley's writings. The salaries still reflected wartime inflation, ranging from $2,000 to $2,500. Lindsley, as always, listed himself as a teacher of natural science. The income from the endowment was sufficient only for the principal. Paying students funded additional teachers with no problem (77 the first year, 125 the second). The tuition for the three terms each year was sixty dollars in the grammar school and eighty dollars in the high school, which had a four-year classical track to fit students for Harvard and Yale and a three-year English track sufficient for entrance to most other colleges.[14]

Lindsley's other hope, which he first enunciated the same year, was to add a normal school to the university with support from the new Peabody Education Fund. By request of the board, he wrote to the former president of Brown, Barnas Sears, the new general agent of the Peabody fund, whom Lindsley had met in Nashville. Sears pointed out that the fund could not support a normal school until the state established a viable public school system under a board of education and was willing to help fund such a school.[15]

Within two years, Lindsley revealed the next step in his plan for the University of Nashville: to grow a college within MBA. In 1869, he proposed an annual extension of one year to the level of courses offered, building up to a four-year college course to follow high school, with both B.A. and B.S. degrees and the gradual addition of college-level professors (eight instructors in all). The combined endowment of the former literary department and Montgomery Bell was close to $100,000, enough to yield around $6,000 a year. Tuition would provide approximately $10,000 in additional funds. The plan could succeed if enough students would pay the projected $100 annual college tuition. Lindsley also dreamed of opening a law school. But even as he planned, an ominous threat took shape. The Methodist Episcopal Church, South, announced preliminary plans for a great central university, most likely located in Nashville. Lindsley hoped that such a university could somehow become part of the University of Nashville.

Lindsley wanted his new Department of Science, Literature, and the Arts to be separate from MBA. A cautious board, in a divided vote, eventually accepted the plan. Lindsley furnished rooms in the old barracks and advertised for college students. In the fall of 1869, the new department opened. But students enrolled only as freshmen and sophomores, and thus the year ended with public exercises but no degrees awarded. This attempt to create a college with too few resources soon floundered. Lindsley later admitted that the faculty, borrowed from MBA, was not college level. The Science, Literature, and Arts College lasted only one year, because the board received an offer out of the blue to accommodate another proprietary venture, this one headed by two Confederate generals.[16]

Bushrod Johnson of the old WMI and E. Kirby Smith had served in the Confederate army and already enjoyed a degree of fame in the South. In May 1870, they wanted to become heads of a college, expecting to gain both prestige and income from such a venture. This strategy for ex-Confederate generals was now all the rage. Lee at Washington College in Virginia became the model. Now these two generals wanted to lease the two main college buildings for fifteen years (the stone castle and the now largely unused barracks) and operate both the collegiate program and MBA. They promised to provide free tuition for twenty-five students in MBA but rightly asked the board to grant them $2,000 annual income from the Montgomery Bell endowment. They promised to maintain and improve the buildings, add to the library and labs, and allow the board to approve all faculty and courses of study. They contemplated a revival of the military mode of organization but in the end made military drill and discipline voluntary. High school students joined a few college students as cadets, but most local students chose not to participate.[17]

Their proposal appealed to Lindsley, who had a hard time persuading the board. It did not want to surrender so much authority (it would lose control even of MBA), and some board members believed such a surrender of responsibility violated the university charter. When the board voted against the lease, Lindsley offered his resignation as chancellor. (He would remain on the faculty of the Medical School until 1873 but was already devoting most of his time to a crusade for a state system of public schools.) The board, a week later, accepted the resignation, a move that had one intended effect—a barrage of newspaper support for the new plan. Lindsley would never rejoin the board, although his brother remained a member, but he worked for the next five years to establish a normal school for the university. Generals Smith and Johnson, anxious to build new careers in higher education and highly optimistic about the Nashville prospects, improved their offer and released the board from all pecuniary responsibility for the college. A board motion to table the final offer lost by only one vote. After some clarifying amendments to increase the board's role, the board approved the lease by a vote of eleven to six. During the controversy, John Lea, board president and an opponent of the plan, offered his resignation, which the board rejected.[18]

The two generals took command of what essentially had remained a preparatory academy. E. Kirby Smith replaced Lindsley as chancellor; Johnson became principal of the collegiate department. Few college-level students enrolled, and only a few received degrees (eight in the last commencement in 1875). In an innovation that seemed to advance beyond the past practice of M.A. degrees in course, the collegiate department offered an earned master of arts and awarded at least three or four, but nothing indicates a faculty of the quality that could justify graduate work. In 1872, the school moved to a more elective curriculum and adopted the popular system in which each professor became a school and certified the students that qualified in his field. By then desperate to attract students, the college advertised degrees in agriculture and engineering, a ploy that drew few, if any, students. Smith and Johnson, struggling to regain the magic of the old WMI, met with endless frustrations. By 1872, they had 255 students, mainly in the academy, with only 34 in the college and in five years never more than 44, which was below the critical mass needed for a successful college. The generals had promised to raise $7,000 in gifts to improve the buildings, particularly the barracks. They probably raised less but made up the difference and thoroughly refurbished the buildings. Income never matched expenses. By 1873, they had to do what they had promised not to—beg the board to loan $3,180 to pay the teachers' salaries. In the spring of 1874, the Agatheridian boys suspended their literary society because membership was down to only six. In the fall of 1875, they reorganized, but at some meetings, only five members carried on the debates. In their last meeting, on September 21, 1875, they had no intimation that this would be the final year for a collegiate department. (The society would reorganize later at the State Normal College.)[19]

The university board could not come to the aid of the failing literary department . It had no secure income, since Tennessee had suspended interest payments on its bonds. Berrien Lindsley first accepted, then refused, an offer to become an agent to raise a new endowment for the collegiate department. In a new board election, he was nominated as a trustee but lost to other candidates. And by 1873, everyone feared the competition of the new Vanderbilt University. Bishop Holland McTyeire, president of the Vanderbilt board, did negotiate with board members of the University of Nashville during his search for a site for the Vanderbilt campus, but he soon made it clear that Vanderbilt would insist on sole control of any site. The University of Nashville gave up on this possibility and again considered ways to establish departments of agriculture and engineering to win federal land grants. By 1874, a demoralized board often met with no quorum.

In April 1874, with understandable reluctance, the board approved the adoption of the Medical School by Vanderbilt. It did so only because the move was strongly supported by the medical faculty, a group of proprietors determined to protect their own interests. Vanderbilt soon garnered much more prestige than the University of Nashville, and almost all the Medical School's graduates took a Vanderbilt M.D. The faculty also feared the competition if Vanderbilt established its own medical school. But the University of Nashville gained nothing; it was the sole owner of the facilities used by a medical school that everyone soon identified with Vanderbilt. And as Vanderbilt prepared to open for classes in 1875, Generals Smith and Johnson had almost reached the end of the line. The panic of 1873 and hard times threatened their already fragile enrollment. One feels for them, for they tried to build a successful college. In the last year they were unable even to pay their own salaries. As a last friendly gesture, the university board assumed most of their deficit for 1874–75. Even enrollments in MBA had dropped with each passing year. By 1874–75, Smith and Johnson knew that their failed experiment was in its last year, and that the university would shortly end their lease. We do not know how the board handled the final negotiations with the generals. The assumption of debts might have been a concealed bribe to get them to surrender a lease that still had ten years to run. In the last catalogue, in 1874, Smith and Johnson recorded only thirty-one students at the college level, and they awarded only three bachelor degrees that year.[20] The next year, the literary department became part of the new State Normal College supported by the Peabody Education Fund.

In all but a legal sense, the University of Nashville in 1875 once again suspended operations as a collegiate institution. It retained legal ownership of two campuses, but little more. From this point on, the Peabody trustees made all the important decisions for the normal school. The medical department was now more a part of Vanderbilt than of the University of Nashville. After Vanderbilt withdrew from its partnership in 1895 to found its own medical school, the old University of Nashville medical department never regained its earlier glory and soon expired through mergers. Since then, the University of Nashville board has held direct authority only over Montgomery Bell Academy. It is an excellent academy, but scarcely the university anticipated by Philip Lindsley in 1827 in a moment of soaring hopes.

After 1875, Berrien Lindsley remained a patron of the new State Normal. But he all but ended his direct contributions to the university and to public education. Another, and in many ways the most influential, phase of his life was just beginning—public health reform. In 1866, Nashville organized the first board of health in Tennessee. In 1876, Lindsley accepted a full-time appointment as health officer for Nashville, where he served only four years before moving to the state level to continue his reform efforts. In ten years, his efforts and those of his successors had transformed Nashville and drastically reduced its death rate. Lindsley became a missionary in behalf of hygiene and sanitation. With the creation of a state board of health in 1877, Lindsley became its secretary and executive officer and served one term as president. From 1885 until his death in 1897, he edited the *State Board of Health Bulletin.* Eventually, his written reports for various agencies numbered in the thousands of pages. He enticed the American Public Health Association to meet in Nashville in 1879 and later served as its treasurer. He was a member of the National Prison Association, the National Conference of Charities and Corrections, a founding member of the American Association for the Advancement of Science, and a fellow of the American Academy of Medicine. Princeton gave him an honorary doctorate. After 1880, he served as professor of sanitary science and preventive medicine in the new University of Tennessee Medical College in Nashville.

Amid all these honors, Lindsley's greatest achievement in public health was in Nashville. He began by compiling death records, and eventually birth and marriage records. He believed terrible sanitary conditions contributed to one of the highest death rates in the country. He began efforts to clean up the city, gaining broad public support because of the fear of epidemics. He persuaded the city to set up a new, filtered but not treated water system, rebuild and expand its sewage system, outlaw all but carefully designed privies, control garbage collection and the scavenging of dead animals, force the construction of sidewalks and better street drainage, eliminate most stagnant water and swamps, inspect buildings and use new laws to control overcrowding and protect against fires, offer universal free vaccination for smallpox for indigents, plant trees along streets, and improve jails and workhouses (he wrote pamphlets on prison reform). Lindsley seemed vindicated in 1878, when a yellow-fever epidemic that ravaged the South and devastated Memphis spared Nashville. Everyone attributed the city's escape to Lindsley's reforms. As the epidemic spread, willing citizens in Nashville joined in cleaning up every part of the city. No one knew the cause of yellow fever, but Lindsley believed dampness triggered both it and malaria. Nashville in fact owed its escape primarily to its climate, and to the near absence of the mosquito *(aedes aegypti)* that transmits the virus, but Lindsley's control of stagnant water may have helped prevent a few cases of malaria or yellow fever. In any case, his crusade drew enormous prestige, and his sanitation reforms slowly all but ended epidemics of cholera and typhoid fever. This does not mean that Nashville overcame all its horrible sanitation problems, but after the reforms initiated by Lindsley, the death rate dropped by almost half, from 34.55 per thousand in 1875 to 17.81 in 1890, with the highest rates still in black neighborhoods.[21]

Finally, Lindsley tried to redesign school buildings, introduce instruction in hygiene in schools, and get rid of the cruel and harsh discipline that marked public education. He recommended Pestalozzi's approach and rejoiced one year when only one student in all Nashville's schools had been spanked. By the time he died in 1897, still at work on his public-health bulletins, Lindsley had become one of the most honored citizens of Tennessee, and one of the two or three most eminent graduates of the old University of Nashville. His death, at age 75, came as a shock to family and friends. He had not been ill. But a fire in a house next door led him to a desperate effort to move his library from his office, just an alley away from the fire. He obviously overdid the effort, and was frightened by the possible loss of his beloved books. He collapsed, probably with a coronary, and lived only a few days. He left behind a prominent family. He and Sarah had six children, all able students. One daughter married Percy Warner, who donated the land for the city's Percy Warner Park.

CHAPTER FIVE

The State Normal College of Tennessee, 1875–1887

THE NORMAL SCHOOL THAT OPENED IN NASHVILLE IN LATE 1875 eventually became a rousing success story. The school would have an enormous impact on public education in the South. For its time, and given the conditions in the post-Civil War South, its role was fully as significant as that of its successor, the George Peabody College for Teachers. The story of this normal school is a heart-warming example of what idealism, dedication, and hard work can accomplish. And in this case, more than any other in the long history of what became George Peabody College, it would be the students who contributed most to this success.

The opening of the new normal school on December 1, 1875, with only three teachers and thirteen students, all local and all young women, was anticlimactic. To understand the origins and growth of this ungainly educational infant requires some insight into its context: the origins and early program of the Peabody Education Fund and its leadership, teacher education as it had developed in the North before the Civil War, the economic plight and political realities of the former Confederate states, and the problems that faced public education in a biracial South.

GEORGE PEABODY AND HIS FUND

In one sense, the normal school began in the mind of George Peabody, who had lived and suffered through the Civil War at his home in London. By his gift of what became the Peabody Fund, he was the indirect founder of what is now George Peabody College. His name thus joins that of Cornelius Vanderbilt, who endowed Vanderbilt University. Through his fund, Peabody gave more to Peabody than Cornelius Vanderbilt ever gave to the institution that bears his name, but not nearly as much as the extended Vanderbilt family contributed in the next century. Some parallels mark the two gifts. Both came near the end of the lives of the donors. Both were motivated in part by a desire for sectional reconciliation after the Civil War. But Vanderbilt had been ruthless and amoral, while Peabody was an upstanding Yankee merchant and financier. The two men knew each other, but not well. Once, when in London, Vanderbilt borrowed money from Peabody.[1]

George Peabody was born in 1795 in Danvers (now Peabody), Massachusetts, north of Boston and just west of Salem. His Peabody progenitors had immigrated to Puritan Massachusetts as early as 1635. But his branch of the family, unlike those who participated in the transcendentalist movement, was neither famous nor wealthy. His father worked in leather, was never very successful, and died young. George had to leave school at eleven and apprentice to a local merchant. He found his calling. In his late teens he moved with an uncle to Georgetown, in the District of Columbia, and opened a dry-goods store. Two years later, in 1814, he became a junior partner in a dry-goods business owned by Elisha Riggs. They soon moved to Baltimore, where the firm of Riggs and Peabody rapidly developed into the largest dry-goods business in the city. As Peabody became affluent, he assisted his extended family back in Danvers, traveled often to England, and in 1837 moved there. Apart from two one-year trips back to the United States, he lived in England until his death in 1869, although he kept his U.S. citizenship.

In London, Peabody at first largely bought textiles for his firm back in Baltimore. As Riggs's sons took over for their father, Peabody became the senior partner. He made private, often very profitable, investments. He helped sell bonds for the State of Maryland and soon began purchasing depreciated bonds issued by American states that had, after 1837, frequently defaulted on interest payments. It was his belief that these states would eventually honor their obligations. Most did, and he made large profits. Eventually he quit the dry-goods business and became an international financier. He dealt in both public and private securities, loaned money to entrepreneurs, and soon formed the House of Peabody, which he often referred to as a bank, but it was an investment bank only. As his health declined in the midfifties, he took on a partner, Junius Spencer Morgan, who had also grown wealthy as an American merchant. Morgan's son, John Pierpoint Morgan, would follow his father in this firm and turn the House of Morgan, the successor to the firm built by Peabody, into the largest finance company in the world. J. P. Morgan would later serve on the board of the Peabody Fund and contribute to the first endowment of the George Peabody College for Teachers.

After 1850, the wealthy Peabody became the best-known American in Europe, famous for his large dinners, particularly on July 4. He spent lavishly on such entertainments, hosting every famous visitor from America. Privately, he lived simply in a bachelor's apartment and did not own even a horse or carriage. The world's most famous philanthropist, he contributed large funds for the poor of England, particularly for better housing (his housing fund, and the model homes it created, survived into the twentieth century). His major American gifts began with his endowment of a library and lyceum in Danvers, the first Peabody Institute. For its dedication, he sent a toast that included the stricture "Education—a debt due from present to future generations." (These often repeated words became the motto of George Peabody College and are inscribed on its seal.) Eventually, Peabody gave money to every city in which he had lived. In Baltimore, he endowed a much larger Peabody Institute and Library. In Washington, D.C., he contributed funds for the Washington Monument. But he made his largest gifts, all for education, during a trip home to the United States in 1866–67: money for the Museum of Archaeology and Ethnology at Harvard, the Museum of Natural History at Yale, the Peabody Academy of Sciences at Salem, and—the greatest contribution of his life—the Peabody Education Fund, created in 1867.

George Peabody, today usually remembered as a Yankee from New England, actually spent most of his American career in a southern state, Maryland; he loved both North and South. Although he supported the Union, he was distressed by the South's fate at war's end. A prewar Whig in political allegiances, he was never sympathetic with the more radical Reconstruction policies and wanted to help bring about a reconciliation of the country, particularly after a rare visit to the United States in 1866 and 1867. Thus, on February 7, 1867, he wrote to one of his dearest friends, Robert C. Winthrop, a former congressman and senator from Massachusetts, and to a group of other eminent Americans whom he had selected as the first trustees of his education fund. In a letter that would become famous, he noted that he had thought seriously about one subject before leaving England—the educational needs of the war-ravaged South—and had consulted with Winthrop when he arrived in the United States in May 1866. He stressed his attachment to his "native land" and his hopes that after the agonies of war it would have a glorious future as a rich and powerful nation. But his concern was that "her moral and intellectual development keep pace with her material growth." The South, so beset by pressing physical needs, could not, unaided, make the advances in education, in the diffusion of knowledge among all classes, that he earnestly desired. It was, therefore, "the duty and privilege of the more favored and wealthy portions of our nation to assist those who are less fortunate."[2]

Peabody offered these men $1 million. It was "to be by you and your successors held in trust, and the income thereof used and applied in your discretion for the promotion and encouragement of intellectual, moral, or industrial education among the young of the more destitute portions of the Southern and Southwestern States of our Union; my purpose being that the benefits intended shall be distributed among the entire population, without other distinction than their needs and the opportunities of usefulness to them." He gave them permission to use up to 40 percent of the principal during the first two years. In addition, he gave the board Mississippi bonds with a face value of $1.1 million, at that time in default (the state eventually repudiated these bonds). He stipulated Winthrop as chairman of the trustees, Governor Hamilton Fish of New York and Episcopal bishop William McIlvaine as vice chairmen. This board could elect successors, set up bylaws, and appoint agents to carry out its mission. Of great importance for George Peabody College, the board could, after thirty years and by a two-thirds vote, close the trust, giving not less than two-thirds of the remaining funds to educational or literary institutions in the South. Peabody never listed specific states.[3] By later choice of the board, these included the eleven former Confederate states and West Virginia.

The sixteen trustees that Peabody selected to govern the fund were all eminent white men, northerners and southerners. Peabody wanted the ablest and most influential Americans committed to his new project. The trustees included General Ulysses Grant and Admiral David G. Farragut, the two great heroes of the Civil War. Farragut was a Tennessean. Most of the other trustees were either wealthy businessmen or prominent politicians, including the governors of Massachusetts and New York and three southern politicians who had served in Congress or as governors of their states. One trustee was Peabody's nephew, another a close personal friend and widely respected Episcopal bishop. As the first trustees died, the group chose equally eminent successors, among them Senators George Hoar of Massachusetts and Hoke Smith of Georgia; Presidents Rutherford B. Hayes, Grover Cleveland, William McKinley, and Theodore Roosevelt; and such wealthy financiers as J. P. Morgan, Richard Olney, and Morris K. Jesup. The board tried to keep a balance between northerners and southerners. Of special importance for the future State Normal in Nashville, former state supreme court judge and University of Nashville trustee Samuel Watson became a Peabody Fund trustee in 1869. Next to Berrien Lindsley and Governor James Porter, he did more than anyone else to bring the normal school to Nashville. Porter himself became a school trustee in 1883 and served on the board longer than any other member.[4]

Such eminent trustees helped insure continued publicity for the Peabody Fund. The gift itself, the largest in the emerging history of American philanthropy, won praise from all quarters, including a special resolution of thanks from Congress. The trustees' annual meeting, usually in a luxury hotel, made the front pages of major newspapers all over the country. The fund absorbed all expenses of these meetings, and in retrospect the money was well spent. Above all, the prestige attached to membership in what was the most elite private club in the United States insured that such prominent and busy men took their trusteeships seriously. They attended the annual meetings or rendered abject apologies for their absence. The board of trustees was far more than window dressing for the fund. Yet, from the first tentative discussions of the original trustees, it was clear that no one knew exactly how to use a million dollars to aid education in the South. The problems were so intractable that the endowment might seem just a drop in the bucket.

Thus, the trustees decided early on that they had to employ a general agent to help them develop policies and then to implement them. They chose well in Barnas Sears.

Sears's selection was in part accidental. Robert Winthrop simply ran into Sears, then president of Brown University, and began discussing the new fund. The two men knew each other; both had played vital roles in establishing in Massachusetts the first statewide free public school system. Winthrop had chaired the congressional committee that approved, in 1837, the famous Massachusetts school bill. Sears, from western Massachusetts, was a graduate of Brown University, a Baptist minister, and a seminary professor before he agreed, in 1848, to replace Horace Mann, the famous but controversial first secretary of the Massachusetts Board of Education. This move placed him at the head of the early public school movement, where he proved tactful and successful. He had been president of his alma mater since 1855. Aware that he had the perfect candidate for general agent, Winthrop began consulting Sears about the work in the South even before the trustees offered, and

George Peabody (the center person of the five seated men) and his original Peabody Education Fund Board, at its first meeting in March, 1867. Note that both General Grant and Admiral Farragut appear in uniform. Photograph by Matthew B. Brady, the famous Civil War photographer. Frontispiece of *Proceedings of the Trustees of the Peabody Education Fund, 1874–1881,* II (Cambridge: John Wilson & Son, 1881).

he accepted, the position. Sears would spent the rest of his life struggling to improve southern public education. But the job brought enormous prestige, the heartfelt appreciation of southerners, and a good salary, $5,000 a year (comparable to $150,000 today) plus all expenses. To better serve his new constituency, Sears moved to Staunton, Virginia, which became the effective headquarters of the fund during his tenure.[5]

The leadership of Winthrop and Sears insured that the Massachusetts experiment in public education would serve as a guideline for the work in the South. In a letter that preceded his appointment, Sears stressed two aspects of the coming work. First was the use of Peabody funds, not to establish public schools, but to aid state and local governments in the South in developing their own schools. Second was the need to develop normal schools to train teachers. The trustees, in appointing Sears, reiterated this twofold goal—to use whatever means available to promote common-school education, and to promote normal-school education by endowing scholarships in existing colleges and by helping establish new normal schools or aiding those that already existed.[6]

Sears's annual reports to the trustees provide a detailed survey of public education in the postwar South. In brief, except in a few favored cities such as Nashville, there were no free public schools in the South when Sears became the fund's general agent. Those in place before the war had closed. Except for more affluent white families who could afford to send their children to private schools, a generation of children in most rural areas from 1861 to after 1880 grew up with little or no formal schooling. Illiteracy rates soared. Ironically, in 1867 Sears found more good schools available to blacks than to whites, but these were supported by northern funds and largely taught by white missionary teachers, with some protection by federal troops and the Freedmen's Bureau.

From 1867 until after 1878, Sears spent most of his time traveling throughout the South and gradually committing funds. In two years, he had still not spent down the principal by the 40 percent approved by Peabody. As a spokesman or lobbyist for public schools, he worked with state legislatures to get them to enact school laws that created state boards of education and superintendents. By 1875, every one of his twelve states had a state school board, a superintendent, and some form of state funding, although always less than one dollar a year per student. The complications of Reconstruction created endless frustration. Most Republican governments, when the states remained under federal supervision, enacted school laws closely modeled on those of the North, adopting the structure and taxes that Sears recommended. But these governments lacked the support of white elites, some still disfranchised, and had difficulty implementing the laws. In too many cases, beleaguered legislatures diverted school funds to other purposes. Then, when white-dominated Democratic legislatures took over, they often repealed such school laws, as happened in Tennessee, and Sears had his work to do all over again. Only after 1877 did all his states have in place a near universal system. Not that all counties, let alone townships or districts, built schools or hired teachers. Nothing was compulsory, particularly attendance. But by then in most southern states, up to half of school-age white children had at least ramshackle schools available to them and enough ill-trained teachers to conduct classes for four or five months each year. This was a major achievement that was never fully shared in by blacks.

As he worked at the state level, Sears offered small annual stipends to city or municipal schools, which accounted for most of the Peabody expenditures during the first ten years. This represented a deliberate top-down strategy, for Sears wanted models for others to follow. Thousands of schools applied for these subsidies, which began with $1,000 annually for schools of more than seven hundred students and scaled down to $300 for schools of only one hundred. Sears wanted to drive private schools out of business, and he gave them no money. At the peak of this effort in 1875, up to fifty schools in each southern state enjoyed such support, and more competed for it. The conditions were clear. To qualify, schools had to have at least a five-month term, and Sears pushed for longer terms. The schools had to be graded. This may seem an obvious requirement today, but even in the rural areas of the North in 1867, most local, usually one-room, schools were not graded, with no clear progression in subjects studied or instructional difficulty. In Tennessee, Davidson County received Peabody funds, but not Nashville, which had done well on its own. The first high school in Memphis, Peabody High, began with a Peabody subsidy. At least in city systems, Sears insisted that the funding go to black as well as white schools, but he never advocated racially mixed schools, which he feared would preclude the elite white support his reforms needed.[7]

Sears's early work pleased George Peabody, who saw how important his gift was for the South. In the summer of 1869, the last of his life, he moved into a resort hotel in White Sulphur Springs, Virginia. Sears joined him for much of this season, along with leading politicians and nine ex-Confederate generals, Robert E. Lee among them.[8] At the beginning of the summer, Peabody gave a second $1 million to his fund, plus some Florida bonds that proved worthless. Back in England, crippled by gout, he died on November 4, 1879. His body lay in state in Westminister Abbey, a tribute by Britain to his charity and his work for Anglo-American understanding. His friend Queen Victoria ordered a British ship to bring the body to America for eventual burial in Danvers. Winthrop, chairman of the Peabody Fund, offered a moving eulogy.[9]

THE NORMAL SCHOOL MOVEMENT

By 1869, Sears was at work on the second goal of his fund—better training for teachers. This largely involved normal schools, but even these could serve less than a tenth of the teachers in the expanding southern school systems. A secondary mode of training involved a very important, now almost forgotten, American institution—teaching institutes. At these, teachers gathered for instruction in subject areas and teaching methods. Such institutes already thrived in the North, and a few had developed in the antebellum South. In the North, most county superintendents scheduled at least one institute each summer. Attendance by county teachers was often mandatory. Most institutes lasted for only a week, a few for up to four weeks. Three or four outside experts, often from normal schools, taught the courses. In theory, these institutes augmented the former training of teachers, bringing them up to date on new theories or new knowledge. In most of America, these short sessions provided the only contact elementary teachers would ever have with experts in the developing profession of public school teaching.

Teachers came to institutes to learn, to gain inspiration, and to develop a sense of professional identity. The larger public attended evening lectures. Parents gained pride in their schools, and young people committed themselves to teaching as a career. The gathered teachers enjoyed the fellowship with other teachers and the home hospitality offered by local families. Institutes were the camp meetings of the teaching profession, and the ablest, most sought-after instructors the evangelists of the public school movement. Sears, in his last essay, tellingly referred to such institutes as what "whetting was to the mower's scythe."[10] As he worked to found normal schools, Sears increasingly encouraged these institutes, providing at least travel funds for instructors. In Tennessee, after 1876, he stopped subsidizing Fisk University and instead funded fifteen annual institutes across the state for black teachers. He funded ten for whites, who, unlike blacks, could enroll in the State Normal College. In 1877, the University of North Carolina began offering a normal course for teachers each summer. Virginia in 1880, then other state universities, followed suit. In time, such summer-school sessions for teachers, either in universities or in normal colleges, would largely replace the institutes. This was most true for the great George Peabody College summer sessions, which began with the opening of the new campus in 1914.

But summer institutes were no substitute for normal-school training. Here, the need in the South was overwhelming. Beginning in 1867, Sears offered partial subsidies to fledgling normal schools or to other colleges that would agree to train teachers. As early as 1868, he helped fund both a white and a black normal school in Richmond. He also began subsidizing Fisk and Hampton Institute for what he loosely referred to as normal schools at those two black colleges. He also offered small sums for each teacher trained at liberal arts colleges, such as Hollins, a women's college in Virginia. Perhaps the largest normal school was in New Orleans, with branches around Louisiana. Many of these early southern normal schools were fly-by-night institutions, with minimal standards and little funding beyond what Sears offered. But by 1900, all but three southern states had reasonably adequate normal schools, each much influenced by the one southern normal school with standards as high as those of older schools in the North—the State Normal College, and after 1889 the Peabody Normal College, in Nashville, the beneficiary of the fund's largest single expenditure each year after 1875.

The first state-funded U.S. normal schools date back to 1839 in Massachusetts, where they supported the new public school system founded only two years earlier. These schools were much influenced by precedents in Germany and in France. The name "normal" came from a French norm-setting or model school, the Ecole Normale in Paris. In America, almost all normal schools, as well as later teachers' colleges, developed what they hoped were model demonstration schools.[11]

Throughout the nineteenth century, most U.S. elementary school teachers received no special training. Those who completed eight elementary grades, or the few privileged to attend secondary-level academies, won teaching positions by passing state subject-matter exams. Thus, the goals of the early normal schools were modest. The course of training was only one year long, but few students finished the year or earned a diploma. Instead, they enrolled for one term to help them pass the state exam. In New England, normal-school instruction focused on the same subjects then taught in elementary schools, with some attention to methods of teaching. An overwhelming majority of normal-school students were women; two of the first four Massachusetts normal schools were for women only, an early indication that the public schools would largely attract low-paid, usually unmarried women teachers. The level of instruction in early normal schools was, roughly, that of the first two years of the then few public high schools, without the Latin and Greek that remained central to instruction in highs schools and private academies. Normal schools were plebeian institutions. In prestige, they ranked well below the better private academies. They reflected a type of democratic secondary education—free, decentralized, and vocationally oriented.

In the Midwest, early normal schools played a somewhat broader role than in New England. They anticipated later state teachers' colleges. The Midwest did not have the number or quality of private colleges and academies enjoyed in the Northeast. Early Midwestern normal schools thus carried less class stigma and soon served a broader constituency. In 1849, Michigan chartered the first Midwestern normal school, one much influenced by the five already in place in New England. Ypsilanti State Normal opened in 1853, almost in the shadow of the already well-established University of Michigan. Its role resembled that of New England's normal schools, offering what amounted to secondary-level instruction to teachers. In Illinois, a more daring experiment began in 1857 with a charter for a state normal university, which opened for classes in 1861 in what is now Normal, Illinois. Its "university" designation suggested its more ambitious purpose—to offer college-level instruction to teachers or prospective teachers, including the elite few who would become administrators or teach in public secondary schools. Its three-year term included instruction in Latin and Greek, although it did not grant a bachelor's degree and soon dropped the classical languages. Illinois had no other public university, and thus many people expected the Normal University to fulfill the role of early, pre-land-grant state universities in Michigan and Wisconsin.

After the Civil War, the ten or so pioneer normal schools in America influenced imitations in almost every state. By 1900, more than 70,000 students annually were enrolled in well over a hundred schools, with new ones appearing every year. In strength, and in later educational reform, what is now Illinois State University led the way, soon joined by a twin institution at Carbondale in southern Illinois.

In the Midwest, the normal schools had one announced purpose—to train teachers. But they quickly served other, unannounced goals. Much more than in New England, young men joined young women in such schools, although men always remained a minority. Because of the free tuition, the early schools developed a formal pledge that required graduates to teach, and one detailed study shows that almost all kept this pledge; they taught at least for a year or two. But a follow-up study of graduates in four Midwestern states reveals that, by 1880, a vast majority of men soon left teaching for other careers, and most women left at marriage (not always voluntarily, for many states would not hire married women).[12] Many parents used normal schools to provide a free secondary education for their children in a period when few had access to public high schools. Thus, these "people's schools" marked the covert origins of several public high schools in the Midwest and South. Since, by necessity, the bulk of normal training had to be in the elementary subjects (English, writing, arithmetic, geography, history, and civics), the curriculum simply reflected a more advanced, more rigorous, extension of elementary education.

Change came gradually. In the late nineteenth century, a few better normal schools tried to limit admission to high school graduates. Illinois State became intensely involved in the Herbartian reforms, an early version of interest-oriented or progressive education, and helped shift the role of the best normal schools toward more theory and method, and away from what they had until then assumed necessary for prospective elementary teachers, a good grasp of subject matter. In this respect, teacher training moved toward self-conscious professional education, for better or worse. The best normal schools also had to prepare their abler graduates for teaching in the newly developing public high schools, as well as for positions in educational administration. This shift required courses not only in theory, but also in more advanced academic subjects, which in time led to a large arts and science programs.

By 1900, the normal schools faced two alternatives. They could remain the standard training schools for elementary teachers, who by this time in most states needed the equivalent of a high school diploma. If they so restricted their role, state universities, which had already begun to add educational departments, or liberal arts colleges that were willing to meet certification requirements for high school teachers, would monopolize the training of secondary teachers and educational administrators. This path meant a permanent subcollegiate status for normal schools. As one would expect, normal-school administrators, backed by vocal local constituencies, chose a second path. They made a successful bid to retain control over most teacher training, and to some extent even educational policy, throughout the United States. They accomplished this by upgrading standards, improving faculty, adding more and more liberal arts courses, and establishing regional associations to set standards and eventually to offer accreditation. The climax of such reform was the passage of state laws that allowed such upgraded normal schools to offer bachelor's degrees and to change their title to teachers' colleges.

The first U.S. normal school to offer a bachelor's degree was the State Normal College in Nashville. But the University of Nashville, not the Normal College, actually bestowed the degrees. In 1890, the Albany, New York, Normal School began offering a bachelor's in pedagogy, but a full four-year program did not go into effect until 1905. In 1897, Michigan authorized the State Normal at Ypsilanti to confer a four-year bachelor's degree and renamed the school Michigan State Normal College. By then, it was unique in requiring a high school diploma for admission. The first student qualified for a degree there in 1905. In 1907, Illinois approved a bachelor of education degree for Illinois State Normal University. Indiana State soon followed. For the next thirty years, state after state granted degree status to former normal schools (46 by 1920, 146 by 1933). By 1940, approximately 195 teachers' colleges dotted the map of the United States, with three or four regionally located in most states. By then, the label "normal" was becoming obsolete. Last to upgrade normal schools were the New England states, where elite private liberal arts colleges or universities continued to train most secondary teachers.

These all too brief vignettes provide the background and context for the normal school in Nashville. In the total history of normal schools in America, it arguably had the greatest impact of any except, possibly, Illinois Normal University. But such influence was not at all apparent in its first, very difficult ten years of existence.

A NORMAL COLLEGE FOR NASHVILLE

The movement for a normal school in Tennessee began early but soon floundered. The state assembly considered and rejected a bill to establish a state normal school in 1855. Before 1861, and the war, neither Tennessee nor any other southern state would sponsor a school for teachers. In fact, the southern states never developed much more than skeletal public school systems, and even these disappeared during the war. Nashville was unusual in developing a rather comprehensive free school system before the war and continued it afterward. It became in this sense an educational oasis in the state. Berrien Lindsley was partly responsible for this record. He had served as a member of the city's board of education after 1854 and in 1865 briefly served as superintendent of Nashville schools, helping reopen them after the war. As he resumed his wider efforts in behalf of public education, he realized that gaining a normal school for the University of Nashville depended on the state's willingness to match support from the Peabody Education Fund. Thus, Lindsley's work for public education indirectly insured the survival of the University of Nashville.

During his brief tenure as superintendent of Nashville schools, Lindsley had taken the lead in forming the Tennessee State Teachers Association (TSTA). He would serve as its president in the crucial years 1874–75. The TSTA worked to get the state to reestablish a statewide public school system, with local districts and at least minimal state financial support. Abetted by Lindsley's powerful arguments, it also sought at least one white and one black state normal school to train teachers. Lindsley was at the center of an effective lobbying effort over the next seven years, aided by his becoming chair of the education committee of the Nashville Board of Trade. In his advocacy, he took some progressive stands. He wanted to combine a girl's high school with a normal school, and for years tried to get teacher training for blacks as well as whites.

Lindsley's goals thus meshed perfectly with the work of Sears and the Peabody Education Fund. In 1867, at a Nashville meeting of the TSTA, Sears spoke strongly in behalf of a normal school in Tennessee. Aware that the state was facing bankruptcy, a committee suggested that the association seek to affiliate with some college or university and get it to establish a normal department that could use existing facilities. Sears addressed another meeting of the TSTA in 1869. By then, he and Lindsley were co-conspirators. In late 1873, a Nashville delegate to the general assembly introduced a normal-school bill. It entailed $6,000 of annual support from the state, matched by $6,000 from the Peabody Fund (Sears had almost promised this), if located in an existing college or university. If no host offered such facilities, the state was to appropriate $40,000 to build a campus. In fact, almost every college in the state was anxious to bid for such a school. The state senate passed the bill; the house adjourned without action. Perhaps of greater significance, the assembly passed a general school law that offered support for a system of public school districts throughout the state.

The TSTA's campaign climaxed in 1874. Lindsley led the way. It now seemed likely that a commitment from a university to host a normal school would entice the assembly to pass the deferred bill. Nothing could have better played into Lindsley's hands. In the memories of the major participants, the bidding process became a charade after January 1875. The new governor of Tennessee, James D. Porter, a University of Nashville alumnus and brother to a member of the school's board of trust, negotiated an informal agreement with Sears to locate a normal school at the University of Nashville. In the same month, at the TSTA meeting, Lindsley cited New York, Massachusetts, Illinois, and Wisconsin to illustrate the role of normal schools. He hoped the state would help establish the first two normal schools in Nashville, at the University of Nashville for whites, at Fisk University for blacks. Sears not only addressed the TSTA but also spoke before the general assembly. The governor, deeply committed to the plan, proposed that the state draw its $6,000 from the state school fund. Sears spoke for the first time to the board of the university, which appointed a committee to decide not so much whether to welcome such a school, but how best to procure it. In February, Lindsley began a state lecture tour to promote the enabling legislation. All seemed in order.

The general assembly passed a model bill in March 1875. As Sears desired, it established a state board of education (Lindsley would serve as its secretary from 1875 to 1887) and authorized a state normal school for whites and another for blacks. The board was to locate such schools and receive the Peabody funds. But with the state nearly bankrupt, the assembly neglected to appropriate the stipulated $6,000, which would seem to have jeopardized Peabody funding. A new scheme was afoot, however. The assembly amended the charter of the University of Nashville to enable it to suspend college-level courses and arrange with the Peabody Fund to host a normal school. Within a week, the university board began formal negotiations and in April offered a part or all of its facilities, free, to the state board of education for a normal school. John Lea, board president, was one of two trustees to oppose this offer. The board accepted his resignation. In effect, the University of Nashville assumed the responsibility of the state. Sears, on behalf of the Peabody Fund, accepted the offer of the university as a satisfactory substitute for state funds.

By May, the planning for a fall opening was under way, but with a few details still murky. The University of Nashville prepared to transfer the campus, which included MBA, under the conditions set by Bell's will—free tuition for twenty-five students and instruction at a grammar-school level. The board seemed to assume that MBA would become the demonstration school for what everyone had begun to refer to as the State Normal College. Although the board of the university retained the right to approve all faculty and set all salaries, its members realized that it was in effect turning its campus over to the state and, indirectly, to the Peabody Fund trustees. After all, they were providing the money.

In the complicated negotiations of 1875, Lindsley and Governor Porter were the main architects of the final agreement, with the active support of Sears. Left out of the final plan was any provision for black teachers. No one expected black students to attend the State Normal College of the University of Nashville. One suspects that the failure of the state to appropriate its $6,000, and the alacrity with which Sears accepted an alternative arrangement, was a deliberate attempt to finesse the racial issue. The Peabody Fund, after 1868, had allocated $800 a year for the education of teachers at what it referred to as the normal school of Fisk University. In this sense, Fisk opened the first normal school in Tennessee, but not a public normal. It had as strong a legal claim to any state appropriation as had the University of Nashville. Yet, in 1876 the Peabody Fund suspended its subsidy to Fisk, replacing it with teachers' institutes for blacks. Only in 1909 would Tennessee establish the first normal school for blacks, at Tennessee A & I in Nashville, and at the time it also established three white schools.[13]

At its opening in 1875, the official name of the new normal school in Nashville was "State Normal College," a name chosen by the Tennessee Board of Education. The name was pretentious, for in no sense was the instruction at a college level, or even at the level of a good high school. Most people, at least locally, referred to it as the state normal school, a more accurate designation. Its official title made clear that it was a state institution, although one at first not funded by the state. In 1889, the state board of education approved a name change to Peabody Normal College, the official name until 1911. A new president, a course of study that approached college level, and a need to honor its major benefactor all justified the new title. By 1901, the level of work required for a degree was as demanding as that in all but a few southern colleges and universities. Without any formal or legal justification, the school began calling itself Peabody College for Teachers. It no longer wanted to be tied to the reputation of normal schools. Since it had a four-year curriculum and through the University of Nashville granted bachelor's degrees to up to a third of its students, it deserves to rank as the first teachers' college of the South. But the Peabody Education Fund trustees continued to refer to it as the Peabody Normal College, which apparently remained its legal name, although one no longer used on campus or in college publications.

To multiply the confusion over names, the normal school was also the continuing literary department of the University of Nashville. Although now under state control and soon in part funded by the state, the normal school prematurely added what it called a baccalaureate class that led to a bachelor of arts. Eventually it even offered graduate work leading to a master's degree. But the state-chartered normal school had no authority to award such traditional degrees. The University of Nashville did. Technically, those who received them were graduates of the literary department of the University of Nashville, although most never noticed the distinction unless they looked closely at their degrees. This suggests the administrative complexity of the school, which in theory should have caused endless confusion and controversy, but which in practice worked surprisingly well.

Since the opening of Davidson Academy, the University of Nashville and its predecessors had aspects of both a private and a public institution. After 1875, its hybrid character made it administratively unique in the United States. In effect, the university loaned its campus to the state board of education, originally for two years but by intent for as long as the state supported a normal school. The state chartered its State Normal College and had administrative control over it but never owned the campus and buildings. The normal school had no board of trust of its own. Legally, the state board set the rules for the school and had the legal right to control its curriculum. The Peabody funds, and later also state appropriations, went to the state board. The board, in turn, gave the funds to the university's chancellor, who was also the president of the college, to pay all costs, including salaries. The university's treasurer rendered full accounts to the state board at least annually. In a pro forma way, the university board ratified all appointments and expenditures but only by turning such decisions over to its chancellor, who was always also the president of the normal college. For its two other continuing departments, the medical and Montgomery Bell, the chancellor was nominally the head but left all effective decisions to the faculty and administrators of these institutions or to the trustees. To further complicate matters, the university later committed some of its funds from gifts or from earnings on its endowment to its literary department, and even used an endowment fund to pay the salary of its one chair professor, technically a faculty member of the University of Nashville, but otherwise indistinct from the normal-college faculty. As far as I can tell, the university did not have to account to the state for these funds.

Despite these complicated and overlapping roles for the state board and the university trustees, the Peabody Education Fund trustees, with no legal authority at all, made all the important decisions about the normal school. The most powerful person involved with the school was the general agent of the fund, Barnas Sears in the critical early years. Sears selected the first president—technically, the state employed him and the university made him its chancellor. Sears approved all important policy decisions. Money speaks loudly, and the fund paid all the bills at first, and the majority of the bills always. The system worked because of the degree of deference from both Nashville boards toward the northern patrons who made it all possible. On only a few critical occasions did the system require a joint meeting of representatives of all three boards to coordinate policies.

THE TRIALS AND TRIBULATIONS OF PRESIDENT EBEN STEARNS

The newly chartered State Normal College's first task was to appoint a president. The state board of education had to approve such an appointment, and so did the University of Nashville, for the president would be head of a department of the university and also, by the choice of its trustees, chancellor. Fortunately, both boards deferred to Barnas Sears who made the selection before they then gave it their pro forma approval. After two men turned down his offer, Sears finally persuaded Eben Stearns, then head of the Robinson Female Seminary in Exeter, New Hampshire, to accept the position. Stearns would remain as president of the normal college and chancellor of the University of Nashville until his death in 1887.[14]

Though eminently qualified, Stearns turned out to be less than an inspired or fully effective president. Born in Bedford, Massachusetts in 1819, he was in all respects a latter-day Puritan, with a father, grandfather, and several brothers who were Congregational ministers. A rather gentle, kindly, at times humorous man, Stearns was also aptly described as serious, formal, and even cold, like his name, which suggests the frigidity of New England winters, the strict moralism of his Puritan ancestors. He had the best of educations at Phillips Academy and Harvard College, where he graduated in the top third of his class. He taught schools in Ipswitch and Newburyport, Massachusetts, and in Portland, Maine. Most pertinent to his appointment in Nashville was his role, from 1849 to 1855, as principal of the first public normal school in America, established in 1839 at Lexington, Massachusetts, moved in 1849 to West Newton, and during Stearns's tenure moved to Framington.

Almost present at the creation of American normal-schools, Stearns took over the normal school at West Newton just as Horace Mann turned the state board over to Barnas Sears. During his first year, Stearns boarded at Mann's home; Sears was his boss. His years as head of the normal school led to mixed verdicts. Enrollment declined. The school then had a one-year curriculum, which Stearns expanded slightly. In an experiment that failed, he introduced a three-year course for prospective high school teachers. As in a later experiment in Nashville, he had neither the faculty nor libraries to justify such an advanced course. It became not a more rigorous course, but simply a more extended one. As part of a continuing interest of his own, Stearns first introduced required work in physical education. In 1855 he resigned to take a position as principal of the Albany Female Academy. He remained there for thirteen years, including the war years, but his dissatisfied trustees forced him to resign in 1868. The enrollment had dropped after the war, and Stearns was frequently ill. After a failed attempt to create his own girls' school, he accepted a position in the new, well-endowed seminary in Exeter, where his $3,000 salary was reportedly the second highest among New England educators. The seminary proved less than successful, with its enrollment declining by 1875. Although Stearns at first refused the job in Nashville, he may have had compelling reasons to leave Exeter, especially once he had bargained for the same salary in Nashville plus a free house.[15]

In Nashville, Stearns had to begin small. The new normal college shared the stone building with Montgomery Bell Academy. The old library, still announced as 10,000 books, was largely irrelevant to pedagogy and unavailable to students. The old barracks was, as always, in bad repair and unsuitable for classrooms. The school had no scientific apparatus. The campus was barren and uncut. To Stearns's chagrin, he had to share the old president's house with three MBA teachers, who occupied small apartments cut out of this brick building. Because of a late opening, few students applied for the December 1 start date, despite the fanfare and speeches in the state capital. Only twelve young women, all from Davidson County, sought admission, along with Stearns's daughter. Louise Lindsley, Berrien Lindsley's daughter, attended classes but was not yet old enough to register. These original students were not poor girls seeking a chance to teach, but young women from affluent Nashville homes seeking a secondary-level education and a profession. One was the daughter of the white founder of Roger Williams University (the campus of this school for African Americans would later become part of the George Peabody College campus). Another was a descendent of John Sevier. Her sister later taught art in the school. One young woman was the daughter of the state's leading botanist. During the year, sixty students enrolled, but only thirty-five remained to the end of term. In 1877, eight students finished the prescribed course and graduated, five of them women. Lizzie Bloomstein, one of these first graduates and among the original thirteen, joined the faculty the next year and remained for the rest of her career, revered for her instruction in history and geography.[16]

In his first catalogue announcement, Stearns departed hardly at all from his earlier work at West Newton Normal. He had the same admission requirements—sixteen years old, good character, able to pass an examination in elementary subjects, and a declared commitment to become a teacher. In the first year, Davidson County youth had to pay no tuition; others would have to pay fifteen dollars. (It is not clear that any of these others attended, or that any appreciable number of students ever paid any tuition.) In the next year, the state board announced free tuition for one applicant from each county, but almost no one from a distance applied. The state board then decided to admit all state students free, and almost all out-of-state students would have a Peabody scholarship and thus also receive free tuition. The school furnished free textbooks. From the beginning, Stearns announced a three-year curriculum with the somewhat confusing designations he had used in New England: junior, middle, and senior classes. This was a more extended curriculum than in New England's two-year normal schools, possibly duplicated only by Normal University in Illinois. Based on his New England precedents, Stearns announced that graduates would receive a diploma. The next year he changed this to Licentiate of Instruction (L.I.), a degree by then offered by a few northern normals.

The first or junior year involved a review of elementary subjects. The number of students who had to begin at this level steadily declined. All later Peabody scholars would have to enter the middle year. In time, most of the juniors would be young women from Tennessee, usually with little more than an eighth-grade education. From the perspective of the state board, this was a primary role for a state normal, for it helped improve teaching in rural areas. If such students completed two of the three years, they received a certificate attesting to this achievement and in almost any county could receive a license to teach. From the beginning, Tennessee certified for life anyone who received the L.I. degree, and soon other southern states followed suit.[17]

The State Normal, under Stearns, always had a dominant female cast. He brought two female teachers with him to Nashville, Julie Sears and Emma M. Cutter. No relation to Barnas Sears, Julia Sears remained a prominent and well-paid teacher until her retirement in 1907 (she received the first Carnegie retirement in Tennessee and lived on to 1929). Cutter remained for only six years, until her marriage. As Stearns hired additional teachers, approximately two-thirds of these were women. Throughout his tenure, the vast majority of students were women, although by his last year, 1886–87, men made up one-third of those enrolled. By then, a pattern was established. Almost all men entered the middle class (all but three in 1886–87), and women all but monopolized the beginning or junior class (thirty-nine women and three men). Among scholarship students, the gender balance came closer to equal. Stearns had long taught only women and seemed to relate to them better than to men, a stance reversed by his successor as president, William Payne.[18] For its first five years, the heavily female normal school shared a building with Montgomery Bell Academy, an all-male grammar and preparatory school with an all-male faculty. Its faculty was better trained, its upper-level courses more rigorous, and its status in the community higher than the normal school's. This was a perfect recipe for conflict, which erupted by the second year.

I have found no suggestion that anyone connected with the University of Nashville ever considered admitting women before 1875. Thus, the university board had trouble coping with the new, and to it radical, coeducational reality. The board members were careful to offer male teachers at MBA almost double the salaries of Sears and Cutter in the normal school (they did have higher qualifications). Even in the normal school, women teachers were not equal to the men, for they never held an administrative position or received comparable salaries, at least in the early years.

Under Stearns, the curriculum duplicated that of normal schools in New England. In the first or junior class, students reviewed primary and grammar school subjects: English, arithmetic, geometry, geography and map drawing, chemistry, U.S. history, physiology and hygiene, rhetoric, and bookkeeping (bookkeeping was professionally related, since teachers would need to keep student records). These matched courses in grades one through eight and, in the case of geometry and chemistry, often the first year of high school. In this way, even first-year students advanced a bit beyond elementary subjects.

In the second year, students moved into high school subjects: algebra, trigonometry, philosophy, physics, botany, world history, and English literature. Unfortunately, the school never had teachers qualified to offer courses in trigonometry and lacked the apparatus or lab equipment to offer any but the most elementary science courses. The third year matched at least a full high school curriculum. It included calculus, astronomy, the U.S. Constitution, English classics, and the theory and art of teaching. But, once again, the promise far exceeded the reality. Later students complained that no one ever tried to teach trigonometry, let alone calculus. And the students did not practice teach but, at best, observed teachers at MBA. In all of their own courses, according to the catalogue, they had to take over the teaching at scheduled intervals and face detailed criticism from other students. Stearns, as he had years before at West Newton Normal, announced that Latin, French, and German "are taken according to a parallel course." This was mumbo jumbo, for no normal-school teachers were prepared to teach any foreign languages, and none did. A few normal-school students may have audited Latin courses at MBA. Stearns also referred to "attention throughout the year" to composition, reading, spelling, penmanship, and even vocal music, all of which may indeed have been involved in some courses. Later, he did add music as a formal course.

With minor changes, this remained the three-year curriculum from 1875 until 1888. But in 1878–79 Stearns announced the addition of a fourth year, which he called an advanced or baccalaureate class. From 1880 to 1883, some twenty-five students received their bachelor of arts from the University of Nashville. In this group, men outnumbered women. The advanced courses, as listed, included conic sections, analytical geometry, calculus, psychology, plus Latin, French, and German, again "taken according to a parallel course." Although the class remained in the catalogue throughout Stearns's administration, the university stopped awarding the B.A. in 1884. The students, including scholarship students with an extra year of benefits, probably used the degree for professional ends. But they knew that, in most respects, the added class involved largely deceit. They simply spent more time with the same six teachers, taking the same courses. No one was qualified to teach any of the listed languages. Poor Julia Sears, the overly busy mathematics teacher, had only her L.I. degree and no preparation to offer either calculus or conic sections. No teacher had any qualifications in psychology, except in the most limited sense. In fact, apart from Stearns, only one of the six teachers held a bachelor's degree. Able students resented the false claims and the poor excuse for a B.A. and eventually protested. The university board quietly dropped the degree. Only under William Payne, with an expanded and much better-qualified faculty, did B.A. work resume. But through the University of Nashville, Stearns had made his State Normal the first in the United States to offer a bachelor of arts degree.

In 1877, in its second catalogue, the normal school first advertised Peabody scholarships. No one could then anticipate the significance of these scholarships for the school and for public education in the South. Without them, the normal school would have remained a state institution, drawing almost all its students from Tennessee. It could have been a model school because of Peabody support, but its impact would have been limited. Sears surely realized that he needed not only a model normal but one that served the South, not just one state. Without the scholarships and the regional role they gave to the school, it is almost inconceivable that the Peabody Fund trustees would ever have endowed George Peabody College for Teachers.

In 1876, Sears approached the Peabody trustees about scholarships for a normal school in Louisiana ($150 a year, soon discontinued) and the one in Nashville ($200 a year). The board approved, and in the 1877–78 school year, nineteen Peabody scholars (twelve were men) from three states (Georgia, Virginia, and Florida) enrolled, out of 108 total students. Within a few years, scholarship students would make up more than half the student body and account for practically all students from outside Tennessee. In his original announcement, Sears justified the scholarships by the lack of normal schools in southern states. The $200 a year (renewable for a second year) was to aid students from these states. Applicants had to pass an exam at the level of a first-class high school. State superintendents were to appoint examiners and nominate the scholars, subject to approval by Stearns. Each scholar had to promise to teach for at least two years if positions were available, and they always were. Stearns soon required that such scholars be at least seventeen years old and that they enter the middle class, which meant that most scholars stayed for two years and received the L.I. degree. From the beginning, the students were older than the largely Tennessee young women who entered the junior class. In theory, they were professionally committed and well prepared, although state superintendents did not always choose well.

Before Stearns died in 1887, almost 800 scholarship students had attended his school. As early as 1880, they outnumbered nonscholarship students (97 of 137), a trend that continued until Stearns's last full year, 1886 (89 of 153). Most of the nonscholarship students were Tennesseans, most women, and almost the only students who enrolled in the junior class. In a sense, the State Normal was two merged institutions—the state normal for elementary teachers, and a southern normal college for the brightest prospective teachers in twelve southern states. Until 1883, Tennessee students could not compete for the scholarships, largely because the state had not helped fund the college. From 1883 to 1887, all twelve funded states took advantage of the highly valued scholarships, allocated over the years roughly in proportion to population. In 1883, out of 113, Tennessee received 15, Georgia and North Carolina 13, and West Virginia 5. In 1887, the Peabody Fund cut off funds to Florida and Mississippi because the two states, after endless legislative efforts by the fund, finally cancelled the bonds owned by the fund. These defaulting states were reinstated in 1893, and from then until 1905 all twelve states received scholarships.[19]

Even as the scholarships began to transform the normal school, it faced its first crisis. Tennessee almost lost the school, and by all odds deserved to lose it. Stearns, by 1877, was unhappy with his situation in Nashville. The Tennessee assembly, in a not untypical posture that was both ignorant and self-defeating, continued to refuse to appropriate money for its own normal school; the most distressing failure came with the 1879 appropriations bill. Stearns had no money to improve the two main buildings, which lacked adequate space for laboratories and the library, and had no chapel or assembly area large enough to hold all his students. Most annoying to him, he had to share the limited classroom space with MBA. He still resented his living arrangements in what amounted to an apartment house. Finally, MBA never worked as a model school. Its three male teachers, all with college degrees and distinguished careers, did not want a group of young women, some with barely an eighth-grade education, practice teaching in their classrooms. These MBA teachers, who had been part of the literary department under Smith and Johnson, had taught college-level courses in mathematics, the natural sciences, and Latin and Greek. It must have been difficult for them to coexist with a struggling normal school. They also had to protect the reputation of the academy in order to recruit students, for it survived on tuition (the endowment paid the tuition of twenty-five poor boys, but not much more). By 1878, both parties agreed to the divorce that Stearns had recommended in 1877.

For the first three years, MBA had seemed to be part of the new normal school. The catalogue listed it as the model school and listed the three MBA teachers among the normal school faculty. But, while they dramatically enhanced the prestige of the faculty, they did not in fact teach the normal-school students. In 1878 the University of Nashville board separated the two institutions and assumed full control over MBA by segregating the Bell endowment for its use. But the university trustees, who wanted to do everything possible to please the Peabody Fund board, were in a bind. MBA had a contract that expired only in 1882 for use of the stone building and the three faculty apartments. The legal separation still left MBA occupying rooms in the stone castle. Both Sears and the state board of education were unhappy with this arrangement, for the growing number of scholarship students created a severe space shortage for the normal school. But Stearns was on record as accepting the separation, and after all, he was the university chancellor. In 1879, the tension grew, and no one in Nashville seemed aware of how much was at stake. Late in 1879, a frustrated Sears had opened negotiations with the state superintendent of education in Georgia about moving the normal school. For Sears, the lack of state appropriations and space problems at the school seemed intractable obstacles to the further development of a model normal school in Nashville. It was starved for money and for space.[20]

Meanwhile, in Nashville, the university trustees finally became aware that they faced a problem but seemed ignorant of the magnitude of the threat posed by Georgia. In a meeting on January 31, 1880, the board tried to meet most of Stearns's demands. It would seek another home for MBA and by September be able to turn the whole campus over to the normal school, with one exception. It could not break the contract with the three MBA teachers in the old president's home, which unfortunately had become a point of honor with the now aging, remarried Stearns. More important, they selected board member H. H. Harrison to attend the annual meeting of the Peabody trustees in Washington that would begin on February 18. The Peabody trustees postponed any decision about the permanent location of the normal school, but Harrison was alarmed. He pled Nashville's case, stressed the action of the university board, but received no assurances. Back in Nashville, Harrison recommended an all-out effort to keep the school, including a broad public push in its behalf. One problem, in all these hurried efforts, was the lack of commitment from the state, since the assembly would not meet again until early 1881. The anxious state board of education could only stress the likelihood of a state appropriation at that time.[21]

After the Peabody trustees met, the fund's general agent, Sears, left for a critical visit in Atlanta, where Stearns joined him. Although Stearns did not want to move, it had been his frustrations that had led to the Georgia negotiations. His role in Atlanta was critical, although he later claimed too much credit for the outcome. Sears, and by default Stearns, were treated like royalty, staying in the governor's mansion. The state had chartered a Georgia State Normal College, had appropriated $6,000 a year to match Peabody funds (exactly what Tennessee had refused to do), and opened bids for the location of the college. Sears quickly eliminated all sites save Athens and Atlanta. But the aging Sears caught a cold and was unable to make the short trip to Athens. Stearns, while impressed with Athens, decided it was too inaccessible. Thus, in the final negotiations, Atlanta won, and the city offered $25,000 to build a campus. Sears was reluctant to make a final decision. He had many loyal friends back in Nashville, including Governor Porter and Lindsley. He was also concerned about aspects of the Georgia bid. Stearns wanted assurances that he could bring all his faculty, but Georgia would eventually promise them only one year of tenure. Georgia wanted to keep its Peabody scholarships, even though Sears pointed out that Tennessee had none. The greatest fear involved the independence of the new school, and the ability of the Peabody Fund trustees to control its policies and appointments. They wanted the same degree of deference they had enjoyed in Nashville. According to the Georgia constitution, the president of the University of Georgia would have supervisory authority over any state normal school. Yet, as an ill Sears left Georgia in late March, he seemed almost fully committed to Georgia. The worry over this move contributed to his early death. Stearns, according to his possibly self-serving report given after Sears's death, urged Sears to wait until Stearns could consult further with the University of Nashville board. He sent a telegram from Atlanta asking for an emergency meeting.

Stearns appreciated the newly won power Georgia's offer accorded him. He was in the driver's seat in Nashville and could set almost any terms he wanted. He asked the board to agree to remove MBA from the campus by September 1, 1880, raise $10,000 to alter the campus to match the promised facilities in Atlanta, and use income from the university bonds (then $2,700 a year) to pay the interest on this improvement subsidy. More alarming to the board, he asked that the university, or the people of Nashville, guarantee $6,000 a year for the normal school, to match what Georgia had promised. He hoped private subscriptions would amount to $4,000, and the remaining endowment interest would make up the final $2,000. This would be an indefinite commitment, to such time as the Tennessee assembly was willing to appropriate $6,000 a year, which it had promised to do as far back as 1875. Once again, the burden of saving the normal school for Nashville, as in first locating it there, devolved on the university. Board chairman Edwin Ewing gave Stearns quick assurance on all points except the $4,000, conditioning the other concessions on the normal school's remaining permanently in Nashville. Stearns telegraphed the news to Sears, then on a stalled railroad car headed back home to Staunton. Sears, who wanted more assurances of legislative support, deferred any final decision.[22]

Back in Nashville on April 3, Stearns met with the trustees. They feared a long-term commitment of funds, as well as being left with a large debt should the school move in the future. They could not reach a final decision on what seemed a near ultimatum from Stearns. Frustrated in his scheme, Stearns telegraphed Sears that he would consent to the move to Georgia. Although Sears had already finalized an offer to Georgia that required promises of complete autonomy for the prospective normal college, he was reluctant to give up on Nashville and asked Stearns for more detailed comments. Stearns then approached a board member in Nashville and suggested that the city had one last chance before he replied to Sears. On a Saturday, a group of prominent citizens met, heard Stearns, quickly formed a local organization, raised nearly half the $4,000 on the spot, and had it all in hand by Monday. Stearns informed Sears of their commitment, which placed on hold any final decision about Georgia. On April 21, the University of Nashville board and its resolutions met every demand made by Stearns and Sears. Stearns sent the good news to Sears. A member of the local citizens group assured Sears that some of the funds could help build the mansion that Stearns so craved. On May 11, 1880, Sears accepted the terms by letter, announced that State Normal College would remain in Nashville, and, because of the "generous action" in Nashville, promised his "hearty co-operation" in making the "Normal College the pride of the South."[23]

The crisis was over, but not the anxiety in Nashville. Sears died on July 6, 1880, which prompted hundreds of resolutions of appreciation of his work from practically every school board in the South. But would the new general agent, J.L.M. Curry, and the Peabody trustees honor Sears's final commitment? Yes. On February 4, 1881, the Peabody Fund board offered all the desired assurances. The normal school was now permanently located in Nashville. The remaining problem lay with Tennessee. If the general assembly did not appropriate at least $6,000 for Peabody Normal, the citizens' committee and the University of Nashville would be left holding the bag, with $6,000 due each year. The state finally approved an appropriation in 1881 and continued to do so until 1905. But the university could not count on future appropriations and had to assure the Peabody trustees that, if the state did not pay or paid less than $6,000 a year, the university remained legally responsible for the full $6,000 each year, which constituted a perpetual mortgage on its assets. After the state came through, the University of Nashville had full control over its endowment and used the interest to pay off part of its $10,000 debt; lot sales made up the rest.[24]

THE FINAL YEARS UNDER STEARNS

In the three years after the crisis of 1880, Stearns received almost every benefit he had bargained for. He used the new legislated funds to redo the stone building, removing walls to turn one wing into a two-story chapel dedicated in May 1882. He converted residential rooms in the old barracks (now Lindsley Hall) into a library and chemical laboratories. The old chapel became a large lecture room. Perhaps most important, at least to him personally, the university committed its $10,000 to an almost ostentatious new chancellor's mansion—eighteen rooms and four baths in two stories, plus an attic—large enough later to become the first nurses' residence for the Vanderbilt Medical Department. Stearns was now able to add a campuswide, centralized steam-heating system and get rid of the numerous stoves. The old president's home, with considerable alteration, in 1884 became a new gymnasium named after president of the board Ewing, a sop to Stearns's lifelong devotion to physical education. The gym, modeled after those in Europe, had rings, parallel bars, and equipment for floor exercises. Stearns was able to hire a gym teacher for both boys and girls, and soon the students offered weekly gym demonstrations. Finally, since his first year in Nashville, Stearns had worked to beautify the campus. He and students had planted memorial trees and flower gardens around buildings; by 1884 almost everyone applauded its beauty. Still, wandering cows destroyed some of the young trees. The campus needed a fence.

In 1883, Stearns was sixty-four. His health remained infirm. Problems continued to haunt him, some his own fault. He had spent his life as what amounted to a school principal, hiring and firing teachers at will. He expected obedience and loyalty, which he seemed to receive from female teachers and students, less often from men. He allowed the faculty almost no governing role and resented its more independent members. In 1883, he dismissed a male mathematics teacher, Edson S. Wellington, in order to hire a close, able friend, Benjamin B. Penfield from Connecticut, who became acting president at Stearns's death in 1887. Penfield had completed a Ph.D. at Vanderbilt, a degree not quite comparable to the modern Ph.D. Both Wellington and Penfield had M.A. degrees, although probably not earned in either case. The records do not make clear any insubordination on Wellington's part but do suggest that he was critical of deficiencies at the college.

In 1883, in what had to be a related action, a number of alumni from the recently graduated class of 1883 and all the senior male students but one appeared before the Tennessee State Board of Education to present petitions critical of the college. From the context, it is all but obvious that an aggrieved faculty member, or members, was behind the petitions. Wellington seems the likely instigator. A

The new chancellor's residence, first occupied by Eben Stearns in 1883. It was just south of the Castle. Photographic Archives of Vanderbilt University.

majority on the board agreed to receive the petitions. Stearns was mortified and kept silent throughout the extended, and publicized, hearing that soon followed. The alumni petition, inflated into seventeen individual complaints, contained some revealing deficiencies. It backhandedly condemned ill-trained and insufficiently specialized teachers (it desired teachers "of the highest attainment and the broadest culture") and unsuitable or too few textbooks, lamented the lack of scientific apparatus and lack of access to the library, stressed the need for facilities for publishing a student newspaper, and asked that the useless teaching exercises in the classes end. It stressed a lack of harmony and cooperation between president and faculty and the absence of any form of faculty meetings or governance, when eminent faculty should govern the college. It asked for formal courses in pedagogy, for stronger support for the literary societies, and a larger role for alumni. The student petition noted widespread discontent among students. It stressed the

Peabody Normal College women in the new Ewing Gymnasium, probably in about 1888. This gymnasium included parts of the older home of Phillip Lindsley. Photographic Archives of Vanderbilt University.

wide gap between the catalogue and actual offerings (no courses in moral science, spherical geometry, trigonometry, calculus, French, and most areas of pedagogy). It too noted that the library was not open to students, that the scientific apparatus was old and imperfect, and that Stearns failed to support the literary societies adequately.

These were serious charges. Some were unfair, since Stearns was trying to improve the science facilities and apparatus. The students seemed to be relaying the views of disaffected faculty, not their own, in some of the criticisms. But most of the criticisms were on the mark. The state board, and even more emphatically the Peabody trustees, upheld Stearns's authority and competence. Insubordination, or a lack of appreciation for what the college offered, was still anathema to all the boards. Other students on campus, particularly women, rushed forward to denounce the protestors, perhaps in part out of fear. Subsequently, Stearns dismissed the spokesmen for the senior students and apparently denied others their scholarship stipends; a few appealed to the state board on this issue. Two years later, when the spokesperson for the alumni renewed his charges and in a student publication called for Stearns's resignation, almost every student organization rallied to support the administration. The rebellion was over. But it had largely succeeded. In his last five years, Stearns tried to meet almost every demand, including the appointment of the first Ph.D., a chemist to preside over a new chemistry lab. And the state board of education enacted a new set of rules for normal colleges that required faculty government, with at least monthly faculty meetings, a faculty secretary, and full control of individual faculty over textbooks and the conduct of classes. The students had forced the normal school to move a good way from a high school toward a college.[25]

Stearns died on April 11, 1887. By then the normal school had entered a growth spurt, both in enrollment and quality. In 1887 the enrollment, relatively stagnant for five years, grew from 153 to a record 178. Almost everyone realized that the school needed new leadership. Abler students were demanding reforms and a flourishing student culture was abuilding. A golden age lay ahead. But, given the obstacles, the first dozen years laid a strong foundation. And Stearns, despite his personal limitations, had worked hard for the college and was by all accounts a person of integrity. His successor, William Payne, would have all the personal and political skills that Stearns lacked, and soon become the aggressive leader, the empire builder, that the campus needed. But he would lack Stearn's integrity of character and Puritan rectitude.

C H A P T E R   S I X

Peabody Normal College, 1888–1911

THE UNIVERSITY OF NASHVILLE HAD A TROUBLED AND COMPLEX history. Only in two periods, each a generation long, did any of its schools or departments achieve something close to greatness. That is, in only two cases did it have the quality of academic leadership, and the number and ability of students, to rank among the better colleges of the same type in the Unites States, and in each case clearly outrank all its southern competitors. First was the Literary Department under Philip Lindsley, from 1825 until about 1848. Second was the Peabody Normal College as perfected after 1888 by William H. Payne and later led by James D. Porter. It became the strongest normal school in the South, by far, and among the best in the United States.

Only two leaders in the history of the University of Nashville attained national prominence and exerted a broad influence on higher education—Lindsley and Payne. Both came as missionaries from the North. Both devoted the best years of their lives to higher education in the South. Both faced enormous frustrations. Each lost his first wife in the last years of service to the University of Nashville. Each remarried and, disappointed or under duress, resigned the presidency, briefly serving other universities before an early death. Both were successful teachers. Both aspired to much more than they could achieve. Yet, the two had almost opposite personalities. Lindsley remained a reserved, enormously learned, eloquent classical scholar. Payne was an ambitious, driven, egotistic, plain-spoken, but personally insecure educational entrepreneur.

Payne inherited a promising college. Stearns had done his best. But when he died in 1887, the library was not yet open to students, the faculty barely at a high school level, work in pedagogy thin to nonexistent, and student morale low. The school cried out for more youthful and forceful leadership. Payne supplied it.

William Payne was born in Farmington, Ontario County, New York, in 1836, in a Quaker family, although as an adult he did not belong to a Quaker meeting. He attended a local public school with five-month terms and poorly trained teachers. Almost obsessed with reading, he moved to a better, nearby community school at thirteen and soon was able to attend a classical academy fifteen miles from his home. He boarded with a family and spent two sessions at the excellent, Quaker-sponsored Macedon Academy, where he studied Latin, Greek, and advanced mathematics. This completed his formal education, for his family could not afford to send him to college. At that time, attendance at such an excellent academy prepared one to take, and pass, the state exam for prospective teachers. At the not untypical age of seventeen, Payne began teaching in a local school near his home. In 1856, at twenty, he married Sara Evaline (Eve) Fort, also a teacher, who had moved from Ontario County to Michigan before the marriage. The couple taught for two years in a local New York school, then in 1858 moved from New York to near her parents' home in Three Rivers, Michigan, where both taught at a union school for seventy dollars a month. Payne was principal, and thus began his career in educational leadership.[1]

Ability, energy, and writing skill quickly made Payne a leader in the Michigan schools. In 1864, he became principal of a larger school in Niles, Michigan, and in 1866 editor of *The Michigan Teacher* and president of the Michigan Teachers Association. In a critical career move, he became principal of the Ypsilanti Seminary in 1867, one of the most prestigious preparatory academies in Michigan and a neighbor of the oldest normal school in the Midwest. Here, Payne's educational philosophy began to mature; in the process, he became an outspoken critic of the Ypsilanti Normal School, and by implication of almost all normal-school education in the United States. Even in Nashville, he would not be happy with the label "normal" and the associations that usually accompanied it. In 1869, Payne somewhat reluctantly agreed to become superintendent of the school system in the small college town of Adrian. He remained there ten years, during which his writings established him as the leading educational theorist in Michigan, as well as an able and beloved teacher. In particular, he became a valued itinerant instructor in what had become almost obligatory in every Michigan county, a summer institute for teachers. But in Adrian, a demanding, at times overimpatient Payne became involved in a nasty public slander suit brought by a teacher he had censored and finally dismissed during his last year as principal (local newspapers referred to this as his "Payneful decision"). He had publicly referred to her as insane and for a time had to work hard to settle her suit out of court.[2]

At Adrian, Payne established a lifelong pattern of taking time off at intervals from his administrative duties for an intensely concentrated and productive interlude of writing. He published many articles, a little book on school supervision, and a history of Adrian schools. He also completed a draft of what matured into a book on the science and art of education, first published as *A Syllabus of a Course of Lectures on the Science and Art of Teaching* and later as *Outlines of Educational Doctrine.* Always a master of self-promotion, Payne circulated the draft widely before publication, gathering letters of commendation from dozens of leading people in the young field of educational philosophy. The book established his national reputation.

The phrase "science and art of education" became Payne's trademark. His growing reputation led the University of Michigan to award him an honorary master of arts degree in 1872. Sensitive about his lack of college training, Payne rejoiced at this recognition; he kept the diploma among his personal papers for the rest of his life. In 1879, after the University of Michigan had decided to open a small program in education that could lead to a teaching certificate, it asked Payne to become the first and only professor in this new department, a great honor. He reveled in the national publicity, and from then on he proudly claimed to be the first holder of a university chair in education in the United States (by most definitions, the University of Iowa had a stronger claim to priority). The poor Quaker lad from New York, largely self-educated, had reached the apex of his profession at the age of forty-three.

Payne remained in this university position until he came to Nashville in 1887. He proved himself an able promoter, building a large and successful department at Michigan. He also developed a series of courses in pedagogy, and for his students published short texts in most subjects. In these, he further developed his emphasis upon science and art and called himself a professor of the science and art of teaching. These were, in many ways, his golden years. He looked back to them with nostalgia when faced with the frustrations of his job in Nashville. His scholarly output kept growing. To acquire accessible texts for his students, he used his fluency in French to translate four books by Gabriel Compayre on psychology and the history of education, and Rousseau's *Emile.* In constant demand for teaching institutes or public lectures, he became one of the best-known professors at Michigan. He corresponded with everyone in the broader field of education and built a network of loyalists among his graduates, for whom he remained a confidant and career advisor.

But once again—a bit of counterpoint in his successful life—his overweening ambition caused him grief. In 1881, he published a small text called *A Short History of Education,* listing himself as the author. But he had lifted a long essay on the subject from the *Encyclopedia Britannica,* adding only an introduction and bibliography. He acknowledged the *Britannica* source but not by name the author of the essay (only the author's initials appeared at the end of the article). Three years later, someone in England saw his book, and charged Payne with plagiarism. To use this essay as Payne had was presumptuous and ungenerous, yet it did not violate copyright law, even had any applied to an American publication—international copyright protection was not then in place. Payne carefully explained what had happened and defended his innocence, and the British author accepted his explanation. The incident embarrassed but did not humble Payne.

After the death of President Stearns in the spring of 1887, the University of Nashville had to appoint his successor as chancellor, the state board of education his successor as president of the normal school. The local trustees of course deferred to the Peabody Fund board, whose first choice apparently was Payne; it approved him unanimously. After Sears's death in 1880, the board had selected as his replacement a southerner, Jabez Lamar Monroe Curry (always called J.L.M.) from Georgia. Curry was a lawyer, politician, and educator whose family had moved from Georgia, where he was born in 1825, to Alabama. He graduated from the University of Georgia and Harvard Law School; served in the Alabama, the U.S., and Confederate congresses; was an admirer of John C. Calhoun and an aide during the Civil War to General Joseph E. Johnson. After the war, he became an English professor at the University of Richmond, a cabinet member under Hayes, and an ambassador to Spain under Cleveland. In fact, in 1887, he was in Spain, while someone else temporarily served as general agent of the Peabody Fund. Later, Curry would become deeply involved with the Slater Fund and the advancement of black education in the South. It was Curry, from Spain, who wrote to offer Payne the new position (of course, it would be the Tennessee Board of Education and the University of Nashville that legally appointed him). Payne was reluctant. Only after a visit to Nashville was he persuaded to accept. Once again, the Peabody board was generous—a $6,000 salary, with housing and expenses. Payne was inaugurated as president on October 5, 1887.

ACADEMIC REFORM

Between 1887 and 1890, Payne reorganized the State Normal College, which the state board of education renamed as "Peabody Normal College" in 1889. He wanted it to transcend the typical normal school, which he still criticized at every opportunity. What he wanted was a four-year college of education. He did not like the L.I. degree but had to continue it. Even more than under Stearns, the school would now have two tracks, one favored, the other tolerated. After the first year, Payne replaced the old junior, middle, and senior classes with a four-year, freshman-to-senior system. But with this change, the freshman year remained primarily remedial, a review of elementary subjects. Scholarship students entered as sophomores, and those who stopped with an L.I. remained only two years. Freshmen, still largely from Tennessee, remained three years for their L.I. Payne wanted more students who would continue to the fourth year and to a bachelor's degree awarded by the University of Nashville. He reinstituted such a degree in three flavors—arts, science, and letters. Until 1890, he also awarded earned master's degrees in each of the three classifications, but these entailed study under a professor and a thesis, not additional coursework. As he admitted, neither the faculty nor the library supported even bachelor's work, let alone graduate study. But he hoped to so improve the college as to justify such degrees.[3]

Payne also set about creating the infrastructure for college-level work and for professional work in education. He finally persuaded the Peabody Fund to provide $500 a year each for the library and labs. For the first time in the history of the University of Nashville, the library opened daily for students. A librarian and assistant soon began classifying the books under the new Dewey system, including many related to education. They also purchased as many periodicals as their small budget allowed. The new reading room was always crowded. Most of the old library, although it held many rare and valuable books, was of little use to students. And despite all prior claims, these books numbered less than 10,000. Eventually, Payne appointed a library council, prepared lectures on reading and library use, and added courses on library work for prospective teachers. But in spite of all this effort, the library never had more than 25,000 books, the average number for a good high school library today. Surely, many of the new books quickly wore out. In 1901, for example, students checked out books more than 26,000 times, double the number of useful books in the collection.[4]

In 1889, Payne introduced a completely revised curriculum with required and elective courses for each degree. The L.I. was least changed but did require work in Latin, physics, chemistry, and biology, plus at least the first four of six courses that Payne offered in pedagogy. He had brought with him from Michigan this six-course sequence, and the same texts (mainly his) that he had perfected there. The requirements for the three bachelor's degrees compared to those in any good college. The B.A. required both Latin and Greek and a full complement of humanities and science courses. The B.S. required not only Latin, but French or German, plus a heavy dose of science and mathematics courses. The B.L. (bachelor of letters) required only modern languages, but a heavy dose of English and history. All required psychology and Payne's six-course sequence in pedagogy. But despite the range of courses, the level of instruction rarely rose above the high school level.

Payne took full advantage of the gym. Throughout his teaching career, he had been a great advocate of physical exercise. In his paternal opening lectures to new students each year, he always began with an emphasis on health, exercise, adequate sleep, and good clothing. All physically able students had to spend three hours each week in gender-segregated gym classes under the direction of an expert. Soon Payne could boast about the robust health of his students. The era of epidemics, of cholera and yellow fever, had ended. Nashville had cleaned up its water supply, and now only influenza and colds threatened students. The absence of dorms may have helped check epidemics. The students, with the exception of a few boys with rooms in Lindsley, all lived in college-approved boardinghouses near the campus. Faculty members inspected these homes and imposed a few rules—no coeducational homes, and no more than two students per room. The monthly cost for room and meals ranged from fifteen to twenty dollars, with rates slowly falling in a deflationary economy. By 1900, with six hundred students to house, boarding had become a big business.[5]

One of Payne's first priorities was to get Peabody and University of Nashville funds to construct a model or demonstration school. Completed in 1891 and named for the president of the Peabody Fund, Robert Winthrop, it gradually expanded from elementary instruction, to middle school courses, to a full high school, and from one to three expert teachers. In what seemed a perverse decision, even to his colleagues, Payne never allowed any practice teaching in this school, only observation. He wanted a level of artful instruction that far surpassed what a beginning student could offer. The school proved popular with Nashville and suburban parents. In his final campus expansion, Payne gained a long-sought goal—a small administration building, which included a large office for himself. But a soaring enrollment of more than six hundred by 1900 made for a crowded campus. All these students had to take courses in only nine classrooms and the chapel, save for physical education and laboratory courses. The classes had to meet from 8:00 to 5:00, Monday through Friday, with physical education and a few other courses on Saturday morning. Payne could only itemize the needs—a library building, a better gym, a science building, and possibly dormitories and a fence. The campus remained open to any who wandered in, including stray dogs and cows. In 1901, just as Payne left, the University of Nashville completed an impressive stone fence that encircled the sixteen-acre campus and cost more than $8,000, more than some buildings. Much of this fence remains today.[6]

Through his courses on pedagogy, Payne helped shape the educational philosophy of every student in the college. Young, impressionable, they easily capitulated to his views, particularly because of his superb teaching skills and his paternal concern for their welfare. The scholarship students, in particular, carried Payne's beliefs and values back to their home states, where they almost always took the lead in public school reform and in the development of state normal schools. His philosophy thus had enormous impact on southern education. It is odd that, after Payne, neither Peabody Normal nor George Peabody College for Teachers would ever employ even one eminent or widely influential educational theorist or philosopher.

Payne believed that few if any normal schools provided even a modicum of professional training in education. They did not turn out students who could make of teaching what he called a "rational art," an art guided by the "science" of education. Normal schools offered students a high school level of training in key subjects, and some methods to use in teaching them. That was all. Payne, above all, lambasted the emphasis upon methods. Not that a teacher could dispense with methods, but methods, if not based on or even deduced from scientific laws, were usually the result of intuition, trial and error, or some new fashion. They became mechanical rules, a crutch. True professional education required three components—scholarship, methods, and what he often called doctrines or principles. In Nashville, Payne intended to raise teacher education to this level, and thus distinguish Peabody Normal College from other normal schools.

Still, he realized that most students would not be able to rise to the professional level. Only a select group would go on to the bachelor's level, gain a solid grounding in the latest scholarship in each discipline, and be able to move back and forth from scientific laws to the methods suggested by them, or even become critical and innovative creators of new doctrines and principles. These would be the future educational leaders of America. So far, almost none of these leaders

The Winthrop Model School, completed in 1891. In 1911 it became the home of the Vanderbilt University School of Dentistry, but was later demolished. Photographic Archives of Vanderbilt University.

came from normal schools. Instead, they had completed a classical curriculum in a college or university and moved on from there to the science and art of teaching. He did not expect this pattern to change. His university program at Michigan was the likely model for educational leadership. But he hoped, for a select few at least, he could duplicate this opportunity at Peabody Normal College.

Gender entered into his analysis. He expected a majority of L.I. graduates in his college to be women, joined by a few young men who did not have the inclination or money to go on to a bachelor's degree. The two or three years spent in the L.I. program did not allow any depth of scholarship or any philosophical grounding for methods of teaching. These students had to take much of what they learned on authority. Fortunately, with Payne teaching them pedagogy, their training would serve them well, but they were not prepared for educational leadership. Such students were not adequately trained to be principals or superintendents, let alone teachers in normal schools. He welcomed women into the L.I. program, although it is not clear that he wanted them to go on to one of the three bachelor's degrees. They did it anyway. In any case, the professional level of work, from Payne's perspective, primarily existed to prepare men for leadership roles in education, or at least for teaching in the few high schools in the South.[7]

Payne professed no bias against women. Because of the nurturing aspects of their gender, they were the best teachers in grades one through five. Because of certain qualities of mind, he believed, they were not well qualified for higher grades and in no case should serve in supervisory roles, particularly over men. It seemed little less than absurd, from his perspective, for women to become principals, or even to teach such subjects as mathematics or chemistry. Women's minds were not fitted to such abstract subjects. Also, the short period of service expected of women in education—only until they married and had children—did not merit strictly professional training. It was a waste of effort. In Nashville, Payne asked state superintendents, in selecting Peabody scholars, to favor men over women if their performance on exams was otherwise roughly equal. By 1891, men slightly outnumbered women among Peabody scholars, women still outnumbered men in the L.I. program, and men who earned bachelor's degrees outnumbered women by thirty-five to twenty. Payne hired few females for his faculty. By 1891, only four female faculty remained, at least in strictly academic subjects (this excludes physical education, librarians, and a vocal music instructor), compared to nine men plus two assistants in chemistry. This reversed the gender ratio under Stearns.[8]

Yet, despite Payne's preferences, women faculty continued to play a vital role in the school. Julia Sears was soon the senior faculty member, honored by being listed first in the catalogue. Faculty payroll records show that she always had as high a salary as anyone except the president. Since women always outnumbered men as students, these women teachers provided important role models—everyone conceded their skill in the classroom. Notably, none that remained on the faculty for an extended time ever married, a choice that characterized many emerging female professionals at the turn of the century. Of women graduates, almost none could have remained in teaching if they married, took over supervision of a household, and reared children. Most school boards would not hire married women teachers. Yet, many of the Peabody female graduates did stay in education; almost none of these married, as recorded on alumni lists. They followed the path of their mentors—Miss Sears, Miss Bloomstein, Miss Jones, and Miss Carpenter. The college honored Sears in 1905 as the first person in the history of the University of Nashville to serve for thirty years. It placed her portrait in a growing gallery in the chapel that included George Peabody, Philip Lindsley, John Berrien Lindsley, Barnas Sears, Robert Winthrop, and Gerard Troost. Julia Sears retired in 1907.[9]

In the training of teachers, in line with his philosophy, Payne emphasized scholarship and principles, not methods. Ideally, anyone who wanted to become a professional educator needed, as much as did a physician, a classical education in the arts and sciences. It was in university training that a prospective educational professional first learned the sciences that provided the foundation for educational methods. But, of course, students in traditional colleges and universities learned nothing about the art of teaching, or about applying scientific knowledge to problems of learning and teaching. This was the role of professional training in education, in the same sense that medical schools taught the art of medical practice informed by medical sciences. Thus, Payne tried, in his new four-year curriculum, to provide something close to a traditional college education. He wanted a broad curriculum and with typical self-confidence laid out the instrumental, moral, or esthetic benefits of each discipline. But he was honest. In 1890, in an address to faculty and graduates, he admitted that Peabody Normal College, although a notch above most normal schools, offered instruction in most subjects at a level hardly up to the very best high schools, and offered college-level work only in mathematics, literature, and chemistry. (Payne was eventually able to employ men with Ph.D.'s in chemistry and literature, the first at the school.)

Payne deplored the emphasis on ungrounded rules and methods in most normal schools. Some, such as the systems developed by Pestalozzi and Herbart, seemed to offer magical pathways to artful teaching. Fads seemed to follow each other in each generation. But Payne believed that almost none of these were truly scientific, for they were not the deductive implications of known laws or generalizations. Thus, methods taught to prospective teachers faced a dual problem—they could war against the always necessarily individual and contextual aspects of good teaching, and at the same time they could be unscientific. Teachers needed to develop artful techniques tied to their own personalities. While methods required elements of spontaneity and originality, what Payne stood for in educational philosophy was the need to base methods on what he called educational science. In fact, with all manner of semantic problems, he talked all the time about the science of education. Unfortunately, Payne, so confident of his views, was not an able philosopher. He had few analytical skills and simply could not sustain a fully coherent point of view. All his talk about "science," heady as it must have sounded to naive students, was full of sophistry or even deceit. It takes help from a historian to translate his views, published over and over in his books, articles, and lectures, into a clear argument.[10]

PAYNE'S ART AND SCIENCE OF TEACHING

Payne became fascinated with two related terms, "science" and "law," both fashionable in the late nineteenth century. Whatever one meant by the ambiguous term "science," the claim of scientific status seemed almost obligatory in almost any area of study. In many cases, the claim was not only unclear but pretentious. So it was for Payne. Payne did not use the word in the older sense of a systematic body of knowledge, but in the newer sense of knowledge that involved true generalizations or laws. These laws allowed one to predict future events and, in some areas, to gain control over phenomenon. At least for physical phenomenon, such laws seemed to fit and, indeed, had armed humans with new power over natural events. Payne believed that a large body of such laws, at least reasonably well established by experts in several disciplines, was available for teachers. If they attended carefully to such laws, they could deduce from them what they needed to do to teach students. The medical analogy proved most useful to Payne. To help patients, surgeons had to know about anatomy and physiology. This did not eliminate the possibility of individualized approaches to surgery, but such sciences placed clear limits on what a surgeon could do. Skillful surgery, even artful surgery, had to conform to laws.

One could ask: Is medicine a science? Is education a science? Payne had an elusive answer. Both medicine and education are, in reference to lawlike bodies of knowledge, applied sciences. This would seem an awkward way of stating the obvious—that such practices draw upon various sciences but are not in themselves sciences, since they do not reveal any distinctively medical or educational laws. This means that there may well be sciences (bodies of developed, lawlike propositions) that inform medicine and education, but in no literal sense is education or medicine a science, only a scientifically informed practice—or, as Payne put it, a rational art.

What sciences should guide educational practice? Or even allow teachers, with deductive certainty, to prescribe certain methods? Here, Payne was again elusive. Clearly, psychology was the critical science for educators. Without being specific, he argued that psychology was a well-developed science with known laws that were completely reliable. Notably, he never listed a single one. All students at Peabody Normal had to study psychology, at the time a field that, by any contemporary perspective, was just separating from philosophy and still immature. At other times, he listed four other "sciences," each with laws, that had to inform educational practice: physiology, sociology (a late addition by Payne and a subject not taught in his college), logic, and ethics. As he considered the problems faced by teachers, he almost had to expand his list this far, but such an expansion involved him in problems of parallelism and coherence. His appreciation of cultural differences, of the need to fit educational methods to the beliefs and values of a local community, led him, one suspects almost desperately, to sociology. Logic is a heuristic tool in any practice. And ethical standards undergird almost all aspects of education, beginning with the selection of a curriculum. Payne, always a moralist, talked often about the goal of any education: a perfect human, as if all people had the same image of what made a person perfect.

When Payne asked students to move up to doctrines and principles, he was asking them to be scientific. As educational professionals, they were not involved in the inquiry that established the laws they needed. In words that came close to some of John Dewey's later, he was asking well-trained teachers to be critical consumers of such knowledge. The specialists who carried out the inquiry had no interest in educational applications. It was up to educational specialists to discover these, but usually in a context of trust. Payne believed that the various developed sciences provided reliable knowledge because of the methods of inquiry that lay behind them. Thus, he asked his able students to become well informed about whatever scientific knowledge educators needed but not to detour into the inquiry that produced it. They were not to become specialized scholars, but widely informed in all disciplines that informed their art. He believed that at least his more gifted male students, in four or five years, could become connoisseurs of such knowledge.

It is easy, from today's perspective, to ridicule Payne's views as dated and naive. He used the term "law" differently in various contexts. In only one of his sciences, physiology, do open generalizations or laws really fit. To the extent that laws of this type fit psychology, it is at points of overlap with physiology. General propositions in sociology, if at all persuasive, are at best limited in time or space, or to statistical probability. The axioms of logic are formal, with no empirical content; they guide thinking or arguing. And ethical "laws," if one insists on using the term, are normative; they reveal values and lead to prescriptions about conduct but do not parallel propositions about regularities in nature. In short, Payne's laws that were to guide educational practice were a pastiche of physical generalizations, psychological and sociological theories, conventional logical axioms, and self-affirming preferences and values. A glib sophist might easily claim "scientific" authority for any educational practice by appeal to one or another of these purportedly universal sciences. Yet despite his problems, Payne had a point. Teachers did need to know as much as they could about all aspects of their subject matter and of their students, even down to the level of physiology. And the latest, most comprehensive, most carefully verified knowledge in several disciplines might help teachers in their tasks. Despite his sophistic efforts to deal with "sciences," Payne was correct in pushing his students toward a rational art, in the sense of practices guided by careful thought and by rule-governed inquiry. In this, he anticipated John Dewey.

Payne admitted that scientific knowledge did not answer all questions teachers might face. In fact, his list of unsolved problems might incline one to think that every important issue lay outside his scientific loop. These problematic issues included how to relate mental to moral training, how to justify the objectives set for a course of study, and to what degree knowledge determines moral behavior, to what degree student interest or enjoyment should govern what one teaches, and to what degree reading, and books, influence learning. Beyond these issues were all the day-to-day problems of administrative structures, testing procedures, and classroom environments. Here, Payne advocated not applied sciences, but what he called a distinctive educational science, with its own problems and methods. What he meant was simple. He wanted carefully designed inductive inquiries to determine the effectiveness of various teaching methods. For example, one should be able to design experiments to measure the effectiveness of different types of exams. Such focal research could lead, not really to laws of the physical type, but to informed guidelines for teachers. It is not clear if any such inquiry took place at Peabody Normal, but at least Payne tried to teach students about scientific method and lauded the use of statistics.[11]

Payne's professional courses set a tone for the college. He persuaded students that they received an education superior to those offered by other normal schools, that they rose to the level of doctrine and principle, that they were on the way to understanding education as both an art and science. They went back to their local school districts with pride, perhaps at times a bit of arrogance. But this sense of higher achievement lent confidence to their work as teachers and, for most of the men, in time as principals and superintendents. The records reveal a student body fully persuaded that Payne was one of the great educators of America, and that he worked assiduously in their behalf. He helped them get the best possible positions. His files are full of letters from grateful students or those asking for letters of recommendation.[12]

THE WONDERFUL STUDENTS

Payne dominated his faculty and catered to students. He lectured the faculty about its responsibilities, particularly after students complained of harsh treatment or unfair grades. After Payne came in 1887, the college, soon crammed with students on a too small campus, began rejecting more applicants each year, which entailed more demanding entrance exams and tougher grading. Surprisingly, this trend did not please Payne. He did not like entrance exams and wrote and lectured continuously on proper exam techniques in classes. His bent was to give every applicant a chance for admission, and more than one chance to succeed. He felt, quite often, that teachers were insensitive and unsupportive, and that they did not spend the needed time to assure that exams were fair in every sense. Students needed to know what they had attained, what skills they still lacked. Exams were necessary. But he regretted that the fate of a person might come down to one less than "scientific" exam. He suffered when students became discouraged and left, or when they could not make passing grades.

Payne loved his students, and they knew it. They responded with affection to their famous teacher and leader. Morale, in most years, was very high. He noted frequently that the students who came to Nashville, even those on scholarships that never paid all their bills, made great sacrifices to be there. Most were deeply committed to teaching, serious in almost every respect, and wonderful young men and women.

In relative terms, in fact, few of these students were poor. More accurately, the whole South was poor. Average incomes in the eleven former Confederate states were only half the national average. The families of students who came, even on scholarship, did have to make sacrifices in most cases. But it would be misleading to suggest that any but a very few of the students at Peabody Normal were from the lowest economic class. Even discounting blacks, who were not eligible, the poorest white families were almost never in a position to provide even an eighth-grade education for their children, who at a young age had to go to work on a farm or in a cotton mill. In areas of poor soil, counties had not even made public schools available in all too many districts or townships. Compulsory school laws lay ahead, as did the creation of high schools in most rural areas.

Thus, half the students who came to Nashville came from family-owned farms, and most of the remainder from small county-seat towns or villages, with parents involved in the professions (neither lawyers, physicians, nor ministers made large salaries in the South) or in commerce. The few wealthy families in the South would rarely send their sons to a normal school, but their daughters, anxious to find a career for themselves, often insisted on taking advantage of the best educational opportunity available to them. From the first class of 1875 on, many young women from the most eminent or affluent families came to Peabody. And because of the prestige of a Peabody degree, or even of a year's coursework there, students did not have to find jobs in what was still most prevalent back home—one-room, one-teacher rural schools. All the alumni data show that even women students found positions in villages or towns in graded and multiple-room schools, and that men soon moved up to administrative jobs.[13]

Student culture blossomed after 1888 with all manner of clubs and organizations, concerts and art exhibits, and even athletic teams. In 1890, the university fielded its first football team, only to be embarrassed by a 40–0 loss to a regional powerhouse, Vanderbilt, the worst loss in the school's history. Hostilities reached a climax in 1896 when a riot nearly broke out during another game with Vanderbilt. However, intercollegiate athletics was never as prominent at Peabody as at most colleges. The teams were club teams, with no financial support from the college. A student athletic association paid for part-time coaches. The college built stands for a football field immediately back of the main college building but never had a gym for basketball. After 1890, it competed in baseball and track. In 1900, just before Payne resigned, the student managers of the teams faced impossible fundraising burdens. Following the lead of other universities, the college finally assumed responsibility for intercollegiate competitions, under the control of an athletic corporation. The team, with its garnet and blue uniforms, was never dominant and soon stopped playing Vanderbilt, but it competed as an equal with less

The Peabody Literary Society in 1900, in front of the Castle. Photographic Archives of Vanderbilt University.

high-ranked football teams, such as those at the Universities of Tennessee, Texas, Virginia, and Kentucky.[14]

As enrollment surged above five hundred in 1892 and remained in that range for the next decade, students became increasingly busy with extracurricular activities: a lively student newspaper, dramatic and musical presentations, gym exhibitions, literary society meetings, art exhibits, and musical concerts. Full-time music and art teachers, some quite talented, insured that the arts would receive fully as much emphasis as the sciences. The assumption was that future teachers would introduce these subjects into the public schools, as well as the gym skills they learned in physical education. The literary societies not only survived but grew, with new societies assuming a more social role. The two old male societies—Agatheridian and Erosopohian—revived with the opening of the normal school and continued the old debate format. Not to be outdone, women students in 1880 formed the Girl's Chapter, modeled after the male societies but lacking their tradition and well-stocked libraries. In 1889, other young women formed the Literary Society, devoted not to debate of public issues but to the intensive reading and evaluation of great works of literature, beginning with Dante and Shakespeare. In 1889 the men formed a third literary society, the Adelphi. In 1896 the women formed the Alpha Phi Literary Society. All societies were open to anyone who would join.

In the nineties, as on many campuses, the largest organization at Peabody was the Student Christian Association. It would cease to be a coeducational association in 1901, moving to a model that closely paralleled the YMCA and YWCA. Before 1901, it sponsored prayer meetings on Saturday afternoon and a religious service in the chapel on Sunday afternoon. It prepared a list of Bible readings for each day of the week. Affiliated King's Daughters and King's Sons gathered in separate rooms for the Saturday prayer meetings. As a state institution, the normal school never had required chapel services, although special chapel services often had a religious content. But Payne insisted that the school was Christian, although in all ways nonsectarian. His lectures to students in chapel were full of moral instruction and religiously informed content. His was a very loose, social-gospel type of Christianity, with no specific doctrinal content. He encouraged students to attend local churches and assumed that one or another would meet student expectations, but the college could not enforce such attendance. Back in their boardinghouses, students were on their own. The matrons of boardinghouses for females undoubtedly imposed rules, but students were largely in control of their own social life, including how they played the mating game. In fact, this degree of independence, joined to the serious professional commitment of students, may help account for the total absence of major disciplinary problems. Everyone, from Payne to local newspapers to those who owned the boardinghouses testified to the high character and exemplary behavior of almost all the students.

Because of the Peabody scholarships, this was geographically the least provincial normal school in the United States. Around half the students, in any year before 1905, came from outside Tennessee. Eventually, more than two hundred Peabody scholars attended each year, and at least a hundred other students entered Peabody in the expectation of a scholarship in their second year. All were from the twelve scholarship states. Only a handful of northern or foreign students ever enrolled. Even next-door Kentucky, without scholarships, contributed only 99 students to the college from 1875 to 1911, less than three a year. In the same years, 860 attended from Georgia, 692 from Texas, 596 from Virginia, and 620 from Alabama. Even small West Virginia sent 267. These states sent quite diverse students—sons and daughters of coal miners in West Virginia, cowboys in central and western Texas, Creoles and Cajuns in southern Louisiana, tidewater planters in South Carolina, mountaineers in the Ozarks, and orange growers in tropical Florida. Of course, the one missing population was African Americans, who were on campus only in menial roles. Most students were Protestants. No record remains of Jewish students, although President James Porter later claimed that Protestants, Jews, and Catholics found a congenial college home in Nashville. The percentage of Catholics must have been small, mostly from Louisiana. An evangelical outlook pervaded student debates. In the 1904–5 bulletin, President Porter used data from other southern colleges and universities to demonstrate how unique Peabody was: In no other institution did out-of-state students number more than 20 percent, and in most less than 10 percent.[15]

One of Payne's first goals in Nashville was to gain control over the Peabody scholarships. In 1892 he began notifying state superintendents, each year before scheduled exams, of not only the vacancies to be filled by that state, but also the names of nonscholarship students from each state who were already enrolled and deserving of a scholarship. If state superintendents did not object in two weeks (some did), these students won their scholarships. Payne also prepared the exams for the state competition. From then on, at least a large minority of scholarships was earned by achievement on campus, a strong incentive to student effort and an assurance that scholars represented the best students at the college. In 1892 Payne also successfully urged the Peabody trustees to lower the stipend from $200 to $100 plus rail fare. This change equalized the awards and soon almost doubled the number bestowed.[16]

The subsequent careers of scholarship students justified the money spent by the Peabody Fund. About 85 percent at least briefly chose educational careers, as they promised to do when they applied for what became highly competitive awards. In time, a much larger proportion of these students left teaching; men entered business, the professions, and government, but the largest number of defectors, if that is the right word, were women who married. In 1901, 432 former scholars were principals or superintendents, 132 normal-school or college teachers. In 1903, President Porter used alumni records (from all graduates, not just scholars) to survey later professional involvement. Of the 225 students who reported their occupations, 75 were principals, 25 superintendents, 13 college or normal-school presidents, and a surprising 41 teachers in colleges or normal schools, including faculty in such institutions as William and Mary, West Virginia University, Clemson, Florida State University, and the Universities of Denver, Georgia, and Texas. This survey shows that, with few exceptions, male graduates either attained an administrative position, taught in a college, or headed departments in high schools. A few women became principals of elementary schools, but the only higher career that seemed open to most was teaching in a normal school.[17]

THE FINAL YEARS UNDER WILLIAM PAYNE

In 1894 Payne shifted to a standard four-year college. It no longer offered remedial work. Unqualified students were invited to spend a year of high-school work in Winthrop. From then on, the L.I. was essentially a junior-college degree, awarded at the end of the sophomore year. Entering scholars now had to take special exams for admission to higher classes. The bachelor's degrees required, by modern standards, 135 to 140 semester hours of coursework. Only from 10 to 12 of these hours were electives. With each passing year, faculty qualifications improved, and presumably by 1900 most courses were at a college level as Payne defined it. More and more new faculty had at least an earned M.A., and several a Ph.D., although this degree did not necessarily mean the level of achievement now denoted by such a degree. A few took a Ph.D. at Vanderbilt in a graduate program that met no present standards; one earned a Ph.D. at nearby Cumberland University. But after 1900 this changed, as candidates with Ph.D.'s from Johns Hopkins or even German universities were willing to accept jobs at what the locals now called Peabody College for Teachers.

Payne resigned in 1901. This would have seemed to mark a major transition, but it did not, for he had built well. His resignation preceded a strange interlude that began in 1902, when the Peabody Fund trustees announced the early liquidation of the Peabody Education Fund and a commitment to contribute $1 million to endow an advanced college for teachers in the South. This was anticipated. Winthrop, before his death in 1894, had recommended it. Almost everyone assumed that the money would go to Peabody College in Nashville. This led, in 1903, to special efforts headed by the new president, James Porter (he was also a member of the Peabody board), to raise matching donations in Nashville to insure that the college remained where it was. He secured such commitments by 1904, and in 1905 the Peabody Fund trustees approved Nashville. But this marked only the beginning of a complex process that eventually led to the George Peabody College for Teachers, chartered in 1909, and not open to students until the summer of 1914.

Payne had long hoped that the new Peabody endowment would be available in 1897, the date when George Peabody's will allowed liquidation. He was frustrated by the delays. His wife died in 1899, and in 1901 he was offered his old chair back at the University of Michigan (his successor had died). He was also aging, often in poor health. He wanted the quiet life of a teacher, not the endless challenges of a president. But also behind his resignation lay personal embarrassments that involved the state board of education and the board of trust of the University of Nashville and that reflected once again on some of his personal liabilities. Always unable to resist opportunities to promote his own career or financial security, he had eventually claimed, in a listing of the officers of Peabody Normal College, to have a Ph.D. In his first year, he had listed only his M.A., without stipulating that it was honorary, which was typical for the time. But in 1890 and on to his retirement, he listed both a Ph.D. and an LL.D. after his name in the catalogue. This was bold-faced deception. He never earned any degree, certainly no Ph.D. He did receive an honorary LL.D. from Michigan after he came to Nashville and could honestly list it, for everyone understood it to be honorary. Somehow he expanded this into a Ph.D. as well, which made the college look good to prospective students. Because of his LL.D. everyone on campus referred to him as Dr. Payne. As far as I can tell, no one called him on this ego preening, but surely his faculty resented the deception.

In 1898, it became clear that Payne had much deeper problems. These involved conduct that normally would have led to his dismissal. The Peabody Fund board, to prevent damage to the college, chose to ignore Payne's irregular conduct and continued its support for him. The other two boards could not ignore it. In 1898, a state legislative investigative committee, concerned because of the annual state appropriation for the college, reported irregularities in the finances of Peabody Normal College. The sources of information had to be disaffected faculty members. The background is this: President Payne appointed his son as secretary and treasurer of the college (he also appointed a daughter as librarian). This nepotism, while not illegal, was questionable. As early as 1897, the son began some strange manipulations of at least two college funds. He shifted funds from bank to bank, executed notes for some removed funds, mixed his private money with college funds in accounts, and ended up with some funds simply unaccounted for. No one ever determined exactly how much, if any, money he lost or possibly stole, although the college clearly paid unneeded interest on some notes. The legislative committee held the son responsible for these irregularities. He resigned his position, although President Payne appointed his son's wife to replace him. The investigation may have prevented the loss of several thousand dollars for the college, depending upon what the son might have done in the future. President Payne tried to protect his son and may have been more involved in the financial irregularities than anyone could prove. A minority of the legislative committee wrote a report demanding President Payne's ouster, since his "usefulness was at an end."[18] To limit damage to the college, the larger committee required only the resignation of Payne's son, but from this point on the members of the committee harbored deep suspicions about President Payne's honesty and, as it turned out, for good reason.

The board of the University of Nashville, more or less retired from any active involvement in the college, learned about irregularities in the president's office in 1898. The board still approved candidates for its degrees (bachelors, masters, and honorary) and rendered pro forma financial reports to the state board of education, but the conduct of Payne's son alerted its members to problems. Then, in the summer of 1898, members of the board received information about an even more serious misuse of funds by Payne. The source, once again, had to be aggrieved faculty members. Payne always supported a military form of organization for a college. He considered himself the general in command and told his faculty, on

William Payne (in chair) with faculty and students, about 1899. Julia Sears is third from the left (standing) and a young Wicliffe Rose is next to the last in the back row. Photographic Archives of Vanderbilt University.

several occasions, that he would allow no dissent once he had adopted a policy. Any faculty input had to come before he had made his final decision. That he had recruited more able faculty, with earned graduate degrees, made it even more likely that faculty would chafe under his dictatorship.

What the university board learned was that Payne had kept for himself part of the money earned for a declining number of rooms in Lindsley Hall rented to male students. This issue had not been part of the investigation by the legislative committee. That such rentals occurred was not a secret. In fact, the catalogue each year advertised the rooms. As the college had to take over more and more of Lindsley for educational purposes, the number of such rooms declined toward zero. These charges against Payne led to a careful audit by the secretary-treasurer of the University of Nashville and eventually to the appointment of a committee of three to look into the results of this audit. Meanwhile, Payne became aware of the inquiry by the board and as a consequence wrote a long, pleading letter to it in October 1898, in which he clarified what had happened over a ten-year period.

Payne noted that, when he arrived in Nashville as chancellor in 1887, he found much of Lindsley Hall in near ruins (an old story, for it always seemed about to fall down). He reported that he and Edward D. Hicks, then secretary-treasurer of the board, had frequently talked about the unused and unsightly rooms in Lindsley, and that Hicks had verbally accepted a proposal from Payne—if he would assume the risk of repairing and refurbishing these rooms with his own money, he could use the rent in any way he pleased, including a small salary for himself in his capacity as chancellor of the university (his regular salary was for his presidency of Peabody Normal). This claim would have been more persuasive had Hicks recorded such conversations and agreements before his death in February 1894. He had not. According to Payne, he improved the rooms at his own expense and began renting them. In his estimation, this helped save a decaying building. Some rental funds, he reported, went for cataloguing books in the library and for small acts of charity to needy students. In the first years, he kept none for himself and even turned $1,000 over to Hicks to purchase a nearby lot for the university. But as the financial needs slackened, he began to pay himself a salary, with Hicks's express consent and, Payne believed, with the tacit consent of the board. Then, in a long detour, he wrote of his contributions to the college and university—"I have recreated the University of Nashville." He deserved a salary for this extra work as chancellor. But in the final accounting, which he knew would be evident to the auditors, he revealed how little he had given to charity and how limited were his repairs. Out of total rentals of $5,351, he had kept $3,694 for himself.[19]

The board was incensed. Payne had deceived them. For older southerners who valued honor above all else, Payne's conduct was dishonorable if not illegal. On August 1, 1899, the whole board heard a full report from its committee and voted what amounted to a resolution of no confidence in Payne. It concluded: "This

Board declines to ratify the appropriation of any funds arising from the rent of Lindsley Hall toward the Chancellor's salary, it never having been contemplated that any salary should attach to that office." Yet, for fear of losing Peabody Fund support, it never forced Payne to repay these questionable earnings.[20]

Only five days before this meeting, Payne had sent the board a defiant letter based on his extensive consultations with the Peabody board in New York. He announced that it was his wish, and the wish of Curry and James Porter, the local member of the Peabody board and president of the university board, that he fire two faculty members—John L. Lampson, professor of Latin, and Benjamin B. Penfield, professor of biology and one of the few faculty with a Ph.D. In actuality, he also fired a third professor, Julia Doak. Penfield, a close friend of Stearns, had served as acting president before Payne's appointment in 1887 and may have nourished old resentments against Payne and his method of running the university. It seems likely that he was one of the professors who tipped off the board to Payne's financial trickery. Lampson's replacement was Charles E. Little, a Peabody graduate and by 1899 completing a Ph.D. in Latin at nearby Vanderbilt. He would become one of the great professors in the history of Peabody, on both campuses. The University of Nashville board refused to be drawn into the dismissal issue. It would not acquiesce in the action, because it did not believe it had any authority in the nomination of teachers. But the board surely resented Payne's statement that he made these changes "under the direct authority and consent of the Trustees of the Peabody Education Fund, whose appointee and servant I am." He displayed letters of support from both Curry and Porter. The Peabody board in fact had no legal authority over Payne's position as chancellor of the university.[21]

The state board of education was the final authority on all appointments and dismissals in the college (not in the university), an authority it had not exercised in any direct way before 1899. But the three dismissed faculty members appealed their dismissal to the state board. At this point, the developing scandal became public knowledge, to Payne's further embarrassment. Coincidentally, these three faculty members, and these alone, had testified before the legislative committee that had investigated the college's finances. Both legally and morally, they had immunity because of this testimony. Payne justified their dismissal by citing their "disruptive influence" on campus, but the three professors, and members of the state board, were persuaded that their testimony had led to their firing. In a hearing that lasted into the evening of August 2, 1899, the state board heard testimony from both sides in a confidential meeting; concerned faculty and newspaper reporters could only wander the halls and wait for news. In the end, the state board approved the dismissals but mandated that, in the future, only the board would appoint or dismiss faculty. Once again, the state board acted to protect the college and to avoid any embarrassment for the Peabody Fund trustees.[22] But it did not drop the issue, and a subsequent committee carried out further inquiries that led the board to secure from the general assembly a new law applying to all normal schools, which clarified a number of rights enjoyed by faculty. This was not a tenure law, but never again could a president treat the faculty as had Payne.

Much was at stake by 1899. The Peabody Education Fund board was trying to decide whether to liquidate its fund. This is why James Porter wanted to retain Payne. The future of Peabody Normal depended on its endowment by the Peabody trustees. Yet, at the same time, the University of Nashville, which owned the campus, was critical to any effort to procure this endowment for Nashville. In October 1899, a conference committee made up of representatives of the three boards involved with Peabody Normal College met in Nashville. The representatives of the Peabody Fund trustees were wined and dined and greeted like royalty on campus. Out of this meeting came a partial resolution of the developing tensions. The conference recommended a new advisory committee for Peabody Normal College made up of the general agent of the Peabody Fund, the state superintendent of instruction, and the president of the board of the University of Nashville. It is not clear that the committee ever played an important role, in part because the period of tensions was about over. On May 6, 1901, the university board accepted Payne's resignation, probably with considerable relief. A subsequent one-paragraph resolution noted his very important service to the university and even commended his "capability and character as a man and a scholar." No one could doubt his capability, but board members obviously had reservations about his character.[23]

THE BENIGN PRESIDENCY OF GOVERNOR PORTER

On campus, Payne's resignation created great anxiety, especially among students. Payne had always been their advocate and friend. I suspect that many faculty welcomed his departure yet realized he would be hard to replace. A faculty committee petitioned the Peabody Fund board for several needed improvements on campus that Payne had hoped for. It also wanted an expanded program in pedagogy, revealing doubts about Payne's complete domination of this instruction. Payne's successor was a surprise to almost everyone. After Curry, the Peabody Fund's general agent, searched for months and found no compelling candidate, he recommended the appointment of seventy-two-year-old James Porter as temporary president. Porter was a member of both the university and Peabody Fund boards, and no one opposed him. As governor, way back in 1875, he had played a critical role in the founding of the State Normal College. Now, for eight years, as he continued to serve as president and chancellor, he did more than anyone else to insure the creation of George Peabody College for Teachers. Curry decided that, at least briefly, Nashville's college needed no professional educator at its head. He assumed that the old normal school had only a few years of life left. Even in the year of his appointment, the Peabody Fund board made the first official move to establish a new, fully endowed teachers' college.

Porter proved an excellent president. He did not teach or dictate educational policies. A faculty senate formed in 1897 finally came into its own. Under Porter, faculty committees had much more autonomy. Faculty morale soared. Almost none of the faculty already on board in 1902 resigned before the college closed, although some retired. New faculty appointees also remained until the college's closure in 1911, two years after Porter had resigned. Students had no special advocate in Porter, but in almost all ways he kept the existing policies. He failed to win funds for any dorms, and, in fact, because of the school's supposed interim status, no new building was possible in these years. Everyone was waiting for the new college. The unusually independent students continued their clubs, sports, and literary societies, although the turn-of-the-century boom in football diminished. But in the fall of 1904, the Peabody scholarships ended; the trustees had finally committed start-up funds of $1 million to endow a new college. Enrollments declined from the peak of 600 in 1900–1901 to 352 in 1904, and 313 in 1908, but remained as large as the facilities justified. The enrollment pattern, however, shifted. Most students in the final years were from Tennessee, and most were women.

Even before Payne resigned, the faculty had begun planning a summer school. It opened on campus in 1902, Porter's first year, with 448 students, who completed one-half semester of work. But the big demand came from teachers who wanted to maintain temporary teaching certificates, or to pass exams to teach in elementary schools. After this opening demand, enrollments declined for the next four years, then began a slow rise, reaching 376 in 1908. Thus, the combined enrollments approached the peak years under Payne, even without scholarships.[24]

What Porter wanted, in what he hoped would be only three or four years before the transition to George Peabody College for Teachers, was to move as rapidly as possible toward full college status. He also wanted as soon as possible to end the L.I. degree but lost on this point. With Payne gone, he eventually hired four professors in pedagogy and for the first time introduced varied views on theoretical and practical issues in education. This explains why he unofficially changed the school's name to Peabody College for Teachers as soon as he took charge. He did not think the term "normal" still fit the college, but in most respects it did. No more than Payne was he able to get even a fourth of the students to go beyond the L.I. degree. The standards for certifying teachers were so low that few students had a strong incentive to spend four years in Nashville. But in all formal aspects, Porter created a college. He expected only a slow and gradual transition when the endowment was finally available and always dreamed of a George Peabody College on the old campus, with all the new buildings he believed were needed. He had in mind a seamless transition.

By Porter's last year as president, 1909, the institution was far ahead of any of the now maturing normal schools in the South. Because of the imminent closing of its normal school in Nashville, the State of Tennessee had withdrawn all state funding and in 1909 had chartered three regional normal schools, in Johnson City, Murfreesboro, and Memphis. In its final years, Peabody College for Teachers began to look more and more like a typical college. It began recognizing students for honors work, while the students finally adopted an honor code. In 1903, the faculty formed a placement committee to help its graduates find the best possible jobs.

In a series of moves, Porter tried to weed out subcollegiate instruction. In 1906, the college began requiring graduation from a four-year high school for regular admission, with fourteen Carnegie units in serious academic subjects (a unit represented a year of high school work in courses that met five days a week), including four units in foreign languages, but not necessarily Latin and Greek. These requirements matched those of all but a few elite liberal arts colleges. They also were comparable to the requirements, in 1914, for the new George Peabody College. But not until 1910 did these requirements go into effect for all students. Porter created, within the college, what he called a normal school, a two-year program leading to the L.I. Students could enter this school with only 8.5 units, or just over two years of high school. To his dismay, most entering students still chose the normal school. After 1910, in the last year of the college, all entering students had to have the fourteen units. In effect, the L.I., which Porter called a diploma and not a degree, amounted to a junior-college award. Slowly, Porter improved the college infrastructure. By 1909, the library finally held more than 25,000 volumes. The college had laboratories in chemistry, physics, psychology, biology, and even a new Troost geological laboratory. Although it does not appear on any map or later list of buildings, this lab was possibly housed in one of the old stables at the east of the campus.

From Porter's perspective, the glory of his Peabody was its faculty. As new American graduate schools turned out more and more M.A.'s and Ph.D.'s, aspiring new professors with excellent credentials were willing to take jobs at institutions as worthy as Peabody. By 1909, the school had twenty-one professors in academic disciplines, plus three assistant professors and three instructors in physical education. It had seven listed Ph.D.'s, one each from Johns Hopkins, Clark, McMasters, the Universities of Rochester and Wisconsin, Vanderbilt, and nearby Cumberland University in Lebanon. One of the original students of 1875, Lizzie Bloomstein, still taught history. A sister of one of the original students, after extensive training and exhibitions in Paris, taught art. The best-qualified scholar in the history of the college, Herman A. Vance, a Payne appointee in 1889, took three years off to complete his Ph.D. in philology at the University of Jena in Germany, and for two years taught the subject as a part-time professor at Vanderbilt; he died in 1906. Another faculty member that served under Porter in the early years, and as dean after 1904, was perhaps the most famous graduate of Peabody (B.A. and M.A.),

Wickliffe Rose, who became general agent of the Peabody Fund in 1907 and later served in various positions in Rockefeller charities. In short, Porter accumulated a faculty that compared well with that in all but a few southern colleges and universities. But to accomplish that, he may have unintentionally deceived new appointees, for he confidently expected that they would continue as professors in the new Peabody. Only two would do so, in part because of a three-year gap from the closing of one college in 1911 to the opening of the other in 1914.[25]

Only in 1909 did an embittered President Porter finally realize that the new Peabody would be near Vanderbilt. He resigned as president of the college. In the same year, the State of Tennessee chartered a new, independent George Peabody College for Teachers, although it would take five years to get a campus ready for students. By 1909, the old Peabody Normal College was something of an anachronism. The Peabody Fund continued to provide its operating budget through part of the academic year 1909–10, while a faculty member, John Hinds, served as acting president. But largely because so many students needed an additional year to complete an L.I. or even a B.A. (Porter had abolished the three categories of bachelors degrees), Charles E. Little, as chair of the faculty, was able to persuade the new George Peabody board to support a final year of instruction, 1910–11. The enrollment was a surprisingly large 250, in part because teachers in the South realized this was their last chance to return and finish a degree.

The last year was in many ways sad. Little announced the school's closing in chapel in the spring, but by then it was expected. Since the new campus would not be ready for three years, all faculty members received notice that this would be their last year of employment. Little and the staff tried to help students transfer to other colleges and to advise faculty seeking new positions. The final commencement in early June was a special affair, with many invited speakers. Students put on a play, set up an art exhibit, performed the last gym exhibitions, and held oratorical contests. The glee club gave a concert. The six literary societies held their final meetings. The alumni association met, with many speeches celebrating the contributions of their alma mater. In the crowded chapel, alumni looked out, often for the last time, on the beautiful campus. The graduation exercises took place on the lawn, under the trees planted by President Stearns and his students, for the thousand attendees could not fit into the chapel.[26]

Many present were still bitter about moving the campus. When the president of the new George Peabody College, Bruce Payne, came to address the alumni, he stressed continuities, accepted the alumni as alumni of the new college, noted that Charles Little had already received an appointment there (he would continue his employment during the interregnum), and offered to award later George Peabody degrees to the thirteen receiving a B.A. They still received University of Nashville degrees, even though, by 1911, the university did not own the campus. By the time it closed, the normal school founded in 1875 had graduated 2,600 students with the

L.I. diploma or degree, 675 with bachelor's degrees, and 49 with an M.A. It had received $1,126,540 from the Peabody Education Fund, most for scholarships; $429,000 from the State of Tennessee, and $109,800 from the University of Nashville. It had collected $127,000 in student fees, for a total income of $1,793,249.

This commencement marked the end of the historic University of Nashville as a collegiate institution. In 1902, it had deeded the campus to the Peabody Education Fund, and through it to the new George Peabody College. The closing meant the end of its literary department, which dated back to 1806. In the fall, Vanderbilt, which had traded land to secure the old campus for its medical and dental school, wanted access to all the buildings for renovation. Thus, in May of 1911, the university board, which still owned the library, laboratories, and much equipment on the campus, decided to give it all to George Peabody College. On May 29, the president of the medical department, now owned jointly by the universities of Nashville and Tennessee, conceded that the department could not continue operations. It had a large deficit and because of lobbying by Vanderbilt University had been unable to get a bill passed in the Tennessee assembly allowing the transfer of University of Nashville properties to a school operated solely by the University of Tennessee. This transfer would have meant the end of the medical department of the University of Nashville, but the continuation of the oldest medical school in the city. Subsequently, the University of Tennessee would establish its medical school in Memphis. All that was left of the University of Nashville was Montgomery Bell Academy.

The liquidation of assets continued for a few years. The university sold most of the empty medical buildings. In 1913, it faced intense pressure, even from the state assembly, to turn over its endowment to George Peabody College to help it meet matching requirements in a million-dollar campaign. The board, now almost all old men, never made an offer that the new college would accept. It remained loyal to James Porter and those who had tried to continue the college on its south Nashville campus. Within a few years, most people in Nashville had all but forgotten their namesake university. Few knew of its sometimes glorious history.

CHAPTER SEVEN

The Long and Painful Birth of George Peabody College for Teachers, 1897–1910

NO COLLEGE IN AMERICA HAS HAD A MORE COMPLEX AND confusing birth than George Peabody College for Teachers. The intense birth pains left congenital pathologies that would haunt the college for the next sixty-five years. Even Vanderbilt University, which tried to serve as midwife for the difficult birth, suffered from its failure to deliver as early, and as comely, a baby as it expected. For Nashville, for Vanderbilt, for Peabody, even for the whole South, the effects of this difficult delivery would be wide-ranging. On one hand, it produced a strong, independent college of education that had immense impact on the South. On the other, it prevented the early maturation of a great university center in Nashville.

EARLY CONSPIRACIES

Most people had expected the new college in 1897, or soon thereafter. By the terms of George Peabody's 1867 will, the Peabody Fund board was free to liquidate the education fund that year. As 1897 approached, educational institutions throughout the South waited eagerly to see if they could get some of the money. Many did, in the final liquidation, including most state universities and the Slater Fund, which largely worked to improve the education of blacks. To some extent, millions in the South would continue to benefit from the Peabody gift, but nearly everyone understood that Nashville had the most at stake. It was almost certain that the largest portion of the liquidated fund would go toward George Peabody College for Teachers and that the college would most likely be in Nashville, an expansion of, or replacement for, Peabody Normal College.

Just before his death in 1894, George Peabody's close friend and the first president of the Peabody Education Fund, Robert Winthrop, sent a letter, almost a directive, to his board. "In the great Normal College at Nashville, Tenn.," he wrote, "we have already established an institution for the immediate and ultimate benefit of all Southern States. . . . At all events and in every view, this institution has the first and highest claim to our consideration, and should receive the largest share of the distributed fund. It will be the most enduring monument of Mr. Peabody's munificence—it might well have a round million of dollars—perhaps more than a million."[1]

In Nashville, almost everyone expected at least a million. William H. Payne came to Nashville to head Peabody in the expectation that, after 1897, it would become a well-endowed, fully professional college of education. The University of Nashville trustees awaited the largesse and by the midnineties had resolved to give the existing campus to the Peabody Fund. Above all, former Governor James Porter, a member of the Peabody Fund board, expected the gift and devoted ten years of his life to getting it. Other Nashvillians also considered the possibilities of such a gift, but from a different perspective. First among them was the still young chancellor of Vanderbilt University, James H. Kirkland. He believed a new Peabody associated closely with Vanderbilt could assure what he wanted but never had the means to achieve—a major university to match the best in the North. Johns Hopkins University was his model.

Two interwoven strands make up the story of George Peabody College's founding. One involved the extended negotiations to win the $1 million endowment for Nashville. The other involved the exact location of the new college in Nashville, and the type of institution it would become. By 1905, a group of largely young men had decided that it was imperative, for the future of George Peabody College, that it be affiliated with Vanderbilt and thus have a new campus "on, or in close proximity to, Vanderbilt," words that became a litany. One could call these advocates conspirators, for at times they carefully concealed their long-term goals. The four most important conspirators were Chancellor Kirkland at Vanderbilt; Daniel Coit Gilman, the one older man, the soon-to-be retired president of Johns Hopkins, and a key member of the Peabody Education Fund board; Wickliffe Rose, dean of the old Peabody in 1905 and after 1907 general agent of the Peabody Fund; and Wallace Buttrick, secretary of the new Rockefeller-funded General Education Board, which because of its efforts in behalf of southern higher education had a financial stake in the fortunes of both Peabody and Vanderbilt. In time, this small coalition won the support of several key members of the Peabody Fund trustees and of Henry Pritchett of the Carnegie Foundation, and at least limited support in Nashville. Its two most active members would be Rose and Buttrick, who became fast friends as well as leaders in the new world of professional philanthropy.

Wallace Buttrick, born in upstate New York, attended a normal school in his hometown of Potsdam and worked his way through Rochester Theological Seminary, graduating in 1883. He was at the seminary at the beginning of the social-gospel movement in his own northern Baptist church, and the seminary also brought him into a circle of people related to its major benefactor, John D. Rockefeller. Ordained as a Baptist minister, Buttrick served congregations until 1902; his last appointment was in Albany. His leadership skills soon became evident. He served on the board of trustees of the University of Rochester and on the executive board of the American Home Mission Society (important to Peabody later), and he became a close friend of Frederick T. Gates, whom Rockefeller selected to organize and direct his soon extensive philanthropic efforts. It was Gates who appointed Buttrick executive secretary of the new General Education Board (GEB) in 1902. Its work brought him into contact with Rose during the time he served as dean at Peabody Normal College.

Rose, a west Tennessee youth, took both a B.A. and an earned M.A. from Peabody College and became its most distinguished graduate. He would later become the agent of the Peabody Fund, head the large Rockefeller-funded hookworm eradication program (Sanitary Commission), and get involved in several international programs funded by Rockefeller money. He also served, for a time, as executive secretary of the GEB, Buttrick's old position. In this capacity, he would have a continuing relationship with George Peabody College.

The other strand of the story—the site of the new college—involved President Porter of Peabody, a supportive University of Nashville board, most faculty, students, and alumni, and almost everyone in the area of south Nashville surrounding the campus. Porter, for good reason, assumed from 1903 on that the new Peabody would involve an expansion of the old. Despite some troubling evidence to the contrary, he refused to take seriously other proposals, particularly those that would place the college near Vanderbilt. From 1903 through early 1909, Porter spent most of his energies trying to win the new Peabody for Nashville, and building the local support and the funds for a matching requirement set by the Peabody Fund board. This grew into an extended, frustrating effort to which Porter, a locally esteemed politician, was essential. Only after he won his local battle did those on the other side finally make public their much more ambitious plans for George Peabody College, and their belief that only a close working relationship with Vanderbilt would make such a Peabody possible. Secrecy, and sometimes deceit, was a deliberate part of their strategy.

Kirkland and Gilman, as heads of southern universities, became cronies and probably conspirators even before 1897. Gilman visited Kirkland at Vanderbilt in 1894. In 1898, Kirkland spent time in Baltimore at the general conference of the Methodist Episcopal Church, South, and by that date had probably talked extensively to Gilman about the early liquidation of the Peabody Fund. In the next year, he clarified his hopes for a great university in Nashville in a letter to Gilman, suggesting that Gilman, after his planned retirement from Johns Hopkins, become president of the new George Peabody College. Kirkland believed this would assure its location near Vanderbilt, and an affiliation between the two schools. In 1900, he appealed to Gilman to accept this task as a way to uplift the South. He wanted the Peabody Fund trustees to establish a new board of trust for the contemplated college but stressed that a quality college was the first priority, affiliation with Vanderbilt a secondary goal. Kirkland tried to get Gilman to come to Vanderbilt to give the principal speech at a celebration in 1900 of the university's first twenty-five years, but Gilman had to decline. Later, in various discussions, Kirkland sought a way for Peabody to join Vanderbilt's existing colleges and schools in a new, larger university, possibly a reorganized University of Nashville.

In 1901, Gilman retired at Hopkins, highly esteemed among leaders in higher education because of the success of Hopkins's graduate programs and medical school. Kirkland now wooed him with even more zeal. In a 1901 letter, he revealed his dream of an affiliation between Vanderbilt and a new Peabody modeled on Teachers College at Columbia University. Gilman would head the new college and insure the needed cooperation with Vanderbilt. Kirkland even referred to Peabody as a department (college) of Vanderbilt, possibly comparable to Vanderbilt's medical and law departments, which were largely self-governing entities. The Vanderbilt name and the liberal arts courses available in Vanderbilt's literary department would help make the new Peabody a major influence on the profession of teaching in the South. He begged Gilman to enlist support for this scheme among his fellow Peabody Fund trustees. Gilman agreed to do so, dismissing the "unimportant" part of Kirkland's proposal—that he become Peabody's president. This correspondence makes clear that, by 1901, two high-powered educators were ready to do all they could to create a Peabody-Vanderbilt connection that required a new Peabody campus about two miles west of the old one. Kirkland, of course, wanted to enhance Vanderbilt, but he correctly assumed that only such an affiliation would produce a Peabody that could offer the highest level of graduate and professional education. Thus, even before the Peabody Fund trustees made the first decision about liquidation, the possible relocation of the campus was on Gilman's agenda.[2]

THE COMMITMENT TO NASHVILLE

Within months of the Kirkland-Gilman correspondence in early 1901, the Peabody Fund trustees, at their annual meeting in November, began the first, tentative move toward liquidating the trust and founding a new George Peabody College. One has a feeling that these old men were reluctant to give up their club. After Gilman moved to appoint Porter to a full year as president of Peabody Normal College, with the same $6,000 a year Payne had received, William Courtenay of South Carolina moved that the board appoint a committee of three to visit Nashville, "collect all available facts as to the present and prospective status of the Normal College," and report back at the next annual meeting.[3] Curry, the fund's general agent, and Porter joined Courtenay on this committee—three southerners strongly committed to a new George Peabody College as the successor to the old normal school. A second committee of three—Senator George F. Hoar of Massachusetts and two wealthy attorneys, Richard Olney of Massachusetts and Joseph H. Choate of New York, both sticklers for detail—would examine the legal ties of the Nashville campus to the Peabody Education Fund. Olney, one of two board members who did not want to liquidate the fund, would join with Choate in finding legal excuses to delay for six years the incorporation of a new Peabody.[4]

What happened at the next Peabody Education Fund board meeting, in October 1902, would prove critical to the future of Peabody. As one would have expected, after the fact-gathering committee of three (Curry, Courtenay, and the host, President Porter) visited Nashville, it expended great effort to insure that the contemplated million dollars go to the existing Peabody College. The three men easily persuaded the trustees of the University of Nashville to draft a deed that would transfer the sixteen-acre campus to the Peabody Education Fund. Because, if the deed were accepted, as they expected, this would have cut the University of Nashville's ties to the college, the committee recommended that a local council manage the college in the short period before George Peabody College could gain a charter and its own trustees. Finally, it suggested a major building program on campus to prepare it for the new college. But Olney and Choate speedily sabotaged this quick march to a new era. They examined past chartering acts by the Tennessee assembly and concluded that the University of Nashville board had no authority to give away its land. The deed of conveyance was invalid. They thus asked the board to reject the generous gift.

Equally prophetic of future events were some of General Agent Curry's remarks. Of course, he said, he lauded the successes of the Nashville normal school and in all ways supported its elevation to a graduate-level college. But times had changed, and with it the role of the Peabody Education Fund. It was no longer alone in its support of public or higher education in the South. Earlier in the year, as Curry pointed out, after years of effort southern governors and educators had joined to create the Southern Education Board. Andrew Carnegie had just established a new foundation to support original research in colleges and universities. At almost the same time (1902), Gates created the Rockefeller GEB, whose work, Curry noted, would closely parallel that of the Peabody Fund. As a result of Curry's remarks, the trustees appointed a committee to confer with representatives—meaning primarily Buttrick, executive secretary of the GEB—about "feasible and adequate methods of co-operation, including especially the building up of the Peabody Normal College."[5] This meant that Buttrick could become a major player in the events of the next several years, and that the GEB would be a major patron of George Peabody College.[6]

But the most fateful action in 1902, as far as Peabody Normal was concerned, involved another committee. It included the chairman of the board, Chief Justice of the Supreme Court Melville Fuller, plus Gilman, Porter, Hoar, Curry, Hoke Smith of Georgia, and Judge Charles E. Fenner of Louisiana. This group would consider the needs and opportunities of Peabody Normal College and suggest what was needed to increase its efficiency and to make it a "fit memorial to George Peabody and . . . a great Teacher's Training College for the Southern States."[7] Everyone expected the college to receive the famous million dollars as an endowment. As a mark of its importance, the committee was to report to a special meeting of the trustees in late January 1903. Its critical report marked the Peabody Fund board's first commitment to a "George Peabody College for Teachers" somewhere in the South, for it asked the board to use the trust fund or a portion of it to endow such a college. It did not mention Nashville but proposed another committee (one of more than ten committees involved in establishing the new Peabody) to recommend to the regular fall board meeting the best way to carry out this plan. Gilman headed this committee, which also included Smith, Olney, Hoar, and J. P. Morgan. Curry had died, and Samuel Green took the position of general agent until 1907, when he resigned and the board elected Wickliffe Rose. As Hoar's health declined, Judge Fenner joined the committee and would write its key document. Buttrick became an ally of Gilman and an informal consultant to the committee.[8]

The committee controlled events for the next two years. Buttrick often toured the South in behalf of the GEB. When he visited Nashville, his favorite host was Kirkland at Vanderbilt. In fact, Gilman, Kirkland, and Buttrick agreed upon their own agenda: The new Peabody had to be near Vanderbilt and affiliated with the university. But the three worked secretly, for they did not want to disrupt the process that would lead to the support they needed from the Peabody Fund. It was no time for controversy. Increasingly, a very able Dean Rose took the lead in advising Gilman and Buttrick, and in supporting Nashville as the location of the new college. In June 1904, Rose met with the Gilman committee in Washington and suggested the requirements for a new college in a detailed report that had emerged from a series of faculty meetings on the Peabody campus.

President Porter did the political work in Nashville. Local matching funds would be required if the Peabody Fund trustees agreed to the old Peabody as a location. The contemplated $1 million would not build a new college. In fact, the anticipated $50,000 annual income approximated the annual operating budget of the old college. They would need extra funds for the buildings that Porter had already proposed to the trustees and for hiring the better-qualified professors for a graduate-level college. The amount discussed was some $800,000, and this Porter wanted to secure. He counted the deed to the campus as $250,000 (inflated). He secured from a compliant state assembly a bill authorizing the University of Nashville to transfer its property to the Peabody Education Fund. It executed a new deed of transfer in 1904. In addition, the assembly, in its meeting in January 1905, agreed to contribute $25,000 annually for ten years, if the Peabody trustees provided $1 million to endow the college in Nashville. While this appeared to mean a commitment of $250,000, the state also proposed to stop contributing $25,000 each year to the old college, so in fact no new funds were involved.

Local enthusiasm insured that both the city and Davidson County would help. The Davidson County Court approved bonds for $50,000 and the city council for $200,000, both conditional upon the Peabody Fund gift. The citizens of the city, in a required referendum in August 1904, approved the city's gift by a vote of 4,678 to 858, a rare example in Nashville of strong support for bonds to fund education. Thus, before the Gilman committee completed its work, it had before it these local pledges. Elated by the local support, Porter still needed $50,000 to reach the proposed $800,000; he received it from Davidson County. In June, the Gilman committee voted to recommend a Nashville site. Only Hoke Smith dissented—he wanted the Peabody Fund to aid rural schools in the South. Porter had already communicated to the Peabody Fund board what he believed was needed for the new college: a separate board and several new departments of instruction. He demonstrated that his new curriculum was close to his model—Teachers College at Columbia University.[9]

The climactic meeting of the Peabody Fund trustees came in a special meeting in January 1905 in Washington. The location proved significant, for board member Theodore Roosevelt, then president of the United States, attended his first meeting and took an active role. Two years later, in October 1907, President Roosevelt briefly visited Nashville, riding in an open car to review the faculty and students gathered in front of the stone building. In a sense, it was his college. The first resolution he supported in 1905 committed the board to liquidating the Peabody Trust. Only Chief Justice Fuller, the chairman, and Olney opposed. Gilman, as chairman of what was now a committee of six, noted that an extended report written by Fenner would justify the second part of this resolution—to apply $1 million of the trust to a new George Peabody College for Teachers. The resolution's final part established yet a further committee to "prepare and determine the terms and conditions" for applying the gift—Fenner, Gilman, Porter, Courtenay, and Episcopal bishop William Lawrence of Massachusetts, who would soon play a decisive role in the battle over the site of the new college. Lawrence was a graduate of Harvard, a student of Andover Theological Seminary, and a graduate of the Episcopal Theological School, which was next door to Harvard. He later served as professor and dean of this school, as he rose to the position of bishop in his church.

A second set of resolutions specified that "said college should be located in Nashville" and should be "the successor of the Peabody Normal College," to continue "on broader and higher lines the great work which has been done by the said Normal College for the cause of southern education." The resolution specified a matching fund of $800,000, and, aware that this would be available soon, promised that, if it received these funds within a year, the board would move immediately to charter in Tennessee a George Peabody College and turn over to its board the million dollars for its endowment. The wording of the resolution clearly implied that the new college would be at the same location as the old. Porter, who could not conceive of any other alternative, was overjoyed. He had won. In a note that in time would seem almost tragic, he wrote to his dean in Nashville, Wickliffe Rose, that their proposition had carried and that an ever impatient Theodore Roosevelt had helped push the resolution to a quick acceptance. Porter asked Rose to "strip for the fight" and for the hard work that lay ahead.[10]

The wording of this resolution was not fully in line with Gilman's hopes, for it failed to mention a Vanderbilt location. It also dismayed Rose, Buttrick, and above all, Kirkland. The extended Fenner report reinforced the apparent commitment to the old campus. In it, Fenner stated that the new George Peabody College, although with a new organization and administration and with extended purposes,

President Theodore Roosevelt in his brief stop before the students and faculty of Peabody Normal College, Oct. 22, 1907. Photographic Archives of Vanderbilt University.

"will be, practically and to all intents and purposes, the successor and continuation of the Peabody Normal College. It will succeed to its entire educational plant; it will take its site, its buildings, its library, its apparatus and equipment; it will inherit its splendid achievements, its noble traditions, its fine prestige, its body of ten thousand alumni." He probably exaggerated the number of alumni, but he reinforced the continuity further on, stating that whatever "we do for the new Teachers' College will be, practically and substantially, done for the old Normal College"[11] Later, Porter would return over and over again to this language, which reinforced his belief that it included a firm commitment, even a contract, to keep the college where it was. He rightly felt betrayed when a majority of the Peabody trustees later voted to move it near Vanderbilt. The language certainly seemed to preclude any Vanderbilt connection.

Behind the scenes, those who favored an affiliation with Vanderbilt were at work. All was not lost. In the events leading up to the critical vote in January 1905, Chancellor Kirkland had been in continuous contact with Buttrick. As early as 1903, Kirkland promised Gilman and his committee any support he could offer. He met with Buttrick in New York in October 1904 to try to allay any doubts about the nature of Vanderbilt's ties to the Methodist Church. By then, he was involved in a complex struggle with the Church over how much it controlled the policies of Vanderbilt. In 1904, he believed he could limit the Church's role enough to seek new foundation funding and to cooperate with a new Peabody. In a letter to his wife, after conversations with Buttrick, Kirkland wrote that, if Vanderbilt could get Peabody, there was "no telling whereunto we may grow."[12]

After the January board action, Kirkland wrote a long letter to Gilman in April inviting him to visit and again talk about the "grand plans we have had in mind for a long time." He wanted Gilman to investigate the local situation, and if he could not do this, to have the new committee, which included Gilman, hire someone capable of investigating the alternatives. His first suggestion was Buttrick. Kirkland wanted to guide the work of this final committee. He met with Gilman in Baltimore in September and tried to arrange a joint meeting with Gilman and Buttrick. He tried to win over one of the Peabody Fund trustees, Robert C. Ogden, and considered lobbying J. P. Morgan. At this point, Kirkland and Gilman sensed that they might lose, that Porter would win the college for the old site. Although Kirkland hoped the new committee would settle on a Vanderbilt location, he asked Gilman to keep the location issue confidential. Tact and secrecy were essential, not only to foil Porter, but also to prevent land speculators from driving up the value of all plots close to Vanderbilt. He wished he had $200,000 to buy up adjacent land, just in case. Gilman shared this letter with Buttrick, who agreed perfectly with Kirkland's views. He noted that the committee, which included both Porter and Gilman, had no mandate to select a site, but he was confident Gilman would find a way to expand its duties.[13]

By the summer of 1905, for anyone willing to heed them, the signals were obvious—Buttrick would do all he could to support the Vanderbilt affiliation. From the perspective of the GEB, some form of cooperation between Vanderbilt and Peabody was essential for a graduate school of education. Vanderbilt would have to provide the subject courses, leaving Peabody to concentrate on pedagogy. Sometime in the summer of 1905, Buttrick had talked to H. L. Morehouse, head of the American Baptist Home Mission Society (Buttrick was on its board), about buying the campus of Roger Williams University, a black college funded by this society just across Hillsboro from the southeastern corner of the Vanderbilt campus. Morehouse had considered selling the campus as early as 1901, for land prices were rising in an increasingly affluent white suburb. He had thought of moving farther out of the city. A move became almost imperative after fires destroyed the school's two main buildings in January and April 1905. (These buildings were on the site of the later Social Religious Building of George Peabody College.)[14]

In his travels to Macon, Georgia, Buttrick had tried to persuade J. R. Mosley of the Peabody Alumni Association of the necessity of a Vanderbilt connection. A perceptive Mosley found merit in such a move but suspected correctly that Buttrick was not being open with Porter. He begged Buttrick to talk to Porter and thus avoid a tragic controversy in the future—wise words, but unheeded. Mosley wanted cooperation with Vanderbilt, but not affiliation with a denominational school. He wanted a new Peabody free of political or sectarian control, a Peabody that would retain the "wholesome, democratic, and missionary spirit" of the existing college. He also argued that Vanderbilt was not a real university, merely an undergraduate college. It could not do much to enhance the more elevated graduate school Peabody aspired to be, but a nearby Peabody might help Vanderbilt grow along liberal and truly university lines. These were prescient suggestions, for Mosley identified some of the cultural tensions that would undermine the turbulent Peabody-Vanderbilt courtship for the next fifty years.[15]

LEGAL COMPLICATIONS

In the summer of 1905, it seemed almost certain that the Peabody Fund trustees, at their regular meeting in October, would authorize the chartering of the new college. All appeared to be in order. Porter proudly brought to the meeting the deed of the old campus and the commitments of the three local governments. One of the southern trustees moved that the board turn over the million dollars, since a report by Porter revealed that the Nashville supporters had substantially met the terms set in the resolutions of January. This resolution failed. J. P. Morgan noted that what Porter had secured did not meet, in several respects, the terms set by the Peabody Fund, and he moved to extend the period for full compliance to July 1907. This resolution passed. Porter was crushed and stayed angry at Morgan for months. The Morgan resolution began a four-year wrangle over legalities. The timing of the deadlines for compliance were dictated by the Tennessee General Assembly, which met in January in odd years only; the issue was not critical enough to warrant a special session. The next board meeting after the general assembly met would be in 1907.

The legal objections, raised in each case by Olney and Choate, seemed mere technicalities to the Nashville supporters. The major problem involved the state appropriation of 1905 for $25,000 annually for ten years, conditional on the $1 million Peabody Fund grant. Olney correctly ruled that Tennessee had to appropriate the whole $250,000 up front before the fund could make the grant. Although the city and county bond issues were in order, they too were conditional on the grant. Porter easily received the required changes in wording from the city and county and expected the needed legislative changes in 1907. Meanwhile, he could only wait.

The Peabody Education Fund Board in about 1905. It committed one million dollars for a new George Peabody College for Teachers. Note that President James Porter (middle row, second from left), President of Peabody Normal College, is one of the Board members. Photograph by Colvert Brothers. Photographic Archives of Vanderbilt University.

The unexpected postponement in October 1905 removed any need for a report by the Gilman committee on the terms and conditions for establishing the new college. At this meeting, Gilman asked the trustees to engage the services of one or more qualified persons to study the conditions of southern education, and thus the best use of all the Peabody funds. When he asked for a committee of three from the board to select and pay such an agent or agents, the chairman appointed Gilman, Jesup, and Fenner.[16] Gilman's was intentionally an open-ended resolution. In establishing this committee, Gilman did exactly what Buttrick had predicted—he found a way to reopen the issue of location for the new college. Kirkland, who had suggested such a study, also nominated Buttrick as the committee's special agent, and Gilman appointed him. The appointment, at the time in no way suspicious, would prove to be a key move in the founding of George Peabody. Buttrick, who was already surveying all aspects of southern education for the GEB, was becoming an expert on the subject and on what was needed to improve education in the South. Also, with the imminent liquidation of the Peabody Fund, its former support of public schools and state normal schools in twelve states was coming to an end. The GEB would take over this role, and with more funds than the Peabody trustees had ever had at their disposal.[17]

It became immediately clear that Buttrick would spend at least half of his investigation and eventual report on the role and location of George Peabody College. In November, just after his appointment, he wrote to his friend Dean Rose asking to talk with him in Nashville two days later and suggesting that Chancellor Kirkland might join them. From then on, Rose was all but a partner in assessing the needs of a new college, and Buttrick would so recognize him in his final report. On December 1, 1905, Buttrick reported that, at a recent meeting of the GEB, their "dear to heart" plan for the new Peabody was almost the sole issue of an extended discussion. The GEB wanted more detailed information about the cost of land and buildings. Buttrick asked Rose to come to New York for a conference and bring with him a complete plan for the new college—the location and cost of new land, costs of all needed buildings and equipment, maintenance costs, the planned curriculum, number of faculty and their salaries, and needed labs, including those for manual training, domestic arts, music, and agriculture. Buttrick assumed that Rose would be the dean or president of the new college. He emphasized that all these estimates were "to be based on the assumption that the new college is to be affiliated with Vanderbilt University. Such affiliation would, of course, involve much less cost than would the establishment and maintenance of an independent institution."[18] Rose presented his plan, making clear in the process that the contemplated funds for the college (about $1.55 million and the old campus) would not be nearly enough to create a brand-new campus. Whatever the long-term advantages of affiliation with Vanderbilt, moving the campus would mean much higher start-up costs.

Buttrick made a detailed report to the study committee of Fenner, Gilman, and Jesup in 1906. While it included the most powerful argument yet for a Vanderbilt connection, the report's legal status remained unclear. Fenner recorded his disagreement with many of Buttrick's recommendations. Gilman and Jesup endorsed them, and at the October 1906 Peabody Fund board meeting apparently circulated copies of the report to members, although it remained confidential, at Gilman's request, and did not appear in the published proceedings. If he read it at all, Porter apparently considered it nothing more than the views of Buttrick and Rose. He now knew that Rose, his own dean, had deserted his cause. Buttrick, Rose, and Kirkland were very active just before the fall board meeting; Kirkland even traveled Washington. But Buttrick concluded that it was not the right time to push the location issue. Only in 1910 did the Peabody Fund board publish this report in its proceedings, and then as a way of justifying the final allocation of its remaining funds. In any case, when Buttrick completed his report in 1906, the final establishment of George Peabody was on hold, awaiting the action of the Tennessee General Assembly in 1907.

The Buttrick report shaped the later history of George Peabody College. He spelled out what he and Dean Rose wanted: a major university in Nashville that included an advanced teachers' college. They stressed the need for such a teachers' college in a South that finally had a reasonably complete group of regional normal schools. This would be the only graduate-level college for teachers, including those who had graduated from normal schools. Only two such elite colleges existed, at Columbia University and the University of Chicago. It seemed obvious that no such teachers' college could afford to stand alone. The two model colleges did not staff courses in subject areas but had their students take such courses in the liberal arts departments of the host universities. Thus, the new Peabody had to be affiliated with Vanderbilt. Buttrick used Rose's early study to show that a self-standing Peabody would require an initial fund of about $5 million; the Vanderbilt connection would make it $2 million less. Thus, Nashville was the best location, not because of the earlier work of the normal college, but because it had in Vanderbilt the best university in the former Confederate South.[19]

Rose and Buttrick envisioned a new Peabody that in its plant, in the eminence of its faculty, in its range of courses, was qualitatively so far above the old Peabody as to mark a difference of kind, not of degree. They knew firsthand the limited size of the old campus, the inadequacy of its buildings, and the overall mediocrity of its faculty. The Peabody of their dreams could not be grafted onto the old Peabody. The problem with Porter and the local supporters of the old location is that they simply could not conceive of what a quality graduate institution required. But Buttrick and Rose also recognized the start-up costs for new land and new buildings. They thus proposed that the Peabody Fund trustees add $500,000 to the new Peabody. With matching funds, this would suffice. Eventually, the trustees went along.[20]

Early in 1907, the Tennessee assembly did approve the appropriation of $250,000 for the George Peabody College. This seemed to Porter to be the last hurdle. When the trustees of the fund met in Washington on February 20, 1907, most came with the expectation that they could finally accept the Nashville funds and thus soon transfer the promised million dollars to the board of trustees of a newly chartered George Peabody College. But Choate and Olney had other ideas. They argued that the three governmental units in Tennessee had still not met all the requirements, and successfully recommended that the deadline for meeting these terms be moved ahead two more years to accommodate the general assembly's schedule. Three southern members, led by Porter, protested such stalling on the basis of legal technicalities but failed to gain support for a motion to accept the $800,000 on the basis of substantial compliance. On the surface, Olney and Choate did look irresponsible, holding up the transfer for two years when no vital issues seemed at stake. But behind the official proceedings of the trustees, one finds major policy issues. Olney and Choate did compromise on other legal issues. By 1907, they had finally and reluctantly conceded that the University of Nashville could give away its campus. It took several Tennessee lawyers and supreme court judges to gain this concession. Olney and Choate also finally agreed not to press for new action by the city council of Nashville to conform to the unconditional grant required by the Peabody Fund board. Such action would have meant a second referendum, with all its attendant costs.[21]

The published reasons for rejecting the terms of transfer in February 1907 were provisions in both the grant approved by the Davidson County Court and the state appropriation. Davidson County had stipulated that the bonds not be delivered until the Peabody Fund trustees permanently located the new college "on or in the immediate vicinity of the grounds of the University of Nashville" on or before July 1907, a date still in the future.[22] But Olney and Choate noted that this condition on the grant precluded the Peabody trustees from placing the college in the vicinity of Vanderbilt. Nothing in the terms set by the trustees permitted such conditions in the Davidson County grant. This posed no great problem, for the county court could, and soon did, change the wording to a requirement that the college be in Nashville or its immediate vicinity. Porter urged this change, not because he expected a move to Vanderbilt, but as the only way to overcome the objections of Olney and Choate. But the wording of the state bill that appropriated funds for the new college posed an almost fatal problem. The state had tied its appropriation to the same date as the city and county. But at the December 1907 board meeting, as Choate and Olney pointed out, this appropriation was null and void. It seemed a catch-22: Since the state and county had not transferred their funds by the July 24 deadline, the state appropriation was no longer valid. The state would have to do it all over again before a new deadline—July 1, 1909. A series of petitions from Tennessee lawyers would not change the trustees' minds.[23]

What the official proceedings concealed was the main reason Choate and Olney refused to accept the state appropriation. In its innocence or stupidity, the Tennessee assembly in the preamble of its 1907 appropriation act had noted that the trustees of the Peabody Fund had resolved to establish a college for *white* teachers in Nashville. Olney wrote to Porter that this racial reference was "a fatal obstacle" to any resolution of the impasse. He referred to George Peabody, his letters, his expressed concern for all the people of the South, and to past efforts by the Peabody Fund to aid black schools. Olney wrote that he would never vote to support the project under this act. He would not have the Peabody Fund exclude "colored people from the benefit of this portion of the endowment." Choate concurred. Both admitted that the excision of the term would have no practical effect; the college would indeed be for whites. But they did not want the Peabody Fund trustees implicated in a southern caste system.[24]

This new postponement was a terrible blow to Porter, now seventy-nine and unsure whether he would live to see a new college on his campus. Yet he persisted. During the next two years, he attended to every possible detail. In early 1909, the legislators in Nashville practically made Choate and Olney write the new appropriation act, so that it would meet all their expectations. Finally, the end seemed near. At a special meeting of the Peabody Fund trustees on March 18, 1909, Porter could assure the trustees that he had all the funds, bonds, and the deed ready to hand over to them. It was Olney who moved that Porter now notify the several donors that the trustees were ready to receive the donations, and that they would at once proceed to form and organize a new corporation and elect trustees for the new George Peabody College. Bishop Lawrence then moved to appoint yet another committee, to report by July 1 on the form of the charter, the names of persons for election as the original trustees, and guidelines for organizing the college. The committee would be chaired by Lawrence, one of the youngest members of the board, and include Choate, Olney, Porter, and Fenner. Lawrence was the strongest advocate of a Vanderbilt connection. Porter and Fenner opposed any move. At least for a time, Olney and Choate felt that earlier actions of the board had all but committed it to the old campus, much as they appreciated the logic of the Buttrick report of 1906. In any case, sure that his campus would soon break ground for new buildings, a jubilant Porter returned to Nashville to a hero's welcome.[25] The college canceled classes for a day of celebration.

THE CONTROVERSY OVER LOCATION

Bishop Lawrence almost immediately asked Buttrick to assist his new Peabody Fund committee. The bishop visited the campus in Nashville, where he received the gracious hospitality of eighty-one-year-old President Porter. Porter would have been horrified by Lawrence's impressions. He described Porter as a well-intentioned bulwark against progress. He found the campus inadequate, with two buildings (Lindsley and the gym) in such decay as to be of no use. He even made deprecating remarks about the calibre of the students. By June 10, he was ready to report to a special meeting of the board. It is difficult to understand the way the committee functioned. Porter later lamented that Lawrence ignored him and his views. It seems that Lawrence did most of the work and the writing by himself, perhaps realizing that his views matched those of most of the trustees and that a major fight loomed. In March 1909, Lawrence told Buttrick, "I imagine that we are in for a skirmish in Nashville between the old generation and the coming one, such as you have been fighting out all along the line."[26]

Much of the Lawrence report was noncontroversial—a proposed charter and bylaws for the new corporation to be formed in Nashville. The bombshell came in the third section, which included a proposed deed of conveyance by which the Peabody trustees could give the $1.8 million in assets to a new corporation. This conveyance, as prepared by the committee (or at least a part of the committee), listed the property to be transferred and then stipulated that George Peabody College for Teachers be "located in Nashville, in the State of Tennessee, either upon the campus of Vanderbilt University or upon land in immediate proximity thereto . . ."[27] To justify this requirement, Lawrence simply quoted from the 1906 Buttrick report. A Porter faction fought back. Henderson Somerville, a judge from Alabama, offered a motion that the part of the report concerning the location of the campus be advisory only; Porter, Fenner, and Martin Ansel of Alabama supported him. This meant that both Porter and Fenner voted against a part of a report recommended by a committee that included them, at least formally. The issue was clearly sectional. All northern board members present voted to endorse the Lawrence report; the minority of southerners present all opposed.

One has to feel sorry for Porter He had finally won his fight to get the Peabody funds, but now it was all ashes, for the college would leave its old location. He remained silent until Dean Rose began seeking options on land near Vanderbilt. At this point local newspapers learned of the action of the board, which was big news in Nashville. The fight was on. Porter resigned as president of Peabody Normal College, which he had so carefully nurtured to grow into George Peabody College. He remained chancellor of the University of Nashville and lived on into the next year in the chancellor's house. In an attempt to appease the old man, Lawrence persuaded the Carnegie Foundation to grant him a retirement benefit. Not at all affluent, Porter appreciated the money, but it did not have Lawrence's intended effect. Porter openly led the fight against the move to Vanderbilt. At first he gained the support of most Nashvillians. Chancellor Kirkland, or other conspirators, had stolen their campus, and possibly the Peabody endowment.

Newspapers joined in the battle over location that raged during the summer of 1909. To add to the confusion, in the background lay another deepening conflict over the governance of Vanderbilt, a story as complex as the founding of the new

Peabody. By the turn of the century, some bishops in the Methodist Episcopal Church, South, had begun to take a more direct interest in Vanderbilt, founded by Methodists but never financially supported by the Church. The original charter made the Vanderbilt Board of Trustees self-perpetuating and did not specify the rights of the Church in the board. But as an informal rule, the trustees elected some bishops to the board—never a majority—and always elected a bishop as chair. A few bishops, concerned about policies on campus and the purported immorality of students, asserted the ownership rights of the Church and began to meddle in campus policy, including faculty appointments.

The leader of the bishops who wanted to control and change Vanderbilt was Elijah E. Hoss, who lived in Nashville. He had the support of Atlanta bishop Warren Candler. When Vanderbilt chancellor Kirkland guided his board in a 1905 clarification of the role of bishops and set a limit to their number on the board, Hoss was enraged. He entered into what became a nine-year struggle between Kirkland, backed by moderate bishops, and the Hoss-Candler faction. Kirkland had wanted to reduce the role of bishops, particularly if the Church would not give substantial funds to support Vanderbilt. He recognized that the future of Vanderbilt would depend on the new philanthropic agencies, such as the Carnegie Foundation and the GEB, and Carnegie, in particular, restricted his gifts to nonsectarian institutions. Kirkland wanted to demonstrate that no church, no sect, controlled Vanderbilt and thus make the university eligible for outside funds. At first, he seemed to win. His insistence upon only a loose Church tie had helped persuade Buttrick that a Vanderbilt-Peabody affiliation was in order. In the 1906 quadrennial general conference of the Church, Kirkland easily bested Hoss in political maneuvering and refuted allegations of scandals on campus. As Kirkland wished, the conference appointed a commission to inquire into the exact legal relationship of Church and university. To his shock and dismay, the commission report, later in 1906, declared the Church the owner of Vanderbilt, elevated a formerly inactive board of supervisors (all the bishops) to equal status with the board of trust, and, in a probable misuse of a 1895 Tennessee law, assigned the final right of electing trustees to the Church. Kirkland and his board believed the commission report invalid on legal grounds but waited for the 1910 general conference to try and win support for the near independent Vanderbilt that had existed from 1873 to 1906.

This battle was critical for Peabody. If Hoss and the commission findings prevailed, then Vanderbilt was a university directly under Church control. Any affiliation with Peabody would violate the emphatic nonsectarian tradition of Peabody Normal and, before that, Lindsley's University of Nashville. In 1909, when the deed of transfer required a Vanderbilt location, Porter correctly argued that it was by then clear that Vanderbilt was fully sectarian, with no real graduate program and unprepared to offer Peabody students the substantive, high-level courses they needed.

Of course, Kirkland and his Vanderbilt board disagreed with the Church commission and continued to function as before. In the showdown at the general conference of 1910, the Hoss faction won a decisive victory. When the Vanderbilt board chose to disregard what it believed to be illegal encroachments by the Church upon its charter rights, including new board members elected by the Church but not seated by the Vanderbilt board, the struggle moved, as it had to, into the Tennessee courts. After losing the first case at the local level, the Vanderbilt board won on appeal before the state supreme court in 1914. The Church, at its next conference, dissolved all ties to Vanderbilt. Only at that point did it become the nonsectarian institution that Buttrick had believed it to be all along.

But in 1909, Porter seemed correct in his charges. Hoss recognized that he could gain a local ally in Porter and thus joined his fight for control of Vanderbilt to Porter's insistence that Peabody remain on Second Avenue. As early as Buttrick's investigations and report in 1906, Chancellor Kirkland offered to sell some of the Vanderbilt campus to house the new Peabody—the southern part of the campus, a rectangular area north of Garland, and a smaller lot across Garland to the south. Since this was the highest land on the campus, Kirkland liked to refer to it as the best located of any part of Vanderbilt. It included three faculty residences, among them the chancellor's own home, plus tennis courts. In October 1909, the brand-new George Peabody Board of Trust decided to accept Kirkland's offer and buy the roughly fourteen acres involved. Following an earlier suggestion by Kirkland, they offered to trade the downtown Peabody campus, acre for acre, for this land. Since the downtown campus was larger by almost three acres, Kirkland agreed to pay Peabody an added $33,820. He wanted the downtown campus for Vanderbilt's medical and dental schools, which moved there late in 1911. Kirkland, it seemed, had solved two problems—he had insured that Peabody would be on his own campus, with an easy sharing of classes, and he had secured a needed new home his medical institutions.

The details of the swap were perfected in early 1910. Just before the Vanderbilt board approved the deal in October, the Board of Bishops secured an injunction prohibiting such an exchange, acting in accordance with the powers awarded them by the commission. Kirkland was helpless. But by then it was clear that Porter had lost—George Peabody would be near Vanderbilt (it had already purchased land across from Hillsboro)—and the bishops, fearful of hurting the Vanderbilt they soon hoped to control, withdrew the injunction, allowing the exchange to take place. To the chagrin of Kirkland, however, the expected affiliation and cooperation were now in jeopardy.[28]

During the summer of 1909, Porter lost the fight to keep the old campus. He almost won. He rightly emphasized the deceit involved. He noted that he had persuaded three political entities, and the University of Nashville, to contribute to the new Peabody under what had become false pretenses, the expectation that the college would be at the site of the old, as the 1905 resolutions had all but stated. He had the strong backing of almost everyone in south Nashville, including dozens of owners of boardinghouses. The few members of the new George Peabody board loyal to Porter resigned. Two members of the Vanderbilt Board of Trust were among their replacements. Both the state and the city took early steps to reconsider their gifts. The transfer of funds had not yet taken place and was now in jeopardy. Only the county court of Davidson County rescinded its offer of $100,000 in bonds, in January 1910, by a vote of twenty-two to twenty. But on the next day, Christopher T. Cheek, one member who had favored the rescission, agonized over what their vote could mean—the college would go to some other southern city. He successfully moved a reconsideration. After several parliamentary maneuvers, the motion to reconsider passed by twenty to five (several opponents left the room and did not vote). By resolution, the court then voted to deliver the bonds. The final obstacle to an exchange of funds had eroded. On January 31, the Peabody Fund board met in special session, but even then not before resolving a few additional legal technicalities. It approved the transfers of funds. Chartered in October 1909, the new George Peabody received its endowment only at the end of January 1910.[29]

Porter and others still considered legal action. Citizens filed two unsuccessful suits to prevent the county from levying any taxes to pay off the Peabody bonds, and to challenge the legality of the transfer of the University of Nashville deed. Resolutions, protests, and even angry sermons continued in south Nashville. In April 1910, with the fight lost, Porter and his wife went home to Paris, Tennessee, with their new Carnegie pension. Porter continued to attend Peabody Fund board meetings during the final liquidation of the fund. He died in May 1912, at the age of eighty-three. In his last years, he seemed an ogre to the young men who founded the new Peabody. But it is well to remember that he, more than anyone else, secured George Peabody College for Nashville. When the trustees of the University of Nashville gave their valuable library to the new college, they stipulated that it be named the Porter Library. To Peabody's dishonor, it ignored this commitment.

The struggle over location had lasting implications for George Peabody College. Although the young advocates of a Vanderbilt location won, the battle had placed them on the defensive and helped insure that the ties between Peabody and Vanderbilt would not be nearly as close as Chancellor Kirkland had anticipated. During the struggle in 1909, when it was not yet clear that the local governments would transfer the promised funds, Lawrence, as chair of yet another committee, wrote a statement for use by the new George Peabody College board in Nashville. In this white paper, he defended the series of actions from 1905 to 1909, and above all the Vanderbilt location. It was a one-sided, selective account of events, completely unfair to Porter and his allies. But it probably was a necessary condition for the capitulation of the Davidson County Court in January 1910. First, it included a threat: The Peabody trustees would move the college elsewhere in the South if Nashville reneged on the promised donations. Local newspapers took this threat seriously, and many reluctantly decided they had to back the Vanderbilt site if Nashville was to keep the college. One can never know how sincere Lawrence's threat was, or whether the whole board would have backed his self-admitted hard-ball tactics. It is not even clear that he was correct in suggesting that the Peabody Fund trustees had never made a final commitment on the location of the college. The 1905 resolutions suggest otherwise.[30]

Lawrence's other tactic was conciliatory. He emphasized that Vanderbilt would have no direct control over the new George Peabody. The contemplated marriage would never take place, only a platonic relationship. "Such cooperation was never meant and does not now mean any merger, nor even any affiliation. It contemplates nothing more than such arrangements between two independent institutions as shall avoid duplication of plants, of courses, and of instructors, as shall enable each of them, on terms and for considerations satisfactory to it, to supply the other with such educational facilities as the latter could secure for itself independently only at great and unnecessary expense."[31] In fact, not even this degree of cooperation ensued, to the lasting detriment of both institutions.

With the transfer of money and deeds in February 1910, George Peabody College now owned the old campus, pending its possible transfer to Vanderbilt. The state board of education had, after 1905, relinquished any further responsibility for the continuing college, and the state had chartered new normal schools to serve its teachers. After 1905, the Peabody Education Fund had paid all costs, using money formerly committed to scholarships to compensate for the lack of state funds. But in February 1910, the old college was an orphan, with no further Peabody Fund support. For the rest of that academic year, the new George Peabody board paid its costs. For compelling reasons, it also allowed the college to continue in the academic year 1910–11. In a sense, this was the first George Peabody College, owned and operated by the George Peabody board. Its legal name, had anyone thought to clarify it, was Peabody Normal College of the George Peabody College for Teachers. But in 1910, the bachelor's graduates still received University of Nashville degrees, for no apparent reason except tradition. The same was true for the final commencement in 1911, except that the just-appointed president of George Peabody, Bruce Payne, promised the B.A. graduates that they could receive George Peabody degrees as soon as the new college opened (a promise not honored until 1920).

No campus was ready when the old college closed in June 1911, which meant the final of several suspensions of classes in the long history of the University of Nashville–George Peabody College. The next three years had two effects. On one hand, they weakened the feeling of continuity among the alumni of Peabody Normal College. For years, the administration at the new college tried to repair the damage, to create a sense of common identity with the old alumni association, which it adopted as its own. On the other hand, the interregnum made it easier for the new college to develop a new and different identity. This helped establish a clearer demarcation between what had remained a normal school and what became a graduate college, although one without a host university. It allowed the new George Peabody College board to dismiss the old faculty. And these dismissals, more than any other action, helped open the door to a new start.

CHAPTER EIGHT

Creating the George Peabody Campus, 1911–1930

IN MANY WAYS, THE BUILDING YEARS OF GEORGE PEABODY COLLEGE for Teachers marked its golden age. It never had the resources demanded by its aspirations, but nothing seemed impossible in these years of steady growth and enlarged influence. In 1910, the new George Peabody Board of Trust had its original endowment. It took four more years to acquire a campus, complete the first academic buildings, and begin classes. The board had to find a president and then, guided by him, raise an additional million dollars, work out a complex relationship with Vanderbilt University, clarify its academic goals, and design a curriculum. During these exciting years, the campus and the academic and student culture of Peabody matured; it would not change in any basic way until after 1970.

THE GOVERNING BOARD AND A NEW CAMPUS

In 1910, all the major decisions about a new college confronted the just-appointed George Peabody board. It had to decide what to do with the $1.8 million in funds and property granted it by the Peabody Education Fund. It quickly used almost half of its $800,000 of discretionary funds and property to buy a new campus. It also had to supervise the continued operations of Peabody Normal College on the old campus. But the board lacked the expertise to plan campus buildings, or to work out an academic plan. For this it needed a president and began the search for the best possible leader in 1910. Equally important, the new board did not have nearly enough funds to launch a graduate-level teachers' college. Thus, even before the final appointment of a president, the board secured an additional $500,000 commitment from the Peabody Education Fund, but with a required match of $1 million that George Peabody had to raise by November 1913. The anticipated assets of Peabody would then total $3.3 million, enough to create a new college, provided that the needed cooperation with Vanderbilt spared Peabody the need for buildings and faculty to support courses in the arts and sciences.

By the terms of its charter, a majority of the George Peabody board had to come from Tennessee, a minority from other southern states. The governor of Tennessee, an ex officio member, never took an active role. The board could not exceed thirty-three members, but in their original recommendations, the Peabody Fund trustees suggested nine members from Tennessee, eight from other southern states, seventeen in all. Since the early Peabody board would faithfully follow these recommendations, not all southern states would be represented on the board at any one time. In fact, the executive committee provided for in the charter became the main governing body, and thus the Nashville-area trustees, who for convenience usually served on it, had most of the effective power. U.S. federal judge and later Supreme Court justice Edward T. Sanford, from Knoxville, became the first chairman of the board by choice of the Peabody Fund trustees. He lent prestige to the board but was rarely able to attend executive committee meetings. The full board became a ratifying body, with no extended discussion of or dissent from the executive committee's resolutions. Attendance by distant board members was often low. Some out-of-area board members resented their pro forma role and soon resigned.

From a developmental perspective, the all-southern board hurt. Most members were locally prominent lawyers, judges, or businessmen, but few were wealthy. Since the funds for Peabody came almost entirely from northern philanthropists, board members from the North would have made sense. In the early years, four or five Nashvillians dominated the executive committee. For two years, two Vanderbilt trustees served on the committee—Whitefoord Cole, a local railroad executive, and Claude Waller, a lawyer and judge. But when Peabody established its main campus to the east of Twenty-first Avenue, over vehement protests from Chancellor Kirkland, the two men resigned—a loss, for Cole had been very active. Banker James C. Bradford chaired the committee in its early years. James C. Caldwell, a local telephone and banking executive who followed as chair of the executive committee and later of the board after Bradford's death, played a critical role in building the new campus. E. A. Lindsey long served as secretary. Next to Sanford, the most distinguished member of the board was Jacob McGavock Dickinson, soon a federal judge, but too often not in Nashville. He served only briefly on the executive committee. The committee worked most closely with the president, especially during the tenure of Bruce C. Payne. While not a rubber-stamp body, the committee almost always deferred to his recommendations.

The board's first task was to acquire a campus close to Vanderbilt. Representing the GEB, Wallace Buttrick had talked to the American Baptist Mission board about buying Roger Williams University as early as 1905, and that board was still anxious to sell. Dean Rose had scouted out other properties, including a plot on Elliston Place to the north of Vanderbilt. By its first meeting in 1910, the George Peabody board was also interested in a plot of land owned by E. W. Thompson just across Hillsboro from the Vanderbilt campus and adjoining the Roger Williams campus on the south. The board was interested only in the section of the Thompson land south of Edgehill Avenue. Another option before the board was Chancellor Kirkland's offer to sell part of the Vanderbilt campus.[1]

On February 18, the board voted to exchange the old campus for the Vanderbilt plot, pending negotiations over details. It also began negotiating with a real estate agent, A. B. Hill, who acted in behalf of the owners of Roger Williams. By March 2, the board had appointed Cole and Bradford to work out final details on the Roger Williams and Thompson plots. On March 9, the board voted to purchase the Roger Williams property. Some board members were opposed, particularly Cole and Claude Waller, the two who were also on the Vanderbilt board. But this move did not eliminate the Vanderbilt plot or dictate that the main campus building be on the more distant Roger Williams site. Soon, an injunction by the Methodist Church postponed completion of the negotiations with Vanderbilt. On July 5, the board made an offer on the Roger Williams property but was unable to buy the whole plot without legal entanglements along Blakemore Avenue. Thus, on October 12, the board bought only the segment of this property—by then referred to as University Heights—from Capers Avenue north to a line just north of, or in front of, what would soon be the Social Religious Building. The cost: just over $170,000. The board held up the deal until it was satisfied that Hill was not gaining too much in personal fees for the transaction.[2]

The Roger Williams site meant that one college would follow another. The American Baptist Home Mission Society had only closed the campus after the fire in 1905. The society, an agent of the largest northern Baptist denomination, had first opened the Nashville Institute for ex-slaves in 1867 at a downtown site. When in 1874 the society purchased the Gordon estate, a tract stretching north along Hillsboro from present-day Blakemore Avenue, it placed its main buildings on the crest of the hill. It slowly introduced something close to college-level work. Its most famous alumnus, John Hope, later became president of Morehouse College, named after the head of the Mission Society. The society used the purchase money from Peabody to build a new campus off Whites Creek Pike, which it left in 1928 to move to Memphis. Its campus then became the site of the American Baptist Seminary, affiliated with the National Baptist Convention, which became the parent of four denominations that today enroll most African American Baptists.[3]

Also, on October 12, 1910, the board approved the purchase of part of the Thompson property for just over $125,000; this would later be the site of most of the Peabody buildings. The family moved their mansion, Edgehill, elsewhere in the city, but the college would occupy some other buildings on this property, as well as the Roger Williams property, during the construction of the new campus. Only in January 1911 did the board complete the land swap with Vanderbilt. After Bruce R. Payne was appointed president of George Peabody in June 1911, he would make critical decisions about the location of campus buildings. But it was clear, even before he came, that the choice location for a major campus was the large rectangle of land that stretched from Capers north to Edgehill, and from Hillsboro east to Nineteenth Avenue (just east of the present-day Nineteenth as its intersects Edgehill). The eastern border was just behind the present Mayborn Hall and close to an alley named "Appleton Place."[4]

What was unclear in 1911 was the degree and mode of cooperation with Vanderbilt. It was still possible to plan a campus with key classroom buildings along Garland, on the Vanderbilt strip. Had Peabody so chosen, the college would have developed the present site of Medical Center North, the new Vanderbilt Medical School and Hospital as of 1925. This would have so restricted Vanderbilt expansion to the south that it is unlikely the later Medical Center would have been part of the main campus. But the Vanderbilt strip had too few acres (approximately nine, north of Garland) for the campus envisioned by Rose and Buttrick, so they had sought out additional land as early as 1905. The only likely way of joining the two campuses was for Peabody to have purchased additional land south of Garland, most of which was a private residential area and thus too expensive even if available. The next-best possibility for close cooperation involved the rest of the Thompson plot, which stretched north as far as the present-day Scarritt Place (Wesley Garage). Had the Peabody board not purchased the Roger Williams plot first and instead built the main campus from Edgehill to Scarritt Place, the cooperation anticipated by Chancellor Kirkland would have been much easier.

THE SECOND PAYNE

During 1910, the executive committee also struggled to select a president. The unanimous choice was Wickliffe Rose, who turned it down at least twice because of his commitment to the Rockefeller hookworm eradication effort. He remained for the rest of his career with various Rockefeller charities, later serving as chief executive of the General Education Board (GEB). He was an alumnus of the old Peabody, its former dean, a friend of Kirkland, and one who played a major role in the founding of George Peabody College. One can never be sure, but he probably would have been at least as effective a president as Bruce Payne; everyone who knew him applauded his administrative skills. Yet Rose may have served Peabody even better as an arbiter of GEB gifts. From 1910 until 1941, the GEB was Peabody's main patron, contributing at least $4 million, more than all other donors combined. The gifts from the GEB amounted to the yield from an $80 million endowment.

After another candidate turned down early inquires about the presidency, the board formally approved an offer of the position to Bruce R. Payne of the University of Virginia on January 17, 1911. James Bradford, the executive committee chairman, had first learned of Payne the previous July from a consultant who praised Payne highly. By Christmas, when Bradford visited Payne at the University of Virginia, he had become the leading candidate. Perhaps most important, he was a long-time friend of Wallace Buttrick. The GEB paid his salary at Virginia. He also was a friend and scholarly ally of Edwin Mims, an influential English professor at Vanderbilt and an advisor to Chancellor Kirkland. Although Payne at first seemed reluctant to leave Virginia, in March he asked for clarification about the position. The board had stipulated a salary of $5,000; Payne wanted $6,000. By then, the Peabody Fund trustees had approved the extra $500,000, which meant a strenuous campaign for the matching $1 million. Payne wanted to help in the fund drive but not be responsible for it. He wanted to know his title, whether president or chancellor or dean. On April 4, he attended an executive committee meeting in Nashville and consulted about the future of the college, at the very moment the board had finalized all land purchases. He received assurances on all but the salary raise and accepted the position on April 7. He would not be able to assume the new position until August 1911, just as the million-dollar campaign began.

On April 29, Payne wrote a long letter to executive committee chair Bradford in which he recommended the appointment of Charles Little to the faculty of George Peabody. Little was, in effect, acting president of Peabody Normal during its last year. Payne believed him qualified as a professor of Latin but, more important, wanted to establish a continuity between the old and new institutions. He was well aware of the value of loyal alumni. The board concurred, and the appointment had the intended effect when announced at the final commencement on the old campus. The first faculty member of the new college, Little became both an invaluable assistant to Payne during the next three years and recording secretary of the board of trust. His title remained "professor," but he received a salary of $2,500 and the use of a house on the new campus, on Twenty-first Avenue. In August, Payne moved into a rented house, while the board authorized repairs on Chancellor Kirkland's former residence on the land acquired from Vanderbilt.[5]

Born near Morganton, North Carolina, on February 18, 1874, Bruce Ryburn Payne shared a birthday with George Peabody, which later seemed a good omen. His father was a schoolteacher and a licensed but not ordained Methodist preacher. Payne remained a life-long Methodist and in Nashville was active in the West End Methodist congregation, along with Chancellor Kirkland. Payne attended a demanding classical academy in Morganton, then moved on to Trinity College in Durham (later a component of Duke University), graduating with his B.A. in 1896. Back in Morganton as principal of an elementary school, he married Lulu Carr in

1897. They would have only one child, a son named Carr, who later would be a member of the George Peabody Board of Trust. In 1899, Payne returned to Durham as a high school teacher and completed an M.A. at Trinity by 1902. Here he became acquainted with Wallace Buttrick, who helped him win a scholarship to Teachers College, Columbia University, where Payne in two years completed another M.A. and a Ph.D.

At Columbia, Payne met some of the best-known educators in the world, particularly leaders of the progressive education movement. Later, many people would misleadingly refer to him as a student of John Dewey. He took one course with Dewey but did not complete his thesis under him. Also, as a faithful Methodist, he never accepted Dewey's naturalistic philosophy, nor did he embrace the progressive orthodoxy of another famous teacher, Edward L. Thorndike. In fact, Payne was even less a systematic educational philosopher that William Payne had been earlier. He was eclectic and practical in his approach to various theories about education, and never given to abstract theorizing.

Bruce Ryburn Payne, a photograph taken near the time he first moved to George Peabody College. Courtesy of office of the *Peabody Reflector.*

For the academic year 1904–05, Payne taught philosophy at William and Mary. In 1905 he moved to the University of Virginia, to a position in psychology and secondary education funded by the GEB. Buttrick was still his patron. Payne's role at Virginia was critical to the later Peabody. The GEB paid the salary of one professor in each state university to promote its goals: improving rural high schools and country life in the South. Payne proved the most effective of these special professors. He became an effective advocate for an improved state public school system, helped organize and teach in teachers' institutes, helped create a large summer school for teachers at the university, organized a series of conferences on country life, and encouraged instruction in agriculture, home economics, and manual arts in Virginia's high schools. The summer school, open to women in an otherwise all-male university, proved a great success, and soon Payne was well-known in educational circles. The school provided the model for the one he would establish at Peabody, and the beautiful quadrangle at the University of Virginia, planned by Thomas Jefferson, became the model for the Peabody campus.

From the time he arrived in Nashville, Payne was overwhelmed with the critical decisions and hard work that preceded the opening of classes in the summer of 1914. From 1911 to his death in 1937, Payne dominated Peabody. In a sense, the college was his. He devoted himself to its success and probably died from overwork. He soon moved on campus to an apartment on the top floor of the Social Religious Building, supervised every detail of planning and construction, and did most of the fund-raising. During the first twenty years, he delegated few responsibilities. He appointed no dean or even department chairs and selected all the key faculty. Not that he was unusually arbitrary, but he was demanding and never easy to live with. Yet, his passionate commitment to Peabody and his effective fund-raising in the early years won him admiration and support. No rebellions marked his reign. He seemed indispensable.[6]

THE GREAT CAMPAIGN OF 1913

On his arrival in Nashville in August 1911, Payne had two compelling and simultaneous tasks. First was the campaign. Second was completing enough academic building to open classes by what he hoped would be the fall of 1913. It was already clear that the Peabody Fund trustees would approve the $500,000 additional gift for the endowment, largely because of the effective lobbying of Wickliffe Rose. Approval came in November, which set the deadline for the matching gifts at November 1913, although it is unlikely that the trustees would have withdrawn the $500,000 had Peabody failed to meet the deadline. Too much was at stake. By July 1913, when the matching gift was still short $200,000, the trustees were too committed to the college to withdraw the gift. But it served the campaign's purposes to create a sense of urgency in the final months leading up to November.

The Nashville newspapers, which followed the campaign closely, all lamented that Nashville would lose $1.5 million if the drive failed. And, from a local perspective, it did fail, for Nashvillians contributed only a pittance.

The campaign opened with promise. J. P. Morgan offered $100,000 to complete the drive (he would pay up only when $900,000 was in hand). Then the GEB, because of Buttrick's support, offered $250,000 to fund a Seaman Knapp School for Country Life at Peabody (see chapter 9). Finally, after some effective begging, John D. Rockefeller personally, not through the GEB, offered the largest gift of all—$300.000 to construct a social-religious building on campus. This raised the big gifts to $650,000. But by September 1913, the remainder seemed beyond reach. Payne, the trustees, and early faculty appointees sent out thousands of letters. Payne spent more than half a year, at scattered times, in New York working with wealthy prospects. The total return from all such efforts was about $200,000. A campaign across the South in behalf of the Knapp Memorial Fund yielded just over $35,000, a great disappointment. Maria Jesup, the widow of Morris Jesup, eventually contributed $75,000 for a Jesup Psychological Laboratory. Total gifts from the New York area amounted to just over $100,000. Nashvillians contributed perhaps $25,000, most of this to the Knapp Memorial Fund. The State of Tennessee threw in $25,000 to buy a Knapp farm. In late October 1913, as the deadline approached, around $150,000 was still lacking. How Payne raised that money is significant.

One alternative, which led to an extended, well-publicized debate in Nashville, was for the old University of Nashville board to turn over its remaining assets to George Peabody College. When first approached, the board declined, by a narrow vote. It came under enormous pressure. The general assembly even used a legislative act to urge its capitulation. Not public, at the time, were extended negotiations between the old and new boards. The University of Nashville offered several versions of a contract, and the executive committee in Nashville came close to accepting one of these. At stake was the future of Montgomery Bell Academy (MBA). If the University of Nashville surrendered all its remaining assets, George Peabody would have to assume responsibility for continuing MBA on or near its campus. This seemed, at first glance, a way for the new college to acquire a demonstration school, largely with the funds contributed by the University of Nashville. But the University of Nashville board, bargaining for all the guarantees it could get, sought some continued role in MBA—one proposal required two University of Nashville board members on the Peabody board. Financially, the contract would have committed Peabody to continued support of what might have been a costly school. Unstated was the all-male nature of MBA (by the terms of the original gift), and an elite clientele. It was not clear that such a school was appropriate for Peabody, which would have a majority of women students who aspired to teach in coeducational public schools.[7]

In the end, Peabody rejected all University of Nashville offers. Buttrick saw to this. During most of the negotiations in Nashville, Payne was in New York seeking new donors. He corresponded with Little and executive committee members. When Payne and Buttrick submitted the University of Nashville proposals to Choate and Olney, the two trustees did not veto them, but they pointed out problems. By October, James C. Caldwell, chair of the George Peabody executive committee, was ready to sign the final contract offer. When Buttrick read the contract back in New York on October 18, he objected to it and telegraphed Caldwell. J. C. Bradford and several members of the larger George Peabody Board of Trust also were leery. By then, Payne was a pawn in the hands of his New York donors. He did not want people in Nashville to believe he had sabotaged the contract and thus possibly doomed the campaign to failure. At the same time, he wanted to remain in the good graces of Buttrick and the Peabody Fund trustees. He confided to Little that Buttrick was writing all the telegrams Payne sent to his executive committee. Payne thus supported no early action on the contract, even if the campaign failed to reach its goal. It was clear, at this point, that Buttrick would have come to his rescue if, in fact, Payne could not raise the final $150,000.[8]

Payne did get it. He played out one last desperate ploy. He appealed to the heirs of J. P. Morgan, who had died since making his original $100,000 pledge. In 1909, a jubilant President Porter, back in Nashville after the Peabody Fund board had finally granted the $1.8 million to Peabody, reported to journalists that a fellow trustee had expressed his intention of giving the new college a personal check for $250,000. He left no record of this reported conversation, and no one apparently overheard it, but everyone assumed the trustee had been J. P. Morgan. On this basis, Payne had asked the heirs for an additional $150,000, but lacking any proof, he had failed to persuade them. In June 1913, Payne had asked Olney if he remembered such a promise. Olney had not heard Morgan make the commitment, but he recalled that Porter had told him that Morgan had promised $250,000 as a match for a like amount raised locally. At the last moment, on October 23, after a final desperate personal appeal by Payne, Morgan's son-in-law, the trustee of his estate, decided to donate an additional $150,000, consistent with what he believed J. P. Morgan would have wanted. It is not clear that he was ever fully persuaded by the story about Porter.[9] Later, Alfred E. Crabb offered a moving but suspect story about Payne's final and ultimately successful appeal, head bowed in defeat, agonized over his failure to gain the matching funds and thus $1.5 million.[10] In the final listing by the treasurer, by November 5, 1913, Peabody had raised $1,016,026.50.[11] The University of Nashville connection had in the process became moot. Without the compelling need, Peabody did not want Montgomery Bell, and most of the University of Nashville board seemed happy to keep it. It still owns MBA today.

Creating the George Peabody Campus

Even as the campaign took most of Payne's time, he and the executive committee had to build a college. Complicating their task were the expected ties to Vanderbilt, and the question of how to use the land acquired from the university. Chancellor Kirkland was watching every move, for his dream of a unified university center rested on the location of Peabody's academic buildings. From the Peabody perspective, even by 1911 the fourteen-acre Vanderbilt plot was as much a liability as an asset, although no one at Peabody would admit this.

On July 4, 1911, James C. Bradford, chair of the executive committee, first addressed the issue of landscape engineers and architects to help develop the grounds. He referred to some early inquiries in these areas and noted that critical decisions had to be made very soon. The board as a whole granted full power over these decisions to the executive committee.[12] On September 15, Payne noted that the committee needed the advice and counsel of outside academic experts in laying out the grounds. He recommended W. A. Lambeth from his own University of Virginia, Frederick A. Goetze from Columbia, and Ernest D. Burton from Chicago as an advisory board. By this time, Payne was also ready to recommend an architectural firm. He had visited and conferred with presidents or professors at twelve universities or colleges and had corresponded with at least fifteen other academic leaders. He had met with fourteen architects or architectural firms and corresponded with eight others. He conferred with two landscape architects and corresponded with two more.

Payne recommended to a compliant executive committee the architectural firm of Ludlow and Peabody of New York, and landscape engineer Warren H. Manning of Boston. No one could accuse Payne of timidity. Manning, who served for only one year, was arguably the most prominent landscape architect in the country, and one of the founders of the American Association of Landscape Architects. Ludlow and Peabody was one of the three or four most prominent firms in New York, along with McKim, Mead, and White, which would later design two of Peabody's buildings. On his list of four acceptable firms, Payne listed last Cram, Goodhue, and Ferguson. This firm, led by Oliver Cram, specialized in Gothic architecture. Cram designed the quadrangle at Rice University. Payne did not want Gothic at Peabody; his model was Virginia. Thus, in his recommendation of two relatively young but superbly qualified architects, William Orr Ludlow and Charles Samuel Peabody, he stressed that Gothic buildings would require expensive stone and not fit the Nashville climate. He preferred brick, in what he called the southern colonial style. One small factor in the selection of Ludlow and Peabody involved sentiment—Peabody, although southern born, was a distant relative of George Peabody. On September 20, Ludlow and Peabody met with the executive committee and offered a contract, which the board of trust eventually ratified. But before the architects could design buildings, they needed to know where to place them on the campus.[13]

Plans moved quickly. On October 10, 1911, the three-member advisory committee met with the executive committee and architect Charles Peabody. At this critical meeting, the executive committee decided that the advisory board and architects should prepare a layout with the main academic buildings on the campus east of Twenty-first, a decision that by then seemed inevitable. All of Payne's dreams depended on a quadrangle like that at Virginia. By good fortune, the college had secured a perfect plot, the symmetrical rectangle of more than thirty-five acres bordered by Capers, Edgehill, Hillsboro, and a plotted but not yet developed Nineteenth Avenue. Payne was determined to make Peabody a fully independent college. He wanted to keep a distance from Vanderbilt. A romantic, a dreamer, he envisioned a Peabody not just unique in its role, but more eminent and influential than Vanderbilt. On the executive committee, however, were Vanderbilt board members Cole and Waller, who quickly informed Chancellor Kirkland of this dis-

A sketch of the future Peabody campus as envisioned by the architects, Ludlow and Peabody, in 1912. This sketch reveals the Peabody campus before Vanderbilt regained its former campus lots, and before Peabody acquired the site of the later Demonstration School. In 1912, the architects already had a design in mind for the Industrial Arts Building and a Social Religious Building, but all the other forty some building on this sketch were simply part of an almost utopian dream. The original drawing is in the Office of the Dean, Peabody College.

appointing action. A battle was brewing. In a December 4 letter full of disappointment and disillusionment, Kirkland accused Peabody of bad faith and asked to buy back the former Vanderbilt plot, since it was evident that it was no longer "essential" to Peabody's future.[14] After an embarrassing interval, the Peabody board would stress its need for this land and reject any resale.

Kirkland had read about the advisory board recommendations, which probably only confirmed what he had suspected. The advisory board was careful to include the Vanderbilt plot, but not for the purposes that Kirkland had contemplated. To accomplish a difficult blending, though awkward, of a campus divided by Twenty-first Avenue, the board proposed two quadrangles, the main one on the east campus and a smaller one on the former Vanderbilt plot north of Garland. For the small Vanderbilt acreage south of Garland (near the present Veteran's Hospital), it recommended future faculty housing. At the northern border of the two quadrangles at Edgehill, it proposed an entry road into the east campus. This meant a campus that formed an ell, with a long quadrangle stretching north and south, and another long but narrower one crossing Twenty-first and stretching to Twenty-fourth along Garland. As instructed by the executive committee, the board proposed to locate most early academic buildings on the east campus. But in a futuristic drawing of the completed campus by Manning and the architects, a plot crammed with buildings, several liberal arts buildings are on the Vanderbilt quadrangle, with a cluster of dormitories to the west.[15]

What the board proposed for the eastern quadrangle was roughly the present layout of the Peabody campus. It recommended an architecturally dominant building at the highest point of the quadrangle that would be the social and recreational center of the campus. Soon, everyone referred to this as a social and religious building. On each side, it would be flanked by student dormitories. Beyond the crest of the hill would lie the playing fields. The board reserved the lower part of the quadrangle for academic buildings, a gesture to Vanderbilt. The design meant that the architects, in the early planning, would place the first academic buildings at the north end, close to Edgehill, and all student-centered buildings as near the crest of the hill as possible. The campus would fill in from these extremes in future years.

Some of the recommendations did not pan out. The advisory board recommended a chapel near the social-religious building, but Peabody never built it. It recommended placing science buildings on the northeast of the quadrangle, which probably led to the placement of the manual training and home economics buildings, the first two buildings. These involved subjects not taught at Vanderbilt. Peabody would never have a science building, but most science courses would later meet in these buildings. The architects later followed the advisory board's suggestion that the library and administration building lie on the northwest of the quadrangle, but they did not mirror the two original buildings. The symmetry of the campus is flawed because of their siting and would later be destroyed by the location, and architecture, of the Mental Retardation Lab (Kennedy Center).[16]

As the fight brewed with Vanderbilt, the architects began work. At a full board meeting in February 1912, they submitted their layout of the campus, with three slightly different plats. On the basis of what they called plan Z, the board authorized the erection of four buildings—manual training with a basement power plant, domestic economy, and a dormitory for women (later West Hall) on the east campus, and a psychology building on the Vanderbilt plot. Both the alumni association and the United Daughters of the Confederacy were by then soliciting gifts for dorms, but neither was able to raise enough money. Peabody had the funds for the other three buildings but deferred final planning of what became the Jesup Psychology Lab, possibly because of ongoing negotiations with Vanderbilt about its former land. Chancellor Kirkland had raised the issue again in a letter in April 1912.[17]

In July 1912, the executive committee had the completed plans for the manual-training (soon known as the Industrial Arts building) and domestic-science buildings (later called the Home Economics Building). Excavation and foundation work soon began for the manual-training building and power plant. Since it would supply heat to the whole campus, it had to come first. In August, the committee had the final plans for the Home Economics Building. In September, the committee considered bids for construction of the manual-training building and awarded a contract to the Headen Construction Company of New York. Subsequently, it contracted with the same company for three other buildings designed by Ludlow and Peabody—Home Economics, Social Religious, and Psychology. The whole board

Students and faculty of the Peabody summer school in 1914, in front of the first two buildings, Home Economics and Industrial Arts. Photographic Archives of Vanderbilt University.

was intensely involved in these early decisions. Its members even voted on the exact shade of bricks and were bitterly disappointed when the bricklayers at first used a slightly wider mortar than the plan stipulated.

Ludlow and Peabody planned well, at first with little concern for cost. They designed an architecturally unified campus in a style that they somewhat awkwardly described as classic with deference to southern colonial. The Virginia influence was obvious. They planned a campus of relatively small buildings, most with only two stories and a basement, all with classic columns and facings. All would be of brick, although the Social Religious Building would have an expensive, and a bit excessive, marble facing over the columns at the front. If Peabody had ever carried out their plan, the quadrangle, with its outward flair to the north, would have been full of architecturally unified buildings, with arcades connecting them all. But of the four buildings they planned, the gem was the Manual Training Building (today Mayborn Hall). It remains, inside as well as outside, the most pleasing building on the Peabody campus, or for that matter on the present Vanderbilt campus. The Social Religious Building would be more grand, more expensive, but too excessive in its external details and ungainly in size.

Peabody originally accepted a bid of $176,000 for the Manual Training Building, a great deal for a building so small. Unfortunately, the executive committee began cutting details to lower costs, eventually to just over $162,000. The committee substituted tin roofing for copper, gave up a large elevator, substituted beech for oak flooring, eliminated some galleries, opted for a less expensive skylight, eliminated ceilings in the two-story-deep basement (for the power plant), changed granite facings to limestone, omitted a copper penthouse around the steam vent or tower—itself a luxury, the most beautiful smokestack in Nashville—and made changes in

the lights. Even with these alterations, it remained an impressive building, with its large marble entry hall, great staircases, and large reception areas on both floors, with the labs or shops for manual training angling off on both sides. It even had a sky-lighted drafting room on a small but almost invisible third floor. The boilers, supplied by other contractors, added to the cost. Eventually, the building and power plant would run to almost $300,000, close to the cost of the Social Religious Building. It was worth it. No institution in America had better integrated a power plant to enhance, not detract from, a beautiful building. In fact, to the casual visitor, the power plant was invisible and the steam-vent tower an architectural adornment.[18]

The Home Economics Building was simpler, a rectangle with a smaller entry and stairs. It did not have to house the power plant and thus had classroom space in the basement. But even this building had marble floors and an elegant interior, matching its next-door neighbor. From then on, except for the Social Religious Building (SR) and in the twenties the Cohen Fine Arts Building, it was architecturally downhill. Peabody could not afford as many luxuries. Eventually, the obligatory columns seemed only a facade for plain and functional buildings.

But the SR, as the advisory board had suggested, became the architecturally dominant building at the head of the quadrangle and on the crest of the hill. It became the symbol of Peabody and remains the most significant building on the campus. John D. Rockefeller provided the funds for the building, but not for the water and sewer connections or landscaping. Because of his terms, the money was not available until the million-dollar campaign ended in November 1913. Immediately thereafter, the architects began planning. The building would not be completed until the fall of 1915, although the lower floors were used in that year's summer school. During its early construction, the term "social religious" was descriptive only. The board hoped to name the building for Rockefeller, but he declined, in part because he loved the existing name. Emblazoned on its marble front are his dedicatory words: "The glory of God and the Service of Man." In this one case, the architects had more funds than they needed. As Payne noted, this was the most expensive academic building on any southern campus, and the most expensive and luxurious student activities building in the United States.

More than any building at Peabody, the Social Religious Building embodied an ideology hard to recapture almost a century later. The terms "social" and "religious" carried powerful meaning. The closest models for the SR were some new and expensive YMCA buildings. In the early description of the building, everyone at Peabody noted that it would have offices, not for chaplains or ministers, but for secretaries, the title of the person who headed YMCA and YWCA buildings around the country. Chaplains had too much of the flavor of doctrines and creeds. The building also reflected the emphasis in YMCAs upon physical health as a complement to spiritual health. The gymnasium and small swimming pool on the ground floor were thus appropriate. The gym was perfect for gymnastics (early photo-

The beautiful interior halls of the Industrial Arts Building. Photograph by John Halliburton. Courtesy of the office of the *Peabody Reflector.*

graphs show parallel bars and hanging rings) but below the regulation size for a basketball court. Until West Hall was completed in 1922, the gym also served as a student cafeteria. The social areas were clustered on the first floor (today the second floor), with handsome parlors for receptions of all kinds. The second floor housed the offices for the YMCA and YWCA and meeting rooms for student organizations. To the back, under the dome, was the wonderful auditorium used for all student assemblies, for convocations and commencements, for theater and concerts, and for religious services. It was Peabody's chapel. Surrounding the galleries of the domed room (filled with students at assemblies) were rooms for various purposes; Payne converted some of these into his home. Throughout were small meeting rooms or seminar rooms, which served as badly needed summer classrooms. The portico and the huge marble steps hosted receptions and summer-evening performances.

The conception of a social-religious building grew out of liberal Protestantism of the type affirmed by John D. Rockefeller Jr., and what some called a social gospel. This emphasis flowered at the turn of the century, with interdenominational societies such as Christian Endeavor and widespread efforts to imitate Jesus in all areas of life (not that any two people could agree on what that meant). The best-selling book, perhaps in all American history, was Charles Sheldon's *In His Steps.* Particularly in the mainline northern Protestant denominations, including the northern Baptist Church of the Rockefellers, this emphasis on social service as the central motif of Christianity gained wide acceptance. Even foreign missions shifted toward medical and social work and away from overt proselytizing. This explains why Rockefeller wanted a student building that fostered a life of service to others, a motif particularly appropriate for teachers. At the same time, he wanted the rationale for such service to be religious.

In a sense, the SR captured the early mission of George Peabody College, for its teachers, as Payne always stressed, had a much larger mission than communicating knowledge. On July 1, 1913, he told his board that the new building would help Peabody students renew a "democratic spirit and practice." The building was to stand as a monument to the vital necessity of incorporating "in the daily affairs of men all that is excellent in the spirit of religion" and of assuring that all students at Peabody would "be committed, as no other students in the South, to the carrying out of this principle in the daily lives of the people whom they serve after graduating from Peabody." The instruction in the building had to communicate to students that "the supreme purpose of all theoretic learning . . . is social service." Knowledge is futile if not committed to "human betterment."[19]

Classes opened in the summer of 1914 in the first two completed buildings. The daily assembly had to meet under a tent west of them, an area that everyone then called the lower campus. At least half the classes met on the lawn, under the trees. This opening session proved that Peabody would be able to attract even more students than anyone had anticipated. It thus had to keep at its building program and soon struggle to match targeted GEB gifts. In a sense, the new Peabody became an outpost of the GEB, at the heart of its campaign to improve southern education. Even as work began on the SR in early 1914, it was clear that Peabody needed more classroom space, a library building, dormitories for women, a separate building for the Demonstration School, and an administrative building. Fortunately, in these early years, the campus included the one remnant of the Roger Williams campus, the original Gordon mansion, located near today's Gillette Hall. Soon called the Gray Building, its two stories housed all the early administrative offices, including Payne's. But one house was inadequate. Thus, from 1914 until the depression, the Peabody board and Payne worked ceaselessly to raise enough

The Social Religious Building, probably in the early summer of 1924. This shows the terrace and drive-around completed in 1922. East Hall, just to the left of the photograph, was still under construction. The open windows to right, on the top floor, were part of the living quarters of President Payne and family. Photographic Archives of Vanderbilt University.

money for the needed construction. Fortunately, endowment income and tuition largely paid the college's operating costs, along with some targeted annual supplements from the GEB (for higher faculty salaries, for administration, for a library school, and for external surveys and field studies). But before the board could even proceed with the projected Psychology Building, it had to settle the ongoing controversy over the Vanderbilt land.

CONFLICT WITH VANDERBILT

In 1911 and again in 1912, Kirkland had asked to buy back the former Vanderbilt land. Each time, the Peabody board had refused. It had no contractual obligation to sell this valuable acreage, since it planned to use it for Peabody buildings. This was true, but Kirkland sensed bad faith. He placed his emphasis on the reasons Vanderbilt had agreed to the earlier sale, which became an exchange of land. The key word for Kirkland was "essential," for he had offered the land in the belief that it was essential to meet the needs of Peabody and to fulfill the mandate of the Peabody Fund trustees that the college be on or in the immediate vicinity of Vanderbilt. Subsequent events proved that these fourteen acres were not essential to Peabody, in fact almost incidental to its plans for its plot east of Twenty-first. Thus, in good faith, Kirkland felt, it should sell back this land, the best location on the Vanderbilt campus, for what Peabody had paid for it. Obviously, the amount depended upon the evaluation one placed on the old south campus. But at the time of the exchange of deeds, the amount listed on the Vanderbilt plot was $125,000, and this was what Vanderbilt was willing to pay to get it back.

After the Peabody board rejected Kirkland's inquiries about repurchase, informal discussions began. Kirkland noted conversations with board members at Peabody. More important, Dean Wilbur F. Tillett, of the Vanderbilt Department of Religion, began informal discussions with President Payne during the summer of 1912. He had a closer relationship with Payne than Kirkland. It was soon clear that Payne and his executive committee might be willing to sell the land if they could purchase highly desirable land adjacent to their east campus. By then, the Vanderbilt plot was, in most respects, redundant. Peabody was reluctant to build its Psychology Building across Twenty-first. Notably, repairs on Kirkland's former residence ended, and Payne never moved into this house. From then on, both institutions tried to get the best deal possible. The Peabody trustees would not sell the land for $125,000. It was worth more. They felt no obligation to sell at a loss.

At this point, Dean Tillett began contracting options—promises to sell at a fixed price—on land that Peabody might accept in exchange. The value and acreage would have to match those of the land at stake. On October 25, 1912, Tillett was ready to offer three proposals on options that he had secured from seventeen owners, ranging in cost from $125,000 to $130,000. Two involved land north of

Edgehill. The first was a plot two blocks deep—today's University School campus—plus additional land north of it, beyond present-day Scarritt Place. Excluded were two private homes, one on the corner of Edgehill and Nineteenth. The second proposal involved approximately half this plot, plus options on old Roger Williams land between Capers and Blakemore. The third involved the same Thompson offer plus the corner lot, with some lots on the Capers plot excluded.

Peabody rejected all of these options. It countered with an offer to sell the eleven and one-half acres north of Garland, but to keep the two and one-half acres to the south. For the main plot, Peabody agreed to accept the full Thompson acreage only if Vanderbilt also secured the two private lots on Nineteenth. The executive committee at Vanderbilt rejected the counteroffer, which it believed would require Vanderbilt to pay $50,000 above what the land had cost Peabody. Peabody then offered to sell all fourteen acres for the larger Thompson plot, provided that Vanderbilt would move the northern Thompson boundary north by fifty feet. This would have involved land later owned by Scarritt College, and now by the United Methodist Church, and new options for parts of two lots owned by families facing Grand Avenue. The Peabody committee also wanted either Vanderbilt to include the two private lots on Nineteenth, or Kirkland to agree to help Peabody raise money to buy them. Kirkland rejected any fund-raising aid and firmly excluded the prospect of Vanderbilt's expending an additional $36,000 to buy the two lots. Tillett, who saw some progress in this counteroffer, procured options on the additional fifty feet. Excluding the two lots, Vanderbilt would have paid approximately $135,000 to buy back this part of its former campus, only $10,000 beyond its stated value on the deed.[20] At this point, negotiations ended, as the Peabody officials turned all their efforts to the million-dollar campaign.

Only in February 1914, more than a year later, did formal negotiations resume. Payne and Kirkland even talked directly and secured permission from the GEB for a land exchange. Tillett and Isaac Wampler, Peabody's registrar, had tried to find a solution, and finalized proposals to present to both institutions. By now, Vanderbilt had stopped holding out for a maximum of $125,000. It knew it would lose money, although rising land values over the last five years because of Peabody's development might have justified a higher price. Vanderbilt now offered $160,000 in cash, or optioned land that amounted to about fourteen acres worth about $160,000. Peabody wisely opted for the land, which included the smaller Thompson plot of approximately seven acres—the later campus of the Demonstration School (the Wrenn house at the corner of Edgehill and Nineteenth and one other house on Nineteenth remained private)—and a new set of options on a rather narrow strip of land from Capers to Edgehill that amounted to seven acres (one private house was not included). This land later proved essential to Peabody. In effect, it included the platted but mostly undeveloped lots east of Nineteenth Avenue, and backing on an alley behind the lots on Eighteenth Avenue. This strip of land gave Peabody some living room east of its first two academic buildings, allowed it to privatize Nineteenth Avenue and control access to it, and, very important later, allowed it to begin purchasing lots on Eighteenth. The only drawback, from Peabody's standpoint, was that the college would have either to raise enough money to purchase the three excluded lots or live with these quite awkward indentations into its campus. It soon bought the residence behind the Manual Arts Building but had to live without the Wrenn house (and a less essential home farther north on Nineteenth) until it bought the house in 1947.[21]

This exchange of land left hard feelings, particularly at Vanderbilt. Chancellor Kirkland, who felt betrayed, later admitted that the end of his dream of a Vanderbilt-Peabody connection had been the greatest disappointment of his career. Eventually, Vanderbilt had to pay slightly more than $162,000 to fulfill its options; it lost $37,000 in the two exchanges. But in the midst of these negotiations, Vanderbilt bought the northern portion of the Thompson land, part of which it later sold to a YMCA college. When this school folded in the depression, Vanderbilt regained the land and renamed the building Wesley Hall, today the site of the Wesley Garage. When, in 1915, Peabody refused to pay $4,000 of street assessments incurred while it owned the former Vanderbilt property, but which came due after the resale, an angry Kirkland and his board sued in the local courts. This unexpected legal action embarrassed and angered the Peabody board. Eventually, the two neighbors cooled off and settled out of court; each paid half.[22] But the two institutions remained deeply suspicious of one another and often competed for foundation support. For years, with disappointing results, the GEB and other agencies encouraged more cooperation, even to the extent of making gifts conditional on it . Fortunately, the competition and tension did not frustrate early and successful efforts to work out a plan of academic cooperation between the two institutions.

COMPLETING THE CAMPUS

With a now nearly symmetrical campus of about fifty acres, Peabody could focus on its quadrangle. By early agreement, any architecturally nonconforming buildings would lie east of the quadrangle; a temporary stucco demonstration-school building that cost less than $10,000 would be the first of these. Long-delayed were plans for a permanent demonstration school on the plot north of Edgehill, or what would be the northern capstone of the campus. The next project was the Jesup Psychology Lab, north of Manual Training and along a utilities tunnel that stretched all the way to the SR. The first almost average classroom building, it was the last designed by Ludlow and Peabody and built by the Headen Construction Company, which had felt cheated when the board failed to pay for some unanticipated expenses, particularly on the very intricate dome of the SR Building. The Psychology Building was ready for use in the fall of 1915. Relatively simple, it cost about $75,000, the amount given by the Jesup family. As it completed this building, the college began constructing a stone wall along the western edge of the campus.[23]

In just five years, Peabody had built a reasonably adequate campus. Four buildings, two downright luxurious, had cost nearly a million dollars, factoring in water and sewer connections and landscaping. The tunnel to the SR alone cost more than $40,000. Peabody already had all the classroom buildings that it would use until the construction of the Cohen Memorial Building in 1928. Its most compelling need, by 1916, was for a library, but the college had no more money left for construction. It had to move its books, which had been in one of the houses on the Vanderbilt plot, to the east campus. The 20,000 main-circulation books, particularly those related to education, moved into the assembly room in the Home Economics Building; the other 25,000 volumes, including some rare books from the old University of Nashville, went into storage in the basement of the Manual Arts Building, next to the boilers.

By 1916, money was a growing problem. The various gifts had left the college responsible for all external costs, and it was barely able to maintain a balanced budget. New buildings depended entirely on outside funding. This, in effect, meant gifts from northern benefactors or, in most cases, from the GEB. Local gifts remained disappointing, leading to repeated postponements of a badly needed women's dorm that the alumni association had promised, and of a Knapp Country Life School that was supposed to be funded by the Knapp Memorial Association. This school had to occupy temporary crowded quarters in the basement of the Home Economics Building.

Payne first solved the library problem. On February 8, 1917, he announced a successful effort to get the Carnegie Foundation, which had built libraries all over the country, to underwrite a library building. The foundation gave Peabody $180,000, with the stipulation that the college spend $10,000 each year to maintain the library, which would come from a two-dollar student library fee.[24] For the first time, Peabody used new architects from New York and Nashville and a local contractor to fulfill the specifications set by the Carnegie Foundation. Everyone rejoiced at the capacious building, which could accommodate more than four times the books that Peabody had in its library. Vanderbilt did not then have a separate library building, and, in fact, by World War I, Peabody was growing much faster than its neighbor, had accumulated an endowment almost as large as those of all the schools and colleges at Vanderbilt, and enjoyed a more luxurious campus. Only in the midtwenties would this parity erode, with the building of the huge Vanderbilt Medical School and Hospital. The Medical School endowment would soon double those of Peabody and Vanderbilt combined.

The library did not solve the financial problem. Peabody needed more instructors to handle the mushrooming enrollment. This led Payne to recommend a fund-raising campaign to raise $500,000 for the endowment. For the next thirteen years, Peabody would always have a campaign underway. Only one was fully successful.[25] Many floundered and thus overlapped new ones, creating financial confusion. In 1916, the GEB offered $200,000 if Peabody could raise the other $300,000 by January 1, 1921. It promised to begin payments in 1919 toward the total. But Payne was unsure Peabody if could raise that much. He had exhausted his sources in New York and the East. From wealthy private donors, he raised $100,000 in pledges. He believed the other $200,000 would have to come from local supporters, in line with the desire of the GEB. But Vanderbilt too had launched a $300,000 campaign in 1916, also to match a GEB gift. The two institutions would be competing in any local drive. Peabody launched what it would soon refer to as the Nashville effort, a major undertaking that involved the faculty and students. The Commercial Club in Nashville engaged the business community. Since it seemed that Peabody might again lose at least $200,000 if the drive failed, ordinary citizens contributed for the first time ever—more than two thousand made pledges. By 1919, Peabody was able to announce pledges of more than $200,000 from the citizens of Nashville, although some donors probably lived outside the city limits. As in 1913, Peabody had won. By 1920, the college could add more than $300,000 to its endowment, with the GEB matching the pledges as people paid them. By 1920, Peabody's endowment had grown to a par value of $2,395,699.[26]

World War I did not adversely affect Peabody's income. Even its enrollment dropped only slightly. Peabody was less affected by the war effort than most colleges partly because its student body was heavily female and its relatively few male students were often older and married. Five former Peabody students died in the war. Financially, the college gained from a Student Army Training Corps (SATC) of fifty-five men on campus in the school year 1917–18 and from the rent for housing the central offices of the SATC for a large part of the South. The men turned the third floor of the SR into a barracks. For the first time, tuition payments from Vanderbilt exceeded those Peabody paid to Vanderbilt, since 114 students in the Vanderbilt SATC took their coursework at Peabody, which had plenty of classrooms. The Peabody women enjoyed parties and dances on the portico of the SR because of 169 mostly single trainees. All the students entered enthusiastically into mobilization activities and war bond drives. So did the students in the demonstration school. Several alumni served in important government jobs, and a few faculty took leaves for war work. Yet one senses that this exciting time at Peabody carried few risks, particularly because the war ended so quickly. The only serious enrollment drop was one of 195 students in the 1918 summer school.[27]

The war did make even more serious the lack of dormitories, particularly for the young women who made up three-fourths of all students. Local costs for room and board rose rapidly to as much as fifty dollars a month, preventing many deserving students from attending the college. Payne believed that dorm rates would reduce these costs by half. But efforts by both the alumni association and the United Daughters of the Confederacy to fund dorms had fallen far short. Once again, the GEB came to the rescue, donating $200,000 for the construction of West Hall, which included a basement cafeteria. The executive committee carefully supervised the plans for West, working for the first time with a local architect, and found his early plans too ostentatious. The new dorm, ready for use in 1922, was for its time a model of luxury.[28]

With the completion of West Hall, Peabody could at last begin extensive work on grading and landscaping the campus. In 1922, after some small exchanges of land to the southeast, it won City Council approval to close all internal streets, completed a carefully graded terrace in front of the Social Religious Building, and moved some of that dirt farther down the hill, creating the slope as it exists today. It also built a concrete road leading from Twenty-first, under the arcade from West to the SR, north to the front of the terrace, then along the terrace and south to the east of the SR. For many years, automobiles could drive in front of the SR and appreciate the view of its façade across the terrace, which became an outdoor theater. Peabody also built two entrances from Edgehill, creating a circular drive up by the library, over to the Industrial Arts Building, and back to Edgehill across from Nineteenth (now Magnolia Drive). This drive gave visitors a view across the open yard toward the distant SR on the hill. Walkways now connected the lower campus with the upper, but most were still unpaved. With these finishing touches, the campus looked much as it does today.

In December 1922, the GEB offered major funding, mostly for campus construction. Both Buttrick and Rose met with the board and offered up to $1.15 million to Peabody, subject to some matching requirements. Peabody would first have $950,000 to complete three buildings—the new Demonstration School, East Hall, and an administration building. Demonstration classes dated back to the first year of classes. For a time, they met in rooms in the basement of the Psychology Building and in 1922 moved into a temporary stucco building east of the Home Economics Building. The school had a long waiting list of applicants and needed a building to house a thousand students. After years of hoping and planning, the teachers and parents, many of whom considered the Demonstration School the best school in the city, worked with the prestigious New York firm of McKim, Mead, and White to plan a luxury facility, the finest by far in Nashville and probably in Tennessee. Cost estimates soared to near $600,000. Cuts brought it down to $500,000, but the GEB contributed only $400,000. Even without the two wings originally planned, it cost nearly $600,000 when equipped, the most of any building on campus. Construction costs had risen since completion of the SR, but the higher cost largely reflected the size of the new building, the largest at Peabody. The Demonstration School was well named. It allowed experimental course planning and teaching, offered models of good teaching, and to a limited extent provided opportunities for practice teaching. The school gained its reputation from the caliber of its staff, which included advanced graduate students in the college. Even before the new building opened, enrollment exceeded four hundred. In the first year in the new building, 1925–26, almost a thousand attended, counting the summer school; high school students made up about one half. The new building had an auditorium, a gym, and even a swimming pool.

East Hall, designed by the same architect as West, was its twin, minus a cafeteria. With rising building costs, it cost $230,000, more than the $200,000 given by the GEB. Alumni association funds made up the difference. The Administration Building, north of the library, had large open spaces (the bullpen), with desks or cubicles for staff, and cost $190,000. For a time, it also provided extra classrooms.[29]

In 1925 the building program seemed all but complete. The GEB would fund no more buildings but each year contributed $30,000 to faculty salaries. As part of an overly ambitious fund drive that year, Peabody asked the GEB to capitalize this annual gift by a grant of $400,000, with a $200,000 match by Peabody. In 1923, Peabody had begun buying lots on Eighteenth Avenue, beginning with a 250-foot frontage, which provided a campus outlet to the east. Almost every year from then on, it bought additional lots, converting the houses on them into rental apartments for married students. By 1929, the college owned more than half the lots on the portion of Eighteenth that adjoined its campus. This eastward expansion climaxed in 1925, when Peabody purchased the Pullen mansion at the corner of Edgehill and Eighteenth and converted it into nine luxurious married-student apartments. This mansion would later be the president's home.[30]

In 1925, the widow of businessman Meyer Cohen gave Peabody some common stock and valuable business property on Church Street in downtown Nashville. This gift was worth at least $500,000, but the land would transfer to Peabody only at her death. She specified that the gift fund a fine arts building and began transferring some of her art collection to the college—an estimated $250,000 worth. Given her ill health and her expressed desire to see the new arts building, the board took the unprecedented step of funding a building with loans from its endowment. McKim, Mead, and White designed the building, north of the Administration Building, and a new contractor completed the relatively small but elegant structure, Cohen Memorial, in 1928 for $254,000.[31]

Peabody celebrated its semicentennial from February 18 through 20, 1925, fifty years from the founding of Peabody Normal. Planned rather hastily, the festivities seemed to Chancellor Kirkland and others at Vanderbilt a deliberate effort to upstage the university's semicentennial celebrated in October. Charles Little, now the Latin professor, and others planned an elaborate celebration, inviting scholars from around the country. Both Julia Sears, one of the first teachers in 1875, and Lizzie Bloomstein, one of the first students, offered reminiscences. This occasion would, in retrospect, mark the climax of Peabody's progress. The great period of growth was over. But from Payne's perspective, it was only beginning, for he had a hidden agenda for the celebration—to give a boost to a new campaign, the largest so far.[32]

THE PEABODY EDUCATION PROGRAM

Working closely with Charles Little, President Payne planned a great leap forward. It was as if all the prior success went to his head. Nothing seemed impossible. Both the board and the GEB feared for his health, as Payne for the next two years gave up most of his campus duties to direct the new funding effort. He described his new role as "idea man," and his big idea was what he titled the Peabody Education Program. The estimated additional endowment needed to fund this new program eventually rose to more than $20 million. His scheme proved poorly designed, inflated in cost, and too general and elusive to provide clear guidelines for the future. More critical, it accompanied a significant change of policy. Payne and Little for the first time openly proposed a college of education that would offer most of its needed coursework in eleven liberal arts disciplines. They wanted to add a liberal arts college to a professional school of education, the only such blend in the United States. These critical decisions set Peabody on a course that not only proved a dead-end but also culminated in its merger with Vanderbilt in 1979.

This story began on December 26, 1925. Payne wrote to the GEB for help in adding about $5 million to Peabody's endowment. He proposed to use the funds to hire sixteen new professors in eleven arts and sciences departments (English, geography, history, biology, French, chemistry, Latin, mathematics, physics, economics, and government) and to improve faculty salaries. Over the next year, as if to justify the $5 million request, Payne and Little worked out the earliest versions of their Peabody Education Program. Little traveled to New York City in early January to confer with the GEB, but its officers were reluctant to give more until Peabody matched earlier gifts, including the capitalization of the GEB's annual gift for teachers' salaries. It had already turned down a request for $200,000 for a science building at Peabody.

Peabody's new campaign meant more competition with Vanderbilt. From 1914 to 1925, with its more active and exciting campus life, Peabody had fared better than its neighbor. But after 1925 fortune favored Vanderbilt. Largely because of GEB funding, Vanderbilt accumulated a separate endowment (by 1931, more than $12 million) for a new medical school that in 1925 opened in its new building on the part of its campus that Peabody had briefly owned. The Medical School quickly built a strong faculty and soon aspired to establish a Ph.D. program. More critical, the GEB, anxious to begin credible graduate programs in the South, particularly in the natural and social sciences, selected Vanderbilt-Peabody as the best site west of

Duke–North Carolina and east of the University of Texas. It wanted not only graduate-level work in the sciences, but teachers trained to bring this knowledge to the normal schools and high schools. From the GEB's perspective, Vanderbilt could teach the subject courses, and Peabody the professional education courses for those who planned to go into teaching. As so often before, the collaboration required of the two institutions, even at the graduate level, proved difficult. For years, the officials at the GEB were distressed alternately with Peabody and Vanderbilt, but Peabody had the most to lose.

The reason the GEB had refused to fund a science building at Peabody was the lack of any clear need. Why duplicate facilities? Vanderbilt had Furman Hall, an excellent chemistry building with some space for physics. And by 1925, Vanderbilt was ready to begin a modern graduate program. The lack of qualified faculty and of a library had led Chancellor Kirkland in 1912 to suspend what was not very rigorous Ph.D. work, end graduate fellowships, and grant only a few M.A.'s. The university resumed scholarships for M.A. students in 1920, but only after 1925 would outside foundation support lead to a new Ph.D. program. In a funding campaign launched that year, Kirkland stressed new graduate programs, which the GEB wanted for the natural and social sciences. The principal funding came not from the GEB, but from the Laura Spelman Rockefeller Memorial Fund, which gave $750,000 to improve the social sciences and particularly to begin graduate work in these disciplines, and from the Carnegie Foundation, which added $200,000 for new graduate programs. These gifts funded three new classroom buildings at Vanderbilt, two devoted largely to the social sciences (Garland and Calhoun) and one to biology (Buttrick). A decade after Peabody began conferring Ph.D.'s, Vanderbilt awarded its first modern Ph.D.'s in 1928 to two medical school students, in 1929 to a student in history. Although this marked only the beginning of a slowly expanding graduate program at Vanderbilt, one still limited to the medical and social sciences and supported by too few distinguished professors, it ranked among the best in the South.

Peabody was jealous of all the funding that went to graduate education at Vanderbilt. For a decade, it had enrolled the largest number of M.A. candidates in the South and had offered a small but growing number of Ph.D.'s. At least in the area of professional education, it was as well qualified to provide such graduate work as the new Vanderbilt Medical School was in the medical sciences. That is, it had its share of academic leaders in education and psychology, and a library at least as well stocked. But it had no real strength outside these two areas and by later standards its doctoral degree might have better qualified as an Ed.D.

These realities led Payne and Little to cook up the Peabody Education Program. Although they assumed that graduate work in the proposed eleven new subject areas would address issues of pedagogy, they wanted no limit placed on the extent of work specific to an academic discipline. For example, a Peabody Ph.D.

graduate in history would know the field as well as a Ph.D. from Vanderbilt and in addition would know how to teach the subject in normal or high schools.[33]

The Peabody Education Program was comprised in large part of hot air and ineffective promotion. Payne and Little set out a purported new agenda for Peabody in distressingly awkward and jargon-filled prose. By comparison, Kirkland was a model of precision and eloquence. In an endlessly repeated formula, Peabody would first launch new research efforts—"scientific studies" of what a modern society needed from its public schools, and what a child could hope to gain from such an education, viewed from a total or holistic perspective. Second, it would gather appropriate educational materials to meet these needs and shape them into the most teachable forms, all "organized around natural thought and interest centers." Third, it would test such materials until they worked under practical conditions. Fourth, it would "teach, publish and otherwise disseminate such results."

Payne developed an ever-expanding estimate of how much endowment such muddy goals would require. In his final target for the new campaign, Payne listed $2.1 million to hire professors to teach graduate courses in the eleven subject areas, $2.43 million to endow research and field work in the "science of education," $2 million to operate the Demonstration School and a new Library School, $558,000 to support fine and industrial arts, $3,724,000 for health education, including a public health nursing program, and $1,336,000 for its vocational programs in home economics, industrial arts, and agriculture. Administrative costs ($3,335,000) and money for new buildings ($3,525,500) brought the total to just over $20 million, more than Vanderbilt would have in its total endowment after completing its parallel campaign for a modest $4.1 million. One big difference: By 1931, Vanderbilt successfully concluded its campaign; Peabody raised less than $1.5 million, despite a prominent advisory committee that included Herbert Hoover and a huge assortment of glossy promotional materials.[34]

That Peabody's great campaign never raised even a fifth of its goal was not from lack of effort, but from poorly focused academic plans and an unrealistic—or as one critic said, fantastic—financial goal. The college opened campaign offices in New York and Houston and briefly, with no justification, hired an expensive New York City public relations firm, which recommended a prominent national advisory panel that produced no revenue at all. The college sent out more than fifty mailings that brought in some substantial gifts. Two donors gave $100,000 each for what became, in 1929, the Graduate Hall, fronting West Hall (today, this is known as North Hall), the only building funded by the campaign. One of these donors was Benjamin Duke of the tobacco family, whom Payne had known when he lived in Durham. Payne wore himself out in this campaign. His executive committee, which periodically urged him to take vacations, also rewarded him for his dedication. It raised his salary from $12,000 to $15,000 and then $17,000, more than double the salary of Peabody's most distinguished professors.

By the end of 1927, Payne reported pledges of more than $700,000. For the first time, many of these came from board members. No one listed the exact amounts, and by all the evidence, most of these remained unpaid because of the coming depression. The main focus of the campaign was an endowment increase from around $2,856,000 to more than $20 million. In fact, by 1930, the effective end of any fund-raising efforts, the endowment had grown to only $3,760,000, including annuities. Briefly, in 1928, Payne estimated it at over $4 million, but appraisals of annuity properties soon lowered it to a more realistic $3,760,000. As a campaign for a sustaining endowment, the effort failed. Once again, and for the final time, the GEB proved the only large donor. In 1927 it gave $1.1 million, some of which fulfilled earlier promises. Only $200,000 went to the general endowment, and $900,000 to capitalize annual contributions to faculty salaries and administrative costs. The campaign thus gained needed funds for the college's annual operating budget. Peabody in the late twenties was fully solvent, with no annual deficits. It just could not do all it wanted.[35]

A 1926 campaign model of the Peabody campus at the beginning of the great campaign suggests the extent of Payne's dreams for the future. Cohen Memorial and what became the graduate dormitory (North Hall) were complete by 1929. Additional dorms, the long-deferred agricultural building, the science building rejected by GEB, an auditorium-music building, and a building for the graduate school went unbuilt. These would have completed the original quadrangle designed in 1911. Despite these gaps, the west side of the quadrangle, from the library south, was now complete. The major gaps were on the east side, spaces filled today in part by Gillette Hall and Payne Hall. On the northwest, the space for two buildings north of the library also remained vacant. Despite unbuilt dreams, the campus in 1929 reflected a remarkable achievement over a period of only eighteen years. The next question is how Peabody used these buildings.

CHAPTER NINE

The Academic Side, 1914–1930

STUDENTS GATHERED FOR THE FIRST TIME AT THE GEORGE PEAbody College for Teachers on June 25, 1914. Before an abbreviated six-week summer school ended, 1,108 students had enrolled, many more than expected. Even larger numbers would come in the following summers. Whatever their expectations, hopes, and dreams, these students were pleased at what they found on this brand-new but chaotic campus, which featured two new and luxurious buildings. Peabody was thus an almost immediate academic success, in part because it was unique, not just in the South but in the United States. From 1914 until the Great Depression, it would build upon this early success, taking on an expanding array of educational missions. In most respects, this would be Peabody's golden age.

DUAL MISSIONS

At the outset, Peabody had two complementary missions. The first reflected the reasons for its creation by the Peabody Education Fund trustees, who wanted Peabody to serve as "the educational crown" of the new public school system of the South. It was "for the higher education of teachers for *all* the South." It was to send out into these states "men of trained ability to build up and administer state systems of education." In a statement of purpose, Payne and Little elaborated on this broad mandate. Peabody would train educational leaders for the South in the same sense as its two northern peers (Teachers College at Columbia and the School of Education at Chicago) and in the same sense that Johns Hopkins trained medical leaders and Cornell and Wisconsin trained agricultural leaders. They listed the targeted students: normal-school teachers, state and county superintendents, professors of education in colleges and universities, graduate students from normal schools or colleges, leaders in the emerging high school movement, and supervisors of elementary schools. They stressed educational research, a center for educational advice, the recruitment of exceptional talent in the field of education, and surveys and investigations.

Peabody's second mission, which originated with the Rockefeller-funded General Education Board (GEB) and Wallace Buttrick, made the college unique. In 1911 the GEB offered $250,000 to endow a Knapp School for Country Life at Peabody. This helps explain Payne's selection as president, for he had been a pioneer in an emerging country-life movement and held what was probably the first country-life conference in the country, at the University of Virginia in the summer of 1908 (three more would follow). The Seaman Knapp Memorial Association promised to raise at least $150,000 for a building to house this school. Consistent with this aspect of Peabody's mission, Payne and Little cited some pioneering goals for a college of education: to train teachers who could enhance rural life and rural schools, improve southern agriculture, teach various industrial arts, and promote health and hygiene. No teachers' college anywhere had accepted such challenges. For Payne, this mission was more central, more full of possibility, than simply training teachers or educational administrators in traditional academic areas.

At the turn of the century, educators, agricultural reformers, and journalists began to expose the problems of farmers and rural people. They seemed to be losing out on the promise of American life. Those who, like Buttrick, had spent years visiting all parts of the South realized that the problems of rural folk were worse there. The South remained more rural than any other section (over 80 percent). Per capita incomes were half the national average. The South had a worsening racial problem and lagged far behind the North in almost every index of human welfare—educational attainment, social services, health and mortality, conservation, and housing. Both Buttrick and Payne believed that the great hope for the rural South lay in the public schools. But the schools could lead the rural South to a gradual redemption only if they expanded their mission beyond the usual academic subjects. This dovetailed with the position of most rural-life reformers and of the organized Country Life Movement led by Liberty Hyde Bailey, dean of the New York State College of Agriculture at Cornell University and both a scientist and the poet or philosopher of the country-life cause. Almost all self-professed southern progressives supported this movement. Payne, with connections to Bailey, Cornell, and the Country Life Movement, invited Bailey to give the key lecture at his 1910 country-life conference at Virginia.[1]

In February 1909, a Country Life Commission appointed in 1908 by President Theodore Roosevelt and chaired by Bailey submitted a lengthy report. It received widespread publicity, because the country-life issue joined conservation as one of Roosevelt's pet concerns. The report included a long analysis of rural problems and then made recommendations for progress. Its section on rural education could well have served as a mission statement for Peabody, for it proposed a complete redirection of education in rural America. Education had to relate directly to the way people lived, which meant that in rural areas, the schools should emphasize agricultural and country-life subjects. The schools' failures were in large part responsible for ineffective farming and the drift of rural people to cities. Rural schools should become community centers, teaching adults along with children. Teachers should no longer be migrants but part of the total community. The schools should teach home subjects—home economics, health, and sanitation. The commission also had several related recommendations for rural churches and inspired many country-life initiatives by the social agencies developing in the mainline churches.[2] Along with Bailey, another member of this seven-member commission was also a hero of Payne's and a fellow North Carolinian, Walter Hines Page—author, critic, southern progressive, and future diplomat. Page was also an original trustee of the General Education Board and a friend of Buttrick. These multiple linkages make clear that a conspiracy among a small group of southerners who supported many types of reform lay behind the early goals, and the academic culture, of George Peabody College.

The Country Life Commission endorsed increased extension work to aid farmers and homemakers. In effect, it endorsed the work of Seaman Knapp, who in 1909 was a bit of a hero in rural America. His death in 1911 led to the establishment of the Knapp Memorial Association and to the fund-raising for a Knapp School of Country Life. Knapp grew up on a farm in western New York State. He attended a classical academy in Vermont, then graduated from Union College and began his career as a teacher and as a part-time Methodist preacher. He moved to Iowa, where he headed a school for the blind and operated a small farm. He soon made the growing of well-bred hogs his vocation and set off on a career in agricultural reform, publishing a farm journal in which he touted "scientific agriculture." In 1879 he moved to Iowa State Agricultural College as professor of practical and experimental agriculture and superintendent of a college experimental and demonstration farm. In 1885, after he moved to Louisiana to help develop a huge farm and timber colony, he helped introduce rice as a crop, soon the most capital-intensive and most profitable in the South. He edited a rice journal and soon made a fortune. Working for the federal government, he helped introduce new rice varieties and modes of cultivation borrowed from East Asia.[3]

In 1902, as an old man, Knapp gained limited government support for an experimental rice farm. He soon landed a Department of Agriculture appointment as special agent for the promotion of agriculture in the South. In this role, he began introducing demonstration farms, first in nearby Texas, then in Louisiana. These farms were privately owned, but local subscriptions covered any losses by a farmer who followed directions offered by Department of Agriculture agents. All nearby farmers were supposed to visit these farms and learn new techniques. Above all, these Knapp demonstration farms guided farmers in crop diversification during the boll weevil disaster for cotton. Excellent at promoting his demonstration farms, Knapp became famous for them and his work, a point of pride in a South that had few recent heroes to applaud.[4] In 1906, when the GEB became interested in extension work, Buttrick visited Knapp. The result was GEB funding for county demonstration agents. At the same time, Buttrick urged the GEB to fund professors of secondary education in southern state universities (Bruce Payne had this role in Virginia) to help develop courses in agriculture, home economics, and industrial arts for rural high schools. Wicklilffe Rose, then the agent of the Peabody Education Fund, supported this goal and worked closely with Buttrick. Eventually the GEB contributed more than $200,000 a year to pay these agents, aided indirectly by Department of Agriculture funding.[5]

Knapp became known as the father of county demonstration work. In 1914, Congress funded these county programs nationally with the Smith-Lever Act, which established an Extension Service in the Department of Agriculture. It soon employed farm and home demonstration agents in all agricultural counties. Ironically, this new program, which began just as Peabody opened for classes, would in time make Peabody's experiment in agricultural education redundant. It would also reduce the need for the Knapp demonstration farm soon purchased by Peabody, with funds gladly donated by the State of Tennessee.[6]

This background explains why Peabody's first two academic buildings housed industrial arts and home economics laboratories. Lathes and drills for wood and metal filled one building, sewing machines and kitchen counters another. The next building completed, the Social Religious Building (SR), housed an extensive health and physical education program. Had Peabody completed a building for the Knapp School, as planned, it would have been the fourth building devoted to the improvement of country life. As it was, agricultural work filled much of the basement of the Home Economics Building. It included the latest cream separators and other dairy tools. To the east, and up the hill from the Industrial Arts Building, lay an acre or more devoted to vegetable gardens, a barn, and at least two chicken coops. After 1915, about five miles east of downtown off Elm Hill Pike, Peabody operated its agriculture laboratory and the first demonstration farm in Tennessee—the Knapp Farm. No other teachers' college in U.S. history began with such assets. Any principal of a high school under pressure to introduce courses in agricultural or industrial arts or home economics had to come to Peabody, which for a few years had a monopoly in these areas. In the first summer, courses in agriculture attracted 115 students; industrial arts, 110; drafting, 193; home economics, 308. Other courses, such as those in economics, primarily involved rural subjects. Payne praised the students who chose these courses, for in most cases they enrolled not to learn how to weld or sew or cook to improve themselves, but to pass these skills on to their students back home. They did it out of a spirit of service.

The Academic Side

In Payne's vocabulary, two words—"service" and "democracy"—defined the spirit of the new Peabody. The Social Religious Building symbolized these ideals. The early students, many of whom could barely afford to attend Peabody, exemplified these ideals in their dedication to an ill-paid but vital calling—teaching in the public schools. Their task extended far beyond the classroom and teaching the traditional academic subjects, for they were to be agents of change in their home communities. Through the children, or working directly with parents, they were to help improve rural and village life by spreading the gospel of sanitation and hygiene, even sexual hygiene; by communicating the latest improvements in farming and homemaking; and by making school shops or canneries available to the whole community. The walls between school and everyday life would have to come down. In language drawn somewhat loosely from John Dewey and other progressive educators, the life of the school would have an intimate tie to what was most familiar to rural children, to what most concerned them, and to the subjects that would inform their most likely career. After all, 97 percent of southern youth would never go to college. All the young women would be homemakers; most of the young men would farm. This did not mean a displacement of such skills as reading and writing, but rather a rapid decline in the teaching of classical languages. The end goal for this type of education was a new, efficient, prosperous, healthy, and "democratic" South.

Payne's highest praise for his campus was that it was democratic, more democratic than traditional elite colleges and universities such as Vanderbilt. By this hopelessly loaded term, he did not mean that Peabody students, or even faculty, were self-governing. He made all the major decisions. What he meant was that Peabody had no hierarchies, not even department chairs. Payne never grasped the irony. He was determined to force democracy on Peabody, and he did, in his sense of the word. County superintendents and beginning teachers met in courses as complete equals. Every student organization, apart from gender distinctions, was open to anyone who wanted to join. The early George Peabody had no social fraternities or sororities. With one dramatic exception (the best women's basketball team in the South in the twenties), it had no interscholastic sports. Entry requirements were so low that almost anyone with minimal qualifications could enroll. In the summer, even minimal standards did not apply. All were welcome who could benefit from courses and the wonderful social life, and who were committed to take what they learned and share it with the larger society. Peabody graded students, but in the first forty years almost no one made a D or an F. For example, from 1925 to 1929, only 1.9 percent of Peabody students received a D, and only .05 percent an F. In these four years, one fourth of the departments gave no Fs at all; in fourteen of twenty-nine departments, more than half of all grades were As and

Bs. Three years later, in 1932, 53 percent of instructors gave not even one C to graduate students.[7]

The first Peabody summer school combined elements of a Methodist camp meeting and a Chautauqua assembly. A loose, nondoctrinaire, socially oriented Protestantism set the tone, although the campus welcomed Jewish and Catholic students (many nuns in teaching orders took degrees at Peabody). Peabody students, largely from Baptist, Methodist, and Presbyterian families, heard frequent sermons in their assemblies, some from Payne. (A tabulation of religious preferences in 1937 revealed the continued dominance of Methodists, Baptists, and Presbyterians, in that order, but by then Catholics were fourth.)[8] Payne was an evangelist for the type of socially oriented education that Peabody exemplified. Thus, more than at most colleges, being a student at Peabody made one part of a great and noble cause. Students felt this, gained confidence from it, and carried it with them as they went back to what amounted to their mission field—a benighted South awaiting the redemption that depended on their dedication and commitment, on a type of learning that was fully integrated into all aspects of daily life. At times this sense of calling led to arrogance or moral condescension, particularly when Peabody students—often older, already into a career, and mostly women—compared themselves with the largely male, elitist, frivolous, and immature Vanderbilt students. They shared more with, and developed their greatest appreciation for, Vanderbilt students in the School of Religion.

ACADEMIC POLICIES

In every way, the new Peabody tried to meet the special needs of teachers. It pioneered the quarter system. The school year included four equal quarters, with the summer school by far the most important. In the early years it enrolled more than three times as many students, and a more diverse population, as the other quarters. Even during the regular year, students often stayed for only one quarter. Thus, most Peabody courses were quarter-length, and until well after World War II some of these were divided into two terms (one could enroll in the middle of the quarter). The Peabody catalogue listed hundreds of courses—more than 575 by the summer school of 1929. During the summer quarter's two six-week terms, students attended courses five days a week and received three quarter-hour credits in each course. They often enrolled for only one term, completing a maximum of nine quarter hours. This meant that the total summer school enrollment overstated the number on campus at any one time. Vanderbilt adopted the quarter system to mesh with Peabody, but its professors normally taught yearlong courses and in some cases would not grant credit for a part of such courses. This created difficulties for Peabody students, particularly those who did not plan to attend for the whole year.

As a professional school, Peabody in the early years sought only students who were already in education, or who planned a career in education. Payne liked to use the analogy of medical schools. Peabody was to be the most advanced professional school of education in the South, a model for normal schools and a source for normal-school teachers (by 1932, 6 Peabody alumni headed normal or teachers' colleges, 12 were deans, and 625 teachers).[9] This role meant that Peabody needed the best faculty and teaching facilities in the South. The college liked to compare itself to the best law and medical schools, as well as to its only two educational rivals at Columbia and Chicago. As a corollary of this aspiration to excellence, one might expect high entrance requirements and thus highly able students. Not so at Peabody.

Payne was in part responsible for creating a college with an elite teaching corps and a student body with a wide range of abilities. Southern realities almost necessitated it. Payne argued from the beginning that Peabody should place almost all of its emphasis on the ability of its professors, not of its students. Such an eminent faculty had much to offer teachers or would-be teachers, whatever the deficiencies in their prior education. His emphasis was upon value added, on what students could gain at Peabody, not on what skills they brought with them. This outlook reflected his almost instinctive egalitarianism. He wanted to recruit abler students for teaching, to plunge teachers into such an intellectual environment that they would set higher and higher standards for themselves. But the reality, at least in the South, was that most teachers, and even most prospective teachers, had not enjoyed the advantage of excellent high schools. Many, in fact, had entered teaching without completing high school. Despite this, many had risen to administrative positions, often becoming school principals. Higher educational administrators, such as school superintendents, often lacked the best academic preparation and were ignorant of innovations in public education. But these leaders, above all, needed what Peabody could offer. The reform of public education in the South, and the progress of the South in all other areas, depended on them. Why reject them because they did not meet formal and demanding entrance requirements? And why give struggling students, who were often older than college age, failing grades? Why not encourage them, try to push them to their limits, try to engender new expectations, and send them back to their school districts to do the needed mission work? As Payne said repeatedly, a commitment to a life of service, a conversion to progressive ideas, was much more important than academic achievement.

Payne's concern for character and potential over existing skills found expression in what became Peabody's most prestigious graduation honor, the Sullivan Award. This was a certificate, a medallion, and $50, or the equivalent of the Founders' Medal at Vanderbilt. Supporting funds came in 1925 from George Herbert Sullivan and his family in memory of his late father, Algernon Sydney Sullivan.

Throughout the 1910s and 1920s, the Sullivan family contributed not only funds for this award, but works of art and funding for undergraduate scholarships. A faculty committee chose the recipient of the Sullivan Award on the basis, not of scholarship, but of "such qualities of heart, and conduct as evince a spirit of love for and helpfulness toward other men and women." In fact, however, the award soon also reflected excellent academic performance.[10]

The entrance requirements listed in the early George Peabody catalogues were models of equivocation. They were lower than those in the final years of Peabody Normal. Open to white men and women on equal terms, the college required, not a record of academic excellence, but evidence from reputable educational authorities, including both former teachers or school supervisors, that the applicant had the health, scholarship, intellectual capacity, and moral character needed to profit from the courses offered at Peabody. The early catalogues stressed that, in evaluating prospective students, Peabody would give as much weight to individual aptitude and demonstrated ability as to formal academic requirements. Admission to a degree program required fourteen high school units (soon raised to fifteen), standard even for the most prestigious colleges. But, unlike Peabody, such institutions as Vanderbilt carefully specified the fields for academic units that had to be part of the fourteen: classical and modern languages, English, history, the sciences, and mathematics. Peabody had no such qualifications at first, and by 1929 specified only three courses in English. The catalogue stressed "training, maturity, and ability," stipulating that successful teaching experience could count in lieu of high school units. The implication was clear: Peabody would reject very few applicants, and no experienced administrators such as county superintendents.[11]

In the early years, Peabody also accepted special students who did not seek a degree. In some cases, particularly in the summer, students did not even take final exams, in the few courses that required them. Almost all these special students were women, and most were already teachers. Most came to Peabody in the summer quarter, at times with their tuition paid by local school boards, and many for only one six-week term. Local school boards accepted such attendance as the equivalent, or better, of often mandated summer teachers' institutes. Payne rarely publicized these students, and gradually more of them enrolled as degree candidates, although many would never graduate. To aid these special students, Peabody for a few years issued certificates that attested to the coursework they had completed, which often enabled teachers to maintain at least temporary teaching licenses.

THE EARLY FACULTY

Peabody fulfilled its early commitment to employ an eminent faculty. From 1914 to 1930, its faculty in the primary fields of study at the college was more distinguished than the faculty in the College of Arts and Science at Vanderbilt, and at least comparable to the faculty of the university's new Medical School, which opened in 1925. Payne was aggressive in identifying the faculty he wanted, persistent in wooing candidates, and willing to pay the going market rate to get them. Top salaries were thus consistently above those at Vanderbilt, but for twelve months, not Vanderbilt's nine. Because all of Peabody's top professors had some connection to professional education, the college lived up to its professional identity and to the terms of its loose affiliation with Vanderbilt. It did not yet compete in fields in which Vanderbilt excelled.

In the first decade, Peabody had a regular-year faculty that grew from about twenty-five in 1915 to around sixty in 1929. The definition of faculty is slippery, because of the number of instructors in such fields as physical education, music, and industrial and fine arts. But in any given year, eight to ten full professors were the faculty leaders, Payne's pride and joy. They provided the visibility and fame the college enjoyed, particularly in the South. Notably, Payne's first subject priorities in hiring were agriculture and health and hygiene. In part, this reflected the early hopes for the School of Country Life. Charles Little, technically the first professor, was appointed largely for other duties. Almost as soon as Payne arrived in Nashville, he asked the executive committee to appoint Kary Cadmus Davis as professor of agriculture, two years before classes would begin. Payne wanted to get Davis on board before another institution hired him. Davis accepted the then high salary of $3,500 (Payne received $5,000). He had earned the first Ph.D. in horticulture under Liberty Hyde Bailey at Cornell, and at Peabody he would head the program in agriculture and country life and provide most of the guidance for Knapp Farm. By 1925, Davis was as well-known in his field as Bailey had been. He published or edited forty books and became the dean of agricultural educators in America.[12] Davis spent the rest of his career at Peabody.

Payne's next two appointments were equally critical. The first, John Lee Coulter in agricultural economics, had his degree from the University of Wisconsin, which for years trained almost all the leading agricultural economists. When Coulter left Peabody in 1916 for a better position, Payne turned to Lewis C. Gray, another agricultural economist from Wisconsin. He remained only three years, but his subsequent career made him one of the two or three most eminent scholars ever on the Peabody faculty. While at Peabody, he was just beginning a project that ended in 1933, a two-volume history of southern agriculture up to 1860, still a pioneering classic. He moved from Peabody to the Department of Agriculture, eventually heading the Bureau of Agricultural Economics. In the thirties, he would chair Franklin Roosevelt's famous committee on farm tenancy. After Gray, Payne hired a third Wisconsin Ph.D., Otho Clifford Ault, who remained at Peabody for the rest of his career.

The other key early appointment was Fletcher Bascom Dresslar in health education and school-building design. His Ph.D. was from Clark University. Invaluable in helping design and landscape the early Peabody campus, Dresslar loved trees and wrote a small book on them. He became the leading national expert on schoolhouse design and had an enormous influence on the South (see chapter ten), in part through the work of one of his early graduate students, Samuel L. Smith.[13]

In the first year of instruction, Payne added several important faculty. In professional education, his first appointment was Carter Alexander, a Ph.D. from Columbia University and recently a professor at the University of Missouri, who taught key courses in school administration. For the first summer school, Payne recruited Charles Alexander McMurry, a professor at the educational school of the University of Chicago. Payne loved him and hired him as a full-time faculty member for the 1915–16 year. A professor of elementary education, McMurry would become one of the most revered professors at Peabody and the author of at least fifteen books in his field.[14] In home economics and industrial arts, no one yet had earned a Ph.D. Payne's first choice in industrial arts education was Robert W. Selvidge, who had a master's degree from Teachers College, Columbia, and had been a professor of manual arts at the University of Missouri. William Knox Tate, a special appointee in rural education, was an alumnus of Peabody Normal and served as the early treasurer of the college; he died after only a few years. None of the women who taught home economics held a full professorship, although some later became associate professors. None received salaries equivalent to those of male teachers. Only one woman taught outside home economics and physical education, Lula Ocillee Andrews, an associate professor in the teaching of English. A graduate of Teachers College, she had no Ph.D. In fact, in Payne's whole reign, no woman ever attained a full professorship save the head of a small program in public health nursing, and the women M.D.s who taught physiology and served as physicians to women on campus.

During the twenties, other professors became leaders on campus. These included Thomas Alexander, who began as an instructor in elementary education, rose to full professor, and took the lead in the development of the Demonstration School. In 1918, J. J. Didcoct became not only a leading professor in education but a valued advisor to Payne. His unexpected death in 1927 was a great blow, one of many early deaths of important faculty members over the next decade. Didcoct, more than any other professor at Peabody, was both a student and disciple of John Dewey. He turned Dewey's *Democracy and Education* into his bible.[15]

In 1918, Peabody appointed its most distinguished pre–World War II professor, Joseph Peterson in experimental psychology. He replaced the first psychologist at Peabody, Edward K. Strong, who would later achieve great distinction in his field. The son of Mormon immigrants from Denmark, Peterson grew up in near poverty in Utah. By dint of brilliance and a commitment to hard work, he eventually received his Ph.D. from the University of Chicago. He resigned from his first teaching post, at Brigham Young, in protest at the university's lack of academic freedom, and then from the University of Utah in protest over the treatment of a colleague. When he was an assistant professor at Minnesota, Payne invited him in 1918 to the Peabody summer school and there offered him a regular professorship. Peterson accepted, probably because he knew that he would have full academic freedom at Peabody and be able to conduct his sometimes controversial research there. He pushed himself relentlessly, demanded more of graduate students than any other professor at Peabody, and did pioneer research in learning and child development, in intelligence testing, and in race and intelligence. His most successful Ph.D. student would be Lyle Lanier, later a professor of psychology at Vanderbilt and one of the Southern Agrarians who published *I'll Take My Stand*. Peterson's publications gained him national fame. In 1933–34 he became the first professor from a southern institution to serve as president of the American Psychological Association and the first Peabody professor to hold the presidency of a national academic association outside the field of education.[16]

In a pattern soon repeated almost every year, Peabody employed one of its own first Ph.D.'s in 1919. Shelton Phelps, who began his career in school administration, became Payne's key academic advisor and later the director of instruction. Before leaving to become president of Winthrop College, he earned the highest salary of any Peabody professor.[17] Alfred I. Roehm, who came to Peabody in 1919 with a Chicago Ph.D. and additional work at the University of Leipzig, was active in campus government and the first professor to lend distinction to Peabody's modern languages program.[18] All these professors had national reputations, and all were involved in scholarship and seemed to attend almost every professional meeting in the country. Payne delighted in their publications, which he listed in most years in his annual report to the board of trust.

Below these professors were an equal number of well-trained scholars working their way toward full professor. Also in the middle ranks were several faithful teachers who did not carry on any significant scholarship. At the bottom were a number of instructors and assistants. Faculty salaries ranged from $1,000 and even less to as high as $7,000 by the late twenties. Both merit and market competition seemed to determine raises, which Payne initiated and the executive committee ratified. Almost without exception, faculty appointments were for twelve months, since summer-school teaching was obligatory. But during the other three quarters, classes typically had small enrollments or in some cases no students at all, if none signed up for a course listed in the catalogue. Peabody offered no sabbaticals, but top faculty had reduced teaching loads during the regular year. A grant from the Carnegie Foundation gave the Peabody faculty retirement benefits (5 percent from the college, 5 percent from their own salary), if they so chose, in what is today the Teachers' Insurance and Annuity Association (TIAA).

The permanent Peabody faculty provided the instructional core, but over any given year at least half the listed faculty were summer-school visitors. The abbreviated first summer school in 1914 had a faculty of 78. At least 97 taught in 1915, with the number rising each year. By 1929, the summer faculty numbered about 184, with some teaching for only six weeks. Critical to Peabody's early success were Vanderbilt professors who gladly accepted appointments in the summer school to augment their low salaries, and key Vanderbilt professors who taught one course during the regular academic year. In the summers of both 1914 and 1915, eleven Vanderbilt professors taught at Peabody, among them its most distinguished. Of these eleven, six also taught a Peabody course during the three other quarters of 1914–15, and four during the 1915–16 school year. These four included Dean Herbert C. Tolman, a classical and Sanscrit scholar, the most eminent professor at Vanderbilt, who taught both summer and regular courses at Peabody for ten years, until his death in 1923. For the ablest students in classics, he provided advanced courses to back up the courses taught by Little, who had been his student at Vanderbilt. Also a regular, summer and winter, was Payne's old friend Edwin Mims, a leading scholar in southern literature and longtime chair of Vanderbilt's English department. Another regular was St. George L. Sioussat, history chair at Vanderbilt and another distinguished scholar. When Sioussat left Vanderbilt, Walter Fleming—a prominent southern historian and Tolman's successor as dean—took over the advanced history courses at Peabody. These professors, arguably the ablest at Vanderbilt, gave advanced students at Peabody an excellent choice of humanities courses. At least in the summer, Vanderbilt professors strengthened Peabody's weakest programs, in mathematics and the natural sciences. By 1929, fifteen Vanderbilt professors taught in the summer school, including Dan McGugin, Vanderbilt's famous football coach. But by then very few taught at Peabody during the rest of the year.[19]

THE GREAT SUMMER SCHOOL

The summer quarter was the glory of George Peabody. Payne had developed the first summer school at the University of Virginia; Little had done the same for Peabody Normal. The first, abbreviated summer school of 1914, confused and crowded as it was, established some traditions that matured in the wonderful summers of 1915 and 1916. From then until the depression, the summer school changed little, except that it grew year by year, to two thousand students by 1922, and almost three thousand in 1928 and 1929. The summer quarter offered a smorgasbord of hundreds of courses in almost every conceivable subject offered in liberal arts colleges, teachers' colleges, and agricultural and mechanical colleges. Teaching these courses was a staff drawn from all over the United States and increasingly from Europe (up to five each summer by the mid-twenties). By 1915 Payne could rightly boast that he had recruited the largest and most distinguished faculty ever assembled at one place in the history of the South. It would have been difficult to find its equal even in the North. Besides the Vanderbilt contingent in that year, twenty-eight instructors came from twenty-two colleges and universities, at least fifteen more from normal schools, and an equal number from federal and state educational and agricultural agencies.

When Payne had employed Davis in his summer school at the University of Virginia, he learned several lessons he applied at Peabody. Not only was a summer school a perfect tool for evaluating and recruiting full-time faculty, but also that even professors from elite schools were easily tempted to teach in a summer session, especially a six-week session. More important, they came cheap. For $200, almost anyone might come. Many had no summer income and at Peabody they could teach their regular courses without any extra preparation. The atmosphere was relaxed and informal, standards low, grading loose, and the classes of ten to twelve students of varied ages often easy to teach. The cultural life on campus was rich. For a professor and his family, the Peabody stint could serve as a summer vacation. And nowhere else in America could one mingle with so many other and varied professors in a rich intellectual exchange. Some came back year after year, despite rock-bottom salaries. For teaching the three regular quarters in the 1914–15 academic year, Dean Tolman of Vanderbilt received $200. The whole budget for the summer school of 1915 was only $30,000, which included salaries for ninety-seven instructors, an average of less than $300 each. Much later, Payne boasted that he had never paid as much as $200 a week for any invited lecturer at Peabody, however prominent.

The second key to the summer school's success was the cooperation of nearby Vanderbilt and Ward-Belmont, an all-women's college. Because neither offered summer work, their dorms and cafeterias were deserted in the summer but still required maintenance. Thus, Payne virtually took over the Vanderbilt campus in the summer sessions before 1927. Peabody men students moved into Kissam Hall, the only large dormitory at Vanderbilt. Women students rented rooms in Wesley Hall, the home of the Vanderbilt School of Religion, or walked a bit farther to the dorms at Ward-Belmont. Peabody students had access to the Vanderbilt library, and in 1914, Peabody held some of its concerts and assemblies in the Vanderbilt chapel in what is now Kirkland Hall.

Why did students flock to this summer school? The rich array of courses and the eminence of the faculty were prime lures. In the early years, the school offered the only opportunity for students to prepare for teaching agriculture, fine arts, or home economics. For a few years, Peabody was the only teachers' college anywhere to train home demonstration agents. For some students, particularly young women trying to earn teachers' licenses, Peabody was the obvious choice, given its combined prestige and low entrance requirements. But Payne recognized that academic lures were not enough. He wanted the summer to be not only intellectually challenging but fun. And even for the first summer session of 1914, the catalogue advertised the recreational and cultural opportunities at Peabody and in the Nashville area.

By the summer of 1916, the pattern of activities during the summer had already become a tradition. A student newspaper reveals an almost frenetic tempo. Beginning in a tent in 1914, but by 1916 held in the auditorium in SR, a general assembly took place each day, varying over the years from 11:00 to 12:00 (most normal schools or later teachers' colleges featured such assemblies). The early summer assemblies were open to all, required of none; all summer students could not fit into the auditorium. A faculty committee worked hard to secure exciting programs, with lectures, sermons, and musical recitals. Distinguished visitors to Nashville often spoke. On Sunday evening, all students were invited to a vesper service held outdoors in front of the SR, a tradition that drew visitors from Nashville. Local or visiting ministers and at least one rabbi lectured or preached at these vespers, while YMCA and YWCA secretaries arranged religious programs for men and women, including daily morning prayers and a Sunday-morning worship service. Payne usually invited touring dramatic groups to campus each summer to perform plays, some indoors, some outdoors. The yard in front of SR, and after 1922 a graded terrace, became the summer outdoor theater.

Peabody also sponsored a series of excursions each summer. These included cruises on the Cumberland, weekly visits to the Hermitage, two or three railroad tours to Mammoth Cave or Chattanooga, and several local tours, including those to Knapp Farm. Student organizations, including state clubs, held receptions or dances. A watermelon cutting and stunts on the Fourth of July became traditions. In the evening, as the air cooled, students (and soon townspeople) gathered in the grove of trees on the lower campus for a twilight play hour. For two weeks each summer in the early years, this included storytelling by the president of the National Story Telling League, who also offered a course in storytelling. Physical education majors put on exhibitions of folk dances. The home economics and agricultural students held exhibitions in their buildings or on the lawn. Home economics majors also organized and ran the cafeteria in the gym at a small profit. Interest-related clubs soon supplanted the three older male literary societies, which re-formed on the new campus but seemed to evaporate during the first three years. The two women's literary societies from the old campus—the Literary Society and the Girl's Chapter—survived and thrived. So dominant was the summer school that, after 1915, Peabody held its second annual commencement at its close, always graduating more students then than in the June commencement.[20]

The fall, winter, and spring quarters began small and grew slowly, compared to the summer school. Overstaffed and overbuilt for these three quarters, Peabody worked at increasing regular-season enrollments. From an average of just over 200 in 1914–15, it rose by around 100 each year to near 375 in 1916–17, 800 by 1924, and 1,000 for the first time in 1929, but regular-season enrollment remained at only one-third that of the summer school. The students were increasingly diverse. In 1914, in the first summer school, Tennessee students made up 50 percent, which fell within three years to around 40 to 45 percent. It took longer to achieve such balance in the regular year. From the first, students came to Peabody from thirty to thirty-eight states and five to ten foreign countries, with China leading the way because of foreign mission schools. In most years, 60 percent of students had some previous college or normal-school experience. In 1915, they represented ninety-seven institutions, a number that grew with enrollment, as did the percentage of graduate students. By 1926, Peabody enrolled 768 graduate students, more than any other teachers' college except Teachers College, Columbia. In 1928, their number rose to 1,295, including 1,200 who attended summer school, many of whom also attended during the year. By then, Peabody had by far the largest number of graduate students of any institution in the South. In 1928 the college awarded almost as many graduate degrees as bachelors of science (224 to 297)—211 M.A.'s and 13 Ph.D.'s.

Payne was always concerned about the gender mix. He wanted more male

Prayer at a Vespers service in the summer of 1927. In the background, left, is the Gray Building, the old Gordon mansion and former administration building for Peabody, but just converted to married student housing. To the right is East Hall. Photographic Archives of Vanderbilt University.

students at Peabody, for they gained most administrative positions after graduation. In the first five years, males made up less than one-fourth of all students. But the proportion of males rose among those who sought a degree or began graduate work; M.A. candidates were equally male and female. Males dominated the Ph.D. program by a margin of at least six to one before 1930. Females dominated in the first two years and in nondegree work. In 1924, the year's enrollment included 2,461 females to only 733 males; in 1926, 1,712 females to 861 males; in 1929, 2,898 to 1,049, with men still only 26 percent of the total. For young women who came to Peabody looking for a mate, the pickings were relatively slim, although student publications abound with marriage notices. The relatively few male students were more often older and married; through the twenties, all concern for married housing assumed that the married students would be men. Across Twenty-first, most undergraduates at Vanderbilt were male, but it is not clear that the two student bodies interacted much. The women at Peabody, apart from home economics, gender-segregated physical education courses, and nursing, largely took courses from male professors, for the faculty's gender ratio almost reversed the students'. Of the sixty faculty in the academic year 1929–30, about twenty were women, but this number includes librarians who taught courses in library science and several instructors in English, music, and physical education, whose salaries were less than $2,000. Approximately ten were assistant professors; the only two women professors were in nursing and physiology. Three women associate professors were in home economics, one in elementary education. Women at the professorial level probably received salaries comparable to men, but only a much more detailed knowledge of qualifications and achievements would allow a reliable comparison. It is ironic that a man held the one partially endowed chair, the Julia A. Sears Chair in Mathematics. Sears left much of her lifetime savings to the college.[21]

THE VANDERBILT CONNECTION

From Peabody's perspective, the affiliation with Vanderbilt proved invaluable. In 1914 the two schools worked out the terms of academic affiliation, with Vanderbilt geologist L. C. Glenn supervising from one side, Peabody's Charles Little from the other. The two worked together well, even as one controversy after another soured relationships at the top. By agreement, any student at Vanderbilt or Peabody could enroll in courses in either institution. Each year, beginning at $1.95 per credit hour, the sending institution paid its students' tuition, a system of annual exchanges with payments made at the end of each quarter. Except for one year during World War I, more Peabody students enrolled at Vanderbilt than vice versa, a favorable exchange each year for the university. Except for physical education for women, few Peabody courses appealed to Vanderbilt students. In the arts and sciences, Peabody had no courses that did not duplicate ones at Vanderbilt, but Vanderbilt had any number of courses not duplicated at Peabody, including most advanced courses in the arts and sciences, particularly graduate courses. In its catalogue, Peabody proudly listed correlated Vanderbilt courses, tremendously enhancing its advertised curriculum.

Yet few Peabody students enrolled at Vanderbilt. The early peak came in 1919–20, with 104 Peabody students taking 153 courses at the university. No Vanderbilt courses were available during the summer, when three-fourths of Peabody students were in residence, but Vanderbilt came to Peabody in the form of many of its ablest professors. In the regular year, distance was an obstacle. The academic culture at Vanderbilt, and its yearlong courses, also hurt. Finally, many enrolled at Peabody feared the grading standards at Vanderbilt or suspected a prejudice against Peabody students. Except for 1918, when Student Army Training Corps students at Vanderbilt crossed over to the Peabody campus, the number of Vanderbilt students taking courses at Peabody never exceeded forty-two during the first six years, numbers that grew only slowly until 1927, when the whole affiliation became a subject of controversy. By then, Peabody had signed similar affiliation agreements with a new YMCA College and Scarritt College. The YMCA College, which trained secretaries for YMCA work, opened in 1920; it held its early classes in Vanderbilt's School of Religion. In 1927, it completed its own building on land bought from Vanderbilt just north of the Peabody Demonstration campus. Scarritt, a Southern Methodist training college for missionaries, moved to Nashville in 1924 and rented classrooms from Peabody while it completed its beautiful campus on Nineteenth Avenue. Peabody had more in common, in its educational goals and social service emphasis, with these two new colleges than with Vanderbilt and maintained harmonious relationships with both.[22]

Peabody's curriculum was particularly strong in five areas—all aspects of pedagogy and educational administration; health and physical education; vocationally oriented work in agriculture, home economics, and industrial arts; psychology; and English, history, and geography. Only the liberal arts courses duplicated Vanderbilt offerings, but they were necessary for any school of education. One critical discipline for teachers, geography, did not even exist at Vanderbilt. English, history, economics, and modern languages did, yet Peabody faced such enormous student demands in these subjects that it almost had to offer them on its own campus. Vanderbilt came into the picture largely through its professors who offered advanced courses at Peabody, although English, history, and French still drew up to forty Peabody students to Vanderbilt each year. Had Peabody students enrolled en masse at Vanderbilt, the university would not have had the faculty, or facilities, to teach them.

Peabody was weakest in the natural sciences, except for chemistry, a backup for agriculture and home economics. The college had limited work in physics and geology but gradually developed a range of courses in biology, a subject taught in most high schools. Such a breadth of offerings at Peabody meant that almost all Peabody students could avoid the rich offering at Vanderbilt, if they so chose. Most did. Particularly at the graduate level, they suffered from such avoidance. But the availability of Vanderbilt's courses and library, although seldom used by Peabody students, still added academic respectability to Peabody and enabled it to advertise an impressive range of courses in almost every field.

From the beginning, Peabody had a core curriculum. In the first years it only involved a required number of courses in psychology, education, and health and physical education. By 1924, this rose to 20 quarter hours in English, 16 in psychology and education, and eight in health and physical education. Students also had to take 20 quarter hours in four of seven clusters, three of which overlapped the core requirements. The other four included social studies (history, economics, geography, and sociology), mathematics and the natural sciences, the three vocational fields, and fine arts (music, fine arts, and landscape design). This left only 72 quarter hours of electives for the 198 required for the only bachelor's degree Peabody offered, the B.S. By 1929, it had increased requirements in English, maintained extensive requirements in psychology and education, had limited requirements in the social sciences (one course for three quarters) and in mathematics and natural sciences (twelve quarter hours), but required all students to take four years of physical education and six quarter hours in health. Yet such was the flexibility of these requirements, and the options so many in each, that students must have felt relatively free to choose their own course of study.

Peabody students almost every year confronted some new area of study, some new department or school. Guided by Payne's sense that Peabody could and should do almost anything, the college soon tried to do everything. The college began operating Knapp Farm in 1915, added a Correspondence School and a School of Public Health Nursing in 1918, opened a Department of Religious Education in 1920, launched a Department of Race Relations in 1922, expanded courses in library science into a Library School in 1928, and added a major Division of Surveys and Field Studies in 1929. By the depression, Peabody was engorged with programs, some ill-funded and poor in quality. By then, it lacked a clear academic focus.[23]

KNAPP FARM

Payne loved Knapp Farm. When the GEB decided to endow a Knapp School of Country Life at Peabody, it allied itself with the independent Seaman A. Knapp Memorial Committee. This committee, with representatives from all over the South, began raising funds for such a school, which was to include a Knapp demonstration farm. Such a scheme engendered all but unanimous enthusiasm throughout the South but never the funds to carry out the plan. The Knapp Memorial Fund endowment at Peabody never amounted to more than $30,000. But when the State of Tennessee appropriated $25,000 in 1913 to buy land for the Knapp Farm, Peabody bought 141 acres on Mill Creek just northwest of the present airport, the site of the historic Buchanan's Station at the time of the early Cumberland settlements. This land, which bordered today's Elm Hill Pike, was on the railroad line to Lebanon, which soon established a station at Knapp Farm. Davidson County contributed $8,500 for farm equipment. Although a rundown farm when Peabody bought it, it had some good bottomland and soon boasted a large dairy barn and silo, numerous smaller barns and sheds, and a farmhouse for the manager. Subsequently, Tennessee appropriated an additional $30,000, which enabled Peabody to expand the farm to over three hundred acres.

On a Knapp Farm tract purchased in 1922, Peabody built what everyone always called a clubhouse. On Elm Hill Pike and bordering Mill Creek, this two-story farm-type house was fronted by obligatory columns. It cost about $18,000 and served largely as a recreation center for faculty and students. The *Peabody Reflector* makes clear that almost every organization at the college held retreats and meetings at the club house, with a scheduled group every weekend by 1927. Students and faculty came to camp, picnic, or share meals in the large dining room with its two huge fireplaces, or to roast wieners at the outdoor fireplaces. Use declined after World War II. By the late fifties the clubhouse was poorly maintained, as student preferences shifted from inexpensive wiener roasts and campouts to more expensive urban forms of amusement. For those without automobiles, it was now less accessible, for the city had eliminated the streetcars that formerly carried students to Knapp Farm for a fare of five cents.[24]

Knapp Farm was a demonstration farm, the first of its type in Tennessee. It was open to anyone who wanted to observe its operations and learn new and better farming techniques. Kary C. Davis, as the senior professor of agriculture on campus, headed a faculty committee that gave overall direction to the farm manager. The farm was Davis's laboratory, and during each quarter he and the two other agriculture professors frequently brought students there to observe a working farm. The Tennessee legislature gave Peabody the right to sell the farm's products, but, as a demonstration farm, it could not regulate production according to market demand. It diversified by choice, with almost every type of crop and livestock that would thrive in middle Tennessee.

The first task was land improvement, attained by planting legumes and cover crops. Students helped plant a twenty-five-acre hillside orchard with every kind of fruit that would grow in Tennessee; this was Davis's speciality. The manager, guided by Davis, purchased a herd of purebred Holstein cattle and long operated a dairy farm supported by local sales. The farm soon owned purebred Southdown sheep, Duroc-Jersey hogs, and Shorthorn beef cattle, as well as Percheron draft horses, which later gave way to tractors. Using all the latest machinery and pioneering in supplemental irrigation, the farm grew corn, tobacco, potatoes, small grains, fruit, and alfalfa, and sold vegetables, meat, milk, and fruit to the Peabody cafeteria. Even without counting the expected returns from a capital investment of at least $80,000, the farm still lost money (it had a rare operating surplus in 1926), requiring a small subsidy from Peabody each year—in 1928, for example, $1,126.[25]

The educational, but not the recreational, value of Knapp Farm slowly declined in the twenties. In 1918, Congress enacted the Smith-Hughes Act, which subsidized agricultural, industrial arts, and home economics education in high schools. Qualified vocational teachers received twelve-month salaries, in part from federal funds. For a few years, Peabody tried to meet the varying state requirements for Smith-Hughes certification. Although it offered the large number of courses required in each area, it soon could not compete successfully against agricultural colleges in land-grant universities. By 1925, even the GEB had given up on the Knapp School of Country Life, advising Peabody to drop its program in agriculture. Unwilling to close down the program, Payne watched it decline until Kary Davis died in 1936. Above all, he would not give up on Knapp Farm. Every chance

Knapp Farm with its herd of Holstein dairy cows. Courtesy of the office of the *Peabody Reflector.*

Knapp Farm Club House, showing the large dining hall to the rear. Photographic Archives of Vanderbilt University.

he had he visited it, walked the fields, applauded the work. He enticed students to visit. The farm must have reminded Payne of his childhood on a farm in the shadow of the Blue Ridge Mountains of North Carolina. It remained a symbol of his original dream for Peabody. After Payne died, the farm continued, but with little educational purpose. It had simply become one of the college's income-producing assets.[26]

NEW SCHOOLS AND NEW PROGRAMS

In 1917, Peabody began offering correspondence courses. Teachers who attended the summer quarter could continue their education by mail during the academic year by signing up for courses tagged in the catalogue as available by correspondence, most in education. Already burdened by four quarters of teaching, usually four courses each quarter, Peabody professors now had to work out assignments and grade final exams for distant students. By 1921, 800 a year enrolled; by 1924, 930; by 1928, 1,426. Around two-thirds of such students had already enrolled on campus, most in the summer quarter. Peabody hoped that the remainder would enroll, for only in this way could they complete a degree. Large numbers of correspondence students lived in Birmingham and Paducah, where Peabody faculty met with them in local assemblies, creating small outlying Peabody centers.[27]

During World War I, Peabody secured funding to begin a program in public health nursing. The original funding, in 1917 and 1918, came from the Red Cross and indirectly from the Metropolitan Insurance Company, which helped subsidize a Nashville Council of Public Health Nursing. The GEB backed this initiative. The Red Cross provided an endowment of only $20,000, plus $5,000 a year in supporting funds. Payne, who hoped to raise this to $500,000, was never able to find a new sponsor. The new school met a local need, and reflected Peabody's continuing concern with health and hygiene. It is difficult, today, to understand the importance of health and physical education courses to the early Peabody and most other southern colleges. Poor health ranked among the South's most pressing problems, as the terrible health records of southern draftees in World War I indicated. The hookworm campaign reflected one aspect of this concern. At Peabody, every student underwent a complete physical examination. As soon as he was able, Payne hired a female physician to work with women on campus. Every set of core requirements included courses in health and physical education. The concern was twofold—for the Peabody students themselves, and for the students they were to teach. To an extent, every Peabody-trained teacher was to be a public health nurse.

The health of entering female students at Peabody, some of whom were middle-aged teachers, matched that of the World War I draftees. Payne's 1921 report on their physical exams almost defies belief: 59 percent were underweight; 76 percent had eye or vision problems; 41 percent inflamed tonsils; 16 percent defective hearts; 15 percent hearing loss; 18 percent goiter; and most some spinal or postural disorder. Because Peabody referred such students to physical education instructors for corrective therapies, physical education courses were deadly serious matters. The assumption was that teachers, particularly in rural areas, would confront the same health deficiencies. By World War I, the need for public health nurses was growing. In much of the South, physicians were not available. Teachers, aided by nurses, would have to bear much of the burden for improving health. No one in the Nashville area had moved to meet this need, which, added to the wartime imperatives, explains the support of the Red Cross. In the twenties, a few better-funded county health departments began visiting-nurse programs in schools. For most southern counties, only federal subsidies in the Great Depression made possible such efforts in public health.[28]

As so often, Peabody responded to a need, but with inadequate resources. The college hired one woman (soon this would be an able and enterprising nurse, Abbie Roberts) to head the nursing program, which enrolled students in 1919. Roberts at first taught all the public health nursing courses, plus a course on nursing education available to all prospective teachers. Other courses in health and hygiene, and some courses by part-time instructors, made up the limited curriculum. Still, this was the first southern graduate program for public health nurses and the first accredited in the South by the National Organization for Public Health Nursing. When the Red Cross withdrew its funding in 1922, the school would have closed had not Peabody itself decided to fund it. Not until the end of World War II did the school again receive outside support, this time from the Rockefeller Foundation. After Roberts, the most notable director was Aurelia Potts, who guided the school from 1930 to her death in 1944. The program was open to all registered nurses who wanted to enter the public health field. At the time, most nurses had graduated from hospital-owned schools of nursing and had gained all their clinical experience in hospitals. Only a few of the best schools, such as Johns Hopkins, offered training in public health. Thus, the program at Peabody was supplemental to nursing schools. It did not train registered nurses.[29]

The nursing program did its clinical work through the Nashville Public Health Nursing Council. It had close ties to the City Health Department in Nashville, and to a few local settlement houses. Those who completed the prescribed courses, usually in a year, earned a certificate and qualified for public health nursing positions. Others, if they so chose, could pursue a B.S. in public health education. This small program was hard put to keep up with rising requirements. In 1925, the new Vanderbilt Medical School and Hospital created a nursing school, and for five years a joint committee directed a joint public health nursing program, with courses at both schools. Still, Peabody's program remained weak and within a year was embroiled in controversy over what Vanderbilt believed to be inflated statements in the Peabody catalogue. When Vanderbilt reorganized its nursing school in 1930 and moved away from the hospital model, it severed all connections with Peabody and instituted its own courses in public health nursing. Peabody struggled on with its department, which revived during World War II and boomed in the years just after the war. By 1937, it had awarded only 85 certificates to graduates, but this number soared to 696 before the college dropped the one-year certification program in 1948. By 1956, it had awarded 509 B.S. degrees and 63 M.A.'s in public health nursing education. Its nurses, in highly responsible positions, led in the development of public health agencies in the South.[30]

In the fall of 1920 Peabody began offering courses in religious education. Payne hired Leonidas W. Crawford as professor of English and religious education. He had an M.A. in English, no Ph.D., and no degree in religion, but he had taken graduate work in religious education at Northwestern University and taught courses in the field at Emory and Henry, a small Methodist college in Virginia. Payne most valued his work in religion and brought him to Peabody for this purpose. Crawford offered courses on the problems of biblical and religious instruction in both public schools and Sunday schools. Summer school students may have enrolled in his courses better to prepare for Sunday-school teaching, a job that fit the Peabody view of the overall role of public school teachers. The course descriptions reveal a clear Christian orientation, but not a sectarian one. At the time, particularly in the South, Bible readings and opening prayers were not only commonplace in schools but required by law in many states. Crawford included discussions of church-state relationships in his courses. From Payne's perspective, these courses also served to build stronger moral character in students. In this sense, Crawford's small department related closely to YMCA and YWCA work in the college. Notably, the GEB did not support this department and later tried to get Payne to drop it as unrelated to the college's central purpose.[31]

Payne believed religion a prime motivator for a life of service. Religious language and themes pervaded Peabody, meshing comfortably with the students and the culture. But Payne joined Dean Tillett of the Vanderbilt School of Religion and his old friend Edwin Mims in an effort to move the South away from what many called fundamentalism and from a literal biblicalism. Payne favored a liberal Protestantism open to doctrinal diversity and to various interpretations of Scripture, and a Christianity primarily committed to service and reform, to a kingdom of righteousness. He brought to campus representatives of liberal Christianity. Shaler Mathews, dean of the Divinity School at the University of Chicago and among the most radical of Christian modernists, helped open the 1915 summer school. On campus, students read the devotional books of the best-known critic of fundamentalism, Harry Emerson Fosdick. Such a religious outlook led Payne, even more vigorously than Vanderbilt chancellor Kirkland, to condemn Tennessee's 1925 Butler Act, the anti-evolution law that led to the Scopes trial in August of that year. He even suggested that the state legislature had no right to legislate on curriculum issues in the schools, for the sovereign people had delegated this responsibility to school boards and superintendents. One of his most prestigious board members, Judge Jacob M. Dickinson, took him to task on legal and constitutional grounds for such an uninformed and legally untenable view.[32]

In the fall of 1924, a type of revival took place on campus. A Presbyterian minister and a master of campus crusades, David Bayless, preached for five days in the campus auditorium, morning and evening. Students packed his services. Since Bayless was not doctrinaire or sectarian but moralistic, orienting his sermons toward a life of service, Payne applauded his effect on students and bragged that Peabody was the only teachers' college in America to present such a lecture series. By then, he was appealing for an endowment of $125,000 in segregated funds for Crawford's religion department, something like the outside funding that partially supported YMCA/YWCA secretaries. In 1928, the board insisted that Payne and his wife take a break from their exhausting fund-raising and travel to Switzerland for a conference on character training in higher education. He came back even more enthused about formal coursework in religion (Bible teaching was common in European public schools), rejoicing that in 1927 Peabody's courses in religious education drew 335 students, and that Crawford had already supervised one Ph.D. dissertation in the field. Payne considered a new appointment in student welfare, something akin to a college chaplain.[33]

Like religion, race was an omnipresent topic at the college. In 1915, the Phelps-Stokes Foundation gave $500 for the library to acquire books on what everyone referred to as "the Negro problem."[34] Later, Payne would boast that during his entire career in education he had tried to aid Negro schools. His colleagues at Peabody later celebrated his efforts to gain equity for blacks, particularly in education. Every year, some assembly speakers addressed aspects of race, among them James H. Dillard, president of the Slater Fund, which supported better schools for blacks. But Payne and most other friends of improved Negro education assumed that the goal was separate but equal opportunities. It is difficult, today, to understand this perspective and, above all, to appreciate how radical it was. In hindsight, it is clear that integration is a more attainable goal than equality.

By World War I, black public schools were falling further and further behind white schools, in large part because almost all school reforms applied only to whites. In the Deep South, black schools often met for only four months, black teachers rarely had a high school diploma, and the per capita expenditures for black schools, except in Texas, were less than 50 percent that of whites, and in some counties as low as 10 percent. The story, while complicated by regional differences, is dismal in every case. What could Peabody do, and how central were concerns about this issue at the college? The record yields an incomplete picture.

Bolton Smith from Memphis, a board member and Payne's most frequent correspondent, wanted Peabody to address the racial issue in education and all but forced a somewhat reluctant Payne to add coursework in this area. On his own, Smith was able by 1922 to raise enough funds to support a small program in race relations. At Smith's request, Payne hired R. H. Leavell, a rural sociologist, who for three years headed a separate academic department and offered several courses about blacks, their culture, their talents, and their problems. From the early twenties on, Peabody held a two-day conference on race relations each year. Most of the discussions dealt with the role of white administrators who supervised black schools.[35]

Without further subsidies, Peabody ended its courses in race relations by 1926. But in 1928, the Julius Rosenwald Fund gave Peabody $7,500 a year for five years to hire a faculty member to offer courses on the problems of a dual school system and on the problems facing Negro schools. Instead of setting up a separate department, Peabody used this fund to pay the salaries of two professors who devoted at least half their time to racial issues and dual education. Ullin W. Leavell held most responsibility for this Rosenwald program and the annual conferences. He taught courses on black education and cited research to demonstrate the enormous gap between white and black schools. After funding for this work ended in the depression, Leavell became an expert on children's reading problems and helped found the first clinic to diagnose learning disabilities, the nucleus of Peabody's later strength in special education.[36]

Payne was part of a group of southern progressives who wanted to improve opportunities for blacks in a context of continued social segregation. He assumed that blacks differed from whites in essential traits, above all in intellectual aptitude and ability. Much empirical inquiry on this issue at Peabody and Vanderbilt involved tests to prove these differences. Such race-specific characteristics, as well as the black role in the southern economy, meant that black education should not be a copy of that offered whites. Booker T. Washington was a hero to people like Payne, who usually stressed that educational programs developed for blacks were primarily a problem for white school administrators. They needed to know as much as possible about blacks, for, according to Payne, superintendents of schools in the South "have always been and will always be white men."[37] Thus, Peabody graduates in educational administration needed to know all they could about blacks: their intelligence, as determined by IQ tests, the social and economic environment in which most lived, and their problems with inadequate school buildings and ill-trained teachers. Unlike northern teachers' colleges, Peabody had to train people who would administer two school systems. The tone of such discussions was paternal and constructive. Payne gave strong support to Fisk University and even joined in its fund-raising. But the working assumptions were still very much in the southern tradition, and even Payne, on rare occasions, referred to "niggers," as did students in their literary productions. No one conceived of a time when Peabody might educate blacks.

Peabody's Joseph Peterson directed the most careful statistical studies of racial differences. He did not draw any precise conclusions but set a model for research in this area. A critic of the usual misuse of verbal IQ tests, he worked out several nonverbal tests that compensated for educational differences. His various tests of Negro and white children in Nashville, Chicago, and New York at least raised serious doubts about innate inferiority among blacks. Negro students in New York City sometimes excelled whites, but not in any statistically significant ways. As usual, Peterson simply presented the results of his data, which were never extensive enough to allow easy inferences, and offered a model of psychological research in an area in which opinion, not knowledge, had long prevailed.[38]

In addition to the racial problem, the south suffered from too much illiteracy and a lack of libraries. Thus, by 1928, Payne and the board of trust were persuaded that Peabody had to develop an accredited library school; they had petitioned the GEB for funding in 1926. All along, the librarians at Peabody had offered the courses in library science needed by teachers who would have to develop school libraries. But by 1928, with the move to universal high school education in the South, the larger high schools needed trained, full-time librarians, and the South's only library school was not oriented to public schools. Working with representatives of the American Library Association, a Peabody committee determined that the college needed an endowment of $500,000 to fund such a school. The GEB agreed that the need existed and in 1930, instead of an endowment offered $25,000 a year for three years to pay for the new school, which established itself on the top floor of the library. It began offering classes in 1929, and earned provisional accreditation in 1930. As Payne had predicted, the need was great. Even in the depression, the school's graduates immediately found jobs.[39]

Apart from such forays into specialized areas, Peabody's continuing forte was training students in all areas of professional education and in psychology. Except for Davis in agriculture, its ablest faculty were in these departments, most faculty publications in these areas. In 1923, this faculty launched the *Peabody Journal of Education,* its first scholarly journal and soon the best educational journal in the South. In 1927, Peabody merged an alumni journal with the student newspaper, *The Reflector,* creating the *Peabody Reflector and Alumni News,* a model publication with most of its content devoted to serious essays and articles. It supported the continuing education of both students and alumni.

Peabody also had an able, although not outstanding, faculty to teach the courses in the humanities and social sciences, as a backup to the purely professional courses. In these areas, the college continued to draw upon the ablest of Vanderbilt's faculty in the critical summer school. But even in these areas of strength, Peabody tried to do too much, particularly in graduate work, and by 1925 could claim the largest number of graduate students of any college or university in the South. Some of these students were able, as their subsequent careers demonstrate, but not all were qualified for graduate work. The standards enforced in the graduate program were almost scandalously low; anyone with a B.A. could enter the graduate program, and no one seemed to flunk out because of grades. Every graduate student, with rare exceptions, earned As and Bs.

Graduate students at Peabody needed only three quarters of coursework and a thesis to earn an M.A. Most completed the residential work during three summer quarters. It is hard to believe that overworked faculty effectively supervised so many theses. Some professors directed more than ten each year. The topics mainly involved education, although some dealt with home economics, agriculture, or typical topics in English or history. Most were narrow empirical studies, many carried out in the schools in which the M.A. candidates taught. Some involved broader policy issues in a local educational system. Others drew upon the Peabody Demonstration School for data. A surprising number involved Negro education. Some of the titles are entertaining—"Manual Arts as a Home-Making Subject for Girls," "A Poultry Survey of Northeast Missouri," or "The Weeds on Knapp Farm"—but all were serious studies and introduced students to methods of inquiry.[40]

The Ph.D. program was demanding, at least in its listed requirements, but probably not as demanding as the standards suggested. To enter the Ph.D. program in 1923, one needed a year of graduate work at Peabody or a comparable university, and to submit to a standard mental test. To be admitted to candidacy, those without an M.A. had to demonstrate research capabilities to a faculty committee and pass preliminary or qualifying examinations in their major and minor. Candidacy required competence in whatever foreign languages, or statistical tools, a given course of study demanded, which meant that most candidates did not have to take any foreign language. After candidacy, students worked primarily with a single professor on a dissertation. They could take half of the coursework at Vanderbilt, and in graduate bulletins Peabody listed all the advanced courses offered at the university. In the early years, Peabody required each student to publish the dissertation and deposit one hundred copies at the college, which for long dissertations could mean a cost of up to $500, a strong incentive to keep them brief. In a later humane gesture, the college allowed bound typescripts in place of published books. These dissertations are still on file in the Peabody Library under the general category *Peabody Contributions to Education.* Almost all the early dissertations, some of which informed this book, involved some aspect of education and reflect much research, but few are sophisticated in content or eloquent in style. They do not reveal rigorous supervision or editing by mentors, yet they nevertheless measure up to dissertations completed in the same years in other graduate programs. The few Ph.D.'s earned by students of Joseph Peterson in psychology reflected as demanding work as any in the country.[41]

UNCLEAR MISSIONS

By the mid-twenties, Peabody had enjoyed a decade of steady growth, thanks in large part to the support of the General Education Board for new buildings and new programs. Yet, officials at the GEB increasingly felt that the college was losing focus. Payne's aspirations knew no limits, which accounted for his launching the unrealistic campaign in 1926 for $20 million in new endowments. When he, as usual, turned to the GEB, the board sent one of its agents, Frank Bachman, to Peabody in July 1926. Bachman, with a Ph.D. from Columbia University, headed the division of public education in the GEB and had conducted surveys throughout the South. Three years later, he would join the Peabody faculty, but at the time he seemed an ogre to Payne and key members of his faculty. Peabody might well have fared better had it heeded much of Bachman's advice, much of which involved Vanderbilt.[42]

Bachman found a Peabody that was trying to do everything for everyone, and often not doing it well. Proposals in the college's new campaign threatened to draw resources away from its core mission—training educational leaders for the

South. Bachman was not tactful. He so offended Payne, Little, and several professors that they appealed over his head to Wickliffe Rose, now head of the GEB. Bachman was correct in one respect—the new dreams and proposed initiatives would retard, not promote, further foundation support—but he was wrong in thinking they would end GEB support. Bachman wanted Peabody to become more like Teachers College at Columbia University, a single-minded professional school. Although its mission required some courses in the liberal arts, like psychology, its program mainly should involve courses in methods of, and theories about, teaching. Such a program would require educational research and the application of work in the sciences and humanities, but not discipline-based inquiry, which was the task of universities like Vanderbilt or Chicago. This focused mission could tremendously aid the South, as Peabody already had demonstrated. But the more diffuse goals of the campaign—the so-called Peabody Education Program—would so dissipate Peabody's resources, and cost so much, as to sabotage Peabody's mission and destroy what the GEB had pushed for back in 1914: fruitful, complementary, and mutually beneficial cooperation with Vanderbilt.

Bachman was blunt in setting what he believed would be the conditions for further GEB support (fortunately for Peabody, Rose would disagree). He all but demanded that Peabody suspend its now superfluous programs in agriculture, home economics, industrial arts, and religious education. He suggested the phasing out, as soon as possible, of its freshman and sophomore classes. Peabody had no business trying to offer a core or junior curriculum to beginning college students but should become an advanced professional school. This meant that Peabody should not only abolish programs but also fire a good share of its faculty, which would free up funds for what it did well (everyone at the college was horrified at the prospect of such faculty thinning). Beyond these radical proposals, Bachman argued that in no arts and science fields except possibly psychology and geography should Peabody hire scholars to do research or teach graduate students. Vanderbilt could do this better. Peabody needed distinguished scholars in professional education. Even though they should be well-grounded in various disciplines, they should direct their research to the best means of teaching such subjects. Only in this area should Peabody offer graduate seminars. If its graduate students did not have a firm grounding in the disciplines they were to teach, they should take the required courses at Vanderbilt. After all, that was why the Peabody Fund had required Peabody to be adjacent to Vanderbilt.[43]

Payne and his faculty protested these prescriptions with vigor and at points with compelling logic. Payne had long advocated the critical importance of, and logical precedence for, a strong grounding in the disciplines one was to teach. He noted the overlapping boundaries of subject matter competence and pedagogical skills. One could not absorb the subject and later graft on a veneer of pedagogy. The two analytically distinct but complementary fields of knowledge and practice had to develop together. He believed that none of the academic universities in their graduate programs blended the two. Thus, the Ph.D.'s trained at a Hopkins or a Chicago almost never taught in normal schools or high schools or had any interest or competence in such teaching. What had prevailed so far had been normal and secondary teachers trained largely in teachers' colleges, with a deplorable lack of depth in the disciplines they taught. To serve the needs of these schools and of public school officials in the South, Peabody had to offer both content and methods. His models were the scientists employed by medical schools. If Peabody were to attract distinguished scholars in the major disciplines taught in secondary and normal schools, then it would have to allow them to offer instruction, and train graduate students, in their own specialties (Peterson was the perfect example, for much of his research did not directly involve education). Otherwise, they would not come to Peabody, which would ultimately impoverish public education. In these discussions, Payne vented his distrust of most academically oriented universities, and his rejection even of the pattern of course exchange at Peabody's two main competitors, Columbia and Chicago. While he rejoiced in Peabody's independence, he failed to foresee the costs it entailed.[44]

Why not have Peabody students gain their disciplinary depth by taking courses at Vanderbilt? To Bachman, this seemed the all but obvious answer. Payne still hoped that many would continue to take such courses at Vanderbilt, but implicit in his arguments was a confession—the contemplated ties between Vanderbilt and Peabody had not worked as planned in 1909. Most Peabody students, including graduate students, never took Vanderbilt courses, although many took courses at Peabody from Vanderbilt professors. The reasons so few enrolled at Vanderbilt at bottom reflected the enormous cultural differences between the two institutions, and to a lesser extent, the distance. The distrust between Payne and Kirkland did not help. In retrospect, the original plan involved several illusions. Kirkland was probably correct—only if Peabody had become a college within Vanderbilt would full coordination have been possible. Payne had jealously protected Peabody's autonomy. The result at Peabody: different and lower admission standards, a different type of student (older, less elitist, professionally involved, and mostly female), and the elevation of social service to equal importance with intellectual achievement. Those who taught courses and seminars at Vanderbilt ignored problems of teaching and were, Payne believed, completely ignorant of pedagogy and often lacked respect for this area of knowledge. Peabody students at Vanderbilt often felt like aliens, especially women students in an almost entirely male institution.

On the other side, Vanderbilt was increasingly unhappy with the Peabody connection, which it had tried at first to make work. Vanderbilt had changed to the Peabody calendar and quarter system, leased its dorms in the summer to Peabody students (not entirely for friendly reasons, for it gained income from these rentals), and for many years offered no competitive summer school. At least half of its social science and humanities faculty taught in the summer at Peabody. But each year, the number of Peabody students at Vanderbilt exceeded, often by three times, the number of Vanderbilt students who took education courses at Peabody. And it had become hard to predict the courses Peabody students would desire. Vanderbilt increasingly exercised its right to close heavily enrolled courses, thus denying entry to Peabody students. Finally, Vanderbilt professors almost unanimously agreed that Peabody students were academically less qualified than Vanderbilt students, particularly the M.A. students who came to Vanderbilt to take graduate-level courses and seminars. While true of many, this outlook easily led to low expectations for and unfair judgments about the abler Peabody students, who sensed the prejudice. These attitudes reinforced Payne's desire that Peabody offer at least the essential subject matter courses its students needed. In fact, it had been doing this all along. He now simply wanted to add thirteen new subject matter professors to do it better.

In the late twenties, Peabody-Vanderbilt relations reached their nadir. The situation did not change for the better until 1935, and to some extent not until Kirkland retired, and Payne died, in 1937. The tensions came not from Peabody's effort to establish small disciplinary departments of its own, for Vanderbilt did not fear this competition and in fact found it something of a relief. As Vanderbilt began its new Ph.D. program in 1927, university officials decided to close all Ph.D. seminars to Peabody students. This was a severe blow to Peabody, for it had listed Vanderbilt graduate courses available to its students in its own catalogue. In the thirties, Vanderbilt reversed this exclusionary policy after Peabody protested to the GEB, which was in the awkward position of rejecting gifts for subject matter Ph.D. programs at Peabody because of its access to Vanderbilt. To add salt to the wound, Vanderbilt opened a summer school in 1930, closed its dorms in the summer to Peabody students, and in the same year established a program in education, offering the lame excuse that its students had scheduling difficulties at Peabody and thus needed a certification program of their own. Vanderbilt hired Joseph K. Hart who, on paper at least, was one of the leading educators in America, an educational philosopher who was in almost all respects a disciple of John Dewey and an exponent of some of the more daring innovations of the progressive education movement. Hart proved too radical for Vanderbilt, several notches to the left of Payne, and Kirkland fired him in 1934, ending Vanderbilt's education department. Vanderbilt again needed Peabody, for its summer school also failed to attract many students and soon closed.[45]

After continued discussions with the GEB, Payne in 1929 added yet another department to Peabody, the Division of Surveys and Field Studies (DSFS). He had long advocated surveys and field studies by Peabody faculty as part of its larger research mission and as a service to educational agencies. Since the GEB had been much involved with this type of research, in part by Bachman, it decided to shift the program to Peabody and provide $35,000 each year for a three-member staff headed by Bachman. Not closely integrated with the rest of Peabody, the new division was its first funded research center. Much of its work involved contracted surveys for educational agencies throughout the South. In the midthirties, the GEB capitalized the annual funding, and Peabody would continue the program, under new labels after 1975. Some elements of its research and outreach effort exist today in Peabody's Center for Educational Policy. Bachman headed the program until his death in 1935. His first two assistants would have brilliant careers. Doak Campbell, who had just finished a Ph.D. at Peabody, would later head the division, serve as graduate dean at Peabody, and finally move on to be president of Florida State University. Hollis L. Caswell eventually became president of Teachers College, Columbia University.

This completes a very long but still cursory survey of the academic side of Peabody during its most rapid period of growth. I had to leave so much out. This is only further evidence of how busy, even exuberant, was this first era at George Peabody College. In 1929 and early 1930, the era of growth and expansion seemed to have just begun. The future looked bright. But by late 1930, a great depression lay on the near horizon. As it turned out, Peabody had reached full maturity all too quickly. From then on, it would suffer as much retrenchment as growth, as much frustration as fulfillment.

CHAPTER TEN

Depression and War, 1930–1945

BY 1930, THE U.S. ECONOMY WAS IN CRISIS AND IN THE NEXT year would collapse. Even before the United States fully recovered from the depression, it entered World War II. These were crisis years in all areas of American higher education. Comparatively, Peabody suffered less than most colleges and universities, but suffer it did. Campus expansion all but ended. Enrollment suffered. Bold new initiatives became impossible.

THE GREAT DEPRESSION AT PEABODY

By late 1929 the U.S. economy had slowed. The stock market crash in October, while a disaster for investors, did not immediately affect the overall economy. In 1930, the country suffered a recession, with a steady drop in purchases, increasing but not yet disastrous unemployment, and a sharp decline in the money supply. Farm prices had fallen sharply from 1929 levels, and unemployment caused severe hardships in the winter of 1930–31. For the first time, people began to sense a deepening depression, although no one anticipated that it would last a decade. In the summer of 1931, the international banking and finance system collapsed, and the developing depression spread worldwide.

The looming economic crisis was barely apparent at Peabody in 1930. Enrollment dropped from 4,088 to 3,886 for the combined regular and summer sessions, the summer school enrollment only by 154 (from 2,934 to 2,790). Even in 1931, the enrollment fell by only about 4 percent. Only in 1932 did the depression begin to take its toll on campus, and with a vengeance. Enrollment for the calendar year fell to 2,690; summer school enrollment dropped to 1,709, almost half of that in 1929. This led to a disastrous loss of tuition income. Total income for the college dropped from $660,000 in 1929 to $496,000 in 1932, to $406,000 in 1933, with only slight increases over the next two years. Total enrollment declined to 2,150 in 1933 and began recovering in 1935.

The depression lowered almost all sources of income. Dorm rents and profits from the cafeteria and bookstore (a small building near the Gray Building) plummeted. Income from gifts of property from donors, who retained a lifetime annuity from the earnings from city properties in Nashville and Memphis, yielded almost nothing. Peabody still had to pay the annuities, suffered losses each year, and considered rejecting all such gifts in the future, but after only two or three years, the profits resumed.

Peabody survived this budgetary nightmare by cutting costs to the bone. Unlike Vanderbilt, the college never reduced faculty salaries but, after 1930, offered no raises. Yet, the real incomes of Peabody faculty rose rapidly in the thirties because of the severe drop in prices. Full professors with incomes of more than

The Peabody campus in the early depression years. Twenty-first Avenue is to the right. Photograph by Aero-Graphics Corp., Photographic Archives of Vanderbilt University.

$4,000 lived well, a few with homes in Nashville's most luxurious suburb, Belle Meade, and with maids and hired help. Peabody never dismissed any faculty, despite the decrease in enrollment. In effect, professors had lower course loads. The college did lose faculty through attrition and only in the most critical areas replaced professors who left, retired, or died. It drastically reduced the number of visiting professors in its severely attenuated summer school, down from more than a hundred in 1929 to no more than ten in the dark years of 1933 and 1934. Every other aspect of Peabody suffered, most of all the library, as the college could now barely match the annual $10,000 required by the Carnegie grant. The college deferred all possible maintenance. But after 1933, New Deal acreage controls, price supports, and marketing agreements turned Knapp Farm into a profit-making business.

By its own accounting, Peabody's assets actually rose slightly in the thirties. This was misleading, because it continued to list the value of buildings at their original cost, and of its endowment assets, mainly bonds, at their face value. Fortunately, Peabody had never invested in preferred or common stock. Except for a few gifts of real estate, usually with an annuity provision, the executive committee and Payne had bought bonds, frequently selling and buying to keep the return above 5 percent. Although the bylaws required a finance committee, it had never functioned. As early as 1931, the issuers of bonds began to default on interest payments, but the record indicates that all the defaulting companies, municipalities, or churches eventually reissued such bonds (Peabody had invested heavily in church bonds), but at much lower interest rates. Thus, its income from the endowment dropped from over 5 percent to around 4 percent by the late thirties, and even this level reflected a decision, implemented in 1937, to invest up to 20 percent of the endowment in preferred and common stock. New bonds often yielded less than 3 percent.[1]

NEW STRATEGIES OF GOVERNANCE

Depression retrenchment forced Payne and his faculty to face some festering problems, and to make hard but too long deferred choices. Peabody was a loose ship under Payne, with no administrative structure, no clear rules for faculty, no deans of men or women, no organized academic departments, no formal department or division heads. Payne had continued to hire all faculty and set their salaries, with rubber-stamp approval by the executive committee. Appointments were not for a set time, but open or indefinite. Peabody had no tenure system, no formal promotion process (Payne, influenced by faculty committees, simply decided when to promote), no formal disciplinary procedures. Faculty came, stayed, and enjoyed a great deal of personal freedom in planning and teaching their courses or in conducting research. They had no research support and no paid leaves, but a type of informal tenure. That is, Payne never dismissed anyone for cause. Some professors aged badly, contributed little, and continued to receive their pay. For years, a brilliant scholar such as Joseph Peterson received the same salary as incompetents. Peabody did not force professors to participate in TIAA. When nonparticipants died, the college was almost forced to offer them an annuity. Thus, some faculty remained on the Peabody payroll until they died. In a sense, Peabody was a large academic family, with Payne the father.

Students were a part of this protective and solicitous family. By 1930, entrance requirements and grading standards were so low or flexible as to worry even the egalitarian Payne. With the largest graduate enrollment in the South, Peabody ran what amounted to an M.A. mill, particularly in the summer, when graduate students flocked to the campus. Graduate enrollment dropped rapidly in the early depression (from 1,437 in 1929 to a low of 780 in 1933) but rose to 1,164 in 1935. By the most generous count, thirty Peabody faculty members were at least minimally qualified to teach graduate work. This meant that, on average, each professor was responsible for 38 M.A. and Ph.D. candidates in 1935, with about one-third of these completing a thesis each year. It never worked out this neatly, for some faculty without Ph.D.'s undoubtedly directed M.A. work. But some of the thirty, only minimally qualified on paper, were not competent graduate instructors. This was a scandal.

These shortcoming bothered representatives of the regional accrediting agency, the Southern Association of Colleges and Secondary Schools. In January 1931, before the devastation of the depression, SACSS visitors laid down the law: Peabody had to repent and reform. Particularly concerned about the graduate program, the visitors demanded that Peabody appoint its first dean, largely to clean up the problems in graduate education. It asked for formal candidacy for M.A. candidates, higher entrance requirements, departmental approval for admission, a limited number of graduate students for each professor, and restriction of graduate instruction to professors in the senior college and graduate program. Peabody tried to meet these demands. It appointed the first graduate dean at the college, an education professor and former Peabody Ph.D., Shelton Phelps. It even announced in its catalogue than no graduate instructor could present more than nine M.A. and Ph.D. candidates for degrees each year, with no more than four of these for a Ph.D. None of these changes diminished the number of graduate students, but they may have equalized the teaching burden among the faculty.[2]

The outside criticism bothered Payne. He insisted that the accrediting agency misunderstood the college's unique and informal administrative system, which needed no chain of command. From the beginning, Payne had appointed a full complement of faculty committees and referred most important issues to them. The whole faculty met regularly and could recommend academic policies. It was a loose system, but from Payne's perspective a democratic one. Everyone at Peabody was gratified that in 1934 the American Council on Education judged the college qualified to offer Ph.D. work in psychology and education, two of thirty-five fields evaluated. Few southern schools qualified in any field. Vanderbilt qualified in none.[3]

Peabody's unique faculty government seemed well established by the Depression. In 1915 the faculty had adopted a form of organization, with bylaws governing all its operations. As amended in 1920, these bylaws required bimonthly meetings of the total faculty, with additional meetings at the call of the president. By the depression, the faculty served on eighteen standing committees. The bylaws covered all aspects of academic policy (these changed from year to year), including such key areas as curriculum, entrance requirements, and appointments. The catalogue listed, each year, the members of these faculty committees. Some patterns show up in their members, all appointed by Payne: The most eminent faculty members chaired all the committees with major policy responsibilities; women chaired no committees, and in most cases women served on such committees as dorm life, health and sanitation, public exercises, and social activities.[4]

The formal structure concealed the informal nature of the college's administration, particularly the role of President Payne. He not only presided at regular faculty meetings but also was an ex officio member of all committees. While this was not unusual, the extent to which Payne involved himself in the details of the committees was. Faculty members often resented not his policy preferences but his attempt to control even small details. They could not get away from his ever-present eye, for Payne lived in SR, arose early every morning, seemed to monitor every activity on campus, and tried to attend every event. As one faculty member later remarked, if Payne heard that a calf was about to be born on Knapp Farm, he jumped in his car and drove recklessly, as always, to be there. He praised his faculty in lectures and to alumni but pushed them hard in his personal interaction with them. One faculty member recalled telephone calls from Payne before six in the morning. He drove everyone, largely because he was driven himself, completely absorbed in Peabody. He created guilt by his example. The faculty often breathed a sigh of relief when Payne was off on a fund-raising trip. One could relax for a few days.

It was during the deepening depression that Peabody tried a new form of organization that looked important on paper but had no major impact on academic life. With executive committee consent, Payne tried to separate the first two years, which he now called the junior college, from the professional school (junior and senior years and the graduate school). Peabody had developed two student bodies. In the summer, most students were at the graduate level or at least in the last two years of undergraduate work. Almost all were teachers or school administrators, on average in their thirties, and serious about professional advancement. Approximately 60 percent came from outside Tennessee, mainly from the South but with a growing number from all over the country and from abroad. Even the Tennessee students were from all sections of the state. During the rest of the year, no more than half the students were such advanced, professional types. From 1914 on, regular-year students had entered Peabody just after high school, were largely from the Nashville area, and by 1930 were often not seriously committed to teaching. It seemed to Payne and others that these more typical undergraduates did not match the main mission of Peabody, to train educational leaders. This judgment led to the division between the senior college and the junior, and unsuccessful efforts to raise funds to build a separate campus for the junior college.

In 1931, Payne appointed a director for the junior college. He announced separate admission requirements and a general education curriculum not that different from the one in the College of Arts and Science at Vanderbilt (in 1931, Vanderbilt created its own junior college). Notably, and this was new at Peabody, junior-college students did not have to take any courses in education. In conception, the junior college was to function much like the Demonstration School—a resource for local students and a possible site for educational experiments by professional students at Peabody. It would be another laboratory. The junior college also listed its own faculty, though it was never completely separate. Graduate instructors were not supposed to teach junior-college classes. In 1933, in what turned out to be largely a paper change, the junior college joined the Demonstration School, with the same director over both—another former Peabody Ph.D., Joseph Roemer. Briefly, Peabody even advertised a consolidation of the senior year in high school and the junior college. In spite of these plans, the catalogue each year noted with a touch of embarrassment that, for the present, junior-college students would have to take regular courses on the main campus. An imperceptive student might never have noticed that anything had changed. But whatever the administrative structure, Peabody would continue to face the problem of how to blend its largely local, youthful students into a professional school of education. It was as if a medical school included an undergraduate adjunct. From time to time after World War II, Peabody came close to abolishing either its undergraduate program or at least its first two years of instruction, but the college could never afford the loss of tuition.[5]

MONEY PROBLEMS

In the depression, Peabody suffered from the desperate plight of public school teachers and from a lack of funding for teachers' colleges. Public education depended on tax revenues. Particularly in the South, public finance almost collapsed in 1933–34. The Tennessee legislature talked about suspending its teachers' colleges. All suffered severe funding cuts, at times having to cut their budgets by more than half. States cut teachers' salaries, forced teachers to take on more duties, fired married teachers, and in many school districts stopped paying teachers altogether. In place of money, they received warrants, promises of future pay. This meant almost no new jobs in education. Peabody Ph.D.'s who had easily obtained faculty positions in teachers' colleges now found no openings. To help students in their job search, Peabody for the first time set up a placement service and widely advertised its students in need of work. A survey of the alumni records for the thirties reveals a drop in opportunities for graduates who could find work. Students with a B.S. degree more often ended up in elementary schools, not high schools, and M.A.'s found jobs not in normal schools, but in high schools.

By 1933, almost no teachers could afford to come to Peabody. Unemployment might have encouraged applications, which to an extent happened at the graduate level, for a graduate degree might enable one to find a position. But most applicants could not afford Peabody, even when they came. In every way, Peabody tried to help students in need, which soon meant almost all students. Payne noted how many went hungry to make ends meet. In 1933 Peabody had only about $11,700 in income from various scholarship funds, and spread this over 156 students. It made loans to 503 students and, in a daring move, allowed students at admission to execute a note to cover tuition and room rent (most would be repaid at 6 percent interest, double what Peabody could then earn on its investments). It made 203 such tuition loans in 1933. It also accepted warrants offered by states in lieu of salary at a discount of only 6 percent, much more than their market value. Peabody found part-time jobs for an additional 190 students and, in all, aided 1,366, well over half. This pattern of aid continued in subsequent years, supplemented after 1934 by Federal Emergency Relief Administration and, later, National Youth Administration work-study grants of $15 a month for deserving students. For two years, Peabody received less than half the tuition its enrollment warranted.[6]

Hard times warred with student morale. Each quarter, student turnover increased, as many students had to go home because of a lack of funds. As early as the summer of 1932, Payne asked all faculty members to "take time to speak a sympathetic and helpful word to each student in our classes." Professors reported that "students have never needed more a personal word of encouragement . . . than at this time."[7] In 1933, Payne wrote a letter to faculty asking that they exempt all students from routine laboratory fees, except those that paid for actual material consumed.[8] The Peabody faculty also sympathized with the much worse plight of beleaguered teachers in normal or teachers' colleges. The *Reflector,* over several years, carried detailed and favorable stories about practically every teachers' college in the South.

The early thirties took their toll on Payne. He worried continuously about finances and never gave up on future expansion, although he could do nothing in the present. The GEB remained helpful, but its only major initiatives in the thirties were the steps that led to new Peabody-Vanderbilt cooperation, and to the Joint University Libraries (JUL). Construction all but ceased on campus, with one exception. The Tennessee chapters of the United Daughters of the Confederacy

(UDC) had since 1913 tried to fund a special home or dormitory at Peabody. While Payne had welcomed their initiative, he must have concealed some reservations over the terms of the early offers. The UDC wanted something like a girls' home for the daughters of Confederate soldiers. Perhaps fortunately, their fund-raising efforts went slowly, as local chapters in Tennessee contributed only small amounts each year. As time passed and early leaders died, the goal shifted toward a typical dormitory, with perhaps half the rooms reserved for the descendants of Confederate soldiers. In the intervening years, the UDC women pushed Payne to hire a historian of the South, by which they meant a historian who would celebrate the glorious history of the Confederacy. Payne pointed out that Peabody had historians who taught about the South, and in fact for a few years, Donald F. Fleming, of Vanderbilt, offered very scholarly courses on the region that were at least not hostile to the Confederacy. More pertinent, Peabody education professor and popular writer Alfred E. Crabb wrote dozens of articles on the great heroes of the Confederacy in glowing language that matched that of any custodian of the Lost Cause.[9]

The plummeting building costs of the depression came to the aid of the UDC. By 1934, the women had collected $50,000 (held in a trust fund by Peabody), at least a third of the total needed for a dorm. They offered the funds if Peabody accepted their proffered contract, which stipulated a building to cost not less than $50,000 that Peabody would design and build. The only limiting condition was that up to fifty financially needy girls of Confederate lineage receive free rooms, and that the UDC have the right to nominate these occupants. The Peabody board would manage the hall and take care of all maintenance and upkeep, but the UDC promised to appoint an advisory committee. Completed in January 1935 on the east end of the small quadrangle north of East Hall, Confederate Hall was the only major addition to the campus between 1930 and 1945. (Peabody completed a nursery school building near Edgehill just before World War II). In style, the UDC structure conformed to the earlier dorms. Each room bore the name of a sponsoring UDC chapter in Tennessee.[10]

Peabody tried to get federal funding for another dorm, but failed. For years, it planned a dorm near West Hall, on Twenty-first, that would face Confederate to the east. Arguing that Peabody was really a public college, Payne and Little applied for funds from the Public Works Administration. Created in 1933 in the early New Deal, it granted money for campus buildings at public colleges and universities. Their claim, based on past funding by the state and local governments, did not fool the PWA staff, who classed Peabody as the private college it was. This was disillusioning to Payne, who, as one would expect was a great fan of Franklin D. Roosevelt and of New Deal programs. He even began to refer to his own radio addresses over WSM as fireside chats. The *Reflector* carried numerous articles on New Deal programs such as the TVA. To the glory of Peabody, FDR briefly visited Nashville on November 17, 1934, and drove through all the city's campuses, black and white.

At Peabody, he did not get out of his open car but made a short stop in front of the SR before cheering students and photographers, then sped away, behind schedule. This brief visit matched the equally hurried one by Theodore Roosevelt to the old campus in 1907.[11]

SHIFTS IN FACULTY

Peabody suffered a series of unexpected deaths from 1929 to 1937. Some involved Payne's closest friends and advisors. In March 1929, Charles McMurry, the beloved professor of elementary education, died of a heart attack while at work on a Sunday-school lesson. With McMurry's death, only four of the original faculty remained—Charles Little, Fletcher Bascom Dresslar, Kary Cadmus Davis, and Payne. In 1929, Julia Sears died in Massachusetts, the only surviving faculty member from the opening of Peabody Normal in 1875. In the same year, Nashville alumni of the old but no longer active literary societies—Agatheridan, Erosophian, and Adelphi—held a homecoming of former members, most of whom had fond memories of Sears. Not to be outdone, in 1930, the continuing women's literary societies—the Girls Chapter and the Literary Society—held a homecoming for their alumnae.[12]

In January 1930, Dresslar died. Payne, who had loved him, must also have sensed that the early Peabody concern for rural life was at stake. In March 1930, Judge Edward Sanford, the first chairman of the George Peabody Board of Trust, died in Knoxville.[13] In October 1931, Wickliffe Rose died—the most eminent alumnus of the old college, an architect of the new George Peabody, and, through the GEB, Peabody's greatest patron. He was not personally close to Payne but had continued his friendship with his old colleague from the turn of the century, Charles Little. In February 1934, Frank Bachman died. Although he had offended Payne in 1926, he had been the able head of the Division of Surveys and Field Studies since 1929.[14] In the fall of 1935, Peabody lost its ablest scholar, Joseph Peterson, who died of pneumonia in Berkeley while visiting a son after attending a meeting of the American Psychological Association in Michigan.[15] Because of the critical importance of psychology, Peabody began a search for his replacement, one of the few searches conducted in the depression.

The worst blow, and the last before Payne's own death, came on March 4, 1936, when Kerry K. Davis died, Peabody's first and for several years also last professor of agriculture. Payne mourned Davis's death in his report to the board in its May meeting, noting that he had brought Davis to the campus and enjoyed a longer association with him than with any other man; he would "miss him every day as long as memory lasts." Davis for years had offered agricultural courses to a dwindling number of students, in the process keeping alive a shadow of the old Knapp School of Country Life. Payne knew his death marked the end of this early dream.[16]

Peabody had no justification for replacing Davis and did not try. The 1936–37 catalogue listed no courses in agriculture. With Knapp Farm's instructional and demonstrations functions over, manager Ray Appleton could now specialize only in the most profitable crops and would use the dairy herd to earn annual profits. In the depression, students continued to flock to the clubhouse; it cost them almost nothing. Other departments continued courses on rural education. The aging Otto Ault still taught courses in agricultural economics. During the war, students and faculty renewed the gardens to the east of the psychology building, their version of Victory Gardens. But what had most distinguished George Peabody College back in 1914 was gone, and Payne would soon join his closest friends in death. So quickly, the giants of the early years had passed.

Who replaced them? No one of equal ability. Even on campus, the myth of the great founders and of the subsequent decline became an axiom. Peabody recruited no one with the national eminence of Davis and Peterson. No one in education rivaled McMurry, although Lucy Gage, who came in 1920 to teach in the field of kindergarten and early elementary education, rivaled McMurry in popularity. She even converted a green shed into a small elementary school to demonstrate new ways of teaching very young children, the progenitor of Stallworth Hall, the nursery school built just before World War II.

One reason Peabody failed to maintain its early faculty eminence was that, for reasons never publicized or even made clear, it hired too many of its own students. This inbreeding, or nepotism, made the college ever more provincial. In 1937, the year Payne died, both deans held Peabody Ph.D.'s, and so did seven out of about twenty-five full professors. Two more had M.A.'s from Peabody. Sidney C. Garrison, Payne's successor, one of the first four Peabody Ph.D.'s (in 1919), was able, and so were other Peabody graduates on the Peabody faculty, but none had the scholarly distinction of Davis or Peterson. Recruiting distinguished professors from the outside also became more difficult with each passing decade, for few wanted to teach in the South, or to remain there if they began their career in southern institutions. Not only did the low incomes, the cultural backwardness, and the poor public services of the South keep them away, but also the problem of race. John Dewey, who published two essays in the *Reflector*, could not in good conscience have taught in a segregated southern college.

Who were the faculty leaders in the second generation at Peabody, during the depression and war years? Garrison, who taught educational psychology in the shadow of the great Peterson, moved into full-time administration at Peterson's death. Some of the ablest at Peabody worked in the Division of Surveys and Field Studies, but they did not normally teach and received their salaries, at least indirectly, from the GEB. A group of professors in the field of education published continuously, were active professionally, and gave numerous lectures off campus. These included Norman Frost, who in a sense took Dresslar's place, offering courses on rural life and publishing dozens of articles on that topic. A special professor, Michael Demiashkevich, a White Russian in exile from the Soviet Union, taught in the twenties and thirties. He wrote articles and books on comparative education and one book on comparative politics. Unusual for Peabody, he ridiculed progressive or child-centered theories of education, instead supporting an educational system that would screen for an intellectual elite. An outspoken enemy of socialism and communism before such views became a new orthodoxy, he was somewhat isolated at Peabody. He died in 1938, an apparent suicide.[17] Two other professors of education—David Cooke and Ullim W. Leavell—were, for a time, Rosenwald professors who wrote about and directed conferences on race relations.

In deference to Vanderbilt, Peabody made appointments not in the subject areas in the liberal arts, but in the teaching of such subjects. Typically, such professors published textbooks for public schools or, occasionally, for colleges. Alfred Roehm, in modern languages, began this textbook-publishing tradition, and lived on through the depression years. Hanor Webb gained national visibility for his stream of articles on teaching chemistry, as did Frank Wren in mathematics. Webb would become president of the National Council for Research in Science Teaching.[18] Geography was a special field at Peabody, because Vanderbilt had no department in this critical subject and most teachers needed geography courses to earn teaching licenses. Here, Peabody was fortunate. Almon E. Parkins, who arrived in the twenties, became one of the best-known geography educators in the United States, published extensively, and in 1929 presided over the National Association of Geographers. When he suffered a near-fatal stroke in 1939, Joe Russell Whitaker, who had coauthored a textbook with Parkins, replaced him. Whitaker remained on the faculty until the seventies, published extensively, and also served as president of the National Association of Geographers. He lived a century, almost to the end of the 1900s, and wrote several books on conservation and the environment, particularly on the devastation of land and forests. He was Tennessee's first notable environmentalist.

The most successful of these hybrid professors would be Fremont P. Wirth, who came to Peabody in 1925 with a history Ph.D. from the University of Chicago. He eventually published his dissertation on the iron district of Minnesota but gained national visibility with a series of U.S. history textbooks. His first of two high school texts, *Development of America,* featured a new unit arrangement, was adopted in most states, and had sold 1.3 million copies by 1955, when he retired. He also coauthored a civics text, *How America Is Governed,* with his colleague Jack Allen. In 1940, Wirth was elected president of the National Council for Social Studies, one of the highest positions held by any Peabody professor after Peterson's death.[19] Although Wirth participated actively in the major scholarly associations, such was the prevalent disdain for textbook publishing among academic historians that he never gained the recognition he deserved. He could easily ignore the slight, for he became wealthy from his royalties and had more impact on the historical understanding of Americans than any contemporary university scholar.

Finally, another Peabody Ph.D., Alfred Leland Crabb, was by far the greatest booster the college ever had. One of his ancestors had served on the board of the University of Nashville. A professor of education at Peabody, Crabb had no scholarly pretensions in any field of education, but was a prolific writer, mostly on the history of Nashville, the University of Nashville, and Peabody. He edited the *Peabody Journal of Education* and even beyond retirement organized tours of local historical sites for summer school students. In his last years, he published thirteen historical novels. His grandiloquent prose, his embellishment of his sources, his near worship of the old South, and his Confederate loyalties gave flavor to his celebrations of giants of old, reminiscent of the heroes in Walter Scott's novels. A complete optimist, he predicted the future perfection of humankind in the midst of the darkest days of World War II.

It is too easy to caricature Crabb. His work has not worn well. Yet the Peabody records he collected and preserved have proven a gold mine for later historians. I owe him a debt. Locally, he was the best-known professor at Peabody, in constant demand as a speaker. His sentimental and formulaic novels found a large readership and drew glowing reviews—at least locally. But Crabb never gained or deserved recognition in higher literary circles, unlike a 1938 Peabody M.A., William Inge, who became one of America's most distinguished playwrights.[20]

In college histories, the hardworking staff almost always remains in the background, invisible. That is unfair. The staff member who contributed as much to Peabody as any professor, Roy Appleton, came to Peabody as a student in 1916. He went on to serve in World War I, and returned to manage Knapp Farm. After a year, he also worked part-time on the main campus. In 1921 he moved from Knapp Farm manager to superintendent of buildings and grounds (his brother Ray remained as manager of Knapp farm until its sale in 1965). Soon indispensable, Appleton supervised the care of the campus for nearly forty years. He helped develop large gardens of iris, his field of expertise. He deserves most of the credit for the gradual improvement of the grounds from a barren sweep of thin, rocky soil (except for a grove of mostly young trees on the lower campus) to today's contoured campus, which Appleton created from excavated soil from the basements of new buildings. Appleton also lined with trees the walkways to the east and west of the main quadrangle.[21] At his retirement in 1959, his son, James, replaced him, having completed an engineering degree at the University of Tennessee. Ten years later, irregularities in accounts and a suspected loss of college funds, forced his resignation.

Another staff person, Samuel L. Smith, was a major figure in Peabody history. Director of public relations from 1938 to 1945, he eventually held the almost honorary title of provost. Smith grew up in rural Tennessee, graduated from the University of Chicago, came to Peabody in 1914 as a part-time student, and received his M.A. in 1918. As a school superintendent in Clarksville, Tennessee, until 1913, he had tried to equalize educational opportunities for whites and blacks, including identical eight-month school terms and equal teacher salaries. He introduced work in industrial arts and home economics. Such fairness for blacks was unusual in the South, but Smith was an unusual southerner. At Peabody, he took every course offered in rural education with William Knox Tate, and all courses in schoolhouse design, hygiene, and sanitation with Dresslar, who became his hero. Wallace Buttrick was impressed with Smith's record in Clarksville. When the GEB agreed to pay the salaries of state agents who worked in behalf of improved Negro education, it chose Smith in 1913 as agent for Tennessee. He began work in 1914, even as he began his work at Peabody, His half-time assistant was an African American, the first employed by the Tennessee Department of Education. In his promotion of

Roy Appleton, longtime superintendent of buildings and grounds, supervising work on one of his famous iris beds. Photograph by Tucker Studio, Photographic Archives of Vanderbilt University.

better black schools, Smith developed a concern, shared by all state agents, about the unconscionably poor quality of Negro school buildings.

Also concerned about black education was the northern philanthropist Julius Rosenwald. He joined with the GEB to fund the construction, beginning in 1914, of what eventually became one hundred model Negro schools in Alabama. Smith attended the dedication of the first in 1914. These model schools, supported by Booker T. Washington and Tuskegee Institute, so pleased Rosenwald that he established a southern office in 1920 to supervise a major program of Negro schoolhouse construction in all southern states. Samuel Smith headed this program, with offices in Nashville. Dresslar, who contributed most of the school plans, designed a group of one-story buildings to accommodate from one to seven teachers. He had two set of plans for each, one oriented north-south, one east-west, so that windows would best take advantage of natural light, for almost no rural schools had electricity. Each plan, even for a one-teacher school, included two cloakrooms and a community room for adult education. (Dresslar also designed model sanitary privies for rural schools and for the hookworm campaign headed by Wickliffe Rose.)

From 1920 to 1932, Smith supervised this building program. He continued as director of the southern office of the Rosenwald Fund until its closing in 1937. The fund contributed a small amount for each Negro schoolhouse, all based on Dresslar's community school designs. The fund required matching funds from counties and gifts and work from the black families who would use the new schools, or as much as seven-eighths of total costs. Most local whites, who believed the schools were a gift, felt not hostility but, often, envy. They demanded similar schools, for which the Rosenwald Fund provided free plans but no assistance for construction. In addition to schoolhouses, the fund subsidized school libraries, teachers' homes, and shops for industrial arts. In all, the fund expended $28,424,520 on these buildings, with some additional personal funds from Rosenwald—a lot of money in the twenties and early thirties. The payoff: 5,358 model Negro schools in 883 counties in fifteen states.[22]

The last Rosenwald school would be the Eleanor Roosevelt School outside Warm Springs, Georgia, completed in 1937. Smith talked at length about his program with Franklin D. Roosevelt when he was governor of New York and promised to build a model school for Negroes in Warm Springs. The white school there had used a Dresslar plan, and Roosevelt described it as the most attractive school he had ever seen. Local support evaporated in the depression, but in October 1934, Roosevelt requested a meeting with Smith at the White House, where he demanded that Smith fulfill his earlier promise for a school in Warm Springs. When the president visited Nashville the next month on his way to Warm Springs, Smith met with him briefly at Fisk (before the motorcar briefly stopped at Peabody), and Roosevelt again asked about his promised Rosenwald school. Although the program had ended, the Rosenwald Fund made an exception and contributed $2,500, and a compliant local school board and the Works Progress Administration chipped in about $12,000. In 1937, Roosevelt attended the dedication, Smith introduced him, and Roosevelt gave a short speech, the stenographic transcript of which Smith kept as a prized possession. Smith wrote a powerful letter to Roosevelt seeking relief funds for school construction and to some extent was responsible for more than a billion dollars going toward public school buildings.

Smith also became a benefactor of Peabody. He persuaded the Rosenwald Fund to contribute $7,500 a year for two professors to teach and conduct annual conferences on dual education and race relations. In 1938, after his position with the fund ended, Smith joined the Peabody staff as public relations director. He taught only in the summer conferences on dual education, which began in 1933. They were well attended by white superintendents from all over the South, for Smith had persuaded the GEB to offer scholarships to allow county superintendents to attend, and in all more than five hundred did. Smith invited the eminent black sociologist Charles S. Johnson of Fisk University to address the thirty white superintendents at the 1939 summer conference. All were impressed, including those Smith knew to be members of the KKK. Soon afterward, Marian Anderson, in Nashville for a concert, visited Smith at his Peabody office and then in President Garrison's office. Students lined up outside to get her autograph.

Since school construction was so vital for the South, the GEB in 1929 established a Division of Schoolhouse Planning and Construction and located it at Peabody. This was in honor of Dresslar, who died the next year. The GEB also paid the salary of a director of this program in each state. Each of these had to attend Peabody for one year of coursework. These directors, along with county superintendents, held annual conferences on schoolhouse construction at Peabody during the summer quarter. When the Rosenwald Fund ended its southern work in 1937, it turned over all its school plans and its bulletins to this division, by then the leading clearinghouse in the South for school construction for both whites and blacks. The Rosenwald Fund supported the division until 1948, when the GEB took over its funding as a part of the Division of Surveys and Field Studies, where it remained until Peabody's merger with Vanderbilt.[23]

THE POLICIES OF PRESIDENT SIDNEY C. GARRISON

Just after dinner on April 21, 1937, Bruce Payne dropped dead from a heart attack. Completely unexpected, this was a stunning calamity for the campus, where classes did not meet for two days. Peabody had been so inseparably tied to Payne that its very identity seemed threatened. What next? No one knew. Payne had been at the center of every event at the college. Students and faculty saw him daily as he walked about campus. For twenty-three years, every student at Peabody had met Payne, heard his frequent homilies, received a degree from his hand, and, often, received counsel from him. Apparently, almost all had loved him or at least honored what he had given to Peabody—all his devotion, all his energies, and now his life. Thousands of letters poured in from his former students. His funeral took place in the auditorium, under its beautiful dome, just down the hall from his apartment. His minister at West End Methodist Church was joined by the minister of First Baptist Church in the services. Vanderbilt's Chancellor Kirkland was among the honorary pallbearers.[24]

Although he was sixty-three, no one expected Payne to retire early. Yet late photographs show him a bit puffy and tired looking. For several years, he had not been at his best. His speeches became more stilted and repetitious. He struggled with the problems of the depression but missed the great challenges and the fund-raising successes of the early years. His closest friends had died. Had he lived, he should have retired by sixty-five, but he would not have done so. He had no life apart from Peabody. The board of trust allowed his widow to live on as long as she wished in the SR and gave her a lifetime annuity. As the executive committee began to search for Payne's successor, they had few guidelines to follow. For a few months, Peabody fell into a state of suspended animation. Payne had not served even half as long as Chancellor Kirkland at Vanderbilt, who would retire in a few months, but, unlike Kirkland, Payne had not only served as the first president but also planned the campus and defined Peabody's early mission. It would be difficult to locate another founding president of a college or university who so dominated an institution, or who, in the early years, was more successful (possibly Gilman at Hopkins, Harper at Chicago). Although some leaders at George Peabody would be more brilliant, some better focused, all better organized, none would achieve half so much. None would have Payne's magnetic influence over others or believe more firmly in ideals that he usually lumped under that overworked label "democracy."

Of the original faculty, only Charles Little remained. The executive committee asked him to be acting president until the board's scheduled May meeting, at which time it appointed Dean Sidney C. Garrison as acting president, while it searched for a successor. A committee of the board evaluated several names, seriously considered three, but awarded the position to Garrison, the only inside candidate and the only one educated at Peabody. This was not a wise decision, as it turned out, but was in no way a disastrous one. Just as the newly appointed professors did not match the earlier giants, so Garrison was not Payne. He served less than eight years before illness and an early death. In a sense, he was an interim president.

Garrison, like Payne from North Carolina, was a graduate of Wake Forest. He served as a high school principal and a county superintendent before entering Peabody in 1914. He received his M.A. in 1916, immediately joined the faculty as a graduate student assistant in psychology. He rose to the rank of captain in World War I, and helped develop the soon famous but later much criticized army IQ test. He earned his Ph.D. in 1919 and became the leading educational psychologist at Peabody. An active scholar, he never matched the achievement of Joseph Peterson. Garrison wrote books on child development, as well as textbooks, particularly on spelling. He published articles in major educational journals and gained some national visibility, although he was not an outstanding scholar. In 1931 he became director of instruction, and in 1934 dean of the Senior College and Graduate school. He had strong faculty and student support for the presidency. A former professor, H. L. Caswell, noted in a letter that only two professors at Peabody opposed Garrison's appointment.[25]

Although he always acknowledged his great debt to Payne, Garrison differed from his predecessor in philosophy, personality, and educational goals. Payne was expansive and idealistic, Garrison controlled and realistic. Payne ran a loose ship. Garrison was about as organized as the Peabody culture permitted. Payne wanted to train teachers as reformers, agents of change. Garrison wanted teachers who would preserve the always-threatened moral and spiritual ideals of the past. In social and economic outlook, he was much more conservative than Payne except in one area of race relations. Garrison was a member of the board of the Southern Education Foundation, the successor of the Slater Fund, and in 1943 invited this foundation to hold a biracial meeting at Peabody, but not join in biracial meals. (It met in Philadelphia, in one of the few first-class hotels in the United States that would admit blacks).[26] While he wanted to aid black education, Garrison had a deep fear of racial conflict and apparently never contemplated integrated schools for the South. As World War II came along, Garrison at times reflected an almost conspiratorial outlook. He paired the dangers of European totalitarianism with what he perceived as an even more dangerous threat at home, one never precisely defined, that involved radical thinkers, utopian or socialist dreams, and challenges to social order. Although as overtly religious as Payne, Garrison was not as doctrinally loose or as generous and tolerant. He could not conceal his contempt for Roosevelt and many New Deal programs, sensing a whole civilization ready to crumble. In February 1944, he argued that "education must emphasize authority and unity from within, motivated and made dynamic by certain spiritual values."[27]

In May 1938, Garrison's first report to the board of trust must have shocked many present. Never before had they confronted such a detailed and realistic appraisal of Peabody's weaknesses. Although he had admired Payne as a person, Garrison had chafed under his loose administration. He now wanted to create clear lines of authority and clear personnel policies. In meetings with his faculty, he had easily won agreement on a general policy: Peabody would focus only on its teacher education program. Some departments, including fine arts, industrial arts, home economics, music, religious education, and physics, contributed only indirectly to that core mission. Garrison wanted to suspend, reduce, or better focus work in these departments. Peabody excelled in such subjects as psychology and geography that related directly to teacher training. If it duplicated courses in these subjects at Vanderbilt, then Vanderbilt should consider dropping its courses. In English, social studies, and possibly biology, Peabody could provide vital service courses more cheaply than by paying Vanderbilt for them. Otherwise, Peabody needed to take advantage of Vanderbilt's strengths. Most sensitive was his desire to screen out the deadwood on the faculty. He had found plenty. Above all, he wanted, as humanely as possible, to get rid of these unneeded or incompetent faculty members who contributed almost nothing to the core mission of the college. In almost all respects, Garrison restated to the board of trust the recommendations Frank Bachman had made in 1926.[28]

Garrison was blunt. He had compiled supporting data, and he named names. He believed the personnel problem at Peabody was more serious than at any other institution of similar size or like character in the United States. He wanted to dismiss, as soon as possible, no less than 10 percent of the Peabody faculty and divert the funds saved to what the college did well. By an analysis of instructional costs per hour of work, he identified the efficient and inefficient departments—costs ranged from just under $3.00 an hour in English and history to $9.39 in music, $10.47 in religious education, and a scandalous $17.24 in physics and $30.66 in classical languages. Few students took courses in these subjects; professors taught too few students to justify their salaries, particularly since, apart from music, these subjects were no longer critical to Peabody's mission. Garrison asked the board to eliminate physics and religious education. In the presence of Charles Little, he could not ask to end instruction in Latin. Little would retire with great fanfare in 1941, ending Latin instruction except in summer, when he still taught his ill-subscribed course. Garrison wanted to get rid of the present ineffective head of music and then try to rebuild that department. The older, inept physics teacher was an easy target, since few students at Peabody planned to teach physics, and a recent course had only three enrollees. In some semesters, listed courses had no takers at all. Anyone who needed physics could take Vanderbilt courses.[29]

Garrison was particularly hard on religious education and its aging chair, Leonidas E. Crawford. Payne had loved Crawford, who had a large following at Peabody and in Nashville. His generous, albeit a bit fuzzy, Christian witness had won him friends everywhere. Crawford had become, in a sense, the campus chaplain. Garrison did not share this admiration. He pointed out that Peabody had no business offering a few inferior courses in religious education, when both Scarritt and the School of Religion at Vanderbilt offered a fully professional program in these areas. In response to these specific complaints, the board abolished the department of religious education and offered early retirement benefits to the head of physics and, by 1939, to the weak head of the music department. Garrison hired a new and effective head of music, Irving Wolfe, who in the next five years built a music program for Peabody that some referred to as the strongest in the South. Garrison soon hired two young, and more effective, women in home economics. The board did not dare fire Crawford. It allowed him to teach courses in English (biblical literature) and education. After retirement, he continued to arrange all vespers services for the summer and to open each with a prayer, soon a memorable tradition in itself. Garrison appointed Peabody's first sociologist in 1939.

Other academic changes did not as clearly improve Peabody's quality. Garrison asked the board to approve an M.A. without thesis, arguing that because most M.A. candidates had no scholarly commitment, it was as well to replace the six hours of thesis research with coursework; Peabody thus became even more an M.A. mill. Garrison also proposed two new degrees, a bachelor of arts and a master of education. No one knew why Peabody had never offered the popular B.A. degree, but beginning in 1943, students who majored in languages, social studies, music, and art automatically received a B.A., all others a B.S. The M.Ed., which had few takers, went to those with an M.A. who took an additional year of coursework in a specialized field of education. It was the precursor of the later education specialist (Ed.S.) degree. Garrison also established a new department, business education, in response to the needs or desires of a growing number of young women in the Nashville area who entered Peabody straight from high school. The new department, in the war years, primarily taught secretarial skills.[30]

Garrison wanted policies in place that would ensure faculty accountability. He did not propose a formal tenure system, a comparatively new option in the United States. He indirectly accused Payne of hiring good people, those he admired, without too much concern for what they could contribute to Peabody's core mission. Once at the college, they stayed not just to retirement but until they died. Many did not join TIAA, presumably because they did not want to pay the 5 percent from their own pay, thus sacrificing the 5 percent contributed by Peabody—a foolish decision, but no one forced them to join. Very quickly, the board made membership in TIAA obligatory in the first two years of employment at Peabody; failure to join meant dismissal. For uninsured old-timers at retirement age, Peabody used the 5 percent it would have contributed during a professor's tenure to buy a life annuity. To Garrison's dismay, Peabody had never had a retirement policy, with the result that professors taught long beyond their usefulness. The board now made retirement at sixty-five standard, apart from a few special appointments, and in 1946 made sixty-five mandatory, with no exceptions.[31]

Finally, Garrison wanted a rational salary policy. Salaries ranged from $2,000 to $7,000, with no equity at all and—for Garrison the worst crime—no rationale or order to the system. Unlike almost all other universities, Peabody had continued appointments for four-quarters with no free summers, no time off for research. The salary for twelve months made summer school costs much too high. Peabody, in effect, paid its own professors up to $1,500 for summer school work, when visitors would do the same work for $300. The board on May 9, 1940, switched Peabody to a three-quarter salary system and set up a prescribed range for nine-month salaries—$3,000 to $4,800 for professors, $2,400 to $3,600 for associate professors, and $1,800 to $3,000 for assistant professors, or roughly the same as at Vanderbilt. This did not relieve most professors from summer school teaching; it only reduced their summer pay. Most faculty continued to contract for four quarters, but a few soon received one quarter off from teaching every three years.

JOINT UNIVERSITY LIBRARIES

When Garrison took over, Vanderbilt and Peabody moved closer. The suspicions and jealousy of the early Payne-Kirkland era abated. At the heart of these changes had been Dean Garrison. In fact, it is likely that the developing cooperation with Vanderbilt helped win him the presidency in 1937. Again, the GEB almost mandated this interinstitutional cooperation. In 1930, Vanderbilt officials pled with the GEB for $500,000 to build the library required by a modern graduate program (its existing library was in the old chapel of what is now Kirkland Hall). Peabody also asked the GEB for library funds, for the depression had almost ended financial support for its library. Kirkland, who realized that Vanderbilt would never win foundation support for a library reserved only for its needs, proposed a library owned by Vanderbilt but open free of charge during the regular year to the students of Peabody, Scarritt, and the YMCA College. Since Vanderbilt had no summer school, Peabody students would have to pay a special fee for summer use. Payne objected to a library fully owned by Vanderbilt and asked for a joint library, a position the GEB supported. Yet no one seemed to know what form a joint library might take.

In February 1931, when the GEB paid two eminent librarians from the University of Chicago and North Carolina to survey the library situation in Nashville, they found little to praise. Neither Peabody nor Vanderbilt had a library adequate for graduate programs. In 1934, after at least approving Peabody for Ph.D. work in psychology and education, the American Council on Education found not one adequate graduate library in the South. Prepared to help fund some joint scheme, the GEB left the planning to the institutions involved, with the major policies the responsibility of Peabody and Vanderbilt. For two years, a joint Peabody-Vanderbilt committee wrestled with the problem but failed to resolve it. Vanderbilt wanted to retain ownership; Peabody wanted to be joint owner. The GEB rejected the one agreed-upon plan, that a separate corporation own the library. As the depression deepened, momentum slowed, with talks resuming only in late 1935. Payne wrote a key letter, and then boasted that he had taken the initiative on a new era of cooperation. He had asked for a closer affiliation and the elimination of duplicate courses in the two institutions. But a necessary condition for resumed cooperation was the presence of Dean Garrison at Peabody, and of a new vice-chancellor and aspirant chancellor at Vanderbilt, Oliver C. Carmichael. Garrison and Carmichael became an effective team, and after 1937 each headed his respective institution.[32]

In 1935 the American Library Association sent A. Frederick Kuhlman, associate director of the University of Chicago library, to survey the libraries of the four Nashville institutions. He did more. He realized that moves toward academic cooperation would necessarily underlie any foundation support for a new library. He soon presented to representatives of all four institutions a vision of a great university center in Nashville, an experiment in regional cooperation. He developed a prospectus for a joint library system, which he believed to be the new frontier in library work.

By 1936, a joint Peabody-Vanderbilt committee had surveyed all courses on each campus and selected 280 hours of duplicate courses for elimination, some on each campus. No one enforced the agreement. It is almost impossible to prevent faculty from teaching the courses they want. Peabody failed to restrict its courses to education (which included psychology), fine arts, and practical arts. But for the first time, all courses in the two institutions were fully open to all students on both campuses. Undergraduates had to major in their home institution; graduate students had to complete their dissertations at their home school. Graduate students who took more than one-fourth of their work away had to have members of the host campus on their Ph.D. committees. Until the merger of Vanderbilt and Peabody, such complete course sharing remained the rule, but after 1957, when Vanderbilt moved to the semester system, the lack of a common calendar made such sharing difficult.[33]

In 1936, the four institutions began planning a joint library system. The GEB gave Vanderbilt $15,000 a year for library development and $18,500 for a new catalogue of all Nashville libraries. Also in 1936, without final plans on the details of ownership, the cooperating institutions created the Joint University Libraries (JUL), a consolidation of all libraries on the four campuses. A library board with three members each from Peabody and Vanderbilt hired Kuhlman away from the University of Chicago to direct JUL in August 1936. He would also become a professor in Peabody's library school. In the next two years, the two institutions worked out a unique form of ownership, with Scarritt as a junior partner (the YMCA College had closed). In 1939, with state recognition, the three institutions established a trust indenture of nine trustees, with five from Vanderbilt, three from Peabody, and one from Scarritt. The trust (or trustees) would own the new general library, the land deeded by Vanderbilt on which it sat, the books in the general library, and the JUL endowment. Faculty members from all participating institutions served on a board of libraries. The owners of the trust, Peabody and Vanderbilt, could terminate it at any time, but not without respect for the rights of Scarritt, which would recoup all funds it had contributed. A library fee of $25 from each student paid for library operations. Every library, even including that of the Demonstration School, became a part of JUL, although branch library buildings, such as the one at Peabody, remained the property of the home campus. The trust provided that, should either Peabody or Vanderbilt close, the property of the trust reverted to the surviving institution. When Peabody became a part of Vanderbilt in 1979, the JUL ended.[34]

These arrangements pleased the GEB, which had finally achieved the cooperation it had sought as far back as 1914. By early 1938, the GEB had offered the three institutions $1 million for a new central JUL building, provided only that they raise an equal amount by December 1. For the first time, the three institutions cooperated in a fund drive. James Stahlman of the *Nashville Banner* headed the local drive, which inspired contributions from more than five thousand people in a continuing depression. The Carnegie Corporation helped insure success with a gift of $250,000. By early 1939, Kuhlman and a local architect, Henry Hibbs, began planning the central library in Vanderbilt's college-gothic style. Vanderbilt deeded a plot of land to JUL, the closest possible to Peabody and Scarritt (it reverted to Vanderbilt with the termination of JUL in 1979). The *Reflector* carried monthly photographs of the emerging library, virtually complete by the late summer of 1941 and dedicated on December 5–6, just before the attack on Pearl Harbor. For the first time, Peabody summer school students, who suffered through heat waves each year, had a pleasant air-conditioned place to study. In the summer, it was mostly a Peabody library. For the rest of the year, Vanderbilt students dominated. As Kuhlman pointed out, had the two institutions delayed, the war would have postponed construction, and after the war no one could build such a library for $2 million. The Education Library remained at Peabody as a part of JUL, continued to house the Library School, and was distinguished by its collection of older textbooks and its unrivaled Collection of Books on Children (over 4,700 items). In the same pattern, Vanderbilt soon owned several branch libraries in law, medicine, and science, while the Divinity Library moved into the Central Library, which everyone soon called the JUL.[35]

Two other less important joint initiatives followed the creation of JUL. In 1942, to meet a long-felt need in middle Tennessee, the GEB offered funds for a Nashville School of Social Work. Although Vanderbilt received and disbursed the funds and accepted primary fiscal responsibility for the school, it was jointly owned by Peabody, Vanderbilt, and Scarritt, which supplied its first director, Lori Lee Pederson. In a house on Twenty-first Avenue, across and north from JUL, the school could draw on courses in each of the three institutions. Some of its students lived in Peabody dorms. When GEB funding ended in 1951, Vanderbilt ended the partnership. The school continued as a branch of the University of Tennessee, and today of Tennessee State University. Again largely with GEB funds, the three institutions, plus Fisk University, established a Southern Rural Life Council in 1943. In this case, Peabody housed the council, which met during each summer, and in effect made it a part of its Division of Surveys and Field Studies. It was the first legal entity, for either Vanderbilt or Peabody, to include a primarily black institution.

WORLD WAR II AND PEABODY

By 1940, war seemed imminent. Students on campus debated whether the United States should come to the aid of Britain, an argument settled by Japan at Pearl Harbor. Selective Service, instituted in 1940, took some Peabody students and others who might have enrolled at the college. Defense expenditures soared, unemployment plummeted, depression-level state budgets recovered rapidly, and public schools grew. In 1940, the 3,891 enrollment at Peabody fell only 131 short of the peak enrollment of 1928–29, numbers it would not reach again until after the war and the invasion of veterans. With mobilization slow in the United States, not until the summer and fall of 1942 did the war begin to threaten colleges. At Peabody, it soon posed almost as many problems as the depression, but different ones—students no longer needed loans, teaching jobs soared, and morale remained high among what became an almost totally female student body, but enrollment and funding dropped as the college increasingly depended upon tuition as its main source of income.

Despite the severe drop in summer school enrollments, the entering class in the fall term of 1942 was the largest in history. These students were almost entirely women, most from the Nashville area and just out of high school. They helped shift the student profile of Peabody toward the Vanderbilt undergraduate pattern. With the war on and employment high, Nashville families took advantage of Peabody. The College of Arts and Science at Vanderbilt admitted only fifty women each fall and tried to draw many of these from areas outside middle Tennessee. Both its admission standards and tuition were very high. At Peabody, by 1943, only a handful of male students remained on campus. Only five or six men graduated that August, and, for the first time in Peabody history, women Ph.D.'s outnumbered men (six to five).[36] Women now held almost all class offices, dominated all clubs and organizations, and won almost all honors.

A welcome effect of this feminized Peabody was assured enrollments each year. The downside was that Peabody had too few male students to qualify for any of the military training programs available on most coeducational campuses. The large navy and naval reserve programs, for instance, allowed young men to enroll as civilian students but enlist in a speeded-up academic program that led on completion to advanced military positions. While Vanderbilt took advantage of several such programs, Peabody could qualify only for programs that brought military units to campus. It had to import its men. For sixteen months beginning in March 1943, the college hosted two closely related military training units, a fascinating interlude in Peabody history. The federal government rescued the school from budgetary shortfalls that would have created grave problems during full mobilization.

Peabody first signed a contract with the Army Air Force 333rd College Training Detachment. Its first six hundred trainees arrived on March 21, 1943. On campus for just under a year, the program brought 1,752 trainees to campus, of which 1,360 completed training. The 2185th Army Air Force Base Unit arrived next, continuing the same type of training but with a reduced command force. These trainees left in late June 1944 after one training cycle. In all, more than 2,300 trainees were on campus, and at any one time at least fifteen officers and enlisted men in command and training roles. This was the first stage of training for these young men, some of whom were married. They had passed tough screening tests, often had prior college training, and were on their way to flying for the Army Air Force. Besides academic work and military training at Peabody, they spent half days in the last four weeks of a twenty-one week training cycle at a nearby private airfield for twelve hours of dual flight training. They did not solo. In the winter, the smog

Army Air Force troops and Peabody coeds at the first formal dance, April, 1943. George Peabody College Records.

that hung over Nashville prevented morning flying. Everyone in the city still heated with soft, high-sulphur coal, turning winter-time Nashville into one of the unhealthiest cities in the United States. Soot covered every building, even when the air cleared.

These units occupied almost half the Peabody campus. By contract, they had full control of West and Graduate Halls. They turned the cafeteria in West into an army mess. Several female students, displaced from their dorms, moved to dorms on the Ward-Belmont campus. The units leased 80 percent of the SR for their command center and for physical training, 50 percent of Home Economics and 60 percent of Psychology for classrooms, and 80 percent of the library, where twice daily the troops gathered for supervised study halls. Except for the dorm-mess complex, the troops shared the rented academic areas with the regular students, who had to adjust their schedules to the times when classrooms or library spaces were vacant. One suspects that the army never used all the space it rented. The Library School, for example, continued to flourish on the top floor of the library, while female students joined the trainees in the use of recreational spaces such as the gym and pool.

Peabody profited from the excellent contract it negotiated. Although the army insisted upon a close accounting of every detail, in determining costs Peabody was able, for example, to list its buildings at their original value, without depreciation. For the first month, April 1943, it received $15,193 for instructional costs, and $9,671 for all subsequent months, which included salaries actually paid plus administrative costs. The college received $1.20 a day for each of the 611 persons who ate in the mess, and it rented building space for $3,889 a month. The army spent more than $25,000 for supplies (mess equipment, bunks for the now overcrowded dorms, textbooks, and, important for Peabody, several newly equipped science labs). Much of this remained after the troops left, down to silverware and trays in the cafeteria.

College life went on, and the coeds seemed to cope well with the inconveniences. None of the student publications reflect the expected griping; one coed rejoiced in the excitement, the sense of participation in the war effort, and the social gains on campus. The army command wanted to maintain high morale during this demanding training and supported a dance every Saturday night in the gym, a formal dance when each of the four training groups graduated, communal singing in the parlors of SR, and, in better weather, carefully orchestrated variety shows in front of the SR. At least two students became engaged to soldiers. An almost all-women's college offered unique social advantages for an army unit. In a history of the 333rd, the last officer in command had only high praise for Peabody hospitality and cooperation.[37]

Peabody had no easy task. Five professors planned the academic program to match army requirements. In a training cycle, each soldier had to complete 80 hours in mathematics, 180 in physics, 60 each in history, geography, and English, and 20 in medical aid. Peabody paid for seventeen full-time instructors, twelve part-time. It had to hire temporary help in mathematics and physics, the key subjects from the army perspective. Here the level of instruction may have suffered; one of the three temporary physics instructors was a Peabody junior. Yet, the army boasted that eleven instructors had Ph.D.'s—these were the regular Peabody professors. Wolfe, the head of music, even directed an army band, which played for all the dances and for the August 1943 commencement. The troops divided into two groups. While one took military drill in the morning, the other attended classes, and then they switched. This required instructors to be on duty all day and through the usual September vacation in 1943. In the evening, some had to supervise formal study periods in the library, even helping students with course material. Few students flunked out; only two left for "mental disabilities."[38]

The last unit marched from the dusty, hot campus in late June 1944, headed for Union Station, off to further their flight training. After the Normandy invasion, as it became clear that the Allies would win the war within the next year or two, the military began to wind down most campus programs and even began an early release of older draftees. By the fall of 1944, regular enrollments began to rise, making the loss of the troops easier to bear, at least financially. By early 1945, colleges began to prepare for veterans, now sure to attend college because of the GI Bill. Only in the June 1946 commencement was Peabody able to certify that twenty-seven former Peabody students had lost their lives in the war and to honor them with special recognition.[39]

As the troops trained in the spring of 1944, President Garrison was ill, unable to work. John N. Brewton, former director of the Division of Surveys and Field Studies (supported by an endowment of over $500,000 from the GEB) and by 1944 dean of the Senior College and Graduate School, took over as acting president. He negotiated the contract with the second army unit at Peabody. Garrison returned to work in August, and at that point Brewton chose to resume the directorship of DSFS. One of Garrison's last decisions was to appoint a new dean for the Senior College and Graduate School, William C. Jones from eastern Kentucky Teachers College. As Garrison began developing plans for a new building program on campus, he succumbed to what apparently was cancer on January 18. The board appointed Brewton acting president once again. He served until the May meeting of the board of trust, when it appointed Henry Harrison Hill as the president needed to guide the college through the difficult and challenging postwar years.

But the death of Garrison, a mere administrator, is not the proper ending for Peabody's story in these years of crisis. On September 11, 1945, Charles Edgar Little died in a Nashville hospital, two months short of eighty years old. He was seventy-six when he finally retired in 1941 as professor of Latin and the first secretary to the board of trust. His was the last campus tie to Peabody Normal. He had enrolled as a Peabody student in 1885, known every president of the college, beginning with

Eben Stearns, and spent sixty years at Peabody. The last acting head of Peabody Normal and the first appointed professor at George Peabody College, he had helped Payne plan the campus. Since 1937 he had been the only surviving member of the original George Peabody faculty of 1914. He, like Payne, always lived on campus, in a college residence. As an emeritus professor, he continued to teach summer courses, roam his beloved campus, and work on a final writing project. Little was the last professor of classical languages at Peabody, ending a tradition stretching back to 1785. Peabody students, from then on, had to enroll in Latin and Greek classes at Vanderbilt or do without. Almost all did without.

CHAPTER ELEVEN

The Peabody of Henry H. Hill

AT THE END OF WORLD WAR II, GEORGE PEABODY COLLEGE for Teachers faced many challenges. For the next fifteen years, it met most of these quite successfully. In many respects, this was a golden age at Peabody, comparable to the twenties. Enrollments were high. The College never suffered a single operating deficit. The campus expanded to the east of Eighteenth Avenue. Three major new buildings met most, although not all, physical needs. For the first time in its history, Peabody used some new admission requirements to create a better qualified student body. It began, finally, to move toward clear rules for faculty selection, promotion, and tenure, and developed some aspects of faculty governance. Without major controversy, it integrated the campus. Among at least one hundred faculty appointees, at least ten were highly accomplished. Finally, Peabody made its first concerted effort to develop a few strong research programs, primarily in psychology and human development.

Yet, throughout the period Peabody was haunted by anxiety and by often realistic fears about its future. By 1964, after the most detailed self-study in its history, it seemed as if the recent success had somehow rested on a foundation of quicksand. And, indeed, the problems were many and growing, as the following story will make clear. In one sense, the mission of Peabody was clear. In study after study, faculty and administrators reiterated it—to be the best professional school for teachers and educational leaders in America. It was to be for teachers what medical schools were for physicians. It was never this simple. It occupied a unique niche in American higher education, but it was not clear that a fully independent, private, and largely graduate professional school for teachers could gain the support it needed to survive. Such an achievement would have required exceptional leadership, from both faculty and administrators. This it did not have. After 1962, the College found that it could not meet its annual costs, could not retain the needed enrollment, and thus it increasingly floundered in desperate efforts to find a viable role. By the inflation-haunted seventies, the story of Peabody became a sad story, a story made sadder still by the confession of failure that lay behind its voluntary annexation by Vanderbilt in 1979. But this later story, informed by the advantage of hindsight, should not conceal its successes after 1945. To an extent, it owed these successes to a new chancellor.

HENRY HARRISON HILL

Just after World War II ended, and before the first wave of veterans inundated the campus, fifty-one year-old Henry Harrison Hill became president of Peabody in the fall of 1945. Next to Bruce Payne, he would serve longer, and have more impact on Peabody, than any other president. Less passionate, impulsive, and imaginative than Payne, Hill proved a much better administrator. Tall, slender, a bit formal in bearing, and in all ways a gentle man, he was instinctively cautious, moderate on most issues, and an expert at building consensus. He was not a scholar. After some early teaching, he spent his career in educational administration, and by 1945 no one in the field was better known or more respected. He would eventually hold every top elected position in his profession. His aversion to risks may have prevented Peabody from faltering much sooner than it did. On the other hand, such caution may have prevented Peabody from making the difficult early choices that could have allowed it to continue as an independent college.

Hill was no ideologue. He worked well with an increasingly business-oriented board of trust, winning their full respect and almost reflexive support. The board honored him in every possible way: a starting salary of $11,500 (followed by a series of major raises), a refurbished presidential mansion, a large expense account, and free membership in the exclusive Belle Meade Country Club. His willingness to accept this membership symbolizes not only a shift away from the progressive, even populist, stance of Bruce Payne but also Hill's realization that he had to cultivate wealthy Nashvillians to win local support for Peabody. While highly conscious of developmental strategies, Hill did not have Payne's persuasive ability and he did not like begging. At times he backed away from the demands of major campaigns.

Hill stood for a position in the field of education. He was an eloquent spokesperson for the American public school system, which he viewed as a great experiment in universal education, at least through high school. Hill defended the system against a growing cacophony of criticism during the cold-war years and during the concern about mediocrity that followed Sputnik in 1957. Although he did not oppose special attention for gifted students, most students in the public schools hovered around the average, and Hill became their advocate. With universal attendance, most students could not match the achievement of the select students in earlier schools. Now, for the first time, public schools had at least to baby-sit all children (Hill noted that the schools excelled in this custodial role) and try to provide knowledge and skills to a diverse group. Hill defended social promotions, favored vocational courses for those who needed them, and rejoiced in what so many critics lambasted—the hundred or more courses offered in large high schools, courses that were necessary if all students were to receive a worthwhile education, whatever their level of intellect and prior learning. He, like Payne, referred to this as a "democratic" system. He loved it, and in literally dozens of speeches at Peabody, around the country, and abroad, he defended the type of schools the United States had developed and the demanding goals set for them. In his term at Peabody, he also supported a critical expansion of the scope of public education to encompass children who were physically handicapped or academically retarded. Peabody would soon lead in the field of special education.

No one knew the public schools better than Hill. Like his two predecessors, he was born in North Carolina, at Statesville. He first studied in a private elementary school, then moved to the Statesville Male Academy, a demanding school formerly headed by his father. He matriculated at Davidson College before he was sixteen and after three years at Davidson spent an interlude farming. In 1916, he accepted a teaching position in Walnut Ridge, Arkansas. After a summer term at the University of Virginia in 1918, he moved up to school superintendent in Walnut Ridge, returning to the University of Virginia to complete his B.A. and then his M.A. in 1921. He became principal of a Little Rock high school, and then again superintendent in Walnut Ridge. In 1927–28, he completed his Ph.D. at Teachers College, Columbia. He served as state high school supervisor in Arkansas for a year before moving to the University of Kentucky as a professor of education. In 1930, he became superintendent of the Lexington public schools, where he remained for ten years, continuing his affiliation with the university. In 1941 he became assistant superintendent of the St. Louis school system but after a year moved back to the University of Kentucky as a dean. In August 1942, he accepted one of the most honored jobs in public school administration, superintendent of the Pittsburgh school system. His salary of $15,000 was the second highest in the country for superintendents. By then Hill was active in national educational organizations, and when he came to Peabody in 1945, he was president of the American Association of School Administrators. His only remaining step upward in educational administration was as president of a major teachers' college such as Peabody. He not only remained at Peabody until his retirement in 1961 but also came back as acting president in 1966–67. He lived to see, and suffer, the merger with Vanderbilt in 1979 and died eight years later at the age of ninety-two.[1]

When Hill came to Peabody in the fall of 1945, he found plenty of problems. The physical plant, although structurally sound, was in desperate need of maintenance to take care of leaking roofs, cracking or dull paint, leaking plumbing, an aging heating plant, and antiquated lighting. The campus, from an administrative perspective, seemed to him little short of anarchy, despite the efforts of President Garrison to impose order. Everyone reported to the president, who faced an impossible workload. Peabody still had no organized academic departments with heads or chairs. No one had tight control over business affairs. Almost any student was welcome, and almost anyone admitted could graduate. Grading standards remained low. Beyond all this lay the problem of identity or mission. Essentially, Peabody had two student bodies. Recent high school graduates, most local and young women, comprised at least half of the regular-season enrollment. They soon demanded a typical undergraduate experience, with fraternities, clubs, athletics, and publications. The other students were either teachers or educational administrators, serious, older, from all over the South and increasingly from northern states, with a focused, professional goal. They dominated the summer school. Could Peabody serve both student bodies? Hill doubted it.

SELF STUDIES AND REVIEWS

Like most new college presidents, Hill appointed a special committee to consider, in his words, the unique function of Peabody. It went on to conduct the most through examination of Peabody ever attempted, and produced a statement of mission and 148 specific recommendations for change. Hill asked the faculty to nominate members for this committee and from their suggestions chose eleven. Soon everyone referred to the group as the Committee of Eleven. After it completed its report, in June 1946, Hill decided to continue the committee as the Faculty Committee on Planning and Policy, soon with both appointed and elected members. For a time, many still called it the Committee of Eleven, regardless of how many members served on it. This strategic planning committee remained until a new administrative organization went into effect in 1963, when many of its functions shifted to two new councils, one on academic affairs, one on administration.

The original Committee of Eleven was about as distinguished as the Peabody faculty permitted. Its chair was Joseph R. Whitaker, the distinguished geographer. The deans of both the undergraduate and graduate schools served, as did three of the best-known older professors—Alfred Crabb in English, Fremont Wirth in history, and Frank Wren, the Julia Sears Professor of Mathematics. John Brewton, who had been acting president, was on the committee. For the first time in the history of Peabody, an important committee included a woman, professor of elementary education Maycie Southall, one of the first women outside nursing and physiology to gain full professorial rank.

With special funding from the GEB, the committee involved every faculty member in the process via twenty-two subcommittees. It used consultants from around the country—board members, several Peabody alumni who held college or university presidencies, representatives of foundations (including Vanderbilt's just departed chancellor, O. C. Carmichael, president of the Carnegie Foundation), bureaucrats from the Department of State and the U.S. Office of Education (including Harold Benjamin of the Office of Education, who would later move to Peabody), and leaders in other colleges of education. Of particular note, the advisors included H. L. Caswell of Teachers College, Columbia, and a former Peabody professor, and John Dale Russell from the Office of Education. Caswell would return as a member of a critical external review committee only three years later, while Russell would direct a major 1962 study of ways to insure closer cooperation between Peabody and Vanderbilt.

In its 1946 report, *Peabody College Looks Ahead,* the committee began with the problem of function or mission. It succinctly reaffirming Peabody's traditional role—"to provide the best possible instruction and educational guidance for the schools and colleges of the nation." It repeated an earlier statement of purpose, "the selection, education, and continuous development of those who are to teach."[2] It noted Peabody's distinctive heritage, private and independent status, relationship to Vanderbilt and Scarritt, and special role in graduate education. Thus, Peabody should become, more than in the immediate past, a purely professional school and give up its role as a liberal arts college for local undergraduates not committed to teaching.

The committee recommended that Peabody approve no more social fraternities and discourage the continuation of the three already on campus. (Beginning with a sorority in 1926, students had by 1946 organized two social sororities and one fraternity, although these were not affiliated with any national organization, had no separate houses, and were not very exclusive.) The committee also rejected any move to intercollegiate athletics. Unfortunately, but perhaps necessarily because of financial constraints, Peabody would never fully implement these suggestions, remaining ambivalent about its undergraduate program. The college permitted two additional sororities and one additional fraternity to form in the next few years, as well as some intercollegiate or extramural club sports. Failing to give undergraduates what they could get at other colleges, Peabody also never managed to move to a fully professional program. It had the worst of two worlds. Only annexation by Vanderbilt in 1979 solved this dilemma, when Peabody's undergraduates joined the larger Vanderbilt undergraduate culture.

The Committee of Eleven offered some quite prescient recommendations. One group involved the almost chaotic state of administration, another the lack of standards, and a third badly needed new or improved academic offerings. Its very recommendations attest to how out of step Peabody was with other colleges. The committee asked for a new office of student personnel; for someone to oversee or direct student teachers; for a policy handbook or faculty manual to provide guidelines on appointments, promotions, and, tenure; and for formal academic departments with appointed or elected chairs. Until now, only the catalogue's course listings suggested disciplinary boundaries, and on the basis of these listings, the committee identified twenty departments. It asked for some recognition of, and guidance for, faculty professional activities and research. Finally, it recommended one quarter off every three years for any professor who taught for twelve months each year (Hill and the board accepted this), and extra leave for faculty with research proposals or planned publications.

Regarding standards, the committee ventured onto new ground. It wanted Peabody to stress quality, to institute standards for student admission and graduation that compared to those of its main competitors—Teachers College, Harvard, Chicago, and Stanford. Through its open-admission policies, Peabody had attracted plenty of able students, but also many mediocre ones, almost all of whom could graduate, such were the grading standards. The committee dared to reject this tradition, and to ask for selective admission, at least to the extent of excluding largely C and D high school students. Without specifying the standards, it also wanted tighter graduate admission requirements. For undergraduates, it proposed the early development of a core curriculum that required fifty-one hours of work, not just in the first two years but spread over all four. This would render meaningless any further references to a junior college. It recommended the elimination of nonprofessional degrees and asked for very high qualifications for departments that offered a Ph.D. Finally, on an issue that proved intractable throughout Peabody's history, it asked for higher grading standards. It recommended annual reports from the registrar to all faculty that revealed the grades for each department and professor. Apparently, the committee believed this would shame lax professors into tougher student evaluations. It also demanded that all courses at Peabody terminate in final exams of more than an hour, scheduled so that no student took more than two in any given day, exams that professors would actually grade. It is doubtful that half the teachers of large summer courses ever graded any final exams. Again, what is so remarkable about these proposals is what they reveal about what had prevailed before.

Finally, the committee dealt with Peabody's academic program. It suggested new courses in human growth and development, a learning aids center, more clinical laboratories, and expanded work on exceptional children, with as much emphasis upon mental as physical disabilities. It identified weak areas or those with insufficient faculty. Peabody, it believed, needed faculty and coursework in anthropology and philosophy, additional psychologists (depleted during the war), a rebuilt physical education department, a political scientist interested in world problems (a key concern at the end of the war), improved work in the natural sciences, more scholarship aid for needy students, and some special courses for veterans.[3]

Peabody College Looks Ahead guided policy making for the next decade. Aided by the continuing Faculty Committee on Policy and Planning, Hill tried to implement most of the report's recommendations. One nagging problem remained—what to do with the undergraduate program. The faculty did adopt a broad and demanding general education or core curriculum for undergraduates that remained, with only minor changes, until 1979 and beyond. But it did not force all undergraduates to commit to a career in education, and it continued to enroll (but to a large extent not retain beyond the sophomore year) undergraduates not clearly committed to teaching—by some reckonings, up to 30 percent of the total.

Hill also wanted the advice of an external panel. Such a panel could not resolve the undergraduate issue, but it did stimulate a further reorganization of the Peabody academic program. It led, indirectly, to the recruitment of four of the best-paid and most eminent professors in the postwar era. In part with GEB funds, and with GEB encouragement, Hill appointed a three-member external review committee, which visited Peabody in April 1949. It consulted with key faculty and board members and tried to digest the work of the Committee of Eleven and other more recent surveys. Hill deliberately selected three men who knew Peabody but were in the North: Dean H. L. Caswell of Teachers College, who had consulted with the Committee of Eleven and had been a Peabody professor just before the war; William F. Russell, president of Teachers College and also a former Peabody professor; and George Stoddard, president of the University of Illinois and former director of the Division of Child Study at Iowa State University. As usual, such outside panelists wanted to see the big picture, make daring proposals, and leave the hard task of implementation to the locals. The brief report, a bit cavalier and at points patronizing, triggered a critical period of agonized decision making at Peabody comparable to the debates in 1962 over cooperation with Vanderbilt and in 1979 over merging with Vanderbilt or some other university.

The committee's conclusions about Peabody's undergraduate college echoed some already voiced by Hill. To some extent, its findings were shaped by the unique 1948–49 enrollment pattern. In the regular fall term, 1,370 undergraduates overwhelmed the 579 graduate students. Most were just out of high school (with the exception of some local veterans), 71 percent in commuting distance, and 84 percent from Tennessee. Only 20 percent of freshmen ended up as teachers, in part because half had dropped out by the junior year. The summer school reversed these patterns, with graduate students in the majority and almost all the students committed to a career in education. The committee noted that Peabody's undergraduate program was less conservative than most in the South but otherwise undistinguished. It took up most of the faculty's time in the regular year and diverted resources from the professional areas but admittedly also contributed two-thirds of the tuition in the regular year. Peabody could continue the undergraduate program, even improve it, and become largely a liberal arts college. But to do so would violate its traditional role and the mission reaffirmed by the Committee of Eleven.

This led to a daring proposal. Peabody should phase out its junior college over two years and limit its junior and senior years to students already committed to education as a career. Only such a strategy would make it, once again, a professional college. Professional educators could acquire a general education background before entering Peabody. The committee believed that Peabody could effect the transition in five years and lose about $500,000 to $600,000, but that it should be able to get foundations to cover this loss. Gradually, this new, better-focused mission should increase graduate and senior college enrollments enough to make up for the lost tuition. The visiting committee did not explore the problems the transition would create—how it would effect such departments as art and music, how the program in public health nursing could continue without lower-level courses, how the possible reduction in numbers or major shifts in teaching assignments would affect the faculty. And Hill and his faculty knew that the estimated loss of income was too low.

Along with this narrowed focus on professional education, the committee suggested a restructuring of the curriculum into four "educational task forces." Peabody soon referred to these as divisions. The committee did not necessarily envision an end to disciplinary departments but wanted to group the small departments at Peabody into four functional divisions with a head for each: teaching and curriculum development, school administration and community leadership, human development and guidance, and education and social progress. While this organization resembled most liberal arts colleges' divisions of humanities, social sciences, and natural sciences, in Peabody's case the divisions would have a more directive role over departments, including curriculum development and faculty appointments. The committee also suggested more in-service training of teachers, some of this off campus, and closer ties to Vanderbilt. Peabody adopted the new divisions, but because their role remained unclear the change had little effect. Note that the four divisions did not include the Library School, the School of Public Health Nursing, and the rapidly expanding Department (later School) of Music.[4]

Peabody came close to abolishing its freshman and sophomore years. The crucial determinant turned out to be the GEB rejection of a proposed $500,000 grant to fund the transition over five years. Although the GEB was open to a revised and better-clarified request in 1950, by then the Peabody faculty and Hill had decided the risks were too great. Most university presidents had advised Hill to be cautious, for no other college had tried such a radical experiment. This advice played into Hill's natural timidity. His faculty and the board would have gone along had he wanted to push it, as an extended debate in the summer of 1949 revealed. When key faculty members and board members met at a special dinner at the Belle Meade Country Club in June, most faculty present spoke in favor of the shift, voted overwhelmingly to apply to the GEB for the $500,000, and seemed to believe that this move might make Peabody once again a pioneer.[5]

By early 1950, Hill and the Peabody faculty had decided to keep the undergraduate program and even expand it. It now advertised Peabody as both a liberal arts college and a professional school of education. In 1951, the board authorized up to a hundred scholarships of $150 each to attract abler high school graduates. In 1956 it stopped requiring all undergraduates to take courses in education before graduation. In 1958 it devoted an issue of the *Reflector* to the benefits of a Peabody education for new high school graduates, whatever their proposed career.[6]

THE BOOM YEARS

In his report to the board in 1950, Hill announced that Peabody would remain, permanently, a four-year college, but that it would implement the second part of the report, the new division system. Hill applied successfully to the GEB for $250,000 to make these structural changes. He also announced that Peabody would develop more work in special education and would soon lead the nation in this field (see chapter 12).[7] By then, Peabody was in the midst of the greatest boom in its history. From 1949 to 1954, almost everything went right. It enjoyed its highest enrollments, recruited its ablest postwar professors, and conducted the college's most ambitious and exciting summer schools.

In many ways, federal policies underwrote this boom. Most important was the G.I. Bill, which funded higher education for World War II veterans. They flocked to Peabody, just as they inundated colleges everywhere. By 1949, almost half of Peabody's tuition income came from veterans. In that year, 833 veterans enrolled in the fall quarter, 1,259 in the summer school. The numbers dropped off in the fall of 1950 but continued to grow in the booming summer school, reaching an all-time high of 1,905 in 1951. Unlike those at Vanderbilt, the veterans at Peabody blended into the general student population. Older, serious, often married, they matched the profile of graduate students who had attended Peabody all along. Many veterans who returned to teaching or supervisory positions in southern schools took advantage of the G.I. Bill to attend Peabody's famous summer school. Their intermittent enrollment meant that the veterans' rush continued well into the fifties, after it had subsided at liberal arts colleges. One effect was gender equity. For two or three years, for the only time in Peabody history, men outnumbered women. In the fall quarter of 1950, for example, men outnumbered women by 1,167 to 942. When veteran enrollment declined, the old pattern of three women to one man resumed.[8]

The second federal boon involved facilities. By the fall of 1946, the Federal Public Housing Administration had provided most of the funds for fifty prefabricated apartment units for veterans, plus eighteen single efficiency apartments in two barracks. Contractors moved these from a military base in Georgia to the far southeast campus, along Capers and Nineteenth, an area that had grown up in bushes and small trees. Soon dubbed Veteran's Village, it housed more than three hundred people, with a grocery, laundry facilities, and nursery school. This was a gift to the college, except for the expense of connecting utilities and building streets and sidewalks. Peabody received four additional buildings from the Federal Works Agency, all moved from the now closed Camp Forest near Tullahoma. One became a dining facility at the H. G. Hill Camp in Cheatham County, one was located next to the Demonstration School, and two large, U-shaped frame buildings were placed along Eighteenth Avenue, just east and north of Confederate Hall. One of these, Smith Hall (after Samuel Smith, who negotiated the transfer), contained classrooms. The other became a temporary but badly needed Student Center, with a snack bar, a second campus cafeteria, and a bookstore and post office. These plain wooden buildings tided Peabody over its period of highest enrollment. Twenty-six of the veteran's apartments remained on campus as late as 1967.[9]

The growing music department at Peabody helped make the summer school a major cultural event in Nashville. Irving Wolfe, who became head of music in

Veteran's Village. Photographic Archives of Vanderbilt University.

Smith Hall, an Army surplus, prefabricated classroom buildings along Eighteenth Avenue, named after Provost Charles Smith. Photographic Archives of Vanderbilt University.

1940, built a small empire. By 1950, his was the largest department at Peabody, with nine professors and four instructors, some part-time. The music program had taken over the top floor of SR, with its growing music library and full-time librarian on the east wing. Soon, the music offices and performance rooms spilled over into the anterooms around the auditorium. By 1951, more than half of the musicians in the new Nashville Symphony—fifty-one—had a Peabody connection. The symphony gave at least one Peabody concert during each summer quarter, joined by other musical events such as performances by the Fisk Jubilee Singers. In a tradition that continued for two decades, the music department also presented one opera or operetta each summer. Its choir performed at each Sunday evening vespers. For two summers, 1950 and 1951, the musical presentations included six to eight weekly concerts by some of the most eminent musicians in the United States, most from New York or northern cities. On Saturdays, NBC broadcast these concerts on radio. The person responsible for these concerts, Roy Harris, was the most eminent professor ever to teach at Peabody, although he remained for only the 1949–50 year and the summers of 1949, 1950, and 1951.

After the loss of one of the two full professors in the music department in 1948, Hill pulled off a coup in the spring of 1949. He hired both Roy Harris, then at Utah State University, and his wife, Johana Harris, a well-known concert pianist.

He paid Roy Harris $5,000 as professor and composer in residence, Johana Harris $4,000 as associate professor and performer in residence, and also helped them finance a home purchase. At Peabody, everyone soon referred to Roy Harris as America's preeminent composer, and he was in fact one of the three or four most active and honored composers in the country. Born in Oklahoma and proud of that heritage, Harris grew up in Los Angeles and graduated from Berkeley. In 1926 he went to Paris, soon supported by a Guggenheim fellowship, to study the new trends in music, particularly those that broke with the older Germanic tradition. There he joined at least thirty other young American expatriate composers studying at the American Conservatory, among them Aaron Copland, Marc Blitzstein, and Virgil Thomson. Contrary to their expectations, all these young composers studied with a relatively young woman, Nadia Boulanger, who soon became famous for her American students. Back home, most of them tried to create a distinctive American music by blending aspects of regional and folk music and jazz into their compositions. None did more to search out American themes than Harris, although Copland would become better known for his folk adaptations.

By 1949, all the major orchestras performed Harris's symphonies. While at

The summer opera for 1954, *Die Fledermaus*. Photographic Archives of Vanderbilt University.

Peabody, he completed, and at its opening directed, "Kentucky Spring" for the Boston Symphony Orchestra. He had a second income from commissions and royalties and was often away from campus. In the summer of 1950 he helped establish the Cumberland Forest Music Festival at the University of the South at Sewanee, with the major concerts repeated at Peabody, the festival's cosponsor. In the spring of 1950 Harris and his wife asked for a five-year leave of absence to assume a Mellon-supported post in Pittsburgh that included a college position but primarily reflected an effort to stimulate a musical renaissance in that city. In the summer of 1951 the Harrises returned to their festival and to Peabody, but few believed by then that they would ever return permanently to Nashville, although the catalogue continued to list them for the next few years. The music department would never again recruit a composer of such ability, although Copland and Randall Thompson later taught short master classes at Peabody.[10]

The second Peabody composer of note, Charles F. Bryan, moved even closer to the folk music tradition. In 1952 he composed the haunting music for a play, *Strangers in the World,* presented by the Vanderbilt theater department during its golden age. The story of snake handlers in Appalachia, which included live snakes on stage and singing by a church choir, probably ranks as the most memorable play ever presented at either Peabody or Vanderbilt. After this acclaimed composition, Bryan wrote the music for a folk opera, *Singing Billy,* with lyrics by Donald Davidson, the Vanderbilt Fugitive poet, which Peabody presented as its opera for 1955. The work celebrated the life of William Walker, one of the founders of the shaped-note or old-harp church music in the South, a genre that fascinated both Davidson and Bryan. But Bryan's best-known composition was probably "Bell Witch Cantata," performed at Carnegie Hall.[11]

The summer school's intellectual fare matched the musical. Each summer brought eminent lecturers in education (William Kilpatrick and James Conant), on literary issues (Jesse Stuart, Howard Mumford Jones, and John Mason Brown), and on world affairs, all of whom shared one characteristic: All were men. But change was in the air. In 1948, the board of trust elected its first women trustee, Eleanore H. Meade from Louisiana, who served until her death in 1969, although in the early years she never received a single committee appointment. In 1952, the commencement speaker was a woman, the president of Vassar, a first for Peabody. A few years later, Margaret Mead was a featured summer speaker.[12]

The summer schools of the early fifties continued all the older traditions. The daily assemblies on the lawn in front of the SR had declined to one a week, and after 1948, the stunt nights became square-dancing contests among the state clubs. The annual watermelon cutting posed a logistical challenge as the number of melons required grew from 800 in 1948 to 1,200 in 1951 and 1952, all brought by truck from a Texas farm and smothered in crushed ice on the day of the squishy feast. The Sunday evening vespers services retained the old format but gained in quality and became a valued Nashville asset. A year went into the planning of each of the eight to ten services. Only a few Nashville pastors and one rabbi now participated, for most speakers were nationally known theologians or preachers. Thousands attended the services, and the *Reflector* in its December edition each year published the addresses. Few could forget the opening prayers by the beloved but now aged L. C. Crawford, or the concluding choir presentation of "Now the Day Is Done," followed by a reception in the SR. The weekly summer excursions now involved buses, not trains. These summer schools infused the Nashville economy with more than $1 million each year.

Another tradition continued for both the May and August commencements. On the morning of graduation, the Peabody faculty served an outdoor breakfast to graduates and their families. The breakfast featured lectures, usually light—Sarah Cannon (Minnie Pearl) was a favorite, and author Jesse Stuart a perennial

Roy Harris (at head of table with a cup in hand) conducting a music seminar at Peabody, probably in 1951. Photograph by Knutson-Bowers. Photographic Archives of Vanderbilt University.

speaker. Eminent alumni received the Sullivan Award and, later, other awards, and each graduate received an iris bulb from the gardens planted by Roy Appleton, so that they could take home a part of Peabody.

By 1951, the summer school numbers were staggering. The enrollment reached 4,303 in 1950, 4,338 in 1951, the two largest summer enrollments not only at Peabody but at any institution in Nashville. Hundreds more people attended at least a dozen summer conferences and workshops. These students, some with families in tow, filled all Vanderbilt's dorms and nearby boardinghouses. Peabody assigned three students to rooms intended for only two. The campus hummed, as multiple activities filled almost every evening, with evening concerts drawing more than three thousand. Peabody had to rent two large tents and five hundred chairs as overflow classrooms. By 1953, the enrollment began to drop—something of a relief, but a threat to tuition income—yet the general pattern of the summer school continued for the next two decades.[13]

The years of record enrollment allowed Peabody to catch up on long-delayed maintenance and to plan new buildings. By 1950, the college had paved all campus roads, expanded sidewalks, created new parking lots (including the spaces around Magnolia Circle), and dumped a hundred truckloads of fill dirt to grade and grass much of the campus, until Peabody looked much as it does today. Guiding these improvements was Herbert F. Clark, director of business and finance. Hill recruited him in 1946 from the executive offices of John D. Rockefeller Jr. in New York City, paid him more than any professor, and relied on him completely. Next to Hill, Clark wielded the most influence on campus. Self-confident and tough-minded, he rendered detailed financial reports each year, guided investment by the board of trust, and even at times made recommendations about academic policies.

Guided by Clark, Hill postponed any permanent new buildings until maintenance was complete. Only in the spring of 1951 did the board approve two major projects, a new classroom building and a complex of forty-four married-student apartments (later named for former president Garrison), a commitment of $650,000. Both cost more than expected. Since the apartments would be self-liquidating, Peabody borrowed the money from the Federal Housing and Home Finance Agency and easily made subsequent payments on the bonds. It had accumulated enough surplus to pay for Payne Hall, dedicated in 1952, the first centrally air-conditioned building on campus. It lay just southwest of Industrial Arts, and just north of the site that Bruce Payne had reserved for a Knapp School of Country Life.

With Payne Hall, Peabody had enough classrooms to accommodate future enrollment, but critical space problems remained. The college needed a physical education facility (planned in detail but never built) and a music building with a large auditorium (discussed but never funded). Another need was new and better laboratories. This led, at first, to a refurbishing of the top floor of Psychology and later to two large research buildings (the Human Development Lab immediately behind the Psychology Building, now Hobbs Hall, and the Learning Disabilities Lab). With Payne Hall up and running, Peabody could tear down Smith Hall. In 1956, elaborate planning got underway for a new Student Center to replace the temporary one. Since this was also an income-producing property, Peabody received a federal loan for its construction, which began in 1958. The center, ready for use in June 1959, was the most costly building on campus, close to $1 million. It was also one of the ugliest, with no hint of the traditional classical style. Located south of Confederate, it was fortunately well east of the main quadrangle, but by choice Peabody decided to maintain an open mall from the Student Center to the Administration Building, which left a gap between the Psychology Building and the last dorm built on the Peabody campus—Gillette Hall in 1963. Gillette also cost almost $1 million, as inflation sent construction costs soaring, and involved federal loans for a self-liquidating asset. The last Peabody building to conform to the original campus master plan and to reflect the classical style, it completed the east side of the quadrangle. Not long after its completion, regular-year student enrollment failed to fill Peabody's five dorms (four for women and West Hall for men).[14]

The SR also underwent modification. In 1958 the Student Christian Association needed a home. It had temporarily occupied two college-owned residences, one on the site of the new facilities of the Bill Wilkerson Speech and Hearing Center. The widow of former board member William Hume provided the funds to convert the SR's west parlor into beautiful little Hume Chapel, and the Stallworth family funded a pipe organ, used by the music department as well as students. Notably, organized religious life on campus was still confessional and Christian. No facilities existed for non-Christians. A new, staffed international house on Eighteenth Avenue did offer a meeting place and an area for small religious gatherings for the growing number of Asian students.

Hill and Clark decided to cooperate with Vanderbilt and Scarritt in an urban-development scheme. This could have reshaped the Peabody campus, had the college continued to grow. It did not, and Peabody's elaborate plans became pie in the sky. At Vanderbilt, which desperately wanted land to the south and west of its campus, urban-renewal schemes dated back to 1957. Not until 1961 did the three schools jointly apply to the Nashville Planning Commission for an urban-renewal district that would allow expansion for each campus. Under federal legislation, local governments could apply to the U.S. Housing and Home Finance Agency for grants to support the renewal of decaying areas of cities. If the agency approved, local governments could use eminent domain, if necessary, to force property owners in such designated areas to sell at a fair market price. Preliminary federal approval for the schools' scheme came in 1962, but renewal work would have to wait until after 1965. Peabody's urban-renewal area, as shown on 1962 maps, extended from the campus east to an alley beyond Sixteenth Avenue. Peabody could have acquired this land for more than $3 million, but probably not without the kind of extended legal battle with the owners that Vanderbilt had to fight to get its new land.[15]

Peabody never used eminent domain to purchase land and bought only lots, when they came up for sale, as far east as Seventeenth Avenue. It remained on good terms with its immediate neighbors. The college eventually acquired full ownership of both sides of Eighteenth Avenue from Edgehill to Horton, most lots on the west side of Seventeenth, and a few scattered lots on the east side of Seventeenth that it eventually would sell to buy land closer to the campus.

RACIAL INTEGRATION

During this period of campus building and modest expansion, Hill had to confront new racial policies, an issue that led to prolonged and bitter controversy at Vanderbilt. Nashville became one of the most active cities in the civil rights movement. The always moderate and cautious style of Hill meant that, in admitting blacks, Peabody at every stage would lag behind a hesitant Vanderbilt and a more forward-looking Scarritt. Under Payne, Peabody had tried to lead the South, not in overthrowing segregation, but in giving more than lip service to the idea of separate but equal. It had been more daring than most southern colleges. No more. Hill, with his apprehensions about the future and his fiscal conservatism did not dare risk losing students or income by taking a leadership role. He favored gradual desegregation and not, he often said, complete integration. He foresaw its inevitability and knew that foundation support would soon depend upon it. Yet, while he was president, Peabody took only the first, limited step toward integration in 1954 and would not take another step for a decade, under President Felix Robb. The story of racial integration at Peabody stayed low-key, in part because Peabody worked hard to prevent outside publicity of its early initiatives. Board of trust records note the discussion of racial issues but never include any details. No campus publications aired the issues until Peabody implemented a new policy, and even then the *Reflector* offered only the briefest reports. Integration at Peabody was almost a secret.

As early as 1951, Hill had begun discussions with his executive committee about admitting selected black students to Peabody. The issue was very much in the air among southern institutions, since federal courts had, under the equality doctrine, forced many southern public universities to open their professional schools to black applicants. In a few cases, such as Louisiana, the courts would mandate integration of undergraduate colleges and universities by the early fifties. Many private colleges and universities had already integrated. In 1952 Scarritt admitted two black students. These students, according to course-sharing agreements, could enroll in courses at Vanderbilt and Peabody and use all JUL libraries, or a type of backdoor integration for Peabody. In 1953, Vanderbilt admitted its first black student to its

Divinity School. Such local precedents made it easier for Peabody to admit its first black graduate students in the summer of 1954.[16]

Hill tried to prepare all constituencies for each new step. In August 1951, he conducted a confidential poll of the faculty on two options: continue as a segregated college, at least for the next decade, or admit by general consent a handful of Negroes to the Library School or to post-M.A. work but refuse admission at all other levels to avoid competition with Fisk or Tennessee A&I. Of the sixty-three faculty who responded, only four voted for no integration at all. Some wanted full integration. Although in general the faculty believed that only a small minority of students would oppose such a policy, Hill could not poll the students and at the same time keep the issue confidential. In May 1952, in a new five-point program for Peabody, Hill simply stated that "Peabody should move ahead as rapidly as possible to remove racial barriers to graduate study in this institution."[17]

In an introduction to the confidential faculty poll, Hill listed several assumptions that not all faculty accepted. He assumed that blacks would soon be admitted to graduate and professional schools whenever equal facilities were not available in black schools. He believed that, within three, five, or ten years, all state universities would admit blacks to some professional or graduate schools. But he also believed that few blacks would apply to such schools or qualify for admission to such advanced study (an argument he would use before his board of trust). He also assumed that Peabody could confine the admission of blacks to a few deserving, modest, and well-behaved students, and that segregation, whether "legal" or "natural," would remain the norm for years in public schools and undergraduate colleges. Finally, Peabody had a responsibility to lead in education (already too late) but an equal responsibility "not to destroy her leadership by poor practical judgments or poor timing of any changes." It is difficult to imagine a more disarming approach to those who did not want to see racial patterns change.[18]

Hill faced considerable resistance in his executive committee, although he never identified its source. Opposing pressure came from those who had provided funds for new Peabody programs, particularly the Kellogg-funded Southern States Cooperative Program in Educational Administration, which was, in principle and by the desire of the Kellogg Foundation, open to black school administrators. If Peabody rejected black applicants, it might lose further funding. More critical, the Southern Education Foundation (SEF) in Atlanta, the successor of the Slater Fund, was willing to fund selected black students in Peabody's graduate programs in school administration. It pushed for the first Peabody initiative in 1954, and with a great deal of moral authority on its side. The Peabody Education Fund, after endowing George Peabody College for Teachers, left the remainder of its money to the Slater Fund and thus directly abetted the cause of black education. Implicit in this, in the wishes of George Peabody to aid all people in the South, and in the refusal of the Peabody Fund to accept a statement in early versions of the Tennessee appropriations that denominated George Peabody College a "white" institution—was Peabody's obligation to admit blacks as soon as such admissions became legal. The question, from the standpoint of the SEF, was why the college waited so long.

Working with SEF officials, Hill drafted a proposal to submit to his board in December 1953. Peabody would admit, in the summer of 1954, fourteen carefully selected principals of black schools, one each from thirteen states and the District of Columbia. State departments of education were to choose the students, and the SEF to provide them fellowships. Hill announced that Peabody would admit only school principals with an M.A. degree, a condition dropped in subsequent years. The board members present voted unanimously for this proposal but on such a sensitive issue polled absent members by mail ballot; this vote was never recorded, although Hill hinted that some voted against it.[19] Hill also noted that at least one black student would enroll in the Library School, assuring the SEF that Peabody would most likely continue the program in subsequent summers and would in fact admit a few of these fellows to regular-year coursework, even in some cases beyond their outside funding. But these first students received second-class treatment. They could not live on campus, for the first year could not eat in the cafeteria, and were never able to use the gym or swimming pool. They had a difficult time finding housing and had to pay too much for what was available. Even as late as 1966, Hill doubted that any college should force the full assimilation of black students or remove certain restrictions on their social life on an almost totally white campus. To him, very able black students—and he wanted no others—had to win their equality, not gain it by mandate.[20]

For nine years, during the early and dramatic civil rights struggle, Peabody did not move much closer to open admissions. In 1961 it admitted three black Woodrow Wilson fellows and a few blacks each year to the Library School. From 1954 to 1962, 146 blacks enrolled at Peabody, 89 in degree programs. By 1962, 35 had received degrees, including one Ph.D. and two Ed.Ds. The first doctoral candidate, Malvin M. Moore Jr. from Arkansas, enrolled in the first group of 14 in 1954 and received his Ed.D. in 1959. Most of the degrees were in educational administration and library science.[21] The black students were all but invisible on campus. No Peabody publications mentioned them, although a few black faces began to appear in graduation photographs. After the first year, black students could eat in the cafeteria but still could not live on campus.

A cautious Hill considered new initiatives but never acted and did not himself favor a fully open admission policy, particularly for undergraduates. When some faculty members continued to push for open admission, Hill rebuffed their proposals. In 1961, Nicholas Hobbs, a new and already successful chair of one of the four main divisions at Peabody, and thus with enough clout to argue with Hill, pointed out several powerful reasons, beyond moral concern, that mandated that

Peabody move forthwith to open admissions at all levels. In particular, he wanted immediate integration of the Demonstration School as a way of supporting the gradual integration of Nashville public schools. Now near the end of his tenure as president, Hill offered a revealing response. He wanted justice for blacks. He was proud of Peabody's selective admission policy and of the achievements of its black graduate students. But for the foreseeable future, he said, he wanted to keep the door ajar but not open all the way. Concerned faculty realized that the old man would not budge from this position, and he never did.[22]

Only well after Hill's retirement in 1961 did President Felix Robb propose to the executive committee, in April 1963, that it approve the admission of all students to Peabody without regard to race, creed, or color. The committee unanimously accepted this simple resolution: "Admission to all programs of the College shall be based upon competence, character, and merit." In its May 1963 meeting, by unanimous vote of those present, the board simply approved this action. The resolution's wording came from Nicholas Hobbs, who had pushed Robb as forcefully as he had Hill. Robb, as dean, had favored further integration but dutifully followed Hill's wishes. When he became president, his first order of business involved new cooperation, and possible merger, with Vanderbilt (see chapter 12); the integration issue could wait. He noted that several board members resented the increasing federal pressure for open admissions and believed the open policy adopted by Vanderbilt in 1962 was a sham. Vanderbilt did not really want black undergraduates (in part true) but acted purely to insure foundation and government funding.[23]

Robb wooed his board in 1963 with compelling practical arguments. Almost all southern universities were now integrated, he noted. At least two Scarritt undergraduates had already enrolled in courses at Peabody. Many blacks already attended conferences and workshops. He cited irreversible national trends, the need for Peabody to provide international leadership, and the costs suffered by universities that still resisted integration. Without integration, the ablest faculty would refuse to come to Peabody. Grants would dry up, and soon even government funding would end. But like Hill, Robb tried to soften the blow for anyone still opposed. He noted that higher admission standards and rising tuition at Peabody would mean very few black applicants. Newly required ACT test scores, he believed, would eliminate most blacks (Peabody did not in fact set a minimum score for admission). Robb even suggested personal interviews for prospective undergraduates. He promised that Peabody would only gradually admit black undergraduates to dorms and cited special but unspecified procedures to govern their use of the swimming pool.[24]

Although the new policy took effect in 1964–65 and applied to all Peabody programs, the head of the Demonstration School objected. The executive committee promised not to require black admissions until the director of the school approved (this came the next year) and the board agreed. Back of this, in all likelihood, were parents who paid the tuition at the Demonstration School to escape the integrated public schools of Nashville. But the decision came so late as to obviate much controversy, and within a few years Peabody was recruiting black students. The first black undergraduates enrolled in both Peabody and Vanderbilt in the fall of 1964. Before 1974, Peabody hired only one black faculty member, who remained only briefly.

THE FACULTY

After the war, faculty turnover increased, as able young professors found better, and better paying, jobs elsewhere. The market was tight for about five years, and Hill hard-pressed to find enough new faculty to teach the influx of students. Peabody's teaching loads were excessive and its salaries not competitive despite almost annual raises, some supported by the GEB. After the war, most courses were for four quarter hours and met Monday through Thursday. Local students were often free to go home on Thursday evening. The usual teaching load was three courses, or twelve contact hours, per week for twelve months. Now, for the first time, the heavy enrollment during the regular year meant no slack time and fewer low-enrollment courses. The new leave every three years helped (one-half the faculty did not request it), but the teaching load otherwise left little time for research and writing. In the postwar years, the average amount of serious scholarship dipped lower than in the twenties and thirties. Professional involvement continued high. Most of the faculty participated in professional organizations, in off-campus speaking, and in consultations in Europe and in a large Peabody project in Korea. During the boom years, faculty morale seemed high. Many professors felt a deep loyalty to the college.

It is difficult to offer a fair evaluation of the faculty. In the immediate postwar era, no brilliant scholar stood out from the now growing faculty (from 59 of professorial rank in 1946 to approximately 80 in 1952 to approximately 130 by 1964). No Joseph Peterson graced the campus. But during the decade after the war, at least a dozen professors exerted leadership on campus, gained a measure of recognition nationally, and wrote a number of textbooks and articles on educational or psychological issues. The mission of Peabody assured that most writing would involve not the major academic disciplines, but the teaching of such subjects. Thus, productive professors such as Whitaker in geography, or Wirth and Jack Allen in history, gained comparatively little recognition outside education colleges. The one telling exception, after 1964, would be in psychology, which by the seventies was the research tail that wagged the college dog. In no other field did research come close to rivaling teaching as central to the role of Peabody faculty. Yet, despite all the talk about the importance of teaching, little hard data exists on teaching performance. A few beloved teachers stood out, according to student accolades. But Peabody never adopted any formal evaluation of its teachers, and the high attrition rate among undergraduates (more than 50 percent by the junior year) and random student comments suggest that, in all too many departments, the teaching was deadly boring, simplistic, or undemanding. One reason may be that an active involvement in serious inquiry did not inform the teaching.

In these boom years, some programs moved outside the mainstream. Music, for example, taught future composers and performers as much as future teachers. The School of Public Health Nursing sent only some of its graduates into schools, or even to county health departments with school visitation programs. The accredited and popular Library School prepared other than school librarians. Two other branches of Peabody did not, except indirectly, teach students but contracted services to outside clients. The Division of Surveys and Field Services made money for Peabody, with more than $700,000 of committed endowment (given at different times by the GEB), and was in great demand for contracted surveys. The Child Study Center, which opened in the thirties with a focus on reading problems, offered both diagnostic and therapeutic services to children in the Nashville area.

In the field of education, Peabody had a few nationally recognized leaders, if not great scholars. Among these were William Alexander in elementary education; Robert Davis in educational research; Lloyd M. Dunn, who coordinated special education in its years of rapid growth; educational theorist Clifton L. Hall, who was also an expert on birds; and Truman Pierce, who headed the Kellogg-sponsored Cooperative Program in Educational Administration. Early childhood education's James L. Hymes wrote books about child development that gained a large lay readership. By the very nature of Peabody, it could not recruit eminent scientists, but after 1958 its natural scientists directed the well-funded Institute on the Teaching of Natural Sciences. Two historians—Jack Allen and Prentice Cooper—were prolific writers of textbooks and active in college governance. James E. Ward, Peabody's only economist and not a scholar of note, became a student favorite. An active Methodist layperson, he worked with the primary religious organization on campus, the Student Christian Association. The perennially weak departments included business education, modern languages, and home economics. Gradually, psychology became the strongest and soon the dominant department, under the direction of Nicholas Hobbs.

Finally, women rose to leadership positions at Peabody, but none as yet to scholarly eminence. Maycie Southall, the Committee of Eleven member, also helped found and lead an honorary fraternity for women in education, Delta Kappa Gamma. After her retirement, she became president of the college alumni association and thus served two years on the board of trust. Susan B. Riley chaired the English department (the first woman chair, I believe, outside home economics and nursing), served as the first woman dean of the Graduate School during her last year before retirement, and was for one year president of the American Association of University Women.[25] In psychology, Susan W. Gray worked in developmental psychology and later held leadership positions on campus. But Peabody lagged both in appointing women and in elevating them to equal rank and salary with men. When it later had to file affirmative action reports, it admitted this lag.

Peabody usually did not have the funds to hire academic stars. Roy Harris was an exception. But in 1951, with $250,000 from the GEB, the Peabody faculty approved the new four-division system suggested by the outside reviewers in 1949 and had the funds to lure eminent division directors, positions as much like deanships as departmental chairs. In 1951, Hill announced the appointments of four distinguished men. On campus, they would soon be known as the Four Horsemen (a reference, I assume, to Notre Dame football, not to the Apocalypse). Of these, William Van Til, chair of the new Division of Teaching and Curriculum Development, would remain for the shortest period. He moved to New York University in 1957. Van Til, from the University of Illinois, was an expert on curriculum development and consumer education, had published three books, and was a member of the John Dewey Society. He was a strong supporter of racial integration and a bit alienated on this usually conservative southern campus. His was the core division at Vanderbilt, but his leadership was too brief to make much impact on the division that was on its way to becoming the weakest at Peabody.[26]

The first and eldest of the Four Horsemen hired was Harold Benjamin, a top name in education. He headed the division of Foundations of Education, which included such areas as the history and philosophy of education. He left the deanship of the College of Education at the University of Maryland. A veteran of both World War I and II, he flew his own airplane while at Peabody. He may have been the best-known author in the field of education, not for his three or four almost scholarly books, but for his satire, *The Sabertooth Curriculum,* a long-lived best-seller. Benjamin had been a member of half the important national educational commissions of the last thirty years, had traveled widely abroad, had lectured at most universities, and knew everyone in the education establishment. He became Peabody's ambassador to the larger world, frequently on the move. He helped prepare the way for the college's extended program in Korea. But Peabody's most eminent professor was aging, lost his wife while teaching at Peabody, and retired in 1958.[27]

The third horseman, Willard E. Goslin was distinctive in a different sense than Benjamin. He was not a scholar, had no doctoral degree, but was a great teacher. He came to Peabody after a nasty battle in Pasadena, California, where he had been superintendent of schools. Vicious assaults from the political far right, or from Protestant fundamentalists, threatened the schools' continued existence. At the height of McCarthyism, Goslin fought back with rhetorical brilliance and gained a national following for his eloquent defense of the public schools, winning the 1952 American Education Award for his courage. At Peabody, he headed the Division of School Administration and Community Development. He received speaking invitations from all over the country. He published a ringing defense of the public schools and joined Van Til's push for the admission of blacks at Peabody. A lover of controversy, he wrote sharp, biting, effective prose. Later, he headed the Korean project, came to admire Korean educators, and became almost a hero in Korea. The goodwill he created helped insure a long-term Peabody connection with that country, not extinguished even today. Benjamin and Goslin, two of the Four Horsemen, would die within a few weeks of each other in 1969.[28]

The fourth horseman, Nicholas Hobbs, headed the division of Guidance and Human Development. A clinical psychologist who moved from Louisiana State University, he specialized in counseling and guidance. He was a graduate of the Citadel, received his Ph.D. from Ohio State University, and worked as an Army Air Force psychologist during World War II. A convert to the client-based psychology of Carl Rogers, he was a contributing author of a text with Rogers and had taught at Teachers College, Columbia University. The least experienced and least known

In 1955 Peabody celebrated the fortieth anniversary of its suddenly booming psychology department. It first psychologist, E. K. Strong, is at the right. On the left is Lyle Lanier, the most eminent Ph.D. student of the great Joseph Peterson. In the middle are two of the key architects of the new department, Susan Gray and Nicholas Hobbs. Photographic Archives of Vanderbilt University.

of the four new division heads, Hobbs would have the greatest impact on Peabody and also on Vanderbilt, where he later served as provost. Although not well suited for administrative details, he was a charming and persuasive man and proved adept at grantsmanship. He successfully wooed federal agencies, and won more grants for Peabody than anyone in its history. He soon made the psychology department the strongest at Peabody, helped create a Department of Special Education, and eventually helped procure the grants that underwrote the Kennedy Center (see chapter 12).

PEABODY ABROAD

One characteristic that distinguished the Peabody faculty even from its Vanderbilt neighbors was its involvement in international issues. As perhaps befitted the college's educational mission, particularly in the post–World War II era, it had a well-traveled and cosmopolitan faculty. Several professors advised U.S. Occupation officials in Germany. Fremont P. Wirth not only spent leave time there, but also became an expert on postwar Germany. Joseph Roemer, dean of the college just after the war, left Peabody for a full-time position in Germany's American zone. The Korean War, and Hill's internationalism, led to one of the two largest international programs in Peabody history, or what amounted to a Peabody in Korea. In 1952, Hill proposed a five-point program for Peabody. His fifth point was a proposal for more international education, with Peabody taking the lead. Unclear and ill-conceived, the other four points would have limited effect on campus. They involved an organizational tightening, more creative teaching, a more select student body, and more research and in-service training. The fifth point suggested that all faculty members and advanced-degree candidates become experts on some culture beyond their own. M.A. candidates would complete a course of study and research involving one country or cultural area. Doctoral candidates would spend nine months of their training in the cultural area of their choice, an ambitious goal largely ignored by the faculty. But for a dozen or more doctoral candidates, Korea provided such an opportunity.[29]

The Korean War had limited impact on Peabody. College students usually received draft deferments. No military units trained on college campuses. But the armistice that ended the war in 1953 left South Korea devastated, and the United States undertook a major aid program that included help in education. Harold Benjamin first led a small advisory group on education to Korea in 1955–56, and his contacts prepared the way for Peabody to receive a contract from the International Cooperation Administration (soon the Agency for International Development) to set up a staff in Seoul in 1956 and provide advice and help to Korean institutions involved in teacher education. This soon meant a large budget, more than a dozen staff members in Korea, and a small administrative staff at Peabody. William Goslin first directed the program, and other Peabody professors followed. The staff included secretaries and graduate students from Peabody along with a faculty hired in part from other U.S. universities. The faculty traveled all over South Korea to advise teacher-training schools. Each year, up to a dozen Korean educators came to Nashville for conferences or study at Peabody. Many Koreans enrolled as students, creating a Korean community in the university-center area. Hill visited Korea. Dean Felix Robb went there to formalize the original contract. Several Peabody professors advised the project or spent time in Korea. And, best of all, the federal government funded all these activities. The contract expired in 1962, but by then Peabody had more than a hundred alumni in Korea and maintained academic ties for the next two decades.[30]

RETRENCHMENT

As expected, enrollments declined in the early fifties, but less than President Hill had anticipated. In the early fifties academic positions dried up. Higher education entered a period of retrenchment. But at the same time, the baby boom sent elementary school enrollment soaring, which soon meant a high demand for teachers. Hill was again correct in expecting college enrollments to rise rapidly by 1960 or soon thereafter, but Peabody would not share in this boom.

At Peabody, summer enrollment declined from 4,338 in 1951 to 2,860 by 1955 but stayed close to that level until 1960 (2,760). Fall semester enrollments fell from 2,109 in 1950 to a low of 1,372 in 1954, then gradually rose to 1,679 in 1960. One explanation for the rise was Peabody's appeal for undergraduates in the Nashville area. Still, these enrollment figures, particularly by 1960, were deceptive, for Peabody counted all part-time students, a few in evening and off-campus courses, and increasingly, in the summer, students who enrolled in conferences or a midsummer intersession. Thus, by 1960 it still had an annual enrollment of more than 4,800 but a full-time equivalent of at least a thousand less. For example, in the fall of 1960, of its listed 1,637 students, only 1,192 were full time.[31]

The declining enrollments accompanied gradual increases in tuition, which meant that the college's income remained stable. But Peabody's survival still depended on a continuous flow of funds from foundations. By 1960, the GEB was close to liquidating, but the Ford Foundation, the Kellogg Foundation, and federal grant agencies made up the difference. While Hill was president, the college never came close to an annual deficit. Tuition now accounted for more than 70 percent of operating costs. The endowment, in real dollars, scarcely grew at all—from around \$4.8 million in 1946 to \$9.1 million in 1960, if one adds almost \$1.7 million in restricted funds (such as funds the GEB had given to endow the Division of Surveys and Field Services). In 1960, income from all investments totaled only \$463,000 of the total \$3.13 million budget, just under 15 percent.

By 1960, grants had begun to replace foundation gifts. These did not add to the endowment and, in most cases, directly supported educational or research programs. Some overhead helped pay nonresearch professors. But a steady decline in funds to augment faculty salaries, to increase the endowment, or to add new buildings, hurt. Private gifts were never enough to compensate. Here Hill failed, as he admitted. It is doubtful that alumni ever gave enough to pay even the expenses of the alumni office. Annual alumni gifts in the early fifties ranged from $5,000 to $10,000 in what Peabody, like Vanderbilt, called a living endowment. In 1947, Hill and the board approved a general campaign with a long-term goal of $4 million, which included foundation gifts. In the next ten years, Peabody undoubtedly received this amount. But it set a short-term target of $500,000 from local contributors. Solicitors invaded Nashville in 1948, but won only 313 pledges for about $175,000. Some never paid what they pledged. In the next year, a disappointed Hill announced a suspension of the local campaign. The time seemed inauspicious. Peabody simply could not depend on Nashville benefactors.

Hill never asked the board for another campaign until the construction of the Student Center in 1958–59. The college then needed $300,000 beyond the government loan to complete the building and furnish it. Both alumni and local citizens proved rather generous, although this was a timid goal. Eventually, they pledged more than $400,000 (the board raised the goal), and more than $300,000 came in. But Peabody had a disappointing begging record under Hill, and later, more ambitious campaigns would prove even more disappointing. Peabody had no constituency willing to contribute large sums. A few generous board members offered gifts in the $50,000 range (the sum Jesse Jones contributed for a lectureship and scholarships), but no larger. Private gifts remained a minute part of Peabody's income, an ill omen.[32]

Some of Peabody's off-campus properties added to the pot. But a camp near Peagram, inherited during the war from H. G. Hill Sr., proved as much a burden as an asset. Right after the war, a teacher in the Demonstration School established a well-managed camp for middle-school students. Later, the state leased the camp in summer for a joint exceptional-children program it sponsored along with Peabody. By 1960, the camp was a liability, unlike Knapp Farm, which in the postwar years became a profitable enterprise, with one of the best dairy herds in the United States. Well-managed, it yielded more than $5,000 in profits each year. But with the steady increase in the value of its land, this was a small return on capital. In 1959, the Knapp Committee of the board of trust decided that Peabody should sell the farm as soon as it received a good offer. An act from the Tennessee assembly granted it full title. It auctioned the dairy herd in 1959. The sale proved a major event in dairy-breeding circles. The herd of fifty-three prize Holsteins (some calves) sold for $23,290, well over $400 a head. One champion cow brought $885. The board also authorized repairs on the seldom-used clubhouse.[33]

Most people at Peabody did not know it, but the college went into the warehouse business in both Nashville and Chattanooga. This reflected a deal worked out by Clark and board members with ties to the Nashville, St. Louis, and Chattanooga Railroad. The railroad allowed Peabody to buy warehouses (first on Charlotte Avenue in Nashville in 1954, and in Chattanooga in 1958) and then lease them to the railroad for twenty-three years in Nashville, twenty-five in Chattanooga. This combined certain tax advantages for the railroad with a guaranteed 5 percent return on its investment for Peabody, similar to investments in mortgages but more secure.[34]

One sad event marked Hill's last year as president. In 1961, Peabody's School of Public Health Nursing, which had consistently made money for the college, learned that it would lose its accreditation the next year. In the fifties, under its capable chair Edna Lewis, this department had seemed to thrive. With only two full-time professors and a few part-time lecturers for many courses, it earned up to three times as much in tuition as it expended. After the war, it became only a degree program, without one-year certification students. Registered nurses came for a B.S. in public health nursing in order to gain better jobs. They usually arrived with up to a year of academic credit from nursing school and took general education and professional courses in their three years on campus. In their final year, they spent at least three months in fieldwork with public health agencies in Nashville and throughout much of the South. From its founding to 1962, the school had enrolled 3,421 students and awarded 656 B.S. and 113 master's degrees. Its graduates held positions all over the country, participated in an active alumni association, and received newsletters from the department. This made for an especially close-knit body of graduates, with perhaps greater appreciation for Peabody than any other group of students.

In all these ways, the school was a success story. It had enjoyed grants from the Public Health Service, for two years directed a program in Oklahoma to train public health nurses, had met all accreditation standards, and even received scholarships from nursing associations. But by 1961, the National League of Nursing decided to deny further accreditation to such supplemental public health nursing programs and instead to support new, integrated college nursing schools. Lewis, aided by Hill, tried to reverse the league's action or at least postpone the termination for two years, to no avail. Still, eighty-one students in the program were able to complete their work in the next two years. Disappointed, even bitter, Lewis had to retire. Her colleague in the school continued to offer courses in health education.[35]

In August 1960, President Hill announced his impending retirement in August 1961. Board rules required a year's notice. By the old retirement rules, he would have had to retire in September 1959, when he became sixty-five but, conveniently, the board at that time raised the mandatory retirement age for faculty and admin-

A sad ending. President Henry Hill presided at this final banquet of the Peabody Nurses Club in 1961. Next to him, to the left, is Edna Lewis, the last chair of the School of Public Health Nursing. Photograph by Tucker Studio. Photographic Archives of Vanderbilt University.

istrators to sixty-eight, with two additional years if the college agreed. By 1960, Peabody faced a range of problems. Its relationship with Vanderbilt was again under discussion, and before he left office in 1961, Hill knew that closer cooperation, even a merger, was under study. Early in his tenure, he had sought such cooperation himself. In 1953, the Ford Foundation granted $300,000 to Vanderbilt and Peabody for a joint Master of Arts in Teaching program for students from liberal arts colleges with content courses at Vanderbilt, professional training at Peabody. Students received generous scholarships from the Ford Foundation, and the program recruited excellent students into teaching. The Carnegie Foundation had already funded up to twenty annual scholarships at Peabody for much the same purpose, but without a Vanderbilt connection. In 1956 the Ford Foundation withdrew its annual support. In this case, it was Peabody that decided not to continue the joint degree. Vanderbilt continued on its own to admit students to an M.A.T. program and send them to Peabody for some needed courses.[36]

The big blow to cooperation came in 1956, when the Vanderbilt faculty voted to move to the semester system in the fall of 1957. The Peabody faculty resented this shift, although Peabody could have made the same decision and would move to the semester system in 1966. At the time, its large summer quarter made a shift difficult. The change reduced the number of students who chose courses on the neighboring campus but did not end such enrollments. By then, and particularly after this decision, the number of Vanderbilt students enrolling in Peabody exceeded those going in the other direction, a change from earlier years. From 1930 to after 1950, the number of Peabody students who took courses at Vanderbilt remained at around two hundred, while the number of Vanderbilt students at Peabody rose from less than a hundred to six hundred, mostly in education or music courses. But the sense of estrangement and the resentment continued, once again to the despair of foundations that had to sort out what amounted to competing applications from the two schools.

Peabody faced not only a major study of its relationship to Vanderbilt, but also scheduled accreditation visits by both the Southern Association of Colleges and Schools and the National Council for Accreditation of Teacher Education. Originally scheduled for 1962, these did not take place until 1964. Each required an intensive self-study by Peabody, an arduous and time-consuming task. Hill wanted to turn these jobs over to his successor, who would almost certainly be his long-term assistant and dean, Felix Robb. The Southern Association report would lead to major reforms at Peabody, as well as major new expenditures and a budget crunch, the first in Peabody history. The response to the accreditation reports continued until 1966, when Robb left Peabody to head the Southern Association. Thus, Hill, who returned as acting president, would not escape some of the difficult decisions. By then, the golden age was over, the difficult years underway.[37]

In at least one respect, Peabody until 1962 led a charmed life, untouched by controversy, let alone scandal. It had faced its share of frustrations and disappointments. Heavy teaching loads and poor salaries had distressed faculty and led many to leave. The heavy attrition rate among students revealed unhappiness. But compared to almost any other college or university, including Vanderbilt, Peabody was an irenic oasis. From 1914 to 1962, no one at Peabody, including the faculty who conducted the 1964 self-studies, could recall any abuse of academic freedom, any faculty member censored or penalized for a belief or opinion. Major student disciplinary problems were all but nonexistent. And even though Peabody had no formal tenure system, no one could recall any professor who came to Peabody on an indefinite appointment ever being discharged (although some deserved it). Burdensome teaching assignments or low salaries may have disheartened inept faculty, but they faced no disciplinary action or dismissal. The faculty had no elected faculty council or senate before 1961, yet it is almost impossible to find any serious or extended faculty alienation. Most seemed happy to leave most major decisions to their president. The first two George Peabody presidents died in office, while Hill retired with no sign of opposition and came back when needed. Unfortunately, in the lean years ahead, this irenic Peabody would dissolve in the midst of endless controversy.

A Troubled Decade, 1961–1972

By 1961, anyone who was at all perceptive realized that it might be impossible for Peabody to survive as an independent school of education. Whatever the legal arrangements, it needed to become a fully integrated unit within a university cluster, with Vanderbilt the dominant institution. Even before his retirement in 1961, Henry Hill knew this. So did his successor, Felix Robb. The problem was in finding a formula that would be acceptable to Peabody's faculty, students, board of trustees, and alumni, one that preserved as much independence as possible. In the critical years after 1961, the Peabody board and presidents made the critical and costly decision to reject a merger with Vanderbilt, doggedly to maintain the college's independence. In so doing, they missed the last realistic opportunity for a merger of near equals and left a struggling Peabody that later had to accept annexation by Vanderbilt, largely on Vanderbilt's terms. In only one area—special education—did Peabody gain new strengths and plenty of new research support. The Kennedy Center became the enduring token of this success in a period of otherwise weak leadership and low morale.

FELIX ROBB AND MERGER TALKS

The new Peabody president in 1961, Felix Robb, faced more challenges than he at first realized. By 1961 Peabody was gradually losing its earlier preeminence in teacher education. Before World War II, Peabody had not only supported the largest graduate program of education in the South, but the one with the most eminent faculty. It had a near monopoly on M.A. and Ph.D. work in education and related fields, and was a mecca for graduates of state normal or teachers colleges. Even its relatively undemanding M.A. program assured graduates excellent jobs and leadership roles in public schools; its Ph.D.'s dominated normal-school faculties throughout the South. But after World War II, state teachers' colleges became multipurpose state colleges or even state universities. By 1961, many had joined colleges of education in state universities in offering M.A. work in education, with low tuition. Peabody could compete for such graduate students only on the basis of reputation and faculty quality. By 1961, it retained the prestige but in many fields no longer led in quality.

Peabody had even less to offer its undergraduates. It competed directly with Vanderbilt, as well as Ward-Belmont, Fisk, David Lipscomb, Tennessee A & I, and Middle Tennessee State. Yet, as the college learned in the fifties, its survival depended on undergraduate tuition. No longer did prospective teachers have a compelling reason to come to Peabody. All the surrounding undergraduate colleges trained teachers. For undergraduates unsure of their career choice, Peabody offered nothing special except in music and never developed the social amenities of its neighbors. It could not claim superiority in teaching, and its standards for admission and grading fell well below those at Vanderbilt, and perhaps were no higher than those at some state teachers' colleges. Peabody was even gradually losing its long-term claim to fame—the eminence of its faculty. It simply could not recruit or retain faculty stars outside psychology and human development.

Felix Robb set ambitious goals for Peabody. He believed it could become the premier college for educators in the world by 1975. In his brief five years as president, he revised the administrative structure, urged closer cooperation with Vanderbilt, helped guide the most detailed self-studies ever conducted at Peabody, formed a Development Council to stimulate a pattern of annual giving, and rejoiced in the creation of the Kennedy Center. But these were also frustrating years. Robb must have felt like Sisyphus, for an advance in one area accompanied a retreat in others. By 1965, in the midst of mounting problems at Peabody, he had lost much of the support of key board members. Idealistic, he was in the crunch not a forceful or decisive leader and could neither implement a new administrative structure nor bring any clear focus to the campus. Thus, under increasing board pressure, he felt that he should accept an offer to become director of the Southern Association of Schools and Colleges. He must have left in May 1966 not only tired but with some sense of relief, for Peabody by then faced more intractable problems, including looming deficits, than in 1961.

Robb recognized that short of closer cooperation with Vanderbilt, Peabody could not realize his ambitious goals. He had the advantages of being a Vanderbilt M.A. graduate and knowing many of its faculty and administrators. His elevation from dean of instruction to president surprised few on campus, as he had seemed the heir apparent. A native of Birmingham, a graduate of Birmingham Southern, a devoted Methodist layman, and a World War II veteran, Robb also had longtime Peabody contacts. During and after his Vanderbilt studies, he took courses in education at Peabody, and later, while employed at Peabody, completed a Ph.D. in education at Harvard. In 1947, Hill invited Robb to Peabody as his assistant. He became an immediate leader on campus and in 1951 became dean. Indispensable to the aging Hill, Robb probably assured his position as president when, in 1958–60, he took a leave from Peabody to serve as chief of staff on a Carnegie Foundation–sponsored study of the college and university presidency. The Peabody board advertised the position, evaluated more than a hundred applicants, and seriously considered six, but Robb emerged as its unanimous choice. He started with a salary of $18,500, a $3,000 expense account, membership in the Belle Meade Country Club, and a presidential mansion refurbished at a cost of $23,000. The first unmarried president in Peabody's history, his mother served as hostess at the presidential home.

Robb represented a new generation of college administrators. An able and imaginative young man (one thinks of Wickliffe Rose), he was organized, reasonably articulate, and hard working. He lacked the burning passion of Bruce Payne and was more liberal or progressive on most issues than Hill. He believed that Peabody needed more forceful leadership, and that he could dramatically move it forward. He had to plunge directly into the most sensitive policy choices that Peabody had faced since 1914: the college's relationship with Vanderbilt, its academic policies and standards, and accreditation by the Southern Association. Although his leadership on these issues proved relatively ineffective, it is possible that no one could have resolved the problems or avoided the political snares.[1]

On May 11, 1961, the day that the Peabody board elected Robb, it also voted to cooperate with Vanderbilt in a major foundation-supported study of new patterns of cooperation. The origin of this study went back to the fall of 1960, when Walter Stokes Jr., chair of the Peabody Board of Trust, along with one other member, Reber Boult, traveled to New York City to consult with people in the Rockefeller charities and the Ford Foundation about candidates for the Peabody presidency. As in the past, the foundations pushed for a closer tie to Vanderbilt, a message they had often communicated to Vanderbilt officials. Back in Nashville, conversations among members of the two boards led to a joint committee that petitioned the GEB and the Ford Foundation to fund a major study of possible new forms of cooperation. The two boards agreed on a statement of purpose to guide such a study, which they stipulated should be carried out by a panel of leading educators. To give the panel the utmost freedom, the statement by the two boards did not rule out any strategy, including full merger. But it did stress that each institution recognized "the previously existing independence and autonomy of the other," and that any new form of association should not needlessly submerge "the tradition, identity or purpose of either."[2]

Three trustees each from Peabody and Vanderbilt monitored the study. The director, John Dale Russell (back again), on the verge of retirement from the Office of Institutional Research of New York University and the director of many earlier such studies, did most of the work, with his offices and staff located in JUL. The study committee responsible for the final report included only three educators (two others declined to serve): John O. Gross, the chair, who was general secretary of the Division of Higher Education of the United Methodist Church; Carey Croneis, chancellor of Rice University; and Lindley J. Stiles, dean of the School of Education of the University of Wisconsin. Russell and his staff began work in the fall of 1961 and completed a report by May 1962. Accompanying the report were three book-length staff studies on the two institutions' use of instructional space, courses offered, and past patterns of cooperation.

Peabody sabotaged any merger or near merger. Both the *Nashville Banner* and the *Tennessean* carried generally accurate stories about the projected study, but the *Tennessean* led with a provocative headline: "Peabody, VU Merger in Air." Board members had to stress in interviews with reporters that all options were open, since any other response would have seemed to place limits on the study. Equally unfortunate were remarks by the usually blunt Chancellor Harvey Branscomb at Vanderbilt, who talked about merger as a possibility, typically throwing out the suggestion to provoke a response. An unconcerned Vanderbilt faculty anticipated something like a merger, and so did many members of the Vanderbilt Board of Trust. They assumed that Peabody held the inferior bargaining position and that effective cooperation would require the college to become a school within Vanderbilt's cluster of professional schools.

Unlike Vanderbilt, Peabody had much at stake. It is not surprising that talk of merger created fear and anxiety among the Peabody faculty. Almost any form of merger threatened the jobs of faculty members in the arts and sciences. Very quickly, the alumni began to bombard Peabody with opposition to a merger, incited by their main contact with Peabody, the *Reflector.* Its editor, John E. Windrow, took his Ph.D. at Peabody, joined the education department, and for years headed the Demonstration School before he became director of public services and the voice of the *Reflector.* As much as his friend Alfred E. Crabb, Windrow loved the traditional Peabody of Bruce Payne. Many faculty viewed him as a reactionary, since he opposed almost every innovation for twenty years—higher admission standards (a betrayal of the older, democratic Peabody), any emphasis on research at the cost of teaching, and the new trend toward corporation- or government-sponsored research. But above all, he defended the autonomy and independence of Peabody. In the January–February 1961 *Reflector,* Windrow published some of the founding documents of 1909. In the next issue, he wrote a fervent editorial entitled "Our Peabody Guardians Have Kept Us Free." Peabody had followed its own independent path and thus had served as a unique model, for even at Columbia or Harvard, captive colleges of education had become unwanted and ill-treated stepchildren. "For 86 years Peabody's trustees, faculty and friends have kept it free. It is difficult to believe that any set of circumstances could develop that would change this." He and his *Reflector* would lead the fight against any loss of freedom to a resented Vanderbilt.[3]

It was soon clear that Robb would defend Peabody's autonomy. In a long confidential memo to Russell in March 1962, he tried to explain his position on institutional cooperation. He equivocated. He wrote vaguely of a broad, bold vision, of meaningful cooperation that could lead to one of the strongest centers for higher education in the world. He listed the obvious goals of such cooperation. He stressed the importance of a school of education in any cluster of colleges and universities. He listed the distinctive contributions Peabody could make to a university center. He argued that Peabody had always been and was now financially secure (a bit of a stretch). He clearly wanted to reverse recent trends away from institutional cooperation, blamed Branscomb for much of this, and noted the fear of and hostility to merger at Peabody. He listed 39 areas of possible future cooperation. But on the issue of structure, he advised against merger or a superboard with authority over both institutions. Instead—and here he was most general and vague—he suggested an interadministrative council, a university-center faculty advisory council, and a series of agreements between Vanderbilt and Peabody that in some cases could include Scarritt. Voluntary cooperation, backed up at times by compacts like that for JUL, had to come before a tighter union. Robb made it clear to Russell that Peabody would not compromise its independence, a stance that considerably reduced the options open to the Russell staff.[4]

In the final report, Russell recommended the strongest Peabody-Vanderbilt relationship he could devise short of merger. He stressed the liabilities of the old hit-and-miss pattern of cooperation. He listed the advantages and disadvantages of a merger, to which the opposition at Peabody posed the most important deterrent. It was clear that the word "merger" suggested various images, and as a result functioned as the awful "M" word among Peabodians. Russell clarified two models that might fit Peabody and Vanderbilt. The first, the annexation model that would be followed in 1979, would end Peabody's legal autonomy. In Russell's scenario, Vanderbilt would accept Peabody into its federation of self-financing professional schools, leaving its educational mission unchanged, its endowment to support it, and possibly a continued Peabody board to manage the endowment. The second model involved a merger of equals that would lead to a larger university comparable to Case-Western Reserve, possibly with a new name such as the University of Nashville or Vanderbilt-Peabody.

Russell's more modest plan proved unacceptable to either Vanderbilt or Peabody trustees. He proposed a self-perpetuating, nine-member Nashville University Center coordinating board, with some members drawn from the Peabody and Vanderbilt boards, and at least a few members representing the larger community. Most people soon referred to the proposed body as a superboard. Both Vanderbilt and Peabody would remain autonomous, with their own boards, chief executive officers, endowments, degrees, and faculty. The coordinating board, which would have such powers as the Peabody and Vanderbilt boards agreed to assign to it, would resemble a political confederation whose members could secede if they wished. The board would select, as its executive officer, someone referred to as either chancellor or president—whatever title was not in use by Peabody and Vanderbilt—have its own budget, and require no annual contributions from Peabody and Vanderbilt. It would be responsible for arranging all types of cooperation between the two institutions, in some cases providing funds to support such cooperation. Russell, as had Kuhlman for the JUL, became deeply committed to this model, hoping it could show other universities and colleges how to form their own university centers.

As Russell conceived it, this superboard would require an operating budget of about $100,000 a year, mostly for salaries. But it needed much more money for three essential functions. First, it needed the authority from the two institutions to establish and maintain a common calendar including the time for opening and closing each term, final exams, holidays, and vacations. Students could then select courses at either institution guided only by their needs and interests. Second, this superboard needed the authority to review and approve each institution's annual budget. Russell equivocated on this point, stressing that the board could not control the allocation of resources by either institution but needed the budget figures to determine where it should add supplementary funds. Third, the new board needed the authority to approve all new instructional, research, and service programs. This was a powerful but essential tool. For example, Vanderbilt could not unilaterally establish a school of education, or Peabody a law school. Russell, as had Robb, suggested dozens of other cooperative ventures that the board should develop and supervise (a center for the performing arts, a university press, joint intermural and intercollegiate sports, common musical and dramatic productions, joint professorial appointments, common testing and counseling centers, merged maintenance and purchasing). But only in three essential areas would Peabody and Vanderbilt have to surrender critical decision-making powers and thus give up some autonomy.

Russell realized that neither institution would buy into such a plan unless it offered clear benefits. To work, the coordinating board or University Center had to have outside funding, primarily from foundations. Russell believed the new board should from the outset fund three services: student course exchanges, subsidies for faculty salaries, and a common faculty club. With course exchange, neither Peabody nor Vanderbilt would suffer financial loss from teaching students from its neighboring institution. If Vanderbilt taught more students than it sent to Peabody, the fund would reimburse it. Students at either institution could enroll in any course, since the plan would entail a common class schedule at registration time. Faculty salary subsidies were most critical for Peabody. Russell hoped the new board could, in five years, equalize Peabody salaries and teaching loads with the level of those at Vanderbilt. Finally, a common meeting place or club for the faculty of both institutions would encourage cooperation. These costs would amount to more than $2.5 million over the first five years. Russell believed the new board could secure these funds from foundations and even develop an endowment. While the major benefits would seem to go to Peabody, Vanderbilt would gain a great deal from a Peabody with salaries, course loads, and benefits comparable to its own. Such equity would produce a more eminent faculty at Peabody and higher standards in admissions and grading, clearing the way for all types of joint programs. Russell's goal was a great graduate research center equal to any in the nation.[5]

Idealistic, even utopian, Russell's proposal was a pig in a poke. Too much depended on contingencies such as foundation funding, and on a full commitment by both faculties. However sugar coated, the new plan compromised the independence of both boards of trust, promised a whole new level of bureaucracy, and, even with start-up funding, raised a nightmarish specter should outside funding end. The Vanderbilt board, hoping to find an acceptable way to merge with Peabody, and to gain more control over the college, was deeply disappointed with the final report. On June 9, 1962, it rejected the new structure as neither feasible nor workable.[6]

At Peabody, Robb had already informed Russell of his opposition to a superboard. On May 10, a special board committee began its study of the report, soon joined by a faculty advisory committee. The Peabody Executive Committee first reviewed the report on May 31, but the whole board did not act on it until its meeting on December 6. At meetings on November 16 and December 6, a board committee on cooperation with Vanderbilt developed the final motion for the board as a whole. Board discussions lasted two days. At least two members, Maxie Jarman and Arthur Johnson, wanted either merger or some other plan to help Peabody raise faculty salaries. But, in what members recognized as one of its most critical votes ever, the board rejected the Russell plan twenty-one to one, with one abstention. It then rejected Jarman's countermotion by twenty-one to two. Jarman resigned from the board as a result, as did Johnson later. The board noted that it fully concurred with only one part of the report—its rejection of merger. It recommended that the heads of Peabody and Vanderbilt appoint a joint faculty and administrative committee, with board representation, to consider areas of mutual interest and possible cooperation, and that the heads of the two institutions appoint a coordinator to chair the committee and guide such cooperation. It thus advocated a junior version of the Russell plan.[7] But for Windrow and the old-timers, the decisive action had been the board's rejection of merger, or what soon became, in the perspective of the *Reflector* at least, a second courageous, memorable declaration of independence for Peabody.[8]

In the summer of 1962, the two board chairs, Walter Stokes Jr. of Peabody and

Sam Fleming of Vanderbilt, tried to find a basis of cooperation that resembled the Russell report's recommendation. Fleming proposed a joint board committee with a large sphere of control over cooperative ventures, made up of three members from Peabody, three from Vanderbilt, but with Chancellor Heard of Vanderbilt as chair. This committee could have assumed most of the functions of Russell's coordinating board. Stokes rejected a committee with the Vanderbilt chancellor in control and suggested a rotating chair. Discussion soon stalled.[9]

But the Russell report did inspire new cooperation over the next fifteen years. This included major ties between the Kennedy Center and the Vanderbilt Medical Center, a faculty club in 1967 (largely funded by Vanderbilt), a Peabody-Vanderbilt marching band, and in 1972, a new concord, worked out by a committee representing both boards, on cooperation in physical education and intercollegiate sports. The last turned out to be more important than it seemed at the time. With approval by the National Collegiate Athletic Association, Peabody students could now join any of Vanderbilt's athletic teams and soon made up half the football team (forty-eight in 1976). Vanderbilt could now recruit athletes who planned to enroll in an academically less demanding Peabody. The second part of the agreement allowed Vanderbilt students to take a spectrum of art, music, and physical education courses at Peabody as part of a new B.S. degree.[10] In the negotiations that led to merger in 1979, the athletic agreement gave Peabody its most important bargaining chip. What all this cooperation never led to was a much talked about and badly needed pedestrian bridge to unite the two campuses and to help overcome the physical and psychological barrier of Twenty-first Avenue. Also, none of the cooperative arrangements helped raise Peabody salaries or rescue Peabody from its developing financial crisis.

With hindsight, it is easy to see the 1961–62 Russell study as a lost opportunity for Peabody. It needed some form of merger to solve its problems, as a few tough-minded faculty members already realized.[11] New faculty without earlier Peabody connections, or faculty connected to the Kennedy Center, were usually those most persuaded that some form of merger was essential to Peabody's future. Certainly, Peabody held a stronger bargaining position in 1962 than it would have in 1979, and could have asked for more in any merger agreement. For example, it could probably have saved its Music School, perhaps made Peabody the center for fine arts at Vanderbilt, and at the least orchestrated a gradual elimination of arts and science faculty. From Vanderbilt's perspective, a merger in 1962 would have gained for a combined campus the Demonstration School lot, land needed for a performing arts center, possibly a physical education building, and a departure point for a wide pedestrian bridge. This was the land that could have glued the two campuses together. But in 1962, the secret of a successful merger lay in all the details. Without a sense of duress at Peabody and strong faculty support at Vanderbilt, negotiations could have gone on for years and still failed.

As Russell worked on his report, Peabody entered a period of frenetic activity. President Robb wanted to move the college forward at a rapid pace through "hard-driving, relentless, zestful work for Peabody." He outlined his dreams in a special meeting at a motel in Gatlinburg, Tennessee, September 15–17, 1961. Almost every Peabody faculty member attended. Robb was the John F. Kennedy of Peabody presidents, young, inspiring, ambitious, but in the end unable to achieve many of his goals. He would stay less than five years, at which point many of his new programs began to bear often bitter fruit. When he spoke to the faculty the omens seemed promising. College enrollments seemed destined to soar as baby-boom children entered college. The Sun Belt phenomenon made a southern location now seem a blessing, not a curse. Nashville was entering a period of rapid growth, after both the city and county approved a new, unified city-county government. In his report, Robb indirectly identified weaknesses at Peabody. His first priority, he told the faculty, was developing an exciting, stimulating intellectual campus life. He wanted to increase enrollments, particularly for males. He wanted to change the image associated with "teachers' colleges." He believed that Peabody was underadministered and announced plans for a tighter structure. He accepted Peabody's primary mission as training educational workers but acknowledged that it would continue its liberal arts program for undergraduates. He wanted to improve dorm life and social life, tighten admission standards, and challenge the ablest students. He knew Peabody had to improve faculty salaries, and that this would entail new sources of money, which he assured the faculty would be forthcoming from alumni and other donors and from increased foundation and federal research grants.[12]

The midsixties proved the worst possible time for faculty development. Soaring enrollments, as baby boomers reached college age, created the tightest academic market in U.S. history. Not enough new Ph.D.'s entered college teaching. At Peabody, not a top competitor in this tight market, faculty turnover became an annual problem. The vital new post of academic vice president remained unfilled for most of Robb's tenure. In one year, the deans of both the college and the graduate school left. In 1967, the most distinguished professor in education, Samuel Wiggins, moved to Cleveland State, and the longtime head librarian, the diminutive Isaac Copeland, moved to North Carolina. Desperate for talent, Robb moved C. B. Hunt Jr. from the music school to head of the graduate school. Robb's successor as president would move the ablest senior professor left in education, William McClurkin, to academic vice president. In less than a decade, the number of tenured faculty shrank to no more than a third, and the flood of junior faculty included a large contingent of mediocrities, many of whom would not gain tenure, although too many did. By 1970, the overall quality of the Peabody faculty was lower than ever before; only the psychology, special education, history, and English departments had strong overall faculties. In the schools of music and library science, a few able specialists mixed with too many weak junior professors. The one clear disaster area, as two presidents in a row freely acknowledged, was the Department of Education. When in 1972 the president at last recruited the young and promising Roy Alcorn to head the department, he died the following April in an automobile accident.

Despite recruitment frustrations, Peabody expanded in several new directions in the early and midsixties. Robb reorganized the divisional system to increase faculty density in key graduate fields and established vice presidencies for administrative and academic affairs. He formed a development council of prominent and affluent local men and women and through it conducted a continuous fund-raising campaign. Peabody instituted its first, very small, faculty research fund, upgraded the music division to school status, added a new music preparatory academy (Blair, funded by the Potter Foundation, and located in a Peabody house on Eighteenth Avenue), committed itself to a semester system to share a common calendar with Vanderbilt, appointed from thirty to forty-five new faculty each year (most as replacements but some for new programs), and attained a record fall enrollment in 1965 (2,133). Most important, it created the Kennedy Center.

The history of the Kennedy Center dates at least to 1937, when Peabody established its Child Study Center. Soon located in the Wrenne House, it dealt with reading disabilities. It added speech therapy in 1944 and soon gained strength from its cooperation with the Bill Wilkerson Speech and Hearing Center. In 1953, with a grant from the American Federation for the Blind, Peabody began a training program for teachers of the blind, headed by Samuel Ashcroft. In the same year it hired Lloyd M. Dunn to coordinate a growing number of initiatives in special education. By then, Nicholas Hobbs headed the new division that encompassed psychology and special education. In 1954, Susan Gray began teaching courses in developmental psychology. Her early work in special educational programs for disadvantaged preschool children, or what she called the Early Training Project, would directly influence the creation of Head Start.[13] In 1956, the National Institute of Mental Health funded a study of mentally retarded children headed by Dunn and Hobbs. By 1959, twenty-four faculty were to some extent involved in special-education teaching or research, and Peabody was a nationally recognized leader in working with exceptional children. Politically important for Peabody was Hobbs's move to Washington in 1961 to help select the early Peace Corps volunteers, working with Peace Corps head Sargent Shriver. Shriver's wife was Eunice Kennedy Shriver, President Kennedy's sister, who shared the Kennedy family interest in mental retardation because of the affliction of one of the Kennedy children. Hobbs became a close friend of the Shrivers, who visited the Peabody campus in October 1962. In the same year, Hobbs assumed the presidency of the American Psychological Association, a position formerly held by Peabody's Joseph Peterson, and the only such disciplinary achievement by any postwar Peabody professor.

These strengths began to pay off as early as 1962. Peabody received a grant of $160,000 from the Joseph P. Kennedy Jr. Foundation to support visiting Kennedy Foundation professors, support later extended to permanent professors.[14] In part because of effective grant writing by Hobbs and Dunn, in 1964 the National Institute of Child Health and Human Development granted Peabody $1.5 million to fund the Institute on Mental Retardation and Intellectual Development (IMRID), the first of six centers or institutes that would later comprise the Kennedy Center. In the same year, a Carnegie grant funded a research project on individual differences in elementary school children, while Peabody, again led by Hobbs, supervised a Project for the Reeducation of Emotionally Disturbed Students (ReED) funded by the National Institute of Mental Health. This project led to the state-funded but Peabody-supervised Cumberland House School in Nashville.[15]

May 1965 was the greatest month in Peabody's premerger history. On May 26, the National Institutes of Health announced a gift of $2,404,000 to help fund a program in human development at the college, conditional on $1 million in matching funds. On May 29, Rose Kennedy, mother of the late president, along with Sargent and Eunice Shriver traveled to Peabody to announce in a public ceremony an immediate Kennedy Foundation gift of $500,000, plus $100,000 in each of the next five years, to fund a Center for Research and Human Development at Peabody to be named for the late John F. Kennedy. This gift resulted directly from conversations between Hobbs and Eunice Shriver. The center would become possibly the most successful of twelve in the United States. The two coordinate grants also funded construction of the Human Development Laboratory (HDL) behind the Psychology Building (later Hobbs Hall), and the Mental Retardation Laboratory (MRL) north of the Peabody Library, which housed the administrative offices of the Kennedy Center. Matching the first grant proved easy. The $500,000 from the Kennedy Foundation counted (it came three days later), and the Knapp Farm finally made its last contribution to Peabody. It sold for $1 million, net. Although the sale involved annual payments, the first to arrive only in 1966, the mortgage was an endowment asset, and thus Peabody used existing endowment funds for the final $500,000. The Knapp income also paid Peabody's share of a new graduate wing for JUL.[16]

Robb had left Peabody before completion of the two luxurious (by Peabody standards) labs. Hobbs and Dunn had realized their greatest dream. Hobbs directed the new center, which soon dwarfed every other program at Peabody. In the last years of Peabody's independence, at least nine-tenths of all funded research would be tied to the Kennedy Center. Almost all federally funded graduate fellowships would have center support, with eventually more than a hundred each year. The research labs were state of the art. The MRL even housed, on its ground floor, an experimental school for younger children with disabilities (later the Susan Gray School) and provided a new home for the Child Study Center. By the terms of the grants, Peabody had to share these facilities with other universities and colleges in the university center, and soon several members of the Kennedy Center staff held joint appointments at the Vanderbilt Medical Center, including one later director. On campus, the center was supposed to enhance the research activities of other departments, particularly education. But perennial weakness and lack of leadership in the education department limited the collaborative work. The Kennedy Center soon had many more useful ties to the Vanderbilt Medical School than to other departments at Peabody, except for special education. For obvious reasons, less well-paid and well-housed professors on campus envied their colleagues in the center. Most resentful of all would be the next president of Peabody.

In December 1963, just as these efforts began to pay off, Hobbs wrote a revealing memorandum to himself, agonizing over whether to remain at Peabody or move to a better-paying position in North Carolina.[17] He realized that he and Dunn were on the way to creating a nationally prominent research center on mental retardation and special education. They would accomplish this, not because of the

On campus for the presentation of the Kennedy Foundation gift, May 29, 1965. From left, Governor Frank Clement, Rose Kennedy, and Eunice and Sargent Shriver. Photographic Archives of Vanderbilt University.

institutional strengths of Peabody, but because a newly generous federal government wanted to spend educational money in the South, and Peabody fortuitously was in the best position to receive it. Yet the funding was fragile, and if it dried up, Peabody would have either to merge with Vanderbilt (Hobbs had favored this in 1962) or settle for mediocrity. Neither Hill nor Robb, although supportive, had become vitally involved in Hobbs's and Dunn's project and, outside the psychology and special-education departments, neither had other Peabody professors.

Overall, Hobbs judged Peabody to be weak and without forceful leadership. He listed only five professors—himself, Dunn, and Ray Norris, all from his division, plus two others—with the ability, drive, and stature to push Peabody ahead. Only about ten other professors could credibly support such progress. Beyond this, the pickings were slim. Peabody was cursed by inbreeding. Hiring its own graduates for almost all leadership positions had given Peabody a comfortable sense of achievement, and had concealed the enormous gap between the college's reality and its barely glimpsed potential. In summary, Hobbs recognized that a world-class research center largely appended to Peabody, a gift from without, could not sustain the entire college. More ambitious leaders recruited from outside the smug Peabody community, and a much fuller integration of programs with Vanderbilt, were a prerequisite for Peabody's survival as a national leader in education. In all these views, Hobbs was prescient, as preparations at Peabody for reaccreditation visits demonstrated.

SELF-STUDY AND ACCREDITATION

The Kennedy Center constituted a unique success story for Peabody. As Hobbes had noted, it benefited from an early start, from location, and from effective leadership. Unfortunately, the traditional departments and schools at Peabody fared less well. The two schools—music and library science—maintained accreditation, but faced such limitations of space as to jeopardize such a status in the future. The departments in education and the arts and sciences fared even worse. The best way to explore these weaknesses was through the all-important accreditation process that preoccupied the administration and almost all faculty from 1962 through 1966, and then again in 1974–75. In 1957, the two accreditation associations of greatest importance to Peabody, SACS and NCATE, adopted a new procedure. This involved a campus visit, made up of prominent educators, every ten years. Beginning two years before the scheduled visits, institutions had to conduct a very detailed self-study. Guiding this was a set of standards adopted by each agency. The visitors used the self-study as a guideline to what they looked at most closely in their visit. It had to be searching and honest, or the visitors would quickly discover deception or apologetics. Since the Southern Association accreditation process involved all aspects of Peabody, not just its training of teachers, I will use the final

Peabody report as a guide for the following assessment of Peabody strengths and weaknesses in the mid-sixties.

Problems far outweighed strengths. That the problems often had their roots in the distant past and had been perennial only increased their seriousness. Now, often for the first time, Peabody professors and administrators had to confront them directly. One opening gambit in the self-study was to note that Peabody was still implementing a new and tighter administrative structure. The self-study committees, which involved most faculty, found no major problems in Peabody's administrative organization, library resources, faculty quality, or student services (judgments that reflected wishful thinking). It noted needs in campus buildings, excessive teaching loads, low salaries for faculty, and the need for more secure funding, but at the time Peabody had a balanced budget. The committee's main concerns involved undergraduate and graduate education. Despite problems, which the SACS visitors also noted, the undergraduate program met its accreditation standards, just as its role in training teachers met those of NCATE. Just the opposite was true for the graduate program.

Despite recent changes, undergraduate admission standards remained low for a college with Peabody's aspirations. They were higher than the average for teachers' colleges, but far below those at Vanderbilt. High school graduates could enter Peabody without any courses in at least one of the following: mathematics, foreign languages, physical science, or social science. They normally had to have a grade point average (on a three-point system) of 1.5, a C plus. They had to submit ACT scores, but Peabody had no rules for evaluating these and no required minimum score. The Peabody retention rate was a scandal. In recent years, only around 40 percent of entering freshmen graduated. The dropout rate did not vary according to student ability or grades, suggesting that few left because of academic failure. In 1959, only 57 percent of freshmen survived the sophomore year. Despite this, a matter of concern on campus, no one at Peabody had initiated a careful study of its causes. Some later studies leading up to a new accreditation visit in 1975 suggests that none of Peabody students' complaints about dorms, food, the lack of enough males, or aspects of social life seemed closely tied to attrition. What most concerned them was the academic program, admission and grading standards, uninspired teaching, and the lack of intellectual challenge.

Grades were a perennial problem at Peabody. It is unfair to refer to grade inflation, which suggests that grades in the past had been lower. Not so. If anything, grading was more rigorous than before World War II. By 1963, a few departments had such high grading standards that students sometimes complained about too much rigor, as in economics, physics, chemistry, and sociology. But most faculty seemed to limit grades to the A to C range, with almost no Ds or Fs. Within this range, they did discriminate, leading to a C+ to B- overall average. The education department, with the most students, did not award a single D or F in 1963, a shocking statistic from the department that, more than any other, was the gateway into the teaching profession. In all, seven departments gave no Fs. But the few rigorous departments brought the numbers of Peabody students who received a D to 4.9 percent. Low grades were even rarer for graduate students. Library Science gave nothing below a B in 1963. The self-study committee, embarrassed and apologetic at this grade profile, promised that the grade average would go down in the next few years. Instead, it went up.

The self-study committee was most evasive or defensive about the graduate program at Peabody, the college's central emphasis. By 1963, it had awarded 16,002 master's degrees, 658 Ph.D.'s, and 226 Ed.D.'s, far more than all its undergraduate degrees. It led the South in sheer numbers. It had awarded more than 1,000 M.A.'s each in 1951 and 1952 alone. Yet it had not kept up with graduate education, had failed to adjust to a new era of collegial rather than apprenticeship training of graduate students, and had for years violated the minimal standards required by SACS. Peabody had no separate graduate faculty. Almost all professors with a doctorate taught both graduate and undergraduate courses, except in psychology, which had not yet begun to offer an undergraduate major. As in the past, Peabody had an inbred faculty. Of its fifty-nine professors with doctoral degrees, twenty-seven were from Peabody. If one counts those with any degree, the number rises to over 50 percent. The percentage of Ph.D.'s on the faculty was still, for the South, comparatively high, but the organization of graduate work did not take best advantage of these well-trained professors.

Since World War II, the M.A. program at Peabody had meant, in effect, come for three quarters and collect your degree. The M.A. program allowed credit for but did not require a thesis. It required neither a qualifying exam along the way (candidacy) nor a final comprehensive exam. Admission to the program required a college GPA of only 1.5, with 2.0 in the major. One had to maintain an average of only 1.5 to receive an M.A. In many departments, M.A. (and at times even Ph.D.) candidates took more than half their work in courses open both to junior-seniors and graduate students, as was the case in other universities. But in most departments some instructors without a terminal degree taught these courses. As the SACS report would make clear, these embarrassing weaknesses did not begin to probe the deficiencies in Peabody's graduate program.[18]

The 1964 SACS report on graduate education hit Peabody like a bombshell. It pulled no punches. Peabody lacked stable central leadership in graduate education, had wide differences of quality in its graduate programs, revealed no recent restudy of program purposes and degrees, and had lost sight of some of the minimal standards set by the association. Peabody had awarded a "fantastically" high number of graduate degrees, most in the summer school. The granting of degrees seemed largely to depend on the number of hours accumulated. Peabody had paid little attention to the level of courses, had not tied course patterns to specific degrees, and had made no distinction between fifth-year work and graduate-quality work. It did not meet standards in its M.A. requirements and had several graduate programs of "questionable quality."[19] The new dean of the graduate school (Phillip Bacon, who soon resigned) wrote the self-study section on graduate work and promised reform but offered not much more than a promise of future study and planning. Yet in conversation, he was candid with the SACS visitors, which gave them some hope of early improvements.

Peabody, from the perspective of the visitors, had lacked strong central leadership, a slap at both Hill and Robb. Its graduate deans had lost contact with the regional association of graduate deans and had not been alert to new and higher standards. Its graduate programs had drifted according to enrollment demands, with no uniform quality. Peabody had not required departments to evaluate their programs critically. In too many graduate departments, the staff had fallen well below accreditation standards. The committee did commend Peabody for suspending some weak programs, but noted that modern languages continued with a staff of only one qualified graduate professor. Other departments had only two or three graduate-level professors, when the standards required at least four. Heavy teaching loads retarded needed research activity by faculty. Despite these failures, Peabody remained a graduate mill, handing out more than five hundred graduate degrees each year. If it had complied with standards, such as candidacy and final exams for the M.A. and required at least half of all courses in graduate-only courses, it could not have manufactured nearly as many. The visitors were appalled at the 1.5 grade point requirement for M.A. graduates, and the failure of the graduate dean to set standards for graduate admission.

Because of these problems, SACS denied Peabody accreditation for its graduate program, mandating that it continue its self-study and reforms until it met all standards. This meant, not that Peabody lost its accreditation, but that it had only two years to reform its whole graduate program. Its accreditation was in abeyance. Robb and the board of trust, embarrassed by the SACS report, did not publicize it on campus. But it had its intended effect. Very quickly, Robb sent a memorandum to the faculty that included a new set of guidelines for graduate education based on the SACS guidelines, particularly for the M.A.[162] After two years of work, a follow-up report in 1966, and a new visitation, Peabody had so corrected most of the problems that the association granted full accreditation in November 1966, when Henry Hill was acting president. But problems remained, and the Committee on Graduate Instruction, looking ahead to the visit in 1975, rendered another harsh evaluation of graduate programs in 1969–70.[20]

By 1969, the SACS standards had risen even higher. What most challenged Peabody was the required four or five full-time graduate faculty members in an M.A. candidate's subject area, and four or five in a more narrowly defined scholarly field for a Ph.D. An institution could not offer graduate degrees without graduate-level work, not just in one discipline but in closely related disciplines, and not without direct outside funding for graduate students. In view of budget deficits and low morale, the committee concluded that, of the eleven divisions or departments still offering graduate work (several gave up after the 1964 evaluation), only two met or exceeded SACS standards—psychology and special education. Some departments did not approach the required full-time-equivalent faculty, including art, biology, physical education, and mathematics. Even with the required number of faculty, music's severe space problems threatened its reaccreditation, and it still had nondoctoral faculty teaching graduate courses. Library science had the needed faculty but faced problems of accreditation because of lack of facilities. English had the needed faculty for graduate work only in English education, not in disciplinary subjects. The social sciences met the minimal requirements only if the whole division, not individual departments (history came close to the standards on its own), offered graduate degrees in social science education. Most troubling, the Division of Education had plenty of faculty but too few in specialized fields. Biology lacked the required professors and barely made the goal even when combined with physics and chemistry. Business education had only the equivalent of one qualified professor devoted to graduate courses. The conclusion: The Graduate School was in serious trouble and without major changes would not earn accreditation in 1974.[21]

KING CLAUNCH AND TIGHT BUDGETS

When Robb had to leave Peabody for a foreign trip less than two months before his July 1, 1966, resignation, the board asked Henry Hill to serve briefly as interim president. "Briefly" lasted until July 31, 1967. In the interim, the board suspended the implementation of Robb's new organizational plan, and Peabody was unable to move forward in any clear direction without a permanent president. A board committee considered dozens of applicants for Robb's successor and brought three candidates to the campus. The candidates acceptable to a faculty advisory committee turned down offers, a discouraging result because none of the candidates were eminent scholars or from major universities. For example, the candidate almost selected by the board committee, despite limited faculty support, was the president of Kansas State Teachers College at Emporia.

Admittedly, 1966 was a hard year to recruit new administrators. But, clearly, Peabody had lost the prestige it once had. Because of impending deficits, the board in 1965 had announced the largest tuition increase in college history—from fifteen to twenty-five dollars per quarter hour. In the midst of an enrollment boom around the country, Peabody lost students. Summer enrollment was down by 556 over 1965; the fall 1966 enrollment was down 19 percent from its 1965 peak. The board anticipated a deficit for 1966–67. When Hobbs announced that he would become provost at Vanderbilt, devoting only one-fifth time to Peabody and the Kennedy Center, a rumor spread of an imminent merger with Vanderbilt. John Windrow tried without success to scotch this rumor in the *Peabody Reflector.* None of these realities helped attract candidates for the presidency.[22]

The original search committee resigned at the board meeting in May 1967, and Hill announced he would not remain as interim president beyond July 31. The board had no alternative but to appoint a new search committee, chaired by a board member and banker from Dallas, Arthur Young. In this now almost desperate search for a willing candidate, two faculty members participated on the committee and with some reluctance ratified the final, disastrous decision. Soon after the May meeting, Young persuaded a close friend, John M. Claunch of Southern Methodist University, to consider the presidency. In view of the delay and rumors that were damaging Peabody's reputation, the new committee rushed into a hasty courtship. Claunch interviewed with the search committee and the board's executive committee, visited the campus, talked with Hill, and quickly emerged as the only candidate. The letters in his behalf were strong but not always enthusiastic. The board, by unanimous vote, approved him on July 10, 1967; he took office on July 31.[23]

Claunch grew up in Louisiana, received his bachelor's degree from Stephen F. Austin State Teachers College in Texas, and after some years of teaching in public schools received his Ph.D. in political science from the University of Texas. An expert on county government, he wrote a book on the subject early in his career. He went to Southern Methodist University in 1938 but took more than three years off to serve in the Army Air Force during World War II. After the war, Claunch chaired the Department of Government and was dean of Dallas College, an adult education college established by SMU. At the time of his Peabody appointment, he had just become director of a new institute on urban research. Notably, his extensive administrative experience involved a college that largely offered evening courses for adults, most taught by part-time instructors. In this role, Claunch was in full control of his empire and may have developed the administrative habits that so marred his tenure at Peabody.[24]

Why select Claunch, a junior-level administrator with no experience in teacher education? Why choose a president who was sixty-one years old, when Peabody seemed, above all, to need youth and vigor to attack its almost overwhelming array of problems? One of the two faculty members on the final search committee, psychologist Raymond Norris, posed these questions to committee chair Arthur Young, who admitted that he was greatly concerned about Claunch's age. He justified the appointment by the need for a mature person able to take charge and restore morale, a man who could bring the trustees more into Peabody's governance. He believed that Claunch had superb administrative or managerial skills. Finally, he wanted someone who could bring Vanderbilt and Peabody into a much closer relationship. He noted that, if Claunch accepted, the board would make clear to him that he and a board committee should begin grooming a prospective successor within two or three years. Claunch stayed for six troubled years.[25]

It would be unfair to attribute Claunch's ineptitude as president to his age. He did not lack energy and worked seven days a week. But age may have helped solidify certain aspects of his personality. He was rigid, insecure, protective of his authority and status, and about as authoritarian as a college administrator could be and survive in his position. He expected deference and loyalty from the faculty, whom he treated as employees. When beleaguered, he tended to boast of his past achievements, to berate the conspirators who were out to get him, and to assume what struck the faculty as a monarchical eminence as he drove around the campus in his new college-owned Cadillac. In constant fear that students and faculty were trying to undermine his authority, for years he complained of faculty or faculty committees that sent letters and memos to the board without his consent and approval. He wanted a quasi-military system with a clear chain of command. Soon his vice president for administrative affairs, William Force, had more credibility with the faculty than did Claunch.

During the years of student activism and radicalism, Claunch was about as far right on the political spectrum as one could go. A pro-America, free-enterprise patriot, he felt contempt for labor unions, welfare advocates, and anti-Vietnam crusaders. He aired such views in public, to the embarrassment not only of the faculty but of board members, who often shared many of his political views but recognized the dangers of identifying Peabody with any partisan position. Ironically, a traditionally conservative Vanderbilt was now headed by Alexander Heard, a political liberal and Democrat. Henry Hill had always identified himself as a moderate conservative, but his views were far to the left of Claunch's.

A college president has two essential roles. The first is to represent the institution to the outside world, to excel in public relations and fund-raising. Claunch had few skills in these areas. He was not an eloquent speaker, nor could he detach himself from partisan and thus divisive advocacy. On many social occasions, he proved embarrassingly inept. The second critical presidential role is to mediate between the faculty (usually abstract, principled, culturally avant-garde, and politically liberal) and the board of trust (usually practical, business oriented, and conservative on most political and cultural issues). A president needs to interpret the position of one for the other and find areas of commonality, usually tied to a shared loyalty to the institution. Claunch completely failed in this role. At times, his attempts approached the pathetic. He did not relate to Peabody professors, could not understand their position, at times feared them, and created tension and even conflict for no reason. He did relate to his board, deferred to it, and wined and dined its members but could not translate board priorities into the language of his faculty, even when he was willing to communicate it to them. In fact, within a year of his assuming the presidency, the board had to assume a mediating role between Claunch and his faculty—to moderate his more dictatorial directives, drag its feet on his ideologically loaded initiatives, and eventually find subtle ways to bypass Claunch in order to deal with the most able and constructive faculty committees. The most critical issue that confronted Claunch after 1967—deficits—reveals this unusual three-way relationship.

Through no fault of Claunch, who had just arrived, the college suffered a small deficit in its 1967–68 operating budget, the first since the depression. Only last-minute cuts in spending kept the red ink to about $30,000. But a budgeted 1968–69 deficit of more than $700,000 rose to $758,000. More alarming, the projected and approved 1969–70 budget included a deficit of more than $900,000, although recalculated later at around $500,000. The board clamped down, approving a 1970–71 deficit of only $142,000, and mandated that the administration submit a balanced budget for 1971–72 with a built-in 5 percent reserve fund to begin paying down the accumulated deficits, all taken from the endowment. This required cuts in support staff, a freeze on faculty salaries, the elimination of travel budgets, and even a suspension of the small research fund. A 1972–73 budget surplus allowed a 5 percent increase in faculty salaries, but the 1973–74 budget (Claunch's last) allowed only a few merit raises, just as inflation began to soar.[26]

The deficits were in part due to the expanded faculty and new courses required to meet the SACS standards for graduate work. Had enrollment increased as predicted in the mid- and late sixties, no budget crunch would have developed, for tuition covered about 70 percent of all costs (it would have been even more without the grants to the Kennedy Center). Enrollment grew slowly, hitting a historic regular-year high in 1965–66 of 2,046. But in 1966–67, when Peabody radically raised tuition for undergraduates, with a lesser increase for graduate students, enrollment dropped off to 1,825, and summer enrollment to below 2,000 for the first time since the war. Enrollment stabilized in the regular year at around 1,800–1,900 but fell slowly in the summer, which in the past had been Peabody's cash cow, to an appalling 1,324 in 1971, well below the regular-year enrollment. Even these summer figures are inflated, since nearly half the listed students attended part-time, and others for only one term or for short pre- and postsession terms. The old and glorious Peabody summers had ended. The vespers services ended after 1967. The lectures and musical events decreased, and few outside professors taught (Peabody could not afford them).[27]

Regular tuition increases kept the loss of enrollment from lowering tuition income. In fact, with each raise, the income increased. From a purely income perspective, Peabody could have afforded to increase tuition even more. But lower enrollment created a problem with degree programs and particularly graduate programs. Low enrollments also meant fewer faculty, not necessarily by dismissals but by attrition. Yet, at Peabody, the faculty continued to grow by six or eight each year. The Kennedy Center accounted for about half the increase in the midsixties, with most of its new appointees supported from grants. In almost all departments, including the education division, a viable graduate program required more faculty to cover the growing number of disciplinary subspecialties. From the perspective of Claunch and the board, this meant a productivity problem. Several professors taught low-enrollment courses. Despite the desperate space shortages for music, library science, and physical education, classrooms were underutilized. In the midsixties, Demonstration School classes moved into college classrooms. Despite the pressing need for more married-student apartments, some dorm rooms remained empty in most semesters.

One obvious solution to a budget crisis is a major campaign. Peabody tried it, with sad results. In the fall of 1969, the board launched a campaign to raise $34.5 million by the centennial year of 1975. To head up the campaign in 1970, it hired outside fund-raising experts who insisted on a major publicity effort. Board chair H. C. Hill Jr. offered $500,000 on a one-to-four matching basis. In one year, the campaign seemed to have produced $2 million. A mobilized campus tried every strategy anyone could think of, including the awarding of Peabody's first honorary degrees. Yet within two years, campaign costs rose to an embarrassing level: one campaign dollar spent for every $4.87 in gifts. After 1972, the campaign shifted into low gear. Faculty, students, and alumni gave, perhaps generously, considering their means. The more than $14 million raised by 1973 seemed impressive, but the amount was deceptive. More than two-thirds reflected grants, most to the Kennedy Center, and some reflected deferred gifts, realized in many cases only on the death of the donor. By a rough estimate, the campaign brought in not much more than $2 million of non-government, or non-deferred funds, about $1.4 million of this contributed by trustees.[28]

The budget crisis created morale problems on campus. Buildings needed maintenance. All capital improvement ceased, except for a new group of fifty-two married-student apartments funded by self-liquidating and insured bonds (north of the original Garrison apartments on Eighteenth Avenue). Continued accreditation at the next SACS and NCATE visits, scheduled for 1974, depended on an enhanced academic program now threatened by budget constraints. By 1969, as deficits grew and as the faculty faced a salary freeze in an inflationary economy, the crunch was on. Scarcity always creates tensions, and Claunch did nothing to alleviate faculty anxiety and at times became a convenient target for its frustrations. Peabody's faculty, almost as much as those of other colleges in the sixties, began to assert itself, usually in a constructive way, but not from Claunch's perspective. In 1960 a faculty committee had for the first time petitioned the board for a minimal salary scale for each rank. The board acceded to what seemed a fair and reasonable request. In 1961 the faculty proposed, and again the board accepted, a faculty-elected Faculty Advisory Council (FAC). The FAC became the voice of the faculty, at first working mainly on such issues as salaries and fringe benefits. Its role expanded in 1969, in part because the board had asked all constituencies at Peabody to offer suggestions on how to escape the financial squeeze.

Claunch had tried to use the faculty to resolve Peabody's problems. He organized a weekend retreat near Kentucky's Mammoth Cave in November 1968 for selected faculty, administrators, and board members. This followed requests to faculty for recommendation. At the retreat, he divided participants into three groups and asked each to come up with answers to five groups of questions, one each in five seminars over two days: Should Peabody provide a respectable undergraduate program for nonteachers? How could Peabody develop a program of distinction in early childhood education? What should Peabody include in a possible curriculum for junior-college teachers? Which academic departments should Peabody add, expand, or drop? How should Peabody relate the regular departments to the Kennedy Center, Demonstration School, and the Division of Surveys and Field Services?

It is difficult to summarize the range of opinion, both from the faculty letters and from the retreat. Generally, faculty talked much more about expanding departments than about reducing or eliminating any, although some raised the possibility of dropping the Demonstration School. Almost all conceded the necessity of a strong liberal arts college, but possibly not in all disciplines. Only Kennedy Center faculty were willing to move entirely to a graduate-level institution. One professor said, quite bluntly, that as presently constituted, Peabody had no future. A common concern was the weak Division of Education. Many wanted closer cooperation with Vanderbilt, but no one proposed a merger. On the whole, participants felt frustrated at the lack of time to do justice to the issues.[29]

In 1969, two concurrent committees addressed the financial crisis. The first, established by the board in May 1969, was a task force of three persons each from the students, faculty, alumni, administration, and board, all with one charge: Identify new sources of income and indicate what program reductions could cut costs with the least damage to essential operations. By then, the accumulated deficit approached $1.25 million, with almost $100,000 in annual interest. The task force had a hard time going beyond the obvious. It recognized that curtailing expenses would mean eliminating programs and faculty, stressing that such reductions could violate AAUP guidelines and hurt more than they helped. As for new income, it suggested a range of possibilities—better recruiting techniques, new in-service training programs, some tuition increases, more opportunities for adult students. Above all, it recommended a study of Peabody's whole academic program, including degrees offered, which would require a great deal of research. (Such a study would produce the radical 1974 *Design for the Future.*) The task force largely finessed the issue critical to the board and Claunch, increased faculty productivity. Data from surveys of instructors were so flawed, the task force found, that it did not dare suggest a formula for teaching loads, which Claunch was already developing. In fact, so broad and general were the task force's recommendations that the board subsequently ignored them to focus on the concurrent study by the FAC, *Peabody Plus.*[30]

In November 1969, after months of committee hearings, the FAC submitted its proposal, by far the most important faculty initiative so far in Peabody history. It fanned faculty enthusiasm, raised morale, and possibly helped initiate policy changes. The executive committee of the board was wise enough to congratulate the faculty on its work, and to recommend that the administration try to implement as many of its recommendations as possible.

Secretly, Claunch tried to undermine the FAC report. He felt threatened by it, although he had met with the faculty to discuss it. He was angry because the FAC sent the report to the faculty and the board at the same time it went to him, which he argued eroded "away the effectiveness" of the chief executive officer. He wanted the practice to stop. He was in charge. Citing his record as a student of politics, he said he found nothing in the report that he and the board had not already discussed. He received several letters that contained language in common from psychology and Kennedy Center faculty, whom he correctly believed were out to erode his authority. A conspiracy was afoot. He resented recommendations for closer cooperation with Vanderbilt through a suggested Nashville University Center Council. One by one, he went through the recommendations, in each case insisting that he was already on top of the problem, or that he and the board had already initiated action. To Claunch, the subtext was clear: The faculty was trying to ensure that the administration and board did not adopt a pattern of retrenchment. On this, he was correct. He also believed that the faculty had changed course on the possibility of closer cooperation with Vanderbilt, to the point of threatening Peabody's autonomy, which he had come to Nashville to preserve. Above all, he expressed his distaste for the endless studies and reports, citing a dozen since the end of the war. He lamented that a school founded in 1875 had not yet established its goals and sense of purpose. Now an all but impudent faculty wanted to change its course.[31]

In some respects, Claunch was right. It was hard to come up with a completely new proposal. But as a political scientist, he should have appreciated the importance of the faculty's coming to feel a sense of ownership for needed policies. In *Peabody Plus,* the FAC announced that this was Peabody's moment of truth. It began by stressing one simple point: Peabody could prosper, possibly even survive, only by closer cooperation with the other institutions in the university center. It needed access to the resources of a major university. It therefore recommended that Peabody do all possible to strengthen its lagging program in education, so that the division could become the educational school for Vanderbilt. It wanted Peabody to lead the way in creating a university center school of fine arts to link not only Vanderbilt and Peabody, but also Fisk and Scarritt, in music, drama, and the fine arts. It proposed a university center school of health and physical education for Peabody and Vanderbilt. Finally, it wanted to tie the Library School more closely to JUL. Already, a joint Nashville University Center Council (NUCC) was considering such cooperative efforts and more. The FAC report implied strong faculty support for this council at the very time Claunch began trying his best to sabotage the entire NUCC effort.

Beyond this academic program, *Peabody Plus* laid out a long series of nonacademic proposals much resented by Claunch, who was already at work on most of them. The FAC wanted a larger development office, improved faculty recruitment, more vigorous public relations work and better alumni ties, higher-quality publications (the *Peabody Journal* was in decline), an improved business office (Kennedy Center staff had lost grants because of delayed processing in the business office), a review of investment polices (a bit unfair), more collaboration with Vanderbilt in support services, and efforts to find new sources of funding, some made possible by NUCC initiatives. Although not new and not full of magical possibilities, these proposals meshed with board priorities.[32]

THE NASHVILLE UNIVERSITY CENTER COUNCIL

The Faculty Advisory Committee placed great hopes in the NUCC. Yet, it was too early in 1969 to tell how the council would work out in the long run, for it was just getting under way. In late 1968, representatives of Peabody, Vanderbilt, Fisk, Meharry, and Scarritt had begun exploring closer cooperation, again with the urging of foundations. In early 1969, the Ford Foundation gave $50,000 to fund a Nashville University Center Council for fifteen months, for planning new programs. Made up of the chief executives of each of the five institutions, the council had a paid half-time project director who ran the central office. One representative from each institution served on the three major committees or "secretariats," with partial central funding for the chairs of each: resources and facilities, academic programs, and community programs. Jack Allen of Peabody chaired the secretariat on academic programs. In the next three years, dozens of other committees worked under the NUCC umbrella, some at the level of departments or disciplines. In the first year, the council approved a common calendar for all five institutions, including summer schools—no mean feat. It also approved a small shuttle bus to run between Fisk and JUL. It began planning some joint purchasing by different combinations of the five schools, and each secretariat outlined a wide array of possible joint activity. But in the following years, most of the important cooperation would involve Peabody and Vanderbilt, and the NUCC may not have contributed much to such bilateral agreements.[33]

Claunch, who chaired the council during its first year, at first seemed enthusiastic. But within a few months, he believed that all the busywork would not amount to much. The Ford Foundation reduced its funding for a second year to $25,000 and asked the cooperating institutions to contribute $10,000 each (later, $5,000) to make up the remainder; Peabody also had to contribute to the shuttle bus. Even for the financially beleaguered Peabody, this seemed not much more than a token cost. But by February 1971, Claunch had doubts about the NUCC and proposed to his fellow executives an alternative. While he did not make its acceptance a condition of continued Peabody membership in NUCC, this was a clear threat. His preference was that Peabody withdraw from the council. His concern was not cost, but authority. In fact, Claunch was mostly correct in his analysis but politically naive. His action proved disastrous for him, a source of distrust that lasted throughout his tenure as president.

Claunch proposed a new and inexpensive alternative to the existing NUCC. He wanted to abolish the directorship and in effect eliminate most costs. The council would continue, made up of the five executive officers with a rotating chair and, he suggested, other representatives from each of the five schools. It would meet periodically to consider forms of cooperation. He suggested an annual contribution of $1,200 by each institution to provide a fund of $6,000 to cover unforeseen developments. The staff of the institution that furnished the annual chair would also furnish secretarial help. Claunch believed consortiums had become a fad with no proven usefulness. He wanted to save money and protect the independence and autonomy of each institution. University life was too complicated, and too many committees spent too much time in talk. He wanted no corporate superstructure, no "authority between the chief executive officer and his institution," no authority "even over the chief executive officer." Characteristic of Claunch, he feared that the emerging staff of the NUCC would forget about its coordinating role and "begin performing a line function, trying to shape the programs and direct the policies of the member institutions."[34]

The other council members rejected Claunch's proposal, and the NUCC continued unchanged. But the news of Claunch's action spread like wildfire. At the time he made the proposal, Claunch shared his views with his cabinet of vice presidents and deans but justified it entirely on the basis of cost.[35] His action created dismay among the faculty, for it seemed to sabotage the main proposals in *Peabody Plus*. Robert P. Thomson, the new FAC chair, relayed the faculty's response in an open council meeting attended by Claunch. He noted with sorrow that the board's academically disastrous decision to move to a balanced budget in one year, with all the retrenchment that would require, and then Claunch's negative views on the NUCC, had brought faculty morale to an all-time low. He admitted that no magic lay in a consortium, incorporated or not, but Peabody simply had to pursue whatever benefits in economic savings and academic improvements the NUCC might bring. Massive retrenchment, particularly in graduate programs, would "squeeze dry" Peabody's government and foundation support.[36]

CLAUNCH VERSUS THE KENNEDY CENTER

Nicholas Hobbs was more dismayed than anyone by Claunch's apparent betrayal of NUCC. He had clashed with Claunch soon after he arrived on campus because of what he saw as threats to his beloved Kennedy Center. Claunch viewed Hobbs as a threat to his own authority. As the new provost at Vanderbilt and with only one-fifth of his salary from Peabody, Hobbs continued as director of the Kennedy Center, which had more and more ties to the Vanderbilt Medical Center. Even for a president less insecure than Claunch, this created a problem. A small universe to itself, fat on federal grants, with faculty investigators paid by soft money, and supported by a prestigious National Advisory Committee, the center was a locus of power almost immune to Claunch's micromanaging. Yet Peabody increasingly depended on the center's financial resources. The only graduate programs with a claim to national eminence were in psychology and special education, and both relied almost entirely on Kennedy Center grants and facilities. The board had tried to strike a balance between keeping Hobbs happy and preventing Claunch from declaring war on the center. In what turned out to be futile attempt to gain some control, Claunch appointed the College Committee on the Kennedy Center, which largely remained inactive. At Hobbs's suggestion, the board of trust also had a committee to monitor the center, and soon this committee found itself in the middle of a battle royal between Claunch and Hobbs.

The first major confrontation came early in Claunch's regime. Claunch wanted full control over his faculty and did not welcome the arrangement that gave Hobbs a dual role at Peabody and Vanderbilt. In early 1968, Claunch seemed uncooperative with the Kennedy Center, had done little to dissuade able staff from leaving Peabody, and never made Hobbs a part of his informal executive staff. Budget tightening and poor business management threatened the center, although Hobbs magnified every small slight or mistake. The issue that led to open warfare was his desire to appoint Donald Stedman as the center's associate director. A former Hobbs student who took his Ph.D. in psychology at Peabody, a child psychologist with strengths also in psychiatry, Stedman was in 1968 an associate professor of medical psychology and psychiatry at Duke and a visiting professor at the nearby University of North Carolina. He seemed the ideal person to take over day-to-day operations at the Kennedy Center and would also have a joint appointment in pediatrics at the Vanderbilt Medical School. Claunch resisted the appointment, which he felt Hobbs was almost forcing on him. Claunch seemed to use a rigid enforcement of nepotism rules at Peabody to threaten some key staff employees and the wives of key professors in the psychology department and Kennedy Center, a complex controversy that revealed the resentment and envy of faculty who did not share in the center's special funding. Claunch risked losing center faculty and impeded strong appointments by mandating equal salaries for faculty on hard and soft funds. For about two months, the sides fought it out. Hobbs, in effect, forced both the board and Claunch to capitulate, take the center very seriously, and cooperate with its staff. To this end, by July 1968, Hobbs had used every weapon at his command, lobbying the Shrivers and inviting officials of the key funding agencies to Peabody, then persuading them via tours and conversations that the Kennedy Center was in jeopardy. Concerned letters went out to Claunch from Washington. Hobbs even drafted a sharp letter for Ted Kennedy to send to the chair of the board of trust that intimated a withdrawal of Kennedy Foundation funding. But before Hobbs and the Shrivers turned Ted loose, Claunch had a supportive conversation with Hobbs and agreed to most of his demands. The president had already approved Stedman's appointment, and he now made Hobbs part of his inner cabinet. The more able gut fighter, Hobbs had won this battle, leaving the field with nothing but resentment and ill will on the part of a soon beleaguered Claunch. The focus of campus conflict shifted to budgets, curtailed raises, and faculty efforts toward faculty governance.[37]

By the summer of 1970, Hobbs wanted to retire as director of the center but stay on the Peabody faculty without pay and continue to chair the college committee on the Kennedy Center. Already close to firing him, Claunch welcomed his retirement. But much was at stake. A prolonged fight over control of the center could jeopardize its outside funding. Hobbs's conditions for leaving the directorship included choosing his successor—Donald Stedman—and the early appointment of the chair of psychology as a badly needed dean of academic affairs. The ensuing controversy was the most dangerous in Peabody's history.

Claunch was not about to let Hobbs dictate his appointments and in particular did not want a director with a joint appointment at Vanderbilt. Aware of the stakes, H. G. Hill, speaking personally and not for the board, asked Hobbs to resign, making it clear that the board might otherwise remove him from his directorship and one-fifth faculty appointment. Hobbs even drafted a letter of resignation but decided to fight it out for the sake of the Kennedy Center's survival. His colleagues who made up the coordinating committee for the center (the heads of all institutes and the chairs of psychology and special education) petitioned the board on May 27 to meet all Hobbs's demands. These became the demands of this faculty group, the most powerful at Peabody, and which included Ray Norris, Susan Gray, Bob Newbrough, and Carl Haywood. Sargent Shriver, who had just consented to be a member of the Peabody Board of Trust, wrote a strong letter to Claunch on June 2 expressing his concerns about the survival of the center. After several appeals, Hobbs received a hearing before the board's executive committee on June 5,

1970. The committee could hardly refuse to hear from the provost of Vanderbilt, next to Chancellor Heard the chief academic officer on that campus.

Hobbs began by expressing his despair at Peabody's present course toward mediocrity, his apprehension for the future of his center, and his embarrassment at having to intervene. He tried to discount any personal conflict with Claunch and to place the responsibility for Peabody's recent calamities on the board. He projected two futures for Peabody. It might continue as an average undergraduate college for any student it could graduate, with a limited graduate program in a few fields, or what Hobbs meant by mediocrity. He and the Peabody faculty had another scenario in mind—Peabody as a leader in all fields of education, with continuous experimental programs and research on new knowledge and methods, all largely funded by foundations and federal grants. He believed that the Kennedy Center, with more than $2.5 million in such funds each year, was a model for the rest of Peabody, but one not followed so far. In its area, it was the equal of Harvard or Wisconsin, and, contrary to rumor, it was in all ways self-supporting, not a drain on Peabody's finances, which he had the figures to prove.[38]

While he believed that with proper leadership, Peabody could regain a premier position in education, now it seemed destined to become bankrupt. Hobbs almost cavalierly noted that there was plenty of money available if Peabody had the talented leaders, the confidence, and the imagination to get it (a claim in part unfair, in part arrogant). The Kennedy Center could not survive without a more purposeful, dynamic, and productive Peabody. It needed leaders like Bruce Payne and Henry Hill, who built the Peabody that allowed the Kennedy Center to develop, but the college was now increasingly uncongenial to the center. The deficits and proposed retrenchment could destroy it. Inept business accounting threatened its grants. Jealousies and factionalism hurt, despite the unity displayed by the faculty in support of *Peabody Plus.* Above all, the center had to be part of the large, integrated university center just sabotaged by Claunch.[39] Never had the committee heard such a devastating attack on Peabody leadership and policies. Claunch, who had to sit through the presentation, must have felt deep embarrassment as well as anger.

The executive committee, which did not support Claunch on many issues, mandated that he and Hobbs meet until they resolved all differences. When confronted with authority, Claunch usually submitted in good grace. Several tense meetings ensued, the last in early July 1970, when the distraught Claunch begged Hobbs to resign his directorship and Peabody appointment. If he did not, the executive committee was prepared to fire him (Hobbs knew that he had no more than three supporters on the committee). His refusal to resign would not only imperil the start of Peabody's fund drive and the future of the Kennedy Center, but also create deep divisions in the board of trust. Hobbs submitted his resignation on July 14 in exchange for Claunch's concession to all his other demands but one—he did not allow Hobbs to remain on the faculty. Claunch appointed Stedman and made the center director a member of his cabinet. He agreed to appoint Hobbs to the center's National Advisory Committee. He promised an early appointment for vice president for academic affairs, but not Hobbs's candidate; he turned to the aging William D. McClurkin, thereby further undercutting the strength of the education division. He appointed a person in the business office to work directly with the center and promised that Peabody would remain a full participant in the NUCC.[40] Perhaps the crux of the difference between these two powerful egos had been Hobbs's belief that only closer cooperation with Vanderbilt could insure the future of both Peabody and the Kennedy Center.

The center did not in fact suffer from this infighting. Stedman proved an able director and was able to appease the bitter Claunch, promising in his appointment contract never to contact the board of trust directly. But Stedman left after a year, returning to an excellent position at the University of North Carolina, in part because the central administration had rejected his promotion to full professor despite the recommendation of his department. With Stedman's support, Carl Haywood took over as director and brought stability to the center. Its centers and institutes continued to shift, almost year to year, but three held constant: the Institute on Mental Retardation and Intellectual Development, first headed by Lloyd Dunn and later by a series of directors when Dunn left Peabody in 1967 for the University of Hawaii; the Demonstration and Research Center for Early Education, headed by Susan Gray until 1972; and the Center for Community Studies, headed until merger by John R. Newbrough. Claunch saw no reason for such an outreach effort and worked unsuccessfully to abolish Newbrough's center.[41]

FACULTY AND STUDENT ACTIVISM

Faculty and student efforts to take a greater role in college government plagued Claunch's presidency. Such demands peaked across the country between 1967 and 1972, the years of Claunch's tenure, and nothing in his personality prepared him to meet them with good grace. He was willing to accept and even applaud FAC efforts in one area only: to clarify rules on academic freedom, tenure, and promotion. The FAC for years worked on the exact wording of a faculty manual that adhered to AAUP standards, but until merger the board of trust never formally adopted any version of the manual or made it contractual. While the administration never violated the manual in areas of academic freedom or in awarding tenure, the faculty believed that in the 1971–73 period of austerity, the administration did violate the manual in its effort to force added teaching hours on the faculty during an intercession required by the new joint calendar.

The faculty came closest to rebelling against Claunch in 1972, over the issue of teaching loads and faculty productivity. For more than two years, Claunch had fretted over professors who did not do enough teaching or had low enrollments. Hand-drafted notes indicate that he constantly sought a formula to use to guide the faculty, always based on the number of credit hours taught, not the number of classes. On January 31, without consulting his deans, let alone department chairs and faculty, Claunch mandated a new set of guidelines based on his belief that a professor at Peabody should teach the equivalent of five hundred undergraduate credit hours each year, less time for administrative duties. This meant a typical Peabody professor who taught six four-hour courses each year would have to average twenty-one students per course. If Peabody adhered to this formula, then it could reduce its faculty to about ninety-three teachers, a savings of about one-third in instructional costs. Aware that graduate teaching took more time, Claunch suggested modifications for such courses, although he refused to let student advising or thesis direction, functions of every faculty member, lower anyone's teaching load. For 1972–73, he made the teaching-load requirement either four hundred credit hours (to rise to five hundred over three years), or twelve semester hours

A Playboy Party in 1964, or about as daring as one could be at Peabody. Photograph by L. L. Tucker, Photographic Archives of Vanderbilt University.

with no freshman-sophomore course of fewer than ten, and no advanced course of fewer than six. He demanded that teachers submit their total enrollment at the end of registration each semester. If too low by these guidelines, teachers would take on extra but unspecified duties for the college. The size of each departmental faculty, henceforth, would be based on credit hours taught; those that fell below the formula would lose a proportionate number of faculty.[42]

His edict raised a storm of protest. The FAC denounced it in an open meeting. The Student Government Association and the Graduate Student Council wrote letters of opposition to the board. Even the two academic deans, more gently, pointed out its problems and noted that they had no way to implement it for the coming fall, because the catalogue already listed the course schedule. The department chairs met and protested. No one favored the formula, but the protests above all involved the process. The president had imposed from above a radical new departure in academic policy. Once again, Claunch had created a storm unnecessarily. Busy board members resented all the mail but in November 1972 did what they had to: They endorsed Claunch's guidelines. No one seems to have paid the edict any heed after 1972.[43]

Claunch's arbitrary and threatening action convinced the Peabody faculty that it needed a faculty senate, whatever its title. The Vanderbilt Board of Trust in 1967 had set up a strong University Senate. Although ultimately advisory, board concurrence gave it a dominant role on academic issues. The Peabody faculty, with more at stake, wanted the same. In 1971, the FAC began petitioning the president for a plan for college governance that involved more faculty participation, particularly in areas of educational policy. Complicating their early proposals was the issue of student participation. Many faculty, particularly junior faculty, wanted student members in any new faculty advisory body. Claunch shot down all such proposals, often with ridicule. The college already had too many committees. Horrified at student participation outside the sole area of student affairs, he pointed to the radical policies, such as cohabitation, successfully pushed by students at many northern universities. Under Claunch, Peabody would not have a faculty senate. And his board consistently backed him on this issue.[44]

The FAC continued to work on a constitution for what it called the Council on College Policy. In September 1972, the whole faculty met and overwhelmingly endorsed a rather standard faculty senate, close in most details to Vanderbilt's except for two members each from the undergraduate Student Government Association and the Graduate Student Council. The six academic divisions, including the Demonstration School faculty, would have elected members, while administration officers, save for the president, would serve ex officio as voting members. The council, which would elect its own officers, was to make recommendations in several policy areas—admission, degree requirements, student affairs and student aid, curricula, the grading system, instructional and research standards, criteria for faculty involvement in selecting the president of the college, and standards of ethical and professional conduct for faculty and students. Although never accepted by the board, this plan directly influenced the development of a college council after merger.[45]

Compared to most universities, even to Vanderbilt, the student movement at Peabody was relatively tame. Perhaps less than fifty of the undergraduates, who were three-fourths women, were political activists or susceptible to most aspects of the counterculture. Claunch publicly denounced hippies on campus in September 1970, suggesting that they deterred other students, or their parents, from selecting Peabody. The SGA formally protested his remarks as hostile to human freedom.[46] Drugs were on campus and in the Demonstration School, with at least one Peabody student arrested for drug use. Campus crime rose; two junior faculty were arrested for breaking and entering. But the student newspaper noted that only a handful of students, apparently men, had long hair or dressed sloppily. What the students wanted was more social amenities, and the administration, led by dean of students Arthur H. Cook, tried to meet their demands. The administration now encouraged social fraternities and sororities, but with so few men on campus, the fraternities usually folded in a few years. Peabody finally established a small program of intercollegiate sports, with a budget of only $3000 as late as 1972; only the women's gymnastic team won any laurels. Women also competed in volleyball and tennis, men in golf, tennis, and soccer. The students raised $800 on their own to buy athletic equipment. Only gradually did undergraduates achieve their other goals, such as open dorms (in 1973), but never the freedom to invite any speaker they wanted to campus, to have alcohol at campus parties, or to have students on the board of trust.

Political agitation by what students always confessed was an apathetic student body surfaced only in 1969, tied to Vietnam protests. In October, the students voted to join students around the country in a moratorium, with much faculty cooperation, although Peabody did not cancel classes. In May 1970, at the time of the Cambodian incursion and the Kent State deaths, the students received support, in a called faculty meeting, for a two-day suspension of classes. Even Claunch reluctantly accepted the suspension, and the students applauded him for it. They held a memorial service for the dead at Kent State and gathered for an afternoon speak-out against the war. Yet, most Peabody students probably did not take part. Some enjoyed the days off; others, of a different political orientation, protested the suspension.[47]

In the midst of the most violent student protests in the North, Claunch decided to speak out. He offered his extended and divisive speech to the graduating class of August 1970. Poorly written, but at points passionate in conviction, his speech revealed Claunch at his best and worst. He opened with a list of twelve changes that had transformed twentieth-century America. Most of these he chose well: the country's creditor status in the world and its deficit financing (that pressure groups kept boosting spending reflected the economic illiteracy of this generation); the shift from rural to urban, from rugged individualism to a welfare state (he deplored this), from a militia to a large standing military force, from state rights to centralized government, from laissez-faire to state capitalism and a regulated economy, from a real dollar to one worth only forty cents, from a seventy-hour to a forty-hour work week. He condemned the shift from a nonunion labor force to the giant AFL-CIO; union demands for more pay without increased productivity were a sure road to insolvency, while public employees, even teachers, were now organizing and even striking, changes that Claunch believed reprehensible, a cause of the sorry state of U.S. society. He never missed an opportunity to attack unions. His next to last described change was from a "nation of relatively sane people to a nation of drug addicts." He wrote perceptively of the new world order, of the pace of change, of the need for students to learn to cope with a complicated society.

After this catalogue of changes, interspersed with his personal reactions to them, Claunch ended with an evaluation of the dangers threatening American democracy. To the concerns of Americans revealed by a Gallop poll (Vietnam, drugs, crime, race relations, inflation), he added his own, which included unions and pressure groups, irresponsible demonstrators leading the country toward dictatorship, the tendency of courts to defer to minority groups at the expense of the majority, radicals and extremists who did not know the history of the nation's venerable rights, and, in a different mood entirely, the erosion of the environment. He wanted change to arrive through an enlightened evolutionary process, not a revolutionary one.

Claunch summed up his concerns in a final charge to graduates that perfectly expressed the outlook of an old man alienated from almost everything happening in 1970: "It is my hope and my prayer that this graduating class understands that our country is pitted against the shrewdest agitators of history—that they will not overlook or pass up any opportunity to foment unrest among us, to undermine our religious faith, to deride and belittle our patriotism, to erode away our institutions, to divide us into warring factions, to make us a nation of drug addicts, to neutralize our influence among developing nations, to weaken our resolve and ultimately to dominate and destroy us."[48] Published in the *Reflector,* the speech gained widespread attention, for better or worse. Many board members agreed with and applauded Claunch, but they must have felt apprehensive about the address's political effect. James Stahlman of the *Nashville Banner* predictably praised the speech, as did old John Windrow, the recently retired editor of the *Reflector.*

In his final two years as president, Claunch joined a few board members in addressing the festering sickness he saw all around him. In December 1971, officials of an advocacy group called the American Viewpoint and Council for Citizenship Education (AVCCE) contacted Claunch. They wanted to affiliate with Peabody, although it never became clear exactly what affiliation would entail. The executive committee set up a committee to explore the possibilities. A small group, largely made up of faculty members, reviewed the organization's literature and met its president. In January 1972, Claunch and a board member, Frank Farris, met in New York City with some of the AVCCE trustees. Founded in 1922, just after the red scare that followed World War I, the AVCCE was comprised of public school administrators, college administrators, faculty, and civic leaders. It reflected a more sophisticated version of many organizations that had long supported Americanization through education. Its avowed purpose was to promote citizenship and the founding ideals of America. Claunch liked what he saw, for he wanted to make Peabody a bastion of patriotism. No one on the board seemed opposed, but one suspects they were leery of such an alliance, which apparently promised no extra funding for Peabody.[49] In February, Claunch again went to New York to talk about terms of affiliation with the AVCCE staff. On March 17, the executive committee approved a resolution toward what it called merger, emphasizing that such a merger must not impose additional financial burdens on Peabody. It agreed to a joint committee of trustees from each institution to serve as a liaison between the two and asked for a realistic budget proposal. The merger required a resolution of procedural issues and an amended charter for the AVCCE.[50] Apparently, the two institutions did not work out the problems before the meeting of the Board of Trusts in May. The issue never came before the board of trust again, perhaps in part because Claunch was now on the way out as president, and his initiative had lain behind the proposed merger.

Soon Claunch launched a new and more serious campaign, this time with the strong support of board member John S. Bransford. In his 1972 presidential report, Claunch had advocated one program improvement that would "capture the attention and excite the interest of both parents and prospective students who desire to identify with a college that provides a wholesome environment, a pro-American philosophy."[51] The key proposal, less innocent than it sounded, was a three-hour course on the principles of economics and a second on comparative economic systems. Bransford was horrified that militant, misinformed teachers across America were hostile to a corporate free-enterprise system. He had read a survey that showed that a majority of college students had little but contempt for business institutions, that they were completely misinformed about levels of profit, that 53 percent favored government ownership of banks, railroads, and steel companies, and that a horrifying 62 percent believed that the government should guarantee everyone employment. Such students had been bombarded with "leftist falsehoods and socialistic myths." Some churches were in part responsible for such crazy ideas, but most of the blame lay with schools.[52]

These two courses, if taught well, might have improved the Peabody curriculum, but only one point of view would have met the expectations of Claunch and

Bransford. In February 1973, the executive committee held a special meeting to develop a proposal for a Center of Economic Education that, rather than serious work in economics, would provide all Peabody students with a proper understanding of the free-enterprise system, and of socialist and other competing systems. The language was ideologically loaded. Nonetheless, the executive committee voted in favor of such a center, which would require three professors, a summer workshop for teachers, and efforts to spread the enlightenment to school systems, all at a projected cost of more than $130,000 in a year of no faculty raises. Fortunately, saner heads prevailed. Vice President McClurkin pointed out that the six additional hours required of all students would overload the general education requirement. Chairman of the board H. G. Hill Jr. expressed approval, but only if new funds were available. The final recommendation, developed by an ad hoc committee chaired by Bransford, removed the requirement that all students take the courses, but the full board never mandated implementation, and the whole scheme died with Claunch's retirement in 1973. In his last address to the board, Claunch lamented the failure to get the new program underway. Pathetically, this was the only important new program he conceived and promoted during his presidency.[53]

By early 1973, the board had decided to accept Claunch's retirement by the end of the year or early in the next, when he would be sixty-eight, the mandatory retirement age without special extensions. They began a carefully orchestrated process of easing him out with all possible ceremony and words of appreciation. Claunch by then had little authority. Not even many board members took him seriously. They humored him by agreeing with his principles but never got around to implementing his programs. They became masters of delay, of more study, and of no final action. Although not entirely Claunch's fault, Peabody was in even worse shape when he left than when he had arrived in 1967.

CHAPTER THIRTEEN

Merger

IT ALL BEGAN WITH A GAMBLE IN 1974. THE NEW PEABODY president, along with the board of trust, decided that an independent Peabody could not survive without major changes. While it might not survive even then, this was its last chance. The first essential for survival was reaccreditation. In the spring of 1975, both the Southern Association of Colleges and Schools (SACS) and the National Council for the Accreditation of Teacher Education (NCATE) teams would visit the campus. At the same time, the Library School would be under review by the American Library Association. To retain accreditation from these three bodies, Peabody had to reorganize its academic program and commit funds it could not gain from tuition, investments, or grants. The board decided to use $1.8 million of Peabody's endowment (approximately $13 million in 1974) to bridge the next three years and avoid harmful retrenchment. Program improvements, a higher enrollment, and more successful fund-raising, the board hoped, would justify the borrowing and, after 1977, more than pay back the deficits.

It did not work out as planned. From 1977 to 1979, Peabody used funds from the sale of capital assets and from nonrestricted gifts to balance its operating budget. But it was apparent by the spring of 1978 that the college would face large deficits in succeeding years unless it so cut programs as to move toward mediocrity. The last private independent teachers' college in America had reached the end of the line.

JOHN DUNWORTH AND A DESIGN FOR THE FUTURE

The person most responsible for the financial gamble, and for a new academic program on campus, was Peabody's new president, John Dunworth. He was forty-nine, politically gifted, and an experienced administrator. Thus, Dunworth resembled Henry Hill. He was the incoming president of the American Association of Colleges for Teacher Education. He came to Nashville from Ball State University in Indiana, where he was a very successful dean of its largest unit, the Teachers College. Although not a prestigious school, Ball State had developed into one of the strongest of the new comprehensive universities. Dunworth was a native of Los Angeles, an Episcopalian, an undergraduate at Berkeley, and an Ed. D. graduate of the University of Southern California. Again like Hill, he cut his teeth on public school teaching (speech) and as a county school superintendent. Before moving to Ball State, he served as superintendent of the Department of Defense's Pacific and Far East school system, with his home base in Hawaii. His reputation was unsurpassed in educational administration, and his letters of recommendation from Ball State were glowing.[1]

Because of events, and of policies he adopted, Dunworth became a controversial figure at Peabody. Evaluations of his talents and character soon varied immensely. He arrived with a mark against him, but not because of any fault of his own. On August 20, 1973, President Claunch had not only announced his pending retirement but also the name of his replacement. A board committee had worked in secrecy for more than a year to find a new president. Not even all the board members knew the details of this search, which involved no faculty, a slight that made them suspicious of Dunworth. Later, because of the need for confidentiality, Dunworth seemed to many faculty to be duplicitous, a slick politician who publicly celebrated the achievements of Peabody while behind the scenes he plotted a merger or even considered turning Peabody into a research institute. But he was not at all like Claunch. Charming, vain, an expert at self-promotion, and superbly self-confident, he communicated effectively, was secretive but not authoritarian, worked well with faculty committees, and successfully promoted the college. In other times, in other circumstances, he might have been a popular president.

Beginning early in 1974, Peabody would enjoy a year or two of high hopes. Dunworth believed he could remake the college, despite its looming problems. He inherited a Peabody that still retained a high reputation in its field. In 1975, a national magazine rated Peabody twelfth among teachers' colleges, largely on the basis of judgments by educational deans. This was a comedown from the postwar years, when it still aspired to rank alongside Columbia University's Teachers College, Harvard, Chicago, and Stanford (all in the top five). In another ranking of overall college strengths the same year, College Rater, Inc., listed Peabody as twenty-fourth among eighty-four colleges in the South Central United States (Rice was first, Vanderbilt second).[2] The bridging subsidies from the endowment allowed Peabody to "balance" its annual budgets, to improve faculty salaries slightly as inflation of up to 8 percent a year outpaced such raises on almost all campuses, and in a weak academic market to recruit much abler faculty than a decade before. An observer in 1975 or 1976 might have thought that Peabody was again on the move. But waning enrollments and a disappointing campaign for funds told a different story. Peabody was living on illusions.

When Dunworth took over in January 1974, the faculty was deeply involved in the required self-studies for the two main accrediting agencies, and still haunted by memories of the 1964 visits. Graduate accreditation might still be at stake. Dunworth, like past new presidents, wanted a probing self-study not directly connected with accreditation, for he believed that Peabody's survival depended on drastic academic reforms. He thus appointed a Select Committee on Peabody's Second Century, which completed its report in August, well before the outside visitors arrived in March 1975. "Select" is a good label for Dunworth's committee. It included only three experienced and able professors—historian Jack Allen, psychologist Raymond Norris, and Peabody's expert in higher education, Ida Long Rogers. The three consulted widely and asked all constituencies for advice but completed a daring report that largely reflected their own thinking. They met periodically with Dunworth, who did not directly shape the report's content. But he refused to allow a faculty review of the final product, which was so radical in its proposals that it would have ignited heated protest and endless faculty discussion. This lack of further faculty input disappointed Rogers and Norris. Instead,

John Dunworth, the last president of an independent Peabody. Photographic Archives of Vanderbilt University.

Dunworth enthusiastically endorsed the report and took it directly to the board of trust, which approved it on August 29, 1974, with only minor word changes and one dissenting vote. The board was not about to second guess a new president. Entitled *Design for the Future,* this was by far the most influential and controversial of all the self-studies in the college's history. It changed Peabody and moved it at least a third of the way toward the more narrow focus necessitated by the later merger with Vanderbilt. Later, in all the controversy over merger, Peabody's angriest faculty blamed the college's plight on *Design for the Future* and even saw in it a conspiratorial tool for forcing merger. In 1975, the reaction varied according to the impact of the report on each discipline or professor.

The select committee recommended that Peabody become, once again, a college devoted entirely to the training of professional educators. This invited a sense of deja vu, for this had been a perennial theme of earlier self studies. According to *Design,* every student at Peabody would have to learn about schools and the learning process. This meant that Peabody would drop all nonprofessional degrees (bachelor and master of arts, master of music, and doctor of music education) and offer the Ph.D. only as a research degree in education-related fields. Retained would be the bachelor and master of science, the education specialist degree, and the doctor of education. The M.S. would be a strictly professional degree, and no longer have to meet the SACS graduate requirements. It would be the terminal degree in a five-year basic program in preservice educational training. This refocused mission threatened the departments of art, music, and health and physical education, which would now have to drop courses not directly related to the education mission. In particular, this meant a sharp abridgement of offerings and a reduction of faculty in the school of music.

To facilitate the new professional emphasis, the committee recommended a new administrative structure, the third in three decades. Here Dunworth's preferences were critical. In the new plan, which was fully implemented by 1975, only four officers reported directly to the president. The most important of the four were an executive dean for academic affairs, a post soon filled by Thomas Stovall, a Peabody Ph.D. most recently with the Tennessee Higher Education Commission; and an executive dean for administrative affairs, soon filled by James Whitlock, a professor of education and former director of the Division of Surveys and Field Services. Stovall assumed the functions of both undergraduate and graduate deans. In the years before merger, Dunworth, Stovall, and Whitlock became an executive team. Arthur Cook, the dean of students, assumed responsibility for all aspects of student life, including admissions and placement. The fourth position was a new executive director of development and college relations.

In what became a source of more confusion than of significant change, the *Design* also supported a new organization of academic programs. It simply updated the older divisional system. It eliminated departments as administrative units, replacing them with four basic and four advanced multidisciplinary "programs," each headed by a director. The four basic programs included the traditional general education program, the education of children (from preschool to middle school), the education of youth (secondary school), and educational support (art, music, physical education, and library science). The advanced programs included some fancy terms for what amounted to programs in administration, curriculum development, human development (psychology and special education), and education policy (history and philosophy of education, educational psychology, and broader social policy issues). The committee wanted each program to reach beyond the campus and directly involve education officials or lay people in advisory councils (a goal unmet by the time of merger). Individual faculty members would identify with one or more of the programs based on what they taught or their research interests (most would be part of at least one basic and one advanced program). The plan did not abolish departments but renamed them as "faculties." It reduced their number from seventeen to eleven, and provided for elected chairs (with no reduced teaching load). It stripped these faculties of any real power in such critical areas as curriculum development and faculty appointments, promotions, and tenure. In fact, the new programs, like the old divisions, never quite functioned as intended, and the departments never really went away.

This seemed to be a highly centralized and hierarchical administrative structure. Program directors worked directly with the academic dean, who reported to the president. What about input from faculty, students, or staff? The plan took care of this problem by placing four councils (academic, personnel, student, and fiscal policies) between the bottom and top, with intricate appointment and selection schemes to bring administrators and constituencies together to shape policy recommendations. A plan intended to simplify administration had only made it more complex. For the faculty, the two most important councils were the two involved with academic policies and personnel decisions. The council on academic policy included the eight program directors, six elected faculty, two students, and the academic dean; it elected its chair from among the program directors. This council had responsibility for every academic issue—degree requirements, grading polices, curriculum development, research standards, standards of professional conduct, and admission standards. But the vital issues of appointments, promotions, tenure, faculty evaluations, and salary guidelines resided with the personnel council, which included three elected faculty, three elected staff, and the academic and administrative deans. Its chair, ex officio, was the chair of the Peabody faculty, which implicates another aspect of the new administrative order.

The faculty had long struggled in vain to get a faculty senate. When the board in the fall of 1974 ratified the entire *Design for the Future,* it in effect approved a new system of faculty governance. The faculty had a dominant role in the academic and personnel councils, since the program directors were all members of the faculty. The new plan eliminated the old Faculty Advisory Council, triggering some resentment among the faculty, and replaced it with a new, powerful faculty organization. Faculty meetings that in the past had served for little more than information exchange took on new significance. The regular faculty now elected a chair, vice chair, and recorder each year, as well as faculty members on the four councils. The deans, but not the president, were ex officio voting members of the faculty. The three faculty officers, who held ex officio positions on various councils, began to refer to themselves as the executive committee of the faculty and gained significant clout. The faculty also appointed ad hoc committees. This organization served the faculty well during the merger controversies, eclipsing the authority of the councils, which were tainted by their presumed deference to Dean Stovall. The new organization was in effect for less than five years, too briefly to judge how it might have worked in the long term.

It was not these structural changes, but their implementation, that invited controversy. In designing the eight programs, the select committee decided that three small departments, with collectively only eight faculty and twelve student majors, no longer met a vital need. Of the three, home economics was a dying discipline, business education a pale imitation of the many competing schools in the area, and foreign languages redundant because of larger departments at Vanderbilt. Only two continuing faculty in these three departments were tenured, and the committee noted that they would receive alternative assignments. Until the merger, Peabody never terminated a tenured professor. Nontenured faculty would simply not be reappointed at the end of their contract period. This meant eight less faculty at Peabody, or a prospective reduction from 155 to 147.

But the committee wanted to weed out even more faculty, which would mean higher teaching loads for those who remained. Thus, the committee dared tread the path taken by Claunch only three years before and even upped his ante. It recommended, and the board of trust accepted, a new workload formula. Though never fully implemented, the plan predictably created anxiety among the faculty. Professors teaching in basic programs or courses up through the master's level were expected to teach six hundred student credit hours each academic year (summer excluded), advise up to twenty students, and serve on at least one major college committee. In their spare time, they could carry out their research and write their books. This formula meant that the average professor, who taught no graduate courses, would teach a hundred students each semester, or an average of twenty-five in each three-hour course. (To meet the new University Center agreements, Peabody had modified most courses from four hours to three.) Only nine professors at Peabody already met this quota. One who taught only graduate courses had a quota of three hundred credit hours and only ten advisees. Since most professors taught at both levels, their quota fell somewhere between these two extremes. The committee hoped that this formula, gradually applied, would reduce the instructional staff to around a hundred, but this excluded forty-one largely research professors funded by grants. In all, the committee expected the faculty to fall from 155 to about 141, a savings of only 10 percent in instructional costs. It did fall to roughly this number by merger.

The committee believed that Peabody had a large enough but poorly allocated physical plant. It suggested a new professional evaluation of space use, leading to new survey which only identified the obvious problems. The select committee recommended a new home for the library school. It believed Blair Academy should no longer serve as a preparatory academy for the now reduced School of Music. Blair would thus be completely independent, except that the college would pay for the instruction of Peabody students. Two years later, Blair asked for a complete separation from Peabody. For the city of Nashville, the most controversial proposal was that Peabody close its Demonstration School. The committee documented the school's marginal contribution to Peabody student teachers and noted

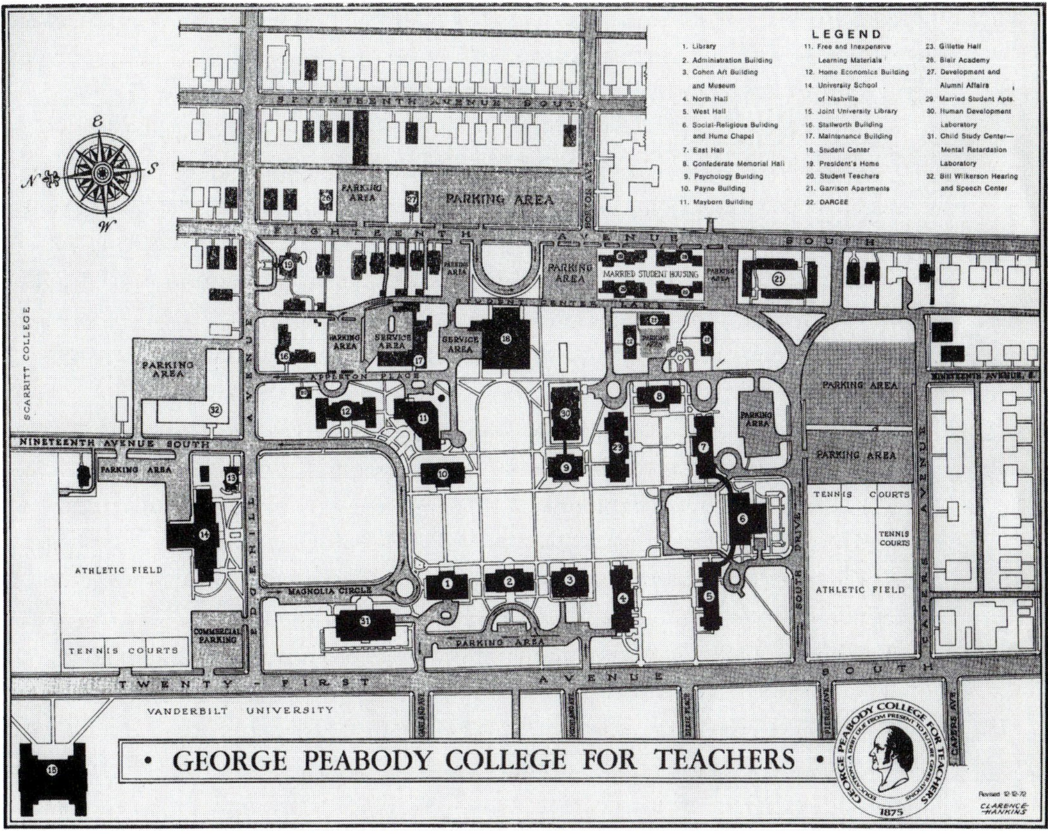

A map of Peabody at its greatest extent, or just before it sold the Demonstration School. George Peabody College Records.

that in all but one year over the last decade, it had run operating deficits (traditionally, Peabody had accepted these as payment for services to its students). In effect, the school was a popular, much loved, and very successful college preparatory academy for the children of mostly affluent parents. Its student profile did not match that of the diverse Nashville public school system, which now provided most opportunities for observation and practice teaching. Because of fiscal needs and the fear of losing local support, this recommendation led Peabody to sell the Demonstration School building and seven acres of land to a new University School Committee. Peabody thus lost its most valuable acreage, the land that provided the best link to the Vanderbilt campus and to JUL.[3]

SELF-STUDY AND REACCREDITATION

As Peabody began implementing its new design in 1975, the self-study committees completed their reports for the SACS and NCATE. The self-studies, which had to reflect the current Peabody, not the one projected in *Design for the Future,* included a critical, honest assessment of strengths and weakness. No one feared the loss of accreditation, except possibly for the graduate program. In fact, largely because of the promise of *Design* and full adherence to formal SACS standards, the visiting SACS committee found Peabody in full compliance.[4] The *Design* had eliminated earlier problems with the M.A. by replacing it with a professional degree. The new programs, which replaced often small departments, eliminated concern over the number of graduate faculty in each degree program, while the conversion of all subject matter Ph.D.'s to education degrees finessed problems with graduate faculty qualifications. These self-studies represent the last full profile of Peabody before the merger. Most of the 1974 problems would remain in 1979.

Many weaknesses identified in 1974 had been perennial. Peabody still did not offer clear guidance to undergraduates not committed to a career in education (the *Design* cured this by requiring all undergraduates to commit to some area of education). Admission standards remained the same as in 1964, higher than most state colleges of education, much lower than more select private universities. As measured by test scores, students ranked slightly above the national median. Retention rates were still low, but Peabody had still collected no exact data on this critical problem (a typical oversight). Two limited surveys indicated that most students left because of perceived deficiencies in academic programs and teaching. Grades were even more inflated than in 1964, a result attributed to national trends. Yet a few departments, most notably in social studies, were more rigorous than in 1964; grade point averages in history and political science were a low 1.37 on a 3.0 scale. Education, the sickest department over the preceding decade, had a scandalous average of 2.41 for beginning courses, 2.71 (A-) for advanced courses. High grades meant that 27 percent of students made the dean's list, with the effect that no one seemed to notice. Graduate grades were even more inflated. For all practical purposes, every graduate student received As or Bs. In 1973 the education department did not award a single graduate student a grade under B.[5]

Peabody still had some serious problems with faculty quality and with its graduate program. Faculty attrition was way above national averages. In 1973–74, twenty-two faculty left Peabody, 80 percent for better salaries. The tenured faculty had declined to just over one-third. From 1970 to 1974, Peabody lost fifty-nine faculty, with only fifteen of these terminated junior faculty. At the level of full professor, Peabody salaries fell well below national averages, or a C level by AAUP standards. A full professor at Peabody averaged only $17,581 in 1973–74, compared to $26,100 at Vanderbilt. The haphazard evaluation of professors varied widely from department to department. Some departments used student evaluations, others did not. The committee had to admit that Peabody gave "little recognition to excellence in teaching." In only one area did Peabody faculty excel—professional involvement and outside consulting. The college had also reduced the number of professors with terminal degrees from Peabody from 45 percent in 1964 to 23 percent in 1974.[6]

In the self-studies, the Peabody faculty did not score well on research and publications. Most research remained in the Kennedy Center. Except in psychology, only three or four professors published a steady stream of scholarly books or well-placed articles, which helped explain why psychology had the only competitive graduate students. In 1973, when the psychology department rejected 526 of its graduate applicants, or the vast majority, the other departments rejected only 11 percent of theirs. Finally, Peabody failed to meet new affirmative-action guidelines. Despite a largely female student population, its female professors, at 25 percent, did not reflect the proportion in the job pool, while Peabody had not a single minority professor (it had employed only one temporary African American professor in its whole history). These realistic judgments about Peabody contradicted the stream of publications that emanated from the campus. The college retained a reasonably high reputation, and had many dedicated professors. But such dire realities made it difficult to attract the support needed to keep Peabody afloat financially. Donors like to back winners, not rescue losers.[7]

FUZZY BUDGETS

The period from 1975 to 1977 was a testing time for the new reforms. Would the reorganization allow Peabody to survive financially? To do so, it needed a combination of increased enrollment to raise tuition income; a more efficient use of resources on campus; and an unprecedented level of outside gifts. Peabody gave it a good try, but by 1977, Dunworth doubted that the college could make it, a conclusion he shared only with Deans Stovall and Whitlock. Evidence of these early doubts was in a memo Dunworth wrote for board chair H. G. Hill Jr. in May 1977.

This is the first thoughtful evaluation of merger possibilities in Dunworth's files. Dunworth argued that merger with another university "could be the very best way to retain our identity" as a college of education and reduce high support costs. Peabody needed to negotiate a merger from a strong position to insure that it retained "reasonable programmatic, policy, and personnel control." If a merged Peabody came under the "tyrannical control of the typical university faculty senate, it would be disastrous," for then Peabody would retain its name but no influence. He preferred a merger with a private university that needed and was willing to support a college of education in a federation of schools and colleges. Because of a downward trend in undergraduate students in all education colleges, a merged Peabody might become "predominantly, although not exclusively, a graduate school of education and human development." It could continue most of its graduate programs and services. "Such a merger with the right university could strengthen both institutions and their potential for impact on the future of the nation's educational system." In this almost eerie anticipation of what would unfold in 1979, Dunworth did not mention Vanderbilt. He did urge the board to study merger as an option.[8]

Dunworth also pointed out the difficulties of a merger. Experts, he wrote, had suggested that the merging college should consider it not as an evil but as a potential good; expect faculty, alumni, and student opposition; expect no miracles; and realize that the benefits of a merger would come slowly. If merger under these conditions proved impossible, Dunworth believed that Peabody should consider closing as a college and using its resources for a Peabody Institute of Education modeled on the Brookings Institute, or a Peabody Education Foundation that could support research and influence national educational policies. Dunworth submitted these drastic and painful alternatives for discussion purposes. They would be better than a weak and mediocre Peabody. A Peabody that was not "strong financially and academically, or a Peabody that has compromised its independence and freedom of action . . . in order to just 'survive' would not be a major force in American education."[9]

Why, as early as 1977, did Dunworth seem ready to give up on the 1974 gamble on survival and renewed growth? Because of financial realities and Peabody's failure to maintain its enrollment. The last half of the seventies marked a low ebb in the fortunes of schools of education. The baby boom had ended in the early sixties. Birth rates declined, and by the late sixties a much smaller cohort of children entered elementary schools. By the midseventies, even high school enrollments began to drop. The nation suddenly had a surplus of trained teachers. Teaching jobs were scarce, particularly in secondary schools, so fewer young people chose teaching as a career. This meant that education schools lost favor, often ran deficits, and were a financial burden in most of their host universities. The image of professional educators was never lower. But as components of a larger university, such schools could survive the downturn. Peabody, as a fully independent college, had no such security. Its enrollment declined at roughly the national average for teachers' colleges, as Peabody officials emphasized all the time. But this was small consolation, with the college's financial well-being so tied to tuition. It had to maintain its own campus, provide its own dorms and student support, and employ a considerable faculty to teach arts and science courses.

By most measurements, enrollments at Peabody dropped steadily after 1975 and the changes mandated by *Design for the Future.* The new professional emphasis probably discouraged some undergraduates from enrolling. From 1968–69 to 1974–75, regular-year undergraduate enrollment remained around 1,100. It dropped to 1,078 in 1975, to 850 in 1976–77, to 778 in 1977–78, and to only 649 in 1978–79. Tuition increases meant that total tuition income did not decline as much, but it could not keep up with inflation. The tuition each semester for undergraduates rose from $850 in 1974–75 to $1,300 in 1978–79; graduate costs per credit hour rose from $80 to $115. Fees, and charges for room and board, rose at similar rates. In sheer numbers, graduate enrollments rose after 1975, but such figures are deceptive. More than half the graduate students were part-time. Graduate students in 1975–76 numbered 998, and 1,402 by 1978–79. But more than four hundred of these were part-time students in a graduate program in human development counseling begun in 1975 and offered on bases in Britain and Berlin for the U.S. Air Force. On the Nashville campus, the total graduate enrollment in 1978–79 was only 980, more than half part-time. The summer enrollment, mainly graduate students, remained around 1,400 from 1970 to 1978, but after 1975, some three or four hundred of these reflected off-campus enrollment.[10]

Behind the Air Force program lay a terminated program in Europe operated by Dunworth's Ball State. In 1975, Peabody signed a contract with the Air Force to provide a graduate program in human development counseling that paralleled a similar but new professional program on the main campus. The Air Force paid the costs of the program, which involved military and civilian personnel in about equal numbers. Raymond Norris spent the first year in Oxford as director and organizer of the operation and supported it from the home campus for the next six years. He was followed as director by Richard Percy, also from Peabody. Of the six or so professors each year, all employed by Peabody, many came from other universities, usually for a year. Most were very able, for a year in England proved tempting. The program had access to English university libraries. In 1978–79, as an example, the director and six professors offered twenty-nine different courses, over four quarters, at six British bases and at Templehof in Berlin. The students could work for an M.S., Ed.S, or Ed.D. More than four hundred completed degrees by the time the program ended in 1981. The focus of the program, human development counseling, reflected its close identification with developmental theories in psychology, particularly those of Carl Rogers. The program emphasized the role of counselors at all stages of human development, not just those related to formal education. It won plaudits from the Air Force, featured annual commencement ceremonies, and, far away from the problems and internal bickering of the home campus, enjoyed high morale.[11]

The Air Force students paid their own way but did not appreciably improve the college's overall finances or compensate for the problems created by a gradual decline of undergraduates on the home campus. Some dorms were half empty. In 1978–79, Peabody rented East and Confederate Halls to Vanderbilt. Organizations suffered. Too few men remained on campus to keep the two fraternities going. Sixty students with Vanderbilt athletic scholarships accounted for nearly half the 1978–79 male enrollment. The intercollegiate athletic program almost expired, and even intermurals were ill supported. It was increasingly difficult to recruit students for clubs, honors fraternities, music ensembles, and the student newspaper. Tuition paid by the six hundred Vanderbilt students who took courses at Peabody each year was now indispensable as were athletic scholarships. In directed student teaching in some semesters, Vanderbilt students made up more than half the enrollment, and as much as half in some art, music, and education courses.

By 1977, the Peabody board had no alternative but to engage in reckless financial gambles. From 1974 to 1977, the $1. 8 million borrowed from the endowment almost balanced the operating budget. H. G. Hill Jr. committed $600,000 of his own money to help pay back this debt. For colleges, the great inflation of the seventies was almost as threatening as the Great Depression of the thirties. Most colleges operated at a deficit. Even Vanderbilt, hard pressed, tried to use a reassessment process to trim programs. Like Peabody, Vanderbilt launched a centennial campaign, and it exceeded its $150 million goal. Peabody could not raise half of its projected $25 million. To keep budgets balanced, the college steadily drew down on its resource base. This was not public information, and even some board members outside Nashville were in the dark about what was happening. Most critical, the faculty—aware of financial problems and anxious about Peabody's future—had no access to the budgeting process or the annual audited financial reports. As Peabody moved toward bankruptcy, the campus seemed normal. The faculty continued to collect annual raises. The college increased its research support for faculty, continued to award sabbaticals, and expanded fringe benefits. Dunworth avoided the confrontations that Claunch had invited a decade before.

The board used several strategies to keep the budget balanced. It raised tuition and fees as much as it dared; in addition to the Air Force program in Britain, it launched off-campus programs in several cities that seemed profitable. But unexpected expenses hurt. In 1975, to win reaccreditation for the Library School, it used more than $600,000 to recondition the Industrial Arts Building as the school's new and almost luxurious home. Meeting city code requirements for various utilities meant repairs that would eventually cost more than $500,000. The board met these expenses in part from the sale of assets—the remainder from Knapp farm, $45,000 from the H. G. Hill Camp (sold to a board member at what many saw as a give-away price), and $1.5 million from the demonstration school lot, sold to the new University School in 1977. Income from the sale of assets would normally go into either the endowment or a capital fund for future expenditures. Peabody used it all up in two years, or more than $2 million in nonrecurring income. The game could not go on much longer.

Equally reckless—and a burden passed on to the future—was the management of the endowment, which scarcely grew at all, peaking at just over $13 million in 1974. Peabody needed all the income it could wring from the endowment, hoping for some $800,000 a year. It shifted some endowment investments from stock funds to bonds. This was a wise move because of the stagnant stock market of the inflationary seventies. High interest rates sent the value of older bonds plummeting. But in some years, new corporate bonds yielded as much as 15 percent. These proved an excellent investment, even though the real yield, given cost-of-living increases, was no more than 6 percent in most years. Later, such bonds sold at a high premium. The problem at Peabody was that, in an inflationary era, it paid out the total yield of its investments each year. It did not use a prudent pay-out rate (say 4 percent) and use the remainder to grow the principal, and thus try to keep the real value of the endowment stable. From 1970 to 1979 the endowment lost by inflation approximately 45 percent of its purchasing power. In the long term, this was a more insidious gamble on the future than using up capital resources. Peabody was rapidly depleting both its capital and investments. Yet, in none of the financial reports to the board have I found any acknowledgement of this doomed strategy. Even the value of the endowment, in current dollars, declined to approximately $11.2 million by 1979.

By 1975 foundations had all but stopped funding Peabody. The GEB had expired, and the Ford Foundation had almost stopped funding higher education. Now all the college had were grants, most federal and most for the Kennedy Center. By 1977 these averaged $3 million a year. The endowment contained $700,000 of restricted funds for the still very active Division of Surveys and Field Services. Interest on this, and payments for services, yielded what seemed a nice profit each year, which went into the operating budget. But the grants and restricted funds paid only for research or services. By 1979, most federal grants for Peabody contained just over 50 percent for indirect costs (a contracted amount). Clearly, at this time, Peabody gained needed money from these grants, but at least in theory, if the costs were fairly established, the indirect costs paid for the long-term costs of services rendered. By 1977 the seeming surplus gained by Peabody largely reflected the fact that it was not even beginning to keep up maintenance on its buildings. Once again, it was borrowing against the future.

By 1977, the new campaign was Peabody's last hope, short of a drastic reduction in faculty and staff. In a pattern that repeated itself almost every decade, the campaign never came close to its goal of $25 million. In 1976, a blue-ribbon board committee completed plans for the campaign, with clearly defined targets for endowment, capital expenditures, and operating budget. The committee seemed to do everything right. It utilized an outside consultant. It wanted to have 30 to 50 percent of its $25 million goal in hand before announcing the campaign, a standard strategy. Events did not allow it to wait so long. It announced the campaign in 1977 as the bridging money ended. H. G. Hill Jr. offered $1 million in a matching gift (one for four), much as he had done in the campaign under Claunch. By March 1977, largely because of board commitments, the campaign had netted almost $1 million in cash and $1.25 million more in pledges. It had to have $1.6 million to balance the budget. Thus, it did what it had to, and used all unrestricted gifts to fund the operating budget.

Some good news leavened the bad. In the fall of 1977, trustee Frank Mayborn pledged $1 million over ten years (the appreciative board renamed the Industrial Arts Building for him). His first installment went into the operating budget. By the fall of 1977, cash gifts in hand totaled $1.2 million and by the end of the fiscal year covered that year's deficit. The total cash gifts beyond those given by the board, the local development council, and the alumni (more than $300,000 each year) never amounted to even $1 million. Without Hill and Mayborn, the college could not have survived through 1978. By budget projections made in 1977, the college might raise enough from the campaign to balance its 1978–79 budget but would face up to a $5 million deficit in 1979–80. By 1978, the campaign had contributed $2,898,000 to operating costs, 58 percent of that target, largely because the board chose to use the funds for this purpose. But it had raised only $184,000 for capital improvements (4 percent), and $4,127,352 for its endowment, largely in pledges or deferred payments (estates, trusts). Almost none of this would be available in the next two years. By the fall of 1978, the college had spent or committed almost all cash raised in the campaign. It used the remaining cash and a declining flow of new gifts to fashion a balanced budget for 1978–79. Beyond lay bankruptcy or drastic policy changes.[12]

MERGER TALKS

This bleak financial picture explains why, by September 1978, Dunworth began serious discussions with his executive committee about Peabody's options. On September 8, the committee met to hear a depressing report on the campaign and on the college's fiscal future. Dunworth gave an equally somber report on enrollment trends. That afternoon, the committee debated three alternatives: closing the college and using its assets for a research institute; trying to remain independent, which Hill most strongly defended; and merger talks with Vanderbilt, a possibility somewhat mysteriously referred to as option 3. On September 14, the committee again met for serious deliberations, unfortunately with none of the details recorded in the minutes. By lunchtime, the committee had reached a majority but not unanimous decision: to authorize the administration to determine if option 3 was a viable alternative. Dunworth would have to make the initial approach to Vanderbilt. The committee reconvened on October 6. Notably, the page containing the minutes of its opening deliberations is the only page missing from the 1909–1979 board records. The discussions had to be intense and emotional. The committee approved the following strained motion: "Keeping in mind that it is the consensus of the Executive Committee that preserving the integrity of our mission is of primary importance, and that in order to achieve this it may be necessary to assume a pragmatic stance insofar as the corporate structure of the College is concerned, the Executive Committee directs the President to negotiate with Vanderbilt University, looking toward affiliation with that university, and report the results of such negotiations to the Executive Committee for approval, and if approved, to the Board of Trustees for adoption and implementation."[13]

This was a major turning point in Peabody history. Note that the executive committee acted on its own without consulting the full board. In fact, it voted to postpone the regular fall meeting of the board (a bylaw required only one meeting a year). Hill cast the lone nay vote. Bernard Werthan, the vice chair of the committee, mailed a letter to all board members announcing a conflict of schedules that required the postponement, a ruse to prevent what could have been a deeply divided board meeting. The board did not meet until March 19, 1979, at which point it would vote to merge with Vanderbilt. But a lot of rapidly moving water flowed under the bridge before this. On September 15, H. G. Hill Jr., Peabody's greatest benefactor after World War II, resigned as chair of the executive committee. He gave no reasons except that it would be "in the best interest of all."[14]

Unfortunately, a merger with Vanderbilt had to take place quickly. Even by the end of the 1979–80 academic year, with a large deficit and a small endowment shrinking toward zero, Peabody would have little bargaining clout. At Vanderbilt, Chancellor Alexander Heard was aware of Peabody's mounting problems and had stressed to Dunworth his willingness to talk about some form of merger. By 1978, Vanderbilt had both a chancellor, responsible for external relations, and a president, responsible for the local campus and academic policies. Because Heard had to be out of town for much the fall, he turned most of the early discussions over to President Emmett Fields. In the next three months, Dunworth and Fields wrestled over merger terms, the opening scene in one of the most fascinating and complex stories in the history of Peabody. I can only recount the highlights of that story.

Talks between Fields and Dunworth went badly, at least from Dunworth's perspective. Their interchanges were not entirely confidential, for Dunworth involved his two main deans, and Fields consulted on campus and sought advice from university presidents around the country. Any interested reporter could have found out what was going on, but none did. Some Vanderbilt and Peabody faculty knew about the discussions but not the details. Fields was in an awkward position. He had masterminded an ongoing reassessment of Vanderbilt's academic programs and as a money-saving strategy had hoped to eliminate weak programs. If Vanderbilt were so pressed financially, why would it want to absorb a financially beleaguered Peabody?

Fields, who prided himself on being tough-minded, bargained for the best possible deal for Vanderbilt. After an internal study on the implications of a merger, he decided that Vanderbilt should not commit itself to the indefinite continuation of Peabody as a college of education, although possibly as a small graduate center or an educational policy institute. If Vanderbilt absorbed all Peabody's assets, he would commit himself to a continued college of education only for eight years, after which the university would be free to abolish the college if its financial plight required such a drastic action.

After a break in November, the talks reopened in December. Heard, who was now back on campus, became increasingly involved. He would not reverse Fields's hard line but privately was much softer on merger possibilities. Dunworth ended the discussions. Vanderbilt had set impossible conditions. His bottom line, at this point, was Peabody's survival as a college of education. Heard later excused this impasse not on the basis of Vanderbilt's offer, which he said was still open for negotiation, but because the secrecy desired by Dunworth made it impossible for Vanderbilt to proceed, since it could not approve a new college or school, or even any new academic program, without faculty involvement and approval by the faculty senate. This was disingenuous.[15]

Dunworth reported the dismal result of his talks to the executive committee on December 8. The committee reconsidered option 3 and postponed further discussion to early January. It accepted Hill's resignation from the committee and his subsequent resignations as chair of the board of trust and of the campaign's blue-ribbon committee. For all practical purposes, this ended the campaign. At the January 5, 1979, meeting, Carr Payne, Bruce Payne's son, resigned from the executive committee, and John Bransford, a major benefactor, resigned as vice chair of the board. Peabody's most fervent supporters were jumping ship, making it possible for Dunworth to win near unanimous approval for later actions taken by the committee. By this January 5 meeting, he was almost ready to submit new options. Significantly, he called attention to a report on research and policy institutes in the United States and Canada, which encompassed their purposes, their success records, and their endowments. Clearly, as in 1977, he still saw a Peabody Institute as a fallback position.[16]

In January, both Fields and Heard expected negotiations to resume. They both assumed that Vanderbilt offered the only plausible partner in a merger. But

Dunworth, like a wounded suitor, argued that merger with Vanderbilt was dead and even suggested that the university would be a poor match, since it would not sustain Peabody's long-term commitment to service. He would not approach Vanderbilt again, as he began exploring other options. He and his two deans visited George Washington, which had no school of education, and Duke, which needed to improve its small department of education (it would abolish the department in 1982). Both universities expressed interest, but only George Washington seemed serious. Later, when the issue became public, Dunworth frequently referred to merger possibilities with these two universities. How serious he was is unclear, as is how much real interest was present on the other side, for negotiations never began. And in this case, the details were all important. Peabody's small endowment was not an enticement; its reputation was. Had the college seriously confronted a move, it would have faced almost insurmountable problems and intense faculty opposition. The only way it could have gained the needed assets was from the sale of its existing campus. Although Peabody listed its value at more than $42 million, this does not mean that it could have found a buyer at this price. Vanderbilt, the only likely purchaser, would have bargained for a much lower price. Later, everyone said Dunworth had been bluffing to get Vanderbilt to come back to the table. I suspect that he did explore outside possibilities, at least in part to gain better options in Nashville. He wanted not only officials at Vanderbilt but also Nashvillians to contemplate what losing Peabody would mean.

No one expected the next turn of events. In early January, Peabody's Dean Stovall met with the vice chancellor of the state board of regents, which governed all the state colleges and universities except the University of Tennessee and its branches, to discuss how Peabody faculty might help Tennessee State University (TSU) develop doctoral programs in education. When Stovall could not offer the support needed, the representative of the board of regents suggested the possibility of merger, which would give TSU the doctoral programs it wanted. This new possibility appealed to Dunworth and soon had the enthusiastic support of Roy Nicks, chancellor of the board of regents. By February 1, the two sides had agreed on the outline of a merger document. From Nicks's perspective, a merger with Peabody served two purposes: to add enormous new strength and doctoral programs to TSU, and to save the assets of Peabody for Nashville and Tennessee. The talks remained confidential for at least a month. The official minutes of the February 2 Peabody executive committee meeting, in the very middle of the Nicks-Dunworth talks, record only extensive discussions about a course of action that would enable Peabody to fulfill its mission.[17]

Except for Dunworth and his deans, no one on campus knew about the TSU talks. Beyond the executive committee, few board members knew about them. This created future hazards for such a merger, but Dunworth apparently wanted the best offer in hand before alarming the campus. The secrecy ended on Tuesday,

February 13. It could not have lasted much longer, because the state board of regents needed approval for the merger from the Tennessee Higher Education Commission (THEC), and eventually from the state assembly. The *Tennessean* carried a long article with the page-wide headline "TSU, Peabody to Join?" This was unbelievable news. All hell broke out on the Peabody campus. For the next month, both Nashville newspapers carried almost daily items on the proposed merger. The *Tennessean* enthusiastically supported the merger, while the *Banner* urged caution.

The merger made sense. TSU provided the best remaining option, one that would preserve Peabody as a college of education, save the jobs of most of its faculty, and provide enough state support to lower tuition and attract more Tennessee students. With Vanderbilt out of the picture, the more faculty and students thought about the merger, the more appealing it appeared, given a favorable final agreement. In one respect, this merger was preferable to one with Vanderbilt. It would preserve the egalitarian and service culture of Peabody.

Now the ongoing bargaining was in the public spotlight. Enterprising reporters or Peabody faculty usually found out about confidential meetings within twenty-four hours. When the executive committee held a special meeting on February 26, several other board members attended, in part to find out what was going on. Some had not even known that the committee had concluded the previous fall that Peabody could not continue as an independent college. They had been as shocked by the *Tennessean* article as had students and faculty. At this meeting, Dunworth reported that he should have a merger document by the scheduled March 19 meeting of Peabody's board of trust, its first such meeting in a year. The executive committee concluded that the negotiations with TSU should continue. As in all the issues related to merger, the committee included no details of the discussions in its minutes.[18] On March 10, the board of regents approved the merger plan in principle and recommended its acceptance by the THEC and assembly.[19] The board of trust would have this document before it on March 19, which gave faculty and students less than a month to try to influence the outcome.

And try they did. The campus was in constant ferment. Not a day passed without multiple meetings of faculty and students. It seems unlikely that any students kept up with coursework. Professors were distracted. Careers were at stake. The sense of betrayal stemmed first from the secrecy of momentous decisions already made. Dunworth and his deans had not consulted with the faculty. Of course, no one had made a final decision, but the executive committee had committed itself to a merger and, if this failed, to closing the college. Such decisions threatened the dismissal of even tenured faculty, contrary to 1976 AAUP guidelines. The Peabody board had neglected to accept those guidelines (as usual, not a policy choice but an oversight). Surprisingly, the Peabody faculty never openly rejected TSU as a possible partner in an academic marriage. In a campus poll, the faculty voted ninety-four to eleven in favor of a merger with TSU if all existing faculty retained their academic positions, rank, and, tenure. The vote for a comparable merger with Vanderbilt was ninety-seven to nine, no appreciable difference. Should less than 50 percent of the faculty retain their positions, only ten favored a TSU merger, twenty-six a Vanderbilt merger (most of these professors would have been in psychology or attached to the Kennedy Center).[20]

Professors were most concerned about job security. Students wanted assurance that they could complete their degrees. These issues overshadowed the problem of academic prestige. TSU could not compare to Vanderbilt. But the proposed merger document offered by Nicks seemed likely to be more generous than any future offer from Vanderbilt. TSU, formerly Tennessee A & I, was in a period of rapid transition. Under court order, it was absorbing the University of Tennessee, Nashville, a downtown center for commuting and largely white students. As a historically black university and a land-grant institution, TSU seemed to some to offer the basis for an expanded urban university, fully integrated, with multiple campuses. This was the dream of *Tennessean* editor John Siegenthaler. Indeed, TSU's main campus had a mostly black faculty and student body. It had low admission standards. Its students scored low on objective exams, as did students in all the traditionally black southern public colleges and universities. But it could improve, and it was trying to. Peabody would give it new prestige and its first doctoral programs. A few Peabody faculty, enthusiastic about the prospect of building such a university in Nashville, publicly supported this merger as preferable to one with Vanderbilt. Some black students at Peabody agreed.

Race had to be a factor, although apart from a few letters to Dunworth, no one mentioned it. The key term in the letters was "standards." Racially stigmatizing statements were no longer acceptable. At times, this language clearly concealed racial content, but in fact such universities as TSU did lack both high standards and academic prestige. Thus, such emphasis could—but did not necessarily—represent a concern about Peabody's becoming identified with a mostly black university. The letters to Dunworth from lay people and alumni about a TSU merger were overwhelmingly opposed, later letters about a merger with Vanderbilt largely supportive.[21]

The Peabody faculty quickly adopted its strategy. Publicly, it expressed its sense of the possibilities in a TSU merger; privately it crucified Dunworth for his secret plotting. The faculty met at least weekly. It appointed two ad hoc committees, one on merger, one on alternatives to merger. It assessed dues, formed a faculty action committee, and hired an attorney. It besieged Dunworth and the board of trust with position papers and procedural demands. The Peabody chapter of AAUP became more active than ever before and prepared appeals to the national headquarters. The mildest demands came from the Council on Academic Policy, made up largely of deans and program directors. Stovall, a loyal advocate of the merger, was on this council, yet next to Dunworth the devil incarnate to many faculty. The council asked, first, that all students in a combined university who were preparing for careers in education and human development matriculate at Peabody. Second, it wanted Peabody to retain, or offer jointly, courses that were designed to improve teaching or to explore the history, philosophy, and nature of educational systems. Third, it wanted all existing Peabody faculty who were teaching and advising students in education and human development to become voting members of the TSU faculty, whether on full or joint appointment. This statement was notable for what it did not ask—retention of all existing faculty and programs.[22]

As one would expect, the position of the whole faculty was much stronger. This position emerged from daily meetings of the ad hoc Merger Committee. The committee sent copies of a developing set of demands to Dunworth and the board of trust. For example, the faculty demanded that a representative designated by the faculty participate in all continuing negotiations with TSU and have a voice in approving any plan. It made, as a condition of merger, retention of all tenured faculty at current rank and salary. During a five-year transition period, tenure-track faculty would remain and be assured a fair review for tenure. TSU should make every effort to move tenure-track personnel into permanent positions. It asked for a continuation of the JUL (necessary for accreditation of graduate programs); the School of Music; the new Center for Economic and Social Studies Education; the faculties in science, social science, mathematics, and English; the Kennedy Center; the Child Study Center; and even the Interuniversity Psychological and Counseling Center shared with Vanderbilt. It demanded some form of participatory faculty government for Peabody as part of TSU.[23]

When the faculty learned of divisions on the board, it set out to exploit them. One professor on the Alternatives Committee arranged a meeting with H. G. Hill Jr., who told the professor that he still believed Peabody could make it on its own. Letters written in response to faculty position papers revealed that many outlying board members were as shocked at events, and as uninformed, as the faculty. One letter from a special board member, Sargent Shriver, received plenty of local publicity (and condemnation from the *Tennessean*) and focused attention on one of the likely results of merger with TSU—the loss of the Kennedy Center. Shriver wrote to acting chair of the executive committee Robert E. Gable, noting his astonishment that at the next board meeting the trustees would be asked to vote on consolidation with TSU, with no advance notice or any opportunity to consider such a merger. Shriver could not attend—he never did—but noted that he would cast his proxy against the merger, particularly since he had no time to consider it intelligently. More important, he promised that, if Peabody so changed its structure, he would want his beloved Kennedy Center to affiliate with Vanderbilt. He felt that it was extraordinary for the board to consider such a change in the status of the center without consulting the Kennedy Foundation and the external committee that oversaw and gave it guidance. He asked for postponement of any action respecting the center until persons beyond the Peabody administration could come together to consider its future.[24]

With its complex involvement with the Vanderbilt Medical Center, the Kennedy Center was one of two critical issues in a merger. The other was JUL, since Vanderbilt might legally void the trust indenture if Peabody became part of another university. No one could mark out a clear legal pathway to a continuation of the trust, and some predicted that the sorting out of rights to JUL would lead to interminable lawsuits.

Nicks and his regents had offered Peabody an appealing merger contract. Peabody would have to turn over its campus to TSU and use the early earning from its endowment to pay transition costs. Otherwise, its endowment was to go to a new legal entity, the Peabody Foundation, and the existing board of trust would continue to manage this fund to augment Peabody's program—some $400,000 of extra funds each year. Peabody would absorb the existing TSU College of Education (a threat to TSU faculty). If TSU subsequently sold any of the Peabody campus, half the returns went to the Peabody Foundation. All Peabody degree programs would continue for at least one year. Peabody would keep the Kennedy Center, the Child Study Center, and the Center for Economic and Social Studies Education, plus all viable off-campus programs. Peabody would have exclusive control over teacher certification and over library science, psychology, special education, and health and physical education. Abundant guarantees protected the rights of existing Peabody students, who could, if they chose, get a degree in the name of Peabody College (but at the current tuition and fees). The agreement did not guarantee the continuation of arts and science departments, and particularly the School of Music. Which, if any, Peabody faculty would lose their jobs remained unclear.[25]

By the time the Peabody board met on March 19, the TSU merger faced major hurdles in the THEC and state legislature. Dunworth later claimed that he was persuaded by March 19 that the merger could not win legislative approval in the 1979 session. Peabody could not stand by while a long, drawn-out political fight ensued. Governor Lamar Alexander withheld his support or opposition until the merger came before the legislature. The strongest support came from Nashville, the clearest opposition from Murfreesboro, the home of a somewhat threatened Middle Tennessee State University. The one member of the board of regents who voted against the merger on March 10 was from Murfreesboro, while Representative John Bragg from Murfreesboro led the early fight against the merger in the state house, lining up fifty-five votes in favor of extensive hearings before any vote on merger. Prior commitments to higher education had jeopardized the further commitment of the funds a merger would require, an estimated $3.4 million of additional annual appropriations. Further, Dunworth and his amenable executive committee might not win the required two-thirds vote of the full board, not just those present and voting.[26]

In retrospect, the brief courtship between TSU and Peabody raised dozens of "what if" questions with no clear answers. Action by Vanderbilt kept the issue from coming to a vote. But based on political developments in the two weeks before March 19, I believe that the state would not have approved the TSU merger in 1979. I have some doubts that two-thirds of the total membership of the Peabody board would have approved it. The Peabody faculty lobbied board members; by their count, far fewer than two-thirds of the forty board members would have approved the merger.

VANDERBILT'S OFFER

The February 13 *Tennessean* article had hit the Vanderbilt University campus like a bombshell. While a TSU merger seemed unbelievable, it looked as if Dunworth and his executive committee were serious. During the month of negotiations with TSU, Dunworth scarcely paid any heed at all to Vanderbilt. That story had ended the prior December. Vanderbilt suddenly faced the prospect, not of more negotiations with Peabody, but of losing all its cooperative arrangements with its neighbor. In particular, local members of the Vanderbilt board were dumbfounded and apprehensive.

A February 14, 1979, editorial by John Bibb, the sports editor of the *Tennessean,* triggered their concern. His headline identified the problem: "Vandy-Peabody Tie-Up In Peril." Boosters of Vanderbilt's athletic program were in shock. Hundreds of anxious letters came to Bibb. Could the athletic cooperation continue if Peabody merged with TSU? Without Peabody students, the Vanderbilt teams would be devastated. Of sixty scholarship players at Peabody, three were starters on the basketball team; more than fifty played on the football team. Bibb's answer: The NCAA could not permit the students of one NCAA member university to play on that of another. Vanderbilt might have difficulty fielding football and basketball teams in the fall of 1979, for most of the Peabody athletes could not meet Vanderbilt's admission requirements, were majoring in subjects not taught at Vanderbilt (primarily physical education), and cost Vanderbilt $1,000 less than if they were Vanderbilt students. If any prospect stunned the local Vanderbilt board members, this was it. Immediately, Heard and Fields were inundated with questions and concerns. Had they blown it back in December? In particular, Fields, who had stood firm against any commitment of the type offered by TSU, was now the bad guy to many board members and athletic boosters.[27]

Athletics packed the most emotional dynamite, but it was only one issue. Vanderbilt had postponed its own dorm construction because it now rented two

Peabody dorms. It had no easy answer to the JUL problem. More than six hundred Vanderbilt students depended on Peabody courses, particularly in music and secondary education. The joint counseling program drew extensively on Peabody psychologists and on the Kennedy Center. These were only the major areas of cooperation; the TSU merger also threatened dozens of smaller joint projects. As quickly as he could do it without embarrassment to Fields (tensions already plagued their relationship), Heard began a flirtation with Dunworth and Peabody. He knew it might already be too late. On February 13, the day the *Tennessean* article came out, he and Fields issued a statement, by far the most conciliatory in months. In it, they noted how much they valued the longstanding relationship with Peabody, and how much they had appreciated Dunworth's initiatives about merger. They claimed that these discussions had ended because they could not consult the Vanderbilt faculty and pursue the matter as they wished (only partly true). Vanderbilt, they said, had interests in Peabody and in TSU and, now that the issue was public, would be glad to take part in any further deliberations that Peabody would like.[28]

With a good bit of publicity, Heard announced on the Vanderbilt campus on February 22 an inquiry to be carried out by Fields. He was to develop an inventory of Vanderbilt's relationships with Peabody and explore the implications of its proposed merger with TSU. Heard telephoned Dunworth, sent him a copy of the questionnaire, and, in a letter later published in the March 6 *Vanderbilt Gazette,* noted his regret that the fall discussions had not moved on to a conclusion. He was sad that the partnership with Peabody might be nearing an end. He wished the best for Peabody in its negotiations. Then, Heard almost begged for more talks: "President Fields and I will welcome the opportunity, when it becomes appropriate, to renew earlier discussions." In a public response that struck some Peabody professors as almost rude, Dunworth rebuffed this overture, insisting that Vanderbilt was not serious about annexing a college of education. Nothing in the record indicates that, at this point, he did anything to entice a new proposal from Vanderbilt. If he was playing coy, he did it well. He afterward insisted that he was always committed to the TSU merger, and only became receptive to Vanderbilt when the TSU alliance seemed unlikely to win state approval. Robert Gable, acting chair of the Peabody board, even reprimanded Vanderbilt for pursuing the issue, fearing it would torpedo the TSU negotiations.[29]

By now, Heard and Vanderbilt board chair Sam Fleming were anxious to prevent what they increasingly saw as a potential disaster for the university. Heard met with the Flemings at their home in Gulf Stream, Florida, to plot strategy, and Fleming informally consulted with other trustees. By March 17, the two had drafted an offer to go from Fleming to Gable and the Peabody board. They had cleared the draft with administrators, the leadership of the faculty senate, and even student leaders. On March 17, the Vanderbilt executive committee approved it. Heard hand-carried the letter to Peabody on March 18, a Sunday, a day before the Peabody board meeting. It included the outlines of a proposed merger with Peabody, which, if Peabody was agreeable, could go to the full Vanderbilt board on April 27.

This critical letter began with a flattering commentary on Peabody's distinguished history and stressed the importance of joint relationships. Vanderbilt valued Peabody for its contribution to the city and nation and its significance to Vanderbilt's future. Fleming noted that Vanderbilt would consult with the THEC concerning the future of TSU. Then he presented Vanderbilt's terms, less generous than TSU's but much more generous than Vanderbilt had offered in December. Fleming invited Peabody to become a professional school of Vanderbilt under the cumbersome name of George Peabody College for Teachers of Vanderbilt University. It would be a college of education and human development, comparable to the other schools and colleges in the Vanderbilt cluster. Vanderbilt would invite four Peabody trustees to join its already engorged board; the remaining Peabody trustees could serve as a team of visitors. Peabody could have full use of its remaining endowment (as did the other schools and colleges), enlarge it by future gifts, and use it to support Peabody. Vanderbilt would absorb its campus, but if it ever sold part of it, the proceeds would benefit Peabody College. Peabody would have to pay the costs of merger, including the cost of terminating faculty and staff. The letter referred to particular areas of academic specialization and distinction in addition to educational training, but it did not specify which would survive the merger. Fleming hoped the merger could be completed by July 1, 1979 (it was). He invited the Peabody board to appoint trustees to work with Vanderbilt trustees on what amounted to a merger committee.[30]

That was it. Peabody for the first time had a firm offer. It could take it or leave it. It accepted the offer the next day, taking advantage of one golden moment. Briefly, Peabody had the psychological edge. Even a week later, it might have been clear that the TSU merger was off, and then Vanderbilt might have offered less. If Dunworth had been bluffing about a TSU merger, he had played the game perfectly. If not, he was incredibly lucky.

Vanderbilt's offer represented a considerable gamble on its part. Colleges of education were at a low ebb. The trend in elite universities was either to abolish or sharply curtail them. Yale abolished its school of education in 1958; in the early eighties, Michigan sharply reduced the size of its school; Duke dropped its department. When Fields asked university administrators what to do about Peabody, almost all warned against taking on the burden of a school of education or lamented the problems that plagued their own schools. Since Vanderbilt was bucking the trend among elite universities it wanted to emulate, the merger offer reflected less a commitment to teacher training than a bid to maintain invaluable cooperative efforts with Peabody. That such cooperation was well established insured Peabody's survival in Nashville. As no one could anticipate in 1979, however, Vanderbilt placed itself at the forefront of a new shift of national priorities apparent by the mideighties. This led to a new, positive evaluation of education colleges and their role. Federal funding, educational reform efforts, a reevaluation of professions largely staffed by women, and rapid enrollment increases in public schools set off a boom in professional education. Not that education colleges gained the prestige of law or medicine, but they would be in a position to raise external funds, upgrade faculties, and become respectable, even if they were still patronized by other schools and colleges in the best universities.

Peabody had planned carefully for the March 19 board meeting, possibly the most critical in its history. The executive committee knew it would face opposition from board members outside the inner circle. On March 12, it elected Gable chair and decided to exclude the press from the meeting. Special representatives from faculty, student, and staff associations were to make presentations concerning the TSU offer. On the big day, thirteen of the forty-one trustees were absent; some sent proxies. Board member Brooks Hays offered a specially written and moving invocation that referred to the founding ideals of Peabody. Instead of proceeding to the main item on the written agenda—the TSU merger—Gable moved to modify the agenda to include Fleming's letter, which he had received the day before and now presented to board members. They already knew about it from newspaper reports. The various campus leaders made their presentations, now almost irrelevant. With some embarrassment, Dunworth reported on the previous year and in particular tried to justify the difficult decision in September that led to merger talks. His deans used overhead projection to prove the necessity of such a move. Gable explained that it was now almost certain that the general assembly would vote down a merger with TSU (his certainty seemed contrived; no one had argued this way before the Fleming letter).[31]

The complex motion submitted to the board began with an endorsement of merger with Vanderbilt under the general principles outlined in Fleming's letter. It named the trustees to serve on a joint merger committee with Vanderbilt trustees and authorized them to appoint subcommittees to work with Peabody faculty, students, alumni, staff, and friends in developing the final merger document. The motion also directed Dunworth to appoint the Peabody members of an institutional merger committee, which would draft the final legal document by April 27. Finally, the motion stipulated the issues that had to be included in the merger document: areas of academic responsibility assigned to Peabody, criteria for faculty staffing, employment status and benefits of faculty and staff, provisions for those displaced, the status of all students as related to degree requirements or options, and such items as tuition and fees. This motion passed, with thirty-one in favor and one abstention justified by a possible conflict of interest. Approval required twenty-seven votes. The board commended the work of Dunworth, Stovall, and Whitlock, who for a month had suffered almost unendurable strain. They would now suffer even more.[32]

The faculty and students now faced a fait accompli. The one remaining issue was the merger document. Fleming's letter suggested that Peabody would be a college of education and human development. What, exactly, did that include? Almost certainly not most arts and science departments. This had been a working assumption as far back as 1962. While no one expected Vanderbilt to reject Peabody's strongest asset, the Kennedy Center, other threatened constituencies lobbied for survival, including the off-campus programs, the library school, the art department and its Cohen Museum, and the music school. In a March 27 memo to Dunworth, the program directors and department (or faculties) chairs first endorsed the merger, then tried to guide it via a moderate position paper. They noted Peabody's special strengths, not only in teacher training but also in psychology, library science, and music. They argued that a detailed self-study comparable to those prepared for accreditation agencies should precede any major reduction of course offerings and faculty.[33]

The faculty met on March 21 and 27 and of course took a tougher stand. It reaffirmed its earlier position on the TSU merger: involve faculty in developing a merger document; retain all tenured faculty and retain faculty rank, salary, and tenure status. Most important, Vanderbilt had to agree to terminate no program or faculty until after a yearlong self-analysis.[34]

On campus, anxiety filled the days leading up to April 27. That a large number of faculty would lose their jobs, and that certain programs would terminate, was now certain. A faculty steering committee and other campus groups held seven meetings on campus with a subcommittee of trustees, who listened, read position papers written by faculty committees, and were deeply affected by the plight of terminated faculty. They had some difficulty either grasping the nature of a tight academic market or understanding why faculty could not move to some other "industry." They promised to do anything possible to help such faculty, and they indeed did just this. But Vanderbilt would largely determine which programs and faculty would continue. The local AAUP continued to emphasize procedural issues and looked forward to national AAUP intervention, as if the threat of an investigation and even censor might preserve all tenure positions. Earl T. Hutchison, an English professor almost certain to lose his job, was president of the local AAUP and by far the most passionate advocate of faculty rights. He and the faculty attorney persuaded an official in the Washington headquarters to write to both Heard and Dunworth about the AAUP position on the discontinuation of programs not mandated by financial exigencies. The one AAUP requirement to which Peabody could not adhere was full faculty involvement in the decisions to terminate programs.[35] At least two weeks before the vote by the Peabody and Vanderbilt boards, the faculty knew what the merger document would contain.

On April 27, the Peabody board met in a called session to vote on the memorandum of understanding developed by the joint merger committee, and some legal articles that accompanied it. This was the point of no return, the last opportunity for Peabody to remain independent. It was a strained gathering. The appeals from faculty and students deeply affected many board members. The vote on the merger documents was not unanimous. Two trustees, Hal Ramer and Albert Rose, voted against them and tried unsuccessfully to win support for the faculty position, including a year of self-study. Five absent trustees voted no by proxy. But twenty-eight present voted yes, one more than the twenty-seven required for approval, even without the three proxies in favor. Then the board approved the terms and procedures for terminating faculty and staff.[36]

The merger document was necessarily complex. It transferred all the assets of Peabody to Vanderbilt and ended the legal existence of Peabody as an independent institution. Six trustees (more than the four originally proposed) were invited to join the Vanderbilt board. Vanderbilt annexed or absorbed only a college of education and human development, which it defined broadly enough to embrace research and services to outside agencies. It thus retained the Kennedy Center, the library school, the child study center, and a few smaller programs. It authorized the new Peabody to offer only four undergraduate majors: elementary education, early childhood education, special education, and health and physical education (this last a concession to athletes on Vanderbilt teams). Except for degrees in music and art, it could continue to offer all professional degrees, but the M.A. and Ph.D. would come under control of the Vanderbilt Graduate School. It abolished Peabody courses in art, music, English, the humanities, mathematics, the natural sciences, and the social sciences. Peabody students would take such courses in Vanderbilt's College of Arts and Science. Peabody had to dismiss all faculty not directly related to its now more focused mission, and at the same time to improve its financial position. Many staff members would also lose their jobs, since Vanderbilt would take over support services. Most continuing Peabody students could finish their degrees at Peabody, at a tuition much lower than Vanderbilt's ($2,850 to $4,260 in 1979–80). (This provision would raise the summer enrollment, as students rushed to sign up before an August 15 deadline.) But music students, for whom Vanderbilt provided no substitute program, had to move to other colleges. If they had fewer than sixty-two semester hours left, they could, with Peabody approval, transfer and still get a Peabody degree. Music graduate students simply were out of luck, although some would be able to finish by the spring of 1980 and the final departure of the music faculty.[37]

Only one issue had plagued the approval of the merger documents—Peabody's campus. As Peabody understood the Fleming letter of March 18, Peabody would be able, not to own, but to use all its resources. The document did not include such an assurance. When challenged, Heard and Fleming offered Peabody the right to continue to control and maintain its campus. It could then rent space to other Vanderbilt schools and colleges. On the other hand, if Peabody gave up these assets, Vanderbilt would pay it a rent of $700,000 for each of the next ten years. The Peabody executive committee quickly, and wisely, took the money. Thus, Vanderbilt bought the campus and controlled its use. But, as in the case of other schools and colleges, it gave Peabody control of all the space it needed for its programs. At first, this meant that Vanderbilt absorbed the dorms and retained control over Cohen, the Administration Building, and the Home Economics Building. The fate of SR remained for future determination, although the physical education department would continue to use part of it. Peabody had no responsibility for its maintenance.[38]

THE FALLOUT AT PEABODY

The merger documents confirmed the worst apprehensions on the Peabody campus. Most of the faculty went into virtual mourning; it had not prevailed on any major issue. The faculty received a tentative version of the memorandum by April 17 and in a defiant meeting overwhelmingly passed a resolution of no confidence in Dunworth and Stovall. The resolution noted that Dunworth no longer commanded the respect of his faculty, had failed to consult the faculty on two merger negotiations, and had repeatedly violated AAUP guidelines. Stovall had served and supported him in those actions. The faculty called for a protest the following morning and dismissed classes. Some five hundred students and faculty gathered in front of SR on April 18, the faculty in academic regalia, and marched to the Administration Building for a silent vigil followed by remarks by various members of the campus community. They recited accounts of Peabody history, sang the alma mater, then silently disbanded. This was the high-water mark of resistance; the faculty soon became engaged in transition politics and gradually worked toward more constructive goals.[39]

By the terms of merger, Peabody had to terminate faculty by July 1. Vanderbilt did not want to be responsible for this messy and sad process. Peabody funds had to pay all settlements. All settlement options required a waiver of future claims against Peabody or Vanderbilt. Tenured faculty could continue their regular appointments through 1978–79, if they preferred, or withdraw their service. Either way, they would receive their normal salary, including the raise already committed for that year, an average of 7 percent. They would also receive 2 percent of this base salary for each year of service at Peabody, and 1 percent for each year remaining to the normal retirement age, up to a maximum of twenty years. Finally, they received $2,000 for relocation, retraining, or readjustment. Nontenured faculty received a final year appointment, which met the AAUP requirement, plus the $2,000 relocation bonus. Dismissed staff received a lump payment of 5 percent of annual salary for each year of service. Faculty who accepted reduction to a part-time status received their proportionate share of the severance benefits.[40]

Had Peabody simply dismissed all the faculty in the terminated departments, the process would have been almost automatic. It had good reasons for not doing this. In each of the arts and science disciplines, it needed faculty to continue working with students seeking certification in secondary education. Before merger, such students had to major in a subject area at Peabody or Vanderbilt, add a series of professional courses at Peabody, and finish with observation and practice teaching. After merger, all such students would major in disciplines at Vanderbilt, but they needed the same supervision at Peabody. This meant that Peabody needed to keep at least one specialist in subject-area teaching in each arts and science discipline. These would transfer to the education department. The responsibility for choosing this small elect fell on Dean Stovall, assisted by anyone he wanted to consult. The board set up the general criteria: experience in teaching consistent with the new mission, teaching experience in elementary or secondary schools, an appropriate education for the new mission, appropriate professional and scholarly experience in the area of the new mission, and possession of an earned doctorate. Those not chosen were jealous and resentful.

In part to meet AAUP requirements, the board also set up an appeals and hearing process for terminated faculty. This turned out to be a fiasco. The first step in the review, for the six faculty who wanted to appeal, was to go before a review committee of seven nonterminated faculty. Hardly in a position to be impartial, the committee judged four of the six appellants worthy of an appointment according to the board criteria. Stovall denied three appeals and modified one to a minor part-time appointment. The board committee on appeals upheld his decisions. Accepting the appeals would have meant either surplus faculty in those disciplines or the termination of some faculty already retained. But hard feelings were inevitable, and it was easy to argue either that the faculty committee or Stovall played favorites. The review committee faced pressure from the faculty. Even after its report, it submitted an addendum, noting that all the dismissals violated AAUP criteria.[41]

Did Peabody violate AAUP standards? Not any that the Peabody board had approved, and not any in the final version of the Peabody faculty manual (never made contractual by the board). The Peabody chapter urged the national AAUP to send an investigating team and found some support in the Vanderbilt AAUP and from the state organization. After Earl Hutchison resigned as president, his successor, Elizabeth Goldman, went to the national AAUP meeting in June 1979, where she found sympathy. The AAUP tried to clarify policies for such mergers. But she did not win support for an early investigation by the AAUP's Committee A, which could have placed Peabody and Vanderbilt on a blacklist. One of the national officials, concerned about the failure of Peabody to accept the findings of the faculty review committee, kept asking for more information. But the AAUP took the case no further, unsure if it had grounds for an investigation. After July 1, there was no Peabody to take action against. After April 27, the Peabody board had certainly followed AAUP procedures. Yet, the merger created a frightening precedent: A still solvent college had terminated twenty-three tenured faculty.

The fate of the terminated faculty remained a sad and slightly confused story for more than two years. The board officially terminated fifteen nontenured and twenty-three tenured faculty, but also reduced three tenured professors to part-time. The part-time appointees could choose to resign. Thus, by the legal merger on July 1, everyone listed thirty-nine terminated faculty, the number that became official. Because of one part-time appointment from the review process, only thirty-eight lost their full-time jobs. But if one counts reductions to part-time, roughly forty-one jobs were lost. For a few faculty in their sixties, the settlement was generous and led to normal retirement. A few faculty around the age of sixty had to accept the generous settlement and retire earlier than planned. Younger faculty had to seek new jobs and, in the terrible job market, few found comparable positions.

Everyone tried to help. After August 15, the Vanderbilt board was as concerned as the Peabody board had been. A transition committee at Peabody in the fall of 1979 recommended that Vanderbilt set up a well-funded office to help such faculty, including funds for travel to interviews or for the costs of advertising for jobs. Vanderbilt in October opened the Office of Faculty Services in the Psychology Building at Peabody, which worked with unemployed faculty until the fall of 1980. It was almost impossible to find academic jobs, since the majority of seekers were not eminent scholars.[42] When their Peabody employment ended, as the *Tennessean* reported on June 30, twenty had found full-time jobs, but many not in academia; three were in retraining programs; nine were not looking (spouses or older people); and seven still sought academic positions. By the fall of 1980, according to the fall *Peabody Reflector,* twenty-nine faculty had new positions, only eighteen in academia. Often overlooked was the plight of graduate students, who were usually part-time, some several years away from completing an Ed.D. or Ph.D. Some in music had to leave, others lost their mentor, and all who remained more than three years faced sharply higher Vanderbilt tuition rates. In the entire merger controversy, the most literate, eloquent, and moving letter came from a graduate-student coordinating committee.[43]

By common consent, the greatest loss in the merger was the already much-reduced Peabody music program. Hundreds of letters of protest flowed into

Peabody, then to Chancellor Heard at Vanderbilt. Nashvillians were concerned, most of all those connected to the Nashville Symphony. Nine key performers in the symphony had adjunct appointments at Peabody. Vanderbilt students had depended on the music program, since Vanderbilt had none. But music was not part of Peabody's new mission. Both Heard and his musically talented wife, Jean, wrote thoughtful letters to those who pleaded for a continuance of the program. The Heards pointed out that music at Peabody had a glorious past but had fallen on hard times since the 1975 *Design for the Future.* Able faculty had left, enrollment had declined, and lack of space had reached crisis proportions. The last head of music, Larry W. Peterson, tried to save the program by making it private and even received a few donations, but he found the venture hopeless.[44]

What Heard could not reveal is that he and key members of his board of trust had decided that Vanderbilt's musical future lay with Blair Academy. In 1979, Blair began building a new home for its music program on land leased for a mere token from Vanderbilt. It was self-supporting, well endowed, and already offered performance courses to Vanderbilt students. Del Sawyer, its director, wanted to move to degree programs as soon as possible. In a carefully planned step-by-step process, Vanderbilt adopted Blair as a non-degree-awarding school in December 1980, approved degree-granting authority in 1983, and first offered degrees in 1986. Vanderbilt also monitored the plans for the new building, assuring space for the Peabody music library, which Vanderbilt now owned; it moved to Blair in 1985. Blair gladly agreed to move and protect the musical instruments from the old school, including pianos. Most important, it moved the Stalworth organ from Hume Chapel in SR. Several of Blair's ablest faculty had formerly taught at Peabody, at least part-time. Blair thus became the successor to the Peabody School of Music.[45]

Peabody became part of Vanderbilt on July 1, 1979, but the effective merger took at least one more year. Because many terminated Peabody professors continued to teach in 1979–80, only in the fall of 1980 did the faculty drop to the approximately ninety-two who retained their jobs. Even tenured faculty who chose not to teach in their final year still advised students or helped graduate students complete dissertations. The music faculty tried to get as many of its majors through their coursework as possible. For one more year, Peabody students lived in Peabody dorms or apartments. They were not always happy. Their post office was not open for as many hours as in the past. Pool hours were skimpy, while the Peabody library closed too early in the evening. Integrating the student bodies took time, although the three Peabody sororities became part of the Pan-Hellenic Council at Vanderbilt. Most aggrieved were the married students, whose apartment rent soared by as much as a third. Vanderbilt calculated rents by the same formula used elsewhere on campus. In the wake of dozens of angry protests, it instructed its aid office to suspend normal criteria and make up the difference in rent for most students, a one-year expedient. In the fall of 1980, all Peabody students joined the undergraduate pool on the larger campus. The five Peabody dorms became the home of most Vanderbilt sophomores, regardless of their college or school.

The faculty merged more easily. Peabody had five delegates on the Vanderbilt Faculty Senate, finally winning what the faculty had struggled for at Peabody. During 1979–80, a Peabody committee on faculty governance developed an elected council, much like the one in the College of Arts and Science. Early in the year, a search committee for a new dean began work; notably, it contained several members from other Vanderbilt units. In the meantime, Hardy Wilcoxon, a psychology professor who had been sufficiently militant in the merger battles to gain the trust of faculty, became acting dean. Dunworth, whom the Vanderbilt board had assumed would be Peabody's first dean, realized that the faculty would never accept him. As he liked to point out, he had informed Gable as early as April 2, well before the vote of no confidence, that he would not continue. He announced the decision on May 2 but remained at Peabody until the beginning of August, when he moved to the

Peabody students preparing to entomb the 1980 Time Capsule. Photograph by Charles Wang, Photographic Archives of Vanderbilt University.

deanship of a new college of education at the University of West Florida. An equally stigmatized Stovall simply became a regular member of the Peabody faculty.

Contrary to fears, the fall enrollment at Peabody dropped by only 8 percent, although this figure reflected the students who had come to summer school to retain the lower Peabody tuition. It would drop more sharply in 1981 and only begin to rise in 1983. The future became clearer in October 1980, when the search committee chose the first dean of Peabody College of Vanderbilt University, Willis Hawley, a political scientist. He was already close by, for he had just arrived from Duke as the director of a center for educational policy in the Vanderbilt Institute for Public Policy Studies. With his appointment, the merger was essentially complete. The story of Peabody became, at that point, part of the much more complex story of Vanderbilt University, with its now eight schools and colleges, plus the Graduate School. For Hawley, it was a time for hope.

For others, it was a time for endings. Many old-timers retired just before or at the time of merger, among them Susan Gray (1978), Dean of Students Arthur Cook (1980), and Jack Allen (1980), the Peabody faculty member who had been most involved with college governance. Sue Eagin, a blind secretary who spent her whole career at Peabody, died in 1979, and so did the widow of one of Bruce Payne's most beloved professors, John J. Didcoct, who had died fifty-two years earlier in 1927. At the commencement in May, the faculty served breakfast to graduates for the last time. The faculty held its final meeting in June. On July 4, the venerable Peabody Women's Club served a picnic lunch for faculty on the lawn in front of SR.

Finally, it was a time for memories. In 1980, Jack Allen published in the *Reflector* a brief but accurate history of the Peabody that was. Almost a year earlier, John Windrow, the most emphatic advocate of Peabody independence, had collected many of the earlier historical essays of his close friend Alfred L. Crabb in a book, *Peabody and Leland Crabb.* On October 1, 1979, Crabb died; his wife had died in the spring, after sixty-eight years of marriage. One would like to say that he died of grief over the death of his beloved and independent Peabody, but since he had been ill for months and was 96, this would be a bit of a stretch. On April 18, 1980, sentimental Peabody students dug a six-foot-deep hole in front of the SR and buried a time capsule that contained largely letters from the students, faculty, staff, and friends of the Peabody that was passing. They hoped a new generation of students and faculty would rediscover the spirit of their beloved Peabody when they retrieved the capsule on April 18, 2000.[46] Unfortunately, before students sought out the capsule in 2001, construction crews renovating SR had found the strange object, badly deteriorated, and destroyed it.

CHAPTER FOURTEEN

Peabody as a Vanderbilt College

AFTER MERGER IN 1979, PEABODY'S FATE WAS LINKED TO THAT of Vanderbilt. In most respects. Peabody gained prestige and financial stability from the connection. After a few difficult years just after merger, it played a viable role in the larger university, and in two decades became one of the strongest and consistently the highest rated unit in the Vanderbilt cluster of nine colleges and schools. This success story is full of irony. At merger, everyone expected Peabody to become largely a graduate and professional school of education. For three years, its undergraduate enrollment dropped. It seemed that it might follow all the other colleges of education in elite universities in concentrating entirely on professional and graduate-level work. It would then have joined the Vanderbilt Schools of Law, Medicine, Divinity, Management, and eventually even Nursing. In fact, today Peabody's undergraduate enrollment is double that of its graduate, and its income from undergraduate tuition as indispensable for its survival as any time before merger.

The merged Peabody was supposed to limit its focus to the training of teachers and other educational professionals. But once again, the more things changed the more they remained the same. Peabody could not enroll enough prospective teachers to sustain a viable undergraduate program, provide employment for its surviving faculty, and assure financial stability. Thus, by a backdoor route created by its being a "school of human development," it invented substitutes for its former arts and science offerings. Today, more than two-thirds of its undergraduates are not prospective teachers, a proportion higher than in the premerged Peabody. Sixty per cent of its undergraduates enroll in one program—human organization and development—which began as a fledgling major for a few special students. This ungainly program, belatedly organized as a department, has also replaced a soon-suspended physical education department as the home of choice for more than 60 percent of Vanderbilt athletes.

VANDERBILT'S PEABODY

Contrary to the fears on the Vanderbilt campus in 1979, Peabody became neither a financial drag nor, after a few years of rebuilding, an academic embarrassment. Contrary to the fears at Peabody, Vanderbilt's central administration and board of trust did not treat Peabody as an unwanted stepchild but worked to insure Peabody's success. The surviving Peabody faculty was determined to prove that as a new, annexed province, Peabody could become the jewel in Vanderbilt's crown. The administration and board were just as determined to prove that it had not made a mistake in the risky decision to annex Peabody.

In the immediate aftermath of merger, Peabody undergraduates indeed lowered the overall quality of entering Vanderbilt undergraduates. This helped lower Vanderbilt's perceived rank among private universities, particularly after *US News and World Report* in 1983 began annually ranking colleges and universities. Overall, the Peabody faculty, immediately after merger, was weaker than that of any other Vanderbilt school or college. On the positive side was Peabody's nationally recognized leadership in special education and, in large part through the Kennedy Center, its immediate success in winning more external funding than any Vanderbilt unit save the Medical School. These were enduring strengths, since the special-education department at Peabody remains one of the two strongest in the world, and Peabody still ranks among the top five educational colleges in external funding. Peabody's grant income helped Vanderbilt cross the threshold in research funding that enabled it, in 1987, to become a Class I Research University in the now widely accepted Carnegie system for classifying universities.

Structurally, merger brought major changes. Peabody no longer owned a campus. It did not control or have financial responsibility for half the premerger buildings and none at all for the grounds. Like all colleges and schools of Vanderbilt, Peabody had primary responsibility for maintaining the buildings it used for instruction and research, for funding new buildings for its own use, and for the space it rented from other units or from the central administration. Like all units, it paid its share of the costs of the central administration and the range of services it provided faculty and students. It received the income from all endowment funds committed to Peabody but turned over their management to the central administration.

A merged Peabody continued to receive payments for students it taught from other units of Vanderbilt, according to a tuition exchange rate. But it now paid out much more than it received because of the large number of courses its students had to take in the College of Arts and Science, a compelling financial reason for Peabody to enroll as many students as possible in its own courses. Peabody establishes the standards for undergraduate student admissions (handled by the Vanderbilt Admissions Office), controls admission to its professional programs, and sets its own academic policies. But any new degree program has to have the approval of the Vanderbilt central administration and ultimately the board of trust. Peabody has no direct responsibility for student affairs or student life. Its students are simply Vanderbilt students, subject to all Vanderbilt's rules, and subject to the traditional honor system.

Like all academic units at Vanderbilt, Peabody College is supposed to live on its own income from tuition, investments, gifts, grants, and contracts. At Vanderbilt, everyone refers to this as "every tub on its own bottom." If Peabody suffers a deficit, this remains a debt owed to the university. It is supposed to repay such debts when it has a surplus in its budget. On the other hand, any surplus beyond debt repayment goes into a reserve fund to cover future deficits or to fund capital improvements. The system is not rigid. For more than a decade, both the Divinity and Engineering Schools suffered annual deficits and incurred debts that it is unlikely they will ever be able to pay back. The university has also absorbed debts accumulated by the athletic department. Peabody suffered small deficits in most years during its first decade after merger but from 1990 on enjoyed annual surpluses, repaid its accumulated deficits, and accumulated enough reserves to assume control over, renovate, and finance the expansion of the Social Religious Building. In the two decades after merger, only the College of Arts and Science, among the seven nonmedical units, enjoyed as much financial stability as Peabody. This stability, however, was possible only because of the ten annual payments of $700,000 from Vanderbilt, the phased-out rent payments for the campus assets Peabody had turned over to the university.

Because it merged with Vanderbilt and did not develop as a college of education within the university, Peabody has remained distinctive among colleges of education. Its undergraduate teacher-training program has insured its close relationship with area schools and its continued ties to educational accrediting agencies. It is the only college of education with its own psychology department not tied directly to education. It is the only college of education so dependent on noneducational undergraduate programs to help fund its professional work. Except in psychology, Peabody has not been able to make joint appointments with the College of Arts and Science in such fields as history, the social sciences, and the humanities. This has helped discourage work in such traditional areas as educational history and philosophy and in sociology. No other highly rated college of education has so few overlapping faculty, but at present several such joint appointments are at the planning stage.

Peabody as a Vanderbilt College

Peabody joined a Vanderbilt that, by 1979, was poised for a period of growth and increased academic prestige. At its opening in 1875, Vanderbilt was the best-funded college or university in the former Confederate states, had the ablest faculty, and soon gained the best scientific apparatus. But at that time, its southern location explained and excused a great deal, for no university south of Johns Hopkins compared to the best private universities in the North. Yet, Vanderbilt took the lead in improving standards for both colleges and secondary schools in the South, even as Peabody Normal trained the ablest teachers through its Peabody scholarships. In the early twentieth century, Vanderbilt maintained its lead over other private colleges or universities in the former Confederate South but faced competition from a few flagship state universities. Its major funding still came from northern foundations or individuals, mostly the Vanderbilt family, foundations supported by Rockefeller funds, and the Carnegie Foundation.[1]

Northern recognition of Vanderbilt's strengths led Rockefeller's General Education Board to fund the model medical school that opened across from Peabody in 1925. Several foundations supported a modern Ph.D. program in select departments by the early thirties. The strength of the Medical School, of several scientific specialties connected to it, and of English and social science departments helped Vanderbilt gain membership in the prestigious American Association of Universities in 1949, which many locally interpreted as a shift from a regional university to a national one. Already members of this elite group were Duke, Virginia, Texas, and North Carolina. This membership attested to the fact that the postwar Vanderbilt was, by national criteria, the fifth strongest university in the former Confederate South.

Immediately after World War II, Vanderbilt was one of only eight southern universities that could support graduate programs or professional schools that competed with those in the North. The others were three state universities (North Carolina, Texas, and Virginia) and four private ones (Duke, Emory, Tulane, and Rice). All would remain Vanderbilt's strongest southern competitors, although Tulane has not kept pace with the others. But in 1979, at the time of merger, Vanderbilt's competitive strength in the South could not conceal the still large qualitative gap (in financial resources, faculty eminence, and student quality) that separated it and all other southern universities, save possibly Duke, from the Ivy League, the great private outlanders (Hopkins, Chicago, Stanford), and the stronger state universities of the Midwest and California.

By 1979, the strongest southern universities were already on the move, struggling toward parity with their northern counterparts. They were competing nationally for students, and they would soon have a few departments or professional schools among the top ten in the nation. In the last two decades, all have moved closer to parity. Duke now ranks among the ten strongest private universities in the United States, while North Carolina is as strong as several Big Ten schools. Necessary for these southern gains were the racial integration of the sixties and the shrinking economic gap between North and South. That Vanderbilt has held its own in this bid for national prominence means that its pattern of growth has paralleled that of its southern competitors, although it has not necessarily gained ground on any, save for Tulane.

These facts have led to both celebration and frustration at Vanderbilt. The marks of progress are clear. Peabody is now the strongest educational college in the South, and among the top ten nationally. The Divinity School is also among the top ten in its field. Other Vanderbilt professional schools—Law, Medicine, Management—rank at least in the top twenty-five, as does the College of Arts and Science at the undergraduate level. Yet these remarkable achievements have simply matched gains at other universities. Location and financial resources have helped Duke outpace Vanderbilt, and recently so have both Emory and Rice. Thus the frustration.

In the merger year, Vanderbilt still faced plenty of problems. In the inflationary seventies, it had fallen behind many of its competitors. Its undergraduate students were less qualified than those of the sixties. Budgets were tight. The new Graduate School of Management (now Owen) foundered in the midseventies and without a complete reorganization would have succumbed. The Nursing School still faced problems with accreditation, student dissatisfaction, and student quality. The Divinity School, in the fifties one of the strongest in the United States, recovered only slowly from the devastating effects of an integration battle at Vanderbilt in the sixties. When it rebuilt an able faculty in the midseventies, it faced mounting deficits as enrollment in its professional program declined (these deficits continued every year until 1998). Engineering, after some daring but controversial academic experiments in the seventies, remained a comparatively weak school; in the eighties, after enrollments did not expand to match a risky expansion of faculty, it too fell into a pattern of annual deficits. Medicine, the strongest school, had to keep expanding its expensive hospital facilities (it opened a new hospital in 1979) and threatened to dominate the rest of the university. The College of Arts and Science, at the core of the nonmedical units, suffered from financial constraints in the midseventies. Although it prided itself on the quality of its teaching, faculty salaries could not keep up with inflation, it could not attract the ablest students, and too many faculty were not involved in major research. Relative to other university libraries, JUL had fallen behind. Vanderbilt had to suspend its university press.

Yet in that merger year, Vanderbilt had reason to hope. A new period of growth and of qualitative gains in most of its units was underway. Responsible for this, as always, was money. Like Peabody, Vanderbilt had to adjust to the new era in university financing, particularly in the South. In the sixties, it had benefited from the latter-day benevolence of the Vanderbilt family via Harold Sterling Vanderbilt and from continued foundation support from GEB, Ford, and Carnegie. This mode of funding all but ended in the seventies. Peabody could not overcome this loss. Vanderbilt recovered, but it took some time. National trends in college enrollment allowed it to raise tuition. Its prestige as an elite southern private university attracted a pool of applicants that grew in spite of the increasingly higher tuition—at times, affluent parents seemed to place more value on a university as its costs soared. Encouraging this parental support were the lower inflation of the eighties, the Reagan tax cuts, a steady shift of income and wealth toward the top percentile of incomes, and the rapid rise of per capita incomes in the Southeast.

Paralleling tuition increases was Vanderbilt's success in tapping new sources of gifts, now largely southern and alumni. In the centennial campaign from 1976 to 1981, the university exceeded its then daringly ambitious goal of $150 million by just over $31 million; members of its own board of trust gave $60 million.[2] This level of support reflected the increasing wealth of southern businesspeople and professionals and of many Vanderbilt alumni. One product of the campaign was a much higher level of annual support from alumni. Vanderbilt would be blessed during the next two decades by, arguably, the most talented and successful business and investment managers in any U.S. university.

Coming at a crucial time, the centennial campaign was more critical to Vanderbilt than later, much larger, fund drives. For example, it allowed the College of Arts and Science to begin recruiting senior scholars, some to fill new centennial chairs. This pattern of senior appointments has continued, and has led to some stronger graduate programs, a higher level of faculty research, and new tenure standards that institutionalized high research expectations for all professors. Only in the eighties, outside the Medical School, did Vanderbilt become a fully research-oriented university. Despite all the problems facing the newly merged Peabody, its Kennedy Center and its strength in clinical psychology and special education meshed perfectly with this new emphasis. But Peabody, and then Blair after 1980, created a continuing challenge for Vanderbilt—the dispersion of resources. It now had nine schools and colleges that ran the gamut of academic fields, or as many as in most state universities. A continuing joke at Vanderbilt revolved around how soon it would create a college of agriculture. Thus, in the eighties and early nineties, Vanderbilt's challenge became how, with its always limited resources, it could promote excellence in so many areas. At times by choice, at others by necessity, its colleges and schools remained small. Always, some were struggling. Consistently, Peabody was among those improving.

Peabody College

In 1980, as the merger took full effect, everyone at Peabody knew that the college had a ten-year grace period to prove its viability. In 1989 it would lose its annual subsidy and be on its own financially. In only a decade, it had to create graduate and undergraduate academic programs that would attract a growing number of students willing to pay its now high tuition. It needed to expand the strong research base in the Kennedy Center to all departments, so that external funding would supplement tuition income and the limited income from its still small endowment. In fact, as now prudently managed by Vanderbilt, the endowment income dropped because of lower pay-out rates. In the early years, Peabody had to be tough. Programs that did not pay for themselves had to go. This led to the difficult decision in 1987 to discontinue the library school in the spring of 1988, and to convert a declining undergraduate major in physical education to a few courses in health education. Above all, the college had to innovate and experiment. It juggled its professional programs to find those with broadest appeal. In what turned out to be the one most important secrets of its financial success, it had to win Vanderbilt approval for new undergraduate majors.

Leadership was critical, and here Peabody was fortunate. Willis Hawley proved an almost ideal dean in the perilous first decade, although one not always loved. Personally reserved, at times distant in direct contact with professors, he was an eloquent, even dogged, advocate for Peabody. An accomplished scholar in political science and educational policy, he exemplified the type of faculty Peabody needed. While dean, he directed a major study and report on the effects of desegregation in the public schools. He worked out a persuasive theory about a lack of cultural overlap among families, communities, and schools to explain the difficulties of so many public schools, particularly in cities. He had a national reputation not as a dean, but as an expert on educational issues. He consulted widely at the federal level. While his cheerleading for Peabody on occasion approached puffery, the gains during his administration almost justified his belief that Peabody in 1990 was in many respects the strongest college of education in the country.

Equally critical was the support of the central administration at Vanderbilt. In 1982, when Alexander Heard retired as chancellor, the Vanderbilt board chose to end the dual system of chancellor and president (Emmett Fields, contrary to his hopes and expectations, did not become chancellor). Under the new administrative arrangement, two academic officers served directly under the new chancellor, Joe B. Wyatt, formerly a vice president for administration at Harvard. A vice chancellor for medical affairs was responsible for the Schools of Medicine and Nursing, while a provost was responsible for the other seven schools, including Peabody. Thus, the dean at Peabody reported to the provost. After Wendell Holliday resigned as provost in 1983, Charles A. Kiesler, a psychologist from Carnegie-Mellon,

became the aggressive, egotistic, at times controversial provost in January 1985. Dean Hawley fought his share of battles with Kiesler, and Kiesler even took their disagreements into the public arena. Tensions between the two helped motivate Hawley's resignation as dean in 1989. But overall, he won almost as much as possible for Peabody in the way of financial support.

Most supportive was Chancellor Wyatt. A new breed of chancellor, without a Ph.D., not an intellectual or a scholar, he was a man of great integrity and goodwill. He chose to leave Vanderbilt's academic policies to the faculty, provost, and deans. Some students and faculty resented this deference and Wyatt's remoteness. Jokes abounded about rare sightings of the chancellor on campus. But Wyatt supported an able team of managers, was effective in fund-raising, played a national leadership role among university executives, worked well with the businesspeople who dominated the board of trust, and helped create an almost model campus with less delayed maintenance than any other major university. Most critical for Peabody, he wanted a Vanderbilt more in the Peabody tradition, a university that not only excelled in research but one that also used it to better the larger society. He was deeply concerned about elementary and secondary education, anxious to use new information technology to improve education (his academic training was in mathematics and computer science), and determined to guide Vanderbilt's largely affluent students into greater involvement with social problems. He loved Peabody, what it stood for, its role in Nashville, and the type of students it had traditionally nourished—students like Wyatt, who was from a less than affluent East Texas family. He urged more A&S students to enroll in courses at Peabody and earn teacher certification, although few did. His daughter graduated from Peabody. Wyatt was personally proud of its successes and supported its programs wholeheartedly.

The first three years after merger were the most difficult for Peabody. Freshman enrollment dropped, since entering students had to pay the standard Vanderbilt tuition, which rose from $4,260 in 1979–80 to $6,100 in 1982–83. The continuing undergraduates and graduate students enjoyed the lower Peabody tuition and graduated with Peabody degrees. The ablest undergraduate still received the Sullivan Award. Only in 1983, when the first undergraduates who enrolled in a merged Peabody College received their Vanderbilt degrees, did the Sullivan Award give way to the Vanderbilt Founders Medal, an award for the most distinguished graduate in each school and college.[3]

Peabody shrank to a small, compact group of buildings. West of the mall, it controlled only the Mental Retardation Lab (MRL) and the library, which was a part of the integrated Vanderbilt library system as it had been under JUL. But Peabody owned and funded the Education Library. East of the mall, it controlled Mayborn to the north, with much of it devoted to the library school. Payne Hall, its largest classroom building, adjoined it to the southwest. Farther south was the Jesup Psychology Building and, connected to it in back, the Human Development

Lab, renamed Hobbs Hall in 1983. It paid a nominal rent for other space owned by the central administration—administrative offices in the old administrative building, physical education facilities in SR, and later some office space in the Hill student center. These were all the facilities it needed or could maintain. But Peabody had to use scarce funds for capital improvements to the buildings, all in terrible repair, including a major and early renovation of Payne Hall and over the next two decades extensive work on all its classroom buildings, the library, and Hobbs Hall.

In the early years, Peabody enjoyed an almost balanced budget. It maintained a faculty of around ninety, gradually raising the salaries of its ablest professors to levels equal to those in A&S. It also lowered the normal teaching load of three to four three-hour courses each semester to two or three; for those involved in research, soon a majority, the normal teaching load was and remains two courses. In this transition, it had some leeway. It could allow the salaries of less able faculty to lag and use a merit system to reward those who contributed most, particularly in research and publishing. In particular, it could bid for eminent outside professors. The higher Vanderbilt tuition helped balance its books, as long as enough students enrolled. A rapid expansion in grant income also helped. Over the next twenty years, the college would keep a faculty remarkably close in size to that at merger, never more than a hundred full-time. It would soon hire dozens of research, part-time, or adjunct and adjoint lecturers and professors. The result: a much more able and distinguished regular faculty.

The merger, of course, led to a new self-study. At Peabody, these were an honored tradition, particularly at times of new leadership. This one, in three phases, would last from 1979 to 1981 and guide Peabody until 1987 when, in anticipation of the end of the $700,000 subsidy, it resorted to another major self-study. This would not be the last. In 1979, a Peabody committee began work on phases one and two—the first on the effects of merger, completed quickly, and the second on the status of Peabody programs, completed in the fall of 1980. The critical study was phase three, which had to chart the future path of Peabody in light of national and international needs in education and human development. As always, Peabody expended an enormous amount of faculty time on this effort, inviting seven major outside educators to come to Peabody as external advisers. Subcommittees that involved most of the faculty focused on undergraduate programs, professional education, graduate education, and research and development.

The self-study matured some critical decisions. The committee rather obviously recommended that all regular Peabody professors, in all fields, become vitally involved in research. The tenure rules of Vanderbilt, which now applied to Peabody, assured this involvement among tenure-track faculty. Despite the risk, Peabody made several critical new appointments from 1981 to 1983, even before its enrollment began a gradual climb. It emphasized its professional programs—then more than twenty that led to the M.S., Ed.S. and Ed.D. degrees, all under full

Peabody control. Peabody decided to limit Ph.D. work, under the supervision of Vanderbilt's Graduate School, to two fields—psychology and human development (the department of the same name soon had more Ph.D. candidates than any other in the graduate school), and education and human development, which would involve selected subjects in all the education departments. Although Peabody would focus on professional education, the committee realized that it was still dependent on undergraduate tuition. Thus it recommended that Peabody seek faculty senate and central administrative approval for two new undergraduate majors—secondary education and human development (both approved in 1982).[4]

Secondary education, an obvious choice, had not been part of the merger agreement because A&S already had a professor supervising Vanderbilt students who sought certification in secondary education. They took their subject work in A&S, their professional courses and practice at Peabody. This small program and its attached office in A&S now made little sense. Vanderbilt abolished it and gave Peabody full control. But students in secondary education would continue to take most of their courses in A&S, including their general education requirements and a major in a subject area. A&S students could still certify as before, taking their professional major at Peabody. Not much changed, except a few differences in the general education requirements according to the college in which a student was enrolled. The new major did not promise much additional tuition for Peabody.

Had anyone, particularly the faculty in A&S, foreseen the future of the new major in human development, they might have tried to block its approval. No one was very clear about what the new major would entail, although Dean Hawley supported it. The major was the only handle Peabody had for introducing courses not directed at training teachers. Robert Innes, a young associate professor in psychology and special education, wanted to developed the new major and had some ideas about how to do it. He later admitted that Peabody's desperate need for students, more than any educational idealism, motivated the early planning. At the beginning, everyone at Peabody talked about a special interdisciplinary program that would appeal to a few, very specially qualified, self-directed students who wanted service- and people-oriented careers in government agencies and possibly in private corporations. The descriptions remained broad and inclusive, since the new major apparently offered something for almost any student.[5]

Organizationally, Peabody seemed always in flux. It frequently shifted its departmental alignment, and eventually created a confusing number of centers and institutes. Without funding for endowed professors, Peabody eventually made almost all of its most distinguished scholars the directors of institutes or centers, which in turn provided the focus for research grants and for graduate student employment. By far the two most important centers in the first decade after merger were the Kennedy Center and the new Learning Technology Center (LTS). The first of twelve, and later as many as fourteen, federally funded research centers involving mental retardation and human development, Peabody's Kennedy Center had been the most successful. With its shifting array of research institutes, it gradually became less and less a distinctive Peabody research center, since it drew its investigators from all branches of Vanderbilt. But it remained the main avenue for funding research in both psychology and special education at Peabody.

Peabody first gained national preeminence in special education. After merger it achieved the same distinction in the creation, adaptation, use, and distribution of new learning technologies. In this area today, it is among the top two or three schools of education in the United States, if not the clear leader. Dean Hawley decided in 1982 to consolidate Peabody's Instructional Media Center and all educational technology programs into the Learning Technology Center, which he hoped could facilitate the use of new technology in teaching not only at Peabody but in the larger society. It would become a major research center, with a large staff funded by numerous grants and eventually some income from its own creations. It innovations in educational technology have had nationwide influence.

Administratively, Peabody did not change very much. The dean appointed four associate deans; their number and duties have shifted over time. Following the pattern of the College of Arts and Science, Peabody finally established an elected faculty council with an elected faculty member as chair. It was made up of the dean and eleven members, one from each of the then six departments and five at large (no more than two from any department). The council advised the dean and reported to the whole faculty at its periodic meetings. The dean and faculty council chair appointed the chairs of three vital committees—academic standards and procedures, curriculum and educational programs, and faculty affairs (other committees were added later). Peabody's six departments (the faculty gladly replaced the old division system), unlike those in most liberal arts colleges, did not match up neatly with academic disciplines or undergraduate majors. In this sense, almost all work at Peabody was interdisciplinary, which befits a school of education. Peabody folded the small staff of physical education into the large Department of Teaching and Learning; the other five departments were Library Science, Human Development Counseling, Educational Leadership, Psychology and Human Development, and Special Education. In 1984, Peabody shifted the human development counseling faculty into a new department, Human Resources, which included the new and soon booming undergraduate program in human development (today, human organization and development). In 1987, it eliminated doctoral work in human development counseling. The demise of the Library School in 1987 left Peabody with only five departments.

Peabody had more than enough faculty in 1980 to teach its declining enrollment. What it needed was a stronger faculty, particularly in teaching and learning and in educational leadership. The self-study recommended, and Hawley began building, a more research-oriented faculty even before finances supported such a move. The two strongest departments, psychology and special education, survived intact, as did the professors with appointments in the Kennedy Center. Many of the old-timers with established national reputations were still on board. These included the director of the Kennedy Center, Carl Haywood, the next director, Alfred A. Baumeister, and his associate director, Paul Dokecki. Samuel Ashcroft, a national leader in education for the blind, Ray Norris in psychological statistics and counseling, Roger F. Aubrey in human development counseling, and John R. Newbrough in community psychology all remained for at least the first years after merger. So did the Library School director, Edward Gleaves, H. Floyd Dennis Jr. in special education, and Jules Seeman and Leonard Bickman in psychology and at the Kennedy Center. James H. Hogge, who took the early lead in computer use at Peabody, would serve as associate dean under Hawley. Thomas Stowall and James Whitlock, Dunworth's cronies, remained as professors, as did Hardy Wilcoxon after serving as interim dean. The core but weak Department of Teaching and Learning became the focus of the most intense effort, as it was continuously involved in self-study and planning. It absorbed some of its ablest professors from the former arts and science faculties, including Elizabeth Goldman in mathematics, who became an almost indispensable administrator at both Peabody and in the central administration at Vanderbilt, and Charles Myers, the young historian who soon chaired the department and also served as associate dean. These professors not only directed the training of secondary teachers but also wrote extensively, particularly textbooks for public schools.

From 1980 to 1985, Peabody hired at least a dozen distinguished mature scholars or promising young scholars. This began in 1981 with Terrence Deal and John K. Fogler in the critical field of education, and also as senior research fellows in Vanderbilt's Institute for Public Policy Studies (VIPPS). It recruited John (Jack) Glidewell that year from the University of Chicago, also a fellow in VIPPS and a social psychologist with an outstanding publication record. In the next year, Glidewell helped establish and then direct the Institute for the Advanced Study of Corporate Learning Environments, a Peabody effort to expand the range of its teaching mission. Also new in 1981 was Chester Finn, who soon had a national but controversial reputation in educational policy, served under Reagan as assistant secretary of education, and became a national critic of the failures of U.S. public schools and an advocate of a return to basic education. In 1982, Peabody hired Kathleen Hoover-Dempsey, who became a master teacher and able administrator, and Ann K. Rogers-Warren (later Ann Kaiser), a specialist in early childhood education who soon became the dynamic chair of special education and a master at winning external grants. In 1985, Peabody employed Carolyn M. Evertson, a nationally prominent expert on teacher effectiveness, who would later chair the Department of Teaching and Learning, and Douglas and Lynn Fuchs, who would eventually gain national recognition in special education and jointly direct their own institute in the Kennedy Center. Also in 1985, John D. Bransford, a psychologist at Vanderbilt who had been an investigator in the Kennedy Center since 1980, became the imaginative and aggressive codirector of the Learning Technology Center. Cumulatively, such appointments helped build a strong research base in all the continuing departments, with a 20 percent average annual gain in research funding for the eighties.

These new professors gradually replaced the old-timers. In 1985, Seeman, Whitlock, and Ashcroft retired, as did Ida Long Rogers and Hardy Wilcoxon in 1987. In the same year, Henry Hill died at age ninety-two, as did Peabody's last educational philosopher, Clifton Hall, long since retired, and board of trust member and Peabody benefactor Frank Mayborn. Mayborn left a bequest of $1 million to help fund the first endowed chair at Peabody, in cognitive studies, soon filled by psychologist James W. Pellegrino, who would follow Hawley as dean. In 1990, Ray Norris and Jack Glidewell retired. At a three-day celebration in 1985 to mark the beginning of Peabody's third century, four ex-presidents returned to campus—Hill, Robb, Claunch, and Dunworth. Jack Allen wrote another short essay on Peabody's history.[6]

After 1982, new appointments and new programs began to pay off in the increased enrollments essential for financial solvency. Peabody awarded 631 degrees in 1980 and 508 in 1981, but not soon again as many. The number of graduates dropped to 314 in 1984, when only sixty-five undergraduates completed their B.S. Peabody could not afford to be selective, in the fall of 1983 accepting for admission 168 of 220 undergraduate applicants; only 115 came. Entering undergraduates had an average combined SAT score of 995, the lowest of any school or college at Vanderbilt (A&S students averaged 1176 during what was a low ebb even there). In the fall of 1984, freshman enrollment rose from 115 to 123, the faint promise of a trend. Notably, 36 of these students came to major in human development. The total undergraduate enrollment stood at 367, compared to 641 in professional programs and 44 in graduate programs. From then on, the percentage of undergraduates would gradually rise. By 1988, 182 undergraduates enrolled, almost half in human development (already the largest major at Vanderbilt), the poorly kept secret of undergraduate enrollment increases. At graduation in 1990, for the first time ever, Peabody had more bachelors than masters of education (148 to 138). By then, human development had 450 majors, including six members of a suddenly booming women's basketball team. The lure of this major as early as 1987 brought Peabody more transfers, most from A&S, than it lost to other schools. By 1990, the undergraduates almost matched the number of graduate students; in the next year, they would be in a majority.

Even with its subsidy of $700,000, Peabody struggled toward a balanced budget. With the subsidy, it balanced its 1980–81 budget, then moved to a deficit in 1981–82 as enrollment declined, and to a peak deficit in 1983 of more than $500,000.

The board of trust was very concerned about the financial situation at Peabody, but the Schools of Law, Divinity, and Engineering, as well as Blair, were also showing deficits. By 1986, Peabody's annual budget had grown from around $5 million in 1980 to more than $8 million, and the annual deficit had dropped to just over $200,000, peanuts compared to the Engineering School's $2.4 million and the athletic department's $2.5 million. In 1986, Vanderbilt converted the former Peabody campus south of the SR to commercial development, the Village at Vanderbilt, projecting a 10 percent annual income on the investment, with one announced purpose—to help compensate for Peabody deficits. Rising tuition (to $11,500 in 1988–89), rising grant income, and a growing enrollment in human development allowed Peabody to earn a surplus of almost $250,000 on its 1987–88 budget of more than $9 million. In 1988–89, the last year of its subsidy, it enjoyed a surplus of more than $300,000. In the next year, fully on its own, it had a deficit of only $87,000, and surpluses from then on.[7]

Peabody had made it financially. But it had to work hard, insecure in its dependence on federal grants. It never did as well as other Vanderbilt schools in attracting gifts, particularly from alumni, who had lower incomes than in the rest of Vanderbilt (only 3 percent with incomes over $75,000 in 1985). In 1990, alumni annual giving amounted to only $200,000, and only 18 percent of alumni contributed

Four former presidents of an independent Peabody at bicentennial dinner in 1985, from left: John Dunworth, John Claunch, Henry Hill, and Felix Robb. Photograph by Dan Lofton. Photographic Archives of Vanderbilt University.

each year, less than half the percentage in A&S. In 1984, Peabody revived the premerger Development Council and named it the Peabody Roundtable, made up of those who contributed at least a thousand dollars annually. But Peabody had difficulty attracting large donors and would have modest goals in Vanderbilt's major campaigns. This meant a dearth of endowed chairs, heavy dependence on federal grants for graduate student support, and inadequate student aid, which in turn warred against the recruitment of minorities. Only Vanderbilt scholarship athletes, a joint teacher-training program with Fisk University, and a much-publicized Posse program, which recruited disadvantaged students form New York City, assured a growing racial diversity.[8]

Few structural changes occurred from 1980 to 1987. The Child Study Center merged with the experimental school (soon named the Susan Gray School) in MRL to become the Family and Child Study Center. The Ed.S degree, with few takers, survived only into the early nineties, but Peabody still trained a large number of doctorates in education (seventy-six in 1989). By then it tried to distinguish its Ed.D., largely awarded to school administrators, from the scholarly Ph.D. by shifting the dissertation from scholarly research to more practical types of inquiry. All the changes won the ringing endorsement of an NCATE committee, which in 1985 not only reaccredited Peabody but pronounced it "one of the brightest spots in American education." The self-study of 1987, looking to the end of subsidies, recommended a new undergraduate major in cognitive studies, which the Vanderbilt administration approved. This new major, really a concealed major in psychology, met a new need. Most states, including Tennessee, now required that elementary teachers have a subject major. Peabody wanted as many as possible of its elementary education students to take their second major at Peabody, not in A&S, to keep as much of their tuition as possible.[9] The strategy worked and in 1994 led to a final major, in child development, also tied closely to the college's strong psychology department. It allowed Peabody to offer a double major in special education and child development.

The 1987 self-study, *Plan for the Future of Peabody College,* led to one sad result. Peabody dropped its sixty-year-old Library School, although it continued to offer pioneering courses in information technology. This compared to losing the agriculture program in 1936, public health nursing in 1962, and the Music School in 1979. At the old Peabody, the Library School had been a major lure for students and a money raiser for the college. It was still accredited in 1987, but times had changed and its enrollment was stable or declining. It was difficult to compete with library schools in public universities and to attract able students willing to pay the high Vanderbilt tuition. And higher accreditation standards meant rising costs for faculty and facilities. The school would lose money in the future, and Peabody could not afford to subsidize it. Other private library schools, including one at Emory, made the same difficult decision. Long-time director Ed Gleaves became the Tennessee state librarian and archivist, while tenured professors transferred to other departments. A celebration at its closing in 1988 brought back appreciative alumni and led to a final award to its most fondly remembered but now-retired professor, Frances Neel Cheyney.[10]

In the summer of 1989, Willis Hawley resigned as dean after nine demanding years of work and what had become an untenable relationship with Provost Kiesler. Looking back, Hawley had much to rejoice over. His deanship had been a success story. He admitted that national trends had helped. Education had become a dominant concern in the eighties, educational reform a national commitment, and by the middle of the decade teachers were again in short supply and Peabody-trained teachers in high demand. Federal funding for education increased almost annually. The economy had grown throughout most of the decade. Private universities such as Vanderbilt were thriving. Peabody's faculty, stable in number, had risen in quality, as had the undergraduate enrollment, which had more than doubled. Peabody SAT scores were two hundred points above the national average among teachers' colleges but still more than a hundred below those in A&S. Student aid had also doubled. Peabody led the nation in educational technology. A new LTC computer and video program in mathematics, *The Adventures of Jasper Woodbury,* adopted in many elementary schools, won national publicity for Peabody and Vanderbilt. No longer a drag on the rest of Vanderbilt, Peabody now helped raise Vanderbilt's ranking among private universities.[11]

What Hawley never mentioned were the problems. Peabody undergraduates, although able in comparison to those in most schools of education, still lagged in academic achievement well behind those in other units at Vanderbilt. In its first postmerger decade, the prime goal had been to enroll more students in all areas; selectivity fell by the wayside. Now it was time to limit undergraduate enrollment and focus on quality. This proved difficult. Peabody still could not be selective in some professional fields, in which it also had a dismal record in attracting minority students. In some years, it could not award all its externally funded graduate scholarships. Despite all the efforts at faculty recruitment, Peabody still had too many tenured professors who had not adjusted to the emphasis on research productivity (other professional schools and A&S had the same problem). Some were tenured before the merger, others at the time of appointment. The evidence of this was in the number of associate professors at Peabody who never moved up to the full professor rank.

Balance was another problem. The booming major in human development, now the tail that wagged the dog, was almost incidental to Peabody's primary mission as a college of education. The need for students had supported its often unfocused growth. It now threatened to spin out of control. By 1990, the program had allied itself informally with the Vanderbilt athletic department, a beneficial symbiosis in the eighties as Vanderbilt recruited athletes with marginal academic credentials and placed them in human development. When Peabody tried to stabilize undergraduate enrollment and raise student quality, as it did by the midnineties, all these athletes would constitute a problem.

PEABODY IN THE BOOMING NINETIES

By 1991, Peabody had matured. Ironies abounded, but by then its role and mission was reasonably clear, and would not change in the next decade. First, it was a small graduate and professional school of education with a distinguished senior faculty and somewhat less distinguished graduate students numbering around five hundred. Early in the nineties, it cut all its off-campus programs, which reduced its professional enrollment by about one-fifth. (Professors had been flying to teach weekend graduate courses at widely scattered cities, some as far away as New England.) Second, it was a small undergraduate teacher-training school, the most prestigious in the United States. Third, it supported an undergraduate major in human development (in 1993 more accurately renamed human organization and development, and usually referred to as HOD). HOD is almost a college in itself, unique in both concept and student appeal.

The nineties brought new leadership. During a two-year search for Dean Hawley's replacement, Joseph Cunningham served as a popular interim dean. In the fall of 1991, the search committee selected as dean the holder of Peabody's only endowed chair, James W. Pellegrino. Like Hawley, Pellegrino had fine scholarly credentials, in his case as an experimental psychologist with abundant publications to his credit. At the University of California at Santa Barbara, he had chaired the education department and served as acting dean of the Graduate School. He was a master of quantitative tools and computer innovations. A less aggressive and eloquent leader than Hawley, Pellegrino would focus not on growth but consolidation. In 1997, he rejected a faculty committee proposal to create two small and, he believed, weak departments to replace the Department of Human Resources. Instead, he abolished that department, and assigned its faculty to the remaining four departments, a unilateral decision that led to resentment among the reassigned faculty and even more resentment from professors in departments, such as Psychology and Human Development, who did not welcome colleagues they had not chosen. Under pressure, and lacking the degree of support he wanted from the provost, Pellegrino resigned in 1998 to return to full-time research and teaching. He and his wife left Peabody for new positions at the University of Illinois, Chicago, in 2001, a critical loss for the college.

The next dean inherited a strong college, but faced an imposing array of problems. A successful committee search led to the appointment in 1998 of Camilla P. Benbow, who was a distinguished professor of psychology at Iowa State, with a

Post-merger leaders, clockwise: Deans Willis Hawley (courtesy of the office of the *Peabody Reflector*), James Pellegrino (courtesy of the office of the *Peabody Reflector*), and Camilla Benbow (photograph by Ardon Brown).

special research program involving very gifted students, and who had served after 1996 as an aggressive interim dean of its school of education. She would become the first woman to head Peabody, and, once again, had established her credentials as a scholar before entering administration. Swedish born, the mother of seven children, and very ambitious for Peabody, she quickly became one of the most energetic and forceful deans at Vanderbilt. She was soon very much involved in efforts to improve Peabody's already high national recognition, and to increase it role in, and contribution to, the rest of Vanderbilt.

Benbow walked into a hornet's nest. She faced so many early frustrations as to have driven many new deans to an early resignation. Departmental restructuring, and with it the fuller integration of HOD, remained an almost intractable problem. With very little lead time, Benbow had to complete a new strategic academic plan for Peabody. She had to work out a carefully worded compromise when the board and central administration, in effect, mandated a tenure appointment for the wife of a new Vanderbilt chancellor, even though the faculty of the Department of Leadership and Organizations had opposed tenure. She had to cut budgets as Peabody began, once again, to face possible deficits. She had to struggle for more than two years with a confusing, rumor-plagued, soon intensely personal controversy with the Kennedy Center director. Finally, she had to negotiate a transfer of the Kennedy Center from Peabody to the central administration (the present director reports to the provost and has his academic home in the Medical Center).

While the campus in the nineties remained basically the same, Peabody assumed responsibility for more of its old campus as it gained financial stability and as its undergraduate enrollment soared to more than a thousand. In 1992, with space at a premium, Dean Pellegrino believed Peabody should reclaim and restore the Social Religious Building. For a few years, Peabody also regained control of the Home Economics Building (for the Learning Technology Center), which it returned to the central administration after completion of the new SR. According to a firm promise by the chancellor, Peabody can reclaim both the Home Economics and Administration Buildings when it needs their space. Of the premerger instructional facilities, Peabody will eventually control all but the Cohen Memorial Fine Arts Building. For the new century, tentative plans for the campus included an expansion of the Kennedy Center by an addition to MRL stretching toward Edgehill, while Vanderbilt has finally committed itself to a linking bridge across Twenty-first Avenue.

In 1993, Peabody and other Vanderbilt officials developed the plans for a complete restoration of SR by 1995, and for construction of a new annex at its rear. This was the most ambitious and costly project undertaken by the new Peabody. This grand old building had fallen on hard times. It was half empty after the music library moved in 1985 and Peabody dropped physical education in 1987. The central administration, which controlled the building, used its offices during a renovation of Kirkland (and at the same time dismantled the beautiful Hume Chapel) and placed a few continuing offices, such as Naval ROTC, in some of the rooms; the rest were almost unused except for the old auditorium, still in demand for some campus events. Vanderbilt did maintain the outside of the building, still the dominant structure on campus.

With annual surpluses running as high as $1 million, Peabody could afford to finance the transformation. It committed $14 million (most of it borrowed) and the central administration another $2 million to help pay for the campuswide value of the SR's planned media resources. The annex would house the offices of the Learning Technology Center, which moved from Mayborn (HOD took its place), and the Department of Teaching and Learning. The main building, in addition to some technologically advanced classrooms, would house administrative offices. The old auditorium, or rotunda, became a model multimedia space much valued across the campus. Once again, SR became a symbol for Peabody, not of the religious and service motifs beloved by John D. Rockefeller, but of the new education technology that was transforming so many aspects of both teaching and learning. Only the entrance hall resembled the old SR, but it was without the beautiful stairway to the upper floors.

The nonacademic buildings on the old campus remained under central administrative control. This included the nursery school on Edgehill, which became a daycare center for Vanderbilt, and the former president's home which, with later additions, became part of the home of VIPPS and its affiliated First Amendment Center. In 1999, Vanderbilt completed a plain brick annex behind the Hill Student Center to house its Academic Computing and Information Services. In stages, Vanderbilt renovated the five former Peabody dorms to near pristine condition. But Confederate Hall has twice led to protests about its name and its possible affront to African American students. Because of its original funding by the United Daughters of the Confederacy, the university cannot easily rename Confederate. But despite the SR's heritage and John D. Rockefeller's preference, the board of trust rechristened the building after retiring chancellor Wyatt and his wife, although the old name and dedicatory statement remain on the front. Wyatt's strong support for Peabody and his interest in new learning technologies fully justified the new name. But it might still be appropriate to refer only to the SR and Annex, collectively, as the Joe B. and Faye Wyatt Center, and retain the old title for the original building out of deference to the wishes of Rockefeller, the largest contributor in real dollars to both Peabody and Vanderbilt.

The Peabody faculty remained stable in the nineties, with about one hundred full-time, full-status professors. The end of the decade brought a second endowed chair, not filled as of 2001, a gift of former psychologist and Kennedy Center architect Lloyd Dunn. Another chair, to be assigned to the Peabody dean, reflects the generosity of H. Rodes Hart, a former chair of the Peabody Roundtable. By 2002, funds were in hand for two additional endowed chairs. Three senior appointments stood out in the decade: Robert L. Crowson Jr. in the critical field of educational leadership; Travis Thompson as a nationally eminent psychologist and director of the Kennedy Center; and James W. Guthrie, at first in human resources and then, with restructuring, as chair of the expanded Department of Leadership and Organizations.

Guthrie came to Peabody to direct a new research center on educational policy. It joins the LTC as one of the two most important centers, since the Kennedy Center is no longer under Peabody administrative control. By 2002, the professors affiliated with the Educational Policy Center were increasingly involved, not just with scholarship on educational policy, but in efforts to influence public policy, including educational reform in Tennessee. Such outreach efforts, plus surveys and data gathering, link the center to the old Division of Surveys and Field Studies. Dedicated funds in the Peabody endowment help support its outreach programs.

By necessity, most faculty appointments in the nineties, at a rate of fifteen or so each year, would be in the lower ranks. Young scholars had to prove themselves in two ways—by gaining tenure after seven years, and by developing a grant-supported research program. As one of the top education colleges in America, Peabody had to appoint well and tenure only the very best. With this highly competitive environment came losses. Peabody was no longer the relaxed, loosely governed school of the past. Tensions were greater, jealousies more evident, and faculty stress omnipresent. In part because of so many interdisciplinary and interdepartmental programs, the Peabody faculty is overburdened with committee work. A scarcity of scholarships means that most faculty have to seek training grants to recruit able graduate and professional students. Certification requirements mean frequent, time-consuming reports and self-studies in the three departments that train teachers. The faculty who work with prospective teachers, as well as those who are part of the facilitative and nurturing HOD program, devote extensive teaching time to individual students. Many Peabody faculty feel overburdened and unable to devote enough time to their own scholarship.

Peabody, by the midnineties, had a world-class faculty in special education, a faculty rapidly gaining national prominence and high rankings in educational policy and administration, and a strong psychology faculty that by 2002 was on its way to integrating its programs with the equally strong psychology department in A&S, beginning with a joint graduate program. Peabody also had exceptional strengths in some areas of teacher preparation. As of 2002, its full-time faculty was divided into five departments: Psychology and Human Development (with the largest faculty), Human Organization and Development (with the most students), Teaching and Learning (largely responsible for teacher certification), Special Education (the highest-ranked department at Vanderbilt), and Leadership and Organizations (the most improved department).

Financially, Peabody remained strong, yet lacked the funds it wanted in such critical areas as faculty chairs and student aid. Tuition and federal grants were the twin foundations of its fiscal success, with endowment and gifts lagging far behind. In each year of the decade, it had budgetary surpluses and thus the reserves for capital expansion. Its annual budget of around $35 million at the end of 2000 is projected to rise to more than $40 million for 2002–2003. Yet, early in the new century, Peabody faced severe financial constraints. It projected a continuing but stable undergraduate enrollment of some 1,060 to 1,080, and very limited increases in indirect cost recovery from federal grants. Projected budgets for the years after 2002 are barely balanced. In any given year, an enrollment drop of only ten students could push it into a deficit. Thus, more than anytime in the past decade, Peabody needs an increase in gifts.

In 1995, Vanderbilt completed a major campaign that met its $500 million goal. While Peabody benefited from a stronger university, it did not attract the major gifts it needed for its priorities. In the first campaign phase, it was unable to raise a modest goal of $13 million, and in the second failed to reach its new goal of $18 million. Even by 2001, the annual unrestricted gifts to Peabody remained at only $681,000, and its share of the endowment of approximately $2.2 billion at only about $72 million. What kept it solvent was tuition income, as undergraduate tuition at Vanderbilt soared from $13,975 in 1990–91 to $24,080 in 2000–2001, and the total cost of tuition, room and board, and fees from $20,914 to $34,322.

Enrollment patterns shifted gradually through the nineties. As undergraduate enrollment boomed, professional and graduate enrollment declined until 2000 and stabilized at around five hundred. Peabody needs further increases in professional enrollment, which may depend upon critical faculty recruitment and more graduate-student support. The college also is well positioned to offer more postdoctoral fellowships. In the fall of 2001 it enrolled 217 M.Ed. students, 107 Ed.D., and 154 Ph.D., many of whom were not on campus or enrolled for courses. Its total graduate and professional students (494) dropped from a year earlier. Still a large graduate program, it is almost minuscule compared to an earlier Peabody, when more than a thousand M.S. students attended each summer school. The largest master's programs are in teaching and learning (67), leadership and organizations (56, and up in recent years), and special education (49, down sharply). The number of M.Ed.s in teaching fields is small, declining except in English and reading. In educational administration, the most popular M.Ed. subject is higher education. Despite several reviews and efforts to drop the program, human development counseling continues to draw some forty students each year, in part because of a joint B.S. and M.Ed. program with HOD. These patterns vary in the Ed.D. programs, with special education scarcely involved, few students in teaching and learning, and most in administration.[12]

Undergraduate enrollment has been relatively stable in educational subjects, higher in child development, and booming in HOD. In the fall of 2001, the 1,147 Peabody undergraduates (a record, but the number includes at least 19 students on leave for study abroad) chose the following first and second majors: HOD (690), child development (150, the fastest-growing major in the last two years), elementary education (121), secondary education (104), special education (86), cognitive studies (63), early childhood education (48), and general education studies (4). For those in elementary education, the top choice in second majors was not cognitive studies but child development and special education. Students in elementary, special, and early childhood education almost all took their second major at Peabody, which means the college has retained this part of their tuition. All students in secondary education (required) and most in HOD (optional) took their second majors in A&S.[13]

By 2000, the role of the Kennedy Center had so altered that it was no longer, in any distinctive way, a Peabody center. Its research orientation changed in the early nineties, moving it away from the dominant behavioral emphasis of Peabody's programs in psychology, if not in special education. This shift would have long-term significance for Peabody, eventually depriving it of control over its once most valuable asset. As early as 1988, as the Kennedy Center developed grant proposals that would insure continued federal funding, director Alfred Baumeister decided he had to develop new programs in neuroscience that related most closely to work in the Medical School and the psychology department in A&S. Other mental retardation centers had already shifted their emphasis to physiologically oriented work in the sciences of the brain, and without such a reorientation the Kennedy Center funding seemed at stake. At first under Dean Hawley, then under Acting Dean Cunningham, the center developed major grant proposals for neuroscientific research, struggling to win the support of three deans and the provost. Vanderbilt created the Institute for Developmental Neurosciences in 1989, and its search for a director soon paralleled that for a new director of the Kennedy Center after Baumeister resigned. That new director, Travis Thompson, whose research interests dovetailed with the more physiological orientation of the center, would soon establish his own Genetics and Biobehavioral Development Institute.

The new research in neuroscience was costly, requiring major laboratories that soon spread across half of Hobbs Hall. Some involved animal experimentation. In 1991, Vanderbilt recruited Ford F. Ebner from Brown University to direct the new institute; he also became the Kennedy Center's deputy director. Although Ebner received half his salary from Peabody, half from A&S, his academic appointment and that of his wife were in the A&S psychology department, and in all of his negotiations he rarely if ever mentioned Peabody. With this shift of leadership and research priorities, the Peabody faculty had less involvement with the center, while the Medical School and A&S provided most of its investigators. Dean Pellegrino struggled with the inevitable strains that developed over space allocation. Although federal grants covered most of the costs of the new institutes, and indirect cost recovery roughly balanced Peabody's subsidy , the Kennedy Center increasingly became a university asset with less and less direct relevance to Peabody's mission in teaching and learning. A connection remained via the two Kennedy Center institutes that correlated directly with special education, headed by Peabody faculty members Ann Kaiser and Douglas and Lynn Fuchs, and via some dozen other Peabody investigators or loosely affiliated scholars. But the center of gravity had permanently shifted. Adding to the somewhat alien nature of the new programs was the salary imbalance. Ebner and Thompson were in fields where faculty salaries were often almost double those that prevailed at Peabody, and their six-digit salaries, plus control over so much space in Hobbs, created some resentment among the older Peabody faculty and left the new Peabody dean in 1998 administratively responsible for a center largely tied to other parts of the university.[14]

Increasingly, investigators in the Medical School and A&S were reluctant to seek new grants that technically went to Peabody. Thus, with Dean Benbow's concurrence, the provost in 2001 removed the Kennedy Center from Peabody administrative control. Peabody and the center, after a few shifts of space in Hobbs, agreed on space allocation in the two lab buildings. Special education retains its facilities in MRL, and the Susan Gray School will remain part of Peabody.

This shift of administrative control paralleled a sometimes bitter controversy between Dean Benbow and Kennedy Center director Travis Thompson. Eventually, Thompson's political maneuvering, and some false charges against Benbow that involved Ebner's institute, forced Thompson to resign. He moved to the University of Kansas, but not without a lot of spilled blood and all manner of false rumors. A great loss for Peabody and the center, the nationally prominent Thompson shifted to Kansas his own research effort and with it the center's strongest interdisciplinary program. Actually, not much will change for investigators. The Peabody faculty in the behavioral sciences will continue to receive Kennedy Center funding. But the older faculty, particularly, regretted Peabody's losing control of the Kennedy Center. They fondly remembered Nicholas Hobbs and how it all began.

HUMAN ORGANIZATION AND DEVELOPMENT

The most intractable problem that Dean Benbow faced when she arrived in 1998 was what to do with the Department of Human Organization and Development (HOD). Its two decades of growth and development may well be the top story of the merged Peabody. In a sense, it has been a submerged story, not fully understood in the other schools and colleges of Vanderbilt or even much of Peabody. While the achievements that have brought national distinction and high rankings to the college have been in other programs, HOD has attracted the most students.

A great deal more than an undergraduate major, HOD is also more than an academic department, which it became only in 2000. It is a world unto itself, with its own educational ideology and distinctive academic culture. It resembles in some aspects an academic church or sect, all shaped by the inspiration and leadership of Robert Innes. The closest comparison in Peabody history is the early George Peabody College led by the inspirational Bruce Payne. Payne projected an image of Peabody that set it well apart from traditional colleges and universities, and inspired his students with a heady sense of their unique role in redeeming a benighted South. HOD is also reminiscent of the early progressive education movement, whose leaders believed that they were veering sharply away from outworn older approaches to teaching and learning. Innes has often credited John Dewey with much of the HOD's philosophy.[15] In both these precedents, the idealism often reflected elusive or ambiguous goals and a sense of radical innovations not always justified by the outcomes. The same is true of HOD. Behind the vocabulary of HOD—action or experiential learning, real-world experience, service learning—is a rather soft but reasonably successful career-oriented school, one very close to many undergraduate business schools or departments.

When the fledgling major in human development began in 1982, no one could have anticipated how it would develop. Its goal was to enlist undergraduates in a program aimed not at training teachers, but at preparing students to work in organizations other than schools. They would study human development, much as did education majors, but join to that some courses or seminars on the dynamics of group interaction and the functions of organizations. They would prepare themselves, in a rather unique way, for jobs in private or public agencies or firms.

Within two years, Innes had worked out a scheme that has remained at the heart of HOD. Its majors take forty hours of general education courses in A&S (a third fewer than education majors), with an emphasis on effective communication and economics. All must take Economics 100, an introduction to macroeconomics required of economics majors in A&S. They complete their general education work in their freshman and sophomore years, along with core HOD courses and one-credit-hour labs that help them adapt to a unique academic program. Courses on developmental psychology, small-group behavior, talent development, and systematic inquiry exemplify the unique culture of HOD—supportive and group oriented, with an emphasis on oral and written communication. These core courses often involve outside speakers, case studies, and field trips, and for some, a practicum that includes part-time work experience. As Innes understood it, HOD stood midway between liberal arts colleges, which did not include career-oriented courses or active learning, and vocational colleges, which prepared students for specialized jobs. HOD began with a base in general education, and then moved students into the types of study that prepared them, not for a specific vocation, but for effective work in organizations, particularly those that directly served the public. Innes contrasted HOD with a somewhat caricatured image of traditional liberal arts colleges or research universities—boring lecture courses, passive students, a curriculum unrelated to immediate student concerns or social needs, the separation of teaching and research, no coordination among academic disciplines, and no direct personal concern for individual students. HOD tried to correct for each of these alleged deficiencies.

In the junior year, HOD students shift their work almost completely to Peabody. They concentrate on a specific track or vocational field (one of three today), with courses or seminars specific to each. They also begin planning for a one-semester internship, which involves near full-time work in an agency or firm. The model for this, of course, was practice teaching. Students typically complete this internship and correlated seminars in their senior year or, in increasing numbers, in the summer. This means, for many students, one summer in addition to the usual eight semesters.

Robert Innes has devoted the larger part of his career to HOD. His immersion in teaching and leadership has diverted him from the research and publishing that lead to academic preferment. He remains an associate professor. He has won a slew of teaching awards, and remains the inspirational core of the program. His students admire him. They bond with each other, provide mutual support, and most become loyal boosters of the program. They are the prime recruiters of new students both off campus and at Vanderbilt, where almost half the enrollment in HOD represents internal transfers, most from A&S. At the heart of HOD, from the beginning, has been the involvement of students in broader community problems. Students must inquire into their own values and value formation and become widely informed about social problems. Outside Peabody, HOD's core courses and seminars have a reputation for being mushy, nonrigorous, and indulgent, an image reinforced by the large number of athletes who choose this major and by grades above the Vanderbilt average. But if the program lacks academic rigor, part of the blame lies in A&S, which teaches a third of the courses taken by HOD majors. In fact, the very nature of the program, the group projects that dominate, mitigates against competitive grades. Instead of encouraging competition among students, most of the core courses set threshold requirements that most can meet, often with a great deal of individual help from the faculty. Students end up with a sense of achievement and in the process acquire organizational skills. Whatever the academic standards, and no one is more concerned with standards, particularly in admission and grading, than the present HOD faculty, most students succeed in the job market, and the program generally gets high marks from those who employ interns or graduates. HOD's retention rate is the highest at Vanderbilt. It is more popular among the parents of students than any other program at Vanderbilt.

The internships are the most distinctive aspect of HOD. Peabody now operates what is probably the largest intern program in any university department in the United States, with the numbers each year approaching two hundred. The logistics alone are staggering and require a large staff. Even by the sophomore year, when they select a track, HOD students have to begin thinking about their internship. For athletes, scheduling options are often limited. The staff has worked out agreements with at least two hundred agencies or firms willing, and often very glad, to accept interns, who provide labor free of charge. Students are encouraged to find a placement that fits their interests, which often means finding new sponsoring organizations. The sponsoring agency has to agree to provide detailed supervision, often by employees who have themselves been interns. Peabody cultivates these on-the-job supervisors and in Nashville brings them together each year for a reception. The interns work thirty-two hours a week and attend correlated seminars, which requires Peabody to employ at least a part-time academic supervisor in each city with interns—in 2002, Nashville, Atlanta, Washington, New York, and San Francisco. For fifteen years, until 2000, up to ten interns each year were able to do their internships in Cambridge, England, under the supervision of a now-retired professor at Homerton College, John Murrell, who held a part-time Peabody position. A few prospective teachers could also do practice teaching at this Peabody-affiliated education college of Cambridge University, and other Peabody students went there for a junior year abroad. Peabody staff work full time at enlisting placement sites and helping students choose a site. The internship experience, somewhat like basic training in the military, creates a bond among majors and very often leads directly to employment. It culminates with a student report or thesis tied directly to the internship experience.[16]

After years of growth, HOD was relatively stable by 2002. A newly reorganized faculty tried to limit freshman admissions each year to one hundred and tried to raise admission standards, but the department was still flooded with transfers, an influx over which the faculty had little control. The program will probably continue to enroll 60 percent of Peabody undergraduates (as in 2000) out of some 1,060–1,080. It has had an irregular organization. From the beginning, it drew instructors from all departments, particularly from psychology and educational leadership. Their names appeared in the catalogue under the listings for the major. But there was no HOD department. Those who taught primarily in the program were part of Human Resources, a grab-bag department that also included three or four professional and graduate programs, most related either to counseling or educational policy. The undergraduate and graduate programs merged in only one five-year M.Ed. in HOD and human development counseling. But HOD's growth forced Peabody to employ an increasing number of faculty and staff to teach its courses and direct its interns. To meet the demand, Innes often resorted to part-time instructors and employed an increasing number of teachers who had their appointment in the "practice of HOD," a role that roughly paralleled clinical professors in medicine. These professors are not on a tenure track and teach nine hours a semester; few are involved in research.

In 1997, after a detailed internal study of HOD, Peabody decided to reorganize its departments. Pellegrino, who had long lamented the lack of a coherent mission in the Department of Human Resources and had tried to limit or even reduce enrollment in HOD, in 1997 abolished the department. Finding a satisfactory replacement has proved difficult. For two years, Innes continued to direct HOD without a clear departmental home. He reported directly to the dean. In 1999, under Dean Benbow, Peabody made HOD an interim department, with Howard Sandler as executor and Innes continuing as director of the undergraduate program. In 2000 HOD became a permanent department. Joseph Cunningham moved from special education to chair it. The department today includes not only most of the engorged undergraduate program still directed by Innes, but three graduate degrees—the continuing M.Ed. in HOD and human development counseling, an M.Ed. in human organization and community development, and a new Ph.D. in community research and action. The department has also created two integrated five-year master's programs for HOD majors, one in the business area, the other in health and community relations. In effect, programs in community psychology and in counseling moved to the new HOD department. John Newbrough, who had led in community psychology since he came to Peabody in 1966, moved to HOD for the final years of his long career at the college (he retired in 2002).

To confuse things even more, with this shift the small Department of Educational Leadership expanded to the present Department of Leadership and Organizations chaired by James Guthrie, the most distinguished professor in the former Department of Human Resources. This new department assumed responsibility for the courses in the largest HOD track, leadership and organizational effectiveness. Guthrie is committed to bringing more intellectual rigor and tougher grading standards to his department's HOD offerings. This split in the location of HOD courses has raised apprehension among HOD department faculty, who fear that the leadership and organizations faculty, oriented largely to educational administration and policy, will lack a full commitment to the program and fail to recruit the professors needed for its HOD courses. Thus, HOD remains an organizational challenge, although the restructuring does provide both an undergraduate and graduate program for each of its five reasonably balanced departments. Of these, HOD is the weakest in faculty eminence and research performance, despite recent appointments of a few junior faculty and one full professor with strong research agendas.

These structural changes reflected an effort to increase student dedication to service-oriented careers and community involvement, the more idealistic goals of the early HOD. All students entering HOD take not only the orientation course in applied human development but a course in values and community service. A concern is that the slightly camouflaged business track will keep gaining over the two tracks most closely attuned to the original service and community motifs of HOD—community development and social policy, and health and human services.

No understanding of HOD would be complete without some grasp of the role of athletes in this popular major. As many as 65 percent of scholarship athletes major in HOD, with an even higher proportion among football and basketball players. Such athletes help lower the SAT scores of Peabody undergraduates, which hit a record high 1,239 in the fall of 2001, but still more than fifty points lower than the university average. It is easy to conclude that HOD is the easiest or least demanding major at Vanderbilt—easier to gain admission, easier to earn passing grades, easier to graduate. This does not tell the whole story. Given the background of many athletes—often minorities, overall from less affluent families, and more poorly prepared in high school—this job-oriented major appealed on its own merits. Not all the athletes are poorly prepared or weak students, and still they in disproportionate numbers choose HOD. But in too many cases athletes enroll in HOD, not because of any detailed knowledge of the program or any special fit for it, but because of the advice of their coaches.

After 1997, a new centralized admissions policy created more problems for Peabody than for any other undergraduate school or college at Vanderbilt. Its faculty could no longer control who entered Peabody. The new policy largely impacted HOD, largely involved athletes, and led to continuing and often bitter faculty resentment. The new admissions policy reflected an unprecedented board assault on faculty prerogatives at Vanderbilt, all in order to relax admission standards for athletes and produce winning teams. These in turn might help reduce the large annual deficits suffered by the athletic department, a deficit the board alleviated after 1996 by forcing the rest of the university to pay the cost of 150 athletic scholarships, and to assume financial responsibility for a Stadium Club and parking garage that had also suffered annual deficits. The board concern followed Vanderbilt's much-publicized refusal to admit a woefully unqualified Ron Mercer, a local basketball star. Mercer would in fact have been foolish to choose Vanderbilt over other universities, for he would have had almost no chance to graduate. But his rejection seemed to many athletic boosters a symbol of the perennial athletic mess at Vanderbilt. Its teams were not competitive in football in the Southeastern Conference, a strong conference from an athletic perspective, a weak one academically. In fact, this conference reflected the distorted values of so many southern state universities, in which winning football teams seemed to compensate for a lack of academic excellence.

Vanderbilt had been a conspicuous exception to such priorities. One result was its perennially losing football team. It had resisted, perhaps as much as any NCAA Division I university, many of the almost universal compromises on academic standards, particularly in admissions, that had become part of semi-professional university athletics. Such compromises were a national scandal that Vanderbilt only in part had escaped, and which in our new century has become an issue of widespread concern. Vanderbilt had consistently admitted scholarship athletes who could not compete with the pool of candidates that survived the normal academic screening. In the midnineties, its football students had SAT scores below 1,000, compared to more than 1,200 overall, athletic scores lower than those at Stanford, Duke, Northwestern, and Rice. Yet, in both men's and women's basketball, Vanderbilt consistently recruited players with among the highest academic qualifications of any Division I institution in the United States. Athletes joined other special admission categories, including some minorities; some students with family ties to Vanderbilt's board, faculty, or alumni; and some students from wealthy families with development potential or from prominent families with political power or celebrity status.

In April 1996, the Vanderbilt board established an ad hoc committee on admissions. It worked closely with the board's athletic committee, whose chair stated frankly that admission policies were the key to athletic success at Vanderbilt. In November 1996, the ad hoc committee recommended, and the board unanimously accepted, a new admissions structure. No longer would professors, who had seemed to stand in the way of winning teams, have the final say on admissions. The board gave this authority to a new dean of admissions, who would report directly to the provost. The new rules forced the board to override a provision in the constitution of the College of Arts and Science that gave final control over admissions to its faculty. Under the new plan, the faculty could still establish overall standards and monitor admission decisions but not override decisions by the dean of admissions. While little changed in A&S, which teaches only about 20 percent of scholarship athletes, the rules were a serious threat to a more involved and vulnerable Peabody at the very time it was trying to raise admission standards and the academic quality of its students, particularly in HOD.

For years, the Vanderbilt admissions office had used a vague formula for special students: the ability to succeed at Vanderbilt. The board of trust identified several categories of special students, and applied to them this formula, which it usually interpreted to mean an ability to graduate. It now provided that each category of special candidates have a sponsor or advocate to aid in the admissions process. Its clear goal was to insure that the athletic director be the sponsor of athletic candidates. After careful consideration, the board did reject any direct role in admissions by either the chancellor or the board. But, as in most universities, the coaches and athletic director now would have almost unlimited freedom to recruit any candidate that met the minimal NCAA requirements. Vanderbilt, so proud of its integrity in this area, had capitulated and joined the crowd (the board was most attuned to policies at Stanford, Duke, and Northwestern). The final agreement on admission standards for athletes, accepted by the provost and athletic director in 1997, illustrated this: "An ability to graduate, with help." This implicated the special tutors for athletes hired by the athletic department. With enough help, most athletes could graduate, and graduation rates among Vanderbilt athletes remain as high as for other students. Of course, professors still had ultimate control. They could flunk students who did not meet their grading standards, and they could make any help in the preparation of assigned papers, even from tutors, an honors violation. But Peabody, which now had a further impediment to raising the quality of its HOD students, had a special responsibility to maintain very high grading standards. This flew in the face of Peabody's soft-grading tradition and the serious grade inflation that has affected all Vanderbilt undergraduate units. Exceptional privileges for athletes, as well as for other special categories, warred against another emerging goal of the board: to move Vanderbilt into the top ten of American private universities. Its two nearest competitors in this ranking game, Emory and Washington University, did not have the albatross of semi-professional athletic programs around their necks, or have to justify their policies by pious references to "student-athletes," which had become in Division I universities an oxymoron.[17]

AN ENDURING PEABODY

Identity has posed a problem for Peabody since 1914. Dozens of committees have addressed the issue. The one major impediment to a clear statement of identity and mission has been the college's divided culture. It has always been both a professional school dedicated to training teachers and school administrators, and a more open-ended undergraduate college with many students not committed to a career in education. Even its graduate programs, to a lesser degree, have had a divided personality. In the past, programs in public health nursing, library science, musical performance, and clinical psychology or counseling diverted resources from professional training in education. Not much has changed since merger. HOD has almost nothing to do with professional education. Indeed, most professional programs at Peabody today relate to education, but not all. An M.Ed. in human development counseling, an expiring graduate program in policy development and program evaluation, and Ph.D. programs in both community and clinical psychology, can in each case can lead to careers outside education. No rationale except financial expediency or the protection of faculty jobs justifies some noneducational programs, although one far-fetched argument might be that HOD is a worthy experiment in higher education, a type of laboratory program that exemplifies new ways of organizing courses and teaching.

Another identity issue is more difficult to pin down. This is the widespread belief at Peabody that the college still embodies a special and distinctive academic and student culture. The only common claim that one confronts among both faculty and students on the Peabody campus is that Peabody has not lost this culture since merger. The word that comes up all the time is "service," echoes from Bruce Payne. Tied to it are other terms: free, relaxed, friendly, supportive, community-oriented, practical, experimental, egalitarian. At times, it is difficult to distinguish this overall image of Peabody from the distinctive culture of HOD. In any case, Twenty-first Avenue, in theory, marks a major cultural divide. When alienated students in A&S transfer to Peabody or even take a Peabody course, they are supposed to feel the difference. The culture is warm, facilitative, and not intensely competitive. Courses are more relaxed, discourse more open, and expectations possibly not quite as high. This is the perception. Its constant reiteration sometimes reflects status anxiety, a bit of paranoia based on prevalent and unfair images of Peabody on other parts of the campus—low standards, unfocused courses, less literate students, and fuzzy goals.

The postmerger developments at Peabody would seem to undermine all these images, positive and negative. The faculty looks more and more like the faculty in A&S, equally career oriented, focused on research, and involved in the highly competitive academic marketplace. The convergence among students is even more clear, although perhaps least so among the fewer than three hundred Peabody undergraduates in teacher training, still more than three-fourths women. In 2002, Peabody students are almost as well qualified as those in A&S, although one has to admit that even today those who choose a teaching track at Peabody are rarely the very brightest and ablest students. Yet, Peabody students are far removed from the undergraduates of 1979, who were largely local, often ill-prepared for rigorous college work, and usually from modest economic backgrounds. Today, most Peabody undergraduates major in HOD, where there is almost a gender balance. Many move to Peabody from A&S. Many, apart from athletes, come from as affluent homes as A&S students and are fully integrated into the Vanderbilt undergraduate culture, for better or worse. Peabody students do not, at least by measurable criteria, stand apart from all the rest. The approximately five hundred professional and graduate students may be distinctive when compared to graduate students in A&S or students in the Law and Medical Schools. Peabody students are older, already employed in educational institutions, and at ease in a relatively low-paid profession. But, except for income expectations, these characteristics match those of many management students at Owen, and in all respects match those of divinity students, including even the high percentage of females. Yet, despite all the convergence, the old image of a distinct Peabody culture still has some truth to it. All the protestations of continuity have some merit, as anyone who spends time on the campus will attest. Peabody is different from either A&S or Engineering.

Each professional school at Vanderbilt is distinctive, in part because of the culture of each profession. In its core mission—helping students gain the knowledge and skills to become successful teachers or educational administrators—Peabody has to fit itself into a huge educational establishment, again for better and worse. This limits experimentation and radical new departures. Nothing is more disillusioning than to read the almost illiterate, jargon-filled prose that communicates the standards of such accrediting agencies as NCATE or the state board of education in Tennessee. For professional reasons, all teacher candidates at Vanderbilt must earn a Tennessee license if they plan to teach in public schools, a license that usually works in other states because of reciprocity. Prospective teachers at Vanderbilt (most but not all enroll in Peabody), have little leeway in course selection, and in elementary or special education almost no room for electives if they graduate in four years. Tennessee mandates that at least half of their coursework be in noneducational subjects and has strict guidelines for the professional courses offered at Peabody.

These requirements change through time to reflect new cultural realities or new educational fads. For the visitations and reviews in 1985, 1995, and 2002, Peabody had to expend enormous resources in self-study. Among other requirements, it had to prepare what NCATE, in the 1995 review, called a "conceptualization" of its teacher preparation program. The word made no sense in such a context, and the education departments at Peabody have responded in kind, with all but unreadable gobbledegook about such elusive issues as vision, educational models, and multicultural emphases. For someone trained in logic or philosophy, this is a never-never land of undefined terms, loose generalities, and pious affirmations of conventional and fashionable values. In fact, one conspicuous aspect of the Peabody culture is a certain looseness of language and a lack of crisp and rigorous analysis in its endless series of reports and self-studies. Academic committees are always prone to such imprecision, but the malady is at its worst at Peabody. One explanation may be that Peabody has no professors in either the history or philosophy of education and offers its students no demanding courses in these traditional areas.

Bruce Payne set another goal for Peabody. It was to have a major role in redeeming an impoverished and educationally backward South. His emphasis was reformist and egalitarian. Peabody graduates were to be sacrificial missionaries to the South, servants of the downtrodden. They were to involve themselves directly in the lives of students and in their home communities. Much of this service emphasis remains, without the sectional focus. Historically, Peabody's great contribution has been to southern education at all levels, but today almost no one gives priority to southern improvement. Still, by its very educational mission, its faculty is intensely involved with the schools of Nashville and surrounding counties. Its outreach may not be as extensive as in the past, although the professional involvement of faculty has, if anything, increased. But most research in the college has a practical emphasis, and local communities serve as laboratories for testing new methods or tools. The new Center for Educational Policy reflects a renewed commitment to broader outreach, with one new faculty member in the field of international education.

The present Peabody faculty could not be more involved in their profession. In 1997, Dean Pellegrino identified the following professional roles for his faculty: 10 presidents, vice presidents, or board members of professional societies; 11 on key committees or task forces, 7 recent recipients of distinguished awards; 1 (John Bransford) a member of the National Academy of Education and 7 on its committees; 11 recipients of research or publication awards; 16 on national or state panels or boards; 41 editors, coeditors, or associate editors of nineteen journals, advisory or consulting editors of twenty-five journals, and editorial board members of sixty-three journals. Half the Peabody faculty attend and present papers at the American Education Research Association annual meeting. The international involvement of faculty has declined since the Korean project and the Air Force program in England, but has involved recent joint programs with a Japanese university and close ties to Homerton College at Cambridge University.

The merger added a new dimension to Peabody's service role. What could it contribute to Vanderbilt? In effect, its role has not changed much. In some respects, the areas of cooperation before the merger were almost as extensive as today. Peabody wants a larger university role. In such areas as instructional technology and teaching evaluation it has much to offer. It is best positioned to refine the technology, and train professors, for off-campus education through the Internet. The Internet will enable it to resume off-campus professional seminars of its own, which it plans to do in the area of educational administration. Peabody has set up cooperative programs with Blair and with the Engineering, Nursing, and the Medical Schools and joins A&S in offering five interdisciplinary majors. Its faculty, over the last two decades, has all but dominated VIPPS. Yet, almost no one at Peabody feels that the larger campus has sufficiently appreciated its achievement or utilized its resources. It still faces older, in part well-founded, prejudices against a college of education. Its high ranking on national surveys of teachers' colleges has pleased chancellors and the Vanderbilt Board of Trust but seems to have made no dent in widespread biases against professional education and suspicions about course content and grading standards. In brief, Peabody has not won the appreciation it deserves. Yet everyone recognizes its achievement in the last two decades has been a success story. In no wise is Vanderbilt embarrassed by Peabody.

Some continuities are more depressing. Peabody has never done well in fundraising. Its alumni, mainly in education, are ill paid and not in the habit of giving to any college. Wealthy donors seem hard to recruit for a college of education, a situation that is slowly changing for Peabody, in part because of the career choices of students in HOD. By 2002, unrestricted annual giving to Peabody had reached almost $700,000, more than half the level in the much larger A&S. Yet, taking inflation into account, Peabody's development efforts have not narrowed the gap that separates it from such schools as Law and Medicine. It has largely depended on federal solicitude, on grants from the Department of Education, National Institutes of Health, National Institute of Mental Health, National Science Foundation, and even the Department of Defense. As Vanderbilt launches the public phase of its new fund drive in 2003, Peabody has a great deal at stake but, if the past is informative, it will not receive as large an influx of dedicated gifts as it needs. It may benefit most from unrestricted gifts to Vanderbilt, at least to the extent that it can make essential contributions to interschool academic programs funded by the central administration. Meanwhile, it remains almost completely dependent on tuition (most from HOD majors) and federal grants.

HOD, a huge anomaly at Peabody, is yet indispensable; Peabody cannot survive without its students. HOD has created problems in departmental organization, required such a large teaching staff as to reduce academic quality, embarrassed Peabody because of its appeal to athletes, and contributed little to the college's national reputation. It is equally an anomaly for Vanderbilt as a whole. Neither Peabody's nor Vanderbilt's administration knows how to control its growth, how to raise its academic standards, how to wean at least some athletes from it, or how to integrate it with other Peabody programs. Here, perhaps more than in any other area, the Peabody future is cloudy, but not necessarily imperiled. In an ideal world, Peabody would convert HOD into an avowed experimental or alternative college, open it up to even more radical forms of experimentation in course content and instructional methods, employ able educational theorists (so lacking at Peabody), and better advertise its achievements. A conventional Vanderbilt needs an offbeat or radical presence. The students of such a modified HOD would be ideal candidates for one of the contemplated residential colleges.

Although the decentralized administrative system will remain at Vanderbilt into the near future, the boundaries between schools and colleges will become more permeable. New efforts to change the undergraduate culture, such as residential colleges, may shift the student profile back toward those of an earlier Peabody—less affluent, more involved in social problems, and more egalitarian or progressive in outlook. Interschool programs, many now in the planning or early funding phase, will multiply and lead to more academic policymaking at the center, more flexibility in budget policy, and more central funding of interschool initiatives. Since Peabody is the master of institutes and centers and the most active suitor of other colleges and schools, it should profit from these changes. It has plans and early venture funds for a Learning Sciences Institute, which will absorb and drastically expand the work of the Learning Technology Center. The centerpiece of its new strategic plan, the institute will coordinate inquiry on learning, teaching, the broader social context, and new uses of learning technology. It will develop eight new or expanded research programs and attract new faculty, but above all, it will involve faculty from throughout Vanderbilt. In a sense, it will be Peabody's major outreach effort.

With such coordinated efforts, Peabody may lose a further degree of independence. This is already apparent in its loss of administrative control over the Kennedy Center, and in the difficult problems posed by the planned integration of its psychology programs with that of A&S. All deans will lose some administrative authority, the provost gain more. Peabody will become a more integrated part of Vanderbilt, and face even more challenges to its unique culture. Above all, Peabody will gain or suffer from the fate of Vanderbilt as a whole, which is very much tied to a new capital campaign and to Board of Trust expectations.

Epilogue: Into the Future

NORMALLY, A HISTORIAN WRITES ABOUT THE PAST. IN THESE concluding comments I want to write about the present and rather freely speculate about the future. Obviously, my own personal perspectives shape what I have to say. I hope such comments at least provoke thinking about the future of Peabody College as a part of Vanderbilt University.

The 1979 merger saved Peabody. It brought security and financial stability to the college, and thus preserved its traditions, its resources, and its primary mission. Today, Peabody faces plenty of challenges but no dire threats to its survival as a relatively autonomous and prestigious education college. But, to an increasing extent, the new Peabody will be different. Over the next twenty years, certain changes seem likely. Some will lead to a more complete merger with Vanderbilt, and thus a more focused role for Peabody.

Because Peabody moved full-grown into the Vanderbilt family of schools rather than developing within it, the merger left some anomalies. Peabody's strongest department, psychology, offered far more than the support needed to train teachers and school administrators. The Kennedy Center sponsored research that went far beyond the needs of special education. Both assets made the merger attractive to Vanderbilt, but both created confusing overlaps with other schools and colleges. Vanderbilt now has two almost equally strong psychology departments, although departments whose research emphases complement as much as compete with each other. The traditional autonomy of each school and college at Vanderbilt has not always made it easy for graduate students in psychology to take advantage of the strengths of both. Limits on the courses undergraduates in the College of Arts and Science may take in other schools have often meant they could not take the Peabody psychology courses they needed. The partial solution, so far, has been more cross-listed courses.

Vanderbilt's present commitment to integrating its two psychology departments faces all manner of administrative hurdles and poses some threats to Peabody. Logically, only the A&S Psychology Department should offer all psychology courses not directly tied to education, but present faculty appointments, budgets, and even laboratory facilities on the Peabody campus favor a continued two-department arrangement. It would make sense, in a gradual move to fuller integration, for most of Peabody's psychologists to have a joint appointment in A&S, and for most Peabody psychology courses to have a joint listing in A&S. But in time, such changes would tend to weaken the Peabody connection and could lead to the gradual capture of psychology by the larger and stronger College of Arts and Science. Psychology would still have a presence on the Peabody campus, but, as has already happened to the Kennedy Center, administrative control over psychology would shift away from Peabody. All one can anticipate in the next decade are more joint appointments, more cross-listed courses, more faculty cooperation, and a fully integrated graduate program, all of which could lead to more tension, if not conflict, between the two colleges.

Another anomaly for Vanderbilt, Human Organization and Development, offers powerful competition to A&S and to an extent conceals an undergraduate program in business. It is much resented in A&S. Yet HOD is popular, attracts more students than it can accommodate, creates goodwill for Vanderbilt, and is a critical source of tuition for Peabody and thus indirectly for the university. By administrative logic, it should become a separate experimental college with its own dean and many joint appointments with both A&S and Peabody. Such a shift is unlikely. HOD has too many entanglements with Peabody and is too profitable for the college to give it up. Here, for the foreseeable future, financial need will trump rationality.

It is likely that, within a decade, the undergraduate certification program administered by Peabody will become a mandatory five-year professional program culminating in an M.Ed. This seems to be the wave of the future and the type of program that fits Vanderbilt's superior undergraduates. Such a program matches the teaching careers such students will likely choose. In this training of teachers, and in the professional training of educational administrators, Peabody can realistically aspire to continue as one of the best in the world. These are the two logical missions of Peabody, but if these were its only missions, it would be a much smaller college today, with no more than one-third of its present undergraduates, somewhat fewer professional and graduate students, and not many more than half its full-time faculty.

With more interschool programs, the national reputation of Peabody will depend more and more on Vanderbilt's overall strength. It has all but outlived the separate identity and reputation that date back to Bruce Payne. In this mutual dependence, lamentably, Peabody will earn more prestige from the achievement of the rest of Vanderbilt than it contributes by its own successes. Colleges of education in major universities have little prestige. Weak or strong, they have limited impact on how people evaluate universities. A very weak Peabody would embarrass Vanderbilt and draw outside sympathy but have limited impact on its overall academic reputation. Peabody can best boost the image of Vanderbilt by what it contributes to the other schools and colleges, and at present it is the most eager suitor at Vanderbilt for alliances with them.

The beginning of a new century seems to mark a clear transition at Vanderbilt. While crises and major transitions in universities are always present, academic leaders at Vanderbilt in 2002 believe the next decade will see a critical and positive change in its fortunes. In 1998, the board of trust moved to implement new goals. In the midst of a flurry of self-studies and planning at Vanderbilt, an unprecedented number of administrators retired, died, or resigned, making way for a cadre of new leaders. But above all, Vanderbilt is in the early stages of the largest capital campaign in its history, a campaign almost certain to meet its financial goal but not necessarily raise the funds most needed for critical academic programs. The campaign's success could lead to major changes in student culture, in the eminence of faculty, and in the strength of graduate programs. Peabody, which has fared so poorly in past campaigns, has as much at stake in this new effort as any school or college at Vanderbilt.

The campaign's goal, not surprisingly, is a new surge of qualitative improvements, mostly academic in nature, and in carefully targeted areas. The late nineties was a period, not of stagnation at Vanderbilt, but of slowed momentum and a comparative failure to keep up with such visible neighbors as Emory University. External funding leveled off after 1995 in the nonmedical units, including Peabody. Student quality, except in the Medical School, remained below that of most of the strongest universities, and the number of nationally distinguished professors declined after a series of critical retirements and resignations. These included a world famous philosopher, a nationally prominent political theorist, a gifted poet, Vanderbilt's second Nobel Prize winner, and several key chair professors in A&S. These losses paralleled Peabody's loss of Travis Thompson and James Pellegrino.

Perhaps unfortunately, the board in 1998 was already deeply entangled in the university ratings game. It defined as the goal for Vanderbilt, and one justification for the new campaign, the attainment of such new strengths as to make the university one of the top ten in the country, or at least one of the top ten *private* universities. Chancellor Wyatt had first suggested such a goal in 1989, at the beginning of an earlier campaign, and the idea captured the imagination of the Vanderbilt

Board of Trust. Thus, on February 27–28, 1998, the board met in a special retreat at the Ritz-Carlton Hotel in Naples, Florida. The initiative came from board chair John Hall, an oil entrepreneur deeply committed to moving Vanderbilt into the top ten, whatever that means.

This historic board meeting followed not an open self-study, but a series of staff inquiries on campus. Three of six special papers prepared for board members contained detailed, honest evaluations of Vanderbilt's financial resources, students, and faculty. By invitation, George Rupp, president of Columbia University, gave a keynote address in which he asked the board to identify the core strengths of Vanderbilt and the distinctive niche the university could fill in American higher education. His suggestion led, throughout the board discussions, to old issues: How could Vanderbilt fulfill a traditional mission to the South, yet become one of the top ten national universities? How could it retain what almost everyone believed was its key commitment to excellent undergraduate teaching, yet boost its graduate programs and its level of funded research? How could it keep each unit financially responsibility for itself ("every tub on its own bottom"), yet create what Rupp defined as necessary for a relatively small and wonderfully compact university—plenty of cross-cutting, interdisciplinary, or interschool programs?

The ratings game made clear what everyone at Peabody already knew. In national reputation and visibility, the college led all the other schools and colleges at Vanderbilt. In the rankings published by *US News and World Report,* it consistently stood among the top ten schools of education in America; two or three of its departments usually made the top five. In a different and less reliable survey of high school counselors, Peabody perennially took the top spot in undergraduate teacher training. Wyatt and board members boasted of its number-one standing, although it was first in a universe of one (the only undergraduate college of education in an elite, private research university). In the 2001 *US News* rankings, Peabody was fifth among colleges of education, but dropped to seventh in 2002 (such small shifts are not very significant). In professional fields, in 2001 special education ranked second, both elementary education and administration fifth, educational policy eighth, and secondary education ninth, or five fields in the top ten (true also in 2002), a record no other college or school at Vanderbilt could come close to matching (overall, Owen was twenty-sixth, Law seventeenth, and Medical sixteenth). Vanderbilt's College of Arts and Science largely accounted for Vanderbilt's tie for twenty-first among undergraduate programs at national Ph.D.-granting universities.

Despite Peabody's success and the improved national visibility and rankings of several of its professional schools, Vanderbilt in 1998 was almost as far behind the very strongest universities as it had been in 1989. The papers presented at the board retreat made very clear the gap that separated Vanderbilt from almost any plausible list of the top ten private universities. Comparatively, its greatest strength was financial. It had not suffered an annual deficit in more than fifteen years, and in 2002 ranked twenty-first in financial resources in the *US News* rankings. By 1998, for the first time in recent Vanderbilt history, all academic units enjoyed a balanced budget, although only Peabody and A&S had significant reserves. The campus was a carefully tended jewel; delayed campus maintenance was arguably the lowest among the top twenty-five universities. But Vanderbilt's assets in 1998 of more than $2 billion and its endowment of more than $1.3 billion still fell far short of those of almost all top-ten schools; the board soon identified a gap of about $1 billion between Vanderbilt and the lowest of the top ten. (A surging stock market and major gifts would briefly push the endowment to $2.4 billion at the end of fiscal year 2000 and to around $2.2 billion in the fall of 2001.) In the South, both Duke and Emory had assets roughly double those of Vanderbilt. These realities established a tentative goal for the new campaign—$1 billion—which the board formally approved in November 2000. Success in the silent phase of the campaign led in 2002 to a new goal of $1.25 billion, and a decision to delay the opening of the public campaign until 2003.

The board's second major concern, shared by Vanderbilt's central administration, was the quality and characteristics of Vanderbilt's students, an issue of particular relevance to Peabody and its traditions. In most rating games, student quality is a primary index of overall university strength. Elite private universities like Vanderbilt compete for the best-qualified students and try to keep them to graduation. Such a criterion of excellence might seem unfair. Both Peabody and Vanderbilt originated as missions to the South and for a century used their resources to help the South close the gap in income and culture between it and the rest of the country. Would it not be in order for Vanderbilt to continue this mission, even if it had to work with less well prepared and largely regional students? Not if it wanted to compete with the best national universities, for a regional focus all but insured lower rankings. Thus, an aspiring Vanderbilt, a Vanderbilt always a bit insecure about its identity and anxious to win in the big leagues, had accepted the rules of the rating game but so far had made little progress in enticing its share of the very best-qualified students. With the exception of the Medical School, Vanderbilt remained well behind the strongest private universities in the number and quality of its applicants, in the selectivity of its admission process, in retaining students, and in student diversity and intellectuality. This held most true for undergraduates but posed a problem for all the professional schools except the Medical School. Even Law and Owen did not attract the quality of students justified by their faculty. A highly rated Peabody and Divinity both had trouble recruiting the most competitive professional students, a problem even more critical in many of the graduate programs in A&S. The one clearest reason for Peabody's fall from fifth to seventh in 2002 was the quality of its professional and graduate students. It is now involved in the most energetic effort to recruit professional students in Peabody's history.

A central concern at the board retreat in 1998 was the quality of Vanderbilt's undergraduates. Measurements of undergraduate quality are difficult and always imprecise. But comparative evaluations involve such quantifiable data as the number of applications, numbers admitted, numbers who accept, retention of those accepted, high school grade averages and class rank, and scores on the Scholastic Aptitude Test (SAT), a standardized test required by almost all elite universities. At the time of the retreat, Vanderbilt ranked nineteenth in *US News*. Yet, on student quality it did not approach the top twenty-five. On the most easily quantifiable criteria (though possibly not the most fair or reliable), SAT scores (the top combined score is 1600), Vanderbilt's students scored some 50 points below Emory's, 80 points below Duke's, and 150 points behind Yale's and Harvard's. In 2002, Vanderbilt undergraduates did not match those in the top twenty-five universities in SAT scores, or even those in the top ten liberal arts colleges. In student selectivity, Vanderbilt ranked thirty-sixth in 1998, thirty-fifth in 2002. Only 56 percent of Vanderbilt freshmen had made the university their first choice, compared to around 70 percent in the top ten universities. Vanderbilt accepted 58 percent of its applicants in 1998 (a bulge in applications in 2002 lowered this to 46.6 percent), Emory accepted 44 percent, Duke 31 percent, and Harvard and Princeton only 11 or 12 percent.

Vanderbilt has lower retention rates than most of its competitors (81 percent in 1998 and in 2001), although Peabody leads the way in improving this record. Lower retention seems, at least in part, to reflect some problems—some would even say pathologies—in undergraduate student culture at Vanderbilt. Its student profile may explain this. Among highly selective private universities, Vanderbilt students stand out in several respects. They are, on average, from the most affluent families of any comparable university (in 1998, 57 percent of Vanderbilt students came from families with annual incomes over $100,000, 29 percent over $200,000). They are less likely to be worried about jobs or finances. They are also more white, more English-speaking, more Protestant, and more Evangelical (25 percent are born-again Christians). Fewer are international students, or from still identifiable ethnic American families. Its Jewish enrollment is lower than in any comparable university. Vanderbilt students are more politically conservative, meaning that they are primarily Republicans, but not clearly more conservative on social and cultural issues. They are more likely than the average student elsewhere to volunteer or become involved in community service (a product, perhaps, of Chancellor Wyatt's emphasis on community service and the community involvement of Peabody students). In part because of affluence and the high percentage from stable families, Vanderbilt students are generally tolerant and generous. They remain more provincial than students at Vanderbilt's major competitors, for Vanderbilt offers fewer courses in international studies and about non-Western cultures. In sum, Vanderbilt students are more homogeneous and more affluent than on competing campuses.

Vanderbilt has a reputation, partly deserved, as a party school. It is the most Greek of comparable universities. On enrolling, 38 percent of students plan to join fraternities and sororities, and more than half of all students eventually do. The Greeks dominate social life at Vanderbilt, and, as on many campuses, the weekend parties seem to rely almost entirely on the use and abuse of alcohol. Diversity, now a verbal mantra on campuses, may or may not be desirable. It depends on whether differences serve ethical goals (such as increased opportunity for minorities) and enhance the learning environment. Vanderbilt seems to need more undergraduate diversity in several respects—more intellectually hungry and aggressive students, more from lower-income families, more from non-Protestant cultures, more from abroad, and more from a politically less conservative background. Significantly, such a shift would move the student culture back toward the older Peabody tradition. Among all the departments and programs at Vanderbilt, it is HOD which most values students with a cultural and economic profile radically different from the existing university mix.

One goal of the new campaign will be more funds for scholarships, both honor and need based. Within the next ten years, Vanderbilt will likely move to a new residential college pattern, with much more of the intellectual and social life of the campus centered in clusters of dorms. This will be a momentous and expensive transformation. It may reduce the social role of fraternities and possibly raise the intellectual tenor of the campus. But changes in student culture do not come easily. The 56 percent of applicants who make Vanderbilt their first choice know and appreciate its conservative yet socially intense campus. In fact, Vanderbilt is one of the few highly selective universities of its kind left in America. In the fall of 2001, Vanderbilt enjoyed a rise in applications of almost 10 percent over 2000 and kept more than 94 percent of its fall 2000 freshmen. While its popularity with students grows, most applicants continue to fit the traditional Vanderbilt student profile.

A final major issue that prompted the new campaign was the quality of faculty, along with Vanderbilt's achievement in research and graduate training. Here, closing the gap between Vanderbilt and the top ten universities rivals the difficulty of transforming student quality and culture. Vanderbilt has a well-qualified faculty, most now committed to excellence in both research and teaching. In most undergraduate rankings, Vanderbilt scores highest on faculty quality, in part because of its competitive salaries, its low faculty-student ratio, and its limited use of part-time or temporary professors. In the *US News* 2002 rankings of undergraduate education, Vanderbilt ranked ninth in faculty resources, by far its best showing.

Vanderbilt today is tough in evaluating candidates for jobs, and equally tough in awarding tenure. It has raised the floor of competence in the last two decades and has little deadwood. But it has too few faculty stars, too few professors at the daring frontiers of knowledge or with great national visibility, to join any credible list of the top ten private universities. It has too few Nobel Prize winners, members of major scholarly or scientific academies, presidents of major disciplinary organizations, and prize-winning authors. In part, the push toward faculty distinction in so many colleges and schools has prevented it from moving ahead in a few areas, of gaining the critical mass of eminence needed to attract the best faculty and to create highly competitive graduate programs. It has eschewed the star system, has refused on principle to release highly productive scholars and scientists from undergraduate teaching responsibilities, and often has difficulty recruiting academic stars, in part because of its location away from the two coasts and its relative isolation from other major universities.

Faculty distinction, away from the home campus, comes almost entirely from various types of inquiry and criticism and their published results, or from creative work in such areas as poetry, the plastic arts, and musical composition. A distinguished faculty is highly productive. The volume and the critically evaluated quality of its productions is what gains it recognition, and such recognition in turn attracts able graduate students. Thus, a successful graduate program is an index of faculty research, scholarship, and creativity. The most competitive graduate programs nationwide usually have a critical mass of such productive faculty. It takes time to build such a faculty and to establish a reputation. The two highest-rated graduate programs at Vanderbilt—pharmacology in the Medical School, special education in Peabody—have developed their strength over fifty years. Religion, the highest-rated graduate program in the humanities, draws its strength from the work of an exceptionally talented Divinity School faculty over the same period. The trouble is that Vanderbilt has so few graduate programs in the top ten, as evaluated periodically by the National Research Council (NRC) or by *US News*. Only Peabody has most of its professional programs in the top ten. In the more traditional academic disciplines, including the sciences, social sciences, and humanities, Vanderbilt has not a single graduate program, apart from religion, in the *US News* top twenty-five; English comes closest at twenty-seventh. A top-ten university has at least ten or twelve programs in the top ten. And at the very top, at Harvard or Yale, most graduate departments will rank in the top ten.

Because the NRC evaluations rely heavily on reputation, and because of Vanderbilt's small departments, its graduate programs may be slightly better than their ratings. In any case, Vanderbilt rejoiced that marginal improvements in several graduate departments, from the NRC evaluation in 1982 to that in 1995, resulted in the third-largest improvement (8 percent) of any university in its overall graduate program. Yet, even another 8 percent improvement, as measured by the NRC evaluations in 2002, will not move Vanderbilt near the top ten universities. Clearly, there is no easy or quick solution to its relatively weak position in graduate training. After the board retreat in 1998 and early plans for the campaign, both the Medical Center and University Central (the nonmedical schools and colleges) began major and ongoing strategic academic planning. This joins major studies of student life and the Greek system, of the benefits of residential colleges, and of the Graduate School and the role of a graduate school dean.

Vanderbilt has embraced, almost with a vengeance, Rupp's earlier recommendation of cross-cutting programs to compensate for its small size and to exploit its compact campus and strong professional schools. Earlier interschool programs in the biomedical and neurosciences served as models for a range of academic proposals from all parts of the campus for interdisciplinary and interschool institutes and centers, most oriented to graduate work. A new Venture Fund is providing seed money for new institutes and centers, including the Learning Sciences Institute whose hub will be at Peabody. Many of these draw upon the strengths of professional schools, with Peabody critically located for such interschool initiatives. These major interschool programs at least challenge the "every tub on its own bottom" tradition at Vanderbilt. To succeed, they will need special funding from the center. One goal of the campaign will be gifts dedicated to new interschool programs or, better, unrestricted gifts to the endowment. The campaign's most difficult challenge will be to recruit gifts for often unglamorous academic programs, or for support services such as libraries and computer networks. The largest cost will be for new and more eminent faculty. Vanderbilt had eighty-two chair or distinguished professors in 1998, many not endowed and almost none fully endowed; Peabody had only one partially endowed chair, and it is not yet filled. All top-ten universities had more. It is therefore not surprising that almost all recent proposed academic initiatives at Vanderbilt include requests for such chairs. They make up the most expensive goal in the new Vanderbilt campaign, and the most ambitious goal for Peabody.

Even as the board developed early plans for a great campaign, it knew that Chancellor Wyatt would not be able to complete the effort. When he retired in 2000, the board, with the least faculty input in Vanderbilt history, offered the chancellorship to Gordon Gee, for the previous two years president of Brown University. His appointment, which began in 2000, accompanied a virtual turnover of top administrators at Vanderbilt. In only a three-year period, new deans took over at Peabody, Medical, Owen, Divinity, and A&S. In 2002 Vanderbilt appointed a new provost. Perhaps just as important was a change in board leadership. In 1999, Martha Ingram followed John Hall as president, the first female to head the Vanderbilt Board of Trust. By the time of her election, the Ingram family had become

Vanderbilt's greatest contemporary benefactor. Her role will be indispensable in the campaign, which will succeed or fail according to the contributions of board members. By a decision of the board in 1998, any gifts that came in after that year's board retreat were to count toward the coming campaign.

It may be unfortunate that the board has focused so much on comparative rankings, favorable as they have been for Peabody. What is important is improvement consistent with a university's mission. And this is the rub. The ranking game has, in a sense, already established much of the mission for the top research universities, particularly private universities: to garner enough financial resources to build a magnificent campus, to provide a growing range of expensive student services (the most rapidly growing cost on campuses in the last decade), to recruit the most visible and productive faculty, to attract the brightest and best-prepared students in the world, and to educate undergraduate and graduate students who become national and international leaders in their chosen professions. Certain other goals, including perceived social needs, leaven this profile. All universities give lip service to excellent teaching. Most mean it, as Vanderbilt clearly does. Most are now committed to various types of diversity in both faculty and student bodies, even when this wars against academic preeminence. Vanderbilt is so committed, perhaps least so at the level of economic and ethnic diversity.

In a vast, heterogeneous, and hierarchical body of American colleges and universities, most have to define their mission in more limited, and often more regional, terms than does Vanderbilt. Most students cannot attend elite universities. They have plenty of more welcoming choices. Vanderbilt has come to define itself as one of the best universities, with all that entails. Peabody aspires to be the strongest educational college in the world. But because all the best universities are seeking to improve at least at the same rate as Vanderbilt, the ranking game will always involve moving targets. And to move up in rank, a university has to displace others that are, relatively speaking, falling away from the top. It is difficult to see any social advantage in the shifting of relative strengths, but of course, from the perspective of any single university, this is the very essence of a competitive game.

In the long run, say fifty years, more southern universities will equal in strength the older, established northern ones. With continuing gains in population, wealth, and political clout, southern states and southern universities will close the gap that has haunted the South since the Civil War. The lag effect is greatest in higher education, where older strengths are more enduring, older deficiencies more crippling, than in any other area. But in time, one or two other southern private universities will follow Duke into what, by any fair appraisal, is the top ten, and in 2050 the Magnolia League of southern private universities may compare favorably with the Ivy League, just as more southern public universities will be the academic equal of the best Big Ten universities. To what extent Vanderbilt will share in or lead such a continuing renaissance of southern higher education is an open question. The challenge is intimidating, but present efforts impressive. What is obvious is that Vanderbilt cannot overtake enough other universities to move into any credible list of top ten universities in the next decade. This is of no great importance. From a national perspective, the desirable goal is not a small group of universities that comprise a top ten, but thirty or forty universities, including Vanderbilt, that are so nearly equal in overall assets, despite specialized missions, that close comparisons will be even more misleading than they are today.

It is a commentary on Peabody's success that it is as vitally involved in the new campaign and in interschool planning as any Vanderbilt school or college. Peabody, perhaps as much as any education college in America, has enhanced the reputation of its host. Philip Lindsley's 1826 dream of a great university in Nashville, with one of its colleges dedicated to the training of teachers, no longer seems hopelessly visionary. Chancellor Kirkland's dream at the beginning of the last century of a great university center in Nashville that involved both Vanderbilt and Peabody is now a reality.

NOTES

LIST OF ABBREVIATIONS

GPCR	George Peabody College Records, *Record Group 5812*, Special Collections, Jean and Alexander Heard Library, Vanderbilt University
Board Minutes	*Board of Trust Minutes*, George Peabody College for Teachers, Special Collections
BRP Papers	Bruce R. Payne Papers, Special Collections
Hobbs Papers	Nicholas Hobbs Papers, box 43, Special Collections
Minutes	*Minutes of the Vanderbilt University Board of Trust and Executive Committee*
Payne Papers	William H. Payne Papers, Special Collections
P-VMR	Peabody-Vanderbilt Merger Records, Special Collections
UNBI	*University of Nashville Bulletin of Information, Peabody College for Teachers*, Special Collections
UN Records	University of Nashville Records, *Record Group 5811*, Special Collections
UN Files	University of Nashville Files, GPCR

CHAPTER ONE
DAVIDSON ACADEMY AND CUMBERLAND COLLEGE

1. Francois Andre Michaux, *Travels to the West of the Allegheny Mountains in the States of Ohio, Kentucky, and Tennessee, etc.* , 2d ed. (London: B. Crosby and Co. and J. P. Hughs, 1805), 199.

2. Paul H. Bergeron, Stephen V. Ash, and Jeanette Keith, *Tennesseeans and Their History* (Knoxville: University of Tennessee Press, 1999), 21–46.

3. Ibid.; A. W. Putnam, *History of Middle Tennessee or, Life and Times of Gen. James Robertson* (1859; reprint, Knoxville: University of Tennessee Press, 1971), 36–79.

4. Putnam, *History*, 86; Allen Kelton, "The University of Nashville, 1850–75" (Ph.D. diss., George Peabody College for Teachers, 1969), 10–12; *Laws of Cumberland College*, 1825, University of Nashville Files (hereafter, UN Files), box 2989, folder 6, George Peabody College Records, Special Collections, Vanderbilt University (hereafter, GPCR).

5. Wilbur F Creighton Jr. and Leland R. Johnson, eds., *The First Presbyterian Church of Nashville: A Documentary History* (Nashville: Williams, 1986), 2–5; Putnam, *History*, 234–35.

6. William Henry Foote, *Sketches of North Carolina, Historical and Biographical, Illustrative of the Principles of a Portion of Her Early Settlers* (New York: Robert Carter, 1846), 80–81; Earnest Trice Thompson, *Presbyterians in the South* (Richmond: John Knox Press, 1963), 1:62–64.

7. Douglas Sloan, *The Scottish Enlightenment and the American College Ideal* (Columbia Teachers College: Teachers College Press, 1971), 36–64

8. Paul K. Conkin, *The Uneasy Center: Reformed Christianity in Antebellum America* (Chapel Hill: University of North Carolina Press, 1995), 39–43.

9. Ibid., 42–43.

10. Ibid., 53–54; Thompson, *Presbyterians in the South,* chaps. 1–4, 8.

11. Conkin, *Uneasy Center,* 55–57; Sloan, *Scottish Enlightenment,* 42–64.

12. Paul K. Conkin, *Cane Ridge: America's Pentecost* (Madison: University of Wisconsin Press, 1990), 50–53.

13. Thompson, *Presbyterians in the South,* 113–14, 248, 253–54, 272.

14. Putnam, *History,* 410–11.

15. Kelton, "University of Nashville," 17.

16. Putnam, *History,* 639–52.

17. Ibid.

18. Bergeron, Ash, and Keith, *Tennesseeans and Their History,* 47–67.

19. Kenimer Houze Morgan, "The University of Nashville, 1825–1850," vol. 1 (Ph.D. diss., George Peabody College for Teachers, 1960), 14–15.

20. Thompson, *Presbyterians in the South,* 144–45, 356–58; Conkin, *Cane Ridge,* 52–63, 153–61.

21. Morgan, "University of Nashville," 1:16–17.

22. Ibid., 1:17–18.

23. Ibid., 1:118–20; Putnam, *History,* 648.

24. William E. Beard, "The History of the First Church," in *The First Presbyterian Church, Nashville, Tennessee: One Hundred Years of Service* (Nashville: Foster and Parkes, 1915), 47–48; Creighton and Johnson, *First Presbyterian Church,* 11–12.

25. List of Alumni of Cumberland College and Account of Examinations, UN Records box 2106, folder 8, Special Collections.

26. Morgan, "University of Nashville," 1:18–23.

27. Ibid., 1:123–24.

28. Frank Burns, *The Sesquicentennial History of Cumberland University, 1842–1992* (Lebanon, Tn.:Cumberland University, 1992), 46–47.

CHAPTER TWO
THE EDUCATIONAL MISSION OF PHILIP LINDSLEY

1. Mark A. Noll, *Princeton and the Republic, 1768–1822: The Search for a Christian Enlightenment in the Era of Samuel Stanhope Smith* (Princeton: Princeton University Press, 1989), 16–58; Thomas Jefferson Wertenbaker, *Princeton, 1746–1896* (Princeton: Princeton University Press, 1946), 77–79.

2. Noll, *Princeton and the Republic,* 125–85, 214–71; Wertenbaker, *Princeton,* 118–52.

3. Le Roy J. Halsey, introduction to *The Works of Philip Lindsley, D.D., Formerly Vice-President and President Elect of the College of New Jersey, Princeton; and Late President of the University of Nashville, Tennessee,* ed. Le Roy J. Halsey (Philadelphia: Lippincottand, 1866), 3:8–22; John Edwin Pomfret, "Philip Lindsley: Pioneer Educator of the Old Southwest," in *The Lives of Eighteen from Princeton,* ed. Willard Thorp (Princeton: Princeton University Press), 158–64.

4. Noll, *Princeton and the Republic,* 272–91; Wertenbaker, *Princeton,* 153–83.

5. Philip Lindsley, "On a Learned Ministry: A Plea for the Theological Seminary at Princeton," in Halsey, *Works,* 3: 33–83; Wertenbaker, *Princeton,* 153–83.

6. Kenimer Houze Morgan, "The University of Nashville, 1825–1850," vol. 1 (Ph.D. diss., George Peabody College for Teachers, 1960), 118–23.

7. Ibid., 55, 122–23.

8. "Inaugural Address, Delivered at Nashville, January 12, 1825," in Halsey, *Works,* 1:13–66.

9. Ibid., 32.

10. Lindsley, "Anniversary Commencement, at the University of Nashville, 1837," in Halsey *Works,* 1:326.

11. Morgan, "University of Nashville," 1:137–69.

12. Lindsley, "Baccalaureate Address, at Cumberland College, 1826," in Halsey, *Works,* 1:104–8.

13. Lindsley, "Baccalaureate Address, at Cumberland College, 1827," in Halsey, *Works,* 1:144–48.

14. Lindsley, "Baccalaureate Address, at Cumberland College, 1829," in Halsey, *Works,* 1:203–204.

15. Ibid., 205.

16. Lindsley, "Our First Mother," UN Records, box 2989, folder 4, Special Collections.

17. Lindsley, "Baccalaureate Address, at Cumberland College, 1837," in Halsey, *Works,* 1:347.

18. Ibid., 371.

19. Morgan, "University of Nashville," 1:414–27.

20. Lindsley, "Ministers of Christ, as Stewards of the Mysteries of God, Required to be Faithful" and "The Bible Adapted to Man as He Is," in Halsey, *Works,* 2:631–60, 663–98.

21. Lindsley, "The Bible Adapted," 2:672.

22. Ibid., 2:681.

23. Lindsley, "The Pastoral Office and Work," in Halsey, *Works,* 2:310–11.

24. Lindsley, "Maxims—Sophisms—Dogmas—Fallacies—Themes—Nothings—Suggestions; or, Materials for Reflection," in Halsey, *Works,* 3:572–73; Lindsley, "Thoughts on Slavery: An Extract," in Halsey, *Works,* 3:663–72.

25. Lindsley, "Pastoral Office and Work," Halsey, *Works,* 2:311, 312–13.

26. Ibid., 314, 318–19, 324.

27. For greater detail on topics only touched on here, see David Mathis, "Image, Institution, and Leadership: Philip Lindsley and the Modern University Presidency, 1825–1850" (Ph.D. diss., College of William and Mary, 1985), on Lindsley's leadership style in the context of the developing role of presidents in American universities; Larry Thomas McGehee, "Changing Conceptions of American Higher Education, 1800 to 1860: Ideas of Five Frontier Presidents on Transplanting and Transforming Collegiate Education" (Ph.D. diss., Yale University, 1969), on the theological underpinnings of Lindsley's thought as well as his interest in the study of political economy; and Miles Julian Wickless, "Philip Lindsley and the University of Nashville: An Experiment in Republican Christian Idealism" (master's thesis, University of Georgia, 1996), for a more extensive discussion of Lindsley's education at Princeton, his developing interest in the natural sciences, and his interest in political economy.

CHAPTER THREE
PRINCETON WEST

1. Kenimer Houze Morgan, "The University of Nashville, 1825–1850," (Ph.D. diss., George Peabody College for Teachers, 1960), vol. I, 84–94; *Laws of Cumberland College,* 1825, Box 2989, folder 6, GPCR.

2. On commencements and those participating in them, see Jethro Peyton Gatlin, *Diary,* February 24, 1842, Tennessee State Historical Society, Nashville; *An Account of Commencements*

(microfilm), Ac. No. 153, University of Nashville Records, Tennessee State Historical Society, 1:33–36; Morgan, "University of Nashville," 1:61–69

3. Morgan, "University of Nashville," 1:128–31; 2:580–81.

4. Morgan, "University of Nashville," 2:700–708.

5. Philip Lindsley, "Discourse on the Life and Character of Prof. Gerard Troost, M.D. Delivered on Commencement Day, October 2, 1850," UN Records, box 2991, folder 18, 26–28; *Board of Trust Records* (microfilm), Ac. No. 153, University of Nashville Records, Tennessee State Historical Society, 1: 279; Morgan, "University of Nashville," 2:708–13.

6. Lindsley, "Discourse on Prof. Gerard Troost," 25–26; Morgan, "University of Nashville," 2: 694–700.

7. E. E. Hoss, W.B. Reese, and John Wooldridge, *History of Nashville, Tenn.* (Nashville: Methodist Episcopal Church, South, 1890), 105–7.

8. L. C. Glenn, "Gerard Troost," *American Geologist* 35 (January 1905): 72–94; Priestly H. Manning, "Gerard Troost: Address of Professor Manning," *University of Nashville Bulletin of Information* (hereafter, *UNBI*) 5 (January 1907): 17–29; Henry Grady Rooker, "A Sketch of the Life and Work of Dr. Gerard Troost" (typescript), in "Troost, Girard (or Gerard)," UN Files, box 2116, GPCR.

9. Gerard Troost, *Fifth Geological Report to the Twenty-Third General Assembly of the State of Tennessee, October, 1837* (Nashville: S. Nye, 1837); Gerard Troost, *Sixth Geological Report to the Twenty-Fourth General Assembly of the State of Tennessee, October, 1841* (Nashville: S. Nye, 1841).

10. Lindsley, "Discourse on Prof. Gerard Troost," 29.

11. The biographical sketch of Gerard Troost draws upon Lindsley, "Discourse on Prof. Gerard Troost"; Morgan, "University of Nashville," 2:713–38; and "Troost Lectures," UN Records, box 2995, folder 4.

12. "Minutes of the Erosophian Literary Society, 1841–48," box 2996, folder 1, UN Records.

13. For the list, see *Board of Trust Records* (microfilm), Ac. No. 153, University of Nashville Records, Tennessee State Historical Society, 1:10.

14. Allen Kelton, "The University of Nashville, 1850–75 " (Ph.D. diss., George Peabody College for Teachers, 1969), 103–6.

15. *Laws of Cumberland College.*

16. Morgan, "University of Nashville," 2:763–93.

17. Gatlin, *Diary,* February 24, 1842; *Account of Commencements,* 33–36.

18. *Account of Commencements,* 38.

19. *Board of Trust Records,* 106

20. Morgan, "University of Nashville," 1:58–61.

21. *Board of Trust Records,* 95, 103.

22. Morgan, "University of Nashville," 1:231–45, 2:580.

23. *Board of Trust Records,* 126.

24. The story of this disposition of the land is in "Memorial of the President and Trustees of the University of Nashville to the Congress of the United States" (Nashville: Republican and Gazette Office, 1834), box 2106, folder 12, GPCR.

25. Morgan, *"University of Nashville,"* 2:432–48.

26. *Board of Trust Records,* 243–44; Philip Lindsley, "Anniversary Commencement, at the University of Nashville, 1837," in Halsey, 2:361–71; Morgan, "University of Nashville," 2:585–86.

27. *Board of Trust Records,* 309–13.

28. Ibid., 279–81, 325–27; for a more lengthy account of the struggle over a medical school,

Lindsley's subsequent retirement, and the ending of classes, see Morgan, "University of Nashville," 2:585–672.

29. "Agatheridian Literary Society, Secretary's Book–Minutes, 1848–1856," in folder 4, box 3004, UN Records.

30. Lindsley, "Discourse on Prof. Gerard Troost," 38–39, 49–52.

CHAPTER FOUR
CRISIS YEARS FOR THE UNIVERSITY OF NASHVILLE, 1850–1875

1. Ellen V. Piers, "Gerard Troost: Pioneer Scientist," *Peabody Journal of Education,* March 1953, 30:265–74.

2. John Edwin Windrow, *John Berrien Lindsley: Educator, Physician, Social Philosopher* (Chapel Hill: University of North Carolina Press, 1938), 1–21.

3. *Board of Trust Records,* 1:323–39 and December 5, 1851 (n.p.); Allen Kelton, "The University of Nashville,1850–75" (Ph.D. diss., George Peabody College for Teachers, 1969), 473–500; Windrow, *John Berrien Lindsley,* 22–42 .

4. Kelton, "University of Nashville," 217–455; "Minutes of the Agatheridan Literary Society, 1825–1870," folder 9, box 2994, UN Records; Windrow, *John Berrien Lindsley,* 42.

5. Windrow, *John Berrien Lindsley,* 43–46; *Minutes, Board of Trust, University of Nashville,* a bound folder of hand-written notes in Special Collections, Vanderbilt University, 74–92.

6. Richard Owen, *Key to the Geology of the Globe: An Essay Designed to Show that the Present Geographical , Hydrographical, and Geological Structures, Observed on the Earth's Crust, were Laws, and Analogous to Those Governing the Development of Organic Bodies* (Nashville: Stevenson and Owen, 1857).

7. Although an expanded discussion of WMI appears in Kelton, "University of Nashville," 510–620 (I have drawn heavily from this), no one has attempted a full treatment of this interesting example of the South's affinity for military training. The sources for such a study are extensive. The University of Nashville preserved almost all of its records from this period, now stored in UN Records.

8. *Minutes, Board of Trust,* 172–77, 180–81.

9. Kelton, "University of Nashville," 616–20.

10. Lindsley recorded his views on secession and the war in his diary; for relevant sections, see Windrow, *John Berrien Lindsley,* 60–64.

11. For Lindsley's summary of his activity during the war, see *Minutes, Board of Trust,* 190–93.

12. Kelton, "University of Nashville," 453, 358–85.

13. *Minutes, Board of Trust,* 190–93; Kelton, "University of Nashville," 659–69.

14. *Minutes, Board of Trust,* 201–3.

15. Windrow, *John Berrien Lindsley,* 105–6.

16. Ibid., 214–17.

17. Ibid., 255–56.

18. Kelton, "University of Nashville," 712–50.

19. Catalogues, UN Files, in box 2100, GPCR; "Agatheridian Society Minutes—Roll and Constitution, 1868–77," box 2986, UN Records.

20. *Minutes, Board of Trust,* 330–31.

21. Windrow, *John Berrien Lindsley,* 113–63.

Notes to Pages 102–128

1. The biographical information that follows draws heavily from Franklin Parker, *George Peabody, A Biography* (Nashville: Vanderbilt University Press, 1971), an abridgment of Parker's "George Peabody, Founder of Modern Philanthropy," 3 vols. (Ed.D. diss., George Peabody College for Teachers, 1956).

2. *Proceedings of the Trustees of the Peabody Education Fund, from Their Original Organization, on the 8th of February, 1867* (Cambridge: John Wilson and Son, 1875), 1:1–7.

3. Ibid., 1:1–7.

4. For a listing of the members of the Peabody Fund trustees and a summary of some of their contributions to U.S. public life, see Hoy Taylor, *An Interpretation of the Early Administration of the Peabody Education Fund* (Nashville: George Peabody College for Teachers, 1933), 15–18, 20–21.

5. Ibid., 28–31, 33–34; for Robert C. Winthrop's memorial address after Sears's death, see *Proceedings of the Trustees of the Peabody Education Fund, 1874–1881* (Cambridge: John Wilson and Son, 1881), 2:302–24.

6. *Proceedings, 1874–1881,* 2: 306–8.

7. The summary in the preceding three paragraphs is based on my survey of the reports of Sears to the Peabody Fund trustees, 1868–80; see *Proceedings,* vols. 1 and 2.

8. A photo of these men appears in *The Genealogy of George Peabody College for Teachers,* box 2107, GPCR.

9. The eulogy appears in *Proceedings,* 1:151–67.

10. Ibid., 2:418.

11. The discussion of normal schools that follows draws heavily from Jurgen Herbst, *And Sadly Teach: Teacher Education and Professionalization in American Culture* (Madison: University of Wisconsin Press, 1989).

12. Ibid., 109–39.

13. John Edwin Windrow, *John Berrien Lindsley: Educator, Physician, Social Philosopher* (Chapel Hill: The University of North Carolina Press, 1938). 84–112.

14. *Minutes, Board of Trust,* 359–60; Eugene Melville Waffle, *Eben Sperry Stearns: Pioneer in American Education* (Ph.D. diss., George Peabody College for Teachers, 1939), pt. 3: 766.

15. This biographical information, and much more, appears in Waffle, *Eben Sperry Stearns.*

16. *Proceedings of the Trustees of the Peabody Education Fund, 1881–1887* (Cambridge: John Wilson and Son, 1888), 3: 283–86, 302; Waffle, *Eben Sperry Stearns,* pt. 3:781–83.

17. *Catalogue of the Officers and Students of the University of Nashville, including the State Normal, Montgomery Bell, and Medical Departments,* 1875–76, Special Collections.

18. For information regarding enrollment and curriculum, see the University of Nashville catalogues, 1875 and 1887, Special Collections.

19. Tracy Mitchell Kegley, *The Peabody Scholarships, 1877–1899* (Nashville: Bureau of Publications, George Peabody College for Teachers, 1949), chaps. 2 and 4, and appendix A.

20. *Proceedings,* 2: 232–35, 247–48, 331–32.

21. *Minutes, Board of Trust,* 387–89.

22. *Proceedings,* 2:331–43.

23. *Minutes, Board of Trust,* 395–400, 401–2.

24. *Proceedings,* 2:342–43, 371.

25. Waffle, *Eben Sperry Stearns,* pt. 3:806–29.

1. Unless otherwise noted, biographical information on William Payne is from George Cleveland Poret, *The Contributions of William Harold Payne to Public Education* (Nashville: George Peabody College for Teachers, 1930).

2. Lydia Spencer to Sara Evaline Payne (n.d.); Lydia Spencer to William Payne, July 26, 1879, and August 22, 1879, all in box 6, William H. Payne Papers (hereafter, Payne Papers).

3. See *Catalogue of the University of Nashville: State Normal College,* 1887–88, 1889–90, 1890–91, Special Collections.

4. *Proceedings of the Trustees of the Peabody Education Fund, 1888–92* (Cambridge: Jon Wilson and Son, 1893), 4:278–79.

5. *Catalogue of the University of Nashville, Peabody Normal College for the Year 1894–95,* 73–74.

6. *Minutes, Board of Trust,* 517.

7. A plethora of sources on Payne's philosophy of education can be found in box 1, Payne Papers. Unless otherwise noted, this and subsequent discussions of his philosophy are the result of my survey of these sources.

8. For Payne's views on women, see, for example, William H. Payne, "The University of Nashville: Peabody Normal College, Baccalaureate Address, May 25, 1890," box 13, Payne Papers.

9. *Peabody Alumni Quarterly,* 1897, in folder, "Alumni Lists," Special Collections, Vanderbilt University.

10. Payne, "Baccalaureate Address," box 13, Payne Papers.

11. Box 1, Payne Papers.

12. For examples of these letters, see box 13, Payne Papers.

13. Tracy Mitchell Kegley, *The Peabody Scholarships, 1877–1899* (Nashville: Bureau of Publications, George Peabody College for Teachers, 1949), 61–100.

14. "Athletics," *UNBI,* November 1902, 9–13; on Vanderbilt and football, see Paul K. Conkin, *Gone with the Ivy: A Biography of Vanderbilt University* (Knoxville: University of Tennessee Press, 1985), 135–41.

15. "Students, 1904–1905," *UNBI,* June 1905, 99–108; "Students, 1909–1910," *UNBI,* July 1910, 134–49.

16. *Proceedings,* 4:382.

17. *Proceedings,* 4:214–15; see also Kegley, *Peabody Scholarships,* 44–100.

18. *Nashville American,* August 3, 4, 12, 15, 1899.

19. William H. Payne to John M. Bass, October 1898 (loose insert), *Minutes, Board of Trust,* 502.

20. *Minutes, Board of Trust,* 506.

21. William H. Payne to the Trustees of the University of Nashville, July 26, 1899 (loose insert), *Minutes, Board of Trust,* 506.

22. *Nashville American,* August 3, 1899.

23. *Minutes, Board of Trust,* 509, 514, 521.

24. The enrollment statistics in the preceding two paragraphs come from *UNBI,* July 1903, 113, 115; June 1905, 113; June 1909,145.

25. *UNBI,* June 1909.

26. *UNBI, 1910–1911* (n.d.).

1. *Proceedings of the Trustees of the Peabody Education Fund, 1900–1914,* 6:266–67.
2. On the Kirkland-Gilman correspondence, see Conkin, *Gone with the Ivy,* 126–27, 166–67.
3. *Proceedings,* 6:93.
4. Ibid., 59, 104.
5. On the October 1902 meeting, see *Proceedings,* 6:105–57.
6. Ibid., 144.
7. Ibid., 159–65.
8. On the fund raising efforts, see Ibid., 6: 241–57
9. Porter to Rose, January 24, 1905, in "Rose, Wickliffe / Buttrick, Wallace, General Education Board," box 2107, GPCR.
10. *Proceedings,* 6: 265.
11. Ibid.
12. Quoted in Conkin, *Gone with the Ivy,* 167.
13. Kirkland to Gilman, April 5, 1905, and Buttrick to Kirkland, April 10, 1905, in "Buttrick, Walter (Wickliffe Rose et al)," box 2107, GPCR.
14. Morehouse to Buttrick, Sept 29, 1905, in "Buttrick, Walter (Wickliffe Rose et al.), Box 2107, GPCR.
15. J. R. Mosley to Buttrick, Nov 4, 1905, ibid.
16. *Proceedings,* 6: 285.
17. Ibid., 281, 303.
18. Buttrick to Rose, December 1, 1905, in "Wickliffe Rose," box 2107, GPCR.
19. *Proceedings,* 1900–14, 6:434–483.
20. Ibid., 522–25.
21. Ibid., 317–33.
22. Ibid., 323.
23. Ibid., 335–56.
24. J. W. Brouillette, "The Third Phase of the Peabody Education Fund" (Ph.D. diss., George Peabody College for Teachers, 1937), 152–56 (quote on 155).
25. *Proceedings,* 6: 392.
26. Buttrick to Rose, March 19, 1909, folder, "Rose, Wickliffe / Buttrick, Wallace, General Education Board," box 2107, GPCR.
27. *Proceedings,* 6: 392.
28. I have told the preceding story in Conkin, *Gone with the Ivy,* 149–84.
29. Brouillette, *The Third Phase,* 200–212.
30. The Lawrence document appears in "For All Time to Come, Sacred Duty of Peabody Guardians Interpreted in Document of 1909," *Peabody Reflector,* January–February 1961, 4–9.

31 Ibid., 9.

CHAPTER EIGHT
CREATING THE GEORGE PEABODY CAMPUS, 1911–1930

1. *Board Minutes,* George Peabody College for Teachers, February 9, 1910, 1:191–93, 202.
2. *Board Minutes,* February 18, 1910, 1: 48–52; March 2, 1910, 1: 54–55; March 9, 1910, 1: 61–65; July 5, 1910, 1:91–130; October 12, 1910, 1:131–32.

3. Eugene TeSelle, "The Nashville Institute and Roger Williams University: Benevolence, Paternalism, and Black Consciousness, 1867–1910," *Tennessee Historical Quarterly* 41 (winter 1982): 360–79.

4. *Board Minutes,* October 12, 1910, 1:131–32.

5. The appointment of Payne is recorded in *Board Minutes,* January 17, 1911, 1:156; the extensive correspondence and negotiations leading to his appointment are in *Board Minutes,* June 13, 1911, 1:183–189.

6. William W. Force, *Payne of Peabody, An Apostle of Education* (Nashville: no publisher listed, 1985), 5–8.

7. This whole, complex story is recorded in hundreds of documents in "University of Nashville\Changeover to Peabody College" box 2099, GPCR.

8. Letters from Payne to Little, October 18 and 20, 1913, ibid. These files also contain most of their telegrams.

9. *Board Minutes,* January 20, 1914, 2: 446–47.

10. A. L. Crabb, "Bruce Ryburn Payne—Man of Faith," *Peabody Reflector and Alumni News* (hereafter, *Reflector*), March 1931, 91–95.

11. *Board Minutes,* January 20, 1914, 2: 445.

12. Ibid., July 4, 1911, 1: 191–93, 202.

13. Ibid., September 20, 1: 206–14.

14. Ibid., October 10, 1911, 1: 215; January 15, 1912, 1: 219–22.

15. This architectural and landscape mockup appear in the front of the first bulletin for the college, *George Peabody College for Teachers, Its Evolution and Present Status* (Nashville, 1912).

16. *Board Minutes,* January 15, 1912, 1: 223–25.

17. Ibid., July 2, 1912, 1: 272–74.

18. Ibid., September 16, 1912, 2: 304–08.

19. Ibid., July 1, 1913, 2: 373–74.

20. Ibid., October 31, 1912, 2: 314–17, 322–25.

21. Ibid., February 18, 1914, 2: 495–501; June 5, 1914, 2: 531–34.

22. Ibid., March 25, 1915, 2: 613–14; May 28, 1915, 2: 617–18.

23. Ibid., January 20, 1914, 2: 448–49, May 13, 1914, 2: 526.

24. Ibid., February 8, 1917, 3: 775–76.

25. "Report of the President to the Board of Trustees of George Peabody College for Teachers, delivered, June 13, 1916," in *Reports of the President: George Peabody College for Teacher,* vol. 2, Special Collections (hereafter, presidents' reports to the board will be cited in the notes as: Report of the president, with date, volume). Most of these reports do not have page numbers.

26. Ibid., March 12, 1917, 2:783–86, June, 1920, 2:2–3.

27. Ibid., June 1919, vol. 2.

28. Ibid., June 1920, 2:15–16, June 7, 1923.

29. On the Demonstration School, East Hall, and the Administration Building, see "Demonstration School BLDG.," "East Hall (Dormitory)," "Administration BLDG.," box 2062, GPCR.

30. *Board Minutes,* February 18, 1926, 5: 1559.

31. Ibid., February 18, 1931, 6: 1905–06.

32. *The Semicentennial of George Peabody College for Teachers, 1875–1925* (Nashville: George Peabody College for Teachers, 1925), box 2107, GPCR.

33. Conkin, *Gone with the Ivy,* 290–94; "Peabody Education Program, The," "Peabody Education Prog., 1926–29," and "Fund Raising Campaign–1926," box 2099, GPCR.

34. "Peabody Education Program, The," "Peabody Education Prog., 1926–29," and "Fund Raising Campaign–1926," box 2099, GPCR.

35. The preceding summary draws from Reports of the president, 1927–1930, vol. 2; and *Board Minutes,* 5:1653–1861, 6:1862–1945.

CHAPTER NINE
THE ACADEMIC SIDE, 1914–1930

1. *George Peabody College for Teachers: Its Function, September, 1912* (Nashville: George Peabody College for Teachers, 1912); Philip Dorf, *Liberty Hyde Bailey: An Informal Biography* (Ithaca: Cornell University Press, 1956); Liberty H. Bailey, *The Country-Life Movement in the United States* (New York: Macmillan, 1913).

2. U.S. Senate, *Report of the Country Life Commission* (Washington, D.C.: Government Printing Office, 1909).

3. Joseph Cannon Bailey, *Seaman A. Knapp: Schoolmaster of American Agriculture* (New York: Columbia University Press, 1945).

4. Ibid., 133–68.

5. Rose to Buttrick, April 28 and 30, 1909, "Rose, Wickliffe / Buttrick, Wallace, General Education Board," box 2107, GPCR.

6. J. Bailey, *Seaman A. Knapp,* 244–80.

7. Bruce R. Payne Papers, folder 35, box 3, Special Collections (hereafter, BRP Papers).

8. Henry W. Jinske, "The Religious Influence of Peabody College," *Peabody Reflector,* February 1938, 60 (hereafter, *Reflector*).

9. A . L. Crabb, "Statelier Mansions," *Reflector,* August 1932, 326.

10. "Twenty Years of the Algernon Sydney Sullivan Awards," *Reflector,* October 1945, 324–25.

11. *George Peabody College for Teachers: Announcement of a Second College Year, 1915–1916* (Nashville: George Peabody College for Teachers, 1915), 14.

12. Ashley Van Storm, "Kary Cadmus Davis—Man of Action," *Reflector,* March 1931, 83–86, 95, 98.

13. "Alumni News," *Reflector,* January 1930, 42.

14. "The Teacher Goes Home," *Reflector,* April 1929, 4–5.

15. "In Memoriam, Memorial Services for Professor John J. Didcoct," *Reflector,* November 1927, 14–22.

16. Lyle H. Lanier, "Joseph Peterson—Teacher and Psychologist," *Reflector,* January 1936, 3–4, 7.

17. "Alumni News," *Reflector,* May 1948, 197.

18. "Dr. Alfred I. Roehm," *Reflector,* August 1949, 293.

19. The preceding section derives from a survey of the bulletins of George Peabody College, 1913–14 to 1929–30.

20. For the story of the summer school at Peabody, I have drawn from "Peabody Summer School News—Vol. 1, 1916," box 2060, GPCR; a survey of *Reports of the President: George Peabody College for Teachers,* vol. 1; and the bulletins of George Peabody College, 1913–14 to 1929–30.

21. *Bulletin: George Peabody College for Teachers,* 1929–30, 4–17.

22. For details of the affiliation, see "Peabody / Vanderbilt Affiliation Committee," box 2089, GPCR.

23. The preceding section derives from a survey of the bulletins of George Peabody College.

24. "The Knapp Farm Club House," *Reflector,* July–August 1959, 194–98; Helen White Gentry, "Knapp Farm," *Reflector,* November 1953, 219–22.

25. "Financial Reports, 1928," box 2099, GPCR; Payne to George Reynolds, May 28, 1928, folder 45, box 3, BRP Papers.

26. Report of the president, June 8, 1921, 2:2–5; *Board Minutes*, January 30, 1915, 2:605–6, February 20, 1915, 2:607, March 25, 1915, 2:613–15; "Knapp Farm Readied for Sale at $1 Million," *Reflector*, July–August 1965, 168.

27. Report of the president, June 5, 1922, February 18, 1925, February 18, 1929.

28. Report of the president, June 8, 1921.

29. "Announcement of the Department of Public-Health Nursing, 1922–1923," supplement to *Bulletin, George Peabody College for Teachers*, 1922–23.

30. Report of the president, June 8, 1921; Conkin, *Gone with the Ivy*, 282–87; "Nursing Education Division Report 1961," box 2117, GPCR; Payne to Beardsley Ruml, May 1, 1924, folder 16, box 1, BRP Papers; Edna Lewis, "Public Health Nursing at Peabody," *Reflector*, February 1956, 30–32.

31. *Bulletin, George Peabody College for Teachers*, fall 1920, 5–6, 35.

32. "The Voice of Bruce R. Payne," *Reflector*, March 1953, 51–52; Edward Neely Callum, "George Peabody College for Teachers, 1914–1937" (master's thesis, George Peabody College for Teachers, 1963), 286–89.

33. Report of the president, February 18, 1924, and February 18, 1928.

34. *Board Minutes*, January 19, 1915, 2:585.

35. Report of the president, February 18, 1928, 2:12–13; Callum, "George Peabody College," 283.

36. Editorials, *Reflector*, August 1930, 23, November 1930, 15.

37. Report of the president, February 18, 1929.

38. For more detail, see Joseph Peterson and Lyle Lanier, *Studies in the Comparative Abilities of Whites and Negroes*, Mental Measurement Monographs 5 (Baltimore: Williams and Wilkins, 1929).

39. Payne to Trevor Arnett, April 1 and 10, 1929, and October 23, 1934, folder 16, box 1, BRP Papers.

40. "M.A. Thesis Lists," box 2110, GPCR.

41. "Announcement of Summer Quarter," *Bulletin, George Peabody College for Teachers*, 1922, 15–16.

42. "Payne to GEB, Dec. 26, 1925," "Charles Little to Payne, Jan. 2, 1926," in "Buttrick, Wallace (Wickliffe Rose, et al) Miscellaneous Correspondence," box 2107, GPCR.

43. "Conference between Dr. Bachman and Messrs. Payne, Didcoct, and Phelps, July 2, 1926," "Some Impressions on Extended Conference with Dr. Bachman," "Comments on the Conference between Phelps and Didcoct with Bachman, June 30, 1926," "Questions Arising in Our Minds Resultant from the Bachman Conference of June 28 and 29, 1926," and "Conference of July 12, 1926 between Dr. Wickliffe Rose and Charles E. Little," in "Buttrick, Wallace (Wickliffe Rose, et al) Miscellaneous Correspondence," box 2107, GPCR.

44. Ibid.

45. Conkin, *Gone with the Ivy*, 360–66.

CHAPTER TEN
DEPRESSION AND WAR, 1930–1945

1. The story of Peabody's financial situation during the Great Depression is reflected in Payne's memos and letters, box 1, BRP Papers.

2. For the SACSS report , see folder 1, box 1, BRP Papers.

3. Editorials, *Peabody Reflector*, April 1934, 147 (hereafter, *Reflector*).

4. "By–Laws of the Faculty, 1920," box 2056, GPCR.

5. For the story of Payne's leadership style and the reorganization of Peabody's curriculum, I have drawn from surveys of *Reports of the President: George Peabody College for Teachers,* vols. 1–2, and of *Bulletin: George Peabody College for Teachers,* 1915–16, 1918–24, and 1929–36.

6. The preceding numbers appear in Bruce R. Payne, "Report of the President," February 19, 1934," vol. 2.

7. "Payne to faculty, Aug. 15, 1932," folder 22, box 2, BRP Papers.

8. "Memo to faculty, June 29, 1933," folder 22, box 2, BRP Papers.

9. Most of Payne's correspondence with the United Daughters of the Confederacy is in folder 7, box 1, BRP Papers; on the history professorship, see "Chair of Southern History (UDC and Peabody)," box 2088, GPCR.

10. Box 1, folder 7, BRP Papers.

11. *Board Minutes,* July 19, 1933, 6:2056; editorials, *Reflector,* November 1934, 434.

12. These reunions are abundantly documented in "Peabody-Reunion-1929, 1930," box 2117, GPCR.

13. "Alumni News," *Reflector,* January 1930, 42, March 1930, 37.

14. Editorials, *Reflector,* October 1931, 346, February 1934, 65.

15. "Campus News," *Reflector,* October 1935, 341–42.

16. Bruce R. Payne, "Report of the President," May 7, 1936, 2:22–23.

17. "Campus News," *Reflector,* November 1938, 380.

18. Editorials, *Reflector,* January 1938, 23.

19. "Campus News," *Reflector,* 1941, 21. A personal note: Like most high school students in Tennessee, my text for U.S. history was Wirth's *Development of America,* the first history book I ever read.

20. James W. Byrd, "William Inge: Peabody's Playwright," *Reflector,* February 1956, 55–56.

21. "Four Campus Veterans Reach Retirement Age," *Reflector,* July–August 1959, 149, 151.

22. James D. Anderson, *The Education of Blacks in the South, 1860–1935* (Chapel Hill: University of North Carolina Press, 1988), 153–85.

23. For more on Smith and Rosenwald, see S. L. Smith, *Builders of Good Will: The Story of the State Agents of Negro Education in the South, 1910–1950* (Nashville: Tennessee Book Company, 1950); see also "Campus News," *Reflector,* November 1950, 310; February 1951, 52; and December 1952, 265; "Samuel Leonard Smith, 1875–1956," *Reflector,* September–October 1956, 168.

24. "President Bruce Ryburn Payne," *Reflector,* May 1937, 163–66.

25. On Peabody's immediate reaction to Payne's death and Garrison's appointment see ibid.; Caswell to Hill, September 16, 1937, "Garrison's Election," in "Peabody Presidents—Garrison and Hill," box 2287, GPCR.

26. Garrison to Arthur Wright, Southern Education Foundation, July 12, 1943, in "Southern Education Foundation, Wright, Arthur D.," in "Peabody Presidents—Garrison and Hill," box 2284, GPCR.

27. "President's Page," *Reflector,* February 1944, 43.

28. Sydney C. Garrison , "Report of the President," 1937 (delivered 1938), vol. 3.

29. Ibid.

30. *Board Minutes,* March 17, 1942, 8:2521; June 5, 1942, 8:2539; August 20, 1942, 8:2540; June 4, 1943, 8:2573; Ella Mae Walker, "The Training of Teachers of Business at Peabody College," *Reflector,* November 1938, 370.

31. Sydney C. Garrison , "Annual Report of the President," 1939 (delivered 1940), 3:1–2; *Board Minutes,* May 9, 1940, 8:2434; April 17, 1946, 9:2690–92.

32. Payne, "Report of the President," May 7, 1936.

33. Conkin, *Gone with the Ivy*, 409–11.

34. Ibid., 407–14; "Committee on Cooperation, Vandy, Scarritt, Peabody;" box 2117, GPCR.

35. A. F. Kuhlman, "Progress Report on the Joint University Libraries," *Reflector*, March 1995, 87–90, 94.

36. "Geographical Distribution of Graduates—August, 1943," *Reflector*, September 1943, 335–36, 338–43; *Board Minutes*, August 19, 1943, 8:2591.

37. "Historical Report, 333 AAF CTD (A.C.), George Peabody College, Nashville, Tenn., April 1, 1943–March 15, 1944," 2 vols., box 2110, GPCR; Lexie Ferrel, "A Co-Ed's View," *Reflector*, November 1943, 388; Etha Green, "Aviation Student Program Comes to an End," *Reflector*, July 1944, 249–50.

38. "Historical Report, 333," 1:89.

39. "Peabody's War Dead (World War II)," box 2117, GPCR.

CHAPTER ELEVEN
THE PEABODY OF HENRY H. HILL

1. "Hill, Henry H.—Biographical," box 2057, GPCR.

2. *Peabody College Looks Ahead: Report of the Committee of Eleven* [1946], in "Peabody: Reports Studies and Proposals," box 2109, GPCR.

3. Ibid. An appendix to this 1946 report is filed in "Hollis L. Caswell, George D. Stoddard and William F. Russell—1948," box 2109, GPCR. For related publications, see "Committee of Eleven—Reports," box 2119, GPCR.

4. *Proposals for the Future Development of George Peabody College for Teachers* [summer, 1949], in "Hollis L. Caswell, George D. Stoddard and William F. Russell—1948," box 2109, GPCR.

5. Ibid.; *George Peabody College for Teachers, the President's Annual Report, May 10, 1955*, box 2064, GPCR; "Faculty, Dinner Meeting at Belle Meade Country Club June 9, 1949," box 2101, GPCR.

6. *Board Minutes*, December 6, 1951, 10:3017; "Academic Year, 1957–58," *Bulletin: George Peabody College for Teachers*, summer quarter, 1957, 41; *Peabody Reflector*, May–June 1958 (hereafter, *Reflector*).

7. *George Peabody College for Teachers, The President's Annual Report, May 10, 1955*, in box 2064, GPCR.

8. "Summer Enrollment," *Reflector*, July 1949, 239; "Fall Enrollment at Peabody," *Reflector*, October 1949, 239; *Board Minutes*, July 5, 1951, 10:2990; "Summer in Retrospect," *Peabody Reflector*, August–September 1951, 213.

9. "Veterans Village and Nursery School," box 2060, GPCR.

10. On Harris, see "New Faculty Members," *Reflector*, August 1949, 290; *Board Minutes*, June 16, 1949, 9:2878–2879; and Alan H. Levy, *Musical Nationalism: American Composers' Search for Identity* (Westport, Conn.: Greenwood Press, 1983), 86–99.

11. "Peabody Leadership," *Reflector*, January 1949, 22; "In Memoriam," *Reflector*, June–July 1955, 181.

12. *Board Minutes*, May 6, 1948, 9:2806; Sarah Gibson Blanding, "The Liberal Mind," *Reflector*, August–September 1952, 176–78.

13. I lived less than a block from the Peabody campus and took advantage of the evening programs. For details about these summer schools, see *Reflector*, 1948–52.

14. *Board Minutes*, May 10, 1951, 10:2979; December 5, 1952, 11: 3083; "Student Center BLDG." and "Gillette Hall (Dormitory)," box 2062, GPCR.

15. Documents concerning urban renewal as well as the maps are filed in "University Center—Urban Renewal Project," box 2133, GPCR.

16. On integration at Vanderbilt, see, Conkin, *Gone with the Ivy,* 539–80.

17. The results of this ballot are filed in "Negroes Admitted to Peabody, Summer, 1954," box 2110, GPCR; for an insightful vignette on integration at Peabody, see Sherman Dorn, *A Short History of Peabody College* (Nashville: Peabody College, 1996), 62–66; *Peabody in 1965: A Proposed Five-Point Program for Faculty Study, George Peabody College for Teachers* [1952], in "Peabody: Reports, Studies and Proposals," box 2109, GPCR.

18. "Negroes Admitted to Peabody."

19. *Board Minutes,* December 4, 1953, 11:3157–58.

20. Memorandum, Henry Hill to Sam P. Wiggins and Felix C. Robb, January 10, 1966, in "Hill, Henry Harrington—Peabody College"; "President: Sept. 1945–Aug. 31, 1961, Acting President: July 1, 1966–July 31, 1967," box 2057, GPCR.

21. *Board Minutes,* April 1, 1963, 15:3720.

22. Hobbs to Hill, February 6, and Hill to Hobbs, March 2, 1961, in "President Emeritus—Henry Hill," Nicholas Hobbs Papers, box 43, Special Collections, Vanderbilt University (hereafter, Hobbs Papers).

23. *Board Minutes,* April 1, 1963, 15:3716; May 9, 1963, 3730; Hobbs to Robb, May 5, 1962, and Robb to Hobbs, undated but a response in May 1962, in "Past President—Felix Robb," Hobbs Papers, box 43.

24. Board Minutes, April 1, 1963, 15:3718–22.

25. Dorothy Louise Brown, "Maycie Katherine Southall: Her Life and Contributions to Education" (Ph.D. diss., George Peabody College for Teachers of Vanderbilt University, 1981).

26. "Faculty News," *Reflector,* August–September 1951, 221; "Van Til to Assume Posts at Maryland, New York Universities," *Reflector,* May–June 1957, 136.

27. "Harold Benjamin, 1893–1969," *Reflector,* January–February 1969, 2–10.

28. "Willard E. Goslin, 1899–1969," *Reflector,* March–April 1969, 55–60; Dorn, *Brief History of Peabody College,* 34–35.

29. *Peabody in 1965. A Proposed Five Point Program for Faculty Study, George Peabody College for Teachers* [1952], in folder "Peabody: Reports, Studies and Proposals, in Box 2093, GPCR.

30. Felix C. Robb, "Peabody Goes to Korea," *Reflector,* February 1958, 4–7.

31. For enrollment information, see "Enrollment," box 2093, GPCR.

32. The preceding discussion of Peabody's financial situation has been drawn from the yearly reports of the college treasurer during this period in *Board Minutes.*

33. *Board Minutes,* May 7, 1958, 14:3482–85; October 15, 1959, 14:3519.

34. Ibid., March 25, 1958, 14:3413–14.

35. "Nursing Education Division Report 1961," box 2014, GPCR.

36. On the M.A.T., see Conkin, *Gone with the Ivy,* 470–71.

37. For documents regarding the 1962 study of the Peabody-Vanderbilt relationship, see "Peabody / Vanderbilt—Report on Proposed Merger (1962)," box 2109, GPCR; for the self-studies of the midsixties, see box 2101, GPCR.

CHAPTER TWELVE
A TROUBLED DECADE, 1961–1972

1. I have drawn biographical information from "Dean Robb Named President," *Current Scene,* an insert facing page 78 in *Peabody Reflector,* May–June 1961.

2. *Board Minutes,* May 11, 1961, 15: 3604.

3. The reprinted founding documents are in *Reflector,* January–February 1961, 4–11; "For Eighty-Six Years Our Peabody Guardians Have Kept Us Free," *Reflector,* March–April 1961, 42.

4. Memorandum, Felix C. Robb to John Dale Russell, March 9, 1962, box 2047, GPCR.

5. *Report of the Study of Closer Cooperation between George Peabody College for Teachers and Vanderbilt University, Prepared for the Joint Committee of Trustees of George Peabody College for Teachers and Vanderbilt University* [May, 1962]. For this report, along with numerous supporting documents, such as newspaper articles, letters, and memoranda, see "Peabody / Vanderbilt—Report on Proposed Merger (1962)," box 2109, GPCR.

6. Conkin, *Gone with the Ivy,* 472.

7. *Board Minutes,* May 31, 1962, 15: 3683.

8. "December 6, 1962: A New Era Begins," *Reflector,* January–February 1963, 8–13.

9. Ibid., 11–12.

10. *Board Minutes,* May 12, 1972, 17: 4384.

11. For faculty comments, see Felix C. Robb's memorandum to John Dale Russell, March 9, 1962, box 2047, GPCR.

12. "President Looks at Peabody's Problems, Needs, Aims, Hopes," *Reflector,* September–October 1961, 130–39.

13. Paul R Dokecki and John R. Newbrough, "For the Love of Children," *Reflector,* summer 1998, 18–21.

14 *Board Minutes,* December 6, 1962, 15: 3701.

15. *Board Minutes,* May 7, 1964, 16:3787; "Carnegie Project also Gets Underway," *Reflector,* July–August 1964, 170.

16. Hobbs to Felix Robb, January 16, 1964, in "Past President—Felix Robb," Hobbs Papers, box 43; *Board Minutes,* August 18, 1965, 16:3787; "Editorial Comment," *Reflector,* May–June 1965, 92–93.

17. "Hobbs Memo to Himself," December 5, 1963, in "Past President—Felix Robb," Hobbs Papers, box 43.

18. *Self-Study Report to Southern Association of Colleges and Schools* [March 1964], box 2101, GPCR.

19. "Report of the Southern Association Visiting Committee" [April 5–8, 1964], 32, box 2047, GPCR.

20. "Robb to Members of the Faculty," January 26, 1964, in "Past President—Felix Robb," Hobbs Papers, box 43.

21. For the report of the Graduate Instruction Committee, see "GIC Study 1969–," box 2070, GPCR.

22. For enrollment and tuition data, see "Enrollment," box 2093, GPCR; John E. Windrow, ". . . The Anatomy of a Rumor," *Reflector,* May–June 1966, 89.

23. *Board Minutes,* May 11, 1967, 16: 3952–56; July 10, 1967, 16: 3968–70.

24. "The Story of Peabody's New President," *Reflector,* July–August 1967, 166–76.

25. Smith to Norris, July 5, 1967, in "Dr. Claunch, 1967," box 2063, GPCR.

26. The preceding discussion derives from financial data for this period in Board Minutes.

27. "Enrollment," box 2093, GPCR.

28. I have calculated the numbers based on frequent discussions and reports on fund-raising in *Board Minutes,* 1970–73. See, for example, November 6, 1970, 17:4277–78; January 8, 1971, 17:4291; April 7, 1972, 17:4370–72.

29. "Mammoth Park Retreat," box 2118, GPCR.

30. "Task Force Report," box 2116, GPCR.

31. *Board Minutes,* November 21, 1969, 16: 4096–4100.

32. *Peabody Plus: A Positive Plan for a Greater Peabody in the Seventies* [November 1969], in "Faculty Advisory Council Minutes 1969–70," box 2142, GPCR.

33. Documentation on the NUCC is in unmarked folders in box 2077, GPCR.

34. *Board Minutes,* 5, 1970, 17: 4228.

35. [Claunch memorandum], Feb 12, 1971, unmarked folder, box 2077, GPCR.

36. Thompson's notes for his presentation to FAC are filed in "Faculty Advisory Council Minutes, 1969–70," box 2142, GPCR.

37. The best record of the 1968 and 1970 controversies is in "Hobbs / Peabody / Kennedy Center situation," Hobbes Papers, box 67, which contains dozens of letters, including the draft letter prepared for Ted Kennedy; for the final resolution, see Hobbs and Claunch to Horace Hill, November 4, 1968, "President Claunch—1968," Hobbs Papers, box 80.

38. *Board Minutes,* July 10, 1970, 17: 4233.

39. Ibid., 4235–39.

40. The details of this final resolution are in "Hobbs / Peabody / Kennedy Center situation," Hobbs Papers, box 67.

41. On Stedman's tenure as Kennedy Center director, see "Peabody College Correspondence, Stedman," Hobbs Papers, box 67.

42. Claunch to faculty, January 31, 1972, in "Faculty Teaching Load," box 2093, GPCR.

43. Ibid.; *Board Minutes,* November, 9–10, 1972, 17:4429–34.

44. "FAC Minutes 1970–71," box 2142, GPCR; Claunch to Robert Weaver, July 15, 1971, in "FAC: College Governance," box 2065, GPCR; Claunch to faculty, July 26, 1972, "Governance in the Area of Educational Policy," in "Faculty Governance," box 2093, GPCR.

45. "A Proposal for the Creation of a Council on College Policy," in "FAC: College Governance," box 2065, GPCR.

46. *Peabody Post,* September 28, 1970, in "[Peabody] The Post, 1970–73," box 2060, GPCR.

47. *Peabody Post,* May 15, 1970, in ibid.

48. "Address by Dr. John M. Claunch, President of George Peabody College for Teachers, to the August 1970 Graduating Class," *Reflector,* summer 1970, 101.

49. *Board Minutes,* February 11, 1972, 17: 4364–65.

50. Ibid., March 17, 1972, 17:4367–68.

51. Ibid., November 9–10, 1972, 17: 4432.

52. Ibid., 17: 4434.

53. Ibid., March 2, 1973, 17: 4458–64.

CHAPTER THIRTEEN
MERGER

1. "Dr. Dunworth Will Succeed President Claunch," *Peabody Reflector,* summer 1973, 73 (hereafter, *Reflector*); "Dunworth, John—Newspaper Clippings," box 2063, GPCR; letters of recommendation in black Peabody notebook, box 2048, GPCR.

2. "Ranking Universities," *National Observer,* February 1, 1975; *Nashville Banner,* May 21, 1975.

3. For the complete *Design for the Future* [August 29, 1974], see box 2091, GPCR.

4. *Visiting Committee Report, George Peabody College for Teachers* [spring 1975], box 2091, GPCR.

5. *George Peabody College for Teachers, Nashville, Tennessee, Self Study, Prepared in Accordance with the Institutional Self-Study Program of the Southern Association of Colleges and Schools* [January 1975], 3:38–48, box 2100, GPCR.

6. Ibid., 5:1–104.

7. Ibid., 9:1–64

8. A copy of this memo is attached to a letter Dunworth sent to the executive committee of the board, January 2, 1979, in "1977 merger proposal," in the Thomas Stovall box, GPCR.

9. Ibid.

10. For a summary of enrollment trends at Peabody, 1968–79, see Board Minutes, March 19, 1979, attached to 18:4922. This is a collection of hard copies of charts and graphs reproduced from overhead transparencies in *Peabody-Vanderbilt Merger Records* (hereafter, *P-VMR*).

11. Thanks largely to the work of Raymond Norris, the detailed records of this overseas program are in boxes 2135 and 2124, GPCR.

12. The preceding financial analysis derived from my survey of *Board Minutes,* vol. 18.

13. *Board Minutes,* January 5, 1979, 18:4887.

14. His letter is attached to *Board Minutes,* October 6, 1978, on the unnumbered page following 18:4886.

15. Conkin, *Gone with the Ivy,* 706–15.

16. *Board Minutes,* January 5, 1979, 18:4898.

17. Ibid., February 2, 1979, 18: 4902.

18. Ibid., February 26, 1979, 18: 4906–07.

19. Roy L. Lassiter Jr. to G. Wayne Brown, March 13, 1979, in "Merger," Thomas Stovall box, GPCR.

20. This survey is in folder 2 (March), box 4, *P-VMR.*

21. "Dunworth, John (Letters to, concerning "merger")," box 2048, GPCR.

22. *Resolution* [February 26, 1979], folder 1, box 1, P-VMR. See also the numerous other letters, memos, and minutes regarding faculty response in the same folder.

23. Faculty Committee on Peabody–TSU Merger to Dunworth, February 28, 1979; *Statement of Faculty Position on Merger* [February 26, 1979]; and *Report of the Faculty Committee on Peabody-TSU merger* [February 28, 1979], all in folder 1, box 1, *P-VMR.*

24. Shriver to Gable, March 9, 1979, folder 3, box 1, *P-VMR.*

25. Roy S. Nicks to Members of the State Board of Regents, March 7, 1979, folder 3, box 1, *P-VMR;* "Agreement" [March 2, 1979], folder 2, box 1, *P-VMR.*

26. *Nashville Banner,* February 20, 1979.

27. *Tennessean,* February 14, 1979.

28. *Vanderbilt Gazette,* March 6, 1979.

29. *Nashville Banner,* February 27, 1979.

30. Conkin, *Gone with the Ivy,* 711–12. The Fleming letter is available in several places, including the board of trust records of both Peabody and Vanderbilt.

31. *Board Minutes,* March 19, 1979, 18, 4922; the original overhead transparencies are stacked at the top of Box 1, *P-VMR.*

32. *Board Minutes,* March 19, 1979, 18:4918–19.

33. Memo, Peabody Faculty Chairpersons and Program Directors to Dunworth, March 27, 1979, folder 4, box 1, *P-VMR.*

34. *Board Minutes,* April 16, 1979, 18:4935–36.

35. David Pack to Lesley Zimic, April 13, 1979; Zimic to Heard and Dunworth, April 13, 1979, folder 5, box I, *P-VMR.*

36. *Board Minutes,* April 27, 1979, 18:4940–64.

37. "Memorandum of Understanding," in *Board Minutes,* April 27, 1979, between 18:4961 and 4962.

38. Fleming to Gable, April 15, 1979, in *Board Minutes,* April 16, 1979, 18:4932–34.

39. Folders 5 and 6, box 1, *P-VMR; Nashville Banner,* April 18, 1979.

40. *Board Minutes,* April 27, 1979, 18:4955–59.

41. For this complex story, including the six petitions and the disposition of each case, see "Faculty Review Committee 1979," Thomas Stovall box, GPCR. For guidelines for the Faculty Review Committee, see *Board Minutes,* May 4, 1979, 18:4966–69.

42. Ashcroft to Wendell Holladay, October 5, 1979, folder 6, box 2, *P-VMR.*

43. The Graduate Student Coordinating Committee to the Members of the Board of Trustees, April 20, 1979, folder 6, box 1, *P-VMR.*

44. Jean Heard to Neal Neunschwander, July 26, 1979, folder 5, box 2, *P-VMR;* "A Statement by Alexander Heard, Chancellor of Vanderbilt University, for publication in *Ala Breve*" [July 31, 1979], folder 4, box 2, *P-VMR.*

45. Conkin, *Gone with the Ivy,* 715–18.

46. "The New Book by Alfred Leland Crabb," *Reflector,* winter 1979; "Alfred Leland Crabb: Teacher, Author, 1883–1979," *Reflector,* autumn 1979; "The Peabody Saga,"*Reflector,* summer 1980; "Peabody Buries a Time Capsule," *Reflector,* spring 1980.

CHAPTER FOURTEEN
PEABODY AS A VANDERBILT COLLEGE

1. This and the descriptions of Vanderbilt that follow derive from Conkin, *Gone with the Ivy.*

2. *Minutes of the Vanderbilt University Board of Trust and Executive Committee,* July 28, 1981, Special Collections (hereafter, *Minutes*).

3. Most of the data on Peabody since merger are part of active files at Peabody; none since 1979 have been transferred to the Vanderbilt Archives in Special Collections, so they cannot be referenced here. The annual college catalogues provide information about administrative structures, curriculum, and departments and faculty; most major news about the Peabody campus is in the *Peabody Reflector;* and budget details are in *Minutes.*

4. "Future Directions for Peabody College: The Report of the Phase III Program Review and Self-Study Steering Committee," appended to "1985/86 Self-Study Report, II," Peabody College, 1986, presently located in the dean's offices, Peabody College.

5. Ibid., 19–20.

6. "1785–1985, Peabody, 200 Years of Excellence" *Peabody Reflector* (hereafter, *Reflector*), spring 1986, is devoted to these celebrations.

7. These budget figures appear in the *Minutes* for the eighties.

8. The one subject covered continually, and well, in the *Reflector* is alumni affairs and gifts.

9. For the justification for cognitive studies, see *Plan for the Future of Peabody College,* 1987, Dean's offices, Peabody College.

10. Ibid., 29–30; "Centuries of Influence: A Celebration of Library Science at Peabody," *Reflector,* fall 1987, 9–11.

11. Willis D. Hawley, "Reflecting on the Character of Peabody College," *Reflector,* winter 1989, 2, 41; Nelson Bryan, "The Dean and the Decade," *Reflector,* fall 1989, 12–15; Jean Crawford, "Learning with Jasper," *Reflector,* summer 1990, 26–27.

12. These data are available from the Registrar's Office at Peabody.

13. Ibid.

14. For the fullest account of changes in the Kennedy Center, see "Neuroscience Center—

1990–91, Ford Ebner," a Kennedy Center records folder that will soon go to Special Collections, Vanderbilt University.

15. Robert Innes, "The Application of the Philosophy of Dewey and Research in Cognitive Science to Reforming Higher Education" (typescript), author's files.

16. This overview of HOD draws from interviews, student comments, and several published articles. A good introduction, written at the formative stage of HOD, is Nelson Bryan, "Preparation for Life," *Reflector,* winter 1987, 15–18; also informative is Mary Crichton, "A Desk–Top Education," *Reflector,* summer 1990, 23–26.

17. The board action on admissions policy is in *Minutes,* November 1–2, 1996, 9–12; additional information is in *Minutes,* April 25–26, 1997, 17–18, and in appendix E, "Statement on Admissions for Student-Athletes," and appendix F, "Initiatives to Support Academic Success of Vanderbilt Student-Athletes."

INDEX